The Encyclopedia of
World Folk Dance

The Encyclopedia of World Folk Dance

Mary Ellen Snodgrass

ROWMAN & LITTLEFIELD
Lanham • Boulder • New York • London

Published by Rowman & Littlefield
A wholly owned subsidary of The Rowman & Littlefield Publishing Group, Inc.
4501 Forbes Boulevard, Suite 200, Lanham, Maryland 20706
www.rowman.com

Unit A, Whitacre Mews, 26-34 Stannary Street, London SE11 4AB

British Library Cataloguing in Publication Information Available

Library of Congress Cataloging-in-Publication Data
Names: Snodgrass, Mary Ellen, author.
Title: The Encyclopedia of World Folk Dance / Mary Ellen Snodgrass.
Description: Lanham, MD : Rowman & Littelfield, [2016.] | Includes
    bibliographical references and index.
Identifiers: LCCN 2016010712 (print) | LCCN 2016021732 (ebook) | ISBN
    9781442257481 (hardback : alk. paper) | ISBN 9781442257498 (electronic)
Subjects: LCSH: Folk dancing—Encyclopedias.
Classification: LCC GV1743 .S68 2016 (print) | LCC GV1743 (ebook) | DDC
    793.3—dc23
LC record available at https://lccn.loc.gov/2016010712

Printed in the United States of America

For Berta Bolick and Gretchen Wilson

To the universe belongs the dancer.
He who does not dance does not know what happens.

—Gnostic Gospel of Thomas

To dance then, is to pray, to meditate,
to enter into communion with the larger dance, which is the universe.

—Jean Houston, Sicilian-American author

Contents

Preface

The Encyclopedia of World Folk Dance examines an ephemeral branch of vernacular art—the costumes, steps, figures, and techniques of anonymous choreography, the dance designs that arise from grassroots sources. To inform the dancer, choreographer, student, teacher, librarian, and art historian, the comprehensive survey covers 168 topics elucidating global involvement in musical and rhythmic performance, from processionals to clogging to dragon dance, a common holiday gala in Chinatowns worldwide. Entries exemplify broad terms—terminology, finale, nudity, veiled dance, flowers, animal dances—as well as specific occasions for groups ranging from sword and warrior dances to healing, community dance, commedia dell'arte, harvesting, and worship. Research data follow the evolution of specific dances from folk origins to court presentations, artistic stereotypes, fads, stage showpieces, and elements of such cinema as *The Last Emperor* (1987), *The Big Easy* (1987), *The Mask of Zorro* (1998), and *Salome* (1953). The text covers adaptations as significant as contributions to the *tanko bushi*, the spread of Caribbean mating dances to Europe, and the global welcome of tango, polka, rumba, and waltz to an inclusive education in Western arts.

Essential to any sector of folk arts, public reception generates critiques and condemnations of anatomic movements, particularly after the introduction of closed-position partnering to ancient and medieval circle and line formations, dance drama, and handkerchief dance. The entry on censorship alerts the reader to the shifting socioreligious opinions and exploitation of dance as provocative as the Afro-American slave gyrations of the *calenda* and *bamboula* in Congo Square in New Orleans and as debatable as *ghurei* dance, Wiccan Beltane ritual, and *Totentanz*. The text analyzes nationalistic fervor that either promoted or suppressed major examples, especially Sufi dance, Greek bacchanalia, hora, the *Ländler*, maypole frolics, *mbende/jerusarema*, and the traditional Irish *cèilidh*.

Key to the encyclopedia, the placement of folk dances within world history reveals the significance of peasant expressions of such issues as subsistence, colonialism, bondage, gender equality, and artistic freedom. During the Renaissance, the incorporation of the *volta* at the court of Elizabeth I invited ridicule of the English queen and harsh diatribes against the Tudor Dynasty. The carmagnole stirred public unrest leading to the French Revolution of July 14, 1789, and epitomized the virulent impact of body language and lyrics in explosive times. The complex issues affecting scheduling and performing the *jarabe tapatío*, tango, sun dance, hula, capoeira, zydeco, and ghost dance require perusal of postures and mime for subtle meaning. Overarching questions of legality and public decency are folk concerns about civil liberties.

The 168 headwords alphabetize the crucial terminology of folk arts appraisal, for example, propitiation, Walpurgis dance, *odori*, nuptial dance, galop, and juvenile dancers. Recurrent specifics—farandole, *branle*, zapateado, contradance, galliard, drumming—assert the importance of musical landmarks to a range of subsequent dances, as with Creole dance, polonaise, schottische, and fandango. Shifting values muddy the interpretation of controversial figures, particularly labyrinthine dance, coming-of-age ceremonies, Eskimo dance houses, and exorcism. Broad overviews—sub-Saharan dance, *matachines*, Siberian dance, Indonesian dance—picture multiple creative responses to universal behaviors, from birth and initiation to death and sanctification.

The complete A to Z differentiates modes and styles, for example, story dance, square dance, step dance, and stomp dance. Commentary encompasses similarities and differences within ethnic groups, such as the homeless Kurds, Lakota, West African slaves in Santo Domingo, Tibetans, and Roma, all of whom have borne traditions with them as they shuffled from motherland to extremes of diaspora. Peripheral subjects fill in particulars essential to an understanding of dancers and presentation, for example, disguise, body art, headdress, and jewelry. For visual illustration, the text features photos, sketches, and bas-relief from a variety of civilizations, from ancient Greek, Persian, and Roman artistry to the nineteenth-century struggle of the Mandan, Ojibwa, and Chukchi to maintain the heritage of First Peoples.

A chronology reprises events in folk arts from Chinese shamanic dance to rehabilitate warriors in 5000 BCE to contemporary Islamic suppression of Somali partner dances and the ISIS war on Kurdish freedom fighters. The timeline intersperses origins of resilient dance categories, as with the emergence of the British morris dance in 1448 from the Moroccan *morisca* and the Canaanite or Phoenician initiation of the *dabke* line dance in 2000 BCE to Iraqi, Jordanian, Lebanese, Palestinian, and Syrian folk gatherings. Entries explain the sources of the *siva* Samoa from the aboriginal Lapita, the comic *kochari* mime in eastern Asia, and Etruscan mourning ritual that celebrated a joyous afterlife.

The glossary defines focal terms—grapevine, *carole*, kinetics, allegory, meter, troubadour—and cites examples of usage, specifically the percussive idiophonics that make body music for the hornpipe, jig, and *Schuhplattler*. The initiation of male-female duets links the concept of partnering with execution of the mazurka, *varsouvienne*, and *carabine* scarf dance. Dissension over such facets as ululation characterizes the ethnic significance of high-pitched wails and tongue flutters by Arab women, who mark bridal preparations and energetic Mauritanian gymnastics with vocal rejoicing. Additional listing of national and state dances mentions unique choreography, as with the Toboggan and Trinidadian limbo, Scandinavian *polska*, and Australian corroboree, and the shared enthusiasm of Germany and Paraguay for the polka.

A thorough index of primary and secondary topics alerts researchers to major essays on the history of the saltarello, *mayim mayim*, *halling*, tarantella, and cakewalk, as well as to details influencing world folk performance:

- **dances** Mankon bottle dance, *antikrystos*, berdache dance, shawl dance, *krakowiak*, nautch dance, *hakka*, trance dance, Viennese waltz, Newroz dance
- **people** Liholiho Kamehameha, Tuareg, Rabindranath Tagore, Korekore, Yupik, Ponca, Thutmose III, Mevlevi Jalaluddin Rumi, Nikita Khrushchev, Rama IX, !Kung, Saami, Mustafa Kemal Ataturk, Zulu, Arawak, Josephine Baker, George Catlin
- **accompaniment** yodeling, polyphony, Peter Ilyich Tchaikovsky, Johann Strauss I and II, drum dance, juba, shoe clapping, hoop dance, ululation
- **eras** Ming Dynasty, Napoleonic Wars, Chakri Dynasty, Protestant Reformation, Spanish Inquisition, American Civil War, Byzantine Empire, Nazis, Joseon Dynasty
- **places** Isle of Mann, Abydos, New Zealand, Burundi, Manitoba, Lübeck, Bight of Benin, Paris, Sikkim, Slovenia, Libya, Ukraine, Balkans, Crete, Bali, Laos, Iceland
- **issues** Mormonism, magic, Zionism, cross-dressing, Orientalism, women's gendered dance, *The Spiral Dance: A Rebirth of the Ancient Religion of the Great Goddess* (1979), powwow, physical education, nationalism, Christianity
- **scripture** Mishnah, Song of Songs, Rigveda (ca. 1200 BCE), Job, Black Elk, *Bhāgavata Purāna* (ca. 3000 BCE), I Samuel, Dead Sea Scrolls, Exodus
- **media** *Kristin Lavransdatter* (1919), *Zorba the Greek* (1964), *A Treatise on the Art of Dancing* (1762), *Quadrille and Cotillion Panorama* (1817), *Slave Songs of the United States* (1867), *Pride and Prejudice* (1813), *The Tudors* (2009–2010), *Outlander* (2014), *Hedda Gabler* (1890), *My Antonia* (1918), *Little House in the Big Woods* (1932), *The Hunchback of Notre Dame* (1831), *Out of Africa* (1937)
- **ritual** Inviting-In Feast, stilt walking, jazz funeral parade, All Souls' Day, Patum de Berga, mumming, saber dance, reindeer dance, childbirth, carnaval/carnival, cathartic dance

Acknowledgments

Dale Adamson, president, dale.c.adamson@gmail.com, Surrey International Folk Dancing Society, Surrey, British Columbia

Amarouche Sid Ahmed, manager, ahmed.sid.amarouche@gmail.com, Algerian Folk Dance, Sidi Bel Abbes, Algeria

Monika Amar, marketing coordinator, Morikami Museum, www.morikami.org, Delray Beach, Florida

Curtis Andrews, codirector, Adanu Habobo, www.adanuhabobo.com, Vancouver, British Columbia

Jean Apollon, artistic director, http://jeanappolonexpressions.org, jaexpressions@gmail.com, Boston, Massachusetts

Glenn Bailey, director, Young Audiences of Houston, www.yahouston.org/#!leadership/cxqmHouston, Texas

Alessandra Belloni, founder, I Giullari di Piazza, artist in residence, Cathedral of St. John the Divine, www.alessandrabelloni.com, New York

Berta Jo Bolick, dance instructor, Louis Nunnery School of Ballet, bjobolick@AOO.com, www.louisnunneryschoolofballet.com, Hickory, North Carolina

Cathy Bono, operations assistant, Museum of Fine Arts, www.mfah.org, Boston, Massachusetts

Millie Broussard, production manager, www.jefferybroussard.com, creolecowboys@gmail.com, Lawtell, Louisiana

Nancy Carlin, administrator, Lute Society of America, nancy@nancycarlinassociates.com, www.nancycarlinassociates.com, Concord, California

Manel Carrera, photographer, manel@festes.org, Museu de la Patum de Berga, Berga, Catalonia

Corey Chan, cchan@icnc.com, Kei Lun Martial Arts, www.keilun.com, San Francisco

Chien-Mei, dancer, info@gundkwok.org, http://gundkwok.org/photos/, Boston, Massachusetts

Judith Cohen, webmaster, Ontario Folk Dance, www.ofda.ca/folkscene.html, Toronto, Ontario

Emma Gibbs De Oliveira, director, BrazilArte, info@brazilarte.org, www.brazilarte.org, Harlow, England

Rica Derosier, president, www.filamcultural.com/letters.htm, Fil-Am Cultural Association of North San Diego County, blimoge@filamcultural.com, Oceanside, California

Ghislaine Desmaris, artistic director, Amuséon, www.amuseon.fr, Picardie, France

Carolina Varga "Morocco" Dinicu, morocco@casbahdance.org, www.casbahdance
.org, New York City

Stan Dunn, manager, www.tempoparknews.org/2_BYU_flyer_2PG.pdf, Brigham
Young University International Folk Dance Ensemble, Salt Lake City, Utah.

Jale Nejdet Erzen, erzen@metu.edu.tr, Middle East Technical University, www.metu
.edu.tr, Ankara, Turkey

Margaret Evans, director, Kelly Irish Dancers, www.thekellyirishdancers.com, Chattaroy, Washington

Aurélie Giet, www.folkfestivalmarsinne.be, contact@aureliegiet.be, Folk Festival de
Marsinne, Belgium

Laurel Victoria Gray, artistic director, Silk Road Dance Company, silkroaddance@aol
.com, www.silkroaddance.com, Mt. Rainier, Maryland

Michael Greenwood, communications, www.rscds.org/article/media, Royal Scottish
Country Dance Society, Edinburgh, Scotland

Anne Marie Greymoon, www.wiccantogether.com/profile/AnneMarieGreymoon,
greymoon@wiccanfest.com, Ontario, Canada

Parul Gupta, artistic director, Infusion Dance, www.infusiondance.ca/parul-gupta,
Toronto, Canada

Leslie Herzberg, curator, Hancock Shaker Village, http://hancockshakervillage.org,
Pittsfield, Massachusetts

Victoria Hofmo, president, scandia36@optonline.net, Scandinavian East Coast Museum, Brooklyn, New York

Jonathan Hollander, artistic director, Dariel Sneed, and Richard Termine, jonathan@
batterydance.org, Battery Dance Company, New York, New York

Wakako Imamura and Priscilla Portsmouth, Japanese Tourism Organization, www
.ilovejapan.ca, Toronto, Ontario

Holly Ireland, photographer, info@hollyireland.com, www.hollyireland.com, Carlsbad, California

Niels Mejlhede Jensen, jensen@dadlnet.dk, www.mejlhede.dk, Virum, Denmark

Michael Kempf, engineer, Fraunhofer-Institut of Manufacturing and Engineering,
Stuttgart, Germany

Danny KilBride, director, Music Traditions Wales, www.trac-cymru.org/en, Cardiff,
Wales

David Knowlton, dcknowlton@gmail.com, Utah Valley University, www.uvu.edu,
Orem, Utah

Alex Kropog, president, and Juliano Petho Roberson, Hungarian Museum, akropog@
att.net, www.hungarianmuseum.com, Albany, Louisiana

Kun-Yang Lin, artistic director, Kun-Yang Lin/Dancers, www.kunyanglin.org, Philadelphia, Pennsylvania

Max Markusen, Media Cause, max@mediacause.org, http://mediacause.org/, San
Francisco, California

Maru Montero, founder, Maru Montero Dance Company, maru@marumontero.com,
Washington, D.C.

Charlotte Moraga, director, Chitresh Das Dance Company, charlotte@kathak.org, www.kathak.org, San Francisco, California

Christianne Odehnal, manager, Aché Brasil, http://achebrasil.ca/contactus/, info.ache brasil@gmail.com, Vancouver, British Columbia

Citra Satria Ongkowijoyo, Ksatria Lion & Dragon Dance Troupe, University of Melbourne, www.unimelb.edu.au, Melbourne, Australia

Trefor Owen, clogmaker, Gweithdy Clocsiau, treforowenclogmaker@gmail.com, www.treforowenclogmaker.co.uk, Gwynedd, Wales

Bette J. Premo, White Water Associates, bette.premo@white-water-associates.com, www.white-water-associates.com, Amasa, Michigan

Pedulla Narsing Rao, www.nrityanjaliuevents.com, Nrityanjali Academy, Telangana, India

Steve Rasmussen, high priest, oldenwilde@oldenwilde.org, http://oldenwilde.org/blog/, Asheville, North Carolina

Starr RavenHawk, founder,wordpress@www.wiccanfamilytemple.org, New York City Wiccan Family Temple, New York, New York

Sohini Ray, Manipuri Dance Vistions, www.manipuridancevisions.com, Los Angeles, California

Lucina Rodriguez, coordinator, lucina@loscenzontles.com, www.LosCenzontles.com, San Pablo, California

Silvia Salamanca, Ballam Studio, http://silviasalamanca.com/classes/, Houston, Texas

Keti Sharif, WAMED Festival & Dance Resources, www.ketisharif.com, Perth, Australia

Mikhail Smirnov, mikhail@barynya.com, www.barynya.com, Barynya Ensemble, New York

Keith Stanley, photographer, www.kestan.com/travel/dc/smithson/dance/asiadance, kesta1001@yahoo.com, Washington, D.C.

Jessica Stringfield, marketing, jessica.stringfield@cincyart.org, Cincinnati Art Museum, Cincinnati, Ohio

Roman Strom, president, International Youth Club, cossacks.rus@gmail.com, Krasnodar, Russia

Lulu Tepaeru-Ariki, Anuanua Dance Group, Cook Islands, www.anuanuadance.com, Auckland, New Zealand

Laurette S. Tuckerman, laurette.tuckerman@gmail.com, MINES ParisTech, www.pmmh.espci.fr/~laurette, Paris, France

Barbara Vijayakumar, barbaravijayakumar@yahoo.co.uk, Kala Chethena Kathakali Company, www.kathakali.net, Kerala, India

Helen Winkler, instructor, winklerh@hotmail.com, www.yiddishdance.com, Toronto, Ontario

Chloë Woolley, development officer, www.culturevannin.im/cms/profile_286124.html, Culture Vannin, chloe@culturevannin.im, Douglas, Isle of Man

Lera Yanysheva, dancer, svenko70@yandex.ru., http://english.svenko.net/svenko/bios/lera.htm, Moscow, Russia

Livija Zgurić, marketing, livija.zguric@lado.hr, www.lado.hr/en, National Folk Dance Ensemble of Croatia, Zagreb, Croatia

Special thanks to reference sources on dance from Pollak Library, California State University, Fullerton, California, and University of Georgia Library, Athens, Georgia.

I owe many thanks for the help of reference librarian Martin Otts and the publicity written by Joan Lail. I appreciate editor Stephen Ryan, who leaves me undisturbed while I research and write.

Introduction

Since humankind first gathered around a fireside, occasions for dance have conveyed the geometrics of community. Over millennia, evolving folk pageantry incorporated amateur dancers of varied ages in patterned steps, head and limb gestures, facial expressions, and acrobatic feats set to traditional music; drumming; or the recitation of narratives, prayers, and epigrams. Participants accented rhythms with shouts and imitative body language—from the gleeful, rejuvenating elements of the square dance at frontier North American weddings to the joined hands of Chinese female circle dancers in the Neolithic Yan-shao culture of 4000 BCE.

For social equilibrium, folk choreography conveyed approval of behavior and monitored individuals who strayed from the norm, the purpose of mystic Tibetan chant dance, Nepalese meditative stillness dance, and somber Canadian Cree dances. And as manifested by the Swiss *holderbeerli*, the Finnish *purpuri* (potpourri), and the all-male *shopska petorka* of Serbia and Bulgaria, group participation fostered consciousness, visceral pleasure, and expressions of vitality and belonging.

Around 400 BCE, Plato contended that children were not socialized until they could sing and dance, an educational ideal shared today by Venezuelans, Irish, and Hawaiians. The Spartan version of this was to integrate five-year-olds into a martial society by teaching them the belligerent stance and defensive posturing of the Pyrrhic dance, a preparation for war based on combat tactics. For the approval of the citizenry, accomplished performers practiced the dance in the agora, the public square. In seventeenth-century Europe, parents perpetuated Plato's idea by introducing children to the galliard, just as in Japan it was the *odori* dances, both sources of discipline, confidence, poise, and courtesy. Observing young soloists or performers of line and circle dance or dance drama constituted the source of tribal education and training, as with the clogging education for Irish children.

Traditional dances also enhance a love of history and facilitate an understanding of phenomena, the focus of the Polynesian hula. The most creative dances enact story and myth, honor monarchs and heroes, and dispel ghosts and evil spirits. The latter was the goal of Magyar death rites, Chinese lion dancers, the fright masks of Buddhist monks, and the capers of rustic communal sheep shearers each July in Devon, England. Dance sets retained memories of past sufferings, such as invasions depicted in stilt dances in Yucatán and the Italian re-creations of stoicism and triumph over sorrow during the Black Death. In the New World, the holiday relaxation of West African slaves in the juba commemorated the black diaspora, reclaiming identity with past clans and enriching lives marred by abduction and the flesh trade. Dancers healed the wounds of bondage through rigorous clapping and body slapping, processions, liberating whirls, seduction or courtship rituals, and audacious footwork, forerunner of tap dance.

Body language could express decorum, as in the polonaise or pavane step from Renaissance Venice, or the sweeping away of winter hardships, as in processions from one English village to another. Various symbolic positions—hands crossed, feet close together, head down, lips humming, eyes uplifted, back arched, breasts exposed, fingers splayed skyward—indicated to spectators the intent of chains, double circles, line dances, mazes, and promenades. For the *bharata natyam*, from 400 BCE, Hindu women in India wore jingly bangles and painted their fingertips with henna to draw attention to feminine stance and attitudes.

Folk institutions typically feature working and agrarian classes, such as the oral tradition of India at the core of Manipuri dance and the eighteenth-century frontier American barn dance to "Turkey in the Straw" and "The Arkansas Traveler." Everyday dance also mimicked occupational skills and ethnic identity, as seen in the English hornpipe on English vessels, the rowing and net casting of the coastal Africans of Madagascar and the Comoros Islands, the miner's chores of the Japanese *tanko bushi*, and the female strengths of the Hungarian czardas. During the feudal period, European guilds sponsored individual dances for fishers, coopers, meat marketers, tailors, bakers, copper- and silversmiths, and furriers. As a feature of economic fairs, union members performed dances that illustrated the physical exertions of the trade, as with the stirring of vats by dyers and the sawing of woodcutters, one of the figures of the German *Schuhplattler*. The steps and gestures passed to apprentices and journeymen the folk customs of master artisans.

Participation in folk dances purified emotions, reconciled soul with body, and communicated cultural values—the purpose of highland reels and Ponca fancy dance. Presentations affirmed maturity, wedlock, fertility, prosperity, work, combat, death, and worship, as performed at Athenian festivals to revere the cult of Athena, the Greek goddess of wisdom and war. By improving flexibility and balance, alternative healing, such as that practiced in Bali and among Comanche and Kiowa hoop dancers, relieved stiffness, clarified thoughts, and boosted bone and cardiovascular strength. Folkloric performance might also be body therapy, one purpose of Wiccan Maychant and the trance ceremonies of the Moroccan Blue People. Heritage dances—the Israeli hora, the Egyptian oath dance of 1700 BCE, and the Navajo corn festival—tend to stress muscle memory, traditional figures, and gestures that ally hands with feet. Social stimulus added the bonus of friendships among performers, especially partners, such as the gavotte duos in Canadian Maritimes and paired zydeco dancers of Texas and Louisiana. The most transformative dance interpreted spirituality, often conducting individuals into altered states to glimpse a god, cosmic truth, or the afterlife—for example, whirling Sufi dance in Iran and Santeria rituals in Brazil and Haiti.

Performances of some dances may render physical evidence of beliefs relevant to the clan or tribe, as with the bear dance of the North American Mandan and Lord Rhys ap Gruffydd's Welsh *eisteddfod* (arts session). In some settings, only a privileged sect or caste may participate, a stricture of the Montagnais scalp dance and the *kathak* of north and east India. Whoever does the dance, the individual performance seldom alters the basics—energy, steps, national costume and headdress, instrumental music, and joy or reverence. For example, the rhythmic leaps sanctioned by sub-Saharan Yoruba; the curative gestures of pubescent Apache girls at the San Carlos Reservation of Arizona; and the thigh-high boots, embroidered cummerbunds, vests, and head wraps of male Macedonian *tanec* dancers of Skopje all conform to tradition.

Rhythms and energy level vary depending on the topography and lifestyle, a distinguishing factor in Scandinavia, for example, with variations in performance of the *halling* in Norway and Sweden and the galliard in Denmark. Danish moderation stresses partnering and gentle group activities that invite spectators to join, as with the recitation of rhymes for the *songleik*. In their more frigid clime, however, Swedes inject greater fervor and vigor into large-group dance, such as the maypole ritual, usually to stringed instruments. Likewise, the rugged terrain of Norway influences male athleticism, such as the whirling of partners into the streets for the *polska*.

Africans present unique views of work styles. In Uganda and Burundi, the *igishakamba* ignited herders' voices and bodies in elation to entertain their cows. For the Bakiga of Rwanda, morning warm-up consists of dance that precedes farming in the high country. In Zimbabwe, a tree-planting ritual each December 3 commits farm families to reforestation. Sudanese rain dance propitiates deities to provide nourishment for children.

Unlike professional choreography, folk dance welcomes all to join in, as in the Azerbaijani *kochari*, a comic emulation of head-butting goats. Today one can thrill to the fused Afro-Hispanic heritage of Filipino *jota forlana* and the passion of tango in the harbor districts of Argentina. Drumming, clapping, or percussive rhythms on gongs, bamboo sticks, and cymbals set the speed and cadence and mediate responses of both participants and onlookers on the island of Guadeloupe as well as the Samoan ceremonial dance procession on Tonga. On the Kenya–Uganda border, dances and parades welcome spectators to the all-important circumcision of teen boys. The costumes and adornments also retain elements of the past—the clinking coin belts and bracelets of Peloponnesian dancers, the native jacket and cropped pants of Siamese *khon* mimes, the slap of the dried calabash on the hand in the Central African Republic, and the Inuit dance caps from ermine and caribou pelts and yellow loon bills. Through food, ritual, camaraderie, and melody, outsiders today can still intuit the rhythms, quirks, vigor, and joy of folk life.

Chronology

5000 BCE	Chinese shamans choreograph warrior healing in Sichuan and Shaangzi along the Yangtze River.
4000 BCE	In the Neolithic Yan-shao culture, Chinese females join hands for a circle dance.
3400 BCE	As carved on rocks by proto-Egyptians, circle dance involves humans in the first group activity.
3000 BCE	In the Indus Valley civilization, midwifery protocols prepare parturient women for labor and delivery with sessions of belly rolls.
3000 BCE	Caucasian Kurds, who derive from the Zogros highlands, retain Assyrian and Armenian elements in their kinetic arts.
3000 BCE	Dating to the Neolithic Age, the *Schuhplattler* preserves Europe's oldest surviving choreography.
2500 BCE	Egyptian warriors perform the *tahtib* (stick fight), a sword dance emulating warfare.
2000 BCE	From Canaanite or Phoenician culture, Palestinian and Levantine villagers stamp and kick their joy in the *dabke* line dance.
1600 BCE	As early the Shang Dynasty, the Chinese dragon dance ritual propitiates the gods on behalf of the farmer.
1570 BCE	The Egyptian *bedleh* (belly dance costume) acquires tinkling jewelry and sheer scarves and veils.
1446 BCE	The exodus of Hebrew slaves from bondage impacts Hebrew dance with praise to Yahweh for a safe flight of the Israelites from pharaoh.
1400 BCE	Pottery and murals reflect the twisting, twining patterns of chain dance in Crete and Ionia.
1200 BCE	An organizing place for May Day or midsummer celebrations, the maypole dates to Germanic tribal ritual.
1200 BCE	The Celtic jig and step dance, circle sets, and sword rituals develop in Ireland from the influence of Druids and immigrant peoples.
1000 BCE	Egyptians become the first folk dance specialists.
1000 BCE	Siberia's totemic dances along the Bering Strait engage aboriginal Khanty and Mansi in propitiation of the sacred brown bear.
800s BCE	The farandole follows the style of ancient Greek crane dance, which Phoenicians carry to Marseilles.

800 BCE	The Lapita, the aboriginal settlers of the central Pacific, introduce Samoans to the *siva* Samoa, a couples dance to a gentle rhythm.
800 BCE	Etruscan funereal dance influences a bas-relief on tombs as proof that the deceased can expect a joyous reception in the afterlife.
776 BCE	Before the Pan-Hellenic Games, Greek athletes synchronize steps to the lighting of the Olympic torch at the shrine of Zeus in Olympia.
768 BCE	Etruscan reapers play pranks and organize dance skits anticipating the commedia dell'arte.
March 1, 714 BCE	Under the rule of the Roman king Numa Pompilius, the *salii* (leapers) present a cultic martial dance derived from the Etruscans and Albans who preceded Rome's founding.
589 BCE	The deportation of 4,600 Hebrews from Judah to Babylon inspires a scriptural lamentation dance.
578 BCE	Preceding state-sponsored games in the Circus Maximus, the Roman *pompa circensis* (circus parade) included a dance company performing to the lyre and pipers along the Sacred Way from the Capitolium to the forum.
500 BCE	Cave paintings attest to claims that the Norwegian *halling* is northern Europe's oldest folk dance.
480 BCE	The playwright Sophocles celebrates the Greek victory at Salamis by dancing.
423 BCE	Greek comedy writers arouse audiences with the *cordax*, a racy, ribald masked dance that Aristophanes incorporates into *The Clouds*.
400 BCE	Plato, the Greek philosopher, contends that children are not socialized until they can sing and dance.
400 BCE	Hindu women in India wear jingly bangles and paint their fingertips with henna to draw attention to complex dance gestures.
400 BCE	Hindi storytellers present myths or epics with voice and *kathak* dance.
275 BCE	Pantomime specialists introduce dance drama to the Roman Republic.
April 27, 263 BCE	The Roman observance of Floralia contrasts martial dance with garlanded performers venerating nature.
206 BCE	Chinese performers dance their thanks for ample food from trapping, hunting, and harvesting berries and nuts.
186 BCE	Under Cato the Censor, the Roman Senate bans foreign dances that he considers immoral.
180 BCE	At harvest dances at Nazca, Peruvian reapers wield hoes and sheaves while executing steps.
50 BCE	Julius Caesar, the remodeler of the Circus Maximus, introduces the Pyrrhic dance to Rome.
154 CE	An indigenous folk art form from northeastern India and the Burmese border, the Manipuri dance incorporates percussion with the double-headed drum and cymbals.

300	Marquesas dancers serve as arts ambassadors when the elegant *siva* Samoa spreads north to Hawaii to introduce a late night torchlight procession.
465	In southern Normandy, the Council of Vannes prohibits dance because it ennobles the flesh.
500	The Slavs of southeastern Europe originate dominant folk dance patterns.
600	Rudimentary folk dance permeates worshipful processions when Spanish archbishops make grand entrances to Tarragona.
657	Japanese peasants adopt a dance ritual from India welcoming the dead.
917	At the monastery of St. Gallen, Switzerland, Magyar insurgents combine a war dance with wrestling while grasping weapons in their hands.
1000	In a comic circle dance, the Armenian, Assyrian, Kurdish, Pontine, Greek-Georgian, Macedonian, and Azerbaijani *kochari* (or *kotsari*) mime the bounding, squatting, and butting of heads like goats.
1014	The Gaelic *cèilidh* (house party) takes shape in peaceful times after the Viking raids end.
1023	The foundations of the *Ländler* retain the charm of the *Schuhplattler*, a medieval Tyrolean round dance imitating the courtship of the black grouse.
1100s	The Polynesian *me'etu'upaki*, a mimicry of paddling a canoe, originates on Uvea island. The Kurdish *sexhani*, a face-to-back line dance, dates to a Yezidi saint, Sheik Adi (or Hadi) ibn Musafir of Iraq. In the Balkans, the migration of the Roma northwest from Turkey adds handkerchief waving to ring figures.
1150	A full cast of characters performs the traditional *hahoe byeolsingut* healing drama in Andong, South Korea, where dancers restore psychological wholeness.
1176	In Wales, Lord Rhys ap Gruffydd holds the first *eisteddfod* (arts session), which regularly features cloggers.
1194	The Christian *bergerette* labyrinthine dance parallels the traversing of life, a forty-foot pattern incorporated into the floor of Chartres Cathedral.
1200	For the Kainai and Siksika of southern Alberta, the tobacco dance sustains agrarian communities.
December 17, 1273	After the death of first darawish Rumi in Konya, Turkey, his Sufi disciples introduce a whirling trance dance.
August 26, 1278	At Vienna, King Ladislaus IV honors the combat death of Czech king Ottokar II of Bohemia with a whole day of dance.
1300	An English-Welsh specialty, late medieval morris dancers claim rural exotica and seasonal spectacle as ethnic expressions of unity and belonging.

1368	First executed to mincing steps and frozen facial expressions, the parasol dance gains favor during the reign of Japan's emperor Ashikaya Shogun.
Fall 1374	A psychosomatic frenzy moves geographically to Cologne, Trier, Ghent, Metz, and Flanders, causing European priests to ban all church and public dances.
1392	A form of story dance, the Korean fan dance derives meaning and direction from shamanic ritual.
1404	The tossing of a partner high above the floor and exposure of female legs outrages moralists at Ulm, where authorities ban the *Ländler*.
October 1415	A fall gala in Italy begins with issuance of six hundred invitations to women to even out pairing with men for the entrance saltarello.
1447	The *cachucha* reaches Barcelona and Zaragoza with the nomadic Roma and thrives at Cádiz and Jerez. The bolero derives from a loose fusion of body language, figures, and gestures introduced by the Andalusian Roma.
1448	An Anglo-Welsh specialty, the morris dance derives from the *morisca*, an ancient Moroccan fool's frolic around agrarian boundaries from farm to farm.
1454	The provincial *tirabol* begins in Berga, Catalonia, as the conclusion to Corpus Christi Day processions known as the Patum.
1501	Catherine of Aragon, the future wife of Henry VIII, reputedly introduces a restrained pavane to the English.
1508	Lute composer Joan Ambrosia Dalza collects variations on five pavanes that champion the divine right of kings.
1509	From the reign of Henry VIII, the sailor's hornpipe serves as exercise and amusement on British ships and a competitive display of agility.
1540	At the reception that Francis I arranges to welcome Holy Roman Emperor Charles V, a column of couples performs an allemande.
1546	In France, innovators fuse the Italian saltarello with the galliard.
1550	A slave import to the West Indies from tribes along the Congo River, the *calenda* influences colonial Dutch, French, and English folk dance.
1560	The reformed church proscribes street dances and drinking at the Scots Hogmanay (New Year's Eve), a nationwide *cèilidh*.
1570	For the Iroquois Confederacy of Albany, New York, an elaborate calumet dance reflects native respect for peace.
1580	At Augsburg, German dancers indulge in hug dancing, an innovation in partnering that predates the waltz and *polska*.
1586	In the Awa province, the *awa odori* dance of the dead involves Japanese citizens at the opening of Lord Hachisuka Iemasa's feudal castle.
1600	In Argentina, dancers and drummers evolve the *malambo*, a step dance mimicking gaucho postures and folkways.
1601	Louis XIII schedules the French "*gaillarde*" for his courtiers.

1603	Japanese *odori* evolves from a thirteenth-century all-night community dance venerating ancestral spirits.
1609	At Istria, influences from the Venetian state contribute the European *furlana* to a textured Balkan mix of steps and rhythms.
1631	Playwright Lope de Vega complains that the allemande, *branle*, and galliard disappear from Spain.
1635	Because of a ban on female dancing in Japan, male actors perform a transvestite version of the parasol dance.
January 21, 1648	In token of a Ukrainian victory over the Lithuanians and Poles, hero Bohdan Khmelnytsky grasps his saber and leaps onto a banquet table to perform the *hopak* for appreciative patriots.
1650	British children form a ring and frolic to an appropriate tune, "Oats, Peas, Beans, and Barley Grow," a reflection of their rural musical heritage.
1679	A national couples dance of Poland, the *oberek* introduces frenzied spinning among the peasants of Mazowsze.
1680	In imitation of the sun, the Pawnee calumet dance diffuses smoke in the four cardinal directions.
1682	Tsar Peter the Great forces Russians to abandon dancing to traditional balalaika and zither.
1685	A Vatican censure of dance at Iberian cathedrals generates an uproar and supplication to Pope Innocent XI, who lifts the ban for Corpus Christi Day in Seville.
May 26, 1687	Charlestown dancers return the Massachusetts Bay maypole as an emblem of anti-Puritanical revolt.
1692	Dutch explorer and shipbuilder Nicolaas Witsen summarizes the all-night shamanic dances in northern Siberia and Mongolia.
1700	According to baroque arts theorist Santiago de Murcia of Madrid, the *rigaudon* advances from a peasant figure to a courtly art.
1715	The Hungarian czardas begins as a military recruiting and drinking song in the Hapsburg Empire.
1742	At Yare, Venezuela, African slave groups join white Christians in adoring San Francisco on Corpus Christi Day.
1752	The Spanish Inquisition and the colonial viceroyalty from Spain ban the Mexican *jarabe tapatío* because of gestures suggesting sexual intimacy.
1769	On the bark HMS *Endeavour*, Captain James Cook sanctions the hornpipe as a means of keeping sailors well and free of contagion.
1770	The Seneca, led by War Chief Ganon, perform a pipe dance to sanction peace with the Cherokee.
1782	Siamese court mime involves armed warriors in the Khon masked dance drama from the Ramakien, the Thai version of the Indian epic Ramayana.
1783	In Philadelphia, John Durang introduces the sailor's hornpipe to the United States at the Southwark Theatre in Philadelphia, where he performs in burned cork blackface and clogs.

March 18, 1785	Because of female fainting from disorientation or vertigo, Bohemian authorities ban the *Ländler*, a popular spinning dance.
1789	An instructor introduces Irish step dance in Philadelphia.
1790	Male-female couples perform the *jarabe tapatío* in Mexico City.
1797	A gallant Polish dance provides homeless Poles with a national anthem, "The Dabrowski Mazurka."
1819	London Missionary Society evangelists in Tahiti ban tattooing of flesh and sexually suggestive mating dance. Itinerant dance masters teach clogging and the hornpipe to Scots children in Edinburgh.
1820	At Congo Square in New Orleans, Sunday evening and holiday relaxation brings blacks from Gambia, Senegal, and Congo into a unique frenzy of the yelping, athletic *bamboula*.
1822	The standard fado dates to Lisbon and Coimbra after patriots return home from Brazil following the upheaval of the Napoleonic Wars.
1840	Gallo-Danish soloist August Bournonville fosters eclecticism in Danish ballet by incorporating into *The Toreador* (1840) the zapateado, a Spanish folk dance.
1844	The merengue enters folk history in the wake of the *tumba*, an African beat from Aruba and Curaçao.
1843	At Congo Square in New Orleans, urban whites suppress the frenzied dancing of the *bamboula* and juba.
1849	French colonizers restore the hip-quivering *'upa'upa* in Tahiti.
1850	One spontaneous martial dance, the *cibi* of Bau Island, erupts during a triumphant return home of Fijian warriors. Eskimo villagers of Point Barrow, Alaska, support three dance houses.
February 13, 1850	At Vidauban, France, Jacobins of the Second Republic defy a ban on public dance on Ash Wednesday to dance an infernal farandole that sets a precedent of annual carnival mockery of the pompous.
1855	For the Omaha, harvest dances cease during the Sioux Wars, when farming takes second place to combat.
1864	When clogging develops from folk dance into theatrical fare, four-year-old Dan Leno stages a clogging exhibition in Coventry at the Britannia Music Hall.
1874	Under mythographer-king David Kalakaua, Hawaiian hula returns from hidden retreats to urban display as a respected folk art.
October 1890	Some eight hundred Paiute ghost dancers force themselves into a trance state and summon help from the spirit world.
1895	Cakewalk dancing initiates commercialization of New Orleans jazz.
1896	Shona warriors of Zimbabwe express nationalism and diversionary strategies with the *jerusarema*, a defiance of colonialism.
1896	Exotic dancing generates the first case of cinema censorship, which halts viewings of *Fatima's Dance* on the shores of Atlantic City, New Jersey.

January 16, 1914	A formal censure from the antimodernist pope Pius X declares the tango damaging to the soul.
1916	Bering Sea islanders, Hooper Bay Yupik, and Siberian Inuit observe bladder feasts each January and March by revering slain seals, whales, and walruses with a return to the sea of animal bladders.
1920	At the end of World War I, Kemal Ataturk, founder of modern Turkey, tries to introduce European couples dancing to replace folk arts.
1920s	To preserve the country mode, automaker Henry Ford and his wife, Clara, open a teaching studio in Dearborn, Michigan.
1925	Turkish law bans Sufi whirling in the *sema* trance dance.
1928	American radio popularizes the first zydeco records, a defiance of a ban on Creole French in Louisiana schools. Ponca shawl dancers at White Eagle, Oklahoma, hop, flutter, twirl, and soar with light steps, stretching their arms gracefully to display color and fringe.
1937	The choreography of the *mayim mayim* by Else I. Dublon dates to 1937 after searchers locate water in the Israeli desert.
1942	During the absence of male Lakota from South Dakota during World War II, the first female fancy dancers and butterfly dancers add dramatic shawl sweeps that stir deep fringe.
July 14–15, 1944	Because of a festival performance at Dalia, the dynamic grapevine (or *mayim*) pattern advances from troupes at Israeli kibbutzim throughout the Jordan Valley.
1945	Louisiana zydeco dancers reclaim folk dancing to the rhythm of corrugated tin scraped with spoons and bottle openers.
1946	In San Francisco in 1946, Samoan folk dancer Freddie Letuli emulates a Hindu fire spectacle by pouring gasoline on flaming machetes.
1948	Venezuela's *música llanera* takes on patriotic symbolism for its aggressive beat and lures upper-class men into a predominantly peasant pastime.
1950s	Ewe maidens in southern Togo demand their rights by drumming and performing the previously all-male *takada*.
1954	The Sioux create a new pipe dance to support native soldiers fighting in the Korean War.
1956	The first Tahitian troupe revives heritage dance as the *tamure*, which appeals to amateur performers and tourists.
1960	Islamic-communist dictator Ahmed Sèkou Toutré ousts traditional Baga religious dance from Guinea. A *joropo* competition in Villavicencio, Colombia, discloses intricate variations by the best couples.
1965	Cook Island school systems and youth clubs nurture folk dance through competitions and professional troupes.
July 19, 1980	At the opening festivities of the Moscow Summer Olympics, the charged mood of the *hopak* creates an authentic atmosphere.

1984	The Baga of Guinea reinstitute their annual tribute dance.
1998	The Ivory Coast government bans the *mapouka*, a lascivious bending of the female waist and presentation of the posterior in side-to-side motions.
2000	The appeal of plump female buttocks distracts young Ivory Coast girls from the American craze for thinness.
March 9, 2003	In South Dakota, the Lakota close the sun dance to outsiders.
July 2006	At Acre, 2,743 Israeli Arabs set a record for joining in the longest human dance line for the *dabke*.
November 14, 2008	A Muslim militia invades a folkloric Somali dance, arrests thirty-two participants for intermingling male and female dancers, and flogs them in front of hundreds of observers.
February 2015	As visual propaganda, Kurdish fighters victorious over ISIS dance in uniform in the north Syrian streets of Kobanî.
December 2, 2015	At Bursa, Turkey, presentation of the *kılıç-kalkan* (sword-shield) dance from the fourteenth century emphasizes valor, brotherhood, and peace.
December 9, 2015	At Kerala, India, *kappoli* folk dancers compete at traditional choreography.
May 20, 2016	At a Russian summit at Sochi, a member of the foreign ministry performs the kalinka.

· 𝒜 ·

ACROBATIC DANCE

The merger of gymnastics with dance enhances the dynamics of folk artistry, such as the tumbling and rope dancing of the nomadic Nats of Northwestern India, the athletic *calus* in the Balkan states, and the gracefully balletic *aurresku* in Barcelona. The degree of physical challenge varies in global settings, for example, the double twisting and turning of the Polish *oberek*, the mad whirl of the torch-waving exorcist in the Sri Lankan devil dance, and the sorcery and curative antics of the medicine man in the Eskimo dance house. Acrobatic dynamics mark the *kazhai koothu* of Aryan performers at a Tamil Nadu circus in southeastern India; the thrumming oberek couples dance of central Poland; the Chinese lion dance; and, in Norway, the bounding and hand-to-foot lifts of the *frikar* and the kicking of a hat from a pole in the *halling*. The motivation of athletic folk dance varies by country, enhancing troop and martial arts training, village festivals and receptions, shamanic healing and spiritual trance, recreation, and novelty competitions—the purpose of the turns, springs, and leg circling of the androcentric Russian *plyaska*.

In west Sumatra among the Minangkabau of the Sri Vijayan Empire after 682 CE, dancers combined balancing skills with choreography for the *tari piring* (plate dance) in reverence of the rice goddess. Whether at harvests or for nuptials, young males formed two rings and performed swinging rolls, stamps, and crouches while holding saucers in their outstretched palms. Concentration on lighted candles in the saucers caused performers to lapse into a trance state. To accentuate the finale and rid themselves of negative emotions, they smashed the crockery on the floor and danced barefoot over the jagged edges.

Martial Gymnastics

The Renaissance reclaimed from the ancient Mediterranean world the value of exercise, grace, courtesy, and dance discipline to a complete education. The concept found takers in Germany, Denmark, and Sweden. In 1454, Catalonian troupes at Berga north of Barcelona pledged to complete the Patum, a five-day Corpus Christi procession that ended with the exhibitionist *tirabol*. The yearly masquerade required a community troupe to perform clockwise steps and bounds in 6/8 meter. As part of their devotional war on evil and political suppression, presenters cracked whips to the repeated thump of a single drummer.

Catalonian dancers lighted the Patum parade from the parish church to city hall with torches, a burden that added a shadowy drama to their choreography. Contributing to the level of difficulty, the balancing of allegorical and comic papier-mâché costumes—eagles, crusading knights, royalty, mule-dragons, dwarves, hobbyhorses, Saracen giants, David and Goliath on stilts, horned demons—preserved folk art and group steps that remained in use over centuries.

As solemn as the Catalonian Patum, the running prances, jumps, trots, and kicks of the Turkish and Romanian calus preserve a seventeenth-century martial display. The synchronized show of masculinity united members of a secret brotherhood. A lifetime membership required an initiation to learn the choreography. Costumed in beribboned hats, white tunics, loose pants, and ankle bells, they assembled each Easter for cavorting to fiddles and flutes.

Daring calus dancers specialized in a difficult gymnastic stunt—holding a shoulder-width stick in both hands while leaping over it. By swinging clubs and swords and waving battle flags depicting loyalties and solidarity, they honored a code of conduct similar to that of medieval European knights. Variants of the calus spread over the Carpathian Mountains to Transylvania.

In Luxor, Egypt, in 1978, soloist Osman Balata performs the *raqs baladi*, a stationary belly dance featuring hip undulations to sounds of the horsehair *rebaba* while Osman balances thirteen chairs in his teeth. The black sash draws attention to the rhythm provided by four accompanists. *Carolina Varga "Morocco" Dinicu, morocco@casbahdance.org, New York City.*

Innovative Acrobatics

Across ancient Mesoamerica, the *danza de los voladores* (dance of the flyers) propitiated sky gods to relieve drought. In a performance at the 2009 international summer festival in Washington, D.C., male performers recruited by the Smithsonian Institution climbed a pole and tethered themselves by the feet to a rope twisted around a platform at top. While playing the flute, each man fell backward at a precise moment and whirled within seconds to the ground, a stunning display of courage and control.

North African virtuoso dance currently thrives in Libya and Tunisia, where gymnastic contortions and foot slides to flute and bagpipe amaze spectators. Mauritanian folk rhythms require the twirling of grand embroidered robes that add weight to the dancers' movements. While women clap and ululate, male performers coordinate leaps and leg swings to cymbal, drum, and flute accompaniment. A martial version adds a wood rifle to the display.

See also Balkan dance; *bamboula*; barn dance; commedia dell'arte; disguise; exorcism; fancy dance; *halling*; highland fling; holiday dance; hoop dance; *hopak*; line dance; lion dance; North African dance; *oberek*; *polska*; *Schuhplattler*; sword dance; tango; *tirabol*.

Sources: Craine, Debra, and Judith Mackrell. *The Oxford Dictionary of Dance.* Oxford, UK: Oxford University Press, 2010. Dills, Ann, and Ann Cooper Albright. *Moving History/Dancing Cultures: A Dance History Reader.* Middletown, CT: Wesleyan University Press, 2001.

AFRICAN DANCE

See North African Dance; Sub-Saharan Dance.

ALLEMANDE

A ceremonious procession of pairs, the allemande (also *allewander*, *almand*, or *Deutscher Tanz*) developed in Renaissance South Germany in the 1500s as a mark of social refinement. A post-Reformation advance in tempo and pleasure, the allemande drew its moderate meter and steps from a medieval dance of knights in armor, but left little history of time or place. At its first mention at the 1540 reception that Francis I of France held to honor Charles V, the Holy Roman emperor, a column of couples repeated forward and backward the step-step-step-lift to a 4/4 beat. In synchrony, they thrust their joined hands out from the waist and trod the length of the dance floor. French touches to the figures helped to defeat stereotypes of Germanic culture as lumpish, awkward, and incapable of delicacy.

As a segment of the early seventeenth-century suite, the low-energy, four-part figure was the only dance of the period in which partners held each other's two hands. Named for the French adjective for "German," the dance spread over Europe, yield-

A moderate, ceremonious procession of pairs, the allemande (also *allewander, almand,* or *Deutscher Tanz*) developed in Renaissance South Germany in the 1500s as a mark of aristocratic refinement. *Vuillier, Gaston.* A History of Dancing from the Earliest Ages to Our Own Times. *New York: D. Appleton and Company, 1898, 435.*

ing the *almande* in France in 1546, the *almain* in England in 1550, *almande de Ungrie* in Hungary in 1550, and the *balletto Tedesco* in Italy in 1561. In 1590, musicians adapted the basic choreography to lute melodies performed to plucked strings.

In the mode of the *branle* and other *basse danses,* the measured footwork preceded the sarabande and gigue and anticipated the polonaise, a more balletic processional of step-step-plié and thrust that marked company entrances in stage ballets. For changing partners, the line of parallel dancers advanced only on the right, leaving the left-hand dancer to pair with someone new. A more serious version enacted respect for a deceased dignitary with figures set to a *tombeau* (memorial) melody, a respectful gesture emulating an orderly society.

Adapting the Allemande

For Elizabeth I, the allemande marked a noble evening presented at Kenilworth in 1575 by her court favorite, Robert Dudley, the Earl of Leicester. As the allemande gained stylized touches in the Rhineland, Alsace-Lorraine, Switzerland, Austria, France, Holland, Spain, and England, the innovations amused the courts of Louis XIV, Napoleon, Catherine de' Medici, and Holy Roman Emperor Ferdinand I and Anne of Bohemia and Hungary. For its courtesies and amusing rotations, the original dance received notice in French arts writer Thoinot Arbeau's manual *Orchésographie* (1589) along with commentary on a unique variation, the *branle du chandelier*, in which men performed while holding burning candles.

In the baroque era, the allemande evolved into a livelier sequence at an oblique angle of skip-skip-skip-hop in 2/4 meter, but it waned among French folk dancers by 1636. After the Thirty Years War suppressed folk dance until 1650, the allemande, along with the pavane, minuet, and contradance, replaced the more demonstrative galliard as both folk dance and social art. More complex counterpoint motifs in 4/4 required entwined arms, glissades, and chain and line dancing.

Allemande composers Dieterich Buxtehude, Johann Sebastian Bach, and John Dowland provided musical accompaniment for flute, virginal, and other keyboard instruments. In southwestern Germany, Swabians added the jingle of the tambourine. The rise of the Hanoverian Dynasty in England with the coronation of George I in October 1714 increased references to the allemande at social and court occasions. The mid-eighteenth-century addition of a pirouette allowed each gentleman to add savoir faire to his role by passing the lady under his arm. With introduction of the cotillion in 1750, the allemande joined chains and promenades as parts of called figures, all presaging the quadrille.

New Steps to the Music

For suites, instrumentalists paired the allemande with the courante, a sequence of runs and jumps such as those arranged by Clemens August of Bavaria, the elector of Cologne, in 1759 and for Parisian cotillions and English country dances in 1760. In 1773, commentary on a joined right- and left-hand turn described a bridge motif showcasing harmony and balance, a winsome forerunner of the waltz. By 1808, bridge choreography morphed into a dos-à-dos (back-to-back) sequence. The turns remained popular and received notice in the handbook *The Modern Dancing Master* (1822) by the inventive London instructor G. M. S. Chivers.

Into the nineteenth century in Slovenia, Austria, and Bohemia, a stylized allemande competed at open-air community socials with French and English quadrilles, romps, and the *Ländler* (or *chassé*), a gliding, skipping, and rotating dance mimicking male-female romantic pursuit. For the rising middle class in the regency era, social novelist Jane Austen admired the allemande for the elegant figure in which partners reached over each other's heads. In the North American colonies, the allemande influenced weaving motifs around an axis in square dancing and contradance, a sequence performed by face-to-face partners.

See also cèilidh; contradance; cotillion; *Ländler*; polonaise; quadrille; square dance; waltz.

Source: Thorp, Jennifer. "Pecour's L'Allemande, 1702–1765: How 'German' Was It?" *Eighteenth Century Music* 1, no. 102 (September 2004): 183–204.

ANDEAN DANCE

South Americans demonstrated refinement and enthusiasm for music from the pre-Columbian era dating to 15,000 BCE. Around 180 BCE at harvest galas at Nazca, reapers wielded hoes and sheaves while executing steps. Another example, the Peruvian *huayño*, demonstrated heterosexual standards of meeting and wooing by imitating the grand airs of the Paso Fino stallion with choreography in 2/4 meter. As an honorarium to nature gods, masked Inca troupes imitated the beauty and power of sea terns and the frolic of alpaca with movable false faces, wings, and legs. At Ecuador, frolicking herdsmen's dances to flute and strings displayed the hardihood of high-country stockmen.

After the arrival of Spanish conquistadors under Francisco Pizarro to Cuzco in the Inca Empire on November 15, 1533, colonialism threatened the survival of heritage arts in the distant mountains. Under the influence of Catholic missionaries at Q'ero, highlanders dramatized Andean and Christian legend in costumed dance drama. Looking to their colonial future, the women of Margarita Island, Venezuela, imitated the femininity of Spanish women in discreet flourishes of long skirts and genteel steps.

At Cuzco, masking disguised performers of *taqui* (song and dance) and dance drama, shielding them from reprisals for satirizing their European overlords and instigating revolt. After 1542, Afro-Hispano-Indians merged the region's three artistic strands in the *zamacueca*, a Creole kick dance marked by sub-Saharan hip sways and Caribbean meter. To censor torrid couples dance, Catholic hierarchy prohibited the huayño in 1583 by ending female participation in sensual public display.

Historic Choreography

Priests promoted syncretic religio-historic dances that retained traditional feathered headpieces and woven tunics as elements of performances on Corpus Christi Day. In jungle accoutrements, local converts performed the trial and crucifixion of Jesus and the Iberian reconquest of Christian Spain from the Moors from 711 to 1492. Discreet huayño choreography at Málaga to hymns honoring the Virgin of Carmen, the protector of mariners, and hero dancing to the song "Ollanta" perpetuated an undercurrent of discontent while rescuing from Spanish suppressors the strength and loyalty of Andean warriors.

The combination of dress and theme calmed rebellious spirits of Andean mestizos still outraged by the slaughter of their last emperor, Atahualpa, whom Francisco Pizarro's occupation troops had executed by strangulation on July 26, 1533. Despite the censorship of colonial insurgents, Quechua-speaking Peruvians retained their history in the Carnaval pageantry, which acknowledged a Creole heritage. The focus was the whip-cracking *rucus* (guards) and a spray of fake blood in the *muerte de Atahualpa* (death of Atahualpa), a dance drama in the plaza at Cuzco that promoted pride and ethnic identity with Incan resisters.

For the native press gangs at silver mines in Bolivia and Peru, religious brotherhoods arranged spiritual dances to songs of lamentation. At shamanistic rituals in Arequipa, *curanderos* (healers) uplifted and solaced bondsmen through the Afro-Peruvian *alcatraz* (fire dance). For miners who lived short, anguished lives, choreography and mime became outlets for powerlessness and despair.

Mixed Arts

Folk dance marked the cultural individuality of diasporic peoples. At Lima in 1714, Gallo-Scots explorer Amédée François Frézier outlined the unusual physicality of the zapateado. A brisk competitive footwork in clogs, the repetitious hops and stamps stressed heel strikes in contrast to stooped torso and unmoving shoulders and arms. At Cuzco at the end of the twentieth century, the dance differentiated native and Creole technique, with mestizos lifting the chest and swaying to the beat.

For tourists, Quechua couples perform to the seventeen-note panpipes, flute, and frame drum the rocking, side-to-side steps of the *suri siquris*, a couples dance dating to 800 BCE. While women lift the right and left edges of multicolor skirts, males display caps and neck pieces formed of alpaca yarn pompoms while they skip and stamp. Varied ethnic dances—Colombian and Venezuelan *joropo*, Bolivian *diablada* (devil dance), Ecuadorian *tonadas*, the competitive *danza de las tijiras* (scissors dance) of the Peruvian Quechua, and the graceful, romantic *marinera norteña*, the national dance of Peru—characterize the waves of immigration and conquest that determined the region's history. Each March, a more blatant defiance of colonialism at Tarabuco, Bolivia, the Quechua *pujilay* (play dance), a UNESCO World Heritage art, revisits an 1816 skirmish that defeated the Spaniards. Dancers in animal masks and false faces representing evil mock the Spanish exploiters who tried to despoil the silver mines.

See also huayño; *joropo*; *matachines*; parasol dance; technique; zapateado.

Source: Higgins, James. *Lima: A Cultural History*. New York: Oxford University Press, 2005.

ANIMAL DANCES

An evocative re-creation of bestial stance and instinctual behavior, mimicry of animals recognizes peasant connections with nature. Examples include the courtship of doves in the Mexican *jarabe tapatío*, the llama-herding antics of Aymara dancers in Bolivia, and the avian hand flaps of Ecuadorian soloists in the Amazonian jungle. Bestial representation requires folk dancers to deck themselves in animal remains, puppet heads, hoops, and four-legged regalia, as with the bull either slain or castrated by *matachines* dancers across Mesoamerica, Amerindian hoop dance, and the Catalonian eagle dancer and hobbyhorses of the crusaders masquerading as fighters of the Moors at Barcelona for the annual Corpus Christi festival.

Into prehistory, dancers have emulated animals in hopes of sustaining herds, flocks, and schools of fish for food, an essential of the Pear people of Thailand and Cambodia and the camel-mounted Saharan nomad. For the Australian aborigine, the aping of the dingo began with howling, frisking by firelight, snarling, scratching the ground, and sniffing a trail. The shaman completed the ritual by leading a totemic dance. Variations imitated the owl, lyrebird, and the comic rock wallaby. The Molongo and Pinya of southeastern Australia revered the emu by dancing in feathered headbands and white lines painted on shoulder, chest, and thighs.

In North America, Plains Indians around the Great Lakes reverenced herds of buffalo with a bull dance in which the star performer imitated sniffing the air and pawing the ground while balancing a full buffalo pelt and head. Farther west, the Ute of the Great Basin welcomed spring with a sacred bear dance, a celebration of the end of hibernation and rejuvenation of clans. Choreography began with parallel rows of men and women testing the thawing ground with small steps to the beat of a *morache*, a scraped instrument that emitted growls.

Attack and Survival

In medieval Europe, the tension between wolf and goat inspired duets among herders, whose work relied on shielding the naive, weak kid from the creeping, menacing wolf. A similar chain dance by stilt performers in the marshlands of Les Landes, France, captured the shifts of stance and attitude in a flock of browsing sheep. For each December revival, the flock's survival depended on the ingenuity of a human shepherd, portrayed by the lead dancer.

For more comic appeal, Belgians at Ath trotted in synchrony to a brass band in the guise of Bayard, a six-meter giant horse. Latvian males depicted the quirks of frogs and magpies, predictable characters from Aesop's fables. As early as 1023, Bohemians, Bavarians, and Austrians emulated the cockfights of black grouse with the slap-footed *Schuhplattler*, a precursor of clogging. When the dance extended to couples in the seventeenth century, women danced demure hen behaviors that soothed males during the finale, a cuddly, spinning *Ländler*.

In southeastern India, a similar Tamil Nadu dummy horse dance required swordsmanship and lashes with a whip coordinated with clops of four wood legs. A mesmerizing female dance among the Tamil, the snake mime invoked the divinity and protection of serpents among superstitious country folk. As the women performed in tight snakeskin regalia, they crept, writhed, cupped hands like cobra hoods, and struck with head and teeth as though sinking in fangs. To the east, a less menacing dance, the *robam kngaok pailin* of the Kula people of Thailand and Cambodia, welcomed bird antics in the peacock dance.

Animal Majesty

A range of bestial dance characterizations contributes texture and amusement to story dance and mime, including the capering of herds in the Scots-Gaelic goat dance and the llama herding of the Peruvian *llamerada*. Equine dances flourished among mounted cultures, as with the sixteenth-century Polish *krakowiak*, the gallop of Hispanic steeds in Peruvian *muerte de Atahualpa* (death of Atahualpa) pageants, and horsemanship of the Venezuelan *joropo*. With indigenous fauna, Asian folk dance lures spectators to view yak maskers in Tibet and admire Malay dancers seeking trance states in the totemic worship of mythic hybrid animals. The Balinese *barongan* features a dragon-headed peacock/tiger, which took shape after the curse of fairies mutated a trickster. For avian mimicry, traditional steps and gestures imitate the strutting rooster with the *marghi chdro* (cock dance) performed by male Bhils in India and the full-body tiger costume and choreography to taico drums in Iwate, Japan, and Odisha, Nepal.

Kurdish woman imitate the gazelle in the *xwezale*, a common dance in Kurdistan enhanced with the graceful sways of a sinuous, muscled trunk. A mixed-gender pastoral dance, the *gur-u-pez* (wolf and lamb) presents a visual fable featuring a Kurdish shepherd, lambs, a dog, and a wolf. In Melanesia, dancers at New Ireland impersonated the hornbill by wearing a bird head mask and flapping in alarm at the approach of danger. For the dove totem, a line dance wiggled along after the bird, which hopped to safety.

Another animal imitation from Agri, Turkey, the *kazkaz* depicts the long neck of the goose as he drinks water and hyperbolizes the strength and expansion of his wings when he flies away. In Bulgaria, *kukeri* dancers overleap nature with the furred disguises of magical animal shapes. In each scenario, performers align steps and limb, head, and torso movements to re-create the grandeur of animal life.

See also Andean dance; comic dance; dragon dance; Eskimo dance house; exorcism; hoop dance; hunting dance; *jarabe tapatío*; *joropo*; *Ländler*; lion dance; *matachines*; *odori*; *Schuhplattler*; totemic dance.

Source: Solway, Andrew. *Country and Folk Dance.* Chicago: Heinemann, 2009.

ARAB DANCE

A blend of sound, emotion, and kinetic interpretation, Arab dance incorporates the passion and zest of a broad and varying folk landscape. Sources cover much of Lebanon, Saudi Arabia, Syria, Jordan, Iraq, Turkey, Palestine, Upper Egypt, and North Africa as well as details adopted from itinerant Bedouin, Roma, and Kurds. From ancient times, desert wanderers and traders shared news as well as song and dance around nighttime fires. The first pictorial proofs appeared in tomb murals in predynastic Egypt after 5500 BCE.

From Canaanite or Phoenician culture as old as 2000 BCE, Palestinian, Jordanian, and Levantine villagers stamped and kicked their joy and celebration in the *dabke* line dance. Performed to flute and pipe, lute, tambourine, and frame drum, the quick, light-footed line dance or semicircular presentation on holidays or for competition moved at the direction of a leader of chain dancers who twirled beads or a handkerchief to mark the way. A folk anecdote linked the origin of the stamping dance to community assistance in tamping down a new straw and mud roof. Later performances elicited humorous insults and honored grooms-to-be, circumcisions, and the safe return of travelers and prisoners.

Arab style began impacting the West secondhand in 600 CE, when the migratory Roma moved from the Caucasus across the Balkans, carrying details of costume and music from Arab enclaves through settlements of Greeks, Macedonians, Czechs, Slavs, Serbs, and Romanians. In response, spectators voiced their approval with ululations or vibrations of the tongue, a common praise for the Egyptian dancer of the *shemadan*, a wedding procession adopted by Coptic Christians. Led by a female belly dancer topped by a lighted candelabra, the parade of wedding guests followed the candles to the groom's house.

From the 700s to the tenth century, the Islamic Golden Age, Arab dance and music reached a height of innovation, marked by the ceremonial all-male whirling dervish, the common name for Sufi dance that united a worshipper with God and nature. Social castes performed distinct choreography: the street class dominated outdoor entertainment with earthy moves to folk musicians. From Libyan Arabs came the *hagallah*, a hip-swinging nuptial song and dance that delighted wedding guests as far west as Egypt.

Under 624 years of Ottoman rule after 1299, dance and music veered from folk-loric moves of rural Arab farmers and herders to the classical *raks sharki* in cities. Sumptuous brocades and silk and velvet costumes marked aristocratic presentations. Among the graceful gestures, female soloists developed wrist circling, a component of *naz* (coquetry). The Mevlevis, religious scholars known as whirling dervishes, worshipped Allah with an elegant rotation dance that increased in speed and exhibitionism. At the finale, dancers lapsed into a trance of devotion and praise.

In 1650, the Roma passed through Egypt and introduced the *ghawazee*, a hip-shimmying, strutting showstopper that flaunted spins, finger snaps, cymbal clanging, and backbends as variants of the basic pelvic rotation. In a satire of men's martial *tahtiyb* (stick dance), female dancers of the *raks assaya* wielded canes while mocking belligerent males with hip rolls and mincing barefoot steps. During the Qajar court rule at Tehran after 1779, the solo female performance of the *raks baladi* to African flute and drums elicited slow, tantalizing behind-the-scenes gyrations forbidden for outsiders to watch.

At Marrakesh in 1978, Berber *schikatt* dancers display balance while holding erect posture and performing a muscular hip roll to Arabic music. *Carolina Varga "Morocco" Dinicu, morocco@casbahdance.org, New York City.*

Arabs and Diasporic Arts

In the nineteenth century, Arab dance absorbed the artistic techniques of other races and nations and imparted Middle Eastern movements and rhythms to other choreographies. The flourishing Mozarabic culture of Andalusia passed equestrian elements and contradance gestures to the *joropo*, a jubilant, stamping step common to eastern Colombian and Venezuelan shepherds. The Moors of Granada added rhythms and steps from Algeria, Tunisia, and Morocco to the Hispanic zapateado, a syncopated display of fancy footwork that developed in the 1500s. A century later, the fado combined North Afro-Arabic tunes of the *lundu* with the Brazilian fandango and zapateado for a barrio favorite of harbor dwellers, stevedores, and coachmen.

On wharfs in Middle Eastern lands, Arabs observed the English seaman's hornpipe, a solo step dance that they named the *buk*. At Place Congo in New Orleans, black slaves imported African choreography from the Roma, Moors, and Arabs. Middle Eastern specialties identified the strands of diaspora in public performances of the juba until Louisiana authorities banned the celebrations in 1843. In the 1920s, world tourism introduced travelers to Arab story dance, which visitors photographed for its extravagance and color. Presentations in nightclubs, film, and television programs expressed to the world that regional arts encompassed more than belly dance.

Global Dance

Modern Arabic dance filled the eyes and ears with color and engrossing gallops and sashays, for example, the zesty grapevine step that Yemenite Jews introduced to the Israeli *mayim mayim*. At cafes along the Arabian Gulf, women clad in monochromatic silk scarves and glittering beads rippled the abdominal muscles and rolled their hips and shoulders to the drumbeat while tossing their hair or veils. The arms framed the choreography to impart a holistic view of sinuous torso, undulating spine, and total body involvement.

Ethnic modesty dictated a covering of the legs and restrained foot action, a dominant impression of the all-girl *khaleegy* with its head-tossing, skirt-lifting tease. In obedience of Sharia law, female dancers topped a tight shift dress with a broad tunic of opaque silk. A celebration of femininity, the khaleegy created an illusion of seduction as head rotations, rippling torso bends, and hypnotic hair and arm gestures drew spectators to the performance.

In the twenty-first century, Arab dance entertained spectators at feasts, weddings, and clan gatherings, but conservative Muslims banned male-female touching and limited the styles of men's or women's dances and the audience to family insiders. The ongoing restlessness of Middle Easterners impacted the Kurdish *delilo*, which incorporated both Turkish and Arab melodies and gestures. In North America, Arab immigrants increased the venues of traditional dance to restaurants and dance halls and recreational lessons in belly dance. At Acre in July 2006, 2,743 Israeli Arabs set a record for joining in the *dabke* in the longest human dance line.

See also belly dance; hornpipe; *joropo*; juba; Kurdish dance; line dance; Malay dance; martial dance; *mayim mayim*; Sufi dance; zapateado.

Source: Kaschi, Elke. *Dance and Authenticity in Israel and Palestine.* Leiden: Brill, 2003.

ART, FOLK DANCE IN

For stirring body language, artists choose dancing figures for murals, painting, and sculpture, as with the trance dance of the Tuareg Kel Tagelmousse (blue people) in the mountains of Morocco, Mary Irvin Wright's illustration of the Amerindian ghost dance, and Hindu representations of Shiva, the lord of the dance who created earth, with the spiritual choreography of India. The choice of dance as a subject for decorating pottery, bas-relief, and tapestries is fortuitous for art history and anthropology, specifically the Irish step dance pictured in Christian illuminations after 500 and the enormous quetzal plumage bobbing over heads of Mayan dancers in 976 at the Bonampak Temple complex mural of Chiapas, Mexico. Prehistoric art retains moments in ethnic history—the languid temple processions in pharaonic Egypt, the hypermasculinity of Australian aboriginal rituals, and the crested headpieces and stylized hand flexion of story-dance troupes depicted in bas-relief from 770 on the Borobudur temple in Java and from 900 at Angkor, Cambodia.

A common theme in artistic representation of tribal unity, symbols of hunting, fertility, planting, and harvesting capture ongoing community subsistence, the theme of the Hopi green corn dance sketches and totemic salmon carvings of red cedar masks from the Pacific Northwest Salish/Penelakut. In addition to details of primal worship and blessing of food stores, realistic images preserve unique processions and ceremonial obeisance as well as folk costume, hair styles, and jewelry of Aztec bas-relief and musical instruments and attire found in Nigerian lion disguises. Fiber art from the Balkans and Southeast Asia connects the elevated spirits of dancers with the promise of plenty, a common motif in dance figures on Bulgarian scarves and aprons and in sketches of thanksgiving ritual in Laotian rice culture.

Historic Dance Art

In the late Middle Ages, classical Greek bas-relief and realistic Roman statuary set the tone and atmosphere replicated in peasant artistry. In 1338, fresco artist Ambrogio Lorenzetti of Siena depicted a singer-tambourinist and nine performers of a serpentine figure of the farandole, a prevalent chain dance in southern France and Italy. Essential to motifs of traditional gesture and kinetic flow, the draped garments, graceful necks, and devout expressions draw on austere Byzantine representations of folk art. Examples from two Mediterranean countries include the festive ritual in the linen and wool tapestry displaying the Triumph of Dionysos from fourth-century Panopolis, Egypt, and the cortege of maidens in the mosaics of the Church of St. Apollinare Nuovo in Ravenna, Italy. Despite the lack of sound and detailed movement, in both instances, the figures come alive with gesture and unified concentration on the steps.

Erratic dance epidemics in northern Europe influenced the sketches of Flemish painter Pieter Brueghel the Elder, a significant figure in representational peasant choreography. For *The Dancing Mania* (1564), he followed two bagpipers and fifteen frenzied pilgrims on June 24, St. John's Day, across a bridge near Brussels, where the idiosyncratic marching and hopping rid them of hysterics for a year. The psychosocial St. Vitus' Dance took a traditional form called two-and-one, the prance of a single woman flanked by a pair of male attendants. The disproportion of genders exemplified a Renaissance truth that women lacked autonomy as well as compassionate treatment for epilepsy and chorea germanium (mass hysteria).

In Flemish painter Jan van Kessel's *Gentry at a Peasant Dance* (ca. 1666), the delimitation of caste illustrates a key theme in folk dance history—the observation of lower-class frolics by the privileged, who amused themselves by watching primal choreography. From such encounters with the *furlana*, saltarello, highland fling, parasol dance, and tarantella, aristocrats and the landed gentry derived figures and rhythms that formed the foundations of court choreography and processional dance, including the pavane and *volta*. Kessel set territorial boundaries, placing at the periphery the overdressed matrons who seem drawn to lighthearted folk diversions. Kessel's theme implies the universality of dance to all classes, even those who do not mingle physically or socially.

In a fluid sketch for a tapestry designed to please Maria Luisa de Parma and the future Charles IV of Spain, Spaniard Francisco de Goya created a view of baroque figures with *Dance on the Banks of the River Manzanares* (1777), a river that flows through Madrid. Because of the artful positioning of figures, the four-person ensemble suggests both ring dance and the quadrille, a French creation in 1740. The two-couple choreography added vigor and precision to suites featuring the slower, less vivid minuet, the subject of Goya's contemporary, Venetian painter Giovanni Domenico Tiepolo.

In the exhibition of prim footwork in Tiepolo's *Carnival Scene or the Minuet* (1775), the knee breeches of male dancers framed the muscularity and elegance of white hose. The two female dancers appeared to delight spectators with genteel arm stretches and feet poised to display pointed slippers below waltz-length skirts. In the same era, English printmaker James Caldwell produced *The Allemande Dance* (1772), a social scenario emphasizing the delight of onlookers in an elegant pair dancing with joined hands. The heads inclined toward each other; the synchronized footwork epitomized harmony and grace, a carryover from Renaissance German style.

Amerindian Dance

At a turning point in US racial history, American portraitist George Catlin, the first white artist to paint Indians in their native settings, preserved Plains Indian folk arts from Dakota Territory and Missouri. Over five expeditions to the West out of St. Louis, he intended his portfolios of seven hundred sketches and five hundred oils, portraiture, and regalia to record the customs and artistry of the vanishing Amerindian. Among featured ritual scenarios from eighteen tribes, his image of a Mandan bear dance reprised the mimicry of paws and bestial posture as performers stamped clockwise around a circle. In 1832, he preserved the disguises and synchronized postures of the bull dance and the symbolic body paint of the "day and night dance" performed by the Mandan, who died out two years later from epidemic smallpox.

In other oil scenarios of native life, Catlin vivified Choctaw ball-play choreography, an entire Sioux village during a scalp dance in 1835, an Ojibwa braves' dance in 1837, and four participants in an Ojibwa warrior dance, which featured fringed buckskins, feathered headdress, bows, and a club. Although homosexuality disgusted Catlin, in 1835, he detailed the Fox and Sauk of the Great Plains acknowledging a berdache, or two-spirit, a native term for trans-dresser. A Sioux buffalo dance displayed men attired in buffalo heads and red with green stripes painted on back, chest, limbs, and face. The painting of a first snowfall dance in 1845 also depicted weapons and snowshoes on ten dancers. The combined collection indicated the dominance of males in displays of brawn and ferocity.

A century later, printmaker and artist Anna Barry contributed both romanticized and realistic images similar in indigenous detail to those of Catlin. In 1945, she pictured two Hopi participants in kachina disguise performing with four men in mudhead masks. A dance leader in white kilt edged in native symbols appeared to direct the ritual with a long cane and nods of his feathered headdress. In the same year, she stood in New Mexico opposite Taos Pueblo to interpret the turtle dance, another all-male performance of Indians in plumes and feathers and leafy anklets taking small, synchronized steps to the beat of three types of drums. The dance leader waved two feathers while executing his individualized footwork.

Technical Artistry

European art retains the technique and mode of antique dance. In Pieter Brueghel the Elder's *A Wedding Feast with Peasants Dancing* (1568), country folk appear to enjoy a *branle*, a medieval circle dance simple enough to invite all levels of expertise, from children to elderly. The relaxed postures and loose costumes imply joy as well as uninhibited abandon to the rhythm of a lone bagpiper. A parallel painting by his son, Pieter Brueghel the Younger, *Flemish Fair* (ca. 1620) characterizes community camaraderie in a farandole, a chain dance dating to the ancient Greek crane dance.

In contrast to Brueghel's celebratory images, Flemish baroque artist Peter Paul Rubens's *A Peasant Dance* (ca. 1630) intensified the swirl of human and mythic figures aligned by clasped hands for a thread-the-needle figure. By forming arches from pairs of men and women, a train of barefoot peasants leans into the dynamics of a melody played by a flautist in a tree. In a rustic setting picturing Palladian architecture from Italy, Rubens shaped ivy crowns, bells, and flying shawls and skirts into a panorama of counterclockwise movement and faces tinged with reddened cheeks, a suggestion of group brio. The sensuous postures express the unity of spirit as sixteen participants expend their energy on Bacchic madness.

With a stronger grasp of real people and their dances, French painter Jules Breton's *La Saint-Jean* (1875) refocused typical dance images by highlighting a fire at nightfall and the seven semi-obscured harvesters who encircle it. With primordial relish and friendship, the handholds and upraised feet energize a rural folk endeavor far from town. Breton suggests the rigor of urbanism in the architectural up-thrust of a church tower, which occupies a separate sphere from field work. The city vs. country motif, common to the Industrial Revolution, implies a vast change in folk art during an era marked by the emergence of the waltz and intimate couples dance.

Breton's contemporary, French impressionist Pierre-Auguste Renoir, epitomized the moral quandary over partnering in 1883 with *Dance at Bougival*, a suburban setting on the Seine west of Paris. The intimate male grasp of the woman's waist, the meeting of torsos, and his face lowered to her cheek account for religious and parental disapproval of the waltz and other couples dances in closed position. The ambiguous pose offers no hint to the woman's reaction nor to the man's intent, but the painter communicates motion and energy in the pair's synchronized steps as well as opportunity for erotic contact.

Political Dance

In addition to amusement and pleasure, artists encapsulate the release of tension and the assuaging of despair through rhythmic movement, a motif of sketches of the Afro-American juba. Roman painter Agostino Brunias accepted a commission from Sir William Young, governor of Dominica and St. Vincent, to record island customs evoking the picturesque tropics as a choice place to settle and invest in sugar plantations. By painting enslaved dancers in *Dancing Scene in the West Indies* (1779) bending their bodies and tossing their heads to a jig, Brunias muses on the immediacy of Afro-Caribbean choreography as a transformer of bondage. In an ethnographic scenario of Dominica, five jubilant black Caribs vary body language with raised arms and a partner turn. While the lone male keeps time with a tambourine, the four females raise proud heads topped by the *tignon*, a standard head wrap that bondswomen shaped from rags and flaunted like a crown. A more personal view, Brunias's *The Dance of the Handkerchief* (1779) implies a delicacy and refinement of courtship among people who have little control over their lives. For the sake of luring investors, the artist's jovial dance paintings camouflaged the brutality of press gangs on West Indian plantations.

As folk dance raised interest in tourist locations, poster art featured stylized views of movement and national costumes, especially pre-Lenten carnival in Rio de Janeiro. By turning spontaneous choreography into a showpiece, advertisements for Roma fandango in Barcelona, Sufi dance in Istanbul, hoop dance at Amerindian assemblies, and presentations of Korean fan dance at the Olympic games stereotyped the facial features, jewelry, and props common to indigenous dance arts. The posters themselves established their own authenticity as folk art, a common feature of depictions of Chinatown dragon dance, Turkish belly dance, booted Russian *hopak* performers, St. Croix story dance, and Mardi Gras street parade in New Orleans.

See also belly dance; chain dance; coming of age; disguise; dragon dance; fan dance; farandole; *furlana*; ghost dance; highland fling; *hopak*; hoop dance; hunting dance; jig; juba; lamentation dance; masked dance; music, folk dance; parasol dance; partnering; pavane; processionals; sacrificial dance; saltarello; scalp dance; step dance; Sufi dance; tarantella; *volta*; waltz; warrior dance.

Sources: Catlin, George. *Life among the Indians*. London: Gall and Inglis, 1861. Chico, Beverly. *Hats and Headwear around the World: A Cultural Encyclopedia*. Santa Barbara, CA: ABC-Clio, 2013.

ATTIRE

The costuming of folk companies achieves artistry on a par with musicality and choreography. Rural and amateur troupes schedule lengthy preparation time for applying body paint, wigs, jewelry, masks, shin bells, finger cymbals, feathers, and agave-stalk headgear—adornments of the aboriginal Australian corroboree, New Zealand *hakka*, and Apache mountain spirit ritual. For local color, Mesoamerican companies stress an outstanding element, as with white tunics in Juárez, Mexico; silk capes in San Juan, Texas; and embroidered and fringed aprons in Tortugas, New Mexico. In St. Lucia, the Madras skirt and *tignon* (turban) with sash tied over generous white petticoats and the gentleman's plaid vest add a note of island pride to presentations of the camp-style quadrille.

Featured makeup and accoutrements include such showpieces as the flowered headpiece and embroidered collar of female dancers of the Hispano-Mayan *baile de las cintas* (ribbon dance) of Yucatán, which introduced Mayan circle dancers to the fluttering tethers of the European maypole. For heavily made-up dancers, particularly the mythic characters of *kathakali* troupes of Kerala, India, and the devils and giants of religio-historical *matachines* pageants in Hualuapan, Mexico, each presentation required heavy expenditure on regalia. Less spectacular, the scalp dance of Plains Indians highlighted warriors' dress in leggings, breechcloth, feathered crest, and body paint communicating daring and spirituality, the chief traits of Roman Nose, a Southern Cheyenne performer with fourteen Iowa dancers in London in fall 1845.

Historic Costuming

For global folk dancers in Ontario, Turkey, Czechoslovakia, Siberia, and France, body enhancement has typically foregrounded the athleticism, drama, and passion of choreography. From 33,000 BCE, performers disguised their humanity by pretending to merge with the animal world or mythic deities. Australian aborigines decked themselves in feathers as visual metaphors of the ephemeral nature of prayer. The Aztec of Tenochtitlán painted skulls to turn them into sacred props of blood sacrifice. The Pueblo clans of the Great Basin equipped dancers with clappers, bells, bird bone whistles, and gourd rattles, sound makers that produced both visual and auditory effects.

After 1570 BCE, the Egyptian *bedleh* (belly dance costume) began with bare flesh and advanced with skimpy aprons and loin wraps that left the abdomen unrestricted for undulation. As the dance standardized, costumers matched an abbreviated top with an opaque overskirt or harem pants tied at the ankles, translucent hand and head scarves, finger cymbals, coin necklaces and belts, and wispy veils. Egyptian men and women accessorized with metal armlets and collars set with glittering stones. The Turkish couples version of the belly dance decked the man in a vest over a nude chest, loose trousers, and a plumed turban that dipped and swayed in time to the music.

Under the influence of Druidic worship and waves of immigration, in the Iron Age after 1200 BCE, the Celtic circle sets, jig, step dance, and sword rituals developed in Ireland along with the traditional tartan. For professional contradance in later eras, Highland women topped fitted dresses with shawls and headbands. The male Scots dancer energized drama and sweep by flourishing the brat (cloak) over plain kilt or tight pants, sash, vest, and low ghillies, tongueless lace-up slippers worn with thin hose. The dominant plaid enhanced an atmosphere of clan loyalty and belonging.

Heritage Choreography

In Oceania and sub-Saharan Africa, dancers performed without shoes. For Fijian narrative dance, around 800 BCE, Lapitan mariners from Indonesia sat and danced from the waist up to the clanking of shell jewelry and the sway of blossom collars, painted torso symbols, tattoos, and piercings with thorns or animal fangs. About 200 BCE, dancers at Cook Island, Tahiti, and Hawaii revealed hip sways with grass or ti leaf skirts and bark cloth kilts. Above oiled torsos, presenters contrasted their dark skin tones with flower necklaces, leafy sashes, and ankle, wrist, and forehead garlands.

For the *midimu* circumcision ritual, aboriginal Kaka males of Cameroon and Makonde dancers at Mozambique and southern Tanzania graced trousers and shirt with string netting, bells, and a cloth helmet reaching to the shoulders. The regalia signified admission into adulthood. From the 400s CE, the Sotho of South Africa propitiated rain by gyrating and leaping in black ostrich plumes and a blanket cloak. In the eighth century, Fono dancers of the Ivory Coast gathered raffia from fringes and skirts, pierced beads for jewelry, and detailed their choreography with stilts, fly whisks, and mud or carved masks exaggerated with teeth, antlers, feathers, bones, and cowries. Likewise costumed in found items, from 948, upland troupes in Nigeria performed the *agaba* (lion dance) in shapeless suits made auditory with rattling seedpods and brass bells.

In the late Middle Ages, religious ceremonies based movement on melody rather than idiophonic attire. The shift in styles of dress and instrumentation influenced Danish chain dance, Balkan line dance, Bolognese circle sets, and the Catalonian *estampie*, a solo or two-voice song and dance imported from France by itinerant jongleurs, buskers, storytellers, pipers, and actors and featured in the *Carmina Burana* (Songs from Beuern, 1230). A prime holdout in the late 1300s, the Dance of Death throughout Europe involved street performers during the Lenten carnival. Parades and processionals encouraged the painting of linen dance costumes with the bones and fleshless grimace of skeletons.

Another shift in costuming marked global folk dance in the Renaissance. For French courtiers popularizing the gavotte, pointed toes and stylized steps, crossovers, and pliés displayed expensive buckled shoes. In Kerala, India, kathakali dance drama retained the bold dress and weighty gilded headgear of heritage Hindu arts dating to Sanskrit scripture from the Mahabharata (400 BCE) and Ramayana (300 BCE). To showcase folk choreography amid singing and drumming, cosmetic artists highlighted individuals with henna and kohl facial, hand, and body paint.

For performing Sanskrit epic episodes, wars, and myths in southwestern India, mimes adopted the short-sleeved bodice over gathered skirt. Character dancers individualized personalities by padding wraps and coats into lumpy shapes and impersonated authority figures with starched neck cloths and skirts. For symbolism, presenters completed stage outfits with tiaras, long wigs, tassels, torso beading, shawls, and pointed-toe slippers.

Group Dance

At Rarotonga in the Cook Islands, a couples story dance or symbolic ritual similar to the Hawaiian hula incorporated detailed gestures and profiles of trunk and limbs, a physicality that outraged Protestant missionaries from New England. To display musculature to the beat of slit drums and sharkskin bongos, women topped the wrap-around *pareu* (sarong) with a grass skirt. For naturalistic detail, dancers coordinated shell headbands and flower leis. Additions of fans, stilts, spears, and torches varied the atmospheric figures.

In 1965, school systems and youth clubs nurtured folk dance through competitions, arts festivals, and professional troupes exhibiting traditional dress. At Oak Alley Plantation in New Orleans and Monmouth Plantation in Natchez, Mississippi, women and girls chose the soft-soled kid dance slipper for group presentations of three heritage dances, the sarabande, mazurka, and galop. Flexible footwear enabled contradancers to control crinoline slips and unpredictable hoop skirts while joining exuberant choreography. Folk troupes executing the Austro-German *Ländler* relied on picturesque Tyrolean peasant costume—women in aproned skirts and dresses and men in Alpine hats, knee pants, and lederhosen. A costume called *tracht* by folk troupes from Liechtenstein identifies children's companies, who study folk arts in the Liechtensteinisches Gymnasium.

See also animal dances; body art; contradance; corroboree; disguise; fancy dance; galop; gavotte; ghost dance; headdress; jig; masked dance; maypole dance; nudity; quadrille; scalp dance; shawl dance; step dance; Thai dance.

Sources: Carter, Alexandra. *Rethinking Dance History: A Reader.* New York: Routledge, 2004. Kassing, Gayle. *History of Dance.* Champaign, IL: Human Kinetics, 2007. Knowles, Mark. *The Wicked Waltz and Other Scandalous Dances.* Jefferson, NC: McFarland, 2009.

· ℬ ·

BALKAN DANCE

Balkan folk arts encompass music and dance of Bosnia-Hercegovina, Croatia, Serbia, Hungary, and Romania. From prehistory, outdoor ring dance, an ancestor of the hora, energized Croatian village amusements on the Adriatic Sea at Dubrovnik, at Posavina in the Sava River basin, and at Podravina in the Drava River basin. In 1100, arrival of the nomadic Roma from Anatolia introduced handkerchief dances and sybaritic solos. On the islands of Corsica and Korcula off the southern coast of Croatia, the *moresca*, a sword dance mimicking male competition for a veiled woman, anticipated the vigor of the polka. Based on the historic clash of Christians and Muslims and marking the Feast of Saint Theodore the Martyr each July 29, the dance drama flourished over centuries of religious conflict.

Balkan dancers established the syncopated style of the *kolo* (also *oro*), a typical line dance of the hemp harvest accompanied by recorder. In Croatia, Belarus, Serbia, Slovenia, Montenegro, Bulgaria, and Macedonia, parents approved the group dance as a time and place for teens to court and choose mates. At Lika in central Croatia, mountaineers performed an idiophonic kolo to erect postures and stamping boots rather than to music or singing. In Shoplouk outside Sofia, Bulgaria, troupes of old women danced a coming-of-age ritual for younger women. To two-part harmony over a piper's drone line, the performers encircled each other's waists and stepped counterclockwise.

Similar to the medieval farandole, the Romanian *sîrba* joined men and women in hand clasping and multiple skipping crossovers to back and front accompanied by singing and flute tunes in a minor key. Similarly, the *floricica* from Muntenia in the south coordinated clockwise glissades, toe taps, knee lifts, and forward and angled foot lifts with shuffles and single and double stamps. Handholds varied from the upward W to sudden drops to V shapes and splits of the ring into parallel lines.

A Lasting Tradition

A Slavonic dance, the *tamburitza* (also *tamburica*) anchored the folk choreography of clans east of Zagreb. Taking its name from the tambura (mandolin), the dance migrated from the Ottoman Empire to Croatia in 1299 and reached Bosnia after 1300. Performers locked arms at shoulder level in a line or circle and stepped and shuffled to the left. Rapid bounces, skips, and hops stressed sociability and joy. A slower version involved hand clasping and solo performances to full-voice singing in unison or two-part harmony.

In 1609 at Istria, a Croatian peninsula east of Venice, influences from the Venetian state contributed the European *furlana* to a textured Balkan mix of steps and rhythms. Bulgarians, Serbians, and southern Romanians developed the *calus*, a ritual acrobatic dance dating to the Roman soldier ritual honoring the war god Mars. In the 1600s, the calus accompanied purification and fertility ceremonies based on horse worship. Men in loose white tunics brightened with embroidery and colorful sashes edged with small bells followed the lead of the dance master, who taught youths traditional patterns and stunts. The complicated dance varied leaping and leg swings with stamping and heel clicks to the rhythms of a chant. As the line progressed about a village on Whitsuntide (Pentecost), the calus conferred health and fortune on spectators.

Late in the 1700s along the Adriatic coast, Dalmatian dancers at Dubrovnik adapted the *lindo* (also *lindjo*), a couples duet or line dance favored for wedding receptions. A blend of steps and rhythms from Greece and the eastern Mediterranean, the lindo developed with stamping feet and arms held above the head to bellows accompaniment. Performers followed the calls of the dance master and competed at improvising new steps with lifted knees and hands clasped over the chest. The vigor of Balkan folk art spread north and influenced dance figures at Viennese nightclubs, restaurants, and cafes on Otxakringer Strasse, the "Balkan Mile."

In 1818, an imperial entertainment at the bishop's palace in Zagreb for Holy Roman Emperor Franz II and his consort, Karolina Augusta of Bavaria, boasted peasant musicians. Count Janko Draskovic, the Croatian reformer and poet, led the kolo performers to a melody composed for the visit. To enliven the rising nationalism, dancers reclaimed the choreography of their Balkan ancestors.

The Balkan Diaspora

In the mid-1800s, musicians in the Danube River valley formed musical ensembles to accompany singing and dancing. Beginning with a band formed at Osijek in eastern Croatia in 1847, Balkan musicians rescued folk songs of neighboring clans. In 1882, a large faction of university students at Zagreb capered to folk orchestras composed of medieval and Renaissance instruments—tambura (lute), accordion, bagpipes, violin, and guitar. The migration of farmers, coal miners, construction and railroad laborers, and steelworkers to Ontario, Alberta, Saskatchewan, and the US frontier in the 1880s as far west as Vancouver and San Francisco introduced Serbian and Croatian folk dance to fraternal and church socials, graduations, Easter rituals, weddings, baptisms, and funerals. In 1903, Slavic Roma and Macedonians transported unique musical tastes from Eastern Europe to Winnipeg, Montreal, and parts of Victoria, Australia.

In 1937, the Tamburitzans, a student song and dance troupe at Duquesne University in Pittsburgh, Pennsylvania, revived intricate folk dances that identified the spirit of Eastern Europe. Tours of Czech, Croatian, and Slovak enclaves taught the younger generation the medieval tamburitza and augmented pride with ancestral polkas and mazurkas. Media broadcasts in Croatia from 1941 increased the popularity of Slavonic folk music and dance, which immigrants carried to Lower Canada and Australia after World War II. In August 2015, additional waves of Balkan immigration to Ontario and Australia introduced Slavonic folk arts to new audiences.

See also czardas; *furlana*; hora; mazurka; polka; Sufi dance.

Source: March, Richard. *The Tamburitza Tradition*. Madison: University of Wisconsin Press, 2013.

BAMBOULA

An orgiastic, amorphous dance of slaves and Creoles, the *bamboula* (also *banboula*) united polyglot blacks of the French and Spanish West Indies in a sensuous fertility and mating ritual. The dance appears to have derived from occult West African liturgy and sacrifice and from extempore presentations of story dance by Wolof griots (storytellers). The meter followed the beat of the goatskin membrane on a bamboo or log bamboula drum, which players pounded alternately with fingers and the heels of the hand to alter the timbre.

Because the bamboula mimed the mating of ducks, on August 8, 1672, the dance came under a Danish colonial ban from Governor Jorgen Iversen at St. Thomas. Violators risked imprisonment at the fort at Charlotte Amalie for a public lashing. At Congo Square in New Orleans, as early as the 1720s, thousands of blacks from Gambia, Senegal, and Congo, the largest representative group of plantation slaves, rendezvoused outdoors on Sunday, Christmas, and New Year's Day to celebrate their common joy in procreation. Their unique all-day frenzy of yelping, athletic motion honored ancestors and furnished temporary relief from the stress of bondage.

Unrepressed Style

Art historians compared the style and secular nature of the bamboula with the Haitian *méringue*, the Jamaican *mento*, the Spanish *chica*, and, at Guadeloupe and Martinique, the beguine, a slow rumba featuring contact between gyrating hips. Staccato banjo tunes, satiric chant, and drumming summoned onlookers to a circle, where the lead performer, clad in scanty attire, earned the title of bamboula king. A solo female at St. Croix undulated in erotic pose around a fire while mimicking sex acts with a snake.

A progressive choreography similar in style to the congo dance, the bamboula advanced to a duet by a male soloist, who invited a female to join him to the tam-tam (flour-barrel drum) beat of the deep-voiced bamboula drum, the honk of horns, and the rattle of tambourines, shakeres, and equine jawbones. The partners shared the bounding, singsong gossip-filled ditties, limb contortions, and un-patterned footwork until the duo paused for a rest. The queen of the dance, who often collapsed from heat exhaustion, revived to the rigorous fanning of her attendants. By giving her primacy, black performers empowered the female from devaluation as a drudge or sex toy.

More partners and spectators joined the bamboula exhibition and gyrated freely for hours in a tumult of laughter, clapping, and the shouts of children. The dance spectacle anticipated the introduction of the juba in 1760. Other clamorous dancers arrived after the Santa Domingo Revolution of 1791 from Haiti and Cuba and pressed into the swirl of the bamboula at the finale. In 1816, an influx of Guinean slaves increased the impetuosity of bamboula antics along the Mississippi Delta.

The Bamboula in History

In like manner, free time among blacks in St. Croix in 1845 brought dancers together in their best outfits for a New Year's lark. Later that year, composer Louis Moreau Gottschalk published an Afro-Caribbean dance tune, the "Bamboula: danse de Nègres." One of the famous performers, the legendary Bras Coupé, an amputee featured in George Washington Cable's psychological novel *The Grandissimes: A Story of Creole Life* (1880), epitomized survival and defiance of white oppressors, the motif of the bamboula.

Criminalized by urban police in Louisiana in 1886, the Afro-American slave dance continued to energize duos after harvest in the US Virgin Islands, St. Lucia, Dominica, Martinique, Haiti, and Trinidad and in Mardi Gras processionals in New Orleans. In September 1892, Queen Coziah led two hundred bamboula dancers through Charlotte Amalie, the port of St. Thomas, in a choreographed protest of the devalued pay tokens for female mine workers. Although newspaper features in 1889, 1891, and 1909 connected the dance with convulsive voodoo ritual, such nightspots as the Grand Theatre in New Orleans and His Majesty's Theatre in Haiti perpetuated the dance in the mid-1910s. In November 1921, a US Senate committee investigated the bamboula to determine whether Haitian and Santo Domingan dancers were practicing voodoo.

See also drumming; juba.

Sources: Castellanos, Henry C. *New Orleans As It Was: Episodes of Louisiana Life.* New Orleans, LA: L. Graham & Son, 1895. Francis, Dale. *The Quelbe Commentary, 1672–2012.* Bloomington, IN: iUniverse, 2014.

BARN DANCE

A rowdy neighborhood hoedown or clog fest set to jigs and country music in Scotland in the 1600s, the barn dance derived from the traditional Scots reel and highland fling, a men-only post-combat victory solo. Additional influences ranged from the Scots-Irish *cèilidh* (house party) to the French *branle* and *pas de quatre* (quartet dance) and the English morris dance and harvest home, a traditional ingathering of field produce. At all-night cabin warmings and donor parties to fund the housing of newlyweds, European immigrants to the Americas coordinated their peasant steps to popular rhythms and figures, including the meandering labyrinth of the medieval farandole, reels, step dance, and the exuberant cotton-eye Joe.

During "play parties" in the Appalachian Mountains, on the frontier, and in Amish agrarian communities, the barn dance became a child's introduction to solo steps, dance games, and partnering. For barn-raising socials, workers sometimes completed construction of the board floor before assembling couples and children for circle and line dancing and quadrilles. At established barns, party-givers chose autumn for the sweet smell of new-mown oats hay and timothy, which dancing feet crushed, releasing a nutty aroma.

For a group of sixteen to twenty of mixed ages and backgrounds, a caller warmed up with basic circles and reverses in 4/4 rhythm. Favorites ranged from "Old Zip Coon," "The Campbells Are Coming," "Turkey in the Straw," "The Bear Went over the Mountain," "The Virginia Reel," "The Arkansas Traveler," and "Ole Dan Tucker" to "Foggy Mountain Breakdown," a bluegrass version of a slave-era plantation and juke joint caper involving crossovers, jerky steps, and jumping with feet crossed at the ankle. For variety, the group joined a line dance, wove in and out in the dos-à-dos (back to back), or formed a coil to the center, which the caller reversed in labyrinthine form. Unsophisticated choreography pleased children and youth, who danced along with their elders.

Dance outfits tended toward work shirts, jeans, brogans, and straw hats for men and gingham wash-dresses, slippers, aprons, and sunbonnets for women and girls. In lieu of tables and chairs, guests and chaperones sat in warm lantern light on hay bales and hastily assembled trestle benches for placement around the wall. For such presentations as solos and the couples cakewalk and schottische, all spectators clapped along with the instrumentalists, usually banjo and guitar pickers, fiddlers, bagpipers, juice-harpers, and harmonica players.

Barn Etiquette

Social structure imitated the grander manners and entertainments of the gentry, who confined their entertainments to ballrooms. Barn dance courtesies obliged young men to return their partners to their seats at the end of a set and offer a drink from the punch bowl or cider keg. To spare hurt feelings of wallflowers, chivalrous men selected spinsters and older women for less vigorous dances. At a rural German wedding in 1821, the barn dance was the occasion when the father danced with the bride and presented his daughter's dowry to the groom, a public exchange establishing the honor of both families.

Any disagreements between males demanded fistfights outdoors rather than among dancers. The likelihood of violence caused an anonymous Wallingford minister to issue "A Few Words of Advice to My Flock" (1841), in which he condemned English barn dances for encouraging frivolity and vanity. From a more liberal viewpoint, Scots poet James Stirrat of Ayrshire published "The Barn, O" (1844), a testimonial to the merriment and energy of the highland fling as well as to the cuddling of couples. In "The Dance of the Haymakers" (1847) in *New York Illustrated Magazine,* the anonymous author explained the reason for dancing in a high-ceilinged barn, which was cooler and less noisy than a house or church social hall.

Varied Steps

More experienced barn dance leaders joined two couples in square formation or contradance, a forerunner of the quadrille and cotillion. The percussive buck dancing (men's tap dance) and clogging popular among Appalachian mountaineers introduced energetic solos and ensembles to the mountain dulcimer. Social events often ended with Texas two-steps and slow couples dancing, a preface to courtship and after-dance romancing. In 1926, folk art collectors Henry Ford, his wife, Clara Bryant Ford, and Benjamin Lovett revived amateur groups by publishing a compilation of barn dance styles called *Good Morning: After a Sleep of Twenty-Five Years, Old-Fashioned Dancing Is Being Revived*. Radio broadcasts from Ohio and southern Ontario gave agrarian dancers authentic music for get-togethers.

Dance master Michael Kidd's rambunctious barn-raising in the musical *Seven Brides for Seven Brothers* (1954) incorporated partnering as well as gymnastic male solos featuring Russ Tamblyn on the balance beam. Another film, *Urban Cowboy* (1980), starred John Travolta in line dancing. The popularity of singer Billy Ray Cyrus's "Achy Breaky Heart" (1992) drew a younger crowd into the heritage dances of their ancestors.

See also cakewalk; *cèilidh*; clogging; coming of age; contradance; cotillion; cotton-eye Joe; farandole; highland fling; jig; juba; morris dance; quadrille; reel; schottische; square dance; step dance.

Source: Laufman, Dudley, and Jacqueline Laufman. *Traditional Barn Dances with Calls and Fiddling*. Champaign, IL: Human Kinetics, 2009.

BELLY DANCE

A complex aesthetic of confident, athletic women, belly dance, or *baladi*—which the French call *danse du ventre*—retains its ancient foundation in Mesopotamian, Greek, and North African fertility rituals and mythic femininity. In the Indus Valley around 3000 BCE, midwifery protocols readied parturient women for labor and delivery with sessions of belly rolls, pelvic shimmies, and torso spirals and circles. Companies of women performed their craft at birthing rituals and extended their expression of gender identity in the private women's quarters of harems.

Dancers hybridized style and technique with elements of Earth Mother worship from Phoenicia, Crete, Etruria, Syria, Nubia, Palestine, Ethiopia, and the Sudan. Focusing on the torso rather than limbs, performers framed their movements with graceful arm gestures and used their legs for balance. The cross-cultural touches sensitized performers and liberated kinetic perceptions of self from shame. As a result, creative energy empowered a class of women usually devoid of autonomy, gracing them with serenity, self-esteem, and spirituality.

In Egypt after 1570 BCE, nude presentation gave place to a more modest *bedleh* (belly dance costume), which consisted of aprons and kilts that left the midriff free for muscle tightening. In the first millennium BCE, dancers topped a see-through skirt or harem pants with a breast cover and increased allure with transparent veils, finger cymbals, coin necklaces, and metal belts. Anatolians invented a belly dance duo, featuring a bare-chested male in flowing trousers and a plumed turban that trembled to the musical beat. Males and females decked their bodies with hammered armlets and collars set with colored stones that flashed in torchlight.

In 1998, a Moroccan performer of the *rags sharki* (belly dance) illustrates the clack of small brass finger cymbals to accentuate hip thrusts and belly rolls. *Carolina Varga "Morocco" Dinicu, morocco@casbahdance.org, New York City*

Altered Messages

In Egypt, the *ghawazee*, a harem dance to percussive castanets and brass finger cymbals, evolved into the *raks sharki* (oriental dance), an erotic presentation glorifying female anatomy. Through intricate contortions and backbends, in the Byzantine Empire after 330 CE, roving courtesans created their own versions of belly dance. The carnality of Salomé in Galilean legend raised the scarf dance to an acme of sexuality, which belly dancers perpetuated in Byzantine Anatolia and among the nomadic Roma. In less lascivious presentations in the Jordan Valley, Palestinian women danced at henna parties. The all-female assemblies glorified the bride-to-be with the painting of hands and feet in gynocentric symbols and ended the occasion with a unison cry of joy.

In 600, itinerant Roma dancers brought Arab belly dance across the Caucasus to the Balkans, where it prefigured the passion of the flamenco. Greeks, Macedonians, Czechs, Slavs, Serbs, and Romanians adopted flamboyant Roma execution of Arab modes as nuptial rituals. In Middle Eastern style, audiences voiced their approval with ululations or tongue flutters, a jubilant commendation for the Egyptian performer of the *shemadan*, a wedding procession adopted by Coptic Christians. Preceded by a female belly dancer balancing a lighted candelabrum on her head, the line of guests followed the candle flickers to the bride's new home.

In the seventh century, conservative Islamic gender segregation forbade the mixing of male and female dancers. While men sought amusements outside the home compound by ogling Algerian women dancing unveiled on the streets, genteel women retreated into the harem to dance for the viewing of other females. They developed wrist circling, an eye-catching component of *naz* (coquetry).

After the French seizure of Algeria and Tunisia and the British move into Egypt and Arab lands on the Persian Gulf, historians and artists disseminated the fantasy of the female belly dancer titillating sheikhs and sultans with mesmerizing belly rippling. The atmosphere set with carved screens, filmy drapes, and lush pillows implied intimacy and sexual pleasure suited to male desires. To the uptight, corseted Victorian female, the stereotypical belly dance epitomized scandalous, opportunistic Orientalism, a catchall term that ranked Western mores as more virtuous and undefiled.

Dance and Censorship

In 1834, Ottoman military commander Muhammad Ali Pasha outlawed belly dance by Cairo street entertainers, whom he banished to Esna, an island in the Nile River south of Luxor. In the Sudan, women remained free to perform. They prepared for marriage by learning the belly dance for presentation to the groom and wedding guests. At Balkan feasts and nuptials, the *cocek*, a popular Croat-Serb chain dance for cross-dressing males, perpetuated Roma belly dance mode. While Europeans and Americans parodied the belly dance in stage shows and carnivals in the 1880s, Middle Easterners combated the misconception with prohibitions of immodest folk art.

In the Maghreb, female belly dancing in Morocco ventured beyond Mauritanian drapery to expose flesh and muscular control of abdomen and pelvis. Because tourists sought viewing and participation in folk dance, poster art stylized figures and the erotic hip wraps in Arab and Turkish belly dance. Supper clubs, television, and the film *The Secret of the Grain* (2007) carried the abdominal contortions over the globe, outraging devout Muslims and trivializing Arab culture with a travesty of exoticism.

See also Arab dance; attire; chain dance; flamenco; mating dance; North African dance; nudity.

Source: Fraser, Kathleen W. *Before They Were Belly Dancers: European Accounts of Female Entertainers in Egypt, 1760–1870.* Jefferson, NC: McFarland, 2013.

BODY ART

Gracing the body with paint, tattoos, and piercings distinguishes folk dances worldwide with embellishment and whimsy—for example, Australian aboriginal dancers whitening swarthy skin with moistened clay or coating uninitiated boys in red. Designs shaped with henna, berry juice, saffron, woad, tamarind, clove, tea, annatto, pollen, saffron, mica flakes, lead carbonate, chalk, limestone, hematite, and ground copper establish status as well as spiritual oneness with the divine. Among the Tamil Nadu of southeastern India, young males painted their torsos in yellow ochre (limonite) and black (charcoal) stripes and highlighted animal behaviors with fangs, fuzzy ears and paws, tails, and claws. With the *puli attam* dance, they imitated the movements and steps of the stalking tiger as it approached a tethered goat. For communal blessing, Amazonian tribal dances among the Bora of Peru flaunted facial dots and lines in red ochre (iron oxide) to mark the settlement of a new village.

Body Cosmetics

After 800 BCE, Lapitan seafarers sailed from Indonesia to Fiji, where they told their epic story in narrative dance. In a seated performance marked by strung shells and flower collars, they mimed their adventures with hand and shoulder gestures accentuated by shell bracelets, tattoos, body paint, and piercings with thorns and animal teeth. The adornments anticipated the initiation of the hula at Kaana on Molokai in 300 CE and the sacred tattooing of faces, limbs, and torso with red whirls and symbols among the precolonial Maori *hakka* dancers of New Zealand.

In the 1500s in Kerala, India, *kathakali* narrative dance amazed spectators with bold attire; weighty headdress; and artistic facial, hand, and body paint, a source of emotive expression. For Malayan and Tibetan folk presentations, color coding identified the gender, caste, and profession of kathakali characters. For depiction of Asian aristocrats, dancers tinged their faces green; Amazons dressed in yellow cosmetics. Woodsmen and hermits appeared in blackface. Demon portrayers topped green foundation with red streaks and beards. Gods exhibited their deity with facial hair lightened with a slurry of rice.

Dance Censorship

The concept of body decoration remained a standard of island dancing until March 6, 1797, when the kinetic *'upa'upa* shocked the seventeen prim London Missionary Society evangelists at Tahiti. The proselytizers compared Tahitians to gypsies and, in 1819, condemned anyone guilty of permanent flesh alteration. A year later, Christian missionaries Hiram and Sybil Moseley Bingham from Westfield, Massachusetts, shamed Hawaiian islanders for glorifying the body with oiled torsos, painted face and limbs, and shell and flower decoration.

Amerindians faced the same subjective judgment from missionaries who observed warrior dances for which body paint delineated rank and combat record. At an exhibition of the Iowa scalp dance in London in 1845, Cheyenne chief Roman Nose stripped to the waist and streaked his flesh with red stripes and hand prints dipped in red paint. As Protestant missions gained sway over the North American Indian, pulpit condemnation warned performers that kilts and breechcloths, such as those cloaking Kewa troupes at the Keresan plaza of Santo Domingo Pueblo, New Mexico, turned harmless seasonal dance into scenes of lust. In 1917, the Europeanization of Turkey by founder Mustafa Kemal Ataturk demeaned Kurds for tattoos featured in the Newroz (New Year) dance.

See also corroboree; hula; nudity; Polynesian dance; scalp dance.

Sources: DeMello, Margo. *Encyclopedia of Body Adornment.* Westport, CT: Greenwood, 2007. Jablonski, Nina G. *Skin: A Natural History.* Berkeley: University of California Press, 2006.

BOLERO

A sultry, hip-swaying national dance suited to an adagio beat, the bolero (also *Goyesca* or *escuela bolera*), one of Iberia's oldest folk figures, may date back to the Roman stage performer Bathyllus, a mime from Alexandria who thrilled viewers in the Augustan age. Described by early second-century CE satirists Martial and Juvenal, the bolero gained its name from the Spanish verb *volero* (to fly), which captured the fiery, wanton character of the peasant original. To a 3/4 meter set by guitar, castanets, conga and bongo drums, and vocals, the torrid figures and stamps of the heel originated outdoors in Mozarabic Spain.

Bearing ultra-romantic elements of some two hundred traditional Catalonian dances, the Venetian *furlana*, the Moorish *chica*, and the nationalistic *cachucha*, *contradanza*, and *sevillana*, the bolero emerged in 1447 from *bolero moruno*, a loose fusion of body stretches, figures, and head and arm gestures introduced by the Andalusian Roma. Emotional and sophisticated, the Iberian version began with a languid solo or couples slow-quick-quick side steps and rocks. It increased energy with dips, crossovers, and pivots on the ball of the foot and closed on a posed duo.

A European Favorite

Over three centuries later at Cádiz, dancer Sebastiano Carezo standardized the bolero in 1780, when the choreography thrived in Madrid and southern Andalusia. Art historians placed the dance in the same genre as the cha-cha, rumba, merengue, samba, salsa, and *pasodoble* with less melodrama than the fandango and tango. The bolero rapidly infiltrated Europe and reached London in 1782.

Following the flight of islanders after the Haitian Revolution of August 21, 1791, the *bolero romántico* engaged the imagination of Afro-Caribbean dancers at Santiago in a North American variant, the first Cuban folk rhythm to encompass worldwide audiences. Executed to the poetic Cuban *son* (ballad) played on guitar, bongo, and maracas in 2/4 meter, the bolero quickly outclassed the hip-swaying beguine and *danzón*, an offshoot of the *contradanza* and habanera. During the Napoleonic Wars and into the post-romantic era, the bolero couples dance and the more tempestuous fandango solos outpaced the gavotte in popularity and modified Italian ballet.

At first, the elite criticized the bolero for belonging to earthy, voluptuous underclass culture. Public response altered after the Andalusian rhythm liberated the courtly primness of the European dance floor. In April 1812, an American soldier posted in Salamanca reported on a Spanish woman who fainted from the exertions of the bolero. As the dance reached a peak of popularity in the 1820s, a warning in London physician John Shaw's *On the Nature and Treatment of the Distortions to Which the Spine and the Bones of the Chest Are Subject* (1823) remarked on the dips that endangered the tibia and ligaments and toe pressure that could destroy the arch.

A Social Scuffle

In matters of decency, opinions of the bolero teetered back and forth. On October 6, 1820, the English Parliament discussed sportive male body language and its suitability for female spectators. Neapolitan choreographer Carlo Blasis's *The Code of Terpsichore: The Art of Dancing* repudiated censure of the bolero's glides and beats in 1830, calling the dance nobler and more modest and restrained than the fandango. Refuting censorious Toledan clergy in 1845, travel writer Richard Ford concurred with Blasis, characterizing the bolero as matchless, unequalled, and inimitable. An anonymous arts critic writing for *Littell's Living Age* complained that too many noble Spanish women had rejected the dance, leaving it to servant girls and gypsies.

At the Seville Fair in April 1847, Roma men celebrated all-night galas in bolero costume consisting of boots, tight trousers, and short jackets, which female dancers rapidly adopted. Massachusetts-born transcendentalist Margaret Fuller claimed the dance for her own in 1852 because of its existential lust for life. In 1886, New York local colorist Washington Irving made a positive judgment based on the ebullient steps and optimistic air.

In the Dominican Republic, a Spanish folk arts mania in the 1890s created competition for the bolero from the pasodoble, Spanish flamenco and habanera, the Cuban and Puerto Rican *danzón*, and rural Afro-Caribbean merengue. From Cuba, aficionados carried the graceful, dreamy steps to New Orleans as well as Mexico, Puerto Rico, Brazil, Ecuador, Venezuela, Colombia, Chile, and, after 1910, Argentina. Costa Rican musicians evolved a dramatic bolero-tango mode.

In the twentieth century, radio broadcasts extended the audience for intoxicating bolero music. Students of Hispanic dance added the bolero to classes in zarzuela (operetta), flamenco, and Aragonese *jota*. Classroom teachers incorporated the spicy rhythm into physical training and band programs.

In the 1930s, the US version of the bolero drew dancers to the floor to drum pulsations, creating a demand for pliant cocktail dresses. In Spain from 1939 until his death in 1975, dictator Francisco Franco suppressed folk arts, making the bolero illegal. The danceable music and simple steps returned to popularity, forming the basis of the salsa.

See also cachucha; fandango; flamenco; *furlana*; *jota*; merengue; *pasodoble*; Roma dance; tango.

Source: Matteo, Carola Goya. *The Language of Spanish Dance: A Dictionary and Reference Manual.* Hightstown, NJ: Princeton Book Company, 2003.

BRANLE

A joyous rural ronde or roundelay popularized in cities in the early 1500s, the *branle* (also *bransle, brando, brawl,* or *brantle*) was the original figure dance, perhaps a carryover from such children's circle games as "The Shepherd's Pastourelle" and "The Bridge at Avignon." Inviting to young and old, the steps moved couples side to side via sedate glissades in 4/4 meter, a choreography similar to the allemande. Troubadours spread the swaying cross-front-cross-back (grapevine step) throughout the countryside of Poitou, France, in the 1100s as a farandole chain dance, *carole,* or serpentine figure to flute, recorder, and vielle, a bowed string instrument.

Along with the farandole, the branle invigorated the commedia dell'arte and made France a center of European folk choreography. Similar to the ancient Greek *krinon* (choral dance), the steps evolved from the *basse danse,* a serious, slow line or circle dance. The ease of movement of precision line dancers passed the dance into children's play involving hand clasping or "pinky dancing" by hooking little fingers. In Langres, Avignon, Hainaut, Gascony, and Champagne, as well as Holland, Malta, Spain, Scotland, Sweden, Italy, and the Faroe Islands in the 1600s, the dance morphed from a lifting and lowering of heels into a quick left-right-left-right shuffle, clap, and turn accompanied by lute, bagpipes, and hurdy-gurdy, a stringed lute cranked with a wheel that plucks out a melody as well as a monotonous drone.

Dance Evolution

With more spirit than the basse danse or the pavane, the branle developed twenty-three local versions, such as the Charlotte and *pinagay* branles, which added multiple kicks, and the Brittany *trihory*, which swung heels right-left-right. The branle Cassandra equalized movement to left and right and incorporated a heel-toe-heel-toe shuffle popular with German troupes to accordion accompaniment. For the hermit's branle, participants crossed their hands over their chests and nodded a greeting in the pious style of monks. With *la guerre* branle, a dance at double speed, pairs incorporated a cabriole and couples embrace as a finale. Arrangers of an evening of dance often chose the branle for the couples' entrance and their exit to more passionate activities.

The balanced pendulum-style sway of the branle amused the courts of Louis XIV, Henry VIII, and Elizabeth I and, in May 1560, thrived among ladies-in-waiting at the court of Elisabeth of Valois and Philip II at Toledo, Spain. One innovation described in French dance maven Thoinot Arbeau's manual *Orchésographie* (1589), the branle *du chandelier* (torch branle) began with men carrying lighted candles. In the 1570s, the lighted dance appealed to Margaret of France, who received the flame and passed it to the man she chose as her next partner. Spanish dramatist Lope de Vega regretted in 1631 that the dance had declined in Iberia.

During the English restoration after 1660, the branle returned to popularity at the entertainments of Charles II, who lifted the Puritan ban on frivolities imposed during the Commonwealth. Aristocratic dancers enjoyed the skipping branle and knotted or hay styles in which a leader wound among the other dancers in an S or Z pattern. After 1715, the fad waned under Louis XV, who preferred the slow, sober minuet, and after 1774 under Louis XVI, an aficionado of the gavotte, an offshoot of the branle.

Mime and Romance

To keyboard accompaniment, singing branles permeated the social dance of court masques with the pleasures of country folk. More vivacious varieties, notably the clog branle (or branle *de sabots*) of Poitevin, imitated wooden shoes; the horse branle mimed horseback riding that involved clopping and pawing the ground with the feet, a development shared with the bourrée, a quick-paced dance from Auvergne and Limousin. For the picturesque branle *des lavandières*, women performed a coquettish mime of washerwomen with hands on hips or wagging fingers in the posture of a scold, a humorous admonition repeated by male partners.

More than the courante, the branle absorbed numerous adaptations and gestures, earning a snide slang meaning of "masturbation" for its steady repetitions. Unlike the scandalous *volta*, the addition of lifts in the official branle at Roussillon, a Gallo-Catalonian enclave on the western French Riviera, retained decorum because the man placed his hands on his partner's waist to guide her leap. The gavotte branle carried the lift to extremes with a kiss between partners or a more aggressive kissing of all partners, a custom Belgians added to the clapping, circling, and turns of the *zwierig dansje* (jaunty dance).

See also allemande; commedia dell'arte; farandole; gavotte; gendered dance (women); labyrinthine dance; literature, folk dance in; pavane; *volta*.

Source: Vuillier, Gaston. *A History of Dancing from the Earliest Ages to Our Own Times*. New York: D. Appleton and Company, 1898.

· C ·

CACHUCHA

A variety of waltz named for a captain's or baseball cap or a diminutive boat or canoe, the *cachucha* involves a female soloist in graceful swaying, arched attitudes, foot shuffling, glissades, and crossovers to the bouncy rhythm of castanets and guitar. A holdover from the time of the Roman poet Juvenal, the dance to a nationalistic melody derived from the Andalusian Roma, who added African facets to their dance when they crossed North Africa and Gibraltar. The cachucha reached Barcelona and Zaragoza in 1447, when the late medieval folk dance thrived at Cádiz and Jerez.

Two decades after standardization of the fandango, the cachucha reached its present form in Cuba in 1803, when it became a favorite children's street amusement. Further migration to the Western Hemisphere in 1825 introduced the choreography, curved back, pliant midsection, and majestic head and torso pose in Mexico, Peru, and California. Simultaneously, prospectors transported the steps and undulating abdomen to the Australian goldfields in Victoria and New South Wales.

Hispanic Craze

In France in 1836, Parisians adapted cachucha choreography into a couples dance and the basis of the cancan. The cachucha thrilled spectators at London's Drury Lane Theatre on October 6, 1838, as a segment performed by Pauline Duvernay for *The Devil on Two Sticks*. The two-person version drew couples to Hamburg dance halls and entertained spectators in Dublin, Manchester, and Liverpool on programs executed by Clara Vestris Webster. At the request of Pope Gregory XVI for the Corpus Christi Day procession in Seville in June 1839, Spanish peasants presented the cachucha at the Plaza of St. Francisco as an introit to the sacraments.

Austrian theatrical star Fanny Elssler rifled the Iberian choreography from the scenic music in Jean Coralli's classical ballet *Le Diable Boiteaux* (The lame devil, 1836) at the Paris Opera, where she danced the part of Florinda. At the Park Theatre in New York in May 1840 and the next month at the Chestnut Street Theatre in Philadelphia, her flirtatious execution energized a cachucha mania brought on by waves of espagnolism from France. Because of the burgeoning of cachucha fans, she extended the tour of America over three years and continued south to Havana, Cuba. To Elssler's dismay, the Gypsy infamy of her dance prohibited her entry into polite New York society.

The cachucha proved so infectious that performers adopted it around the globe, especially among West Indian Creoles, south to Guiana, and west to Nicaragua and Costa Rica. While honeymooning in Cuba in August 1842, the author Nathaniel Hawthorne compared his wife Sophia's cachucha allure to that of Salomé. At the Alhambra Theatre in London in 1843, Lola Montez hybridized the cachucha with the Italian tarantella for her debut in *El Oleano*. A snide review on July 16 in *London Illustrated* noted her gift for displaying arms and bust while doing little with her legs and feet.

Executed in 3/4 or 3/8 oom-pah-pah time, the tempestuous cachucha earned the title of Spanish waltz, but demeaned Brazilian women as a pejorative for "loose female." The dance appeared on stage programs after the American Civil War and in Australia in 1867 performed by French actor Céline Celeste. The skipping steps emulated the style of the bolero by gradually increasing speed and emphasis on brisk footwork and the flexibility of a small waist.

Historic Dance

The cachucha retained its appeal to all levels of society. At the wedding of Maria Christina of Austria to King Alfonso VII of Spain on November 29, 1879, two dancers performed the cachucha in Seville's Plaza des Armas. After the inauguration of President Chester A. Arthur on September 19, 1881, he requested a demonstration of the cachucha at the White House. A decade later, the Roma at Granada made the dance a focus of their public exhibitions.

The cachucha marked a high point of William Schwenck Gilbert and Arthur Sullivan's operetta *The Gondoliers* (1891) and returned at the finale. The music and steps influenced the love themes of the *sevillanas* and gestures of the galop and fandango and invigorated the physical education classes of Filipino elementary schools. From the pulpit, Catholic clergy decried the sensuality of the arched back, which emphasized breasts, waist, and hips, and the ardent eye clashing of lovers.

By the early 1900s, the cachucha had become passé in Madrid. While plotting *West Side Story* in 1949, composer Leonard Bernstein proposed a cachucha for the character Maria in the song "I Feel Pretty." In the twenty-first century, Les Ballets Trockadero de Monte Carlo adapted the overly sissified sensibilities of the cachucha for male ballerinas in drag.

See also bolero; fandango; galop.

Source: Matteo, Carola Goya. *The Language of Spanish Dance: A Dictionary and Reference Manual*. Hightstown, NJ: Princeton Book Company, 2003.

CAJUN DANCE

Cajun dance preserves a focal element of a poignant diaspora. A mass exile after 1755 displaced Franco-Americans from the *bals de maison* (house dances) of rural Nova

Scotia, Gaspé Peninsula, Prince Edward Island, and New Brunswick. A brutal deraci-nation deported Acadians and their music culture as far south as southern Louisiana and Mississippi, Guadeloupe, Martinique, Guiana, and Haiti. Under a Cajun flag along the Mississippi Delta, the exiles promoted self-sufficiency, but proved loyal to the United States during the American Revolution.

Strongly Catholic and clannish, the artisans and smallholders reared large families in isolation and commemorated their roots with secular community dances at high points of the Christian calendar. At Little Acadias in Quebec and New England, wed-ding receptions, rites of passage, holiday carnivals and processions, and Saturday and holiday *veillées* (parties) featured eighteen authentic Acadian folk dances, including the waltz, *varsouvienne*, polka, mazurka, two-step, and quadrille. Among the historic chore-ography, the troika, a dance for one man with two female partners, recalled a Cossack occupation force in Paris on March 30, 1814.

Cajun folk arts made a strong impression on juveniles. With lyrics dating to the Middle Ages, peasant children formed rings and danced to "Savez-vous planter des choux?" (Do you know how to plant cabbage). For each verse, the children mimed Chinese and Roman methods by touching the ground with finger, hands, knees, and feet.

Cultural Guardians

Among the three thousand Cajuns and their offspring burned out of their homes and forcibly colonized in southern Louisiana, music bound deportees into resilient commu-nities. Fiddlers brought dancers to their feet with the cotton-eye Joe and the territorial two-step "Allons à Lafayette" (Let's go to Lafayette). Late in the 1800s, musicians ad-opted the Polish mazurka as a party tune. The Cajun waltz emulated Corsican couples dances in counterclockwise direction with the subtle inclusion of shoulder rocks, con-versation figures, and hip sways in closed position. Women added a subtle gesture by turning with left arm dropped to the back.

In a religious contretemps, Catholic prelates declared the two-step and waltz inde-cent for women because of their partner's grasp around the waist and cheek-to-cheek embrace. In the confessional, priests refused to grant absolution for multiple infractions of the ban. Acadians compromised by continuing their chaperoned dances in stately, gliding style but halting at midnight on Ash Wednesday and refraining from the of-fensive closed position during Lent. In the 1890s, commercial interests in Montreal and Quebec scheduled large public costume balls and traditional processions as lures to the tourist trade. In New Orleans, the exuberance of "*laissez les bons temps rouler*" (let the good times roll) turned national and global attention to street dance Cajun style.

In 1900, Cajun dancers at Quebec, New Brunswick, Nova Scotia, and Mont-pellier, Vermont, claimed the stamping, bobbing Scots-Irish jig in 2/4 time and the *lanciers* (lancers) quadrille. As groups of eight formed squares for the reel, instrumental-ists accompanied on spoons, juice harp, harmonica, and fiddle. The five-part quadrille symbolized courtship with the girls spurning suitors before agreeing to their advances. More patterned than the Western square dance, the quadrilles required no caller.

Dance Preservation

Despite the pressures of Anglican Protestant proselytizers, on February 2 in the late 1900s, French Canadians of Quebec and the Maritime Provinces observed Candlemas night in traditional style—with crêpes parties and visits from *la chandeleur* (alms collectors). Young men visited neighbors to beg donations of food, clothing, and cash for the poor. In exchange for donations, the alms collectors entertained with song and dance, including the gigue and the Cajun jitterbug.

The Franco-American tradition raised new advocates on the Texas-Louisiana border and at the University of Southern Maine, where physical education instruction included folk choreography and a campus troupe. In New York City in 1936, the Societé Historique et Folklorique Française (French History and Folklore Society) archived details of dances, costumes, and instrumental melodies as resources for folk clubs. Teacher training programs introduced more Cajun children to kinesthetic exercise from their musical heritage by featuring clogging, ring dance, jigs, chaconne, the lullaby *fais do-do* (go to sleep), and the *belle aire*, a dance mode chosen for social commentary, amusement, and relief of spirit possession. From contradance, children performed the figures *la rose*, *le pantalon* (trousers), *l'été* (summer), *la poule* (hen), *la pastourelle* (the shepherdess), and the traditional finale.

During World War II, when stateless Cajuns volunteered as interpreters and interrogators for the Allies, pride in service eased assimilation in southeastern Texas and the twenty-two parishes of Louisiana's Acadiana. Musicians Americanized Cajun dance tunes—"Jambalaya on the Bayou" (1952), "Mississippi Queen" (1970)—with steel guitars and amplifiers from country-western music, but maintained the traditional slow-quick-quick step in closed or semi-open position. The native rhythms appealed to returning GIs and their girlfriends. Francophone dancers preferred Cajun music and rice festivals to the rock concerts of the late 1950s and the British musical fads of the 1960s, and nurtured an older, more precious choreographic genre.

Laborers migrated to jobs in California and introduced Cajun dance styles in the San Francisco Bay area. Following a 1980 antidiscrimination lawsuit in US federal court, the Cajun craze revived cultural stability and pride in cuisine, language, and dance, a source of tourist dollars and exposure on television documentaries *J'ai été au bal* (I've been to the dance, 1989) and *Cajun Country: Don't Drop the Potato* (1990) and the commercial films *Southern Comfort* (1981) and *The Big Easy* (1987). At Berkeley and Palo Alto, dance classes and instructional videos in *allons danser* (let's dance), *fais do-dos* (church socials), and Cajun coffeehouses kept alive the spirit of Franco-American dance.

See also cotton-eye Joe; Creole dance; mazurka; polka; quadrille; *varsouvienne*; waltz; zydeco.

Source: Daniel, Yvonne. *Caribbean and Atlantic Diaspora Dance: Igniting Citizenship.* Champaign: University of Illinois Press, 2011.

CAKEWALK

A popular evening finale among field laborers on plantations in Florida, Virginia, North and South Carolina, Tennessee, and Georgia, the cakewalk (also chalk line dance or dusky drill) became America's first mainstream folk dance craze. The format dated to Ireland before 1680 before passing to slaves in the plantation South. In the mid- to late 1800s, performances entertained the slave quarters on winter nights. To juice harp, banjo, and fiddle, the cakewalk promenade satirized the egotistical grand march of planters decked out in long-tailed coats, tuxedo shirts, ascots, top hats, and canes.

For fluid processions around circles and squares, men stood on the inside to squire female troupers arm in arm. Featured figures involved bows and curtsies; trots, cross-overs; back kicks; hand walking; and mimicry of shoe tying and shining, the Tennessee walking horse, and driving the buggy. Their partners rustled ruffled skirts, pivoted, stepped high, and rocked back with parasols aloft. In competition for hoecake, molasses candy, or other prizes, the winners gained respect for "taking the cake."

Satire on the March

Mockery fueled enthusiasm for the high-toned antebellum cakewalk among black house staff, who secretly lampooned their owners' dancing the prissy minuet and qua-drille. Whites groomed black duos to dress in secondhand finery of their owners and prance at parties on neighboring plantations while balancing water jars on their heads to steps in 2/4 meter. The momentary fame transcended the burden of servility while concealing animosities toward a dominant and inhumane race.

A test of poise and elegance, the cakewalk derided European stuffiness with cartoonish swaggers of walking sticks and adjustments of monocles. When the music stopped, judges eliminated couples as they wound down to the grand prizewinners. Among first-generation African captives, the dance retrieved from West Africa the balance of women carrying burden bundles or men transporting luggage for white safaris in the Congo. Other sources of figures and gestures included West African syn-copation, Kaffir hand gestures, Scots jigs, Irish reels, New Orleans street marches, and Seminole promenades.

From Plantation to Fame

In 1866, an all-male minstrel burlesque in Brooklyn incorporated the cakewalk in the first years of Afro-American liberation. Under demeaning titles mentioning pickanin-nies, darkies, octoroons, coontown, and Uncle Tom, the procession drew fans to ca-sinos, Chautauqua halls, and nightclubs in New York, Boston, and San Francisco. In synchrony, at the 1876 national centennial in Philadelphia, black couples linked pinkie fingers and demonstrated precision and coordination along with high knee action and athletic somersaults before a panel of white judges.

Stage productions distorted the steps with grotesque gestures set to the first ragtime dance tunes, the grandsires of American jazz. Presenters exaggerated defiant leans forward and bent backs like trees in a gale. White imitators turned the plantation dance into a drag show. Protestant deacons punished church members who took part in cross-dressing. In newspapers, art critics demeaned black dancers for their negritude and humble beginnings through stereotypes and rude diminution.

The black diaspora carried the waggish steps to hotel dining rooms, to the 1889 World's Fair in Paris, and on tour in England, Scotland, Australia, and Russia. In the 1890s, the Creole Show, staged to brass band tunes by Kentucky vaudevillians Dora Babbage Dean and Charles E. Johnson, brought the cakewalk to a pinnacle of European patronage. In imitation of John Philip Sousa's "Washington Post March" and in anticipation of the two-step, high school and college drum majors across the United States adopted the high strut for parades.

At the beginning of the twentieth century, the cakewalk migrated to Buenos Aires, Argentina, influencing the nuances of a stylized tango. The cakewalk appeared in unforeseen venues, including a San Francisco ballet *en pointe* in 1903 and during a Norwegian expedition to Antarctica in 1911. School music classes added the strutting steps to folk dance classes of the 1910s. By the 1920s, the cakewalk lost fans to the Lindy hop and the boisterous Charleston.

Source: "The Cakewalk." *Our Paper* (Concord, MA), December 3, 1904, 780.

CALENDA

A slave-era couples dance imported from Angola, Zambia, and tribes along the Congo River basin to the kingdom of Arda on the Gulf of Guinea, the *calenda* (also *calinda*, *kalenda*, or *congo*) initiated a Caribbean form of all-male stick fighting. The martial art developed into the first model of "dirty dancing" in the New World, by which a line of men faced a line of women and leaped before potential mates to clash thigh to thigh in midair. Performers danced Creole style to call-and-response songs about sexual heat and uninhibited copulation.

After 1550, the pelvis-grinding, head-tossing drum dance diffused colonial Dutch, French, Portuguese, and English folk art with the blatant desires of bondsmen and their lovers. Increased trade in sugar plantation labor introduced West African steps, ring shouts, and rhythms to children and adults in the Antilles. To avoid punishment by censorious white Protestants, slaves slipped away to distant clearings and surrounded the amorous dancers. Pairs shimmied and hitch-stepped forward to Congo-style *bamboula* drumming and banjo thrums and uttered suggestive apostrophes and rumblings.

Fertility Dance

During time off work on Sunday evenings, the fertility and mating dance dramas filled duets with lustful body contact, kisses, and embraces. From observations in Grenada, Guadeloupe, Martinique, Dominica, and Hispaniola, Père Jean-Baptiste Labat, a French Dominican friar and historian, described in *Nouveau voyage aux isles de l'Amérique* (New journey to American islands, 1698) the topping of a hollow log with goat hide or sheepskin to make the bamboula drum, played with wrist and fingers to the accompaniment of shakers, gourds filled with corn grains or stones. While the Catholic hierarchy allowed the calenda as exercise and an emotional outlet, Labat demeaned the libidinous dance as an indecent satisfaction of carnal passions.

After 1550, the pelvis-grinding, head-tossing *calenda* diffused colonial Dutch, French, Portuguese, and English folk art with the blatant desires of bondsmen and their lovers. *Cable, George Washington. "Creole Slave Dances: The Dance in Place Congo." Century Magazine (February 1886): 524.*

At Montevideo in 1764, French Benedictine monk Antoine Joseph Pernety observed the calenda performed by animated mestizos of Amerindian, Latino, and African ancestry. Despite its licentious nature, the infectious rhythm permeated social customs, even worship. Pernety expressed shock that adults allowed children to imitate the steps and gestures. While Pernety promoted solo hornpipes and sedate minuets and allemandes, in 1784, French jurist Médéric de Saint-Méry disagreed. He admired the expertise of the female performer, who flirted with handkerchief and petticoat while keeping her spine erect.

The growing appreciation of black social customs decreased condemnation of the calenda. German playwright August von Kotzebue accepted the ethnic value of the dance, which he inserted into his three-act play *The Negro Slaves* (1796). According to "The Coffee Planter of St. Domingo," a first-person article issued in the April 1799 *New Jamaica Magazine,* French travel writer Louis-Sebastien Mercier witnessed a New Year's Day party during which male slaves darted glances at their favorite women. Imbued with free-flowing rum and brandy, their flirtatious calenda continued until 10:00 PM, when a trickster tripped the last couple and caused them to collapse into a tangle of limbs.

After the Louisiana Purchase on May 2, 1803, and the establishment of the sugar industry along the Mississippi Delta, the calenda added voodoo dance and sexual hexing to the multicultural arts of New Orleans. At Congo Square, freedmen escaping a racial backlash from the bloody Saint Domingue insurrection of 1791 saluted liberty with the jig and juba and the seductive symmetry of the calenda. The intriguing duet drew tourists and students from the College of Orleans and contributed to the city's reputation for multicultural oddities.

The calenda lent an air of liberation to black slaves. Until the firing of the Sunday night cannon at 9:00 PM, the beginning of curfew for urban blacks, women gestured with raised petticoats to men. Males leaped into a face-to-face courtship and rubbed their lower torsos against partners in explicit invitation to coitus. The pairs parted suddenly with a pirouette before repeating the set. Upon exhaustion of either party, volunteers took their places in syncopated figures symbolizing the balancing and circling nature of bestial mating.

West Indian Dance

In the late 1830s, solo African choreography gave place to the wildly popular bamboula, *chica*, and calenda. Performers executed the latter to jeering ballads that degraded privileged, hypocritical whites. The mixing of men and women fostered erotic innuendo with pelvic thrusts, rotating buttocks, and rubbing of pubic areas. Central to the teaming of the genders, an advance-and-retreat figure and clapping portrayed the ups and downs of romance. Church edicts and a ban by polite society in 1843 failed to quell enthusiasm for the throbbing music and titillating choreography.

In February 1886, New Orleans author George Washington Cable composed an essay on Creole dance for *Century Magazine* in which he commented on the addition of a madras handkerchief to the calenda in the Windward Islands. The small separation of partners with a cloth rectangle reduced the wanton, orgiastic nature of the mating dance. Men adapted their role with castanets. The prominence of mulattoes on the dance floor caused whites to stereotype the darker races as self-indulgent and voluptuous.

As the calenda migrated, its cross-rhythms invested choreography as far away as Montevideo, Uruguay, and Lima, Peru, and east to Cádiz, Spain. In 1890, author Lafcadio Hearn noted in an article for *Harper's Magazine* the improvisational style of the dance in Martinique. For the *lundu*, which arrived in Brazil and Lisbon, Portugal, from Angola, a gentrified finale pictured the female awarding a handkerchief to the mate of her choice. The dance evolved into the Cuban rumba, Puerto Rican *bomba*, Jamaican calypso, Spanish fandango and habanera, and the Haitian merengue, the source of the reptilian Congo-Caribbean hip roll.

See also allemande; handkerchief dance; hornpipe; jig; juba; merengue; zydeco.

Sources: Cable, George Washington. "Creole Slave Dances: The Dance in Place Congo." *Century Magazine* (February 1886): 517–31. Jones, Susan. *Literature, Modernism, and Dance.* Oxford: Oxford University Press, 2013.

CARMAGNOLE

An antiroyalist song and victory ronde originating in 1790, the carmagnole stirred and inflamed patriots in exuberant dance similar to the Provençal farandole. The circle dance connects historically to scenes of vicious overthrow of the French ruling class in August 1792 in protest of the royal veto of National Assembly resolutions. Set to a

An antiroyalist song and victory *ronde* originated in 1790, the carmagnole united patriots in exuberant dance similar to the medieval farandole from Provençal. *Dickens, Charles. "A Tale of Two Cities,"* All the Year Round *(November, 1859).*

sailor's ditty from the port of Marseilles, or an antimayoral tune from the early 1400s, or the medieval Provençal crusader song *"Malbrough, s'en va-t-en guerre"* (Marlborough has gone to war, 1709), the dance tune rose to popularity in 1781.

Based on the medieval farandole, the steps to left and right preceded advances to and from the center following a call–and–response pattern, a controlling figure of children's games and square dancing. The title bore the name of a skirted laborer's jacket worn by illiterate red–capped peasants near Turin, Italy, at Carmagnola, a piedmont border town of northwestern Italy and southeastern France. The name also applied to immigrant Italians who took low-level work in Paris, in particular, small Savoyard boys who swept chimneys.

The Carmagnole in History

While the privileged stepped to the minuet, subversive Jacobins chanted the spiteful lyrics to rally hatred for "Madame Veto," the rebels' name for Marie Antoinette. The partisans' colorful vests earned the name "carmagnoles," as did the protesters themselves. At Jemappes, Belgium, French revolutionaries forced aristocrats and church prelates to perform "La Carmagnole" and "La Marseillaise" as a punishment before revelers hanged their victims from lampposts. Wise authorities joined the dance around bonfires to save themselves from the noose.

At the rebel invasion of the Tuileries Palace on August 9, 1792, an all-night orgy of radical song and spinning dance glorified the slaughter of six hundred Swiss Guards, the mercenary squad who shielded Louis XVI. Following the transport of the king and queen, fifteen-year-old Princess Marie Thérèse, seven-year-old dauphin Louis Charles, and eight-year-old dauphin Louis Joseph to a cell in the Temple, guards tormented the five captives' fresh-air walks by singing "La Marseillaise" and dancing the carmagnole. Until the execution of the king on January 21, 1793, revolutionaries burst into drunken song and dance at public debates of the king's destiny.

In delirious joy throughout the ten-month Reign of Terror, jostling peasants greeted executions at the guillotine with "La Carmagnole," including Louis's decapitation at Place de la Concorde. Tormentors capered under the queen's windows, singing "La Carmagnole" and flaunting her husband's head on a pike. On May 21, the French navy launched the forty-gun frigate *Carmagnole*. Throughout Austria and the low country, French rebels forced city *carillonneurs* to play "La Carmagnole" from bell towers.

The Jacobins danced the carmagnole after May 31, 1793, while they seized icons of Catholic fanaticism for burning and made merry on their way to melt silver and gold at the mint. They escorted the cart bearing the queen on an hour's ride from the Conciergerie to the scaffold on October 16, 1793, and frolicked for another hour at her beheading for treason. Carmagnole bands gained recruits when they carried their song and dance to bonfires in French towns. Disciples of the Jacobins danced at a series of plantings of linden saplings that restocked Arles and other cities with sixty thousand "liberty" trees. While they exulted, workmen stripped churches of bells and other sources of metal to be melted down for cannon.

Adapting a Dance

La Carmagnole passed to North America via Great Britain in 1793. The song and dance incited support for the French in Boston, where little children learned the steps, and launched chaos in a New Orleans theater, requiring police intervention. For ensuing events, French peasants added more couplets to their jibes, which soldiers shouted out on maneuvers much as marchers counted out steps to *corridos* during the Mexican Revolution. The song reached thirteen stanzas. In *The French Revolution* (1837), Scots philosopher Thomas Carlyle described the dance as a jig performed before the Notre Dame Cathedral upon the raising of a statue on November 10, 1793, to the Goddess of Reason. Another song and dance accompanied the ragged *sans-culottes* (pantless) revolutionaries after they pillaged the abbey of Saint Denis of eighteen cartloads of religious plate and statuary.

Social novelist Charles Dickens depicted the innocent Lucie Manette's glimpse of the demonic fervor of carmagnole dancers in *A Tale of Two Cities* (1859), where Parisian men partnered with men, women with women, and men with women in a deluge of street vengeance. A revival of the vituperative song and dance on December 2, 1851, greeted the seizure of the press by the repressive emperor Napoleon III. More singing and dancing metered the march of anarchists from 1887 to 1890. A later revival in the 1900s supported silk workers at Lyons in their demands for higher wages and Breton steelworkers during strikes and anticlerical activism in September 1903.

See also farandole; jig.

Source: Kippis, Andrew. *The New Annual Register, or General Repository of History, Politics, and Literature for the Year 1801.* London: T. Davison, 1802.

CÈILIDH

A Gaelic dance party in rural Ireland, Scotland, Wales, and Northumberland, England, from the late Middle Ages, the *cèilidh* (pronounced *kay*-lee) took shape in peaceful times after 1014, when the Viking raids ended across Britannia. The social event merged Gaelic storytelling with folk song, "jig-gid-y, jig-gid-y" step dances, and group choreography that anticipated New World barn dances. House parties and university socials to familiar piper's tunes gave youth opportunities to size up prospective partners and court likely mates. Charitable groups used the occasion to collect donations for the poor.

Itinerant pipers and fiddlers memorized locations of common cèilidh houses and made the rounds. To the music of dulcimer, accordion, penny whistle, flute, fiddle, harp, and bodhran (frame drum), guests circled a central peat fire and performed the polka, eightsome reel, jig, schottische, waltz, military two-step, hornpipe, and strathspeys, a dynamic Donegal or northern écossaise (Scots folk figure) typically danced to "Loch Lomond." Following witch tales and bardic lays of Cuchulain, Ossian, and Finn, partnering and square dance preceded ring dance, such as the "Gay Gordons," which a caller announced.

Dance Styles

At the typical cèilidh, folk figures required little explanation or training, even for youths. In allemande pose with right hands joined over the woman's right shoulder, duos took four walking steps, pivoted, and walked four steps back. After a repeat, the man raised the woman's right hand for her turn. The set ended with partners returning to the standard hold for a polka figure circled around the floor.

Cèilidh celebrants excelled at variety. Solo performances of step dance exhibited individual talent and audacious stunts. The "Dashing White Sergeant" freed each man to squire two women. A circle-to-partner-to-circle dance, the "Canadian Barndance" involved groups in a simple round set marked by skips, hops, and claps in 2/4 meter. A longer figure, the "Orcadian Strip the Willow" raised spirits with laughter. Evenings ended with singing of "Auld Lang Syne."

Colonial pioneers carried Gaelic ring and step dance to Australia, New Zealand, the Falkland Islands, Singapore, and Cape Breton in Nova Scotia. Immigrants from the blustery island of Tyree turned Ontario logging bees into cèilidhs, a deep winter pastime and mutual aid for lumbermen and their families. Because of education in the Gaelic language and culture in public schools, the pub and village hall gatherings along the Pacific coast of New Brunswick earned the name the "Cèilidh Trail."

For the Royal Scottish Country Dance Society in 1990, Pam Dignan performed at the summer school *cèilidhs. Michael Greenwood, communications, www.rscds.org/article/media, Royal Scottish Country Dance Society, Edinburgh, Scotland.*

The Cèilidh in History

Impromptu occasions for the cèilidh ranged from Robert Burns' Night each January 25, Valentine's Eve, Halloween, St. Andrew's Day on November 30, and celebrations of great battles to cèilidh plays, a subgenre of alternative theater. At the Scots Hogmanay (New Year's Eve), nationwide mumming and street dances brought hordes of Scots and tourists from as far away as the outer islands and northwestern Europe for drinking and socializing until 1560, when the Scots Reformed Church proscribed the cèilidh. A half century later, round dancing resumed.

Dance parties fed folk hunger for scandal and political intrigue. Between 1689 and the 1750s, home gatherings spread Jacobite news of the exiled Stuarts. In 1745, Scots mobbed cèilidhs during the clearance, the ouster of smallholders from the Highlands to free land for corporate sheepherding by English investors. Featuring lampoons of

British royalty, satiric song and dance assuaged the bitterness of the homeless and raised funds to alleviate family suffering.

The Gaelic dance party never lost its merit as a nexus of folk concerns. At Croy on the lower Strath northeast of Glasgow in 1748, a Sunday night cèilidh mourned the death of a neighbor until sunrise. At a wake at Milltown in southwestern Ireland in 1798, the nearest of kin led the first reel. Establishment of the Free Kirk of Scotland and New Zealand in 1843 renewed religious protests of the cèilidh, but failed to stifle sources of merriment.

During the famine of the late 1870s, cèilidh gatherings at Castlebar, County Mayo, promoted the Irish Land League, a political organization that opposed English landlords, excessive rents, and the eviction of tenant farmers. In 1879, some twenty thousand protesters met at Irishtown outside Claremorris for speeches, music, and dance that affirmed Gaelic identity. At a religious fraternity in Antrim, dancers received weekly lessons as well as information on the Irish underground. The conviviality of cèilidh dances made their way into urban settings, notably, the socials of the Scots Folklore Society of London in 1888.

In 1926, the structured party ensemble aired dance music over Irish radio, encouraging youths to form cèilidh folk bands. A resurgence of dance during the Celtic Renaissance of the 1990s and the film *Rob Roy* (1995) reclaimed collective Gaelic customs. In 2003, the Smithsonian Folklife Festival in Washington, D.C., honored the roots of Gaelic culture with a traditional cèilidh. To fund clean water in poor countries, the English Folk Dance and Song Society sponsored a Big National Cèilidh at Worcester on October 11, 2011. For the WaterAid charity and as a boost to old-time folk arts, additional settings of the global event included Edinburgh, Manchester, Cambridge, Singapore, and Lisbon, Portugal.

See also allemande; barn dance; community dance; jig; polka; reel; schottische; step dance; waltz.

Source: Henry, Lori. *Dancing through History: In Search of the Stories That Define Canada.* Vancouver: Dancing Traveller, 2012.

CENSORSHIP

Attitudes toward the human body and its personal, cultural, religious, and civic use have precipitated curbs on music and suppression of dance. From the biblical heresy of golden calf worship by Israelites around 1440 BCE, the controversial motivation for footwork to music has aroused serious, sometimes lethal repercussions. At the core of the contretemps lay power struggles between creativity and authoritarianism.

Any encroachment of immigrants brings with the newcomers a foreign aesthetic of folk arts. On the advice of Cato the Censor in 186 BCE, the Roman Senate judged foreign religious dancers as degenerates and disallowed exotic and nude performances that threatened ancestral customs. Some seven thousand people across Italy faced questioning and prompt execution. For the next thirty-five years, Cato asserted his right to oppose the dances at the heart of ecstatic Greek bacchanalia and wielded the death penalty to punish infractions of the civic moral code. Because of his virulent embargo, women performed the dances in strict privacy and left few details to history.

Moral Standards

More controversy over dance resulted in harsh laws and repression of creativity. In southern Normandy in 465, the Council of Vannes under Bishop Perpetuus of Tours barred French folk dance and love songs because they ennobled human anatomy and coitus. Drawing on the philosophy of St. Paul and the patristic fathers, the council labeled peasant performance a decadent cult of the body lacking any redeeming value to the mind or soul. Except for lamentation ritual for the dead, dance remained taboo in Christian history, earning condemnation from Pope Adrian I in 774. In 847, Pope Leo IV singled out women as most at fault for profaning worship with their circle dances and farandoles.

Other issues impinged on attitudes toward folk arts. In fall 1374, a psychosomatic madness encroached on Cologne, Trier, Ghent, Metz, and Flanders. The inexplicable St. Vitus' Dance craze forced European priests to ban all church and public socials that might endanger congregations. Under the crusader pope Innocent III, additional canonical sanctions against dance drama at vigils and saints' days emerged from the Council of Avignon on September 6, 1209, when strict Christians struggled to extirpate secularism and heresy. More injunctions—September 17, 1286, at the Council of Bourge and the 1300 synod at Bayeux—ended folk dancing in religious environs.

In the waning of the Middle Ages, forceful clashes between critics exacerbated the plight of folk dance. At Ulm, consternation in 1404 against the tossing of a partner high above the floor and exposing female legs outraged German moralists, who outlawed the *Ländler*, a popular couples dance in closed position. In 1444 at the Sorbonne in Paris and again during a puritanical wave in 1562 at the Council of Trent, clerics declared the Feast of Fools and other peasant choreography idolatrous and heathenish for its disguises and impromptu gamboling and leaping.

From the high Renaissance into the baroque era, judgmental clergy affirmed their suspicions of carnality and debauchery at folk dances. At Jewish weddings in the 1500s, Venetian rabbis considered forbidding the partnering of women with men, but chose to let the Jewish community set its own standards. After 1560, the reformed Church of Scotland proscribed the Hogmanay (New Year's Eve) street dances and drinking at a nationwide *cèilidh*, a successful tourist attraction. In 1635 in Japan, male actors circumvented a ban on female dancing by dressing as women to perform the mincing parasol dance, a hyper-feminine presentation. With similar aggression, the seneschal of Limoux, France, outlawed the bouncy *volta* in 1666 for the scandalous male role in lifting the female partner to his thigh.

Traditional vs. Modernist

Political intervention in dance aroused folk rebellions. In an effort to update Russia, in 1682, Tsar Peter the Great forced dancers to abandon the balalaika and zither, the traditional accompaniments for peasant amusements. Three years later, Pope Innocent

XI incited such dissent over his ban on dance at Iberian cathedrals that he compromised on a papal edict by allowing the congregation at Seville to process and dance on Corpus Christi Day. In Kyoto, Japan, the 1703 restrictions on Kabuki dance for alleged promotion of prostitution resulted in suicide for censors.

Altercations about deportment rocked the New World as well as Oceania. To spite the Puritan hegemony at Massachusetts Bay, on May 26, 1687, the residents of Charlestown raised a maypole as an emblem of their disgruntlement over prohibition of spring folk dances. In 1752, the Spanish Inquisition and the Spanish viceroy, Don Juan Francisco de Güemes y Horcasitas, outlawed the Mexican *jarabe tapatío* because of suggestive body language and intimate male-female contact.

Adverse points of view on dance lacked common ground. Cuban racists terminated Afro-Hispanic dance at fiestas in 1792 and 1799. The prudery of preachers from the London Missionary Society in Tahiti in 1819 vilified ancestral mating dances and revelations of tattooed flesh by participants. Into the mid-nineteenth century at Congo Square in New Orleans, urban whites demonized the frenzied dancing of *bamboula*, *calenda*, and juba out of fear that uninhibited steps and gestures of liberation might lead to a slave revolt.

Throughout the 1860s, European settlers of North America suppressed the sun dance as a means of forcing Amerindian assimilation by ending seminude displays of Lakota, Ojibwa, Métis, Cree, Potawatomi, Algonquin, Mississauga, Inuit, Oneida, Cayuga, Tuscarora, Seneca, Iroquois-Mohawk, Arapaho, Piegan, Assiniboine, Ponca, Omaha, Shoshone, Kiowa, Blackfoot, Ute, Cheyenne, Crow, Arikara, Gros Ventre, Hidatsa, Mandan, and Pawnee dancers. For decades in Rio de Janeiro, Brazilian police decreed an end to the capoeira, a defiant slave exercise in hand-to-hand combat. In Buenos Aires in 1882, an unrestricted municipal decree regulated actions that offended Argentine customs and morality, which included community folk dancing and choreographed scenes from cinema.

Censorship and the Status Quo

During the mounting class warfare in mid-nineteenth century France, satiric public dance presaged a revolution. At Vidauban in Provence on February 13, 1850, Jacobins of the Second Republic defied a prohibition on folk dance commemorating Ash Wednesday. Peasant rebels lined up an ominous farandole caricaturing the decapitation of an aristocrat, a forerunner of Mardi Gras mockery of the pompous. With parallel contempt for the ruling class, during the reign of mythographer-king David Kalakaua in 1874, Hawaiian islanders reclaimed the hula, which missionaries had shamed for more than half a century.

Ineffectual censorship continued to batter folk arts into the next century with explicit veto of the fandango and *sardana* in Spain, the square dance in Quebec, and the Tanzanian and Kenyan *ngoma* (drum dance), an acrobatic line dance featuring hip rotations that outraged Protestant missionaries and terrified mining authorities with threats of revolt. In *Out of Africa* (1937), author Isak Dinesen disclosed the arrest of dancers for performing the ngoma in the 1910s. In 1896, the first film gag rule shut down theaters showing the film *Fatima's Dance* in Atlantic City, New Jersey. Vatican backlash at modernism erupted from Pope Pius X on January 16, 1914, when he demeaned the tango for undermining the spirituality of dancers.

For political reasons, in the early 1920s, Mustafa Kemal Ataturk, the shaper of modern Turkey, outlawed Sufi dance because of its ancient beginnings. He attempted to force peasants to replace pagan folk dance with European waltzes and polkas. An additional grassroots resistance of Louisiana's ouster of Creole French from public schools resulted in the successful launch of zydeco dance music on radio broadcasts. In 1929, the emerging white supremacy in Weimar Germany criminalized "Negro" dance for its assault on white purity.

In more current times, the free expression of rhythm and dance continues to rile fascists and religious fundamentalists. Examples include the interdiction on Indonesian dance drama in Jakarta under President Sukarno in 1962, Chinese dictator Chairman Mao Tse Tung's control of the arts in the same decade, Chilean strongman Augusto Pinochet's closing of public venues after 1973, and moral censorship in Zaire under Mobutu Sese Seko and Pakistan under Inder Kumar Gujral in 1997.

The price for subverting anti-dance law jeopardizes civil liberties and lives. In Burma in January 1996, a Mandalayan folk dance in Rangoon cost participants seven-year jail sentences. Muslim oppression in Somalia in 2006 resulted in the arrest and flogging of dancers for male-female partnering. From 2013 to 2014, Sayyid Qutb, leader of the Muslim Brotherhood of Egypt, threatened belly dancers with flogging for debasing sexual mores.

See also bamboula; belly dance; *calenda*; *cèilidh*; circle dance; community dance; fandango; farandole; hula; *jarabe tapatío*; Jewish dance; juba; lamentation dance; maypole dance; parasol dance; Siberian dance; square dance; step dance; Sufi dance; sun dance; tango; *volta*; zydeco.

Source: Jones, Derek, ed. *Censorship: A World Encyclopedia.* New York: Routledge, 2015.

CHAIN DANCE

A repetitive peasant figure performed on common ground, chain dance epitomizes the democratic ideals of folk arts and healing and fertility rituals. The style flourishes in northern Panama, among the Choctaw stomp dancers of Oklahoma, and across the Balkans and northeastern Europe. Pottery, bas-relief, and murals from 1400 BCE reflect the twisting, twining patterns of chain dance in Crete and Ionia, where leaders nodded their heads or swung a wand to set the meter. Styles encompassed the sacrificial ceremonies of Carthage, Corsica, Phoenicia, Phocaea, and Tibet and communal European gaiety to trace a magical labyrinth or mark good weather on May Day and midsummer each June 24.

Historically, hand clasping varied with pinky chains linking little fingers, waist encircling, and the Jewish and Romanian shoulder hold used in the Sabbath entrance to the synagogue and in presentations of the *sârba*, *aksak*, and Carpathian and Danubian *brâul*. For grasped hands or interlinking fingers, dancers could stretch out in a simple T shape, cross hands into an X, raise hands into a W, or drop them to hip height into a V. For chains facing forward, dancers often joined hands at back. For the Moroccan *ahwash* and the *dabke* of Jordan, Syria, Lebanon, Iraq, and Palestine, participants extended arms straight across shoulders.

Historic Chain Dances

During campaigns and wars in France and Germany throughout the Middle Ages, women left to their own entertainment in baronial castles often formed a post-lunch chain dance. Moving to the left, they followed the lyrics sung by the leader and joined in the chorus. To flute, recorder, and vielle, a bowed string instrument in Poitou, France, troubadours spread the swaying cross-front-cross-back (grapevine step) in the 1100s as the basis for a serpentine chain or *carole*, a popular after-tournament amusement in Ireland and Finland and on the Continent. In Brittany, the introduction of the gavotte took the form of a chain. In Denmark, chain dancing in farmhouses packed festivities into small spaces.

In Balkan prehistory, nuptials and feasting gave opportunities to form the comic *cocek*, a pumping Croat-Serb chain formed of transvestite men. The weaving cortege joined central European survivors of the Black Death in the *Totentanz*, an existential acknowledgment of mortality after the mid-1300s. As an icon of renewal, the Italian *ridda* developed bridge figures featuring arches from hands joined over the dance path. From Bohemia, Slovakia, and Poland to France, participants wound under the arches, closed ranks, reopened the line, and repeated the cycle, a style that artist Ambrogio Lorenzetti painted at Siena in 1339.

Between 1362 and 1389, when Murad I extended the Ottoman Empire into the Balkans, Evzoni light infantrymen executed mime steps in chain dances reenacting guerrilla resistance in the Greek mountains against the advancing Turks. Once traversing castle halls to ballads in community rings and coils, the late medieval chain dance spread to some thirteen hundred peasant choreographies across Europe, with Slovakia claiming fifty-nine varieties. The pattern reached Azerbaijan and Turkey as the *dilan*, a handkerchief dance set to a heel-and-toe figure at nuptial galas.

In 1503 at precolonial Cuzco, Peru, Huayna Capac scheduled a state chain dance of some three hundred men to honor the birth of a son, the Inca prince Atahualpa. By the time Hispanic freebooters learned of the chain, legend had described it as golden, a metaphor that conquistadors misunderstood as a hidden treasure. The rhythm gained favor with Afro-Caribbean slaves, who ended the sugarcane harvest with a throbbing chain line. In token of a history of legs chained from one to another, dancers named the figure a "conga" from the Bantu word for "uproar."

The chain became the national dance of the Faroe Islands under the name "the crowding dance." Also called *kaededans*, the retinue developed into a favorite in Copenhagen, Denmark. Although Vatican and priestly jeremiads castigated the body language of dance drama throughout the Catholic world, good-natured performances flowed left to right around bonfires during the cold months from September to Lent. The socials reclaimed Nordic heritage cycles of two hundred stories.

In Old Norse tradition in the Faroes, the footwork of two stamps left, one stamp back, and one stamp right derived rhythm and motif from a chant or song sung by the *skipari* (line captain). In kinetic education to the young, gestures acted out thirteenth-century tales from Iceland and Scandinavia depicting Viking sea rovers, vengeful trolls, souls of the drowned united on shore, and triumphs of Sigurd the dragon-slayer. As the verses described battles of Charlemagne and his paladins, participants raised fists; when forces triumphed, the dancers cheered. A variation formed arches of ribbons held by couples for the cavalcade to tread under. At Ólavsøka, the midsummer festival on July 29, Faroese celebrants rounded out boat and rowing races and soccer with chain dancing to folk classics for all ages.

Rural vs. Urban Dance

The individual expressionism emerging during the Renaissance created social boundaries separating peasants from aristocrats. In place of jubilant improvisation among chain dancers, courtly dance imposed the formal patterns of the polonaise and pavane. As a military training exercise, warrior chains set offensive soldiers at the front of the line to counter attacks from the end of the line. By the 1750s, chain dancing incorporated the more elaborate figures of the cotillion, allemande, and promenade, all forerunners of the quadrille.

The arrival of Danish pioneers to Danebod, Minnesota, on September 8, 1872, brought Lutheran holiday customs from Scandinavia to the Great Lakes frontier. In the style of folk arts from the 1780s, families grasped hands at Christmas for a ring dance. In heritage clothes, Danish-Americans readied for the season and directed their steps around the Yule tree, the focus of their Christian celebration.

As a carnival novelty after 1929, Brazilians and Cubans zigzagged to shuffle-shuffle-shuffle-kick, the syncopated Afro pattern of the conga's 4/4 meter. The line snaked through streets and plazas of Rio de Janeiro, Havana, and Santiago. By 1936, the conga revived single-file dance at Montmartre clubs in Paris and in New York at the Stork Club and Cotton Club and in the Waldorf-Astoria ballroom to the beat of Xavier Cugat on the staved conga drum. Among laboring-class blacks and mestizos, in 1940, Cuban politician Fulgencio Batista scheduled demonstrations to staccato drumming that anticipated the third beat.

With the rise of urbanism after World War II, cohesive dance with hand clasping died out in industrialized areas, but the shoulder and waist holds of the cotton-eye Joe persisted. For the physical education and play of children, schools retained the catenated foundations of "London Bridge Is Falling Down," "Looby Loo," "Hokey Pokey (or Okey Cokey)," and "The Bunny Hop," which emerged in San Francisco in 1953. For all ages, the chain dance genre survived in Ukraine, Brittany, Sardinia, and Provence and thrived in Yugoslavia, Hungary, Romania, Slovakia, Bulgaria, Albania, Greece, and the Aegean and Faroe islands. Neopagan gatherings accentuated oneness with Wiccan chain and round dances.

See also allemande; *branle*; community dance; cotillion; cotton-eye Joe; farandole; film, folk dance in; gavotte; labyrinthine dance; maypole dance; pavane; polonaise; quadrille; stomp dance; *Totentanz*; Wiccan dance.

Source: Mullally, Robert. *The Carole: A Study of a Medieval Dance.* Farnham, UK: Ashgate, 2011.

CIRCLE DANCE

A protective geometric, the ring dance epitomizes a prehistoric belief that circles exerted magic over evil and ill fortune. The earliest form of synergy, the circle dance to drumbeats or chant built fellowship around cave fires while offering warmth and exercise during a long winter. Because of social complexities regarding divinity, sorcery, and protective charms, ring steps evolved to propitiate gods, honor the dead, predict the future, and celebrate victory over the elements and enemies.

To ready children for adult responsibilities, outdoor circular games and steps engaged cognitive awareness and taught group reliance during tribal hunting and gathering. At weddings, encircling the nuptial couple blessed the new household, a hallowing of the nuclear family such as that conferred on the featured couple Esteban Trueba and Clara del Valle in the film *The House of the Spirits* (1993), Isabel Allende's dynastic saga based on Chilean history. In Laos, dancers quadrupled the blessing of the ring dance with the *lamvong*, the Lao national dance featuring a circle of onlookers around three concentric rings of dancers.

As epitomized in the art of the Neolithic Yan-shao culture of 4000 BCE and carved on rocks by proto-Egyptians in 3400 BCE, circle dance developed folk significance at the earliest stages of civilization. The need to gyrate and prance permeated the Iberian fado, Mediterranean mystery cults, and Iron Age ring sets created by the Irish Celts. From 1200 BCE, Germanic and Scandic tribes of tree cultists honored spring with the maypole dance, a ring circumscribing a wood post or trunk that has survived in folk art for more than three millennia.

Particularizing Ring Dance

The classical period characterized in art and literature the refinement of choreography as dance acquired clearer purpose and style, for example, arm-in-arm bonding of Greeks at Epiros and the *gorka*, or spring planting dance, of the Old Believers in central Russia. In the *Iliad* (800 BCE), Homer described the Greek and Cypriot *choreia*, a maidenly honor to the Great Mother Goddess Cybele. Dancers encircled a sacred space—a tree or spring, idol, or altar, or the midpoint of the Greek theater, such as the orchestra (dancing place) of Epidaurus, erected around 350 BCE. The Romans reclaimed the ring as the chorea, an impromptu circle dance for women's enjoyment. The Catalonian *sardana* circle dance promoted unity with the lifting and lowering of clasped hands, an aim shared with early Hindu and Christian communities.

The ring dance took distinctive names in Eurasia—*horo* in Bulgaria and Macedonia, *kolo* in Bosnia and Croatia, *khorovod* (choral dance) in Russia, the *anzhao* masked circle dance in northwestern China, the Kurdish shoulder-to-shoulder *kochari*, Manipuri dance in northeastern India and the Burmese border, and hora in Romania, Ukraine, and Moldova. Around 1300, the Slavonic *tamburitza* spread from the Ottoman Empire to Croatia and Bosnia. In the late Middle Ages, the Bolognese and Danes favored ring and chain styles that opened the circle to create a follow-the-leader pattern. Paintings of Dutch country folk captured the simplicity of the *branle*, a round that adults and children performed without training. For bar and bat mitzvahs, Jewish guests joined the hora and other circle dances to klezmer music. From 1396, each Easter Monday, in an ecclesiastical ring dance at the Cathedral of St. Stephen at Auxerre, France, the turn-halt-counter-turn followed twelve concentric circles, an adaptation of circle dance that evolved into labyrinthine dance.

In the Renaissance, rural ronde or roundelay and contradance gained favor in urban areas in the early 1500s. Roma children migrating over the Balkan states taught their peers rounds that originated in India. Elizabeth I devoted middle age to touring rural dance venues, where she first observed the gavotte, a distinctive outgrowth of the medieval round dance.

As indoor couples dance began replacing outdoor ring dance, in 1591 at Cowdrey in Sussex, the queen studied the sequence of circle dancing by farm tenants to pipe and tabor. Because of her rejection of Continental fare as "un-English," she fostered rural enthusiasm for authentic British folk arts. Her choices included steps to "Greensleeves," a love song reputedly written by her father, Henry VIII, and the Rogero, a rural dance similar to a pavane, which playwright Thomas Heywood mentioned in *A Woman Killed with Kindness* (1603) and John Playford described in his manual *The English Dancing Master* (1651).

With the creation of the cotillion rural dance in 1750, callers of figures coordinated a promenade with the allemande and ring dance. Spectators among Native Americans described clockwise circles of the Maya performing the *baile de las cintas* (ribbon dance) of Yucatán and Mandan males in the Dakota Territory imitating a great beast for the bear and buffalo dances. In Portuguese South America, the capoeira (chicken fight) circle dance, an acrobatic bush fighter's mime, expressed the animosity of a brotherhood of Afro-Brazilian slaves.

On the North American frontier, children's "play parties" in the Appalachian Mountains and Amish farm compounds tended toward round capers and games set to two European favorites, "Go In and Out the Window" and "Ring Around the Rosy." For adults, barn dances began with circles and advanced to quadrilles and square dancing. At Scandinavian settlements, families encircled the Christmas tree to perform the *polska*, the national dance of Sweden, Finland, Denmark, and Norway.

Meaning in Ring Dance

In the early 1800s, community dance thrived among agrarian populations, notably Australian organizers of bush dance and Sicilian circle dance and residents of central Russia, the Ukraine, and Siberia, where the village *hedje* (circle dance) welcomed the sun. Sardinians animated gatherings with the *ballu tundu* (also *ballu bardu*), a flexible circle formed around singers. Set to reed instruments and accordion, the choreography in 6/8 time recognized the marital status of performers. Unmarried pairs held hands; husband and wife interlocked fingers.

The *songdans*, ronde, or ring dance remains a standard twenty-first-century genre for children and young adults in Franco-American New England and Canada, in Norwegian enclaves and the Faroe Islands, and among the Zionists of Israel and Sufists throughout the Muslim world. For the Makaraka tribe, a Sudanese circle dance performed three times a day for three days honors the recent dead, a custom similar to the *raksa* circle dance on the Arabian Gulf. In Nigeria, the *gahu* circle dance displays costly headpieces and robes that celebrate prosperity and pride. As a source of satire, the performance ridicules Europeans. Globally, the occupational therapy of round dancing, especially for the elderly, bereaved, and handicapped, promotes healing and wellness.

See also barn dance; *branle*; carmagnole; contradance; fado; film, folk dance in; gavotte; ghost dance; *ghurei* dance; Greek dance; handkerchief dance; holiday dance; hora; labyrinthine dance; Manipuri dance; *mayim mayim*; maypole dance; *odori*; *polska*; square dance; tarantella.

Source: Watts, June. *Circle Dancing: Celebrating the Sacred in Dance.* Mallet, UK: Green Magic, 2006.

CLOGGING

Born from the make-do footwear of the poor, clogging provides folk dance with percussive two-count steps that also clack out music similar to a march, a popular twenty-first-century genre in Franco-American New England and Canada. Dances took their precise downbeats on heels from the sounds of everyday countrymen's footwear on slate floors and cobbled streets. Routines reflect the historic step dances of black minstrels and the hard-clacking jigs of Irish sailors in West Indian and Pacific ports. By dancing in split-sole leather shoes, the cloggers increased the range of steps and intricate toe work.

The nailing of metal heel and toe plates with brass or iron studs to the soles of one-piece wood slip-ons enhanced the wooden thuds of clogging equipment. Another invention, the articulated plate, fit over the front of the shoe for toe touches and foot-pulls over the floor. For a more complex sound, dancers chose hinged taps, cast aluminum flanges, lightly resounding bell taps, or jingle taps, the common term for two-part metal plates, one loose and one stationary. To prevent injuries or harm to dance floors, modern taps are attached with glue rather than studs.

A Medieval Rhythm

Like the Roman *scabillae* (tap shoes), Australian *gabber*, Japanese *geta*, Korean *yuhye*, and Peruvian zapateado, unisex clogs evolved naturally for men in India. They also shod Celts at Bath and London; Korean minorities in China in 618; and herders and farmers in late medieval England, Ireland, Scotland, and Wales. Like British bondsmen, servants, and gardeners, French, Walloon, and Belgian laborers carved their own *sabots* (wood clogs) from springy woods—aspen, alder, willow, birch, or sycamore—that resisted splintering and splitting from hard stamps and toe taps. In cold, blustery weather, wearers secured the tieless shoes by wrapping them in animal pelts.

When British laborers went dancing, one-piece work brogans developed into hand-tooled and colored *neet* (night or party) shoes. Clog makers began offering styles of seasoned woods in varied shoe fronts, advancing from the plain round toe to the duck or square toe and elevated heel. At Deheubarth in southern Wales in 1176, Lord Rhys ap Gruffydd held the first *eisteddfod* (arts session), which regularly featured cloggers. Similar festivals took clogging to British enclaves in Bellarat, Australia; Canterbury and Otago, New Zealand; and Gaiman, Argentina. At Sydney, Australia, seamen and stevedores in the wharf district invented the "Sydney Three-Crack Whip," a three-stamp imitation of the bull drover's lash. Upon viewing a Russian Gypsy *hopak*, the Welsh added a "toby" (squat-kick) to clogging in Cossack style.

In Holland in the early 1300s, fishers, farmers, and animal slaughterers stomped their low-backed ash wood *klompen* (safety shoes) to polka rhythms in the *klompendansen* (also called the *boerendansen* or farmer dancing). For fifteenth-century Dutch dancers, the introduction of wood-soled leather brogans with rawhide ties made clog stomping more comfortable and controllable. The command of motion and sound resulted in the double-toe shuffle and the stamp-stomp-tip, two standard presentation techniques.

The long-lived clog dance thrived in Naples in the 1520s, when dancers called clogging shoes "*zoccoli*" or by the French term "*des sabots*," dancing slippers that fastened in front with a leather thong but were loose at the back for heel rapping. A version of a Renaissance dance, the clog *branle* concluded with stamping and pawing at the ground like a horse. Clogging remained in style into the seventeenth century, when King Charles II requested an exhibition upon his return to the English throne from France in 1660. By 1735, when Welsh Methodist revivalists banned clogging festivals for corrupting Christians, Roma immigrants kept heritage arts alive. Radical Welsh antiquarian William Jones of Llangadfan, Montgomeryshire, preserved tunes, clogging steps, and figures in his histories in 1794 for the Gwyneddigion Society.

In rural North Carolina, Tennessee, and Kentucky in the 1700s, Appalachian mountaineers evolved the "hillbilly tap dance" from square dancing. Identifiable styles emerged from Scots-Irish fiddle tunes and German step dance and *Schuhplattler*, a vigorous mountaineer rhythm marked by syncopated hits on the torso, backside, thighs, and feet and slaps on lederhosen and shoe soles. European newcomers adapted Cherokee and West African slave techniques to banjo riffs, the forerunners of tap dance.

Backwoods flat-footers kept knees bent and accentuated taps with casual flat-footed chug-and-pullback and drags or slides while maintaining a crisply vertical upper body posture and loose arms. Integral to clog figures, the buck and wing named a bounce-and-scuff step to the side and gave male performers the name "buck dancers." Additional technique involved balancing on the ball of the foot and pattering with alternating heel and toe clacks.

From Folk to Stage

In the late 1700s, supercilious British aristocracy scorned the Bavarian Schuhplattler and clogging as rustic and passé. Nonetheless, clog dances flourished among rural folk in Devon, East Anglia, and the Lake District and passed to Scots-Irish enclaves in North America along with the highland fling, jig, and reel. Clog dancers entertained their families at parties and sometimes threatened first-floor ceilings with second-floor galas. Males settled disputes in the nude by outdancing an opponent or leaping in place to kick him in the head.

In northern England after 1773, bargees on the Leeds and Liverpool Canal set a unique 2/4 rhythm with iron-soled clogs to the chug-chug-chug of the single-stroke

Bollinger engine. When wars stripped the barge service of male laborers, women took the jobs and danced as "cloggies." At Bordeaux in 1789, choreographer Jean Dauberval incorporated clogging as a humorous character dance in his popular French ballet *La fille mal gardée* (The poorly guarded girl).

At nineteenth-century collieries and cotton mills in Lancashire, English workers used cheap wood-soled work shoes and warmed their feet in unheated factories by shuffling and tapping. They emulated the rhythm of looms with heel-and-toe steps, such as the "pick the shuttle" or heelless choreography, called "off the toe." During informal competitions at breaks and after-hours workingmen's clubs, judges assembled under or behind the dance platform to evaluate unbroken steps. They awarded the most rhythmic and innovative clogger a championship belt.

In Scotland in 1819, itinerant dance masters taught clog steps, jigs, and hornpipes to urban children in Edinburgh. The best performers introduced street presentations around 1820. Inventive performers developed folk clogging, shepherd's dance, schottische, slip jig, clog rag, step dance, clog polka or waltz, Scots hard-shoe, and clog-hornpipe and furthered global folk choreography with the new combinations.

In 1864, four-year-old Dan Leno staged a clogging exhibition in Coventry at the Britannia Music Hall and in London at the Rotunda. Dan paired with his brother Henry the next year for a clogging duo. At the same time that industrialized weaving burgeoned because of a dearth of raw cotton during the American Civil War, the folk art returned to popularity and passed to dance halls and vaudeville.

Clogging gained fame in the first Broadway musical, Charles M. Barras's *The Black Crook* (1866), and the silent films of Charlie Chaplin, Clara Bow, and Stan Laurel. In the late 1800s, clog buyers paid sixteen cents a pair, from which the carver earned two cents' profit. By 1901, the British kept six thousand clog carvers in business, in part to supply the unemployed at the workhouse and equip street corner dancers, who rapidly wore out wood toes and heels.

British and French Canadian dancers pleased pub goers at a "free-and-easy" (amateur night) by elevating their clog routines to trestle tables, bar counters, and high platforms as varied as packing cases, flat-bed trucks, beer barrels, bass drums, accordion boxes, cellar doors, flagstones, and pony carts. Throughout former English colonies in the 1940s, the descendants of Irish laborers restored traditional mill workers' dancing, called the Lancashire-Irish clog. The rise of interest in folk art in the 1970s returned clog dancing to prominence.

In July 2006, some five hundred teens from twenty-six countries clogged at The Hague to set a world record. Folk performers from Canada, Israel, Jamaica, and Finland presented their regional styles. Another record, set in May 2010 in Pella, Iowa, featured 2,604 Dutch-Americans in a celebration of clogging heritage from the Netherlands. In Wales in 2013, children learned clog steps in school.

See also branle; cotton-eye Joe; highland fling; hornpipe; jig; *joropo*; morris dance; parasol dance; polka; schottische; *Schuhplattler*; square dance; step dance; waltz; zapateado.

Source: Dunmur, Ian. "Traditional Step Dancing" (1984). *Chris J. Brady.* Accessed September 3, 2014. http://chrisbrady.itgo.com/dance/stepdance/trad_step_dancing .htm.

COMIC DANCE

Satire, mumming, and humor mark story dance, totemic rites, and mime; the high point of the post-Easter Berga *tirabol*; the Mexican *el baile de los viejitos* (dance of the old men) of Michoacán; the *yatton bushi* of the unemployed Japanese worker; and the Jamaican *jonkonnu* (also *John connu, John Canoe, junkanoo, Jangkunu*), a prancing parody of slave ownership. In Sri Lanka, the *salupaliya* dance presents a transvestite stand-up soloist performing a comic dialogue while flirting with a shawl and twirling a tiered skirt above ankle bells and restrained footwork. Extravagant and grotesque dance taunts human foibles, such as "Matthew Is Dead," a Polish story dance that depicts so lively a spirit that even a funeral does not end his foolery. By mocking death and fears of entombment, performers reject doom from their folk activities.

From 768 BCE, Etruscan harvesters played pranks and organized dance skits anticipating the commedia dell'arte. In ancient Delos, Crete, and Greece, from 500 BCE, Dorian devotees of Apollo along the Aegean Sea performed the *hyporchema*, or crane dance, a mimetic liturgy that directed dancers around a temple altar to Apollo, the god of the arts, or Dionysus, the god of wine. In an innovation of choreographer Thales of Crete, serpentine steps imitated the myth of Theseus in the labyrinth, where the hero searched for the Minotaur, a bloodthirsty bull. The hyporchema concluded with a half circle of choric dancers singing odes and dithyrambs (hymns). In contrast to serious dance, the licentious *cordax* contributed hilarity to the plays of Aristophanes.

Throughout the Middle Ages, the immurement of European women during lengthy military campaigns left girls and their mothers bored while knights attended to wars. As entertainment in nearly deserted courts of baronial castles, women gathered around the court fool, the royal jokester who frisked about in satiric mockery. Stylized court dance involved French and German women in pre-Renaissance farandoles and chain dances around the spring maypole, two sources of merriment for lone females.

Daily Humor

In India, parody became the focus of thirteenth-century CE Malayalam stage plays and their clownish songs and witty burlesque channeling sarcasm and irony based on social class. In southeastern India, the Tamil Nadu enjoyed the *kali attam*, a fun dance requiring twisting and rotating while swinging sticks tipped with brass bells. A more buffoonish dance, the severe *attam* involved a group in defeating a trickster who performed ridiculous steps behind the king's chariot.

From the 1200s onward, Catalonians let off steam at Corpus Christi Day, a fiesta held sixty days after Easter. The annual five-day roistering in Berga incorporated masking and spiral dance to tirabol music of a drum, tambourines, and bands. Chases of devils and angels and parodied jousting of cavaliers on hobbyhorses moved counterclockwise around the plaza while peasants drank and pranced in a line dance. The addition of satiric bourgeois figures in the late 1700s skewered the foibles of the privileged.

In the 1500s, droll miming upgraded repeated folk choreography with minor skits and gags. For the French *branle des lavandières*, female dancers posed as annoyed laundresses with hands on hips. For stress, they clapped hands like washing bats and brandished fingers in the faces of partners as though scolding the man who dirtied his work clothes. The duet took a gendered turn when male dancers reversed the finger shaking and lambasted the females.

In central Mexico after the conquest of Tenochtitlán by Spanish conquistador Hernán Cortés in 1521, mestizo dancers presented mocking pageants. The *chinelos*, a deriding of Hispanic overlords on Independence Day, blatantly copied the curled beards and light skin of Spanish insurgents. Under huge hats, symbols of egotism, the performers exaggerated the foibles of Spanish colonizers with elaborate footwork and jumps, an allegory of European rationalization of land theft and cruelty to the Aztec. In the seventeenth-century, a parallel lampooning of English royalty and landlords filled Scots-Irish *cèilidhs* with mirth.

Satiric Dance

With more pernicious intent, dancers in southern France derided royalists and their priests with the farandole, a medieval chain dance. As an introit to the French Revolution of 1789, folk line dancers wound through streets and performed the carmagnole around liberty trees to proclaim the downfall of the Bourbon Dynasty and the executions of Louis XVI and his queen, Marie Antoinette, in 1793. Rancorous stanzas and hopping, bounding maneuvers recruited spectators to the rebellion against royalists in 1815 and the Second Republic in 1849. At its most ribald, the farandole burst into Catholic worship and parodied the local curé with obscene ditties and sashaying burlesque.

Around 1880, Malay choreography adapted the *boria*, a humorous skit dance from Persia similar in tone to the Italian commedia dell'arte. By combining a chorus, a solo dance, and a comedy routine, the olio entertained residents of Penang. At Pekan, Endau, and Johor, varied forms of the *labi-labi* (turtle dance) in heritage costumes delighted spectators with the wobbling movements of a crawling amphibian. Variations of the gendered *matachines* dance in Alcalde, New Mexico, and Rio Sucio, Colombia, derived drollery from transvestite males who mocked facets of female vanity and dress. For the *Schuhplattler* in 1890, Bavarian clap dancers added a naughty peek under their female partners' skirts to elicit chuckles from tourists.

See also animal dances; *branle*; cakewalk; carmagnole; *cèilidh*; corroboree; cotillion; disguise; farandole; jig; labyrinthine dance; lion dance; *matachines*; morris dance; *Schuhplattler*; Siberian dance; *tirabol*; totemic dance.

Source: Kassing, Gayle. *History of Dance: An Interactive Arts Approach.* Champaign, IL: Human Kinetics, 2007.

COMING OF AGE

The passage from child to adult inspires its own artistry in ethnic cultures. Dance takes an honored place in the psychosocial adjustment accompanying the Jewish bar and bat mitzvah circle dances to klezmer music, the gyrations of teen boys enduring the stings of bullet ants of the Amazonian Satere-Mawe tribe, and all-night folk dance of courting males in Samoa. Arbitrary dates and landmarks precede scheduling of a maturation dance, as with the sidewalk break dancing of Puerto Rican boys in the Bronx, a daughter's presentation of the *bharathnatyam arangetram* in India, and the *ticuna* fire-jumping dance of girls in Brazil. For the Chinese priest after 1500 BCE, false faces obscured identity during curative treatments and transformative coming-of-age ceremonies for tribal youths.

Public recognition of adulthood can bring teens together in a commemorative dance, as with the playful Libyan and Egyptian *hagallah*, a veiled dance that allows nubile teen girls to strike with a stick any man yanking at her head scarf. To honor adolescence, Arab celebrants at weddings from Libya to Egypt perform the hagallah in token of a woman's self-esteem and readiness for marriage. Surrounded by men, the veiled bride-to-be sways to chants and clapping. In 1835, American portrait and sketch artist George Catlin recorded a Fox and Sauk slave dance, by which young males voluntarily accepted any menial assignment for two years to establish their potential as loyal followers of the chief. Other examples of coming-of-age ritual involved barn dancing and hayrides enjoyed by the Jewish teens of Natchez, Mississippi, in the 1880s and the interethnic salsas and sock hops of California Chicanos in the 1940s.

Begashu youths of the Central African Republic undergo circumcision and tooth extractions at puberty before both boys and girls participate in a beer-drinking and dance festival. Among the Aymara of Bolivia, boys and girls clad in vests and fitted alpaca wool caps with earflaps gather on November 29 for a kachua feast. For a dating dance, boys play flutes while girls gambol in a rigorous choreography aimed at new boyfriends.

Dances of Transition

In a more gendered ritual, a once-in-a-lifetime girl's dance of the Americas and the Caribbean, the gala honoring an Hispanic teen on her *quinceañera* (fifteenth birthday) exalts dance as a symbol of womanhood. In a reversal of emphasis on age and experience, rituals honoring Balkan preteens near Sofia, Bulgaria, feature old women performing for maidens. As the steps move counterclockwise to two-part harmony, the elders press arms around each other's waists and sing of the transition of girl to woman and wife.

The display of dance talents proves to observers that African girls are ready to assume adult responsibilities. To honor pre-adults, the Bambara of Guinea arrange a *focodoba*, a rapid stomping, kicking, and clapping dance similar in acrobatic skill to the Maasai *eunoto*, a jump fest and competition for males of Kenya and Tanzania. The Ga-Adangme of Accra, Ghana, involve girls in the *takoe*, a puberty dance that introduces maidens to mothercraft.

A complicated initiation of boys in Gambia and Senegal introduces them to a secret hunting society. Disguised in masks made from leaves, red fiber, and bark from trees in the sacred forest, in late August, the youths process to a circumcision rite. Staccato dance steps lead into the trees, where older boys and neighbors wield machetes and cry out as they beat on drums with sticks. To ensure community solidarity, the complex ritual dance instructs young males on adult behavior and woods lore.

Makeup and Disguise

Additional examples of costuming, makeup, and masking invest maturation dance with festive elements, as with the leafy crowns and kilts of young men in Manaus, Brazil, and the totemic ceremonies welcoming the children of Nor-Papua, New Guinea, from childhood to adulthood. In northwestern Zambia, the *makishi* masquerade involves Chokwe, Luvale, and Mbunda boys from eight to twelve years of age in adopting disguises to celebrate the spiritual nature of maturation. Upon masking as a plutocrat, supernatural lord, ideal woman, or ancestor, the boys live for up to twelve weeks in a bush camp. Upon return to the village as men, they receive indoctrination into religion, society, and masculinity.

For the Apache sunrise ceremony, girls acknowledge menarche with four days of smearing themselves with clay and performing with a medicine man. In a mask applied by a godmother, each girl dances for hours and mimes the life of White Painted Woman, the first human female. Staining with pollen empowers the budding woman with the spirit of natural healing.

See also corroboree; healing dance; mating dance; mime; shamanic dance; sub-Saharan dance; totemic dance.

Source: Alvarez, Julia. *Once Upon a Quinceañera: Coming of Age in the USA.* New York: Viking Penguin, 2007.

COMMEDIA DELL'ARTE

For commedia dell'arte, upbeat Italian street theater preceded professional drama and opera with an olio of visual comedy and mime, verse, and dance. In the piazzas of fifteenth-century Mantua, Florence, and Venice, amateur troupes raised temporary platforms for presenting skits and scenarios. Performers, whom critic Niccolò Rossi's *Discorsi sulla commedia* (Reflections on comedy, 1590) scorned as "mercenary bands," danced on market day in the style of bucolic Etruscan reaper pranks from the 780s BCE.

Choreography such as the *moresca* dance, or sword or stick fighting dance, gave folk performers and jongleurs opportunities to develop the attitudes and postures of stock figures, for example, the armed *matachin* (Moorish soldier) performing with the tight-fisted capitalist Pantalone at Munich. Presenters mimed local scandals and politics with fixed *lazzi* (gags), such as a court pavane in which the ingenue Isabella eludes all men except her lover. Each represented a social type—the pedantic Dottore, *danzatrice* (dancer), *vecchi* (dotards), buffoonish Pierrot, cooing *innamoratti* (lovers), drunken *tedesco* (German or Swiss mercenary), and the vain general, adapted from *Miles Gloriosus*, the boastful soldier of Plautine comedy from Republican Rome.

Comic Finales

The falling action of chaotic plots typically ended with an upbeat *branle* or farandole, a fantasy finale that lauded good fortune over bad luck. To torchlight, spectators joined performers for the concluding open-air caper or wedding dance honoring the stage couple. Audiences applauded novelty and relaxing humor as well as the improvised dancing that brought them into contact with masked actors.

Boundaries wavered between loud and colorful spectacles, street parade, comic allegory, and dramatic after-dinner song and rope dancing. Presentations ranged from an unplanned encounter of musicians at the White Horse Inn in Verona on December 4, 1565, to the cross-dressing valet who entertained Cosimo de' Medici from the evening of December 26, 1565, until 7:00 the next morning. At Ferrara on January 12, 1566, a pick-up company of mummers arranged a folk dance routine for Barbara and Alfonso d'Este II and Archduke Ferdinand II of Tyrol.

Eclectic Folk Arts

With masking and acrobatics, pre-Lenten street fare drew crowds at Venetian carnivals from 1570, as well as to Verona and Ferrara, where performers gleaned the latest dance figures. In response to the demand for street comedy in Paris in 1571, the Gelosi and Zan Ganassa become the first touring companies. In 1579, amateurs dressed in their exaggerated makeup and costumes and rode through Mantua in search of a dance to watch or a house party to join.

Masks conferred anonymity for farce and serious satire, such as the parodies enacted by the *zanni* (trickster servants), concealed behind long, pointed noses. A partner dance of Columbina, the naif, with Arlecchino, the clown, enhanced her charm while fostering his innovative quirks and pratfalls. The appeal launched the career of amateur dancer Vittoria Piisimi, whom Henry III of France applauded in Venice in 1574. By 1600, the impromptu public shows and itinerant troupes developed into serious drama, opera, and Punch and Judy puppet theater.

See also branle; comic dance; farandole.

Source: Katritzky, M. A. *The Art of Commedia: A Study in the Commedia dell'Arte 1560–1620 with Special Reference to the Visual Records.* Amsterdam: Rodopi, 2006.

COMMUNITY DANCE

Across time, the gaiety of villagers and neighborhoods at plaza *candombe* processions in Uruguay and Argentina; English harvest homes; Provençal communal chain dance; Scots-Irish *cèilidhs*; and frontier contradance and cowboy, cavalry, and Mormon dances animated participants as one. The benefit of democratized activity appeared in the togetherness on Flemish market days painted by Pieter Brueghel the Elder and Pieter Brueghel the Younger, heroic boasting at the Mandan hunting dances painted by American artist George Catlin, and flirtation to the medieval fiddle tunes in Sigrid Unset's Norwegian saga *Kristin Lavransdatter* (1919). The motivation for group dance dwells in the immigrant, nomad, and refugee, all members of displaced groups who bear with them their musical arts, a feature of Greeks and Koreans in multicultural Toronto, Hmong enclaves in the Carolinas, and uprooted Amerindian tribes in Oklahoma. As memories of home, community dance revives joy in song and patterned steps as familiar as the Vedic dances of 1700 BCE revering Hindu deities, the crane dance to Greeks in 500 BCE, the fandango to the Roma, and the *mayim mayim* to Zionist pioneers on Israeli kibbutzim.

From Canaanite or Phoenician culture as old as 2000 BCE, Palestinian, Syrian, Jordanian, and Levantine collectives synchronized the traditional *dabke* in line or ring form. In ecstatic bounds and stamps, the union of disparate ages accentuated felicity in clasping hands and sharing song and rhythm, which passed without formal instruction from adults to children and youth. In the elderly, the repetitive music rejuvenated muscle memory from childhood. Instrumentation attracted spectators to sing and clap and pat toes to the beat.

Propitiating Nature

A fertility rite and assembly activity for the first of spring, the maypole dance dates to Germanic and Scandic tribes of tree cultists from 1200 BCE. For more than three millennia, children and adults have encircled the central trunk or post to weave ribbons to the farandole, schottische, highland fling, or waltz. Whatever the choreography, the dance reunited villagers after the wintry gloom into a May gala as simple as step-step-pause. Dancing benefited the young by teaching the formalities of curtsy and bow.

Among agrarian settlements, plowing and sowing dances revived the hopes of farmers, as with the Zimbabwean tree planters, the *kumi odori* performers giving thanks in Japan, the Navajo rain dancers of the Colorado River Valley, and Breton female furrow stampers in Rennes, France. In reverence to the cyclical nature of growing food, the dancers commemorated ancient spirits of seed and rain and the rhythm of the

In Santiago, Chile, in 1822, a European traveler observed steps of the zapateado imitating the striking hooves of a galloping horse to the 6/8 percussions of a harp. *Schmidtmeyer, Peter.* Travels into Chile, over the Andes. *London: S. McDowall, 1824, 348.*

plow, the focus of the Russian *khorovod* (choral dance) and Bulgarian rain dances. The choreography replicated in a limited ceremony the value of family and neighborhood participation in the toil of gardening, loosening soil, removing rocks, setting out rice seedlings, picking apples and coconuts, and tying grain into sheaves.

Esprit de Corps

Community dance delved deep into shared respect for beliefs, religion, and governance, as with the gift-giving dance and feast of the Akamba of Uganda that endeared a son-in-law to his wife's mother and the honorary dance for aged men among the Kaya-Kaya of Doreh, New Guinea. From 1454, Catalonians at Berga exaggerated the battle for salvation with Patum, a five-day Corpus Christi procession and masked dance to drumming and sizzling whips. The British uprooting of Acadians from Nova Scotia in 1755 endeared to exiles the music and folk dances of their ancestry, which they bore with them into the diaspora. For a comeuppance to the privileged at the French court, carmagnole dancers preceded the French Revolution of July 14, 1789, with a swooping, reversing ring dance based on the medieval farandole. Solidarity pressed peasant malcontents toward destructive acts and the gala ringing of the guillotine during the 1793 executions of Louis XVI and Marie Antoinette, when royal heads plunked into baskets.

Evaluations of the mulatto arts in New Orleans after the Louisiana Purchase of July 4, 1803, lauded music and dance as unifiers of disparate nonwhite people. The slaves with Fon and Yoruba backgrounds from the Bight of Benin and the Kongo tribe members of the Congo River basin formed artistic networks in the Mississippi Delta. Contributing to the resistance of blacks against whites, the *calenda* joined dancers in holiday and Sunday evening jubilation. The uninhibited mating dance flourished at Congo Square, where tourists and college students gathered to observe a multiracial phenomenon—a human struggle against plantation regimentation.

A more forceful circle dance, the Kurdish *kochari* stressed a double bounce on the tremolo, a hand-to-shoulder proof of solidarity within a stateless people with a long history of flight from harm. Unlike written constitutions, music and choreography strengthened cultural survivalism among the preliterate. As a political ideology, the unstructured dance formation emphasized a casteless society and epitomized shared beliefs with exercise and fellowship. The concept influenced a performance of the galop by villagers in act I of Adolphe Adam's playful ballet *Giselle* (1841).

The focus of twenty-first-century folkloric pageantry retains the survivalism and historic commemorations of ancient dance, the purpose of the Bora village ritual in the Amazonian rainforest and aboriginal Australian sorrow ritual. Armenians, Azerbaijani, and Assyrians link little fingers to prance out the *tamzara*, a two-stage figure of three steps forward and three back. The *sardana* circle dance in Catalonia accentuates oneness with the raising and lowering of clasped hands, a feature shared with the Breton *an dro*.

In southern Mozambique, the Chopi rejoice in an olio of recitation, chanting, and song that confers identity on members of a coastal African culture. In Guinea, Malinke women act out the *moribayasa* in the deplorable state of the homeless beggar. A female dance drama, the choreography builds sisterhood among female Guineans by depicting the triumph of the individual over disease, hunger, and spousal abuse.

See also art, folk dance in; Cajun dance; *calenda*; carmagnole; *cèilidh*; chain dance; contradance; fandango; farandole; galop; hula; *mayim mayim*; *odori*; processionals; Roma dance; sacrificial dance; stomp dance; sub-Saharan dance; *tirabol*; totemic dance; worship dance.

Source: Nielsen, Erica. *Folk Dancing.* Santa Barbara, CA: ABC-Clio, 2011.

CONCHEROS DANCE

A syncretic spectacle similar to the Hispano-Mayan *baile de las cintas* (ribbon dance) of Yucatán, the Concheros dance (also Chichimecas, Aztecas, and Mexicas) blends indigenous Aztec artistry with Roman Catholic ritual. The typical dance began with invocations to gods, the patron St. James, and native forebears. Performers gestured praise to the cardinal directions, north, south, east, and west. Leg and foot rhythms agitated the *ayoyotes* (gourd rattles) tied to wrists and shins.

Under the watch of the dance captain, troupe members demonstrated their individual skills at leaps and rotations. The tempo rose, then fell once more as members alternated prayers and songs with instrumental solos in a revival of aboriginal choreography. Between performances, troupes repaired and cleaned regalia and vestments, which consisted of leather anklets, animal pelts, metallic ornamentation, pheasant and ostrich feathers, and fabric tunics and capes painted with religious and historic scenarios. Amateurs came to presentations to learn the dance.

Historic Choreography

The traditional pre-Columbian *mitote* (round dance) coordinates feathered headdresses and tunics with steps to the beat of *huehuetl* and *teponaztli* drums and the sounding of the conch shell. Story dance performances at Bajío and on the periphery of the Aztec Empire as far south as Tlaxcala reflect the overthrow of Montezuma II after the invasion of Hernán Cortés's five-hundred-man force in March 1519 and the conquest of Tenochtitlán in August 1521. Some elements depict Otomi mercenaries from the east who aided the Spanish and the enslavement of the seminomadic Chichimec as mine workers in 1526.

Concheros performed to strums of a lute strung over an armadillo shell. Missionaries countenanced facets of the militaristic dance and adapted the semi-pagan ritual to Christian evangelism. In the 1800s, church brotherhoods promoted dance troupes, who presented their folk art in the *zocalo* (public square) of Mexico City and its environs. Membership reflected genealogical connection to Concheros forefathers.

Repression and Reclamation

During a secular suppression of the church after the Mexican Revolution, from 1920 to 1929, legislation forced the story dance into hiding. Anti-dance factions damaged public arenas and shrines. The reemergence of Concheros performances in 1930 preceded two decades of public support for some forty companies presenting heritage spectacles.

Tourists at Acapulco and Veracruz lauded the cultural elements and artistic competition, which involved bare-chested males for the first time.

To restore authentic folk art, nationalistic performances rid the dance of Catholic influence and stressed the pre-Columbian dance of the Aztec. Concheros troupes toured Tex-Mex communities along the Rio Grande and advanced across Arizona and New Mexico to California. Presentations featured elders, dance leaders, and drummers around an altar smoky with incense. Outer rings separated male and female dancers, who reduced their regalia to fringed loincloths and short kilts.

Source: Rostas, Susanna. *Carrying the Word.* Boulder: University Press of Colorado, 2009.

CONTRADANCE

The first European choreography to delight all social levels and ages, contradance (also *contradanse* or country dance) introduced geometric patterns and changes of partners to grid square choreography directed by a caller. A British original rooted in the Iron Age after 1200 BCE, the basics involved advancing either two or four steps and retreating in the same rhythm. Fiddles and other stringed instruments playing traditional reels and jigs metered the steps. For variety, pairs rotated while grasping both hands and followed a progression of partner changes.

Concentric circles performed parallel advances and retreats at different rates, always generating a new alliance of partners. Star figures required three or four dancers joining four or eight hands across and stepping in a clockwise or counterclockwise direction. Around 1437, the finale for some sets wound a line of dancers in and out of the row, a foreshadowing of line dance and *rigaudon*, a springy solo or capricious couples quickstep in 2/2 or 4/4 meter.

After conservative European Christians exiled dance from cities, peasants initiated their own version in the country. Italian arts patron Catherine de' Medici acknowledged the uniqueness of herders' dances at Bayonne, Gascony, in the 1540s. The contradance developed into a fad during the rule of the rebellious Henry VIII about the time that he broke with Vatican control. With the banning of religious dances during the Reformation of 1534, peasants secularized the Italian *contradanza*, a set of steps set to choral chant or hymns.

Ensembles tended to include anyone who had an interest in rural dance. The community style paralleled the seventeenth-century Finish *ankleesi*, Danish *hopsa*, and the Norwegian *bygdedans*, a genre of district choreography individual to its performers. Among French Canadians, New Englanders, and mountaineers in the Appalachian chain, from the 1600s, parties requested the Virginia reel, a hybrid structuring of contradance figures and forerunner of square dance.

Blending Modes

Set to jig time, contradance was easy to master because it had less exacting patterns than court dance. When Mozarabic music and body language migrated from Andalusia to Colombia and Venezuela during seventeenth-century colonialism, courteous contradance rhythms permeated the stamping, uproarious *joropo*, a common shepherd's dance. In the North American colonies, contradances featured a core around which performers wove stars and allemandes. Late in the 1600s, French dance teachers organized training sessions in contradance that emphasized the swinging of a partner and neighbor and a constant shifting of geometric figures to slow glissades.

Because of the free selection of partners, the contradance version of the waltz made dancer's choice the highlight of the evening. On August 1, 1708, at the proxy wedding of Holy Roman Emperor Charles VI to Elisabeth Christine of Brunswick-Wolfenbüttel in Barcelona, mountain folk from the Pyrenees performed an invitational rural dance with partners in two lines facing each other. In 1740, the contradance evolved into the quadrille, *lanciers* (lancers), and the cotillion, a West Indian—or possibly German—peasant dance. After 1745, Louis XV abandoned the swaying cross-front-cross-back (grapevine step) of the *branle* and replaced it with the courtly phrasing of minuet, gavotte, and rondeau and the playful caprices of the contradance. In 1774, Marie Antoinette imported a Viennese contradance to Paris.

Emigration of Austro-Germans to Hungary, Switzerland, Slovenia, and the Ukraine in the 1780s introduced the contradance and the *Ländler*, a hopping, skipping, turning romantic duo in open position. Because women's costumes grew unwieldy with bamboo or wire hoops, they abandoned heeled pumps for flexible footwear, which displayed their fancy stepping below long crinoline slips. For the opera *Don Giovanni* (1787), composer Wolfgang Amadeus Mozart recounted the shift in dance style from minuet to contradance and waltz. Copenhagen musician Johan Bülow and Jane Austen's novels valorized the polite mode as an appropriate way for young unmarrieds to socialize, whether by invitation or impromptu assembly.

In the West Indies, contradance set a precedent of crossbred folk arts. Whether in plantation manse or public square, a melding of European style with West African line dance kept contradance relevant in the nineteenth century. The multiracial community built fellowship from democratic social interaction inspired by black and Creole musicians, notably, Louis Moreau Gottschalk and Manuel Saumell. By 1815, suites ended the contradance with a racing, cantering round of the galop.

Creole country forms and quadrilles swept Venezuela, Brazil, Cuba, Puerto Rico, Dominica, St. Lucia, and the Dominican Republic. At Montevideo, black males prized their aptitude for the "white man's square dance." Although academicians considered contradance a shameful residue of colonialism, the dance attained a folk primacy among the Afro-French in Martinique, Basse Terre, and Guadeloupe. In the 1840s, the contradance passed through the Caribbean, tingeing the Haitian style *méringue* with bourgeois French elements. The form invested Haitian voodoo ritual and festivals and established identity among Jamaican Maroons and the Caribs of St. Vincent. In Montserrat and Tobago, the dance figured in ancestor worship.

Historical Choreography

In the twentieth century, folk groups alternated open and closed positions and coordinated gestures with sets of salsa, swing, and jive. To preserve the country dance genre—waltz, *varsouvienne*, quadrille, polka, contradance—in the 1920s, automaker Henry Ford and his wife, Clara Bryant Ford, opened a teaching studio in Dearborn, Michigan, and issued their book *Good Morning: After a Sleep of Twenty-Five Years, Old-Fashioned Dancing Is Being Revived* (1926). In 1937, they erected a hall especially for contradance that drew hundreds of couples for the next sixty-eight years.

New interest in refined folk dance flourished in the Canadian maritime and American Midwest, Pacific Northwest, and New England at dance camps and festivals. For the inclusion of more people, ungendered contradances marked the traditional lead partner with an armband. A full evening incorporated variety with alternating sets of polka, waltz, schottische, and Swedish *hambo*. In 2005, Prince William and his future wife, Kate Middleton, took a break from classes at the University of St. Andrews in Edinburgh to learn Scots contradance.

See also allemande; attire; community dance; cotillion; Creole dance; galop; jig; *joropo*; *Ländler*; line dance; polka; quadrille; reel; *rigaudon*; schottische; square dance; *varsouvienne*; waltz.

Sources: Harkleroad, Leon. *The Math behind the Music.* Cambridge, UK: Cambridge University Press, 2006. Manuel, Peter, ed. *Creolizing Contradance in the Caribbean.* Philadelphia: Temple University Press, 2009.

CORROBOREE

An aboriginal Australian trance ritual from New South Wales, the corroboree (also *corrobory* or *caribberie*) ushers tribe members into an animistic mental state known as the primeval dreamtime. First observed by European colonists in the northwest at Kimberley and Pilbara, the dance melodrama, like the powwows of North American First Peoples, incorporated spiritual meditation, worship, mime, and man-making (coming-of-age) ceremonies. A session involved as many as three hundred male dancers and five hundred singers.

A *kamaran* (headman) organized proceedings, which coordinated the whir of the *bondaban* (bull-roarer), beating of rhythm sticks on shields, and application of headdresses. On a flat dance floor topped with a pavilion, choreography united pubescent youth in hand clasping, donning ceremonial feathers, and encircling a fire each night to a monotone chant. Elders mimed the totemic kangaroo and emu, clapped with both hands on the thighs, and performed mock conflict and myths with coordinated knee jiggles, hops, roars, and steps to left and right.

Spirit Dance

American sea captain Charles Wilkes, head of a South Sea nautical survey from 1838 to 1842 and author of *Voyage Round the World* (1849), gave an eyewitness account of the spectral corroboree. Red and white body paint covered faces, limbs, and female breasts with religious icons. By flickering firelight, as dusky male aborigines animated their limbs, the rib markings of white pipe clay appeared and vanished like skeletons.

Male aborigines danced the details of such everyday events as rowing a dugout on a turtle hunt, the revenge killing of a woman stealer, a sailing adventure, and search and lamentation for a drowned man. As boys progressed to manhood, they performed clapping and fire dancing, suffered scarification and circumcision, and accepted wives. Girls celebrated menarche with a group mating encounter.

Gendered Style

For male companies, dance steps began with a widely spaced stance and leg quivers. Singers created comic effect by mixing aboriginal lyrics with popular English tunes. On the serious side of each corroboree, the oldest songs mimed creation stories to rattles, rhythm sticks, and the deep hoot of the didgeridoo. The tales linked participants to the preservation of land, animals, water and weather sources, plants, and healing.

Women accompanied the figures by clapping, banging boomerangs, and pounding opossum-skin drums. A few women danced apart from the men and executed stiffer figures than the wholehearted cavorting of males, who nodded their heads to activate dog tails, parrot and cockatoo feathers, and swan's down. Tribes formed traveling companies that introduced neighboring clans to the dance, which typically ended with storytelling. At dawn the next day, dancers awakened to issue a lamentation and chant for the dead.

Source: Petrie, Tom. "Early Reminiscences of Early Queensland" (1904). Accessed October 9, 2015. www.seqhistory.com/index.php/aboriginals-south-east-queensland/thomas-petrie.

COTILLION

A West Indian—or possibly German—peasant dance named for the petticoat, the cotillion (also *cotillon*) seized the European imagination around 1750 and replaced the minuet. Performers numbered off for eight-person squares and four-couple set dancing, a precursor of the more structured quadrille and square dancing to a caller. As reported in William Wycherley's restoration play *The Country Wife* (1675), the style developed from the contradance and the long chains of the farandole.

From the counterclockwise "Great Ring," dancers advanced to folk tunes in the chain, allemande, and promenade sets. The most common patterns earned the names *la rose*, *le pantalon* (pants), *l'été* (summer), *la poule* (hen), *la frenis* (reins), and *le final* (conclusion), which formed the components of the quadrille. The courtesies of the figures saluted seventeenth-century bows and curtsies, the baroque social norms of the court of Louis XIV.

A comic custom for the cotillion began with women holding candles on their palms. When two men approached to invite her to the floor, she left the second male "holding a candle for her" until her return. For half a century, callers announced the multiple figures, which participants executed in 2/4 meter. In 1760, the Parisian dance teacher LaCuisse recorded in a manual that the basic cotillion blended with the gavotte and graceful glides of the minuet.

The side-to-side cotillion figures and partnered turns acquired realistic names—presentation, columns, rounds of three, gliding line—as well as metaphoric descriptions, for instance, oracle, king's cake, Alpine shepherd, the bridge, serpent, trap, double windmill, star and circle, and thread the needle. The brisk dance intrigued the queen, Caroline of Brandenburg-Ansbach, in 1758, causing a rumpus with the jealous Hanoverian king George II, and fascinated the English majority in 1766. The figures migrated to Ireland in 1770 and North America in 1772 before reaching Australia.

Historically, the faddish dance cropped up in noteworthy places and company. According to *Gentleman's and London Magazine* in 1788, vacationers at Bath joined the cotillion. Guests at Mount Vernon performed the decorous figures with George and Martha Custis Washington. At his inauguration at Federal Hall in New York City on April 30, 1789, the first US president enjoyed two cotillions.

Because of increasingly complex choreography, performances set intricate models of good manners and drew more spectators than dancers. As a model of public decorum, Scots poet Robert Burns reported the introduction of country dance figures in *Tam o'Shanter* (1790). By the nineteenth-century, the slow waning of the cotillion, especially in New England, prefaced the popularity of the quadrille, hoedowns, and rambunctious square dancing. Still, a social must in Richmond in 1814 involved the gentry in the cotillion. An English steps manual, Thomas Wilson's *Quadrille and Cotillion Panorama* (1817), followed the shifting dance with fifty-two schematic drawings of configurations. For the middle class, the quadrille was easier to master and remember than the cotillion, a fact noted in an 1825 issue of *Harmonicon*.

From 1824, Charles X of France reclaimed the stately cotillion for court use and in the programs of military balls. On plantations in the New World, African slaves learned the figures from domestics and performed them for weddings, funerals, Christmas, and Saturday night breakdowns, plantation stunts involving jumping with both feet crossed. After 1830, street marchers in the New Orleans Mardi Gras added the cotillion to parades. As settlers moved into the West, they developed the cotillion into barn dancing.

For Mormons in Salt Lake City, Utah, in 1852, prophet Brigham Young set the example of polite dance as exercise by leading the cotillion. At a state dinner in Norfolk, Virginia, on January 25, 1877, Americans invited Grand Duke Alexis of Russia and officers from the frigate *Svetlana* to join the dance. In the US South, zydeco music and dance at Acadiana, Louisiana, blended cotillion figures with the *varsouvienne*, polka, galop, waltz, and mazurka.

American terminology merged cotillion with quadrille into the 1840s, when a mountaineers' ball at Table Rock, North Carolina, featured the schottische along with the reel and cotillion. The dance acquired the name "the German" in 1844, when the figures gained fad followers in New York and returned to central Europe and Italy as *il codiglione*. According to *Harper's Bazaar* in 1899, the elite Goulds and Vanderbilts perpetuated the term "cotillion" in presentations of debutantes to society and held pre-dance classes to teach teens the steps.

See also allemande; chain dance; circle dance; contradance; farandole; galop; gavotte; mazurka; polka; quadrille; reel; schottische; square dance; waltz; zydeco.

Source: Pittman, Anne M., Marlys S. Waller, and Cathy L. Dark. *Dance a While: A Handbook for Folk, Square, Contra, and Social Dance.* Long Grove, IL: Waveland Press, 2009.

COTTON-EYE JOE

An infectious country-western polka, two-step, or reel in the United States, Saskatchewan, Quebec, Ontario, Nova Scotia, and Newfoundland, the cotton-eye (or cotton-eyed) Joe features a heel-and-toe line dance, counterclockwise spoke-wheel, and couples dancing similar in style to the schottische. Performers move in 2/4 time to fiddles and banjos at Cajun barn dances, hoedowns, square dances, Western saloons, and Southern clubs. While spectators stomp and clap, booted line dancers link up with arms over the shoulders or waists of the next dancer. The figure combines stomp, kick—or cross-kick—and a left-right-left reverse preceding an eight-count shuffle before repeating the set.

Derived from the "quarters" in the antebellum plantation South, the original lyrics about unrequited love blamed a blue-eyed black field hand, fiddler, or beguiler for stealing the speaker's sweetheart. An alternate history depicted the steps as an Irish clog dance adopted by enslaved blacks accompanied by frontier fiddlers. Alabama, Texas, Missouri, and Louisiana slaves sang and danced variant words and steps interspersed with hollers and whoops and a promenade. Mimicry depicted taming a bucking colt, lassoing, and twirling six-shooters before holstering them. The rollicking spectacle flourished in blackface minstrel shows and at community dances and freestyle clogging to Appalachian and Ozark Mountain dulcimer tunes.

Written directions for the cotton-eye Joe appeared in print in 1882 and earned the sobriquets "The Mother of All Texas Honky-Tonks" and "The South Texas National Anthem" for its popularity as a cowboy breakdown. Serious ethnographers analyzed the existential questions—"Where'd you come from? Where'd you go?"—and proposed that Joe represented a venereal disease that postponed wedding plans. During the Great Depression, the classic cotton-eye Joe became the prime warm-up for barn dancing, where couples in gingham dresses and overalls felt right at home. Educators added the catchy rhythm to physical education curricula.

The film *Urban Cowboy* (1980) made the cotton-eye Joe into a US fad. Swedish recordings by Rednex and Irish albums featuring bodhran (frame drum) and tin whistle music by the Chieftains spread the dance to Norway, Switzerland, Germany, Austria, New Zealand, and Australia. Performers mimicked strutting and the slinging of barn muck from shoes. To the caller's question—"Stepped in what?"—dancers yelled, "Bullshit!"

See also barn dance; line dance; partnering; polka; schottische; square dance.

Source: Pittman, Anne M., Marlys S. Waller, and Cathy L. Dark. *Dance a While: A Handbook for Folk, Square, Contra, and Social Dance.* Long Grove, IL: Waveland Press, 2009.

CREOLE DANCE

Creole dance attests to the extraordinary capacity of folk to resist suppression and as-similate contrasting styles, from the Afro-Peruvian *alcatraz* (fire dance) at Cuzco, the Dominican merengue and Haitian *méringue*, and Chilean *cueca* to the French cotillion and quadrille, Iberian fandango, and the Trinidadian *mento*. In the late 1600s, French, Spanish, and Portuguese planters and settlers of the Mississippi Delta adapted to mixed art and cuisine and ebullient patois. The most nationalistic ethnicities rejected the English language and Protestantism, Anglo arts, and intermarriage with whites or people out of their class. In Tobago, communities danced the pre-calypso *kaiso*, a sensual, sa-tiric choreography that fused rhythmic shoulder rolls, back and front kicks, and furious turns with backtalk and scoffing at French planters.

After the arrival of the first black slaves to Mississippi plantations in 1720, Creole dance to Cajun fiddle tunes flourished on the Louisiana plains. Footwork became a statement of race and heritage, as with the Spanish passions released in the fandango and the pent-up African yearnings in the juba, which derived from Bantu and Akan dance from Ghana, Ivory Coast, and Togo. Under French rule, New Orleans hosted public dress balls twice a week and publicized the location by hoisting a flag outside the venue.

On the crowded floor, white and mulatto women executed challenge steps to settle rivalries and elevate their class. As refugees from Haiti and Saint-Dominique es-caped a horrendous slave massacre of the Napoleonic era in 1809, they fled directly to the Gulf Coast or through Cuba. Some eleven thousand survivors—black, white, and mulatto—retained Afro-Caribbean rhythms and combinations and developed engaging styles of quadrilles and contradance.

Mixed Cultures

Creole dance acquired syncopation and brio from strums of the banjo, the twang of the juice harp, and insistent percussion of bamboo drum, gourd, bones, spoons, and triangles, the accompaniments still in use for Franco-American dance in Canada and New England. On Dominica, Grenada, and Martinique, pairs performed the *bélé* (from the French "*belle aire*"), a pure African seduction and fertility ritual, to the boom of the goatskin drum. Dancers added distinctive touches to the elegant French quadrille and *lanciers* (lancers), an offshoot of Scots-Irish reels. In the 1770s, African sailors and Portuguese colonists in Brazil hybridized the Brazilian fado, a pensive ring dance. By the 1790s, Dominican and West Antillean Creoles incorporated the cotil-lion as a coda to the quadrille.

The new citizens performed a jaunty *bamboula* in New Orleans at Congo Square to oversized drums that players straddled. As whites doubled the population from 1820 to 1830, the emergence of the *calenda*, schottische, contradance, and congo from street corner buskers and in proletarian theaters, minstrel shows, ballrooms, and musical comedy halls of the Vieux Carré permeated Southern folk arts. Aficionados danced the convulsive spectacle of voodoo and the eccentric Afro-European style and jeering satire of the *chica*. By 1850, the polka varied Creole dances. Shortly after the Civil War, notation of the crossroads tunes and lyrics at Good Hope Plantation in St. Charles Parish west of New Orleans produced *Slave Songs of the United States* (1867) and archived the foundations of Creole dance.

Refined Creole Arts

In self-imposed exile in Switzerland from Paris, New Orleans artiste Louis Moreau Gottschalk wrote the refrains coursing through his brain. He published piano ballades in 1849 featuring the frenzied *bamboula* and Algerian casbah figures, introducing to Parisians the Creole exotica and brooding, complex tonalities of the New World. In 1853, he arrived in New York to launch a concert tour of his driving, pounding delta music, an impetus to a new wave of popular dance.

Admirers Karl Cherny, Alexander Borodin, and Jacques Offenbach extended the audience for Creole folk art with sassy contradance, habanera drive, and tropical dissonance. Spanish components added the heat of the zapateado and *jota*. Amid various critical interpretations, in February 1886, local colorist George Washington Cable standardized the definition of Creole dance for *Century Magazine* with "Creole Slave Dances: The Dance in Place Congo." He marveled at slave torso twists set to love songs, superstitious chants, and the work plaints of cane cutters. He identified African racial strands—Senegalese, Bambara, Mandinka, Foulah, Guinea, Ibo—and related their gyrations, thigh slaps, chest pats, and ecstatic collapses to the wild dance of Roma, Moors, and Arabs until New Orleans police intervened in 1843.

The demand of the elite for dance lessons increased employment opportunities for dance hall musicians and instructors. In 1934, academic interest in heritage Creole arts derived from the 1934 recordings that Alan and John Lomax made of pulsing, clapping, stomping good times. In Trinidad and Jamaica, Beryl McBurnie and Ivy Baxter promoted postcolonial nationalism through Caribbean Creole dance festivals.

Still vibrant, Creole dance defines cultural affiliation and legitimacy through idiosyncratic motions of the human body, the chief difference between Viennese waltz and *vals criolla*. In Grasse, Dominicans reenacted the feminine bélé, a feminine roll of hips and swish of skirts in token of romance under a full moon. At the 2008 Miss Haiti pageant, Creole dancers stepped and gyrated to an erotic Afro-Caribbean beat. In Opelousas in 2013, Louisiana Creoles contended for the championship against Texas dancers with fast Afro-French zydeco duets to accordion riffs.

See also Andean dance; *bamboula*; *calenda*; contradance; diaspora; fado; fandango; *joropo*; *jota*; juba; merengue; nuptial dance; quadrille; schottische; waltz; zapateado; zydeco.

Source: Cable, George Washington. "Creole Slave Dances: The Dance in Place Congo." *Century Magazine* (February 1886): 517–32.

CZARDAS

A traditional tavern dance for male villagers, the czardas (also *csardas* or *verbunkos*) became the tempestuous emblem of the Hungarian and Slovak spirit. Arts experts trace its evolution via Phoenician traders from the nautch dance of India to exotic tavern dances in Gades (Cádiz), Hispania, and the Spanish fandango. Set to accordion, *tarogato* (clarinet), and violin trios, the medieval forerunner of the czardas dominated folk performances in the Carpathian Basin despite the Catholic ban on Magyar dance in 1279. Style advanced from males stamping their equestrian boots in one spot to couples in closed or semi-open position with the man's hand riding high on his partner's back. To a rapidly shifting tempo, steps involved improvisations on the basics—step-close-step-touch and side-cross.

Based on Slovak rhythms and tenth-century Magyar war dances, the genre took a military turn after 1715 as a *verbunkos* (recruiting) and drinking activity and spread along the Roma diaspora to Serbia, Croatia, Poland, Moldavia, Slovenia, Moravia, Bulgaria, Transylvania, and the Carpathian Ukraine. In a vigorous 2/4 or 4/4 march tempo, the Magyar dance served Hapsburg emperors soliciting manpower in Eastern Europe by bankrolling musicales in agrarian villages. The quickening of the beat from the slow *lassú* (or *lassen*, introduction) to the *friska* (or *friss*, finale) pinpointed hardy plowmen as likely conscripts for the Austrian army.

The People's Dance

In western Transylvania in the 1780s, the exuberant figures acquired androcentric solos while women encircled the exhibitionists. The czardas gained favor across Europe for the performers' heel clicks, boot slaps, and proud torso carriage in evidence of Hungarian nationalism. In 1811 during the romantic era, Jewish violinist Mark Rozsavolgyl earned the title of "Father of the Czardas" for publishing dance songs at Pest, often executed on the harpsichord. At the Budapest National Casino in 1840, Franz Liszt, composer of a suite of Hungarian rhapsodies, promoted a performance of Magyar peasant dance that welcomed both the impoverished gentry and ruling class to the floor.

By 1842, the dance took its standard name after the czarda (roadhouse or hostelry) and flourished to the clang of the tambourine and the hammering of the trapezoidal cimbalom (dulcimer). The merger of peoples in folk art began healing the rift between royalty and upper and lower classes. Along with the promotion of Hungarian industry and agricultural products in 1844, the arts, too, gained new prominence through adaptations of the czardas. Similar in fascinating rhythms to the Bavarian-Austrian *Schuhplattler*, the clapping, stomping, and whirling czardas fascinated dancers mid-century, when Magyar costumes, tight hose, shiny knee-high boots, and spurs became the fashion for balls among law students. In a triumph of nationalism, attendees proclaimed Hungarian the language of the dance hall in place of German.

On November 14, 1847, King Ferdinand requested an exhibition of czardas before his court, where men in crisp, gold-trimmed uniforms contrasted the swish of satin gowns against lacy petticoats. In March 1848, the king's reclamation of folk identity inspired fifteen hundred men to join the army, where dance relieved boredom and inactivity. At the failure of the Hungarian Revolution of March 15, 1848, the loss of independence in October 1849 cut short the popularity of the czardas, a reminder of former liberties.

A mid-nineteenth-century pastiche of racial, national, and social animosities marred the art scene. Because Johannes Brahms composed a suite of Hungarian dances

For the czardas, male and female Hungarians wore peasant dress, hats, and kerchiefs over boots. *Vance, Lee J. "The Evolution of Dancing."* Popular Science *41, no. 52 (October 1892): 755.*

in 1853, he endured the opprobrium of Richard Wagner, who sneered that Brahms was a Jewish imitator of low-brow peasant music. The restoration of Hungarian constitutional rights in 1860 by Franz Joseph I generated a renaissance of salon-czardas along with Magyar skirts and cavalry boots. For its ardent dynamics and formal ornamentation, the dance outclassed the quadrille, polka, mazurka, and waltz.

Politicized Dance

The airs of Italian violinist Vittorio Monti's czardas in 1904 supplied Roma orchestras with a rhapsodic tune. Without scores, musicians improvised melancholy phrases enriched with Bohemian riffs in a minor key. In Eastern Europe under less militaristic sociocultural conditions, the dance epitomized male-female courtship and served school children as physical exercise. The revived czardas opened with a promenade similar to a polonaise and advanced to lateral steps, concluding with spins and vertical figures.

As Slavonic character dance, the czardas maintained its pulsing national temperament at harvest festivals, initiation rites, and weddings. Pre–World War I Budapest cafe society offered lusty Magyar music for the pairing of noblemen with red-cheeked partners. Immigrant Hungarian coal miners recorded czardas tunes in Pennsylvania in 1928. The collapse of feudalism and the rise of Communism in 1946 placed Hungarians once more in charge of their folk arts.

Into the 1950s, the czardas accentuated virtuoso violin programs, revivals of peasant dance scenes from Léo Delibes's playful ballet *Coppélia* (1870) and *Die Fledermaus* (The bat, 1874), an operetta by Johann Strauss II. Troupes scheduled folkloric dance tours in California, Ohio, New Jersey, Michigan, and Washington, D.C. Presentations in Cleveland by Hungarian refugees in spring 1960 featured the essential black boots opposite embroidered vests, wide skirts, aprons, kerchiefs, and peaked Tyrolean hats. Actor-dancer Yvette Mimieux performed nightly in a swirl of orange skirts for the MGM film *The Wonderful World of the Brothers Grimm* (1962).

In the early 1970s, a resurgence of Hungarian artistry returned the "tango of the East" to venues in Budapest and London. Innovations varied from Romanian and Croatian touches to the Jewish czardas, another name for klezmer or Maramaros laments. At the beginning of the twenty-first century, tourists at Budapest nightclubs along the Danube could request an evening of czardas. At the 2013 Smithsonian Folk Festival, experts instructed visitors on Hungarian steps.

See also fandango; galop; mazurka; polka; polonaise; quadrille; *Schuhplattler*; waltz.

Source: Fulemille, Agnes. *Magyar Orokseg Washingtonban: Hungarian Heritage: Roots to Revival*. Budapest: Balassi Intezet, 2014.

· 𝒟 ·

DANCE DRAMA

Theatrical dance incorporates everything from low comedy to bemusing skits, such as Balinese thanksgiving at the royal temple in Ubud, the ambiguous stanzas of the cotton-eye Joe, and tempestuous floor romance of the Spanish fandango. From 33,000 BCE, performers turned prehistoric dance into a mimetic merger of self with the animal world and godhood. Around 1200 BCE, the Celtic sword rituals of Ireland acquired panache from rhapsodic displays of the *brat* (cloak), a parallel to the mummery in Eskimo dance houses and the intense face paint and costume drama of *kathakali* theatrical dance in Kerala, India.

Acting skills enabled dancers to turn ephemeral figures and facial expressions into preservations of history. Around 31 BCE, dance drama honored the military might of the Pharaoh Narmer, Egypt's unifier and sire of the First Dynasty whom tomb seals honor at Abydos. At Hierakonpolis, the capital of Upper Egypt, a painter's plaque in bas-relief pictured a significant episode of royal power. Two female dancers in tableau vivant enacted Narmer's defeat of an enemy with the single blow of a war club.

Advanced Stagecraft

Medieval theatrical dance also tended toward martial episodes, particularly the *moresca*, a mime of swordsmanship on the islands of Corsica and Korcula off the southern coast of Croatia. Additional Mediterranean dance drama depicted the bellicose *tergui* of the Tuareg of the Sahel north of Niger and Macedonian martial arts that prepared stalkers for a manhunt. In the 1300s, Buddhist chant centered shamanic Shinto elements of Japanese *nomai*, a musical dance that began in the sacred precincts of Mount Kumano.

For the coastal Portuguese, from the 1400s, the fado enacted the creolization of dance that reflected tragedy and romantic intrigue. Catalonian mime at Berga, Spain, in 1454 turned Corpus Christi ritual into the Patum. The five-day masquerade elevated the cavorting of eagles, crusading knights, royalty, mule-dragons, dwarves, hobbyhorses, Saracen giants, David and Goliath on stilts, and horned demons into full-blown outdoor theater.

For comic relief, pre-Lenten carnival antics flourished in Venice in the Italian Renaissance from 1570 with processions, allegorical skits, and masked spectacle that turned into a major component of the tourist trade. In the Andes, Cuzco dancers from the Inca Empire imitated the extremes of Spanish colonizers with the satiric *huayño*, a mockery of greed concealed behind masks. By 1705, the melodramatic Spanish fandango merged precision steps and emotional engagement into psychological tableaux. In this same period at Shuri Castle in Okinawa, the creation of *kumi odori* (ensemble dance) imported facets of Japanese Kabuki and Noh and karate to entertain the Ryukyu court of King Sho Tei.

A specialty of Mesoamerican and South American dancers, narrative dance relied on stylized gesture and dance to the samba, tango, bolero, and waltz. The tradition derived from the precolonial Maya and Inca, who valued spectacle for religious and political edification. After seventeenth-century European colonization and Christian conversion, at Q'eros on Corpus Christi Day, Peruvian groups processed in costume to enact Andean legends and Christian history of Spanish wars. Troupes syncretized prehistoric elements with feathered jungle headdresses and woven tunics.

Scenes of Good vs. Evil

Two popular Hispanic story dances, the trial and death of Jesus and combat between Iberian Christians and Moors, enacted legends from the Catholic calendar. Mime conveyed ethics and group attitude toward Hispanic history, which included the African diaspora and European conquests. In the Dominican Republic, the establishment of colonial sugar plantations required migrant laborers, the founders of the *cocolo* (non-Hispanic) dance drama. From 1850 at San Pedro de Macoris, celebrants observed Christmas, Lenten carnival, and St. Peter's Day (June 29), when troupes mimed traditional stories about David and Goliath, the prototypical weakling and strongman.

Narrative drama recorded gendered and universal struggles. For the Malinke females of Guinea, the *moribayasa* reenacts a woman's survival of adversity. Costumed in rags, she danced her way around the community and led village matrons in song. By donning new garments and burying her rags at an intersection, she celebrated a victory in a personal dilemma, for example, overcoming disease or spousal abuse. The corroboree (also *corrobory* or *caribberie*), a trance ritual of aborigines in New South Wales, Australia, created primeval dreamtime, an expressive consciousness of human evolution.

See also Andean dance; Balkan dance; body art; bolero; chain dance; comedy dell'arte; corroboree; cotton-eye Joe; Eskimo dance house; exorcism; fado; fandango; *huayño*; tango; waltz.

Source: Zarrilli, Phillip. *Kathakali Dance-Drama: Where Gods and Demons Come to Play*. London: Routledge, 2000.

DIASPORA

The muscle memory that retains folk steps, mimesis, and postures follows refugees and wanderers the world over, notably, the Filipino *pandango sa ilaw* and *tinikling* dances in Hawaii and Polynesian national dances in New Zealand. Because of allied soldiers in the field, alien occupations spread the jitterbug and Korean story dance during World

War II and the funky chicken during the Vietnam War. In peacetime, from Norway, the *halling*, northern Europe's oldest folk dance, spread to immigrant farm communities in Canada.

The definition of *syrtos*, the body of ancient Greek folk dance, explains its advance in Thrace, Aegean isles, Crete, Ionia, Macedonia, Thessaly, Pontus, and Cyprus. One long-lived folk art, the Greek *antikrystos* (face-to-face) dispersed the Mediterranean concept of welcome to strangers among communities in Persia and Turkey. A cheery, smooth innovation of steps to a 9/8 tempo, the antikrystos thrived through the Middle East.

Wanderers, such as the Tibetan *tsam* (or *cham*) dancers exiled during a disastrous face-off with China in 770 CE, accumulated steps and mime like flavorful herbs in a sparse diet. The advance of Roma folk arts into the Balkans in 1100 initiated seductive solo dance and festive handkerchief figures. Early thirteenth-century troubadours who fled Provence during the Albigensian Crusades carried into the Italian Alps the *volta*, a romantic couples dance that anticipated the *polska* and waltz.

In a three-stage folk migration across Europe to England, the Roma performed a Cossack kick-squat for the Welsh, who incorporated it into traditional clogging as the "toby." In southern Spain during an anti-Muslim sweep by Catholic forces, Arab and Berber tonal scales and rhythms blended with Hispanic dance to create the flamenco, a fusion completed in the 1300s by the Roma. On an Iberian battleground, guitar strums and Arabic drumbeats accompanied universal themes of sorrow, suffering, and mortality.

Dance Treasures

The West African abduction of Benin, Mandinka, and Yoruba tribesmen by profiteers introduced to the Western Hemisphere the *bamboula*, *candombe*, *bomba*, *calenda*, and juba, all elements of black identity and religious rites in the Antilles, Argentina, Cuba, and Puerto Rico. Derived from the three-thousand-mile shore from Senegal to Angola, African ritual gestures and dance exertions restored aesthetics and ethnic and racial identity dating back to tribal origins. Dance education reclaimed the past for displaced generations, creating ties with myth, self-image, and ideology, specifically trance dance among Haitian Santerians, the Tokoe scarf dance by Ghanaian slaves on New World plantations, and ethnic identity in performances in Martinique, Harlem, and French Guiana.

During great periods of diaspora, folk dances nurtured both healing and assimilation, a feature of Irish wharf clogging in Australia and Argentina, exuberant Swahili ritual with the *lewa* dance in Oman, Armenian and Portuguese survival dance in Canada, and Bantu song and dance in the Arabian Gulf. In eastern Colombia and Venezuela, bondage encouraged the combination of steps and gestures for the *joropo* from Afro-Caribbeans with aboriginal Arawak music and the contradance of Arabo-Andalusian Spain. While blacks and Cubans influenced the Caribbean conga, Bahamian quadrille, and *son jarocho* of Veracruz, Mexico, Portuguese sailors spread the fado to North Africa and Brazil in the early 1600s. Simultaneously, the Hispano-Mayan *baile de las cintas* (ribbon dance) of Yucatán introduced Mayan circle dancers to the European maypole.

Roma buskers and street dancers moved from central Europe north and east to England, Scandinavia, and the Ukraine. The wanderers bore with them a host of melodies to which they whirled and clacked wood castanets while asserting their individuality and blended ethnic history. By 1750, the centuries-long Roma dispersal passed through the Austro-Hungarian Empire, where musical troupes found employment along the Danube as entertainers at receptions and costume balls.

Emigration in the late eighteenth century carried Filipino tinikling from Leyte to California and New Orleans, the Cajun quadrille and gigue to Quebec and Louisiana, the hula to Portuguese ukulele strums among the *paniolo* (cowboys) of Maui, and the Ukrainian peasant *hopak* and the Polish *oberek* to the Great Lakes area and Canadian weddings in Alberta. Similarly, Chinese-Americans performed the dragon and lion dances in Chinatown in Manila and Calgary while Irish-Americans introduced St. Patrick's Day (March 17) pageantry and jigs to dancers in Moscow, Boston, Seoul, and Sydney. A variety of ethnicities reaching New Orleans from Cuba following the Haitian Revolution of August 21, 1791, formed the first Mardi Gras cotillions and street processions and carried the sensuous bolero to the United States.

In the 1800s, Hispanic Arawaks fleeing press gangs in Venezuela and eastern Colombia carried the joyous joropo to British Guiana, from which it migrated to Cuba, Curaçao, St. Lucia, Trinidad, Tobago, and western Mexico. In the late 1820s, the Roma trek through Slovakia and France reached Iberia, where India's *kathak* colored the Roma steps and rhythms of the Andalusian flamenco with a fiery passion. After 1830, a parallel dispersal of homeless Poles transferred the mazurka to Russia, England, France, the Philippines, and the United States.

Festivals and Tourist Attractions

In the early twentieth century, the Japanese diaspora perpetuated the *odori* at summer festivals and street dancing in California, France, and coastal Argentina as well as Maui, Hawaii; Penang, Malaysia; and São Paulo, Brazil. Likewise, tourist attractions in Brazil and the Caribbean drew attention to the African basis of carnival pageantry and processions, such as drum dance in Jamaica and Haiti, single-file conga lines at the carnival in Rio de Janeiro and Santiago, and the parade of little pirates among Bastille Day marchers in Guadeloupe. From the 1960s, the University of Wisconsin at Milwaukee, Oberlin College, SUNY, Indiana University, Duke, and the University of Havana encouraged multiculturalism by creating ethnic dance opportunities in physical education and the arts.

Late in the 1900s, immigrant settlements enlightened their hosts on the arts of the motherland, a source of satisfaction and pride among Hmong and Cherokee dancers, Cajun school children, Slovenian polka dancers in Venezuela, and Scots-Irish cloggers and dulcimer players among the Appalachian mountaineers. In Tahiti, sword and fire dancers displayed the merger of Polynesian and French techniques each July 14 on Bastille Day. The draw of jobs in Australia to the unemployed and underemployed in Latin America introduced the *pasodoble* to an Anglo culture. In the 2000s, upheaval in the Middle East displaced Anatolian Kurds, who absorbed disparate Arab and Turkish factors into the *delilo*, a nonviolent protest dance.

See also Balkan dance; *bamboula*; bolero; Cajun dance; *calenda*; chain dance; clogging; contradance; cotillion; cotton-eye Joe; Creole dance; czardas; dragon dance; fado; *halling*; hula; Jewish dance; *joropo*; juba; lamentation dance; lion dance; *mayim mayim*; maypole dance; merengue; *oberek*; Persian dance; polka; *polska*; quadrille; Roma dance; Siberian dance; *tinikling*; *volta*; worship dance.

Source: Harrison, Paul Carter, Victor Leo Walker, and Gus Edwards, eds. *Black Theatre: Ritual Performance in the African Diaspora*. Philadelphia: Temple University Press, 2002.

DISGUISE

Dress in regalia, headdress, and false faces to conceal the human form retains importance throughout world folk arts, as with the witty carnival masquerade to *candombe* music in Montevideo, Uruguay. Asian models include the camouflage of *tsam* (or *cham*) dancers in Mongolia and Siberia, the cow impersonation for the *gai jatra* in Nepal, and the *mayil attam* dance of the Tamil Nadu of southeastern India, who disappear behind beaked puppet headdresses and peacock feathers. In Nor-Papua, New Guinea, the wearing of a disguise begins a child's initiation ceremony, when he or she enters a mystic relationship with a mammal or fish. For exorcism, the Tungus shaman of Siberia retreats under animal pelts and antlers before strutting, brandishing spirit bells and wand, and dancing the magic steps of the trickster.

In North America, Turkey, Czechoslovakia, Siberia, and France, from 33,000 BCE, performers concealed their humanity by pretending to merge with gods or beasts. The ancient tradition survives in the Sri Lankan exorcism rite, which coordinates grotesque animal pelts with the fierce snouts, bulging eyes, oversized fangs, and extruded tongues of a fantastic beast. After 206 BCE, Chinese dragon dancers swathed themselves in green cloth to take on a mythic shape to protect farmers from floods and drought.

Stories and Comedy

Disguise maintained purpose and significance to pagan communities. The medieval *talchum* in North Korea introduced children to costumed story dance. In 1436, costumers' guilds unionized the Venetian shapers of papier-mâché heads and seamstresses who personalized gowns, cloaks, and satin or silk dance slippers. In Wales and England, morris dancers performed from as early as 1448 disguised as blackface riders on hobbyhorses, a representation of Moors in Iberia. After the arrival of Hernán Cortés at Tenochtitlán in 1521, historians characterized Aztec regalia as animal skins cloaking tricksters, priestly dancers who teased spectators with comic skits. Among the Andean Inca at Cuzco, Peruvian rebels retreated behind full costumes to perform comic dance lampooning Hispanic colonizers led by Francisco Pizarro.

English settlers of North Carolina created a low-country oasis at Tryon Palace in the 1760s. Slaves living in nearby Edenton made their own fun with *jonkonnu* (also *John connu, John Canoe, junkanoo, Jangkunu*), a West African and Jamaican yuletide masquerade to secular call-and-response singing and dance theatrics. Leading the mime, two figures, the horned ragman and fancy man, dressed in cloth scraps that covered them from head to feet. The full-body masking, cow tails, and stilt walking reflected obeah ancestor veneration from the Congo that Caribbean laws prohibited in 1774.

In coastal Virginia, Belize, and the Bahamas, the jonkonnu disguises freed slaves to perform buffoonery and ribald verses to fife and gumbay drums. Dancers appeared in the character of a knight, queen, devil, whore, beggar, messenger, greenman, belly woman, maddah lundy, policeman, horsehead, cowhead, Babu the Indian, and pitchy patchy, who performed jumps in a circle. The revelry commented on colonial social news, religion, and politics with seven distinct figures—*gerreh*, *dinki mini*, *comobolo*, *calimbe*, *bélé*, wake, and ring games—as well as a European quadrille, maypole, and a house-to-house procession. The dance grew so offensive that whites banned it in 1841.

From the 1820s to the 1930s on May Day, Easter Monday, Boxing Day, and Plough Monday, the first Monday after Twelfth Night, English boys and men in East Anglia and the Midlands erupted into comedy skits known as Molly *guizing* (or Molly dancing) to pipe and tabor. In blackface and women's hats, dresses, aprons, and hobnailed boots, the rough, earthy folk ribaldry drew spectators to broomstick maypoles erected in village squares of the Fenland. The jigging steps and bawdy lyrics to "Soldier's Joy" and "Gypsies in the Wood" lacked the complexities of morris and sword dances.

The lighthearted dance routines of rural Molly dancers accompanied rowdyism and entreaties for cash. Spectators who withheld donations could find their front yards plowed into furrows. Masqueraders secured anonymity to hide their identities from potential employers. Australian fiction writer Peter Carey incorporated an Irish version of Molly dance in *True History of the Kelly Gang* (2000), in which bushranger Ned Kelly's father and brother dress in drag in November 1868 as a disguise for robbery.

Varied Motivations

Currently, concealment marks a folk ruse in Bulgaria, where *kukeri* performers cloak themselves in fur in the shape of supernatural beasts and imitate bestial movements. With more fashionable items, the Yoruba *egun* (shaman) in Cove, Burkina Faso, covers his body from head to ground in fringe, beads, fabric drapes, and gloves before beginning his swaying dance. Each August in Gambia and Senegal, boys enter hunting brotherhoods during coming-of-age masking. Decked in tree bark, leaves, and red raffia fiber, they follow a staccato meter to a circumcision ceremony. The dance ritual concludes with training in courtesy and survival.

A South American gangster's specialty, the capoeira (chicken fight) circle dance, an athletic bush fighter's contortion, developed during Afro-Brazilian bondage by Portuguese colonials. While dissimulating samba figures at Salvador, Palmares, and Bahía, blacks whom traders had enslaved in Angola-Kongo areas and transported for sale in Brazil reclaimed the *n'golo* from Angolan dance. Choreography concealed their readying for a fight with spinning and arching sweeps of the leg. As a signal to end a practice session, slaves disclosed surveillance from military police by moving to the rhythm of the cavalaria, a mimicry of galloping hooves. Trained scrappers fought well in the 1865 war against Paraguay.

See also animal dances; exorcism; jig; lamentation dance; masked dance; *matachines*; maypole dance; morris dance; processionals; quadrille; Siberian dance.

Sources: Carey, Peter. *True History of the Kelly Gang.* St. Lucia: University of Queensland Press, 2000. Dills, Ann, and Ann Cooper Albright. *Moving History/Dancing Cultures: A Dance History Reader.* Middletown, CT: Wesleyan University Press, 2001.

DRAGON DANCE

A traditional Chinese spectacle, the dragon dance coordinates the steps, snapping jaws, and undulations of a troupe of players under a single costume, the flexible body, swiveling eyes, and outsized head and tail of a dragon. The execution of some seven hundred dance styles and martial arts postures conceals the inner workings of poles elevating the bamboo hoops supporting and wielding a fabric body for the delight of spectators. Attendants accompany the open-mouthed figure and twirl dazzling balls on sticks in time to the music of gongs, horns, cymbals, and drums. As a bringer of luck in the coming year, a deterrent to ghosts, and a curative of plague, the dragon totem venerates Chinese wisdom, dignity, courage, and a long history as an Asian power.

A gendered dance, strict dragon manipulation reverences the yang principle and reduces female participation to cutting the grass, vines, or rice straw for body and head stuffing. No woman may touch the dragon. One arcane regulation allows under the paper or cloth body any pregnant women who have borne two daughters and await the birth of sons.

For fifteen days, dancers in China, Taiwan, Hong Kong, Malaysia, Vietnam, Australia, and Chinatowns worldwide convey their disguises as emblems of Chinese culture and homeopathic healing. Color symbolism links red scales with joy, green with the rice harvest, yellow with empire, and silver and gilt with wealth. Less realistic dragons feature stag horns, carp scales, and tiger paws.

Dragon Dance History

As early the Shang Dynasty after 1600 BCE, dragon dance ritual emerged from snake totem worship and propitiated the gods on behalf of the farmer. Disguises cloaked rainmakers posing as Shenlong, the five-clawed storm dragon; Tianlong, the heavenly dragon; and Yinglong, the mythic flying rain dragon, canal designer, and controller of floods. According to *Abundant Dew of the Spring and Autumn Annals*, compiled by chronicler Dong Zhongshu around 139 BCE, child and adult mimes shaped their dragon costumes out of clay. Around 115 CE, Zhang Heng's *Lyric Essay on Western Capital* described later dragon imitations. Merged beasts produced a carp dragon and a frog dragon.

In a New Year's parade after 618 during the Tang Dynasty, dragon dancers in Zhejiang, centered on the east coast of China, marshaled hundreds of performers and the support of wood stools for a dragon procession as long as seventy meters (230 feet). The artistic extravaganza overlaid the costume with calligraphy, painting, paper cuts, sculpture, and plaiting. The dancers propelled the textured shape through the streets as a model of folk art. By 1000, the dragon dance had lost its agrarian significance and become an East Asian entertainment.

Ethnographer Meng Yuaniao's *The Eastern Capital: A Dream of Splendor* (1047) described the dedication of young men to dancing and drumming. The text named cloth, grass, and candles as the materials for dragon costumes celebrating the Lantern Festival on New Year's Eve. Correct execution of steps and manipulation of the figure ensured good fortune for the next year. At Nanxi, a Sichuan city in central China, after 1127, immigrants from Fujian province invented a miniature dragon dance, a duet coordinating the motions of head and tail. In 1200 at Fenghua City, Zhejiang, dancers coiled and animated a cloth dragon carrying the pearl of wisdom in its mouth.

After 1368 in the Ming Dynasty, performances at Chongqing and Sichuan combined a candlelit dragon with a colored lantern dance, the source of protection and salvation. On a practical note, the flickering lights drew insects, which dancers drowned in a pond after the parade. On Donghai Island off China's southeastern coast, around 1644, lithe dancers formed a human dragon composed of their half-naked bodies interlinked and borne on the shoulders of attendants. The unique presentation included homage to the dragon and ancestors, worship, and a sacrifice to the sea.

In 1880, a *hakka* troupe in Tai Hang southeast of Causeway Bay, Hong Kong, introduced the fire dragon dance at a fall festival. Inspired by a vision from Buddha, for three successive nights, a 220-foot straw dragon showcased firecrackers, smoke, and joss sticks (incense) propitiating the gods to protect villagers from epidemics and typhoons. Contributing to the procession, school children in global costumes synchronized parade steps.

Essential to correct execution of the dance, the serpentine behavior of the dragon required practice at arching the back, crouching at enemies, extending the tongue, and twisting the long body forward and backward. The team of 120 dancers supported thirty-four billowing segments and two dancing pearls. The company concluded the dance by tossing the straw and cloth figure into the harbor. Priests at the Lin Fa Kung Temple rewarded the company with dragon cakes honoring deceased villagers who had previously animated the rippling figure.

In Hanoi, Vietnam, in 1929, celebrants of the Tet New Year holiday enjoyed a dragon performance. Officers of the Red Guard selected strong soldiers for prancing in red shirts tied at the waist and, around the head, red scarves, emblematic of the Communist revolution. Security guards armed with clubs and hatchets marched along at the dragon's sides to shield the troupe from attack. To mock assaults on the figure, the silken body and string beard quivered in fear.

Choreography set to drum rhythms enlivened the fringed or scaly dragon to fly among the clouds, swim in a whirlpool, undulate in a spiral tidal wave, and search for the pearl, an icon of wisdom. To cause the head to rise, dancers stood on shoulders. At Liancheng in the coastal province of Fujian, children flocked along the route bearing paper dragon eggs, another symbol of wealth. Southeast of Hong Kong at Macau, blessing the red and gold wooden head and green tail by a Taoist priest preceded the tying of a gold flower with a red ribbon on each dancer's head as a symbol of divine energy. As the Macau troupe danced their way along the parade route, their consumption of wine and beer reduced dance steps to drunken lurches.

Sources: Visser, Marinus Willem de. *The Dragon in China and Japan.* Amsterdam: J. Müller, 1913. Yang, Lihui, and Deming An. *Handbook of Chinese Mythology.* New York: Oxford University Press, 2005.

DRUMMING

For aboriginal cultures, drumming offers a ritual invocation, the purpose of syncopated beats of the Hutu and Tutsi instrumentalists to a Burundi standing drum line. The sacred beat elicits security and peace by imitating the maternal heartbeat that enwraps the fetus before childbirth. Whether performed on a single conga, *bamboula*, bongo, taiko, cauldron drum, djembe, or a percussive medley, an insistent tattoo unites each human rhythm with the palpating blood flow of Mother Earth, a focus of Nanai sacrificial dance in Russia and China and the shamanic healing of the Tungus of Siberia. During First Nations powwows, the drum absorbs healing energy from sky and land, a facet of the seasonal Yupik rhythm chant in southwestern Alaska.

Anthropologists connect drumming with spirituality and holiness, the basis for the Chinese lion dance. Percussionists, such as the Micmac performers in Nova Scotia and the religio-historic *matachines* instrumentalists in Aguascalientes, Mexico, pledge to remain clean of drugs and alcohol before touching sacred instruments. In northern Norway, the Saami shaman sings, dances, and beats a drum while his spirit soars free of his body. Celestial mapping on the drum membrane guides his soul in its mystic flight.

Preparing for Dance

West African drummers require therapeutic washing before they can begin the nonverbal language of the dance. From their percussive cadence derives the intuitive, ecstatic dance that yields insights into the spirit, a purpose of the Anlo-Ewe and Fon *kinka* drum dance in Ghana. Participants among the Bakiga of Rwanda and Uganda experience kinesthesia and visual, auditory, tactile, and olfactory sensations that transcend reality and project startling perceptions in an otherwise dark world. The most involved dancers achieve glimpses of an unrealized self and an opportunity to awaken inner strengths, such as fertility, creativity, and immortality.

During the Renaissance, acoustic meter honored the primitive roots of dance, often initiating community gatherings, as with a nonverbal invitation to celebrate the Korean *mugo* (drum dance), which originated from a log raft around 1275 during the reign of King Chungnyeol. From 1454, Catalonians at Berga epitomized the primordial battle against evil with Patum, a five-day Corpus Christi masquerade and processional dance to the lash of whips and the beat of a single drummer, a symbol of the persistence of the Christian message. For a less doctrinal honorarium, after 1558, celebrants at the court of Tudor queen Elizabeth I turned and stamped to pipers and drummers around a maypole and jingled bells in celebration of May Day.

Drumming as Communication

In Dutch, French, English, and Portuguese colonies in the New World, the slavery era immured coastal and West Africans in a wretched plantation milieu. In place of shared language, the polyglot cultures of Grenada, Guadeloupe, Martinique, Dominica, and Hispaniola preserved their motherland in dances and ceremonies to distant reverberations. A staccato beat directed the Cuban conga line to step-step-step-kick. In the Antilles, ring shouts and mating rituals to thumping, rainstick, and shakere invited the innovation of the *calenda* and juba, choreography that assuaged homesickness and despair from field labor. In Brazil, the capoeira evolved from the Angolan *n'golo*. An engaging rhythm allowed participants to mark with samba steps a martial art coordinated by a steady meter. The *tamborito* (little drum), a three-drum Panamanian dance, featured a women's chorus and interactive couples dances that drew spectators.

In Bahai, Afro-Brazilian migrant workers at Reconcavo introduced the samba, an amalgam of Portuguese, Bantu, and other West African drum dance traditions perpetuated by slaves. To rejoice in freedom, female participants formed a circle and clapped to spontaneous innovations coordinating the rhythm of hips, thighs, and feet to snare drum and guitar. To strummed melodies, a lead dancer gyrated at the center, then picked the next woman to take the floor. At pre-Lenten carnival in the early 1700s, young girls joined the company and imitated their elders. In the 1940s, dancers extended the range of the samba to Rio de Janeiro, ennobling the samba as an icon of Brazilian nationalism.

An unrelenting beat continues to modulate dance steps and gestures in settings as varied as the *tergui* hunting ritual of the Tuareg of the Sahel north of Niger, prayer ceremonies of the Montana and South Dakota Sioux, and the transvestite *hardah* of Sumatra, the Malay Peninsula, Singapore, the Riau Archipelago, and Borneo. At Belize, Guatemala, and Punta Gorda, Honduras, Garifuna drum dancing invites solo and group invention of shuffles, head and hip rolls, and palm waggling, all evidence of uninhibited involvement in African traditions. Whether a funereal gesture of respect among Creole *bélé* dancers of Dominica and Saint Lucia, taiko blessing on the Japanese New Year, or a rhythmic jubilation during pre-Lenten carnival in Barbados, the vibration of mallet or fingertips on drumheads summons dancers and directs their steps.

See also chain dance; exorcism; fancy dance; healing dance; lion dance; *matachines*; maypole dance; Polynesian dance; propitiation; step dance.

Source: DeFrantz, Thomas F. *Dancing Many Drums: Excavations in African American Dance*. Madison: University of Wisconsin Press, 2002.

· *E* ·

ESKIMO DANCE HOUSE

The Eskimo dance hall houses a series of rituals and galas that bridge family and clan in a mystic universal oneness. Folk dancing allies humans with the animal and plant world and the cosmos. For the Yupik of eastern Siberia and southern and western Alaska, dancing seems as natural as eating and sleeping, especially during the tedium of long, dark winters. The *qasgiq* (dance house) becomes a social hearth for warming villagers with activity and hospitality.

From the 1700s among the indigenous Unalit of Norton Sound on the Bering Sea north of the Yukon River, folk dances paid no tribute to war or violence. Instead, earnest dancing created a continuity that renewed alliances with the Malemute and Unaligmiut at bordering enclaves. At Kotzebue Sound on the Chukchi Sea in north-western Alaska, the late arriving Malemiut performed to the clack of ivory clappers by leaping from their toes in hypnotic synchrony. By exchanging gifts at communal drum dances, participating tribes secured the needy from want, a situation that arose in the mid- to late 1800s with the dwindling of the caribou.

At the village of St. Michael, Unalit masking honored supernatural powers, whose sanctity required the sacrificial burning of regalia after each presentation. At the Inviting-In Feast each January, prayerful dance drew game to the area and kept alive names of the deceased and their songs. The folk ritual ensured a successful hunt as well as food for spirits and the shades of ancestors. After the Russian-American Fur Company opened a trading post at Unalakleet, Greek Orthodox prelates banned the performances. The Unalit retreated to the mountains to dance in seclusion from white authorities.

In Athapaskan communities on the Yukon River of east central Alaska, coiled grass and willow root fans, wolf tails and tassels, and finger masks added drama to movements, which beginning dancers performed on grass mats. Costumes were sewn with snowy owl and swan tail feathers, caribou beard hair, and beading; caribou teeth and tusk amulets emitted sounds that accompanied movement. In the lower Yukon, masked dancing during the heavy snows of February ensured plentiful berries in summer. On the Gulf of Alaska at Icy Cape near the Canadian border, the dance-potlatch incorporated story-dance with gift exchanges. The Igomiut doll festival of the Bering Strait violated more conservative choreography by popularizing a nontraditional local dance.

Farther south, by 1850, Point Barrow, Alaska, supported three *kashims* (dance houses), where the Inupiat practiced each step and gesture to such folk and magic tunes and games as "Song to the Aurora" and "Sparrow Song." When a hall reached capacity, additional guests peered down on the dancers through the smoke hole. Along the Victoria Strait of north central Canada, the Netsilik Inuit packed snow blocks into a beehive recreation center, a functional social and commensal unit in the midst of individual igloos. During the drum dance, drummers passed their hooped instruments from hand to hand for sharing.

For Victoria Island Inuit along the British Columbia–Washington state line, the use of snow knives enabled youths to sculpt a dance hall in mid-May. They shaped a dance floor roomy enough to hold forty to one hundred villagers. To the drum, the only musical instrument in ancient times, a singer began the dance with a solo or recitation suited to the season or to the initiation of young males.

For shape-shifting and propitiating nature on Victoria Island, the nomadic Copper Inuit stitched dance caps from yellow loon bills, ermine and caribou pelts, and red or black bird throat plumage to secure mild weather, good health, and a successful season of hunting and gathering. The shaman wore the cap to free his spirit to fly over the performers and spy infractions of clan taboos. Choreography limited steps and concentrated on swaying trunk, shoulder, and arm gestures, which expressed how spirits could shatter forbidding ice fields and transmute themselves into beasts, fish, birds, and humans.

On the Atlantic coast, the Labrador Inuit, descendants of the prehistoric Thule culture, honored the dead whale with a festival. In a circular snow house sixteen feet high by seventy feet in circumference, the shaman added ritual to folk dance by interacting with villagers. In Newfoundland, the skinning dance starred an Inuit seal hunter in prancing around his kill, played by a child stretched out under a blanket like concealed prey. As the hunter peeled away the woven covering, the child came to life and dashed away. Animal dances ended with sacred gifts to the spirits of meat, drink, and tobacco pushed through chinks in the dance house planking.

Preparing for Dance

According to Kingikmiut Eskimo myth along the Bering Strait between Siberia and Alaska, the first whaler, named Seutilit, assuaged his sorrow at the death of a family member by initiating a grief dance at the coastal village of Kingegan, Cape Prince of Wales. Diarist James Wickersham, a frontier politician and scholar, visited the Kingikmiut Eskimo via snowshoes and dog sled in January 1902. On return, he addressed the Nome Literary Society on Eskimo culture and published a vignette the next year on Kingikmiut dance.

In mythic tradition, Kingikmiut men built and maintained the *kozge* (clubhouse), a dance and gambling hall, workshop, and reception center featuring seats assigned by age and rank. As elements of totemic worship, the shaman constructed wood, fur, and feather puppets and masks with hinged jaws. He painted finished pieces with the five sacred colors—charcoal black, copper oxide green, ochre red, clay white, and ash blue. He encircled stark surfaces with pegs and quills that set feathers and carved icons aquiver with each step. In addition to dancing, the Eskimo brotherhood mended sleds, repaired harness and fishing equipment, smoked, swapped stories, and planned whaling expeditions. In their absence, women performed their own dances, ribald ceremonies and rites honoring pregnant women.

During wintry blusters from November to March, the Kingegan *youwytsuk* (dance) propitiated the powers of wind and weather to ensure bear, seal, walrus, and whales for food, clothing, coverlets, and building materials. Guests entered the twenty-four-foot rectangular dance floor down a forty-foot covered vestibule and through the eighteen-inch entrance hole edged in ivory strips. The visitors, including women and children, exchanged gifts of reindeer skins and dried salmon before seating themselves in a special section. Elders reposed on raised platforms on the west wall alongside singers and drummers and faced performers.

Kingikmiut dancers dressed in deerskin, labrets, and black markings painted on the face performed a variety of steps. To the music of rattles and frame drums, the family solos, lasting up to two minutes, preceded formal seating on a bench. A singer or drummer stripped to the midriff and danced along as vocal, acoustic, and kinetic accompaniment. The program concluded with three jesters masked as three races—Eskimo, white, and black—and garbed in a grotesque outfit. Their farce coordinated off-key songs with ungainly footwork and imitations of the insane.

The Greenland Inuit prepared their *qashe* (singing house), a twenty-by-fourteen-foot snow dome with a lamp at the center of concentric circles that placed matrons behind single girls and men on the front row. Children took seats near the entrance. For the inviting-in feast each January, shamans scheduled totemic and comic muscle dances displaying animal mimicry, feathered costumes, and biceps competitions.

Dance with Purpose

Despite the disapproval of pagan amusement by Greek Orthodox, Moravian, Seventh-Day Adventist, Church of England, and Presbyterian missionaries to west central Alaska, drum dancing retained the mysticism of supernatural songs. In the early 1900s, each December, a somber dance to the dead of the Diomede Inalik on the Bering Strait incorporated a recital of heroic deeds and whale blubber offerings to the deceased. Every decade, the feast of the dead and its folk choreography enabled villagers to requite debts of honor and hospitality, a serious part of family and clan tradition.

Each commemorative dance of the Diomede Inalik ended with a banquet on walrus and whale meat, which drummers and chorus members served to visitors, beginning first with males and continuing to women and children. A subsequent dance set involved guests in the same two songs and choreography that began the session. As each family joined departing visitors, one by one, they slipped out through the entrance hole carrying leftover blood soup and seal meat.

Among Diomede islanders, from 1911 to 1914, American anthropologist Ernest William Hawkes summarized Yukon Inuit amusements in the *kasgi* (semi-subterranean dance hall), a communal gathering place built of driftwood posts and plank flooring. For stability during vigorous dances, builders anchored the structure in rocks against a hill. All villagers maintained and furnished the long entrance tunnel and dance floor and contributed bearded sealskins for carpet. Seating around the interior ranked citizens by worth, with derelicts, the homeless, and orphans given positions along the coldest wall.

Steps and Gestures

Key to Diomede Inalik choreography in the thirty-foot square, dance pantomimes of Arctic animals commemorated the sources of ancient clans from salmon, deer, and orca. In addition to footwork and rhythms, headmen smoked, discussed governmental issues, mourned the dead, and cleansed themselves in sweat baths. By dancing in troupes, males solidified the collective strength of clan hunters. When women and children joined the presentations, they remained separate from privileged males and participated while seated.

Unlike social dancers, Diomede Inalik totem dancers based movement on rhythm and imitation of animals. Limbs throbbed to a 2/4 beat of hoop drums topped with 24-inch circles of seal or walrus bladders tied with rawhide. With laughter and jesting, the drummers held their instruments head high and tapped surfaces or rims with thin wands. On a platform raised shoulder height from the dance floor, drummers sustained the cadence while an elder recited traditional lyrics. As he began a chant, guests rose to limber up and step to the beat.

For the reindeer dance and wolf pack dance, Diomede Inalik males asserted their primacy. A female soloist wearing a deerskin belt and crest improvised steps at the cen-

A community enjoys performers at an Eskimo dance house, photographed in Alaska by Judge James Wickersham in January 1902. *https://education.alaska.gov/temp_lam_pages/library/gold/1000/p277_009_110.jpg.*

ter of a circle of men adorned in wolf pelts. While circling the dance house entrance, the threshold of the spirit world, men gloved in wolverine skin and loon feather mitts set a pattern of stamping, leaping, and forearm jerks, two to the right and two to the left. The stalkers surrounded and attacked the deer with howls and jumps.

Farther inland, the Inupiat propitiated high country and tundra as well as shore animals. On the Unalakleet River in Alaska, dancers depicted the life cycle of the red fox and the mating rituals of the crow or ptarmigan. The drama of walrus life began with an awkward waddle on ice and a quick dive into the sea to escape the hunter's harpoon. A slow kill left the animal jerking its flippers and quivering in death. For ease of movement behind heavy masks, the performers suspended large carved wood false faces from the ceiling and danced behind them.

Gender Dances

When female Inupiat joined in the animal propitiation, they decorated their arms with grass armbands and duck or ptarmigan feathers. Women performers sat or stood in one place and bent knees and swayed the torso in rolls to the music while imitating a seagull's flight with the hands. They mimicked traditional female occupations—curing and dressing pelts and cutting and sewing boots and parkas. After removing their tunics, the women performed a unison line dance by undulating arms and shoulders.

Inuit dances contained no lyrical wooing songs, unrequited love, or broken hearts. For the asking festival, held during a lull in fishing in mid-November along the Bering Sea, Inuit men sought wives who could survive a hazardous climate and frequent hunger. Males stripped and painted their bodies with oil and charcoal before petitioning each potential wife for gifts of food, evidence of Arctic cooking and frugality.

Inuit women choreographed ancient courtship rituals for single girls, which dancers presented with naked torsos. At the end of the presentation, pairs of villagers entered temporary wedlock, which empowered the female as mistress of the household for one night. In the clown performance, a jester satirized the ideal maiden's daintiness and grace with grotesque overstepping and torso undulations.

Each January and March around 1916, Bering Sea islanders, Hooper Bay Yupik, and Siberian Inuit observed bladder feasts by honoring the year's slain seals, whales, and walruses with a return to the sea of animal bladders, the receptacles of animal spirits. By dancing naked on the fourth evening and brandishing lighted stalks, hunters cleansed the spirit of vengeance and greed. The complex ritual ended with folklore and storytelling, anthropomorphic driftwood masks painted with mineral pigments, and a pell-mell rush down the exit tunnel.

Among Alaskan Inupiat, as white culture intruded on indigenous heritage in the 1970s and weakened ties to the past, assimilation sickness required a healing of everyday dysfunction. To instill traditional spirituality, youths resumed hunting and fishing, gathering moss and duck eider, sewing bead-curtain headdresses and belts, and drumming and chanting in Yupik to accompany seasonal dance and coming-of-age rites. The purchase of fine Siberian sable from the Russian Eskimo who visited Kuskokwim Bay in southwestern Alaska enabled dancers to adorn traditional dance hoods made from wolf and wolverine fur, otter pelts, and swan foot skin. The costume restored unity with ancestors and enthusiasm for animistic dance.

See also healing dance.

Sources: Hawkes, E. W. *The Dance Festivals of the Alaskan Eskimo.* Philadelphia: University of Pennsylvania Museum, 1914. Hawkes, E. W. *The Labrador Eskimo.* Ottawa: Government Printing Bureau, 1916. King, Jonathan C. H., Birgit Pauksztat, and Robert Storrie, eds. *Arctic Clothing.* Quebec: British Museum, 2005. Wickersham, James. "The Eskimo Dance House." *The American Antiquarian and Oriental Journal* 24–25 (July–August, 1902): 221–23.

EXORCISM

Exorcism ritual incorporates the folk facets of elaborate wizardry, cathartic dance, and revivalism to cure neurological distress, hysteria, Tourette's syndrome, schizophrenia, anxiety attacks, and unthinkable sorrow, such as that following an epidemic or natural cataclysm. Mystic gesture extends the frenzies and beat of folk dance with stylized waves of the medium's hands and plunges of the head in a battle with evil spirits.

From the dim beginnings of folk dance history, the Chinese choreographed warrior healing in Sichuan and Shaangzi along the Yangtze River around 5000 BCE. Various styles of dance therapy ranged over the globe, as with *hahoe byeolsingut* healing drama in Korea from 1150 CE, the ghost dance in Nevada in 1889, and the Balinese *kecak*, a curative trance scenario involving sorcerers in fire walking. A less manic version in indigenous Korean culture, the *salpuri* exorcism rite generates an altered state of consciousness in the spiritually sick or a release of the souls from corpses by gradually quickening a moderate dance of the neuromancer. Choreography features rolling shoulders, a gesture related to the Chinese scarf dance, and unleashes a fount of inner gladness or ecstasy that calms brain waves.

Psychosomatic Dance

In the decline of feudalistic repression and the aftermath of the Black Death, mass hysteria seized thousands of Rhinelanders in summer 1374 in a dance of death. According to observations in 1386 by abbot and chronicler Peter of Herentals at a Walloon abbey in Belgium, the kinetic mania at Aachen, Hennegau, and Liège filled villagers with satanic urges. In response, victims bounded down church aisles and gamboled in town squares and forest glades while holding hands, vibrating and twitching, and leaping distractedly from invisible provocation.

Hallucinations of rivulets of blood kept hysterics twirling and spiraling until priests performed spiritual cleansing with extensive prayer and incantation, ending their possession by, supposedly, a mischievous demon named Friskes. The psychosomatic obsession moved geographically to Cologne, Trier, Ghent, Metz, Zurich, and Flanders, causing churchmen to ban church and public dances and restrict all frenetic and, at times, carnal displays to private venues until exorcists could intercede. Religious courts condemned incorrigibles to burn alive at the stake.

Epidemic folk dance recurred in the Renaissance—at Strasbourg and Zabern in 1518, at Basel in 1536, and among residents seized by erotic convulsions at the Nazareth convent at Cologne in 1564. In 1531, Swiss occultist Theophrastus Paracelsus recorded eyewitness accounts of a craze he named St. Vitus' Dance. The bizarre mimicry of orgasm tended to strike women in nunneries, notably in 1606 at the Franciscan convent of Saint Brigitte at Lille; the Ursuline sisterhood at Aix-en-Provence in 1609; among Ursulines at Chinon in 1632 and two years later at Loudun; and among Franciscan postulates at Louviers, Normandy, in 1647. Female victims reacted with howling, blasphemous mantras, and naked, voluptuous dancing.

Sri Lankan Exorcism

From pre-Buddhist Sri Lanka, masked exorcism by an *iramadun* ceremony began with grotesque masking and disguising of the shaman's body in heavy fur. To a complex series of rhythms on a two-ended drum, male and female devil dancers with whitened faces trod frantically, rotating heads back and forth and jingling a corona of bells. Over a twelve-hour ritual to multiple chanting voices, rhythms changed sporadically, causing the team of exorcists to sway, whirl madly, and crouch. The combination forced practitioners into a sound-induced trance.

A male Sri Lankan practitioner waved a large wand, which he exchanged for one or two flaming torches, the focus of an eccentric stooping, rotating shamanic solemnity. The fire show heightened with the juggling of three torches, which came perilously close to the mystic's raffia beard and headdress. The exorcist lapsed into abstracted groans, wails, and seizures that required a halt to the dance and ministrations of attendants. Masked priests returned to the floor in the guise of fantasy animals agitating ankle bells and swirling firebrands to induce an ergotropic trance.

West African Exorcism

Exorcism through dance drama retains its powers among the Yoruba of Burkina Faso. To communicate with the world of the dead in Cove, the *egun* (shaman) disguises his body in massive regalia complete with gloves, colored fabric panels over a long tunic, and a fringed and beaded head covering. To the driving pounds on bongos and skin-head drums, participants sink into a hypnotic state that evolves from chanting, clapping, stomping, and swaying. The immersion in sound allows ghostly ancestors to seize living bodies, punish malefactors, and protect the innocent.

Like the Sufi dervishes of central Turkey, the Yoruba priests of Burkina Faso spin with mounting intensity and twitch as specters from the past supplant their living selves. The healing sacrament terrorizes villagers, causing mambos (witch doctors) to attend to the most needy with brandishes of a lion leg bone tipped with cowrie shells. The coordination of mambo first-aid with the shaman's chanting and gyrating wearies the company of performers. After a rest, a voodoo dance resumes with pirouettes and celebration of juju (supernatural power).

See also Eskimo dance house; ghost dance; shamanic dance; sun dance; tarantella; *Totentanz.*

Source: Hanna, Judith Lynne. *Dancing for Health: Conquering and Preventing Stress.* Lanham, MD: AltaMira, 2006.

· ℱ ·

FADO

A traditional Creole duo or ring dance in 2/4 meter, the Portuguese fado derives from musical improvisation among mixed-race African, Brazilian, and Iberian dwellers of Alfama, Bairro Alto, and Mouraria in west central Portugal. A national dance drama based on approach and retreat, the fado takes its name from Latin *fatum* for "prophecy," the theme of fluid quatrains about ill fame and misfortune. The structure and content hint at Moorish tonality and African rhythms and the Occitan lyric renaissance promoted in Iberia by the twelfth-century Provençal troubadour.

The fado shaped a multifaceted national identity. From the walls of the Coimbra Cathedral and Santa Cruz Monastery, men crooned serenades to distant women framed by upstairs windows. From the 1400s, fisher folk and navigators of caravels carried their instruments as they separated from land on the way to elevating Portugal to a modern nation-state. Risking a high death rate from scurvy and shipwreck, seamen filled songs with a blend of sorrow and desire distilled from windswept horizons, solitude, and yearning common to seafarers living apart from mother and sweetheart.

A short-lived Brazilian and North Afro-Arabic version of the fado from the late 1600s melded rhythms and nostalgic tunes of the Afro-Bahía *lundu* and Spanish fandango and zapateado with the African *fofa, gandu, batuque, banzé,* and *cumbé* (also *goombeh, goombay*), a playful Guinean drum dance. A favorite of black sailors, coachmen, and harbor prostitutes, the fado earned a raffish reputation for its connection with poor barrio dwellers. In the Portuguese diaspora, Iberian fishermen's wives clung to their typical dance costume—grim black dresses, kerchiefs, and shawls. Into the 1770s, polished, easy-listening versions of the fado entertained courtiers, who reduced worries about jobs and money to dance at Lisbon soirees.

A National Dance

Born of ethnic exigencies, the standard choreography dates to Lisbon, Porto, and Coimbra and reflects a historical rift during the Peninsular War—the flight to Rio de Janeiro of Queen Doña Maria I and fifteen thousand followers on November 17, 1807, to escape French general Jean-Andoche Junot's march on Salamanca. In 1821, King John VI and his Brazilian and Afro-Brazilian patriots repatriated to Portugal following the upheaval of the Napoleonic Wars. On Copacabana Beach, he left behind a dance motif popularized to marimba music for all ages and ethnicities to enjoy.

In Portugal, sailors, street toughs, and drifters performed at taverns, bordellos, cafes, plazas, private gardens, and bullfights, drawing into the atmosphere more poor urban Iberians. In Alfama, the prostitute Maria Severa, the first fadista, made her reputation by wrapping her shoulders in a black shawl and singing despairing fado in taverns. In the 1850s, the fatalistic dance grew popular with urban laborers, but earned scorn from aristocrats and intellectuals, who dismissed the music as gloomy and pedestrian.

Presentations in the 1870s incorporated the fado in cheap stage shows and operettas. At the University of Coimbra, male singers clad in black performed the fado in bel canto style at dimly lit village centers and cafes. By the 1890s, the fado had shed the African connection and acquired numerous quatrains of poetry about failed romance and pining lovers. At century's end, the dance lost folk authenticity by adopting the sedate partnering and style of the waltz.

In 1920, the socialistic fado offered a cover for Portuguese militancy. Following a coup on May 27, 1926, strongmen Manuel da Costa and António Salazar recognized the fado as the bane of revolution. To maintain the momentum of radical times and subversive arts, Costa and Salazar banned public performance of the fado on June 22 and limited the dance to low vaudeville theatricals. Nonetheless, dancers flaunted the steps and emotive body gestures as visual resistance to censorship.

A Recursive Art

In 1930, touring artists revived the underclass Portuguese rhythms and expressionism of the fado, which flourished in sound recordings and on radio broadcasts dominated by female crooners. In 1931, fado ballads permeated the first Portuguese film, *A Severa*, with a version lamenting the sufferings of the mythic courtesan-singer. From 1939, singer Amália Rodrigues lifted the fado to a soulful artistry. During World War II, folk embrace of the fado strengthened the dance, which enjoyed a faddish upsurge in Europe.

From the mid-1970s, as the Portuguese diaspora took emigrants to Brazil and Canada, global influences weakened the original fado with new steps, melodies heard at fado houses, and a rock beat. Tourism and Portugal's entry into the European Union in January 1986 introduced the Portuguese to aficionados flourishing in other places, including Angola, Croatia, Japan, Canada, Cape Verde, and Holland. By 2000, the "novo fado" derived energy and variety from an extended repertory and innovative instrumentation.

Among folkloric Iberian dancers, the hopping steps alternate men and women with arms akimbo in a circle for slight kicks. As the group rotates clockwise and counterclockwise, the basic hop dominates the melancholy harmonics of accordion, twelve-string guitar, viola, and bass. Women express femininity by swishing skirts with their hands and raising their arms as though summoning their partners.

See also waltz.

Source: Rohter, Larry. "Carving Out a Bold Destiny for Fado." *New York Times,* March 25, 2011.

FANCY DANCE

First Nations in southern Oklahoma created the dance-off, a free-form competition at Wild West shows and powwows and on reservations to acknowledge the most creative and hardy folk performers. Spontaneous and athletic, the presentations stress precision and ability of warrior dances. Audiences thrill to the bone, leather, brass, and silver of breastplates and moccasins and the hawk and eagle feathers making up bustles attached at the waist or harnessed to the upper back.

Developing a proposal by Wild West showman Buffalo Bill Cody from the early 1900s, Lakota and Ponca fancy dancers began the pan-Indian mode in the 1920s. Men revived Amerindian culture and beliefs through traditional choreography under the name "the crazy chicken." A permanent dance floor opened in 1928 at White Eagle, Ponca headquarters on the Arkansas River in north central Oklahoma.

Fancy Style

Jumps, crow hops, ruffles, leaps, splits, flips, crouches, hand taps, and cartwheels demanded stamina in fancy dancers and showcased rhythmic increases in speed coordinated with rapid drumming reaching one hundred fifty beats per minute. Constant movement drew attention to regalia, especially the roach, an ancient style of feathered headdress stitched with porcupine and whitetail deer hair. The headpiece, ribbons, and medallions spun and rocked in coordination with limb and torso movement.

In the 1930s, Comanche, Arapaho, and Kiowa dancers initiated regalia that combined fluffy arm eiderdown bustles on each arm, beadwork on breechcloth and moccasins, fur leggings, and tall nodding roaches. For idiophonic effects, competitors wore long underwear stitched from midriff to knee with bells. In Minnesota, Michigan, and Ontario and at European expositions, the tourist trade kept fancy dancers in cash during the Great Depression.

During the absence of men from Lakota villages in South Dakota during World War II, the first female fancy dancers and butterfly dancers added dramatic shawl sweeps that stirred deep fringe. Drawing on historic models from the 1840s, they displayed tribal icons in bright colors. In the late 1960s, Ojibwa women added the jingle dress dance to their performances.

Fancy Traditions

Spectators cheer twirling quirts and wands and the introduction of trick songs, which stop abruptly, forcing fancy dancers to freeze in space. One version, the Hidatsa grass dance (also Omaha dance) from the 1870s, imitates traditional prairie scouts who reconnoitered buffalo herds and quail and Canadian geese clusters. The folk dance developed practical skills in young men, who added to surveillance tactics the search for advancing enemies and suitable drinking water and camping spots.

Crucial to fancy dance improvisations is the alignment of heels. Humble body movements capture the graceful sway of prairie grass. Fringed costumes move with the wind to enable scouts to blend with the landscape. The totality honors a life balance and tribal responsibility to respect culture and thank the Earth Mother.

See also shawl dance.

Sources: Browner, Tara. *Heartbeat of the People: Music and Dance of the Northern Powwow.* Chicago: University of Illinois Press, 2002. Miller, Heather Andrews. "Dance Reflects Tradition and History." *Windspeaker* 24, no. 3 (2006).

FAN DANCE

A form of story dance and movement education for females, the Korean *bucheachum* (also *puch'ae ch'um* or fan dance) derived meaning and direction from shamanic ritual. Contemporaneous with the importation of Chinese Buddhism to Korea after 600 CE, celibate monks carried fans to shield their eyes from views of women. Female Koreans adopted rigid silk fans and folding paper and slatted cypress wood fans from the mainland as everyday accoutrements.

Fans rapidly acquired everyday purposes, aiding fire starters, sumo referees, tightrope walkers, musicians, and military commanders, which preceded the ceremonial maneuvers of fans by priests and monks. For ritual, shamans wafted square and semicircular shapes as amulets or charms conveying auspicious elements into troubled lives.

Art historians connect fan dancing to the imitation of the lucky flying pheasant among the Hani, a minority ethnic group in China, Laos, and Vietnam. From priestly nature rites, women developed a language of the fan communicating admonition, defiance, welcome, seduction, and warning. Historically, the ceremonial dance applied the gestures to sedate measures of flute and stringed instruments.

Synchronized Gesture

Fan dancers accentuated movement with exhibitions of hand fans formed from palm fronds, vellum, silk, parchment, and handmade paper. For stability, they attached the fan bodies to handles of bone, ivory, mica, mother of pearl, sandalwood, bamboo, or tortoise shell. Like the parasol dance, the flutter of colorful fans enhanced female delicacy, coquetry, and grace.

With the swish of folded regalia opened in unison, female fan dancing troupes honored couples at weddings and the deceased at funerals. Using one or two hand props, during the Joseon Dynasty after 1392, the typically reserved dancer at the Korean court added fan flirtation to pirouettes; solos; and line, chain, and ring dance. At a time when women maintained respectful silence before men, female mimes synchronized running steps, skips, glissades, and wrist spirals that elevated and lowered fans as a form of visual artistry.

Fans and Choreography

Dressed in traditional high-waisted, floor-length *hanboks*, precision folk troupes surrounded themselves with brightly painted parchment or mulberry paper semicircles. In chain dance style, members diversified promenades by holding the sash of the preceding dancer. Much of the performance consisted of shaping geometric wheels, sampans, and dragons or appealing objects from nature—suns, clouds, ocean waves, butterflies, birds, feathers, trees, and hibiscus blossoms.

The Korean fan dance mode influenced martial arts as well as youthful female folk dance in Taiwan, Japan, Hong Kong, Vietnam, Fiji, and Indonesia. In Japan, the two-fan dance took on the mastery of Kabuki theater and emulated the ethnic philosophy of order and modesty in society. For mimicry of coal miners in the *tanko bushi*, performers wielded oilpaper fans like shovels. Filipino dancers added fans and parasols to the athleticism of *tinikling*, an acrobatic dance between clashing bamboo poles.

The fan dance inspired artists to emulate female poise. Intricately painted posters and carved netsukes, the fasteners for obis, exhibited folk admiration of the fan dancer for her adroit management of an inanimate object. On October 12, 1968, a Korean company presented the iconic fan dance at the opening ceremony of the Mexico City Olympics. For the 1987 Olympic games in Seoul, the Korean mint issued a gold coin picturing bucheachum.

See also chain dance; circle dance; line dance; parasol dance; *tanko bushi*; *tinikling*.

Source: Qian, Gonglin. *Chinese Fans: Artistry and Aesthetics*. San Francisco: Long River Press, 2004.

FANDANGO

A taunting, ardent mating dance, the fandango began as an Iberian peasant duet performed apart to a 6/8 or 3/4 beat. First described by the authors Martial, Juvenal, and Pliny the Younger of imperial Rome, the dramatic, pulsing choreography harked back to the languid seminude dancing girls pictured on Egyptian wall carvings. Art historians describe the fandango's passage via Phoenician traders from the nautch dance of India to exotic performances in Gades (Cádiz), Hispania, and the czardas of Hungarian Magyars.

The fandango foregrounded Spanish folk arts, particularly the sixteenth-century caballero, flamenco, and malagueña, a theatrical male-female seduction choreography from Málaga, Spain, marked by heel taps and sensual turns and concluding with an erotic capitulation of female to male. Picturesque fandango steps featured arched backs, raised arms, stomping feet, snapping fingers, and rapid whirls, components introduced from Moorish Spain as well as the West Indies. In comparison to the bolero, the grave facial expressions and unflinching gaze of the fandango intensified its performance above mere folk entertainment to psychological melodrama.

Influenced by the *chica* and *cachucha*, in 1705, brisk fandango footwork and torso sways followed guitar strums and the rhythm of clapping, tambourine, or walnut or ebony castanets. Wary dancers encircled each other, sizing up the prospects of courtship. The exhibition appealed to the Roma, who added the Spanish character dance to their repertoire for presentation on streets and at inns. The dance also thrived among Portuguese cattle herders, who contributed brio and gaiety.

A Changing Mode

Well into the eighteenth century, the fandango deemphasized touching in favor of eye-to-eye communication. The abandon of the lower class emerged among the upper classes of Seville as a dance for adults and children. At formal balls and staged performances, dignity and formal courtesies between male and female replaced the blazing passion exuded during sudden halts and rotations. Critics surmised conflicting modes of improvisation ranging from Guinea to Arab harems.

Travelers introduced the body language of the fandango dancer in southern France, the Philippines, and Latin America. In the 1760s in Cuba and the barrios of Caracas, Venezuela, the open carnality of the *calenda* increased lascivious overtones of the fandango and imprinted the habanera, which flourished long arm movement overhead. At Altaplano, Chile, fandango posturing creolized the *cueca*, a couples handkerchief dance. The immoderate desire of the creolized fandango engaged the imagination of Brazilian stevedores, harbor dwellers, and coach drivers and increased bordello traffic.

A Foundational Dance

In the 1790s, the two-person seduction dance left its mark on the archetypal "Mexican Hat Dance" or *jarabe tapatío* of Jalisco and Zacatecas. Despite the ban of the Spanish Inquisition on lustful performances, Italian adventurer Giacomo Casanova hired an instructor in Madrid to teach him the alluring attitudes. By the early 1800s, the fervor of the Napoleonic Wars suppressed the more decorous gavotte in favor of the fandango. According to Neapolitan choreographer Carlo Blasis, in 1830, demand for the fandango in Andalusia outdistanced attraction to the Venetian *furlana*. Travel writer Charles Rochfort Scott, a British major general, declared in *Excursions in the Mountains of Ronda and Granada* (1838) that southern Spaniards could keep up the fandango as long as dancers had breath and energy.

At the same time that the dance delighted the Spaniards of Cádiz, American settlers caught fandango fever, especially along the Santa Fe Trail. When a wagon train to New Mexico halted for the night, in March 1840, the passengers who had observed the fandango in double-line mode in Santa Fe swapped opinions about the intermingling of men and women in torrid stamping, which dominated nightly entertainment. In Monterey, California, according to Richard Henry Dana's *Two Years before the Mast* (1842), the fandango offered appropriate entertainment for both a wedding and a child's funeral. At Brownsville and Matamoras in 1875, malicious Texas Rangers delighted in disrupting a fandango and terrorizing Mexicans by shooting out dance hall lights.

The dance made its way around the globe to Smyrna, Georgia, and Kashmir and, in Italy, received positive comparison to the Neapolitan tarantella. During resistance to American insurgency in the Philippines on May 1, 1898, islanders flaunted seductive Iberian dance spectacles—habanera, *pasodoble*, and fandango—as proof of their Latino culture. The Catholic hierarchy protested dancing that expressed so barbarous and blatant a sexual intrigue. The elastic steps and romantic style influenced the Dutch *pluggedansen*, similar in rhythm to the schottische and jig, and presented filmgoers with a stereotype of gendered Iberian relations marred by arrogance and power games.

See also bolero; *cachucha*; *calenda*; czardas; *furlana*; gavotte; handkerchief dance; *jarabe tapatío*; jig; *joropo*; *pasodoble*; schottische, tarantella.

Source: Bellman, Jonathan D. "*Ongherese*, Fandango, and Polonaise: National Dance as Classical-Era Topic." *Journal of Musicological Research* 31, nos. 2–3 (2012): 70–96.

FARANDOLE

A Catalonian or Provençal chain or handkerchief dance from northern Spain and Nice and Roussillon, France, the farandole (also crane dance or *carole*) alternated accented springs and bounds on opposite feet to singing. Similar to classic views of the Greek muse Terpsichore dancing with nymphs, medieval dancers held hands to eddy around guests at a wedding, birth, christening, anniversary, or saint's day as well as celebrations of the end of winter. To ensure a successful sowing of seeds or water from a community well, peasants joined in the frolic and twined around orchards and in and out of homes and churches. For magical effect or holy significance, a dance line followed a geometric path—a circle, square, triangle, parabolas, cross, half moon, star, alphabetic letters, scroll, or lozenge.

Dating to the 1100s, the farandole followed the style of the ancient Greek crane dance, a meandering dance in single file that Phocaean colonists imported to Marseilles in the 800s BCE. The farandole may take its name from the Greek term for "chain" or the Spanish *farandula*, a party of strolling players. After winding through paths and meadows, the serpentine column often reached a finale in which performers joined hands for a concluding circle. For a nighttime embellishment, performers carried lighted lanterns.

The Farandole in History

Skipping in a 6/8 meter to the sound of bagpipes, tambourine, fiddle or flute, and frame drum, the dancers followed a leader dressed like a thirteenth-century guardsman carrying a decorated halberd as a staff. At Belvedere on the Gallo-Italian border, performance of the farandole reverenced Saint Blaise, an Armenian physician whom the Roman emperor Licinius I martyred by decapitation at Sebastea, Anatolia, in 316 CE. In a precursor of square dancing, farandole performers sometimes gamboled through a two-person arch. In other variations, such as the Romanian *sîrba*, the group wound through open-ended linear weaving, called threading the needle, and the snail or coil, a maze figure by which the line reversed direction and paralleled its beginning.

As a finale for the disordered plots of the commedia dell'arte, the farandole reflected the influence of transalpine tarantellas, a frantic agitation of the body to cure the bite of a tarantula spider. Fighters of imperial wars introduced the chain dance up the Atlantic coast of Europe, where it acquired the oblique kicks and steps of Breton gavottes and Irish jigs. The chain dance figured in the Italian *basse danse* and images of the danse macabre, or the dance of death, a phenomenon of the bubonic plague. Unlike the stilted pavane processional, German chain dance united the upper class with peasants for the sake of fun. Late in the Middle Ages, the towering headdress and veil limited women's quick movements through doorways during the farandole.

Into the early Tudor period, the folkloric farandole retained its appeal under the name "the hay" (or hey), a festive framework that influenced the Irish *lanciers* (lancers) reel, a forerunner of square dance popular in Denmark and Ireland. Among Cornish villagers, dancers elided the word "farandole" into "furrydance" or "furry." In English poet Edmund Spenser's *Shephearde's Calendar* (1579), a woodcut pictured eight dancers performing a brisk farandole in celebration of May Day. In the mid-1590s, dramatist William Shakespeare incorporated the chain dance in *Love's Labour's Lost,* an early comedy written for a performance at the Inns of Court to entertain Elizabeth I.

As cities imposed governmental and doctrinal control over villages during the Renaissance, the organization of farandoles enabled country folk to revolt openly. Obscene versions of farandole tunes highlighted Protestant charivaris (public derision), which wound through Catholic churches, interrupted sacred processions, and disrupted the mass with dancers baring their backsides to priests. Perhaps for its loss of innocence, the repeated figure—a stamp on the left foot and a jaunty lift—received its first description in a French text around 1776.

A Grievous Art Form

The gay farandole took on a more rebellious meaning after it influenced the carmagnole, a jeering celebration of the French Revolution of July 14, 1789. Dancers inflamed the populace by leading chains around liberty trees to anti-Bourbon taunts. At Toulouse on August 15, 1815, antiroyalists charged General Jean Pierre Ramel with loyalty to Napoleon. To carry out an anonymous assassination, patriots formed a farandole, encircled Ramel, and butchered him in the streets. He lingered for two days before dying of multiple blade wounds.

In Rochemaure, France, royalists arranged a community farandole in 1823 to flaunt their royalist leanings. At Narbonne in 1849 and Vidauban on February 13, 1850, Jacobins of the Second Republic defied a ban on public dance on Ash Wednesday to enact the beheading of an aristocrat, an infernal farandole that set a precedent for annual carnival mockery of the grandiose. The farandole influenced the cotillion and quadrille as well as stage dance in Giacomo Meyerbeer's ballet *Robert le diable* (1831), Charles Gounod's opera *Mireille* (1864), and Georges Bizet's "Fum, Fum, Fum" from the chamber suite *L'Arlésienne* (1872). In Peter Ilyich Tchaikovsky's ballet *The Sleeping Beauty* (1890), the farandole marks the second act with a folk pleasantry, which contrasts with the stiff court scene that opens act I.

In the 1890s, French folk dancers performed the galloping farandole to a call-and-response pattern—a soloist sang a stanza from a legend or ballad and the rest of the company shouted the refrain. The shift from soloist to group incited a bound and a call of "Theseus" as performers recalled the Greek myth of winding the Cretan maze to the lair of the Minotaur. A favorite in Serbo-Croatia and Bulgaria, the farandole sometimes embodied a whole village in versions called the *chorovod* or *kolo.*

See also art, folk dance in; *branle*; carmagnole; comic dance; cotillion; gavotte; jig; labyrinthine dance; pavane; quadrille; reel; square dance.

Source: Mullally, Robert. *The Carole: A Study of a Medieval Dance.* Farnham, UK: Ashgate, 2011.

FILM, FOLK DANCE IN

As a form of cultural archiving, film preserves the classic melodies and ephemerality of authentic folk dance, as with the surmise of historical figures in the veiled dancing by Rita Hayworth in *Salome* (1953), the Bulgarian *rachenitsa* in *The Pauper's Joy* (1958), the Balkan *tamburitza* performed on the Ukrainian steppes by Yul Brynner in *Taras Bulba* (1962), and the Chinese nuptial procession in *The Last Emperor* (1987), a historical event that cost 400,000 yuan for the union of Emperor Puyi with Wanrong. From accessible history, movies have epitomized vernacular performances, for example, the striding, rocking gaucho tango of Rudolph Valentino and Beatrice Dominguez in *The Four Horsemen of the Apocalypse* (1926) and the Plains Indian ghost dance in *Billy Jack* (1971). Other models include the conga line snaking through Desi Arnaz's film *Too Many Girls* (1940) and the gender-bending finale of *The Birdcage* (1996), Cajun partnering in *Southern Comfort* (1981) and *The Big Easy* (1987), and the sweetheart reel from the Colorado frontier in a December 1993 episode of *Dr. Quinn, Medicine Woman*.

Cinema has popularized emerging dance forms—the crossover waltz in *Groovie Movie* (1944), the galop in the TV mini-series *North and South* (1985), and step dancing or soul stepping in *School Daze* (1988) and *Mac and Me* (1988), an appropriate parking lot setting for high-energy stepping. Later movies educated viewers on art history, the purpose of the lion dance in *Once Upon a Time in China* (1991), the affectionate ring dance honoring Chilean newlyweds in *The House of the Spirits* (1993), the sarabande in Stanley Kubrick's *Barry Lyndon* (1995), and the passionate flamenco by Antonio Banderas and Catherine Zeta Jones in *The Mask of Zorro* (1998). In each case, the dance served as entertainment as well as a tutorial in steps and technique.

Renaissance dance found favor on the screen with the galliard and *volta* in the TV miniseries *Elizabeth R* (1971), performed by Glenda Jackson and Robert Hardy in the parts of Queen Elizabeth I and a court favorite, Robert Dudley, the Earl of Leicester. The controversial volta received more careful screen analysis in *Shakespeare in Love* (1998) and *Elizabeth: The Golden Age* (2007), in which Sir Walter Raleigh, played by Clive Owen, leads Bess Throckmorton, played by Abbie Cornish, in the provocative duet. Additional period dance in the television series *The Tudors* (2009–2010) depicted Jonathan Rhys Meyers as Henry VIII in the volta partnering his second wife, Anne Boleyn, performed by Natalie Dormer.

Film archives less common choreography and demonstrates its uniqueness, as with the Amerindian hoop dance in *Apache Country* (1952) and a New Orleans jazz funeral parade in *Live and Let Die* (1973). For *Titanic* (1997), stars Kate Winslet and Leonardo DiCaprio observed third-class passengers at a *cèilidh*, a Scots-Irish dance party common to peasants. A distinct German-Swiss preface to the waltz, the *Ländler* in *The Sound of Music* (1965) displayed a skipping, gliding, and twirling couples dance enhancing the romance of Maria and Captain von Trapp, played by Julie Andrews and Christopher Plummer. Set to 3/4 meter, the charming interlude displayed the delicacy and grace of European refinement in folk choreography.

More recently, a South Carolina seashore nuptial dance in *The Patriot* (2002), the highland fling in the Charles Dickens social drama *Nicholas Nickleby* (2002), and the Druidic Beltane ring dance with torches at the standing stone in the television series *Outlander* (2014) enacted distinct occasions and need for group and ring dance. Outdoor settings connect all three with the origins of folk dance. For *The Patriot,* Anne and Gabriel Martin's outdoor wedding bears the impromptu gala of antebellum white and slave society. In *Nickleby,* the lax execution of the highland fling suggests folk origins of steps before they mutated into competitive dance. The Scots predawn liturgy in *Outlander* depicts a sisterhood protecting and encouraging parturient women with the flame of firebrands and uplifted hands to invisible spirits, the rudiments of Wiccan ritual dance.

See also Cajun dance; *cèilidh*; circle dance; flamenco; galliard; galop; ghost dance; highland fling; hoop dance; *Ländler*; nuptial dance; reel; sarabande; tango; veiled dance; *volta*; waltz; Wiccan dance.

Source: Dankworth, Linda E., and Ann R. David. *Dance Ethnography and Global Perspectives: Identity, Embodiment and Culture.* Basingstoke, UK: Palgrave Macmillan, 2014.

FINALES

Folk dancers accentuate theme and climactic action with grand finales, as with the snatching of fruit suspended off the dance floor at a Hungarian harvest festival, the jettisoning of the New Year's dragon dance totem into Hong Kong harbor, and the disappearance of Inuit performers from a trapdoor in the dance house. In competitive figures, dancers aim for showmanship in the conclusion, the high point in the Norwegian *halling* and the Ponca fancy dance, and the increasingly vigorous foot tapping of Peruvian zapateado dancers at Lima. In the 800s BCE, the Phocaean traders from central Anatolia introduced the farandole in Marseilles, where Gallic dance concluded a meandering chain with a circle, a promenade through an arch, or a labyrinthine "thread the needle," a dual emblem of couple commitment and copulation. When Ethiopians established Christian worship in the first century CE, they rounded out yuletide observations with "King David's dance," a choreography recalling Jerusalem's first Hebrew king, who stripped and danced ecstatically before the Ark of the Covenant.

After 682 CE in the Sri Vijayan Empire of Malaya, acrobats amazed spectators with plate balancing but finished the display by breaking the saucers on the floor and dancing in bare feet over shards. For the Malay *endang*, couples built passion in their wooing to the finale, a permanent union. At Tonga in Oceania, the conclusion of the *soke* stressed synchrony of sound as dance quartets ended their idiophonic stick duels and thudded their weapons butt first on the ground. In Haiti, Afro-Caribbean *djouba* dancers followed a caller, who initiated a series of figures until he reached the last, the long dog scratch, an intriguing title for a dance about which few details remain.

The Renaissance increased the prominence of the frivolous *rigaudon*, which completed stage shows in Italy and highlighted the role of rifles in Algerian warrior dance, which ended with musket fire. For the Roma, the combination of sexual conquest and militarism built ardor with arrogant head thrusts and embraces, an atmospheric finale of the bolero *moruno*. Scorching looks preceded the climax, a ferocious cry of triumph over the coquettish female. At the resolution of commedia dell'arte street shows, confused partner changes end in a joyous folk dance, a fantasy conclusion to real-life dilemmas.

Religious and Carnal Fervor

Around 1690, juvenile Catalonian companies at Berga anticipated the grand conclusion of the Corpus Christi Day celebrations—the allegorical *tirabol*. The burst of fireworks and drunken dancing in counterclockwise mode filled streets with an orgiastic salute to faith and social unity, which sustained them during the suppression of folk arts under the dictatorship of Francisco Franco from 1936 to 1975. Among Bavarians, the shoe-clap dance mimicked cockfighting of the black grouse. The menacing of rooster on rooster concluded with a coda, the pairing of the saucy male with the appeasing hen, a knowing flirt who settled her man's feathers with womanly gestures of the *Ländler*.

In the Carpathian Ukraine after 1715, the czardas (also *csardas* or *verbunkos*) morphed into a military selection tool for the Austrian army. By treating farm boys to free drinks and music at a local beer hall, the recruiters could observe musculature and stamina. As the beat rose from the slow *lassú* (or *lassen*, introduction) to the *friss* (or *friska*, finale), officers chose the most promising males to conscript into service to the Hapsburg emperor.

The complex religio-historic motifs in Mesoamerican *matachines* reached iconic ends in the late 1700s after some fifteen hours of performance over Christmas Eve at venues in New Mexico. The presentation of Hernán Cortés's conquest of Tenochtitlán and the death of Aztec emperor Montezuma II preceded a mock bullfight resulting in either death or castration of a pagan cult by whip-cracking Christian elders. To express the solidarity of a mestizo culture, at Arroyo Seco, Tortugas, Picurís, and Taos Pueblo, versions of the *matachines* presented the plaiting of colored ribbons around a maypole, an agrarian pageant from early medieval Europe. At San Ildefonso Pueblo, dancers added a child-pleasing touch, the arrival of Santa Claus. At Hualuapan, Mexico, the entire iconography removed historic animosities and replaced them with giants and heavily painted devils, an Old World representation of evil.

Metaphoric Endings

The purpose of dance finales encapsulates the theme and vernacular mode of expressions, as with a brisk zapateado to raise spirits during a Día de los Muertos (Day of the Dead) street dance and a jive session relating joy in the life of the deceased for a New Orleans jazz funeral parade. Late in the eighteenth century, the Hussars of Napoleon mastered the mazurka as an emblem of military might and a form of flirtation with local girls, who admired gold epaulets and shiny cavalry boots. When the dance spread from Poland to the Caribbean, emulators of Napoleon's horsemen performed the crossovers amid relaxed shuffles and slides. For a show-stopping conclusion, they rose on the balls of their feet and clicked their heels in the manner of a salute.

In Guadalajara, Mexico, dancing the *jarabe tapatío* aroused disapproval in the colonial Catholic hierarchy and fear of rebellion among Spanish conquerors. After the eleven-year Mexican War of Independence in September 1821, folkloric revivals of the "Mexican Hat Dance" concluded with a sexual metaphor, the presentation of the man's sombrero for the woman to dance around. The courtship scenario concluded with "La Diana"—a kick over her head and a kiss concealed by the sombrero, a combined gesture of discretion and defiance. A less sedate farewell at the end of Parisian balls drew the majority to their feet for a thunderous galop, a dance that released frustrations with energetic trotting.

See also bolero; cakewalk; *calenda*; farandole; film, folk dance in; galop; *halling*; healing dance; *jarabe tapatío*; *tirabol*; worship dance; zapateado.

Source: Nielsen, Erica. *Folk Dancing*. Santa Barbara, CA: ABC-Clio, 2011.

FLAMENCO

A jolting, improvised solo beloved around the globe, flamenco exhibits authentic folkloric passions. Linguists connect the term to flames and the flamingo and Flamenco soldiers, named for their service in the Flemish wars after 1519. Art historians surmise that the dance of southern Spain bore cultural determinants from Egyptian belly dance and the culture of Tartessos, a legendary Greek colony settled in southern Spain during the Bronze Age. Eighth-century facets suggested the sounds of Byzantine and Visigoth liturgical hymns.

The arrival of the Arabic love song to Cordoba in 1400 initiated a more rhapsodic form of the flamenco called the malagueña. At the height of hybridization, in 1425 during the Spanish Inquisition, the nomadic Roma brought west from the Punjab of northwestern Indian the darkly rhapsodic elements of *kathak*, a storytelling dance. On their advance across Algeria, Tunisia, and Morocco to Gibraltar, the Roma acquired North African heel lifts, pivots on the ball of the foot, and an atmospheric meter pounded out on the floor with a staff or stool.

Low-Class Folk Art

Intense and demonstrative, in private sessions of Roma dancing at Cádiz, Seville, and Jerez, flamenco body language developed a curving arm bent at the elbow and flexing of the thumbs and middle fingers. The flamenco marked the pre-Lenten carnival and entertainments on saints' days as well as brothel amusements, where spectators clapped and shouted "olé" as part of the accompaniment. Cave-dwelling Roma troupes living at Granada earned a meager living by migrating to summer festivals and taverns. To dramatize their social stigmatization, they performed plaints of unrequited love and death.

Spain's outcasts—Roma, Moriscos (Hispanic Muslims), and the Sephardic Jews of Granada—added the finger snaps, shawl flourishes, and clapping that exhilarated vocal solos to guitar melodies in a minor key. From the arched back of the bullfighter, the Iberian rhythm developed in the late 1700s with staccato heel and toe stamps, lidded eyes, mouth slightly ajar, and whip turns. Dancing prostitutes appeared to transport themselves through suggestive presentations with shawls, the source of the Spanish tango, which women performed while wearing men's hats.

Reclaimed Art

A notable star of flamenco music, in 1864, Hispano-Italian sailor Silverio Franconetti of Seville propelled the songs into a golden age. After generations of Roma entertainment of the rich with flamenco, in 1869, cafe society shaped the folk dance to strummed music. Presented in 3/4 or 6/8 rhythm, the flamenco was altered during heightened tourist traffic to southern Iberia in the late nineteenth century. From the modest coffeehouses at Málaga and in Seville's Gypsy Lane, aficionados exported the dance to Cuba, where moody gestures focused fluttering hands before the eyes. In France and Russia, composers added the flamenco to longer works, as with Georges Bizet's opera *Carmen* (1875) and the ballet *Cuadro flamenco* (Flamenco scene, 1921), staged by the Ballets Russes.

When cafe flamenco ebbed, in 1922, two arts giants, playwright Federico García Lorca and composer Manuel de Falla, launched a Spanish folk festival, which they expected to revitalize authentic folk music and dance. Over decades of global commercialization of flamenco throughout Catalonia and Castile, the dance devolved into erotic stage spectacle, yet, in 1929, the steps entranced Cuban dance star Alicia Alonso. In 2010, UNESCO listed the dance among the Masterpieces of Intangible Heritage.

See also belly dance; fandango; film, folk dance in; *kathak*; *pasodoble*; Roma dance.

Source: Lorenz, Roberto. "Flamenco Page." Accessed October 18, 2015. www.timenet.org/roberto.html.

FLOWERS

The choice of flowers as adornments and symbols for dance contributes color, fragrance, and texture to global folk performances, from the ferny leis of the Maui hula and the blossom offerings from *ghurei* dancers of Chamba, India, to the sacred flowers marking Yaqui presenters of the *matachines* at Pasqua, New Mexico. For Fijian story dance, around 800 BCE, Lapitan mariners from Indonesia decked themselves in shell adornments and flower collars to emphasize hand and shoulder gestures. Tongan troupes mimed the *taualuga* in lory crests, coconut and nautilus shells, turtle carapaces, and garlands of blossoms and fern fronds.

Florid body adornment and presentation linked natural beauty with the sacred, a feature of Mesoamerican Mayan headdress, which incorporated hummingbirds sipping nectar from flowers for royal entertainment, and with the wild sage garlands crowning sun dancers among the Teton Sioux. Southern Greeks at Laconia revered Artemis with a maidenly choreography requiring dancers to balance flower baskets on their heads, a display of grace that architects copied for the caryatids on the Athenian acropolis. At the height of Aryan civilization in 500 BCE, the Hindu Vedas extolled the cosmic dance of Lord Siva and the shower of blossoms that honored his presence and expelled evil from his shrines. In 200 BCE, the hula artists of Cook Island, Hawaii, and Tahiti adopted the grass or ti leaf skirt coordinated with blossom leis and ankle, forehead, and wrist garlands. The flora exuded fresh scents with each dance figure.

Decor and Settings

As the gavotte evolved from a mountaineers' caper in Gap, France, in the late Middle Ages, it lost its reputation as a kissing dance. At court in Paris and Versailles, refined gentlemen chose to omit embracing their partners and replaced the intimacy with a party favor or gift of flowers. During the 1750 craze for the cotillion, men presented potential partners daisy and violet bouquets and flower staffs tied with ribbons. To accept a partner, a woman withdrew a blossom to tuck into the man's lapel as a boutonniere.

According to eighteenth-century diaries and letters, flowers gave New World dance planners a reason for an extensive outdoor caper. Mazes and knot gardens drew couples and groups to afternoon and late night torch-lit frolics. North Carolina colonists at New Bern enjoyed chain dance and processions over sixteen acres of gardens precisely planted in baroque style at Tryon Palace by Claude Joseph Sauthier, a French draftsman. Glimpses of gatherings at Drayton Hall outside Charleston, South Carolina, and Iolani Palace in Honolulu, Hawaii, stressed the pleasant outdoor settings for dancing among fragrant blossoms.

Costumes and Props

In coastal Veracruz, Mexico, dancers of the *son jarocho* integrate flowered headpieces into a feminine costume featuring white skirts and black aprons. Rapid stomping and twirling spreads fragrance just as Cuban, Spanish, and African choreography and mime tinge Mesoamerican folk arts. Pre-Lenten celebrations of carnival in Rio de Janeiro, Brazil; Matanzas, Cuba; and Buenos Aires, Argentina, feature couples promenading with flower-covered arches, a bold, aromatic touch to street parades. For Día de los Muertos (Day of the Dead) processions and performance of the zapateado, dancers carry marigolds, a bright gold adornment for cemeteries.

Malay devotees honor the spirit of the sea with the *ulik mayang*. A mystic enlivening of betel or areca nut flowers, the kinetics begin with the quivering and undulating of blossom sprays and chains. As the performer grows convinced that the strand bears life, she passes it to the next dancer.

See also chain dance; cotillion; *ghurei* dance; hula; lamentation dance; Malay dance; *matachines*; processionals; sun dance; zapateado.

Source: Barr, Amelia E. "Characteristic Dances of the World." *Lippincott's Magazine* 27, no. 4 (April 1881): 330–41.

FURLANA

A lighthearted wooing dance from the northeastern region of Friuli Venezia Giulia in northeastern Italy, the *furlana* (or *forlane*, *fourlane*, or *forlana*) originated in 1583 among minority Slavs in the Venetian Republic or possibly in Corfu off the border between Albania and Greece. Set to a syncopated 6/8 meter of clapping and accordions, in 1609 at Istria, Croatia, the dance incorporated Balkan peasant rhythms. A circle or double line of couples followed patterns of raised right arms, hops, rotations, drops to the left knee, and repeated shifts of the right foot from front to side.

For street festivals and the pre-Lenten carnival at Venice, dancers incorporated fluttering handkerchiefs as well as doffed hats and apron flirtation for repeated advances and retreats. During exile for collusion with Jacobites in 1695, James Drummond,

4th Earl of Perth, visited Italy and compared the dynamism of the Venetian furlana to Scots highland dances. He confided that women performed the steps better than men. The baroque choreography became the professional logo of Venetian gondolieri and influenced the Spanish bolero.

Court Entertainment

The bouncy steps of the furlana delighted the court of Louis XIV in 1697 as a folk demonstration for troupes of Roma, Armenians, and Slavs. At masked balls to string music by François Couperin and Jean-Philippe Rameau, the furlana combined well in four-part dance suites with the galliard, *rigaudon*, and slow, sober pavane. Along with the bounding steps of the saltarello, the French popularized the furlana for representing the exuberance of the Venetian carnival.

Over the next half century, the furlana gained fame in England and Germany as well as Turkey. Couples danced in open position at a speed approaching that of the frenetic tarantella. At Constantinople in 1744, adventurer Giacomo Casanova, a Venetian military officer, reported in his memoirs that he danced six sets of the vigorous figure. At the age of nineteen, he expressed surprise that the furlana left him breathless and exhausted.

Into the 1780s, the furlana remained a favorite with Europeans. Ballrooms and street fairs as far apart as the island of Hvar near Dubrovnik, Croatia, and Vaasa, Finland, welcomed people of all social levels to the dance. In 1800, Venetian sketch artist Giovanni Domenico Tiepolo pictured the furlana as an activity popular among children, who flung arms and legs in time to the jingle of the tambourine. In Spain in 1830, according to Neapolitan choreographer Carlo Blasis, demand for the fandango and *chica* outdistanced that for the furlana.

After viewing the tango in a private chamber, on January 16, 1914, Pope Pius X fought the body contact of the lascivious couples dance with a statement in Rome's *Il Tempo* newspaper urging reclamation of the less sensuous furlana, which wags dubbed "La Popette," the pope's dance. Dance teachers immediately opened classes at Rome and Paris featuring the furlana. At a presentation at Schönbrunn Palace in Vienna for Emperor Franz Joseph I, Polish-American stage dancer Albertina Rasch defended the propriety of the dance by stating that Venetian children enjoyed furlana breaks to the hurdy-gurdy. The outbreak of World War I on July 28, 1914, ended interest in the dance.

See also galliard; pavane; *rigaudon*; saltarello; tango; tarantella.

Source: Elson, Arthur. "Musical Thought and Action in the Old World." *The Etude* (January 1914): 418.

· *G* ·

GALLIARD

A five-step Italian couples dance popular in Renaissance Europe, from 1480, the galliard attained prominence in Italy both in Lombardy to the north and Campania on the southwestern coast. Under the names *gagliardo* and *Romanesca*, Italian figures suggested the gaited steps of the horse and a dance popularized in Rome. The robust choreography identified the frolics of Scots shepherds and rural dancers in 1541 and spread to dance floors in England, Scotland, Holland, Germany, Spain, and France, reaching Paris in 1529 and London in 1541. Among Tudor courtiers, it supplanted the simplistic skipping of the saltarello by 1546 with more wanton leg thrusts.

A sporting hopping figure in triplets executed as far from northwestern Europe as the Cape Verde Islands, the galliard rounded out performances of the stately pavane. Without a pause, the five-step followed the beats of a tabor and tambourine and the strum of a lute or guitar playing a popular folk ballad or love plaint of the day. It sometimes preceded a sword dance, a chivalric dumb show that created a canopy of crossed sword points under which female dancers could pass. Often accompanied on the spinet, virginal, or harpsichord, the 6/8 rhythm figured in the instruction manuals of Roman dance master Lutio Compasso in 1560, Venetian compiler Fabritio Caroso da Sermoneta in 1581, Giovanni Radino of Venice in 1592, and Milanese writer Cesare Negri in 1602.

Gendered Presentation

For the galliard, women held their partner's hands for the first set, then separated with a coy profile to allow a male solo. At competitive dance-offs, men held hat in hand to showcase the strenuous four kicks and a cabriole with the front leg lifted. As factors in their advancement in politics and at court, ambitious males improvised variations for side, back, and diagonal steps and showy whip turns at the coda to prove themselves both ingenious and able.

Ever certain of her equality with men, after her coronation in 1558, Elizabeth I executed galliard steps each morning for exercise, often to the compositions of John Dowland of London, a master of melancholy airs. The queen admired the tassel kick, which she aimed toward an adornment on her skirt. She excelled at the *volta*, a provocative variation in which the man lifts the woman with one arm, rests her on his thigh, and swings her in three-quarters of a circle. A French painting from the period captured the pairing of Elizabeth with her favorite, Robert Dudley, the Earl of Leicester. Although she allowed him to lift her by breast and hips, the painting displayed her left hand holding her skirts at a modest height.

In 1561, Queen Elizabeth complimented Christopher Hatton's execution of kicks and springs to the point of riling Dudley. In 1579, she discovered that a youthful French suitor, Francis, the Duc d'Anjou, performed the steps briskly. Performing the popular galliard became a test of culture, a fact influencing William Shakespeare's inclusion of the glittering dance to popular harmonies in *Much Ado about Nothing* and *Twelfth Night*. His corruption of the French *cinq pas* as "sink-a-pace" reprised the commoner's term.

A Varied Galliard

By 1589, folk dances incorporated a simplified version of the galliard that ended in a caper, a figure that dance master Thomas Morley found more stirring than the sedate pavane. Elizabeth discovered another partner in courtier Robert Devereux, who rose to the Privy Council in 1593. Devereux went to the block for treason in 1601 at the time when Louis XIII scheduled the French *gaillarde* for his nobles.

At the Jacobean court, James I extended the dominance of the galliard to more modulated melodies and reprises of original compositions by William Byrd, John Bull, Peter Philips, and Orlando Gibbons. John Dowland wrote a special galliard in 1610 for James's brother-in-law, King Christian IV of Denmark. Playwright Lope de Vega complained in 1631 that the dance had disappeared in Spain. The galliard combined well with the *rigaudon*, pavane, and *furlana*, a bouncy Venetian couples dance. As the allemande, minuet, Spanish passacaglia, and rural dances gained popularity, in 1650, the galliard waned among aristocrats and royalty. Milkmaids used the five-step figure as an entertainment for customers in 1667 and awaited tips.

See also allemande; *furlana*; pavane; *rigaudon*; saltarello; *volta*.

Source: Cosman, Madeleine Pelner. *Handbook to Life in the Medieval World.* New York: Facts on File, 2008.

GALOP

An imitation of a horse at full gait with hints of the outdoor life, the galop (also *galop-pade* or *galopede*) retained its ancient beginnings as the *cwal* in rural Hungary. (Minority arts opinions claim Russia or northern Germany for the origin.) The galop derived mobility and propulsion from the czardas, *cachucha*, and *friska*, a fast improvisational Slovak dance dating to the Middle Ages. The impetuous alternation of a glide, skip, and chassé in 2/4 meter anticipated the polka, *lanciers* (lancers), and can-can.

In dance suites after 1815, the galop concluded contradance and the *volta* with an aerobic exertion and offered a welcome break from the mazurka. Added to the polka, schottische, or the Spanish *guaracha*, the reckless bounding for two to a racing tempo invigorated couples in Berlin and Vienna in 1822 and later in Prague and London.

During pre-Lenten carnival season in 1829, Marie-Caroline, the Duchess de Berry, elevated the *galop-folie* to social prominence in Paris, where her guests gathered at the Tuileries Gardens and the Austrian and English embassies.

According to J. S. Pollock's manual *Companion to la Terpsichore moderne* (1830), Princess Maria Theresia Esterhazy of Regensburg, Austria, quickly passed the steps to guests at the royal ball of George IV at St. James Palace on June 11, 1829, where the orchestra interspersed galops with waltzes and quadrilles. At the height of ball season, as a finale at the French Opera, maskers scheduled the schottische and reel before the commoner's galop. As four thousand clomped through the hall, guests broke chairs, rang bells, and discharged pistols.

The galop added a democratic element to public folk dance, which incorporated any and all performers. In the 1830s, Parisian violinist Philippe Mustard developed the public concert, a natural venue for giddy rounds of the waltz and galop. In London at the Lyceum and in Paris at parks and dance halls, his orchestra played for some three thousand partygoers of all classes, who made spectacles of themselves from their pumping, rollicking exertions.

Galop Diversity

Variations compounded the galop with more structured dance, for example, the Czechoslovakian *redowa*, a leaping, rotating waltz, and the Esmeralda glide (a polka-galop), bearing the name of Victor Hugo's Roma protagonist in *The Hunchback of Notre Dame* (1831). By 1833, the galop reached Sydney, Australia, and delighted participants at children's ensembles. At a musical show in Paris, the audience thronged the stage to dance along with performers. In 1838, the Victoria galop, which honored the coronation of England's eighteen-year-old queen, buoyed the career of black orchestra leader Francis Johnson during his tours on both sides of the Atlantic.

Arts critics seized on the galop for its ability to turn couples from formal to delirious. For the piano, Franz Liszt's "Grand galop chromatique" earned from the *Westminster Review* the sobriquet the "demon dance" for its hectic phrasing. The irrepressible galop marked a village scene depicting the title figure dancing with Loys in act I of Adolphe Adam's *Giselle* (1841), a hugely successful ballet.

Newspapers made a sport of collecting exaggerated galop stories. A spectator of the Paris carnival in 1841 saw four thousand dancers of the "*saturnale galop infernal*" roar off the dance floor and down the Rue St. Honoré to the Place Vendôme before shrieking back. At the carnival in Rome on April 12, 1843, one observer gasped that the "*galop monstre*" at the Theatre de la Renaissance exploded into a whirlwind of jostling and contusions that bruised bodies and shredded gowns and slippers.

The addition of the blast of a hunting horn in 1844 signaled the finale of the post-horn galop at a hunt ball. In St. Louis, Missouri, dancers embraced both the Berlin galop and the Czech redowa in 1849, a year before the arrival of the Bavarian schottische. For house parties, pianists popularized a rousing solo, "The Irish Steeple Chase Galop" (1853). For the stage, Giuseppe Verdi added a galop to the opera *La Traviata* (1853).

In 1856, the triplet galop quadrille in Philadelphia fused the two dances by forming four couples into a square. In Virginia during the American Civil War, a boisterous Prussian galop entertained a house party that welcomed military officers. An official dance of the Ontario and Quebec Rifles at Winnipeg, Manitoba, in 1871, balanced the program with four galops, three quadrilles, three waltzes, two lanciers, and one each of cotillion, jig, and schottische. The pounding furor earned the name *Schnellpolka* (fast polka) and, as a forerunner of ragtime, colored compositions of Johann Strauss II, Franz Schubert, Jacques Offenbach, Dmitri Shostakovich, and George Gershwin.

In travel photographer Paul Marcoy's *A Journey across South America from the Pacific Ocean to the Atlantic Ocean* (1875), he reported armed men following a war chief in a funereal galop while women wept and wailed for those fallen in combat. During waltz mania, the madcap galop shared the spotlight with the box step at the Tuileries Gardens and the Prado nightclub in Paris and Tivoli Gardens in Italy. The steps alternated with sips of champagne at exclusive New York socials; among settlers of Saginaw, Michigan; at a dinner dance at the Austrian embassy in Paris; and at the English embassy in Paris to acknowledge Queen Victoria's birthday.

A Global Dance

In the American South, the galop suited hearty pioneer dancers, whom the driving beat transformed into a synchronized mob. In Texas, it contributed to the two-step and earned the name Herr Schmidt (Mr. Smith) from German settlers of the state's heartland. At Oak Alley Plantation in New Orleans and Monmouth Plantation in Natchez, Mississippi, women and girls presented the sarabande, mazurka, and galop in hoop skirts and soft-soled kid dance slippers.

Popular melodies—the *William Tell Overture*, "Ta-Ra-Ra Boom De-Ay"—accompanied dancers in the Gay Nineties. Late in the century, Swedish revelers from Uppsala, Lund, Stockholm, and Gothenburg universities observed Walpurgis Night by encircling bonfires each April 30 to dance the galop to spring tunes. In Upper Murray, Victoria, the Australian galop acquired a new sound with the addition of Conrad "Con" Klippel's Anglo-German concertina playing "The Manchester Galop," a heritage tune from Berlin that came into vogue at dinky di bush balls.

In southern Louisiana, zydeco dance in Acadiana blended cotillion with polka, mazurka, waltz, and galop. For a ball in the 1880s at Napier, New Zealand, the galop shared the program with the mazurka, lanciers, quadrille, and waltz. The galloping rhythm so seized the imagination of E. Woodworth Masters, president of the American National Association of Teachers of Dancing, that he named his monthly newsletter *The Galop*. Still viable in 2012, the galop in the curriculum of the Children's Club in Suceava, Romania, developed strength and rhythm.

See also cachucha; contradance; cotillion; czardas; film, folk dance in; jig; mazurka; polka; quadrille; reel; sarabande; schottische; *volta*; Walpurgis dance; waltz; zydeco.

Source: Schaff, Helene, Marty Sprague, and Susan McGreevy-Nichols. *Exploring Dance Forms and Styles.* Champaign, IL: Human Kinetics, 2010.

GAVOTTE

A distinctive outgrowth of the medieval round dance, the gavotte is one of the world's oldest folk figures. The rustic line or circle dance originated in the early Renaissance at Gap (or Gavots), Dauphiné, in southeastern France as a light, gracious caper for mountain folk. Some art historians place the first gavotte among Britons on the Atlantic coast or the French Basque of Provence.

Choreography for "*la dance classique*" consisted of a polite tiptoeing double step to right and left followed by crossovers or *assemblés* with pliés in 4/4 meter. Individuals left the circle to perform solo steps in the center. Repeated four times with pointed toes and a light spring, the gavotte paired well with shuffles of the pastoral musette, a bucolic folk dance from Marseilles set to bagpipe drones or accordion tunes. In the 1300s near the end of the Middle Ages, soldiers in imperial wars introduced the gavotte and a chain dance, the farandole, up the Atlantic coast.

The Evolving Gavotte

In new territory, medieval aficionados of the Breton chain form of the gavotte and Irish and Scots jigs introduced more kicks, a long stride, and small skips to piper's music. By 1400, guests at weddings enjoyed the gavotte along with the sarabande, pavane, galliard, saltarello, *branle*, and hora. The creation of the *rigaudon* in 1485 gave dancers a choice of a springier quickstep interspersed among presentations of the gavotte.

In the late 1500s, the gavotte migrated from villages in the French high country south to Italy and north to the royal courts at Paris. At Versailles, the stylized steps presented buckled shoes to advantage. By the 1620s, the gavotte emerged from peasant celebrations as a favorite amusement at the court of Louis XIII, who catered to moderate tastes with such restrained figures as the pavane.

Bourbon court composer Jean-Baptiste Lully provided music for the gavotte. Johann Sebastian Bach arranged harpsichord suites to the tempo and style of the gavotte, which formed a third part in suites beginning with the sarabande and gigue, a skipping, bounding dance in counterpoint introduced in 1650. Around 1745, French demand for the faddish branle waned because Louis XV favored the slow, sober minuet and contradances. At court, the gavotte won his approval and concluded with a rondeau, a light-stepping backward-forward line dance. The gavotte entertained Transylvanians, but by 1760, few serious composers wrote music for urban performers.

Rise and Fall

After the coronation of Louis XVI at Rheims on June 18, 1775, the last Bourbon king before the French Revolution created a court stir with the gavotte. An adaptation of the branle, the dance involved kissing between partners. Less amorous dancers chose to present bouquets or small party favors rather than intimate embraces. In 1777, Parisian letter writer Marie Chantal de Sévigné commented on the popularity of the dance among aristocrats.

In February 1779, Queen Marie Antoinette, wife of Louis XVI, admired the gavotte and danced it at an opera ball at carnival time until 6:00 in the morning. She had
such a good time that she reprised the dance at a masked Mardi Gras ball on March 19,
1799, when she traveled by coach to the Paris Opera House in disguise. The queen's
arrest in 1792 and her beheading in 1793 turned the peasantry against any frivolity once
enjoyed by the hated Bourbons. In North America, the wealthy abandoned the gavotte
and took up the galop and waltz.

The creation of new figures for the gavotte on August 16, 1797, for a dance at the
Hotel de Valentinois aroused new interest among Parisians. During the Napoleonic Wars
and into the 1820s, the more passionate bolero and fandango replaced the fusty gavotte
with group dance. In the form of a quadrille, the gavotte returned to popularity in 1887.

See also bolero; *branle*; contradance; fandango; farandole; jig; pavane; quadrille;
rigaudon.

Source: Lord, Suzanne, and David Brinkman. *Music from the Age of Shakespeare: A
Cultural History.* Westport, CT: Greenwood, 2003.

GENDERED DANCE

The gender of performers determines the mode of presentation, whether men alone,
women alone, or both men and women. Early folk choreography featured organized
community dances, as with the medieval farandole or chain dance; seduction or pursuit dances like the Andalusian *cachucha* and fandango and the West Indian *calenda*; and
select presentations for men or women only among the aborigines of northwestern
Australia and the Amerindians of the Great Basin of the United States. The separation
of genders marked the Ukrainian *hopak*, a soldier's display of bravado; the Chinese
dragon dance, a veneration of the male principle of yang; and the Greek circle dance
before the Great Mother Goddess Cybele, a modest liturgy for maidens.

Placement of males with or without females obeyed social strictures about propriety. In Oman, pairs of men danced the bluesy *zaffan*, an Arab dance varying kneeling
with leaping. Kurds encouraged shoulder-to-shoulder dance alternating genders, but
women never held hands with unknown men. To bridge the social situation, adults
spaced children between strangers.

In Fiji, the *meke* group dance involved either women or men. In 1896, islanders
acted out verses for feasts and holidays. For the Mesoamerican male-only *matachines*, a
religio-historical dance celebrating mestizo culture and the Virgin of Guadeloupe, Mexican troupes at Durango and US presentations at Bernalillo, New Mexico, changed focus
to an all-female cast. Variations of the gendered dance in Alcalde, New Mexico, and Rio
Sucio, Colombia, featured transvestite males, who turned cross-dressing into comedy.
Only Zacatecas, Mexico, maintained its traditional Amerindian men-only troupe.

Men

Androcentric dance thrived in ancient times, a custom demonstrated by the plowman sowing seed and fighting a thief in the Persian *carpaean* dance at Magnesia and

in most of the eight hundred paintings and sketches of Mandan and Lakota Sioux by American artist George Catlin. Cretan sailors favored labyrinthine figures. At the Hippodrome, charioteers exulted over winning laps. For a millennium after the formation of the Byzantine Empire, Eastern Greek Orthodoxy inhibited dancers until authorities granted Greeks the right to *bibasis* (gendered ring dance), processions, and street throngs welcoming triumphant armies. As pictured in sculpture, mural, fresco, and manuscript illumination, males grasped wrists in spiritual celebration of holidays and commemoration of ethnic legends.

Nordic dance, first described in the 1000s, honored two high points in the male life cycle—weapon dances reverencing fealty to Thor and the brotherhood of the drinking horn, a phallic symbol at nuptials. Further glorifying masculinity, the chain dances of the Faroe Islands featured a narrative element extracted from heroic exploits, particularly those of Charlemagne and Roland, a legendary Frankish military commander killed in an ambush in the Pyrenees on August 15, 778. Typically limited to bounds and chassés and the chain lines of the dance of death, medieval Scandinavian choreography offered little variety and few surprises.

From the eleventh century, Bavarian men in the Tyrol advanced the stomping, clapping *Schuhplattler* as an exhibition of male agility and stamina. The lusty slapping of lederhosen, thighs, knees, and shoe soles impressed women. The mimicry of professional labors incorporated evidence of skill at milling and woodcutting. A more rigorous mode, the Norwegian *halling* featured male grandstanding in leaps, throws, and backbends.

Among Samoans, the slap dance presented parallel rows of males miming everyday actions, beginning in the early 1800s with the smashing of mosquitoes on the body. The slapping of torso and limbs, stomping of feet, and jumping evolved into a follow-the-leader style of synchronized dance to no music. Performed on patriotic holidays, birthdays, nuptials, and receptions, the slap dance began with a liberal slather of coconut oil, bent knees, and feet a shoulder width apart.

Malay Muslims, influenced by Indonesian worship dance, honored Allah and the Prophet Muhammad with praise song and dance. In the 1930s, presenters altered the all-male performance by adding female roles played by transvestites. The dance began as a religious ritual for marriages and circumcisions and evolved into a harvest thanksgiving or social presentation.

Women

At the ancient Gymnopaedia, Spartan women formed a ring and frolicked unclothed in the *hormos*, a *syrto*-style honorarium to Diana, the Greek goddess of chastity and the hunt. A precursor of the medieval French *branle*, the brisk skipping steps extended into the streets at the leader's direction. Gestures and voices animated the performance, which swayed now left, now right.

According to historian Michael Psellos's *Chronographia* (ca. 1070), in medieval Constantinople, women gained privileges from the Catholic hierarchy to dance in churchyards at Easter and Christmas. Two traditional occasions marked nuptial receptions and banquets with a ring dance and honored weaving at the Festival of Agathe each May 12 with choreographed figures. Miming characterized the labors of carding, spinning, and looming fabric. To plucks on the harp and flute tunes, participants anticipated intertwining, an in-and-out figure that turned the farandole into fun.

Division of genders marked the lives of the families of hunters, fishers, trappers, and expeditioners. Among Hudson Bay Eskimos, women held dance house rituals while men hunted. Also apart from males, Belgian women whirled full skirts in the *dradenspinnen*, a skip-lift-skip-lift female presentation that incorporated line and ring dance and finger turns. To a somber drum tap, Saami girls at Sodankyla, Finland, opened the Christmas season with the bouncing, rotating steps from Lapp tradition honoring the spirits of forefathers.

Women on the Arabian Gulf performed work rhythms depicting wheat milling and bread making. In serious mode, they executed the *murdah*, a lamentation to males on the dangerous missions of sea fishing and pearl diving. The dance drew together two lines of women, who comforted each other by chanting lyrics of solace and hope. At the approach of Ramadan, post-Ramadan Eid al-Fitr, and Eid al-Adha, the feast of sacrifice, women at Qatar withdrew into the desert to perform the *moradah* to lyrics about passion, mating, and war.

Among Malay brides, performance of the *inai* honored the application of henna to the palms before a wedding. Presented by ladies-in-waiting to the royal court, the dance involved lighted candles and refined steps and gestures dramatizing the deportment of respectable matrons. At the end of the performance, women bent backward and picked up coins with their lips.

Currently, women of Burundi form a vibrant circle to honor the bride at a wedding. The synchrony unites raised arms and extended fingers in exhilarating praise. While stamping their right feet in precise double steps, the women repeat vocal refrains and stress feminine moves and body postures. The cheery abstract mime frames female lives with exuberance and commitment to womanhood.

See also Arab dance; art, folk dance in; belly dance; *cachucha*; chain dance; coming of age; contradance; corroboree; czardas; dragon dance; Eskimo dance house; *ghurei* dance; *halling*; healing dance; highland fling; hornpipe; hunting dance; Kurdish dance; lamentation dance; line dance; Persian dance; Pyrrhic dance; *Schuhplattler*; Shaker dance; shawl dance; Thai dance; warrior dance.

Source: Karakeçili, Fethi. "Kurdish Dance Identity in Contemporary Turkey: The Examples of Delilo and Galuç." Master's thesis, York University, Toronto, 2008. http://www.academia.edu/6546183/Kurdish_Dance_Identity_In_Contemporary_Turkey.

GHOST DANCE

The first religious millennialism in the American West, during the Black Hawk War (1865–1872), the ghost dance (also *Natdia* or spirit dance) began in 1870 at Soda Springs, Idaho, on behalf of peace, renewal of the buffalo, and pan-Indian deliverance. Like survivors of the Black Death or Modoc performers of the dream dance on the Klamath Reservation in Oregon, nomadic Indians decimated by typhoid fever in 1867 and tuberculosis and smallpox among Northern Paiute at Pyramid Lake in July 1868 filled a social and spiritual void with silent dance to drumming. In May 1871 at Bear River, Nevada, and again in spring 1872 in Sanpete County, Utah, Shoshone, Bannock, and Ute of southern Idaho converged to perform a ghost dance.

Based on a divine revelation received by the Paiute prophet Wodziwob (or Gray Hair) on January 1, 1889, of a universal apocalypse to come in spring 1891, visionary Ute, Bannock, and Shoshone created the cry dance to resurrect deceased forefathers and inaugurate a messiah similar to the Mormon concept of Jesus. Dancers filtered into the hills to sleep apart and await prophetic dreams. The spiritual renaissance connected the tribes with Plains Indians who longed for a return to native identity and brotherhood. Whites characterized the dance as a peculiar mix of pagan ritual and charms.

At Wind River in 1889, the Paiute of Walker Lake in Mason Valley, Nevada, held hands and executed a ring dance, which white journalists called a "messiah craze." Worshippers as far away as Oklahoma, Dakota Territory, and California syncretized the ritual into their religion. Led by Wovoka (also known as Jackson "Jack" Wilson), a thirty-four-year-old Paiute mystic and pacifist, in early October 1890, some eight hundred Indians danced themselves into a trance state and summoned help from the spirit world to halt the spread of European destruction across the plains.

A Spreading Faith

The ghost dance cult mutated from pacifist to violent after Sioux interpretations envisioned a final standoff between whites and Indians. At Pine Ridge Reservation in western South Dakota, Wovoka's disciples, Lakota Sioux chief Kicking Bear and his brother-in-law Short Bull, promoted the wearing of ghost shirts (or ghost dress), protective attire for warriors based on the temple underwear or endowment robes worn by Mormons in Utah. Into a snowy November 1890, morning ablutions in creeks preceded the dance, which Wovoka ordered followers to repeat every six weeks. For the occasion, women stitched ankle-length cotton robes with flowing fringed sleeves and dyed the neck and waist blue. Dancers painted faces red and drew black half moons on cheek or forehead.

Around a pine tree decked with stuffed birds, claws, horns, eagle feathers, and colored cloth strips, clockwise steps and shuffles with bent knees unified Indians in a slow, meditational pattern emulating the Earth's rotation around the sun. Each step jiggled owl, raven, and eagle feathers tied by their quill ends to robes and leggings. In anticipation of a blessed utopia, some four hundred dancers maintained the rhythm over a five-day period, during which one-quarter collapsed from hunger, exhaustion, and hallucinations. For the December 6, 1890, issue of *Harper's Weekly,* artist Frederic Remington provided a sketch of Oglala Sioux dancers at Pine Ridge.

A Violent End

With hands on shoulders of fellow dancers, ghost dancers wailed, moaned, sprinkled themselves with dust, and chanted, "Father, I come; Mother, I come; Brother, I come." According to Santee Dakota scout Charles Alexander Eastman, the police assassination of Sitting Bull on December 15, 1890, at his cabin at Standing Rock Res-

In late December 1890, two weeks after the death of Sitting Bull, the slaughter of five hundred ghost dancers at Wounded Knee, South Dakota, ended the messianic cult. *Harris, William Torrey, Edward Everett Hale, Oscar Phelps Austin, and Nelson Appleton Miles.* The United States of America: A Pictorial History. *New York: Imperial Publishing, 1906, 291.*

ervation in North Dakota triggered hostilities over suppression of the ghost dance. The devout believed Sioux medicine man Yellow Bird's contention that ghost dance shirts repelled bullets. Sioux faith wavered on December 29, 1890, when 470 soldiers of the US Seventh Cavalry slew 153 Lakota at Wounded Knee, South Dakota.

Whites approved the massacre of women, children, and elderly, especially martyred chief Big Foot (or Spotted Elk), using four Hotchkiss cannons for combatting a subversive cult rumored to be backed by Sitting Bull, leader of the Sioux resistance. The Bureau of Indian Affairs outlawed the ghost dance. Although rejected by the Navajo, holy men among the Sioux, Kiowa, Paiute, Arapaho, Caddo, Comanche, Cheyenne, Pawnee, Wichita, and other US and Canadian tribes perpetuated the ritual, which illustrator Mary Irvin Wright sketched in 1900 for a geological survey.

See also circle dance; worship dance.

Sources: "Ghost Dance." Accessed November 21, 2015. www.ghostdance.us/history/history-messiahletter.html. Vance, Lee J. "The Evolution of Dancing." *Popular Science* 41, no. 52 (October 1892): 739–56.

GHUREI DANCE

A seasonal spectacle for the maidens and women of Chamba, Churah, Pangi, and Bhattiyat, India, the *ghurei* (also *ghurhi*, *ghuri*, or *dangi*) dance unites performers in parallel lines or rings for group presentations at festivals, holidays, and home rituals. The name refers to the princely dynasty of Ghur, an eastern Iranian hegemony of Buddhists and

Hindus in the Himalayas on the border of India and Kashmir. The ceremonial dance also thrives at Bangladesh to the east.

After the fall of the Gupta Empire in 550 CE, the Ghurids controlled Afghanistan, Persia, Transoxiana, and northern Hindustan until the dynasty's collapse in 1383. Performances on a public platform in Saho village honored the consort of Raja Sahil Verma, queen Sunena (or Sunaina), who gave her life in 920 CE to provide water for citizens. To make a stream flow from the Ravi River through a civic water system to end a drought, the rani consented to burial alive rather than let her son be the sacrifice.

Queen Sunena dressed in a wedding gown and walked to the execution site with palace handmaidens in attendance. She and her ladies-in-waiting met their deaths in a walled compound covered with a stone slab, the standard memorial of royalty. At her death in the dark tomb, water flowed to the region. The king named the area Chamba after his motherless daughter, Princess Champavati, whom citizens worshipped as a goddess.

During the Sui Mata fair in early April at the royal Sunena Devi shrine of the Sui (or Suhi) Mata temple, women and girls of all castes dress in national costume and gather for the all-female dance memorial. Before a royal girl representing Sunena, performers clasp hands, which requires reaching over the bodies of fellow dancers to grip right to right and left to left. With only vocal accompaniment throughout a three-day ritual, barefoot participants offer gifts of song, maize, and flowers. They grip their hands in fists, which they move from midriff to shoulders. Components of reverence to the selfless Queen Sunena involve bending the knees, bowing, clapping, and kneeling, all of which heritage murals and paintings authenticate.

In the 1960s, adaptations to ghurei ritual altered gestures, which some dance companies presented to flute tunes and the beat of the *dhol* (frame drum). Sensuous torso movements and pelvic thrusts abandoned the demure staging of ghurei dance from the tenth century. A wedding version of the ghurei dance synchronizes delicate female steps side to side with gentle arm gestures emulating the tasks of women, from rocking an infant and making thread to drying laundry and performing Hindu ritual. More complex footwork for the kite fight dance pairs the mimetic gestures of loosening string from the kite flier's hands.

See also circle dance.

Source: Sharma, Kamal Prashad. *Folk Dances of Chamba.* New Delhi, India: Indus Publishing, 2004.

GREEK DANCE

Syrtos, the body of ancient Greek, Thracian, Aegean, Cretan, Ionian, Macedonian, Thessalian, Pontine, and Cypriot folk dance, represents a kinetic monument to the arts, as exhibited in the *sirtaki* line dance in *Zorba the Greek* (1964) and ring dance in *Never on Sunday* (1965). The Greeks treasured dance as relaxation, athletic instruction, and moral elevation. For centuries, more than four thousand heritage dances impacted the Hellenic world. Specific choreographies gave thanks for the grape and olive harvests, honored holidays and patron deities, and invited the community to take part in the fertility rites preceding betrothals and nuptials.

Around 1500 BCE, Minoan reapers and winnowers at Agia Triada on the north coast of Crete processed from the grain fields with song and dance to a rattle. For the angelica, early Greeks dressed as messengers; for the antistrophe, they performed precise left–right turns to demonstrate form and harmony. In northeastern Greece at Tyrnavos, Larissa, male celebrants of the one–day phallus festival danced the *dionysiakos*, a vociferous orgiastic parade saluting sensuality and fertility.

Following the metrics of classic poetry, Greek lyrical dances presented the whole person, as the poet Homer states in the *Iliad* (800 BCE) in his presentation of the *choreia* (circle dance). Execution of steps displayed the human form at the height of ability, poise, and harmony. Such graceful choreography became subjects of bas–relief, sculpture, and fresco, such as images of the devotees of Terpsichore, muse of dance. Healers diagnosed orthopedic ills and harmful postures, such as scoliosis and lordosis, before prescribing restorative dance.

According to third–century CE Egyptian arts maven Plotinus, the measure of artistic technique lay in the balance of limbs in service to the schemata (steps) as evidence of a body in balance. Agile dancers received the same level of plaudits and rewards as actors, jesters, and acrobats. In contrast, for the acrobatic *cordax*, a licentious masked solo to clattering castanets, country folk performed it in Piraeus and Athens for merriment and low comedy rather than reward.

On a rustic note, during the Festival of Dionysus, the god of wine, Attic amateurs draped themselves in ivy and bore baskets of grape clusters and figs during their cavort-

Exuberant Greek dance in reverence to Dionysus, the god of wine, depicts the flirtatious style of nighttime processions. *Dubois-Maisonneuve.* Introduction à l'étude des vases antiques d'argile peints. *Paris: P. Didot, 1817.*

ing through the streets. Folk challenged each other to stamp up and down in a riotous pila or dance on an inflated goatskin as a kind of trampoline. Those participating in satyr plays presented the *sicinnium*, a dance skit in which male and female dancers made up steps while accompanying themselves with singing and strums on the lyre.

Gods and Soldiers

According to Plato, the gods scheduled festal seasons to relax human toilers. Popular choreography focused on deity worship, including the welcome to Apollo, god of the arts, before the horn altar at Delos for the six months of summer. To incantatory dithyrambs (hymns), lines of dancers approached the shrine to the right, circled around the left, and stood at the foot of the icon to sing and dance the epode. For the Sapphic wedding ritual, source of the hymeneal or nuptial dance from Lesbos, the maidens presented the ladylike *caryatis* to Artemis, the goddess of chastity. For funerals, the *archimimus* (first mime) led a troupe of buffoons to mock death in mourning processions with grotesque mimicry. Leading the hearse, the masked mime imitated the attitude, gait, and walk of the deceased as a moral lesson for the living.

Patterned steps highlighted the styles of male or female, but not men paired with women. For wooing, the Greeks created the *ballos*, a figured flirtation to light, engaging tunes. In Homer's *Odyssey*, the poet detailed the glamour of male dance presented by Laodamas and Halius, youthful Phaeacian gymnasts from an island near Epirus on the Adriatic Sea. Spartans built manhood in recruits by lining up a phalanx before a caller, who ordered them to step up and back in synchronized motions. Through gestures of the thyrsus (wand) and torch, the hunting dance stressed competition for excellence in adult males and *epheboi* (new recruits).

Other occasions for celebration included sportive rope dance, martial and tumbling displays, chamber dance, and mime and staged choreography for banquets, such as the story dance of the wedding of Ariadne and Dionysus in Xenophon's *Symposium* (ca. 368 BCE). Athena, the goddess of wisdom and war, inspired the *corybantum* (or *korybantes*), a military choreography that set armed Phrygians of Mount Ida in mimetic clashing of shields and swords. Phrygian farmers and herders performed to the flute the early ceremonial *aloenes*, a harvest dance in Cybele's temple to Ceres, goddess of grain. Vintners mimed the *epilenios*, the wine-pressing dance.

With sedate steps, regional outdoor dances honored Apollo, the god of creativity, and Aphrodite, the goddess of passion and beauty. For the propitiation of Dionysus, the patron of wine, around 600 BCE, Athenians adopted the grape festival dances of Megara, a town to the west on the Corinthian isthmus. Devotees performed rowdy debauchery that included the waving of torches like batons for midnight processions. Musicians accompanied revelry with cymbals, sistrum, cithara, and tambour. Dancers also clacked stick-like reed castanets. Refinement of Dionysian worship dance elevated tragedies and choral dance, the high point of Greek drama.

Spontaneous Dance

Bits and pieces of impromptu dance mark the history of fifth-century Greece. In 480 BCE, the playwright Sophocles celebrated the victory at Salamis by dancing. Aristippus, a hedonist who visited Socrates in 400 BCE, impressed Athenians by dancing after dinner to settle his meal. A decade later, the Athenian historian Xenophon welcomed the Thracian king Seuthes and foreign ambassadors to his home by hosting barbarian and Persian peasant dances. After folk dance gained acceptability, Greek citizens bragged on their mechanical execution, notably the Theban general Epaminondas around 380 BCE and the ambassador Aristodemus of Miletus in 315 BCE. Critics named consistency and realism as the height of quality folk choreography.

Women, too, acquired fame for their dance, particularly the domestic festivities in which they displayed shapely arms, supple backs, and bare feet. Notable examples included Philinna of Larissa, the Thessalian consort to King Philip II of Macedon after 357 BCE. At Sparta, a Laconian maiden earned a reputation for one thousand performances of the *bibasis*, a leaping step that ended with bending the knees and smacking the soles together.

Greek courtesans were hired out for male symposia, drinking parties where skilled women provided the entertainment. Because refined males preferred to pay dancers rather than participate, demand spawned a cottage industry in dance schools. The Greek style influenced the farandole, an ancient line dance from Provence, France.

See also circle dance; comic dance; farandole; labyrinthine dance; Pyrrhic dance; worship dance.

Sources: Anon. *The Dance: Historic Illustrations of Dancing from 3300 B.C. to 1911 A.D.* London: John Bale, Sons & Danielsson, 1911. Hall, Edith, and Rosie Wyles, eds. *New Directions in Ancient Pantomime.* New York: Oxford University Press, 2008.

· *H* ·

HALLING

A traditional gymnastic dance from Hallingdal and Valdres in central Norway and Sarna and Varmland, Sweden, the *halling* (also *lausdans* or *hallingdansen*) spotlights the vigor and creativity of male soloists in short, repetitive phrases. Reflecting the back-to-back wooing figure of the Austro-German *Ländler*, the halling gained grace from the French allemande and *volta*, German *Dreher* and *Weller*, Basque *arresku*, Irish jig, Bavarian *Schuhplattler*, and Ukrainian *hopak*. For summer night parties and weddings, an acrobatic finale featured the male soloist touching toes to a wall and kicking the barn rafters or a hat from a pole. Art historians compare the variable rhythms and synchrony to Afro-American show dancing.

A rough, earthy creation of Norwegian country folk, the halling is the oldest folk dance in northern Europe, a fact based on cave paintings from 500 BCE. A performance to music in 6/8 meter took place in a barn and replaced fighting with knives, cudgels, and fists that sometimes resulted in death. Each free-form performance began with a heavy-footed circling of the floor with a march tread before launching examples of power and daring. The brisk masculinity of figures and tumbles anticipated the hornpipe and the highland fling.

Martial Dance

The halling serves Scandinavia as a nonviolent form of martial arts set to music. The Nordic figures—*heeling* (crouching), *kruking* (crouch-thrusts), headspins, neck jumps, hooks, shoulder stands, whirls, flips, and forward rolls—required a stamina and agility on a par with Cossack squat-kick dances. Cooperative moves expressed an edgy, cut-throat camaraderie with hand clasps and arms locked over shoulders, body language the dance shared with the Anglo-Welsh morris dance.

In the monograph *Germania* (98 CE), the historian Tacitus characterized the choreography as a war dance. In the 1600s, visual elements served artists as icons of the Nordic spirit. The seventeenth-century halling paired with the *polska*, marked by a promenade and partner spins, and the *springar*, an improvisational couples dance to plaintive Hardanger fiddle melodies that transitioned without warning to a minor key.

Dance Revival

A critical comment by Italian author Joseph Acerbi in *Travels through Sweden, Finland, and Lapland to the North Cape* (1802) depicted the halling spirit as "mad joy," vibrancy in evidence at Østerdalen, Aurskog, and Engerdal. After Norway liberated itself from Denmark on May 17, 1814, a craze for hallingdansen asserted freedom and ethnic identity. Anglo-Danica consul Jens Wolff noted in *Sketches on a Tour to Copenhagen, through Norway and Sweden* (1816) that the halling lacked grace, but held its place in European folk dexterity. In 1843, Swedish novelist Frederika Bremer disclosed the frantic "berserker" elation in the *halling polska*, a Norwegian couples dance.

During the folk art renaissance in the 1880s, the Scandinavian diaspora created a demand for the virtuoso dance in Canada. Even though halling music thrived, because of mounting urbanism in Quebec and Ontario, the rambunctious steps and leaps faded from dance floors in the 1890s. In 1894, author Charles Edwardes found the halling still customary at Hallingdal, where men, young and old, shoved into the competition with knives in their belts. Their female partners did little more than posture and flirt while the men challenged each other with outrageous stunts, for example, flattening an iron hook driven into the ceiling.

In the twentieth century, the riotous Norse fling retained its appeal. In 1901, composer Edvard Grieg included three of the throbbing solos in his *Lyric Pieces*. During World War II, new interest in martial dance among upper- and middle-class Norwegians revived the halling in Scandinavia and at global dance festivals and competitions. For the next decade, the dance became a home front force against a commercialized mass culture. Into the 1970s, partygoers at Elverum and Trysil revived male solo dancing and a couples variation in central Gudbrandsdalen, Møre, Romsdal, and Sunnfjord.

See also acrobatic dance; highland fling; *hopak*; hornpipe; jig; *Ländler*; martial dance; morris dance; *polska*; *Schuhplattler*.

Source: Dodds, Sherrill, and Susan C. Cook, eds. *Bodies of Sound: Studies across Popular Music and Dance*. Farnham, UK: Ashgate, 2013.

HANDKERCHIEF DANCE

The handkerchief serves folk arts as a symbol of order and decorum, two components of refined folk dance, such as the chaste *satecek*, a slow couples dance from Czechoslovakia that separates male from female by the width of the cloth. As early as 2000 BCE, the hand gesture impacted Greek, Palestinian, Jordanian, Syrian, and Levantine ring and line dance. The Athenian *romaica*, a reenactment of the myth of Theseus and Ariadne, depicted Ariadne lifting a handkerchief, which Theseus grasped as though following her into the Cretan maze that concealed the Minotaur, a flesh-eating man-bull. The alternation of male and female partners marked vase art and supplied poets with a dramatic theme of the clever female leading the trusting male.

From 1500 BCE, Mycenaean Cypriots grasped each other by the hand for the *kalamatianos*, a lively dance in 7/8 meter. Participants followed a leader, who waved a handkerchief while setting a pattern of complex twists and acrobatics for dancers to follow. The style emulated the Spartan *hormos* and marked a passage in Homer's *Iliad* (ca. 800 BCE) in which Achaean troops honored Achilles's spear, a symbol of combat excellence.

At Byzantium in 381 CE, Christian converts gained approval from Eastern Greek Orthodox Church authorities to incorporate processions, labyrinthine holiday figures, and the *mantilia*, a ring dance incorporating kerchiefs. With small left-right steps, Anatolian dancers at Thessalonica, Pontus, and Cappadocia held the cloth rectangles above their heads. Performers formed squares of two couples each and wove their handkerchiefs into a star, a symbol of the church liturgical year from the annunciation, Christmas, and Easter to epiphany.

In the 800s, the Phocaeans of western Anatolia transported the farandole chain dance to Marseilles, France. Lines of village performers surged through paths and meadows in a living symbol of oneness. In the Balkans in 1100, the migration of the Roma northwest from Turkey added handkerchief dancing to the traditions of Bosnia and Hercegovina, Croatia, Serbia, Hungary, and Romania. In one medieval couples dance, the *furlana* from northeastern Italy, a flutter of handkerchiefs marked the finale.

Into the Renaissance, English folk dance developed a subgenre of handkerchief choreography under colorful names—country gardens, shepherd's hay, the cuckoo's nest, and the old woman tossed up in a blanket. Jews in the Sephardic diaspora after March 31, 1492, joined men with women in the Czech *sherele*, a nuptial dance honoring the bride. Orthodox believers insisted that a handkerchief separate the genders to shield young wives from lechery.

New World Dance

For the Moche of pre-Columbian Peru, a Western Hemisphere version of the handkerchief dance after 100 BCE varied hand clasping with ribbon flourishing and linking. During carnival at Altiplano after the arrival of Hispanic insurgents, the Chilean *cueca* creolized the Iberian fandango with the addition of fiber art. To unfold the stages of romance, couples waved handkerchiefs to a 3/4 beat.

Farther north, after 1542, the Afro-Hispano-Andean *zamacueca* merged Peruvian ethnicities in a pelvis-tilting seduction dance punctuated with waves of a bright scarf. The cheerful spirit paralleled the Argentine *malambo* from gaucho culture and the *zamba*, a holiday couples dance of slow walking and a tiptoe figure identifying a mestizo culture incorporating Amerindian, Hispanic, and African elements. The handkerchief covering the man's hand in the zamba illustrated a tribute to female purity and delicacy.

In the Mississippi Delta from the 1720s, the *carabine*, performed with the wave of a red scarf, evolved into a pas de deux by slave and Creole dancers in New Orleans's Congo Square. The blatant sexuality of the West African *calenda* took on a less lascivious gesture with the addition of a madras handkerchief grasped by partners. Dramatizing the finale, the awarding of the handkerchief to a solicitous male indicated the female partner's choice of a mate. The infectious drum dance so inflamed viewers that the calenda flourished in the popular *lundun* from the Caribbean shores of Guiana west to Lima, Peru, and east to Lisbon, Portugal.

Current Examples

The handkerchief still holds a symbolic place in folk dance. The Malay *canggung*, adapted from Thai performances, showcases a female duo dancing while holding handkerchiefs and singing folk verses to the music of gong, violin, and drum. As a blessing on departing fishermen in India, wives, daughters, sisters, and mothers dance the *kolyacha*, a departure ritual of the Konkan shore. While male performers mime the thrusting of oars into the sea, females raise handkerchiefs in farewell. For weddings, presenters dance through the streets waving kitchen utensils.

In a feminine display of synchronized line dance and raised arms, the *yang ge* (handkerchief line dance) preserves authentic folk ritual from rural China. Created during the Song Dynasty after 960, the choreography displays adaptations by region for group presentation or solos in which maidens toss handkerchiefs among spectators in hopes of finding a mate. To celebrate the harvest and autumnal equinox at the Fall Moon Festival, presenters in China, Vietnam, and diaspora communities wave handkerchiefs embroidered and adorned with good luck amulets. The dance holds a prime position among folk arts and in the vigorous physical education of school children.

See also Arab dance; art, folk dance in; *calenda*; farandole; *furlana*; Roma dance; tarantella; veiled dance.

Sources: Barr, Amelia E. "Characteristic Dances of the World." *Lippincott's Magazine* 27, no. 4 (April 1881): 330–41. Knudsen, Jan Sverre. "Dancing *Cueca* 'with Your Coat On': The Role of Traditional Chilean Dance in an Immigrant Community." *British Journal of Ethnomusicology* 10, no. 2 (2001): 61–83.

HARVEST DANCE

From preliterate times, dancers have implored nature deities to provide an ample harvest, a common choreography at the Pongal temple sacrifices of the Tamil Nadu of southeastern India, among Slovakian hemp growers, and throughout the Aegean islands for wheat, barley, grape, and olive rituals. In ancient Egypt from 2500 BCE, royalty and farm families danced their gratitude to the fertility god Min at Gebtiu while presenting a temple sacrifice. Around 1500 BCE, Minoan harvesters bore their bounty from the fields and stepped to the beat of a rattle.

From 768 BCE, Etruscan reapers played pranks and organized skits anticipating the commedia dell'arte. At Crete and Santorini after 500 BCE, the *ghassem abadi* line dance enacted the sowing and harvesting motions of female Persians in vests and layered skirts to a strongly measured beat. From western Egypt to Libya, Bedouin performances of the *hagallah* welcomed an ample date harvest. The veiled lead dancer carried a stick as a weapon against men trying to steal her head scarf.

Before the Roman conquest of Britannia, the Celts, Danes, Picts, and Saxons linked tribal thanksgiving to seasonal dancing and songs. Saxon manuscripts illustrated the sprightly kicks and clapping of hands among common folk to tunes of horn and pipe. Soldiers sharpened their fierce tactics with sword dances acknowledging a victory and the boost to self-esteem, an allegorical harvest of enemy dead.

After 263 BCE, from April 27 to May 2, priests of Republican Rome restored gardens, vineyards, apiaries, and fields to productivity by reviving the Floralia, an annual rite that ensured vegetables, wine, honey, and grain. The obeisance to agrarian deities predicated subsequent dances around the maypole and during the Wiccan Beltane, Christian Easter and labyrinthine dances, and the broomstick dance of the East Anglian harvest home, a jolly jig with a homely besom. In Argyll and Perthshire during a full moon, the ingathering of first fruits swept Scots reapers into a ring frolic around the last wagonload of grain. To cries of "*kirny, kirny*" (corn, corn), the pageantry concluded with the bundling of the *cailleac*, the final grain shock, which dancers turned into a nature doll and preserved through the winter.

From 206 BCE, Chinese dragon dancers chose green materials for their disguise as a symbol of agrarian prosperity. A thanksgiving dance acknowledged ample fishing, hunting, trapping, and gathering of berries, mushrooms, and nuts. At Nazca in southern Peru after 180 BCE, the ingathering of foodstuffs to the larder required participants to grasp tools and sheaves in their fists while performing. In Hebrew communities in Semitic Israel, farmers gave thanks for produce with rapid skips, hops, and running steps while female dancers flung samples from round trays.

Tribal Variations

Newcomers to North America discovered nature dances that varied among tribes, as with the two-faced dance masks of the Otavalo in Imababura, Ecuador. When Jesuit priest Jean Nicolet reached Lake Winnebago, Wisconsin, in 1634, he observed the harvest green corn dance. Performers gave thanks for grain and, simultaneously, honored veterans of the Beaver War in Canada. At the Keresan plaza at Santo Domingo Pueblo, New Mexico, performers wore kilts and breechcloths, fur pelts, body paint, and roaches or corn headdresses to entertain spectators and dance to drumming and the clink of rattles. In Hawaiian myth, the forest goddess Laka, creator of the hula, settled on Molokai around 300 CE. She wed Lono, the god of agriculture, and held thanksgivings each harvest featuring expressive Polynesian gestures. The arrival of Calvinist missionaries Hiram and Sybil Moseley Bingham to Honolulu on April 19, 1820, resulted in the suppression of the hula and the imposition of New England–style dress and dance.

On the Great Plains in the United States and Canada, Hungarians made the czardas the center of fall barn dances and village socials, while Poles whirled to the postharvest *oberek* and Italians rejoiced in October with the saltarello. Pinches of tobacco from harvest dancers rewarded the Amerindian Earth Mother for a fine cutting of leaves, an essential of worship and burial services. For the Omaha, harvest dances ceased from 1855 to 1866 during the Sioux Wars, when farming took second place to combat. In 1915, European settlers, shocked by the vigor of the corn dance, raised complaints about the pagan beliefs and nudity of Indian activities.

Europeans individualized rituals to the end of the farm year. In central France, reapers at Auxerre turned harvest dances into competitions for the fastest grain cutter and the first girl to pirouette around the last sheaf. Finnish men and women paired up to perform a distinctive rocking step similar to the motion of the reaper. They wound in and out of the circle like Earth's orbit around the sun. In Austria, farm women chanted while men brandished swords and performed group figures around the threshing floor. At Real, Spain, *jota* dancers welcomed the year's grapes with steps to the music of percussion and *bandurria* (guitar).

Harvest rituals brought out creativity in rural people, for example, the grass-skirted blessing of the boundaries by Colombians in the Amazonian rainforest and the rituals of the Shona of Zimbabwe, who danced the *mhande*, a jubilant quickstep, in the fields of their neighbors to ensure food for the whole community. From the introduction of oversized masks in Borneo, the Dayak dancers have worn banana bark and palm frond false faces of crows, lions, and rats to scare away garden predators. At Nukuhiva, Marquesan males encouraged breadfruit production by dancing simple forward-backward steps before a nature shrine. For a harvest home in West Loathly, Sussex, in 1869, the dance program scheduled two polkas, three each of galops, marches, quadrilles, and waltzes and concluded the evening with "God Save the Queen."

Modern Reaping Festivals

Into modern times, Turks offered up the *galuç*, a prayer dance for rain and grain that brought the devout to their knees. With more rejoicing than reverence, the South Vietnamese chose October for the *ganh lua* dance commending a successful rice season. In Sikkim, adults united without musicians for the *yialakma*, a thanksgiving for full rice paddies. The Lopit Latuka of southern Sudan reverenced agrarian gods with the *ekanga*, a whole-body dance to group chant. Farther east, the Baga of Mali and northern Guinea blessed nature and gave thanks for their stores and a heavy return of fish with the *kakilambè*, a somber masked dance that involves elders in requesting a positive prophecy for the coming season. Male citizens of Senegal and Gambia presented the *lenjen* with sticks symbolizing scythes and rakes while flapping their arms like grain-eating cranes and egrets.

In Malaysia, harvesters on the east shore celebrated farm bounty with top spinning, kite flying, and a thanksgiving dance. For the *wau bulan*, they played the role of kites and swayed to a traditional folk song. Battered by the wind, the kites moved to the sound of flute and drums.

After 1921, Hungarian immigrants to Livingston Parish, Louisiana, initiated an annual Magyar autumn dance featuring pairs in authentic dances—*az a szép, gancsi, kevi, olahos*—displaying aproned skirts, black and red vests, and sleeves and hats trimmed in the patriotic red, green, and white. A variation placed men in an outer ring and women in an inner circle. Adults formed dance rings to teach children authentic heritage dances from the motherland. A similar ethnic ritual in Indianapolis welcomed newly cut grape clusters. Colleen McCullough set the tone of a Queensland sheep shearers' ball at the woodshed in *The Thorn Birds* (1977), a reprise of an outback Australian hoedown marking a successful season in the wool trade. The spirit of diaspora enables Irish settlers of Drogheda to reprise the steps of their homeland to honor success at the herder's trade.

See also Balkan dance; barn dance; galop; Greek dance; handkerchief dance; Jewish dance; *jota*; *oberek*; planting dance; polka; Polynesian dance; quadrille; saltarello; scripture, folk dance in; Siberian dance; totemic dance; waltz.

Source: Royce, Anya Peterson. *Anthropology of the Performing Arts: Artistry, Virtuosity, and Interpretation in a Cross-Cultural Perspective.* Walnut Creek, CA: AltaMira, 2004.

HEADDRESS

Head attire establishes ethnicity and purpose of folk dance, as with the proud white *tignon* of slave women in the dance art of Roman painter Agostino Brunias in Dominica and St. Vincent and the stylized roaches of the Plains Indian scalp dance. Examples range from the complete stag heads on Yoeme performers in Sonora, Mexico, and the reed *sugegasa* (umbrella hat) in Japan to dog tails wrapped around the hair of Australian aboriginal dancers and helmet masks of the Zaouli of the Ivory Coast, which indicate the sanctity of the cranium as the seat of the spirit. The height and glamour of plumes, tiaras, antlers, and animal jaws and skulls create a focus for spectators and set a rhythmic pattern in time with drumming, singing, and instrumental accompaniment, as with the *ram-thai* crown of Thai folk dance and the four-foot feather circlets on the heads of male Aymara dancers in Bolivia.

Historically, headdress enabled dancers to transition into new states of personhood, from fool to saint. In ancient Rome from 714 to 670 BCE, the college of twelve *salii* (leapers) performed a cultic martial dance in pointed headdress tied under the chin, a sacred identification of adherents with Jupiter, the supreme deity, and the war god Mars, the father of founders Romulus and Remus. In the 1500s in Kerala, India, *kathakali* story dance highlighted elaborate costume and body paint with tall gilt headpieces shaped like Hindu temples, ubiquitous reminders of religious purpose and the sanctity of ritual.

Foregrounding the Dancer

In the Western Hemisphere, roaches, real and celestial birds, and animal skulls and tails highlighted Amerindian regalia during shamanic healing in Alaskan dance houses and entertainments for Mayan royalty and the warrior, buffalo, and grass dances of the Sioux, Ponca, Arapaho, Lakota, and Pawnee of the North American plains. The incorporation of deer and porcupine hair, otter fur turbans, beaded bands, and eider feathers legitimized the rank of braves and accentuated the human status in an animistic universe, the purpose of painted derbies in Nicaragua, ermine fur headbands of Inuit in the Aleutian Islands, and the ornamented black wigs of the Tarascan Indians of Mexico's Sierra Madre from Christmas to New Year's Eve. In the seventeenth and eighteenth centuries for the "Dance of the Moors and Christians," Mesoamerican pageantry syncretized traditional Nahuatl worship with Catholicism by masking and swathing villains in Muslim toques to resemble the Islamic insurgents in Iberia.

Spectacular head adornment, facial expression, and inclinations of the head reframe the personality and ennoble folk ceremony, as with the carved antelope fetish propitiating the agrarian god Tyiwara among the Bambara of Guinea, the plaid *tignon* (turban) of the quadrille dancer in St. Lucia, and the shell headpiece for the Samoan *taupo*, which demands poise and stateliness for the kava ritual. Among the Tlingit of the Pacific Northwest, folk art combines choreographic talent and the effect of a head wrap composed of ermine skin, abalone shell, and sea lion whiskers, three elements identifying coastal tribes. With the puppet-like lion and dragon heads with their floppy ears and eyelids and movable jaws, the original Chinese holiday dance heightened cultural significance and humor. With less drama, the Naga seed and fiber semicircle from Assam, India, in the 1890s projected contrast in the meticulous arrangement of orange seeds and the loose edging of dark hair, which caught the sway and stamp of torso and footwork.

Atmospheric Headgear

From Oceania and Sri Lanka to the Ukraine, Balkans, and Scandinavia, headdress shapes movement, anchors style, and sets the tone of ethnic dance. Among the Tuareg Kel Tagelmousse (blue people) of Timbuktu, Mali, and the Moroccan Sahara, the plaits and cowrie shells of the *guedra* trance dance empower the female performer with icons of genitalia and fertility. East of Australia at Tonga, aboriginal Polynesian dancers mimed the completion of heavy tasks with the *taualuga*, an elegant solo executed by royal children. Key to costumes, the heavy coconut and nautilus shell tiara and attached turtle carapace, wig, and lory feathers identified the dancer as a model of island hospitality and spirituality. Fern and blossom garlands and upright combs added a touch of splendor. Dance motions required careful balance of the tiara on an erect head. Modern adaptations incorporated mirrors, sequins, and glitter, which flashed orange and gold from firelight.

For the Sufi of Pakistan, the brown wool cylindrical hat with a flat top derived religious significance from the symbolic phallus of Shiva and represented the creative energy of dancers attempting to unite with God. Another interpretation of the pervasive hat describes it as the tombstone of the ego, which the dancer submerges through trance. A more perilous head adornment, the candelabrum that tops the lead dancer of the *shemadan* in an Egyptian wedding procession required practice at balancing with aesthetics and detailed choreography.

See also attire; Concheros dance; corroboree; disguise; dragon dance; exorcism; fancy dance; lion dance; masked dance; *matachines*; scalp dance; Sufi dance; veiled dance.

Sources: Chico, Beverly. *Hats and Headwear around the World: A Cultural Encyclopedia.* Santa Barbara, CA: ABC-Clio, 2013. Looper, Matthew G. *To Be Like Gods: Dance in Ancient Maya Civilization.* Austin: University of Texas Press, 2009.

HEALING DANCE

The tradition of healing through the arts flourishes among aboriginal Australians, South Africans, Balinese, Siberians, the Bwiti of Gabon, and Native Americans. First Peoples worldwide depend on the revitalization of holistic movement, rhythmic prayer, mimetic bird and quadruped motions, improvisational meditation, and centering of positive energy to drumming, an essential of hoop dancing, the Nanai sacrificial dance in Russia and China, and the shamanic magic of the Tungus of Siberia. In 1374, a seeping choreomania set the Flemish on a frenzied worship of St. John. Historians named their performance St. Vitus' Dance. In Apulia, Italy, tarantism forced ailing maidens to whirl away depressive states allegedly caused by a tarantula's bite.

The curative method of the Alaskan shaman in the Eskimo dance house began with masking, gesticulating to the evil spirit, and chasing it around the hall and out the entrance hole. The melodramatic healing required trapezes and hidden trapdoors for theatrical treatments and sometimes concluded with the performer falling into a trance. Restoration became the purpose of the Tumbuka healing *vimbuza* dance performed by patients in Malawi. In Mongolia, shamanic exorcism dance rid the sick of infectious spirits, guided lost souls, and predicted the state of health to come.

For the *curanderos* (healers) of the Peruvian Amazon, medicine songs and rhythms summon intercessory spirits. At Garifuna wakes in Belize, drumming, pecking of conch and turtle shells, and singing coordinate with processions bearing meals to the dead to determine causes of fatalities. To placate spirits, circular shuffles around a temple floor synchronize dance with the heartbeat and a shaman's rattle.

South Africans absorb universal energy from the repeated leg lifts of the *umoya*. Bété dancers on the Ivory Coast gain strength and vision from the *gbegbe*, which incorporates grass skirts to mark swaying hips, fast footwork, and feathered ankles to dramatize a search for a new homeland as well as messages of the spirit world. West Africans and Haitians call on the sky father Damballa, represented by the seven-thousand-coiled serpent, through the Afro-Caribbean *yonvalu*, a stately women's step dance featuring back and forth swaying, twirls, and an outreach of hands. For special occasions, the Ewe of Ghana perform the *sowu* or dance of life, marked by sideways skips, wavy spins and rolls, and raised arms expressing gratitude for the Earth.

The San Trance

Holistic medicine retains its relevance to !Kung shamans and San bushmen. Among half the males and one-third of the women of Botswana and Namibia, a weekly curative dance sends energy upward from the feet to all parts of the anatomy. The ecstatic experience alters the conscious state to *!kia* (trance) and discloses colors, images, and insights usually shrouded by reality. During all-night participation in the Kalahari Desert, bushmen old and young move to medicinal power songs and the clapping of female supporters, who encircle the sick. Males step around a fire to the offbeat, fling up their arms, wail, and stamp the earth while clacking turtle shells and cocoons tied to their legs with sinew.

The San shaman believes himself called by his ancestors to traditional healing and divination through human transformation. With fluttering hands, he dances alongside the patient, touching, massaging, and directing wholeness from the god Cagn into the torso or to an ailing body part. As an intercessory warrior fighting pain, the shaman aims invisible arrows into sufferers to suppress malevolent spirits from the world of the dead. Communication with the divine and the stars in the firmament increases visual acuity for diagnosis.

In theory, catharsis purifies San patients of hurt. The magic of the shaman's song discloses weakness and corruption in the patient, which the priest battles by sinking into a quasi death. At sunrise, the intense dance reaches its pinnacle and suddenly ends. After a day of rest, both shaman and patient communicate to others the relief of dancing away illness.

Healing Native Americans

By sharing ancestral reverence and reuniting with nature, Saulteaux dancers young and old in the sacred circles at Eagle Lake, Ontario, cultivated their own style of movement. The blend of singing and wailing, sweat-lodge cleansing, pipe rituals, sweetgrass smudging, jingle dress and buffalo dances, home fire ritual, feasting on stew and berry soup, and religious beliefs developed resilience and humor. Participation rid the First Peoples of the residue of European colonialism as well as alcoholism, suicide, murder, disappearances, and violence against women, the urban themes of healing and crying songs performed across Canada. In Chisasibi on the James Bay in northern Quebec, Cree dancers ended the lengthy ordeal with a shared feast and satisfying afterglow.

In Poundmaker, Saskatchewan, seventy-six-year-old Cree jingle dress dancer Evelyn Thom joined the elders as an experienced performer of healing dance and a proponent of dance education for youth. At a powwow in 2003, she celebrated Mother Earth and the curative power of women by reviving traditional modesty and dignified steps for the jingle dress dance, which originated in Ontario. She grew up performing with older women according to protocol—in simple steps respecting other dancers by not passing them or backing up in the circle. On the National Day of Healing and Reconciliation each May 26, relatives of the sick and vulnerable request that women like Evelyn perform the ritual to restore wellness.

In 1947, Evelyn Thom advanced to the healing jingle dance, a symbol of female recovery from spiritual wounds. The choreography dated to a grandfather's attempt to heal his granddaughter by obeying a vision to imitate crow hops and raise arms to receive divine solace. To adorn a healing dress, he formed the first jingles from the lids of snuff and chewing tobacco cans.

To pass on holy knowledge, medicine woman Dorothy Paypompee blessed Evelyn Thom and conferred a feather and the right to join a powwow dance circle, an Ojibwa custom throughout Ontario and Minnesota. Evelyn's regalia of plain or print fabric and yarn had no beadwork, feather fans, plumes, shawls, whistles, or leggings, only smoked leather moccasins and unadorned headbands. Out of obedience to gendered taboo, she did not enter a ceremonial lodge during her menstrual cycle.

Over the powwow circuit, Evelyn Thom performed in a personalized sacred dress marked with four hundred to seven hundred jingly tin cones and raised the lone feather to display its yellow, green, and red ribbons. Forbidden to compete, she danced in humility and unison with other women to combat cancer. The addition of a second beribboned feather encouraged native identity and healing during her dance in the middle of a traditional arbor. Central to the sanctity of jingle dancing, the dress appeared in a dream or vision and remained in her possession as a unique heirloom significant to family and clan. She dedicated her exertions to young people who lacked experience with heritage dance.

Current Therapies

For the University of California San Francisco Medical Center, in 1996, psychotherapist Anne Krantz began offering a program for cancer patients titled "Healing through Dance: When the Body Speaks and the Spirit Moves." Participation fostered revitalization, expression, confidence in wellness, and a creative transformation of inner strengths. Much of the freeing of pain and discomfort and loosening of stiffness derived from articulation of head, shoulders, torso, hips, and knees.

A Toronto psychotherapist, Kathleen Rea, facilitates multidisciplinary treatment through dance improvisation, a source of enhanced body image. At York University and Niagara College, she has taught healing movement and summarized the results in *The Healing Dance: The Life and Practice of an Expressive Arts Therapist* (2012). The text covers the role of the senses in fostering body-based wisdom, well-being, and causes of dysfunction, such as bulimia, anorexia, and personal and communal grief.

A Balinese dance therapy, *watsu*, coordinates healing with flexed motions in warm water. By incorporating acupressure and passive joint movement, watsu enhances health, relaxation, balance, and serenity through buoyancy and freedom of motion in water. Via spontaneous movement, patients anticipate strengthening of the digestive and immune systems, enhanced energy and sleep, and detoxification.

A serious threat to Australian and Torres Strait Island aborigines lies in residential schooling and overrepresentation of black peoples in prison, two attempts by the English to civilize indigenous peoples and suppress their ethnic differences from Europeans. The loss of trust and erosion of cultural roots jeopardizes hope and emotional stability, two essentials to a reintegration into society. Additional trauma from parental neglect, sexual abuse, and ego damage increases the need for ceremonial healing. In an outflow of love for nature, aborigines dance healing steps to revive parched land and restore the power of the Menindee lakes and the Darling and Murray rivers.

In Sydney, the Gadigal perform heritage dances at the Woggan-ma-gule gathering. Reflecting ritual from dreamtime into a more hopeful future, the performance links First Peoples to the land, source of food, and culture. East of Darwin in Milingimbi, Arnhemland, male dancers painted with white clay stripes leap and stamp to the beat of rhythm sticks. In parallel lines, they hop on one leg and run toward each other brandishing sticks representing power over weakness, strife, and bitterness. The dance solicits *riyawarray* (common ground) and acceptance of a despised people disempowered by their British conquerors.

See also coming of age; dragon dance; Eskimo dance house; hoop dance; lamentation dance; pipe dance; sacrificial dance; Shaker dance; shawl dance; sun dance; tarantella; *Totentanz*.

Sources: Hyatt, Ashley. "Healing through Culture for Incarcerated Aboriginal People." *First Peoples Child & Family Review* 8, no. 2 (2013): 40–53. Sexsmith, Pamela. "The Healing Gift of the Jingle Dance." *Windspeaker* 21, no. 5 (2003): 28.

HIGHLAND FLING

An eighteenth-century Celtic reel in 4/4 meter, the highland fling evolved among rural Scots and Danish soldiers from dance games around Celtic monuments. Men performed the figures to ready troops for sword battles and welcome their triumphant returns. Derived from the *ghillie callum* (sword dance) and the staccato strathspey (Scots-Gaelic snap) to fiddle and bagpipe, the nimble highland figure and rapid body turns emulated the gambols of a stag. In mime, infantrymen looked up and stamped, kicked, and leaped in a small ring on the targe, a round shield centered with a six-inch spike. Hands took a distinct shape of the stag antler with little finger elevated and thumb touching the middle finger.

For its vitality and authenticity, the highland fling resembled the vigorous stunts of the Norwegian *halling*. The Scots story dance impersonated folkloric clan episodes. Figures commemorated the defeat of a royal chieftain of Macbeth on July 27, 1054, at the Battle of Dunsinane, which William Shakespeare glorified in act V of his tragedy *Macbeth* (1608). According to the legend of the Scots king Duncan, Prince Malcolm III Canmore (the big head) reputedly crossed his gory claymore (two-handed broadsword) over the weapon of Macbeth, the slayer of Duncan, and pranced over both blades in jubilation.

Although Celtic culture developed English traits during four decades of raids under Malcolm into Cumbria and Northumbria, Scots mercenaries retained the light sway on the ball of the foot as evidence of pride and fitness. Soloists of the highland fling moved clockwise as close as possible to the swords without turning their backs on the lethal edges, a caution ingrained into soldiers. Scotsmen feared a maladroit touch on the blades as an ill omen of defeat or death in combat.

Dance in History

As a show of flexibility and resilience similar to the English hornpipe, Irish jig, and Ukrainian *hopak*, the highland fling demanded a proud head, straight spine, and shoulders aligned, all emblematic of male self-determination and control. The figure entered Scots history on November 1, 1285, at Jedburgh Abbey for the wedding of Alexander III to Yolande de Dreux, the Countess of Montfort. Performances transferring weight evenly from right to left commemorated Robert the Bruce's success at the Battle of Bannockburn on June 24, 1314, a landmark of Scots independence. Recruitment demonstrations became a test of the best candidates to join the royal men at arms.

In October 1573, Swedish baron Charles de Mornay led Scots assassins in a plot to kill John III, king of Sweden, by turning a stationary sword dance into slaughter. At the banquet at Stockholm Castle, the conspirators drew swords for the highland warrior's dance, but chose not to attack. A later version of commoner's highland fling honored Anne of Denmark at her proxy wedding to James I of England at Kronberg Castle at Helsingor, Denmark, on August 20, 1589.

Upon the return of James I to his native Scotland in 1617, the highland fling welcomed him home. At Perth on July 9, 1633, dancers costumed in red and white performed the dance in thanksgiving for their son, Charles I. On recovery of the MacPherson ancestral estate at Cluny, Inverness, in 1745, the landowner, Ewen MacPherson, scheduled a genuine highland fling to pipers after tea and again by firelight on the terrace.

Because the Scots Jacobites incurred a ruinous defeat and two thousand dead at the Battle of Culloden on April 16, 1746, the English Parliament outlawed the costume of the highland fling—tartans, kilts, and swords. In 1768, Scots dancers bypassed the law by substituting a wand, bonnet, or handkerchief for a weapon and staging the

A late nineteenth-century dance manual pictures a child learning the techniques and postures of the highland fling. *Grant, Horatio N*. The Highland Fling and How to Teach It. *Buffalo, NY: Electric City Press, 1892.*

highland dance in mockery of English tax collectors. Following forty-one years of arts suppression, the English rescinded the ban in 1787. By 1799, the highland fling became a popular athletic pastime of Scots boys and served Scots tars as a means of entertaining the Jindoobarrie aborigines in Queensland. Queen Victoria welcomed a revival of folkloric dances before French, Ottoman, and Sardinian allies at the Crimea in August 1855 and as a widow at her Balmoral Castle retreat in Aberdeenshire, Scotland, in the 1860s.

The Fling in the Diaspora

Scots-Irish immigrants transported the highland fling to Commonwealth capitals in Australia, New Zealand, and South Africa. In North America from Nova Scotia and Cape Breton south along the Appalachian Mountain chain, children mastered the highland fling as part of their cultural upbringing. The dance merged with clogging and step and row dancing for rural gatherings and barn dances. When executed to the skirl of the bagpipe over swords laid in an X shape, light crossovers, toe taps to the ankle, and bounds with arms akimbo or raised in graceful curves exulted in a precise technique over iconic blades.

Females made a late appearance in the highland fling. In token of the punishment of the New York Seventy-Ninth Highland Regiment for insubordination during the Civil War, at Beaufort, South Carolina, on Christmas Day 1861, a slave woman volunteered to execute the highland fling. In the 1890s, female dancers took up the highland fling for competitions, which thrived at Charlottetown, Prince Edward Island, and in 1893 at dances arranged by the Caledonian Club. By alternating right leg with left side to side and front to back, the costumed dancer displayed balance, a focus of a staging at the Grand Opera House in 1893 in St. Paul, Minnesota, and in Kansas City, Missouri, in 1910.

In 1934, a female auxiliary of the Mine Workers' Union of Canada escorted strikebreakers to and from the Cumberland mines of Western Canada to a derisive highland fling. When the Volkswagen factory in South Africa celebrated its millionth Beetle in August 1955, a phalanx of thirty-two Scotswomen entertained workers and management with their version of the fling. The event preceded a North American classic, the Grandfather Mountain Highland Games at Linville, North Carolina. First scheduled on August 19, 1956, to commemorate Scots loyalty to Prince Charlie Stuart in 1745, the games reclaimed Scots history and music in the Great Smoky Mountains, where Jacobites once fled to safety.

See also barn dance; clogging; *halling*; *hopak*; hornpipe; jig; reel; step dance; sword dance.

Source: Henry, Lori. *Dancing through History: In Search of the Stories That Define Canada.* Vancouver: Dancing Traveller, 2012.

HOLIDAY DANCE

Dancing on holidays draws communities and congregations into fun gatherings, for example, the Scots-Irish *cèilidh* (house party) on Robert Burns' Night each January 25, the Aruban New Year's *dande*, and rejoicing on St. John's Day on June 24, which coincides with the manumission of island slaves. Jews conclude Sukkot (Feast of the Tabernacles) with Simchat Torah, the dancing and singing of the faithful as they pass Torah scrolls from one to another. Early Christians formed circle dances to the singing of nativity carols, a custom painted by Fra Angelico and Sandro Botticelli. In Taiwan, Teacher's Day honored Confucius on his birthday on September 28 with presentations of music, dance, and sacrifices. A more lavish festival of Taoists at the winter solstice renewed worshippers with holy effigies, gifts, music, and galas. Shintoists in Japan limited their New Year and spring commemorations with the dancing of *miko* virgins (temple attendants) rejoicing at nature's rejuvenation.

The Mexican *baile de los viejitos* (dance of the old men), a parody of Day of the Dead dancing on November 1 in Michoacán, Mexico, anticipated the advance of age with coughing and staggering. Male performers enhanced the satire with canes, which added taps to the stamping choreography. At Chiapa de Corzo in southern Mexico, the January dance of the *parachicos* honored individual patron saints with maracas rhythms, clapping, striped serapes, and wood masks, pageantry that UNESCO declared an Intangible Cultural Heritage of Mesoamerica.

Easter and Mortality

At Verges, Catalonia, the Maundy Thursday mystery pageant preceding Easter enacted the passion of Jesus and the judgment of the soul. Beginning in the afternoon with the strutting Roman legionaries guarding the crucifixion procession to the *plaça major* (town square), the Dance of Death tableau started with the chiming of 10:00 PM and continued through alleys and streets, walls, and towers in Europe's oldest Easter rite. A smaller version on Saturday featured a children's procession.

A form of late medieval street theater north of Barcelona along the Costa Brava, the Verges "*dansa de la mort*" dated to the fourteenth-century terrors of the Black Death and the obligation of potential victims to act out a calamitous event in their ancestral history. The choreography began with the cruciform march of six black-clad skeletons, who sprang and stepped to irregular drumming. A symbolic long-handled scythe carrier pursued a human dancer waving a black flag indicating that life is short. Two child performers transported ashes and a third carried a clock without hands, a suggestion of the unpredictability of death.

Increasing the lurid Dance of Death atmosphere, a quartet of skeletons illuminated the vignette with torches as indicated in Fra Antoni de Sant Jeroni's text from the 1500s, *La gran tragedia de la passió y mort de Jesucrist Nostre Senyor* (The great tragedy of the suffering and death of Jesus Christ Our Lord, published in 1798). Black-robed attendants followed the drumbeat as the dead hopped and pirouetted alongside the weeping Virginia Mary, who harangued Pharisees and disciples. Roman sentinels twirled spears while penitents crept along in cone-shaped hats and eerie white masks.

Immigrant Dance

The Christian calendar schedules a panoply of syncretic dances from the Creole and diasporic milieus, as with the satiric street processions that amuse spectators at pre-

A woodcut from Nuremberg artist Michael Wolgemut in 1493 outlined the partnering of German couples on Christmas night to pipe and drum. *Grove, Lilly.* Dancing. *London: Long-mans, Green, and Company, 1895, 101.*

Lenten carnivals in Cádiz, Spain. At Danebod in southwestern Minnesota, Lutheran families retain a traditional Yule circle dance. In the style of their Danish forebears who migrated to the New World in September 1872, the simple steps encircle the Christmas tree. The same tradition guided the steps of Swedish children in the *polska*, another historic ring dance saluting holiday decorations.

In Miami, Afro-Cuban *comparsa* dancers add color, acrobatic stunts, and knee-bending rhythms to a similar Los Tres Reyes Magos (Three Kings Day) parade each January 6. To brass riffs, drumming, and whistles, troupes costume in feathers and net arm bands to emulate the cheerful turns and step-step-heel-toe of a traditional couples dance from Santiago. The boisterous comparsa energizes similar displays in Argentina, Uruguay, Venezuela, and the New Orleans Mardi Gras.

See also cèilidh; circle dance; diaspora; *matachines*; *polska*; processionals; *tirabol.*

Source: Anon. *The Dance: Historic Illustrations of Dancing from 3300 B.C. to 1911 A.D.* London: John Bale, Sons & Danielsson, 1911.

HOOP DANCE

A centuries-old acrobatic story dance originally for men, the hoop dance manipulates circular props to emulate Amerindian fables that teach humility. Each circlet symbolizes the sacred life cycle, an emblem of wholeness. As many as fifty plastic and wood rounds inter-sect to create the trickster coyote and raven and the mythic eagle and snake. By stepping to chant and drum rhythms, altering head and torso postures, and creating primal images, the performer promotes well-being and generates visions of world harmony and balance.

According to Algonquin lore, Manitou initiated high-energy hoop dancing among humankind to instill appreciation for animal instincts. Performers customized circlets from red willow or *bois d'arc* branches and reeds to whirl in healing ritual. For connection to tradition, individuals marked their hoops in four sacred colors—red, yel-low, black, white—with symbols of the four cardinal directions and forces of nature. From configuring gentle creatures such as the rabbit and fawn, dancers learned to be kind, loving, and loyal.

The dynamic folk mode trained Pueblo children in endurance and agility by teach-ing them to lift hoops one by one from the ground with their feet. From family and ac-quaintances, each dancer developed the hopping, heel taps, crossovers, bending, turning, and crouching that grounded timeless hoop patterns. Fringed and fur aprons and anklets enhanced the impression of coordinated movement. By positioning hoops in the mouth and on limbs and torso, dancers merged circles into wings, tails, cages, and earth spheres. Rapidly, the dynamics spread from Taos, New Mexico, to plains tribes.

The hoop dance attained standard practice at Jemez Pueblo in the 1930s with the formations and designs of Tony White Cloud, a slender, compact dancer. He performed with twenty-four-inch willow hoops in films and at fairs and exhibitions in New Mexico, Oklahoma, and Chicago. At the New Mexico State Fair, hoop dancing reached global significance with the 1991 World Hoop Dance Competition, won by Eddie Swimmer of Cherokee, North Carolina. An all-male panel of judges based their choices on precision, rhythm, creativity, speed, and showmanship of competitors on grass or a cement stage. The 1994 season introduced Navajo performer Ginger Sykes, the first female competitor.

Source: Zotigh, Dennis. "History of the Modern Hoop Dance." *Indian Country,* May 30, 2007.

HOPAK

A martial art derived from the Ukrainian warrior culture, the *hopak* (or *gopak*) demon-strated the Cossack zest for liberty and the cavalryman's contribution to showmanship and European heritage dance. A visually flamboyant regimen for troops similar to the Celtic highland fling and the English hornpipe, the dance emerged in the 1400s near the Dnieper River north of the Black Sea as a pastime for battle-ready mercenaries. Fathers taught sons bare-knuckle self-defense through steps such as jump kicks, lunges, and ankle trips.

A National Dance

In the buffer zones of the Russian Empire, hopak soloists or matched pairs dressed in blue and red silk tunics and black lambskin caps and improvised high-energy leaps, splits, and spins as proof of manhood. Nonstop music accompanied vigorous heel crouches, duck walks, and squat-kicks while the arms remained folded across the chest. For structure, the dancers reenacted wartime feats with saber, lance, dagger, flail, or battle scythe, building intensity to the last note. The masculine exhibitionism paralleled that of the Norwegian *halling*, Sioux sun dance, and the Bavarian-Austrian *Schuhplattler*.

Eastern Slavic cavalry and infantry drew peasants into the leaping, stamping dance to the brisk 2/4 folk melodies of bagpipe, hammered cimbalom, fife, and violin. Dancers punctuated individualized movements with cries of "*hup!*" and "*slava*" (glory). In celebration of a Ukrainian victory over the Lithuanians and Poles at Zaporizhian Sich along the Dnieper River on January 21, 1648, hero Bohdan Khmelnytsky grasped his saber and leaped onto a banquet table to perform the hopak for jubilant patriots.

When Cossack raiders passed through villages, they invited farm girls to join in boisterous spectacles of the hopak-kolom, an adaptation featuring swaying and clapping in a ring. According to author Nikolai Gogol, in their iron-heeled morocco shoes, the girls used the dance as an opportunity to show off chemises embroidered in red silk and headdresses aflutter with blue, pink, and yellow ribbons. By issuing the Statute for the Administration of the Provinces at Moscow on November 7, 1775, Catherine the Great dismantled the Cossack settlement and destroyed the military roots of the Ukrainian national dance by killing soldiers or immuring them in Siberian prisons.

Hopak Survival

The hopak refused to die. Through the Ukrainian diaspora in the late 1700s, companies performed proud steps as a concert dance in peasant and serf theatricals in Karelia, Finland, and at Canadian weddings in Alberta. Professional adaptations in Cesare Pugni's ballet *The Little Humpbacked Horse* (1864) and operas by Modest Mussorgsky and Nikolai Rimsky-Korsakov introduced the muscular dance to gentrified audiences. Mycelia Lysenko placed the dance within its original culture for the martial opera *Taras Bulba* (1890). The Ukrainian composer Peter Ilyich Tchaikovsky added the "Trepak," a ballet version of hopak, to *The Nutcracker* (1892).

Vaslav Nijinsky, a Polish-Ukrainian folk dancer at age five, appeared in *Hopak* (1894), a showpiece produced in Odessa. Folk scholar Vasyl Verkhovynets modernized the steps after 1900 and recorded them along with text in *Theory of Ukrainian Folk Dance* (1919). His tripartite version opened with a breathless martial performance by male dancers and advanced to a sedate women's adaptation and a finale presented by an ensemble of men and women. During the Stalinist purges, exiles in Siberian labor camps and penal colonies retained the leg-thrusting dance under the name "redpoll" as inmate entertainment and exercise.

More good humored than fierce, the hopak became a highlight of Aram Khachaturian's *Gayane* (1941) as well as the background of gymnastic routines of Anna Bessonova and Natalia Godunko. Nikita Khrushchev entertained guests at Josef Stalin's dacha with an exhibitionist hopak. After World War II, amateur folk troupes in Canada and the United States revived the original hopak out of national pride and unity.

In the late twentieth century, the hopak made inroads into global folk art. At the July 19 opening festivities of the 1980 Summer Olympics in Moscow, the charged mood of the hopak created an authentic atmosphere for the competitive games. In 1990, dance master Sergei Makarov formed the Hopak Ukrainian Dance Company, a professional troupe. With the dissolution of the Soviet Union in 1991, Ukrainians reclaimed their combat dance as a salute to the spirit.

See also clogging; highland fling; hornpipe; martial dance; *Schuhplattler*; sun dance.

Source: Nahachewsky, Andriy. *Ukrainian Dance: A Cross-Cultural Approach.* Jefferson, NC: McFarland, 2012.

HORA

A heritage dance in classic Middle Eastern mode, the Israeli hora (or Yerushalimer hora) expresses visceral joy, dynamism, and belonging. Paralleling round dances in China, Russia, and the Balkans, the Jewish hora incorporates facets imported from the Roman *horae*, Turkish and Romanian hora, the Bulgarian *horo*, the Montenegrin and Macedonian *ora*, the Macedonian *oro*, Serbian *kalo*, Slovenian *kolo*, Georgian *khorumi*, and the Russian *khorovod* (choral dance), a celebration of spring and the fall harvest. In traditional folk mode, the hora allies hands with feet and emphasizes muscle memory and traditional swaying cross-front-cross-back (grapevine step) to circular or semicircular figures.

Taking its name from the Greek *choros* (circle), the hora coalesced around 4000 BCE from outdoor ring dance and coronation ceremonies and manifested elements of ancient Dacian sun dances by Indo-European farm folk. Corfu islanders danced the steps around 500 BCE in a wave or whirlpool pattern to honor Dionysus, the Greek god of wine. The dance passed to Denmark in the 600s CE as a *carole*, a medieval church song and dance.

Perennial Circle Dance

At the end of the Middle Ages, nuptial receptions featured the hora in suites coordinating the *freylekhs*, *branle*, sarabande, saltarello, galliard, and pavane. The Romanian folk version of step-step-step forward, pivot, and step back adapted from circle dance to a spiral. Participants joined hands and kicked and stepped to intensely passionate Roma music. Girls who first joined the hora proclaimed themselves marriageable.

The hora reached Israel with immigrants from southern Romania, Poland, and Russia in the form of a rondo, a jolly allegro dance. During periods of famine and malaria in the 1880s, the first Jewish settlers danced the hora in concentric circles to instill hope through love and comradeship. They lifted their heels Arab style as though performing the *dabke*. At Jewish celebrations of births, wedding feasts, and bar and bat mitzvahs, guests typically danced the hora to klezmer music.

The Israeli Hora

For Purim carnivals after 1920, Tel Aviv dancers paraded the streets and danced the walk-walk-step-kick-step-kick or samba step on rooftops and balconies. At Jezreel southwest of the Sea of Galilee in 1924, Romanian Jew Baruch Agadati demonstrated the slow-quick steps and hops of the slower Palestinian hora in 6/8 meter, a derivative of the *hora lunga* from Moldavia. The dance popularized "Hava Nagila" (Let us rejoice), a popular melody of ambiguous authorship.

In the 1930s, Zionists at Israeli kibbutzim clasped shoulders in the circular hora and kicked to the middle in outbursts of pride. Rapt exhibitions of the dance increased tourism in Palestine and at the 1932 Maccabiah Games as a feature of the national dance of Israel. As Nazi Germany usurped Jewish autonomy and deported whole ghettos to concentration camps, in August 1940, fourteen-year-old Ruth Lieblicha of Lodz, Poland, clung to visions of living in a kibbutz in Israel and dancing the hora with other survivors.

Syncretic elements of the polka, polonaise, and *krakowiak* marked the path of the hora as performed in the new state of Israel, proclaimed on May 14, 1948. In rapid spins on Jerusalem streets, the communal circle continued for hours, sometimes lifting participants off their feet. Visitor Eleanor Roosevelt observed that participants enjoyed the dance for its representation of equality and youth.

See also branle; circle dance; galliard; pavane; polka; polonaise; saltarello; sarabande.

Source: Dragomir, Corneliu. "The Sun: Profane Meanings in the Romanian Hora Dances in Northern Mehedinti." *Revista Romana de Sociologie* 1–2 (2012): 133–40.

HORNPIPE

An animated solo step dance or hop-jig dating to the reign of Henry VIII (1509–1547), the hornpipe is an occupational folk exhibition also known as deck dancing. The basic step begins with a hop on one foot and a touch with heel and toe to the ground with the other. It may derive from the British navy in 1694 after the appointment of Charles Lennox, the Duke of Richmond, to Lord High Admiral. Unlike the unstructured Norwegian *halling*, the English sailor's dance followed precise footwork, swings to left and right, and mimetic poses to a 4/4 beat, which an English source from 1815 credited to Roma styles.

Sailors such as those whom novelist Herman Melville described in *Moby Dick* (1851) set records of jigging barefoot in fine weather or in port on the capstan, deck, or bollards on the pier. The vernacular men's dance served as exhilarating exercise and amusement on ships, relief during the tense period preceding sea battles, and a competitive display of agility in pubs to attract women. Legend ascribes the invention of the hornpipe to Welsh sailors whom equatorial winds becalmed in the Atlantic Ocean in the doldrums, a low-pressure zone. The joyous skips, hops, and a three-step conclusion lifted the crew "out of the doldrums."

Similar in technique to the Celtic highland fling, the sprightly skipping step or step-hop involves leg lifts to front and back while the dancer holds torso erect, feet turned out, palms turned in, and arms folded at shoulder height. Variances with heel-to-toe shuffles and glides include cocking the heel on the opposite ankle and slapping the thighs. Hornpipers pantomimed bowing, saluting, hitching up trousers, and rolling side to side in a wave step. They mimicked tasks at sea—manning the wheel, hauling and coiling cables, tying a knot, deck drilling, climbing rigging, rowing, standing on lookout, gazing toward the horizon, pumping water from below, swabbing the deck, and hoisting sails.

Instrumentation

The first hornpipe dancers favored the reed clarinet known as a Cornish hornpipe, or *cornepipe*, a medieval instrument mentioned by Geoffrey Chaucer in *The Romaunt of the Rose* (ca. 1385). Named for the ox horn, the pipes incorporated elements of a Scots or Welsh shepherd's pipe, English shawm, and Welsh seven-hole pibgorn, a common woodwind played at festivals and the Oktoberfest or harvest fair. English poet Edmund Spenser reported in *The Shepheardes Calendar* (1579) how lighthearted rural villagers celebrated May Day in the meadows and woods with ancestral styles of jig and hornpipe.

Descriptions of European celebrations pictured accompaniments to the hornpipe ranging from the bagpipe, panpipes, and penny whistle or flageolet to the tambourine and concertina or squeezebox, forerunner of the accordion. In the pastoral comedy *The Arraignment of Paris* (1584), English dramatist George Peele described villagers sporting with a gleeful hornpipe. The dance gained popularity during England's war with Spain, which ended on August 2, 1588, with the defeat of the Spanish Armada off Portland.

During the early 1600s, Scots dance masters taught solo presentation throughout Northumberland, Nottingham, and Derbyshire of the hornpipe and the high dance, a variant composed of greatly energized prances. In 1607, the dance reached Jamestown in the Virginia colonies in the form of social dance. Performers drew audiences by dancing on pedestals and marble squares. Pure Irish versions to "The Christmas Hornpipe" fiddle tune followed French coureurs de bois and Scots-Irish miners and timbermen who settled the Ottawa Valley between Quebec and eastern Ontario after 1616. They displayed stamina in aggressive lifts of the legs high off the floor, balanced by arms folded out from the chest.

Hornpipe Variations

According to British broadsides from around 1690, southern Irish folk soloists evolved a four-to-the-bar rhythm for the Lancashire clog-hornpipe, which featured heel-and-toe steps set to rapid triplets or "dotted hornpipe" eighth notes. The hornpipe became an official part of training for the Royal Navy and, in 1707, earned prominence at the birthday of Queen Anne, the last Stuart monarch, for symbolizing Scots drive, energy, and work ethic. In 1711, diarist Samuel Pepys declared the dance the "jig of the ship," which a performer presented in Drury Lane Theatre in the guise of Jacky Tar or "jigging Jack," the archetypal English sailor. In 1718, Irish dance master Charles Staunton, a professional hornpiper, earned two guineas in Ballincollig, West Cork, for teaching landlord William Bayly's four children jigs and hornpipes.

In the baroque era, composers George Frideric Handel, William Byrd, and Henry Purcell adapted the hornpipe to artistic settings as elaborate incidental music or entr'actes (interludes) for opera. Folk groups accentuated the rhythmic sounds by trading street shoes for clogs and turned the shipboard rhythm into a Scots highland fling or schottische. The Irish slip jig, a *cèilidh* (house party) or Gaelic folk dance set to 9/8 time, involved heel lifts and the uninterrupted stepping of triplets.

Fiddle music dominated hornpipe execution in 1752, when Scots fiddler John McGill, a teacher from Girvan in southwestern Scotland, described sixteen standard steps in printed dance textbooks for men and women. After bras stabilized jiggling breasts, females joined the street busker's hornpipe by pulling their skirts up to show off feet, ankles, and knees. At Covent Garden, London entertainer Nancy Dawson popularized "Here We Go Round the Mulberry Bush" with hornpipe steps as part of a 1759 revival of playwright John Gay's *The Beggar's Opera*.

The Hornpipe in History

In August 1773, the journal of Captain James Cook compared Russian and Tahitian dance steps to the hornpipe, which the sailors aboard the bark HMS *Resolution* performed to bagpipe tunes to foster good will among islanders. Cook credited low incidence of shipboard disease to regular sessions of the hornpipe to relieve the cramping of legs below deck, especially during bad weather or the boredom of becalming. For similar reasons, Captain William Bligh's sailors on the merchantman HMS *Bounty* in 1787 danced compulsory hornpipes on deck for twenty minutes each. Daily sessions took three hours to accommodate the entire crew. English sailors departing Port Jackson on Australia's first fleet on July 14, 1788, performed the standard steps for exercise on the long journey to Europe of the flagship HMS *Sirius* and the tender *Supply*.

In the United States at the end of the American Revolution, a history of Montgomery County, Pennsylvania, listed the hornpipe as a common community dance. Sixteen-year-old John Durang, an Anglo-American from York, Pennsylvania, introduced the sailor's hornpipe in 1783 to the tune of "College Hornpipe." Before colonial hero General George Washington at the South Street Theatre in Philadelphia, Durang carried a rattan cane and performed the character dance with the Old American Company in burned cork blackface, linen sailor suit, round beribboned hat, and clogs.

The hop-egg or egg dance, based on a German dance from 500 CE, established John Durang's reputation in 1790 for dancing blindfolded among eggs placed at random on the stage. By 1792, dance manuals featured a dozen personalized versions of the dance in double and triple time. By 1796, he was charging a penny a head for seeing him perform the steps in the circus on tightrope, slack wire, and horseback. In the same year on July 30, Australian performers introduced the hornpipe at the Sydney Theatre as a divertissement for drama.

The hornpipe cropped up in Pest, Hungary, in 1797 at a fair when recruiting parties presented a vigorous version to advertise military careers. By 1806, a squib in *The Gentleman's Magazine and Historical Chronicle* complained of fettered prisoners performing a "blackguardly" hornpipe near Westminster Bridge. In London, a black naval veteran named Billy Waters drew crowds in the Strand near the Adelphi Theatre. While fiddling, he step danced the hornpipe, alternating hard-soled sounds with the tap of his wooden leg. Spectators dubbed him the King of the Beggars for his popular tunes. In the 1820s, showmen translated the real Billy into a one-foot-high dancing puppet.

During the search for the Northwest Passage from 1822 to 1824, the arrival of Arctic explorer George Francis Lyon and William Edward Parry's naval vessels, the gun brigs HMS *Hecla* and the HMS *Griper*, among the Sadlermiut of Coats Island introduced the Inuit of the Hudson Bay to the sailor's hornpipe. British solo dance continued to impact Canada, Greenland, and Arctic Alaska through contact between native tribes and whalers from the Shetland Islands. Other harbor exhibitionism introduced the hornpipe in Brittany as the *bombard*, in Arabic lands as the *buk*, among the Boers of Southeast Africa as the *yodlepijp*, and in Russia as the *brelka*.

Simultaneous with seagoing dancers and performances by Lotta Crabtree in California, a steamboat busker on the Thames in London performed for pleasure seekers with hornpipe steps to a concertina tune. For the knowledgeable dancer, John Durang's son, Charles Durang, published a handbook description of the hornpipe in *Terpsichore* (1855). His description particularized pigeon wings, double shuffles, wave steps, double Scotch steps, whirligigs, parried toes, grasshopper steps, and the jockey crotch. On January 7, 1858, an amateur troupe from the British warship HMS *Vixen* performed a hornpipe for islanders at the Royal Hawaiian Theatre in Honolulu. In 1864, men aboard the war sloop USS *Nautilus* danced the hornpipe to the sounds of flute, bones, juice harp, harmonica, and concertina. In the harbor at Rotumah, Fiji, in January 1870, the appearance of hornpipe dancers on the deck of the three-master HMS *Young Australian* inspired natives to dance a competitive jig.

In American taverns and on the streets, black buskers incorporated the hornpipe in tap dancing, a US original cobbled together from European step dance. With *Dancing* (1895), choreographer Lilly Grove proclaimed the hornpipe England's national dance. Among morris dancers in Bromsberrow Heath, Gloucestershire, a concertina player accompanied hornpipe dancers. A report on the Boer War in South Africa in November 1899 described officers as encouraging impromptu crew dancing at the aft hatchway and varying the program with comic songs and boxing matches. From 1933, radio comedy and cartoons perpetuated the link between seamen and the hornpipe by choosing "The Sailor's Hornpipe" as the theme song and dance of Popeye the Sailor Man.

See also clogging; *halling*; highland fling; jig; literature, folk dance in; morris dance; Roma dance; step dance.

Sources: Brady, Chris, ed. "The Hornpipe National Early Music Association." *Chris J. Brady*. Accessed July 1, 2015. http://chrisbrady.itgo.com/dance/stepdance/hornpipe_conference.htm. Hill, Constance Valis. *Tap Dancing America: A Cultural History*. New York: Oxford University Press, 2010.

HUAYÑO

A rural skipping, zapateo (tapping) dance for pairs, the traditional Peruvian *huayño* (also *huaiño* or *wayñu*) contrasts stamping males with twirling females in full skirts. Cloaked in ponchos and embroidered vests woven of llama wool, Andean men maintain an elegant upper carriage and extend an arm politely to women. Males mark their partners by placing a handkerchief on the female's shoulder.

To the music of *sikuri* (panpipe), bamboo or wood flute, harp and other stringed instruments, drum, and accordion, males guide the sharp turns of their partners while performing a right-step-left-toe-tap rhythm reminiscent of the Peruvian Paso Fino horse. Frequent gentle touching on the female shoulder and arm claims her as a sweetheart. A coda heightens the performance with a *fuga*, a syncopated finale punctuated by full-footed stomps.

South American Dance

The indigenous dance expresses the reach of Andean folk arts into Chile, Bolivia, Ecuador, and northern Argentina with lyrics from nature ("The Green Willow," "Hummingbird from Tarma") and aesthetics ("Bonita," "Vanities"). A pre-Columbian choreography of Ayacucho and Serrania tribes in the Mantaro Valley east of Lima, the huayño preceded Incan culture as a funereal dance in 2/4 meter, sometimes accompanied with camelid sacrifice. During a six-day ceremonial around 1450 honoring the rebuilding of Cuzco, guests of Emperor Pachacuti relied on coca and chicha (corn beer) to sustain them during all-night dances.

For galas, the highland huayño became a physical token of the tribal pride of Wanka, Aymara, and Quechua speakers, particularly the Quechua wooing songs "Rosaycha," "Blue Eyes," "My Beloved Mama," "Little Road to Huancayo," and "Valicha." Through leaps and cries, barefoot performers followed a pattern of one strophic beat to two short beats. As more people joined the dance, they encircled the most agile couple and raised hands in an arch for the best pairs to pass through.

According to a chronicle from 1586, Spanish conquistadors adapted the basic pattern with imported Iberian dances and Moorish styles, the sources of the Creole huayño "Imillita." Each February, pre-Lenten carnivals featured the huayño as an animated mestizo dance, such as "The Hill of Huajsapata" from Puno, a town on the western shore of Lake Titicaca. Performers avoided touching and held the ends of a handkerchief. For its gaiety and innocence, the huayño became the most popular mestizo dance.

Dance and Resistance

Catholic priests suppressed the sensuality of the huayño in 1583, beginning with prohibitions against female dancing. Incan caciques (priests) cultivated dance festivals in secret as a preservation of Andean folk art. Subversive presentations of the huayño preceded the composition of *taqui* (song and dance) and dance drama at Cuzco, performed with masks to protect audacious troupes from persecution. To the traditional religious melodies, pilgrims in processions venerating saints, Corpus Christi, and the Virgin of Carmen performed the huayño step as a subtle rebellion against colonialism.

With the importation of sixty-six thousand Africans from 1790 to 1802, a 25 percent bump in the population of bondsmen, enslavement of Indians with blacks creolized the huayño. Consisting in part of unified religious *cofradías* (brotherhoods), the press gangs of central Peruvian silver mines added sorrowful lyrics to huayño songs bemoaning their bondage in dangerous underground shafts. To boost their energy, weary drudges passed around coca, aguardiente (cane liquor), and chicha and gyrated into the night in reenactment of former freedoms.

At Trujillo in northern Peru in 1800, the addition of African syncopation and call-and-response format from the *zamacueca* produced the *marinera norteña*, a more coquettish, competitive adaptation of the huayño. Performed to guitars and beats on the *cajón* (wood box drum), the *marinera* showcased bare female legs under long flowing skirts, frisky foot shuffles and stomps, flutters of handkerchiefs over womanly blushes, stoops to the floor, and flourishes of wide-brimmed straw hats. When the marinera became the national dance of Peru, it preserved choreographic treasures dating to the Moors and Iberian Roma.

In the twentieth century, the huayño genre expressed authentic South American issues. At La Paz, Bolivia, rebels in 1970 revived the huayño as a protest of the military execution of singer Benjo Cruz and the parallel loss of Che Guevara three years earlier. In 1991, filmmaker John Cohen reprised pre-Columbian history for the University of California with the video *Dancing with the Incas: Huayño Music of Peru*. On September 8, 2012, Bolivian vice president Alvaro García celebrated his marriage to Claudia Fernandez publicly in La Paz by dancing the huayño.

See also Roma dance; zapateado.

Source: Higgins, James. *Lima: A Cultural History*. New York: Oxford University Press, 2005.

HULA

Hula, a barefoot, flowing story dance in 2/4 tempo, interprets poetic Hawaiian legends that link island history with Polynesian cosmology and origins. Similar in mesmerizing legato to the Tuvaluan *fatele*, the hula allies body sways, loose skirts and loincloths, and mimetic arm movements with chanted oral history or biography. Presentations are suitable for inclusion in public plazas, church rites, and school curricula.

Precolonial religious and inspirational dance identified the art as the gift of Pele, a volcano goddess. At temples and seaside platforms, movements featured ancient Pacific styles for sitting, crouching, or standing in one place. At hula schools, male and female pupils mastered complex nature symbols for the breeze through palms and sea swells, such actions as sailing and hunting, or abstract feelings of attraction, solitude, or obeisance to the water god Kane, giver of life.

The island hierarchy paid hula troupe members, who wore tapa (bark cloth) skirts, ti leaf coronas, and layers of flowers and bone jewelry. While gazing at their hands, men and women danced bare chested and moved to the music of double gourd and coconut shell drums, bamboo flutes, conch shell trumpets, rhythm sticks, feathered gourd rattles, and lava river rock castanets. Men appended the idiophonic click of toothed anklets, which sounded at the stamp of feet.

Hula History

At the end of a ritual, dancers placed their flower and leaf adornments on the altar to the forest goddess Laka, a Tahitian heroine revered for building a canoe, paddling outriggers north to Hawaii, avenging her father's murder, and honoring his bones. After she initiated the hula on Molokai at Kaana in 300 CE, she taught island aborigines the sacred dance, which they performed in ti leaf drapes and loincloths. Her bones, like her father's, remained in Hawaiian soil.

By 500, Polynesian outriggers brought more dances of the southeastern Pacific to Hawaii. Despite the influence of American, British, and Portuguese seafarers in Hawaiian ports and grog shops, natives retained their aboriginal dances as the essence of Pacific lifestyle. When planters imported Mexican vaqueros to serve as *paniolo* (cowboys) to round up wild cattle on Maui in the early 1800s, the men who married island girls enjoyed solo hulas by their brides.

In 1819, King Liholiho Kamehameha threatened the hula by closing temples and demoting priests, who took their kinetic skills into the wilds for clandestine practice. The arrival of Calvinist missionaries Hiram and Sybil Moseley Bingham from New England to Honolulu, Oahu, on April 19, 1820, introduced shame to hula dancers for glorifying the body. At new churches, American Protestants imposed the harmonics of hymns and the modest pants and muumuus representing the clothing customs of Eurocentric nations.

Under the mythographer-king David Kalakaua in 1874, hula returned to the Iolani Palace in Honolulu from hidden retreats to urban display. At his lavish coronation in 1883, Hawaiian folk dance assumed its rightful place as an authentic form of body art and visible island identity. During the First Hawaiian Renaissance, both Kalakaua and Princess Liliuokalani defied the prudery of outsiders by patronizing the form and ideals of hula as an icon of resistance to white exploiters. Musicians restored gourd drum performances of historic chants, creation myths, and prayers.

An American State Dance

After the US government seized Hawaii and federalized the territory on January 16, 1893, song replaced chant as the impetus to folk dance. Once more, puritanical laws banned the hula and Sunday concerts. Native families still danced at home for entertainment. Privileged whites flouted laws by hiring folk dancers when naval vessels docked and dignitaries arrived.

The Merrie Monarch Festival, first held at Hilo in 1964, honored the nationalism of David Kalakaua with a flashier, more carnal dance and ritual presentations. Under the influence of Mesoamerican cattle herders, musical accompaniment to the hula incorporated the ukulele, bass, guitar, and steel guitar as well as secular gestures venerating the island monarchy rather than deities. Hula companies honored the fertility of chiefs and dignitaries with patterned steps and gentle finger and hand waves. To please an influx of tourists, Hyatt and Sheraton hotels and plantation venues added Samoan fire knife dance and hula spectacles to evening floor shows that featured absurd coconut shell bras and imitation grass skirts.

By the Second Hawaiian Renaissance in 1968, more beginners studied the original hula for the Easter week competition at Ho'olulu Park. The Molokai hula festival, introduced in May 1991, increased the centrality of hula and chant to authentic Oceanic arts. In a model of recursive folk art, hula instruction prospered in Mexico, Japan, the United States, and Europe as an embodiment of island history.

See also harvest dance.

Source: Zhao, Xiaojian, and Edward J. W. Park. *Asian Americans: An Encyclopedia of Social, Cultural, Economic, and Political History.* Santa Barbara, CA: ABC-Clio, 2013.

HUNTING DANCE

A ceremonial or sacred community dance before the hunt permeates music history in much of the world, from 4000 BCE China and fifth-century BCE Sparta to the Japanese masked bird hunters of Nagasaki, camouflaged Djinang tribesmen on the Arafura seashore of Australia's Northern Territory, and the Makua elephant hunters of twenty-first-century Tanzania. For Zulu males, the *guba* stalking ritual emphasizes rivalry. The Ewe of Ghana epitomize hunting with the *adevu*, a reenactment that increases success on future expeditions. The dance episodes symbolize an animistic funeral for the beast's soul. Gestures send the spirit away from Earth before it can retaliate against the hunter. To the north of the Ewe, the Dagarti/Lobi learn the *bawa*, a thanksgiving dance to marimba tunes that expresses thanks for rewarding hunting and fishing seasons.

In Gambia and Senegal, a secret hunting society leads young males to a forest circumcision rite. Into the trees, drumbeats elicit staccato steps by boys gesturing with machetes as they acquire woods lore and camping skills. For Australian aborigines, dance drama begins with clay body paint and grass aprons over loincloths. Each man grasps a spear and creeps carefully through the imagined underbrush. Their ritual concludes with high strides and proud posturing as they haul haunches of meat to their tribe.

Historic Hunters

Ritual and masking highlighted the Amerindian hunting season, as with the bear, deer, beaver, and bison ceremonials before and after hunts of the early Cherokee. At the height of the buffalo culture, the Comanche stationed sentinels to look for dust stirred up by herds. Several nights before the hunt, men and women formed facing lines at the central fire and chose partners for an all-night step dance. The promise of ample meat and hides for robes and blankets raised spirits for the happiest season of the year.

In 1832 at Fort Pierre, South Dakota, American oil painter and portraitist George Catlin pictured the tight circle of Lakota Sioux in a preparatory dance before a bear hunt. While singing to the bear spirit, the medicine chief cloaked himself in bearskin, a disguise that included a full face mask. Mimicking the animal's movements with front and back paw motions, the participants stepped clockwise. The ceremony propitiated the animal world to provide a kill that would restore the tribe's stock of meat and bear oil, the emollient that softened skin and hair.

In the July 1906 issue of *Forest and Stream*, description of a Seminole hunting/harvest dance in the humid summer placed white visitors at the secluded camp at Kissimmee, Florida, of Chief Tallahassee. Rather than perform before setting out on the trail, tribesmen rejoiced on return with a feast and dance thanking the gods for fruit, vegetables, venison, wild hog, bird, rabbit, and squirrel. As models of profusion, women flaunted yards of ribbon on their heads and beads on their necks. For flickers in the firelight, they added silver baubles to their wrists.

Only hunters participated in the Seminole dancing circle. Men clad in turbans, coats, and leggings entered the round in new doeskin moccasins sewn from the recent kill. With hands locked on their fellows' hands, hunters chanted as they began processing in intertwined lines around the sacred fire. Their steps and calls imitated the great horned owl and wild turkey. In an idiophonic counterpoint, terrapin shells filled with pebbles marked the women's movements to the drumming.

A purification rite, the bladder feast of Hooper Bay, Siberia, and the Bering Sea freed aboriginal hunters of guilt for murdering animals. First reported in 1916, naked Inuit replenished nature by collecting animal bladders and tossing them into the sea each January and March. Shedding their hunting clothes, male dancers cleansed themselves of greed and vengeance.

Although hunting ritual typically stressed male plainsong and steps, Inuit women of the Hudson Bay danced while men trailed meat animals of the far Canadian north. The Copper Inuit of Victoria Island readied themselves for the hunting season by dancing in headdresses made from loon bills and soft throat feathers and the skins of caribou and ermine. On Alaska's Unalakleet River Delta on the Norton Sound, Inupiat harpooners turned animal flight into the subject of dance scenarios featuring the walrus, crow, or ptarmigan. Newfoundland hunters emulated the search at a seal-skinning ritual held in the dance house. By cloaking a child with a blanket, each dancer turned the small volunteer into prey and capered around him until the child fled.

Pursuit Mime

Currently, varied hunting rituals mark choreography worldwide, such as the female frolic welcoming Zulu hunters home with their kill and the propitiation of good luck by the Cambodian trot dance, an outdoor dance drama. The Tahitian *paoa*, a reenactment of hunting or spear fishing, involves a troupe kneeling in a circle and singing. By patting their thighs to rhythmic melodies, presenters set the pace for a chosen pair of dancers. Inside the circle the boy and girl eye each other and execute challenging gestures and footwork.

In desert dunes, the Tuareg of the Sahel north of Niger, in the style of their Canaanite ancestors, perform the *tergui* to drumming as a preparation for either hunting or the battlefield. A similar Macedonian training exercise teaches a youthful security squadron the rudiments of a manhunt through a dance drama of swordsmanship, riflery, and tracking. A funeral cortege synchronizes somber liturgy and dance steps for bearing fallen comrades to the grave.

In the mode of the folkloric Yaqui *danza del venado*, the Aztec dance in Mazatlan and Cancun reprises the deer hunt ritual with a solo dance. Naked to the waist, the stalker nods, bobbing the deer head on his scalp and accentuating with rattles his suspicion of human trackers. He sniffs the wind, laps from a stream, and energizes bestial figures with bells from ankle to shin. The approach of two archers begins the coda, in which an arrow to his flank surprises the deer, sending him into death quivers.

See also animal dances; Eskimo dance house; Greek dance; martial dance; masked dance.

Sources: Moore-Willson, Minnie. "Seminole Indian Feast Days." *Forest and Stream* 66, no. 5 (February 3, 1906): 176–77. Weule, Karl. *Native Life in East Africa*. London: Sir Isaac Pitman & Sons, 1909.

· 𝒥 ·

INDONESIAN DANCE

Indonesian dance consists of an array of choreography nearly overwhelmed by specialized attire. In the maritime center of Palembang, Sumatra, after 683, the *tanggai* enacted gestures of hospitality. At wedding receptions, groups of five dressed in bronze nail covers, shimmering brocade tunics and pants, batik sarongs, and gilded buckles and crowns edged in gold fringe displayed the splendor, nobility, and courtesies of ancient Srivijaya, an influential city-state between the 600s and 1100s. As part of state dinners, islanders reenacted traditional court protocol and distributed betel leaves and areca nuts.

Under the Majapahit Empire after 1295, aristocratic Javanese females performed the *bedhaya*, a sacred Buddhist nuptial dance exhibiting the elegance of the monarch and his bride. Each May in Surakarta and Yogyakarta to a chorus of songs, nine presenters honored the prince before a select audience. In accordance with ancient myths about Kangjeng Ratu Kidul, a South Sea deity, the company incorporated steps dating to 300 CE.

Members of the female folk troupe prepared for their appearance by fasting, purifying their bodies, and presenting holy offerings. Bridal costumes covered bodies tinged yellow with medicinal turmeric, a traditional Hindu anti-inflammatory since 1900 BCE. Under the surveillance of deacons, the nine-woman company performed devotional processions clockwise around the throne to the bell tones of the gamelan orchestra and gong. In time of war, the women danced on battlefields to ensure victory.

After 1613, dancers before the throne of Sultan Agung of Mataram east of Bali updated the ancient patterns to illustrate the mystic love between a king and goddess and enact stories from puppet shows. By the 1800s at Yogyakarta in south central Java, performers exaggerated the military significance of communal steps by firing pistols. A version of the warlike dance involved female impersonators.

At a royal Javanese pavilion in Surakarta in September 1983, the ancient bedhaya sanctified the wedding of Pakoe Boewan XII, king of Solo in East Java. Under a salute from the palace guard, the nine dancers advanced to the tones of cymbals, gongs, and a bamboo xylophone. The women trod a red pathway, symbolic of ancient blood ceremonies requiring the sacrifice of animals. Sprinkling rose petals and jasmine, the dancers craned slender necks and bowed in unison.

See also animal dances; lion dance; masked dance; mime; sacrificial dance.

Source: Knutsson, Gunilla K. "The Wedding of Solo's King." *New York Times,* September 11, 1983.

· *J* ·

JARABE TAPATÍO

The archetypal "Mexican hat dance," or *jarabe tapatío*, survives in Jalisco and Zacatecas, Mexico, as a model of anticolonial resistance and autonomy. The famed mating dance evolved among the Coca people of Cocula in western Mexico in the late 1700s. As a charming pairing in open position for females, the choreography merged facets of the *tonadilla*, fandango, and *seguidilla* and the earthy *zambra mora* from Tangiers and Moorish Granada, an Andalusian crowd dance from the 1500s. The bobbing heads and advance-retreat sequences imitated the mating of doves at weddings, anticipating the Roma flamenco and tango.

The dance name suggested three possible origins—the Arabic for herbal blend, Aztec for bartering, and Spanish for sweet syrup, a common finish for desserts in the time of Emperor Maximilian I (1864–1867). In 1790, male-female couples performed the steps in Mexico City, flouting the 1752 Spanish Inquisition edict and a colonial ban from authorities in Spain because of gestures suggestive of mounting intimacy. Another authority figure, Viceroy Félix Berenguer de Marquina, outlawed the dance for its African origins in 1802 on pain of jailing.

Dancing Rebels

For its fractious image, in 1810, the jarabe tapatío served loyal Mexicans as a battle cry. Following the Mexican War of Independence, in 1821, dancers flaunted the high-spirited courtship figures at celebrations in city squares. The steps gained urban popularity in Guadalajara and Mexico City and stimulated wartime chanting during the Mexican-American War of 1846 and the reform skirmishes of 1857. At the direction of President Porfirio Díaz, the jarabe tapatío represented Mexican identity at the 1889 World's Fair in Paris and the 1901 World's Fair in Buffalo, New York.

Along with the *baile de los viejitos* (dance of the old men), another choreographic rebellion against oppression, in 1910, the jarabe tapatío entertained mestizos at peasant theaters in the countryside. During a 1918–1919 tour of the *Fantasia Mexicana* by Russian ballerina Anna Pavlova to raise money for Russian war orphans, she claimed the Mexican hat dance for stage shows. Her presentations *en pointe* of steps on and around the brim of the sombrero retained the symbolic costumes, wooing gestures, and rejections.

At a turning point in its troubled history, the jarabe tapatío became a physical enactment of nationalism and affirmation of mestizo culture. A standard mariachi tune, "El jarabe tapatío" by Jesús González Rubio, in 1924 turned the performance into Mexico's national dance. Children learned the nine-figure choreography in grade school as "El jarabe national."

National Identity

Folkloric troupes adopted the *china poblana* costuming, the stereotypical full beribboned skirt, white peasant blouse, and shawl for women and the silver-edged black *charro* (equestrian) pants, white shirt, string tie, jacket, boots, and sombrero of the rancho foreman for men. To the perky 6/8 beat and phrasing of accented first and fourth beats of trumpet, guitar, harp, and violin, couples swirled, shouted "olé," and curtsied and bowed in dramatizations of formal courtship. The rocking chair step indicated hesitation as the romance failed in its initiation, forcing the beau to mime downing a bottle of tequila. His beloved mediated by serving him tea. The pas de deux spun with color as women flirted with ruffled skirts tiered in contrasting primary colors like those depicted on *Bailarines de Vallarta* (Vallarta dancers, 2006), a life-sized statue sculpted by Jim Demetro.

In contrast to the naive coquetry of the Hispano-Mayan *baile de las cintas* (ribbon dance) of Yucatán, males performing the jarabe tapatío, like snorting stallions, canted forward, stamped boot heels, and kicked a flashy foot flirtation while joining hands behind their backs. The seduction reached an orgiastic finale when the male placed his sombrero on the ground for the woman to cavort around. The wooing ended in "La Diana"—to a 2/4 meter, a final kick over her head led to a kiss concealed by the upraised sombrero. The dance scenario adorned the five-peso coin.

See also fandango; flamenco; Roma dance; tango.

Source: Mendoza-Garcia, Gabriela. "Bodily Renderings of the Jarabe Tapatío in Early Twentieth-Century Mexico and the Millennial United States: Race, Nation, Class, and Gender." PhD diss., University of California–Riverside, 2013. Accessed September 16, 2015. http://escholarship.org/uc/item/8c47k3gm#page-6.

JEWELRY

Metal jewelry and idiophonic adornments shaped from stones, shells, feathers, bones, and teeth heighten the aural and visual impact of folk dance, for example, the Baluchi bracelet dance in Iran and spiked bronze nail covers on Indonesian dancers. For the Armenian, Azerbaijani, and Assyrian *tamzara*, a community ring dance, women wear gold earrings and chains for sparkle and flash by firelight. Among the Bora of the Amazon jungle, modest collar-sized necklaces and chains cover bare breasts and produce a tinkling accompaniment to line dance.

In Egypt around 2000 BCE, tassels, wood castanets, and jewelry accompanied the spare attire of dancers in the Old Kingdom. After 1570 BCE, both male and female performers wore limited aprons and belts and accessorized with metal armlets and collars set with bright stones. Women modified the *bedleh* (belly dance costume) with skimpy aprons and kilts and a crop top. To the transparent overskirt or harem pants tied at the ankles, the tinkle of coin sashes, earrings, and necklaces coordinated with the clanging of finger cymbals by graceful fingers.

Natural Finery

From prehistory, hula troupes in the Hawaiian islands added bone and porpoise tooth accessories, leafy crowns, and flower leis to highlight native sources of dance attire. For Fijian narrative dance, around 800 BCE, Lapitan seafarers from Indonesia wore shell adornments, frigate bird feathers, and flower leis to accent the hand and shoulder gestures of seated miming. At the meeting house on Kiribati in the Gilbert Islands, women and girls began the holiday *ruoia* gala in necklaces and belts woven of human hair and fitted with shell ovals, head wreaths, and breast pendants shaped from whale bone and ivory. To the northwest, Yap women dressed for ritual with beaded neck cords and strings of mussel shells and black discs cut from coconut husks.

Asian folk choreography featured some of the world's most colorful adornment. A mode of embellishment at Mahakala in south central India featured temple attendants wafting jeweled fans and flashing ornaments on their sashes as they performed Hindu story dance. After 618 CE in China, the lion dance paraded five lions adorned with gold eyes and silver teeth, which glittered inside movable jaws.

African dance typically built costuming, masks, fetishes, gilded animal teeth, and luminous brass embellishments from natural sources. Layered costumes for the *midimu* ritual of the Makonde at Mozambique and southern Tanzania topped shirts and trousers with cloth helmets and string netting dotted with metal bells. In southern Africa after 400 CE, the Sotho presenters of a rain dance added black ostrich plumes to mirror their jumps and contortions. On the Ivory Coast during the 700s, the Fon coordinated raffia fringe with pierced beads. Two centuries later, Nigerian presenters of the *agaba* (lion dance) relied on seed pods and brass bells for contrasting rustles and tingling.

European Costume

Early Renaissance dance attire in Florence featured women's hair ornaments that drew attention to heads moving in time to the music. In the 1500s, dance troupes in southwestern India staged Sanskrit tales, dialogues, and myths with mime. Over flounced skirts and short-sleeved tops, character emulators mimicked identifiable authority figures with padding wraps, starched neck cloths and skirts, wigs, tassels, shawls, pointed-toe slippers, coronets, and torso beading. After 1556, peasants ruled by Akbar the Great at Delhi and Lucknow danced the *kathak* in customary saris. Percussive stamping agitated some 150 bells, the featured the sound of the steps. Nobles rewarded folk dancers with gold adornments.

The arrival of Spanish colonists in Oaxaca introduced Mexicans to the pavane, a noble processional that showcased military uniforms, gold braided epaulets, and sabers set with pearls and precious stones and polished for public display. Ladies executed the measured steps in gowns brocaded in gold and silver thread, feathered hats, and jeweled stomachers, hand fans, and slippers, which sparkled with each advance. With similar femininity but less refinement, the Roma in Bulgaria set off dark-toned makeup with heavy chain earrings, medallions, rings, and ranks of bangles aligned to add flash and music to the fandango. For tourists in the Middle East, belly dancers allied jingly coin belts and earrings with ululations, or tongue flutters, two sources of body music.

See also attire; belly dance; circle dance; fandango; hula; *kathak*; masked dance; mating dance; pavane; processionals; story dance.

Sources: Krishnan, Usha R. Bala, Meera Sushil Kumar, and Bharath Ramamrutham. *Indian Jewellery: Dance of the Peacock.* Mumbai: India Book House, 2004. Neich, Roger, and Fuli Pereira. *Pacific Jewelry and Adornment.* Honolulu: University of Hawaii Press, 2004.

JEWISH DANCE

As ritual, relaxation, therapy, and a constantly adapting mode of ethnic identity, Jewish dance marked the highs and lows of two thousand years of diaspora. Hebrew culture embraced music as a facet of the joyous life and blessed the threshing floor with ring dance. At Sukkot (Feast of the Tabernacles) after 957 BCE, priests at Solomon's Hebrew temple at Jerusalem anointed the ground with pitchers of water and leaped in celebration. Summer holidays sent maidens into vineyards to dance before the men of the tribe of Benjamin in hopes of finding a mate. For the annual Simchat Torah, the completion of the year's scriptural reading, a cortege exited the synagogue and continued through streets to family courtyards.

Old Testament scripture cites the dancing daughters of Shiloh in Judges 21:21, the hip-swaying Shulamite woman in Song of Solomon 7:1, and David's religious ecstasy in II Samuel 6:14, 16. After the Israelite exodus from Egypt around 1270 BCE, the prophetess Miriam improvised a triumphant dance at the height of Israelite jubilation over liberation from pharaonic enslavement. The impromptu *simcha* (rejoicing) set a model for women's transformative dance and proved that Hebrew aristocrats sanctioned spontaneous choreography for self-expression and amusement.

Hebraic Style

Although the early Christian era appears devoid of choreography, the evolving dance of Jews bore evidence of ethnicity in the swaying and eye covering accompanying priestly blessing, the graceful welcome of flame by matriarchs lighting Sabbath candles, and the chain dance of males to the synagogue for Sabbath services or around the interior on Sukkot bearing the Torah, palm, willow, myrtle, or citron. At Jerusalem's Western Wall, the devout conducted daily prayer and *kotel* (wall) dancing until August 70 CE, when Roman general Vespasian and his son Titus sacked the city. In Spain, medieval kabbalists honored females as the source of mourning liturgy and steps identified in the Zohar, the basis of Jewish mysticism.

Jews embedded dance in the pivotal moments of family life. From 200, the Talmud decreed *mitsve tansen* (wedding dances) an obligation of guests and family to secure happiness for the bride. In obedience to rabbis, guests processed to the outdoor wedding spot and raised the chuppah (canopy). In Yemen, the women excelled at the female frolics on henna night, the ritual painting of the bride's hands, and at tempestuous nuptial dance.

In the cold regions of Eastern Europe in the 900s, the Ashkenazi maintained a village *tanzhaus* (dance house) as a recreation hall for holidays and weddings, a community center that remained viable until the Napoleonic era. Suppression of liturgical dance in Paris under Archbishop Odo of Sully in 1200 apparently failed to dampen enthusiasm for Jewish folk dance, which continued in Iberia into the seventeenth century. Like the biblical Rachel wailing for her children, Jewish mothers anticipated the hardships and losses of the diaspora of 1492, an exile decreed by Ferdinand and Isabella. As a result, Sephardic communities grieved in steps, facial expressions, and gestures their expulsion from Iberia into an uncertain future.

The Jewish Diaspora

Modes of folk arts followed the diaspora over Turkey and North Africa, acquiring women's solos, swaying cross-front-cross-back (grapevine step), and line dances from Muslim sources and applying them to engagement ritual and bris (circumcision) ceremonies. Jewish originals followed standards for female solos among Sephardic residents in North Africa and the Levant and group dances among the Ashkenazi in Eastern Europe. In the 1600s, Kabbalat Shabbat prayers welcomed the Sabbath queen to the synagogue with elaborate gestures. For authentic source material, folk artists claimed abstract dance movements epitomizing femininity. They chose as models the grace of women carrying water jugs on their heads, serving guests from food trays, and winnowing grain with strainers.

In response to desert privation and sacrifice, in 1882, the *halutzim* (pioneers) of the First Aliyah (immigration) to Ottoman Palestine felt the need to channel their vitality into nationalistic community dance. Settlers relished the rhythms and sounds of the polka, *krakowiak*, *czerkassiya*, rondo, and hora, the national dance of Israel. Into the 1920s and 1930s, female art historians compiled the roots of Hebrew dance from all points of the diaspora, including music, attire, and jewelry. The addition of Jewish arts from Latvia, Lithuania, Galicia, Poland, Palestine, Czechoslovakia, and Russia reshaped the Polish *freylekh* line dance and the Czech *bezeda* and *sherele*, an Ashkenazic quadrille in 4/4 time honoring the shorn bride on her wedding day.

After centuries of influence from anti-Semitic cultures, twentieth-century Jews realized that they had to reclaim the dress and dynamics of original folk arts. For holidays, innovators created new figures from ancient temple rituals. Elementary schools introduced children to the basics of line and ring dance as well as partnering and processions for Hanukkah. In the mid-1930s, Zionists celebrated oneness by clasping shoulders and kicking to the center of the hora, an iconic circle dance. For the first summer harvest, archivists revived the *hag ha-bikkurim*, a thanksgiving retinue that bore olives, wheat, barley, dates, grapes, figs, and pomegranates to the temple.

At Kibbutz Daliyyah of northwestern Samaria in July 1944, the first nationwide festival saluted twenty-two folk dances, including the ancestral *dabke* and *alexandrova*.

The program drew viewers into the rapture of original scriptural and Israeli dances as well as Hasidic, Balkan, Slavic, Arabic, and Yemenite folk music played on authentic instruments. At the amphitheater, five hundred participants demonstrated Jewish figures for the edification of twenty-five thousand spectators.

The formation of the Jewish state on May 14, 1948, increased the prominence of female dancers and juvenile companies at sacred holidays and pageants, including dances honoring sheep shearing, barley harvesting, and fish netting. More festivals embraced historical folk dance in 1951 and 1958 and, in Haifa in 1953, originated a dance parade. By the end of mid-century, Jews had created four thousand folk dances, more than any other ethnic group.

See also circle dance; hora; lamentation dance; line dance; *mayim mayim*; scripture, folk dance in.

Source: Ingber, Judith Brin. *Seeing Israeli and Jewish Dance*. Detroit, MI: Wayne State University Press, 2011.

JIG

An agile folk rhythm that developed as a natural relaxation in the 1300s, the jig (also gigue) retained its appeal among rural Scots, Manx, and the Northern English for rocks on toes and brisk taps below a rigid torso. Identified as the Irish national dance, the fancy footwork and sprightly bounds in 12/8 or 6/8 meter manifested the temperament and outlook of a people who embraced a good time. To the bagpiper's drone, a circle of dancers formed around the soloist and turned toes in and out and crossed hands to the bouncy rhythm.

Along with sword dancing, ring dance, reels, and step dance, the basic jig step acknowledged Celtic influence in the British Isles after 1200 BCE and featured quick steps over *dúidíns* (clay smoking pipes) and flails. At a local *feis* (arts fair), such as the Aonach (great festival) at Tara in east central Ireland, dancers competed at maintaining brisk hopping and switching of feet for the longest period. Following the Dane and Jute invasion of northern Britannia in 449 CE, Celtic jig music blended with Scandinavian reels. At the end of Viking raids on Britannia on February 3, 1014, the jig sparked gleeful assemblies at the *cèilidh*, a Gaelic dance party in rural Ireland, Scotland, Wales, and Northumberland, England.

A Flexible Mode

The versatility of the carefree jig increased its fusion with other dances, as with solo footwork among morris dancers and presentations of the Italian *giga*, a brisk couples dance in 12/8 time. After the 1100s, the crude, sometimes bawdy body language of the jig unified with the farandole, a Catalonian or Provençal chain dance from northern Iberia and southwestern France. The blend of chain steps with solos migrated with sailors up the Atlantic coast. By the late Middle Ages, the Breton chain form of the gavotte gained jig steps and kicks.

At the beginning of the Renaissance, itinerant dance instructors taught jig patterns to the rising merchant class and their children. Precise execution guaranteed increasing sociability in the community, especially for male soloists and instrumentalists. Irishmen added a visual element by twirling an oak stick or shillelagh. The ebullient dance found appreciative knights and dames at the courts of Elizabeth I and Louis XIV. Either holding hands or apart, couples synchronized springy trips into the *gigue à deux* (jig duet), which agitated panniered skirts into engaging jounces.

In the Tudor era, sailors advanced the hop-jig into the hornpipe, a shipboard form of deck pacing to the tin whistle either in hard-soled shoes, clogs, or barefoot. Poet Alexander Pope and playwrights Ben Jonson, Robert Greene, Francis Beaumont, and John Fletcher peppered their works with references to jigs, including a farcical adaptation called fading (also fadding), a rakish figure to an indecent song. In William Shakespeare's mating comedy *Much Ado about Nothing* (1599), Beatrice compared rhapsodic, unpredictable romance to an unstructured jig. In the baroque era, French and Italian dancers adopted the jig as the finale of folk dance suites. Scots jig-a-jig music such as "The Black Rogue," "The Irish Washerwoman," and "Old Gray Goose" set the tone of seventeenth-century barn dances, contradance, and clog fests.

Global Variants

Settlement of the Western Hemisphere introduced clogging and jigs in Newfoundland harbors and on the American frontier. The flesh trade put the sailor's jig to a new use. To keep some forty million West African abductees healthy and ease their despair during the middle passage, after 1650, ship crews "danced the slaves" to hand clapping and the zing of the cat-o'-nine-tails against the deck. The therapeutic movements applied to shackled and unshackled captives from Benin, Dahomey, the Gold Coast, and Nigeria. Slaves in West Indian ports and at Congo Square in New Orleans, the descendants of abductees, incorporated the bounce and toe tapping of the jig in the cakewalk, juba, and clogging.

Baroque choreography embellished the basic steps into the Irish slip jig, a cèilidh (house party) or Gaelic folk dance set to 9/8 time. Dancers aimed for uninterrupted performance of knee and heel lifts, clicks, stomps, and triplets or heavy jigs in hard shoes, sometimes on sand-strewn floors. The Norman French revamped the jig as the *loure*, a slow gigue in 3/4 meter to the scree of the musette, a reedy bagpipe. Galicians created the *muñeiras*, a Spanish line dance in 6/8 meter coordinating back kicks and springs to bagpipe tunes.

The jig fit neatly into emotional community ensembles, notably the Connacht jig as an expression of unity among Ulster Loyalists. The British banishment of Acadians from Nova Scotia in 1755 preceded the evolution of Cajun-style jigs and quadrilles in Quebec, Vermont, Louisiana, southeastern Texas, and the Caribbean. At Monticello, Virginia, Thomas Jefferson rosined his bow to play a jig, which plantation slaves danced in their quarters. At Limoges around 1805, French worshippers ended each psalm with a promise to honor Saint Marcel, the ninth bishop of Paris, with a jig around the choir.

The significance of the jig to history earned scholarly consideration, in particular stage satires of backwoodsman Davy Crockett from the 1830s and the "Red River Jig,"

a breakdown fiddle tune of Amerindians and Métis in Alberta. Irish-Americans introduced St. Patrick's Day pageantry and jigs on March 17 to parades in Boston, Moscow,
Seoul, and Sydney. A German critic, Jacob Venedey, in 1844 compared the jig mode
to puppetry, St. Vitus' Dance, and the national dance of the Savoyards in Sardinia—all
proof of Irish barbarism.

Black dancers focused minstrel shows on hopping steps and shuffles to the banjo.
In the mid-1800s, the popular jig balanced ball programs featuring an olio of the waltz,
galop, quadrille, *lanciers* (lancers), and cotillion. The invigorating footwork raised spirits at home gatherings, such as the after-dinner relaxation between 1841 and 1861 in
writer Charles Augustus Hanna's *Historical Collections of Harrison County, in the State of
Ohio* (1900). In 1893, army wife Elizabeth Bacon Custer's *Tenting on the Plains* reported
jigging as a welcome amusement during dismal posting of the US Seventh Cavalry to
Texas, Kansas, and the Dakotas.

In the 2000s, jigs follow standard patterns. An Irish cèilidh tradition, the hay-
maker's jig aligns two rows of dancers for partnered skips and turns. In contrast, the slip
jig coordinates rocks, bounds, and high skips with kicks to front and rear. The Cape
Breton jig raises the height of figures with bounds and waving arms. The highland jig,
a leaping variation featuring knee-high kicks in Scotland and Nova Scotia, incorporates
uplifted arms, heel and toe steps, flat-footed stomps, and brandished fists. The Ozark
version makes less tapping noise as performers soft-shoe their shuffles and glides along
with loose swings of the arms from the shoulders.

See also Cajun dance; cakewalk; *cèilidh*; circle dance; clogging; contradance; cotillion; farandole; galop; gavotte; hornpipe; morris dance; quadrille; reel; step dance;
sword dance; waltz.

Sources: Pierce, Ken. "Coarse, Odd, and Comic: A New Study of Jigs." *Dance
Chronicle* 38 (2015): 81–86. Venedey, Jacob. "Twaddling Tourists in Ireland." *Dublin
University Magazine* 143, no. 24 (November 1844): 505–26.

JOROPO

An exultant, stamping dance indigenous to eastern Colombian and Venezuelan herders, the *joropo* blends elements of the Afro-Caribbean diaspora and Arabo-Andalusian
horsemanship and contradance with aboriginal South American dance from the Orinoco River basin. Arriving in the 1600s, the origins of the syncopated, contrapuntal
beat dated to sailors on the piers and troubadours in the Caracas barrios. The new dance
coincided with the emergence of the sizzling fandango among Creoles.

The term for the contagious, galloping 6/8 meter first appeared in print in
1749. An easily identified model of miscegenetic art, joropo lyrics of plainsmen
incorporated inchoate cries and vernacular of Indian tribes and black slaves from
multiple West African locales. Eight-syllable quatrains documented historic events,
epic heroes and tricksters, and everyday pastoral rhythms in Aragua, Miranda, Sucre,
Carabobo, and Anzoátegui. By the 1800s, Hispanic Arawak fleeing persecution in
Venezuela introduced the joropo in British Guiana. Less frisky versions, the *golpe*

and *pasaje*, stressed contemplative stanzas, polyphonic harmony, and lyrical form. Although Catholic prelates censured the dance for indecent elements and suggestive phrasing popping in and out of the triple-metered stanzas, by 1882, the joropo became Venezuela's national dance.

In the 1910s, the joropo, sometimes paired with *corridos* (ballads), flourished in rural open-air fiestas and enhanced light theatrical dance and ballet. The mesmerizing choreography permeated street dance in Cuba, Curaçao, St. Lucia, Puerto Rico, Trinidad, and Tobago and at mariachi fiestas in western Mexico. "Alma llanera" (Soul of the plains, 1914), composed by Pedro Elias Gutierrez, served peasants as a national anthem. In the 1930s, Juan Bautista Plaza, chapel master of the Caracas Cathedral, wrote liturgical pieces as well as joropos emphasizing Creole roots and a jig-like double meter overlaid with triple time.

During the regime of strongman Marcos Pérez Jiménez after 1948, Venezuela's *música llanera* took on patriotic symbolism for its aggressive beat and lured upper-class men into a predominately peasant pastime. The joropo invaded radio programming, travel magazine ads, and the film *King of the Joropo* (1978) and starred in grade school introductions to folk arts. By late June 1960, the International Tournament of Joropo, a dance competition in Villavicencio, Colombia, disclosed intricate variations by the best couples as determiners of regional folk culture. In 2012, the city extended the dance festival by inviting performers from Venezuela, Brazil, Costa Rica, and the United States.

Tourists identify the Venezuelan spirit of independence with folkloric executions of the joropo by dance troupes and Colombian cloggers. To an accented first beat, pairs engage hands and launch their feet into complex tapping. Seduction, the focus of the joropo, involves the male in a pulsing spiral that winds closer and closer to his intended. Partnering and turns reveal the female's whirling skirts below a straight back. The style of nasal male vocalists and harp, *cuatro* (four-string guitar), *bandola* (lute), accordion, and maracas accompaniment suits bullfights, tavern entertainment, and celebrations of birthdays, anniversaries, baptisms, or saints' days. Whether indoors or out, the joropo can continue all night, involving children's dance games, wooing, and feasting.

See also contradance; fandango.

Source: Horn, David, Heidi Feldman, Mona-Lynn Courteau, Pamela Narbona Jerez, and Hettie Malcomson. *Bloomsbury Encyclopedia of Popular Music of the World.* Vol. 9. London: Bloomsbury, 2014.

JOTA

The national folk dance of Aragon, the *jota* (also *cota*, *ixota*, or *hotia*), like the fandango, emerged from a Mozarabic fertility ritual and adopted attitudes and light steps from the passacaglia, a sweetly mincing show of footwork. The rudiments of jota permeated worshipful processions from the 600s, when Catholic archbishops made grand entrances to Tarragona in northeastern Spain. The jota served communities as a source of identity and Christians as a street finale for a pious ritual honoring the Christ Child on Christmas Eve.

From steps performed to medieval carols or at wakes, cathedral blessings, and vigils for the dead, in the 1700s, the jota evolved into complex patterns in 3/8 meter.

Valencian folk dancers in Real, Spain, ended the annual grape harvest thanksgiving with bouncy jota toe taps, arm waves, and kicks set to percussion, lute, *dulzaina* (oboe) or bagpipes, and *bandurria* (guitar). On the island of Majorca, an unrefined jota cultivated more modest airs.

Ethnic Expression

Like the Nordic *polska*, the jota individuated peasant character and kinetic arts in specific regions, including Galicia, Navarra, and Murcia. At the fiesta of Our Lady of Pilar in Zaragoza, a remembrance of the Virgin Mary's appearance near the Ebro River on October 12, 40 CE, presentations began at the basilica after 1711 and foregrounded venerations in Uruguay and Argentina. Singers made up droll couplets to accompany the leg lifts, rapid kneeling, and whirling pirouettes set to jota music. Variations added vivacious "olés," leaps, and smacks to the thighs.

Rising nationalism in the nineteenth century invested the Spanish jota with ethnic spirit. The swell of patriotic ardor bolstered Spaniards during Napoleon's siege at Zaragoza from June 15 to August 14, 1808, which ended with a French loss of three thousand five hundred men. In *Revelations of Spain* (1845), English travel writer Terence MacMahon Hughes compared the stirring street dance rhythm to the French Marseillaise for its vigor and inclusion of all ages and ranks. In 1851, the jota lent authenticity to Russian composer Mikhail Glinka's Spanish overtures.

Diasporic Dance

Colonialism carried the jota to Hispanic communities in Australia, Paraguay, Brazil, and Cuba. Canary Islanders turned the dance into the solemn *isa*. At Yucatán, Mexicans based the *jarana* on original Aragonese choreography. In the Philippines, the gestures of the *jota forlana* with shawls and steps to bamboo castanets marked fiestas and weddings. The brisk *jota cavitena* contrasted a feminine skirt dance with arrogant male posturing to zapateado foot taps. For a funeral, the slower rhythm of the jota Moncadeña mimed collapse and death.

New World frontiersmen displayed the exhibitionist jota at opera houses and honky-tonks on the Mississippi Delta, shaping the hybridization of Creole dance. At Santa Barbara, California, from the 1820s, *rancheria* parties brought neighbors from miles around to dance the jota both indoors and under a *ramada* (pavilion) shaded with branches and vines. Along with the flamenco and zarzuela (operetta), students learning Hispanic folk dance practiced the jota in heelless shoes. Still favored in the early 1900s at Andorra and Calanda in northeastern Spain, the jota entered elementary school curricula and, after 1938, enabled dictator Francisco Franco to arouse allegiance through the revival of folk arts.

See also Creole dance; flamenco; harvest dance; lamentation dance; *polska*; worship dance; zapateado.

Source: Dankworth, Linda E., and Ann R. David. *Dance Ethnography and Global Perspectives: Identity, Embodiment and Culture.* Basingstoke, UK: Palgrave Macmillan, 2014.

JUBA

A good-humored yet grotesque West African communal breakdown, the juba (or *majumba*) lacks a clear origin and could derive from a synthesis of slave cultures. In the seventeenth century, juba involved holistic body flexion and amusing tests of endurance that ranged from step dancing and patting and slapping the arms and shoulders to tapping out rhythms on cheeks, chest, thighs, and knees to the beat of the tambourine, spoons, and bone or rosewood clackers. Throughout the West Indies, Dutch Guiana, and Brazil, the juba featured a pair of crouching males performing staccato beats, bird mimicry, and rapid turns to body percussion, which replaced the forbidden drum with slaps on thighs, feet, and chests.

Vernacular and idiophonic sound energized juba dancers. Jingling sheep bells and clacking ox or goat horns tied to raccoon skins and rags and the straw beater's striking with quills or sticks on calabash banjos augmented celebratory lyrics, which South Carolina bondsmen sang during the week of "Krimas" (Christmas) vacation from work. Sung by the ragman, the words "Jump Juba, high en higher" creolized Bantu, Kongo, and Yoruba terms, syncretizing in vernacular authentic West African verses the precursors of children's jump rope rhymes and rap music.

The term *juba* may reflect the historic Numidian king Juba (85–46 BCE) or the name of the Jubba River in southern Somalia as well as a slang term for plantation slops mixed with milk and fed to slaves at a trough. Linguists attach the word to the Bantu voodoo noun *giouba*, a reference to the animistic spirits of soil and farming, particularly the *nguba* (peanut). Additional derivation from the Akan of Ghana, Ivory Coast, and Togo reflects links with the sun and timekeeping, rhythm, and *ijuba*, a chant honoring a deity or master. A North Carolina version, the Wilmington juba from the Cape Fear region, depicted the Yoruba from Nigeria dressed in rags, a possible version of the traditional Dahomean mask of Egungun, a disguise that mimicked the infant-carrying sashes and head wraps of women.

Dance in the Diaspora

As a lifestyle connecting socializing and shamanistic faith and worship, after 1760, African slaves abducted from Benin, Ibo, Mandinka, and Yoruba tribes to the Western Hemisphere maintained the percussive juba frolic in colonial Louisiana, where auctioneers esteemed their courtesy and obeisance to white buyers. The juba or *jiba* of Trinidad and Tobago, the parallel lines of the juba in the Antilles, and the Cuban *moyuba* invoked the Yoruba *orisa* (spirits) of Santeria with unintelligible cries and an enticing Congolese hip roll. In Georgia and Kentucky, dancers formed a circle around Master Juba, the lead performer, and his competitor. Voices called out, "Juba, juba," and sang in call and response in the style of a minister and congregation. All stamped their feet and clicked their heels to a syncopated beat in celebration of jubilee, a joyous break from discipline and a code word for revelry and liberation.

Joyous smiles and vernacular calls concealed from Christian masters the original significance of voodoo and hidden messages in African patois. With emphasis on "pattin' de pat," singers warned of the approach of "paterollers," slave patrols in search of runaways.

Haitians referred to a session as the *djouba* in which a caller named common movements—"the Jubal Jew," "blow the candle out," "yeller cat," "lift the latch," and a finale, the "long dog scratch." On Mississippi River wharfs, keelboats, and plantations throughout the American South and south to the Caribbean, Dutch Guiana, and Brazil, juba dancing solaced the bondsman. At the praise house on Daufuskie Island, South Carolina, the leader of the jumpin' juba lapsed into a trance, melding memory with imagination.

After the planting of a circular park in 1820, the juba dominated black performances at Congo Square in New Orleans, where rich freedmen from Haiti and Cuba took up residence to escape the chaos following the Santo Domingo insurrection of 1791. Poet Langston Hughes honored the dance respites as typical of the black man's Sabbath. One combination, the "pigeon wing," emulated bird courtship with an intricate shuffle accompanied by the scraping and lifting of one foot, extending the neck, and "cuttin' de wings" by the flapping of elbows. A related combination, the "buzzard lope," mimed the circling, shoulder lifting, and pecking of carrion by a carrion bird, the source in 1830 of Thomas Dartmouth Rice's Jim Crow dance.

The Professional Juba

William Henry Lane, the legendary "Sambo" of staged West African juba, flourished in the 1840s at Dickens' Dance House at Five Points in lower New York and in summer 1848 at Vauxhall Gardens in London, where he died four years later. Lane's improvisations impressed novelist Charles Dickens, poets Sidney Lanier and Walt Whitman, philosopher Margaret Fuller, editor Horace Greeley, authors George Washington

A good-humored yet grotesque West African communal breakdown, the juba lacks a clear origin and could derive from a synthesis of slave cultures. *"American Home Scenes: The Breakdown,"* Harper's Weekly *(April 13, 1861): 232.*

Cable and Edgar Allan Poe, and humorist Mark Twain, all of whom recognized the uniqueness and physical demands of African counterpoint. By merging Irish jigs and hornpipes with polyrhythmic African folk steps, in the 1850s, white juba imitators in blackface added to American culture an incomparable multi-ethnic dance that anticipated tap dance, vaudeville, step dance, clogging, buck and wing, jazz, the black bottom, Charleston, lindy, jitterbug, and breakdancing.

An escapist relaxation after emancipation, the rhythmic step dance edged north to Ohio in the 1870s, when journalist Lafcadio Hearn described a session on the Cincinnati levees. As entertainment, itinerant minstrel companies presented the juba under the term "hambone," which coordinated eye rolling, chuckling, spinning, sliding, and finger snapping with steps. Performed in the 1890s to "Turkey in the Straw," the verse and doggerel accompanying juba, "pattin' juba," jumba, and the ring shout released pent-up anguish from slave times and sorrow at the separation of families through the sale and trade of bondsmen. Posturing, gyrating folk dancers earned tips, drinks, and snacks for competing at juba on streets and in taverns and entertaining shoppers at marketplaces.

See also Arab dance; *bamboula*; *calenda*; diaspora; gendered dance; *Schuhplattler*; step dance.

Sources: Brainerd, Mary Bale. "Dinky." *Atlantic Monthly* 53, no. 8 (August 1884): 206–12. Harrison, Paul Carter, Victor Leo Walker, and Gus Edwards, eds. *Black Theatre: Ritual Performance in the African Diaspora.* Philadelphia: Temple University Press, 2002.

JUVENILE DANCERS

Dance impacts children's activities in the form of nationalistic training, physical education, and fun that is as easy to learn as clapping to the Jewish hora and as challenging as the pre-Easter death dances at Verges, Catalonia, and the Aymara children's dance to a brass band in Bolivia. At camp and in classrooms, teachers combine the variant purposes in heritage dances, such as "The Bear Went over the Mountain," a frontier rhythm that immigrated to the Appalachian Mountains from England, Scotland, and Ireland. Participation instructs pupils in geometric patterns based on right- and left-hand partnering, as in the Renaissance *branle*, a useful form of creative play.

While young bodies move through the figures, minds learn the textured sounds of various musical instruments, from drums and clappers to the mountain dulcimer, banjo, and woodwinds. Couples count measures as they alternate walking, skipping, turning, and clapping, all fundamental to the Afghan *attan* dance. An initiation in the physical arts establishes a life pattern of practice and performance of a range of skills—Congo stilt walking, Burmese puppet dancing, or Hawaiian hula.

Childhood dancing reinforces ideals. In the early years of the Roman monarchy after 550 BCE, young boys danced with adult males in an intergenerational spectacle along the Sacred Way. Both groups dressed in purple tunics and crested helmets in imitation of soldiers of Mars, the war deity and patron god of Rome. In Oceania, Polynesian students memorized the kinetic rituals to earth, air, fire, and water, a youth's introduction to teamwork. From Tahitian comics, young presenters mimicked hand gestures indicating hospitality and generosity.

Steps and Rhythms

In the early Middle Ages, masking intrigued children to experiment with story dance, disguise, and mime for the North Korean *talchum*, French cabbage-planting songs, and May Day imitation of frog leaps in Latvia and Great Britain. Late in the medieval era, Catalonian children at Berga joined in the allegorical *tirabol*, the finale of Corpus Christi Day processions. Tibetan Buddhists taught holistic expressionism to children and encouraged innovative steps and gestures with scarves. Among Kurds, shoulder-to-shoulder circle dancing seemed self-explanatory to young participants, who emulated any adult dancer who seemed easy to follow.

Into the Renaissance, knot garden mazes, Italian tarantellas, Albanian sword dances, and labyrinthine church mazes teased the venturesome to master such details as the geometric intricacies of advance-pause-turn-turn again. For Henry VIII in 1510, a child's troupe mimed a morris dance for the royal court. Romani children at Bucharest demonstrated to non-Gypsy children the Roma solo as well as circle dancing and partnering involving backbends, hip rolls, and shoulder undulations, all exercises in motor skills. After 1556, Indian children at Delhi practiced bell work for the evocative *kathak*, working up from 25 to 150 leg bells per dancer.

First recorded by Jesuit prelates in 1585, young Guaraní of the Misiones Jungle of Argentina and southern Brazil joined hands for the back-and-forth sway of folk dance to the tinkle of rainsticks. For young aristocrats in Paris after 1643, practicing the pavane and *rigaudon* became a part of a refined education. Mid-seventeenth-century planting games involved English preschoolers in a ring dance to "Oats, Peas, Beans, and Barley Grow." Sudanese children pondered the importance of a propitiatory rain dance to water fields and subsistence crops of peanuts, cassava, sorghum, sugarcane, coffee, cotton, peas, sesame, maize, and millet. After the restoration of Charles II to the English throne in 1660, youngsters decorated maypoles with garlands and rehearsed the interweaving of ribbons and streamers around the center to acknowledge spring.

Modern Children's Dance

Intergenerational dance welcomed children to participate in adult solos and partnering, particularly the Eastern European czardas, Thai dance myth, Japanese *odori*, Chinese dragon pageants, and North American barn dances, including the cotton-eye Joe. At West Cork, Irish students learned jigs from a dance instructor. From 1819, Scots hired limber teachers to demonstrate the hornpipe and clogging to pupils in Edinburgh. Young participants enjoyed traditional costumes, body language, and songs as well as stepping and clapping to ebullient meters.

More athletic dances, particularly the Ukrainian *hopak*, the Maori *hakka*, and the Filipino *tinikling*, offered holistic exercise as well as balance and eye-foot coordination. In Livingston Parish, Louisiana, after 1921, Hungarian-American youth practiced authentic thanksgiving ring dances that linked the theme with the mores of their grandsires. Young skaters systematized their rink workouts on wheels or ice to standard line dances and mazurka steps. In the twenty-first century, Franco-American adults teach children counting rhymes at family workshops in Canada and New England.

See also barn dance; *branle*; Cajun dance; circle dance; cotton-eye Joe; dragon dance; holiday dance; *hopak*; hornpipe; line dance; Malay dance; masked dance; maypole dance; mazurka; *odori*; parasol dance; propitiation; Roma dance; *tinikling*; *tirabol*.

Source: Bailey, Diane. *History of Dance*. Minneapolis, MN: Abdo, 2015.

· *K* ·

KATHAK

An interpretive dance enjoyed in village marketplace or temple courtyard, from 400 BCE, *kathak* dance followed the bardic and monastic traditions of the Indus-Gangetic belt of north and east India that began in 4000 BCE. A theoretical text, *Natya Sastra* (Arts manual, after 200 BCE), compiled by musicologist Bharat Muni, characterized entertainment of the illiterate with dance. Movements for male and female performers derived from itinerant Hindi storytellers who instructed Indian peasants in superstitions, myths, fables, and epics. Spectators were thrilled by exciting hero stories and the emotional enjoyment of the kathak with its lyrical tunes, body contortions, expository emotional states, makeup, and costumes.

To Hindustani music and scriptural chants, recitals of encapsulated religious episodes and anecdotes marked folk celebrations of holidays, music festivals, births, and marriages. Interpretation relied on heavily kohl-edged eyes, voice, front-back arm gestures, waist bends, and cyclic footwork in triplets to represent joy, pain, devotion, shame, impatience, weakness, or constancy. Dots of perfume on the backs of the hands wafted fragrance around the dancers as they wielded an invisible bow or wove a garland for Krishna. The essential pirouettes illustrated the Hindu belief in cycles of birth, death, and rebirth.

Sacred Kathak

During the Mauryan Empire after 322 BCE, the barefoot, swirling executions stamped heel and toe in demi-plié. Gestures from a half crouch focused on spirituality and the entertainment of royalty. Tinged with temple rites from Varanasi on the Ganges River in northeastern India, the recitation began with an understated invocation to the gods Shiva, Vishnu, or Ganesha and a greeting with raised palm turned out toward the audience. Gliding thrusts of the head and expressive flicks of eyebrows and wrists set an aesthetic or submissive mood. Spectators sang along with the familiar religious songs.

Muslim influence after 800 CE altered the choreographic purpose from didacticism to entertainment. By 1200, kathak followed standard style to the music of the harmonium, flute, sitar, cymbals, and the table hand drum, which the percussionist tied to the waist. Right hand clapping into the left palm, balletic combinations, and facial expressions enacted poetic abstracts, everyday events, or movements in nature of birds and fish. The flash of armlets, necklaces, bangles, and finger and toe rings added sparkle. The rhythm picked up momentum as the narrative approached a stirring conclusion, sometimes with the dancer spinning on the heel and halting in a statuesque pause.

In a golden age after 1526, secular Persian court manners, themes, and kinetic techniques influenced the Mughal Empire, where feudal dance masters trained courtesans like Japanese geishas to sustain kathak as a sincere chamber art. To earn a living, lower-class women performed playful story dance in the mansions of aristocrats and the rich rather than in temples. Blended styles fostered flexibility and improvisation in period repertoires, in which men performed bare-chested or in a long tunic over trousers.

For portrayal of noblemen, Indian actors colored their faces green. Demons added red streaks and red beards to the green base. Gods stood out in white beards. Woodsmen blackened their faces the color of bark. Females wore yellow and outlined the part of their hairstyle with red ochre. As pantomimes of classic myth and historic events, the finished products interpreted ritual, martial arts, and Sanskrit texts.

During the forty-nine-year reign of Akbar the Great at Delhi after 1556, Indian folk dance accommodated Hindu and Muslim elements. Kathak acquired exoticism from musicians and performers captured as prisoners in Mandu to the southeast and migrant performers from Persia. Muslim authorities, at the request of the empress Jodhabai of Rajasthan, invited Hindu dance clans to demonstrate the style of the Lucknow kathak. The themes, extracted from the Mahabharata (400 BCE) and Ramayana (300 BCE), depicted the folk episodes and trickery of Krishna's childhood, adolescence, and maturity. To mediate a religious ritual for non-Hindus, the dancers stretched a propitiatory garland across the floor before they began.

The Lucknow Dance

After popularizing the Lucknow kathak, courtesans taught upper-class women the steps and gestures. In traditional saris, female folk dancing Persian style on straight legs emphasized the whirling of Sufi dance and percussive footwork from the sound of small round bells threaded around the ankles. Children and adults learned the kathak while increasing the number of bells from 25 to 150. By adulthood, women replaced ordinary saris with vest, bare midriff, and trousers and topped the outfit with a transparent veil.

In a climate of competition, royalty rewarded the best performers of the Lucknow kathak with jewelry and gold. During the reign of Aurangzeb, the sixth Mughal emperor, from 1658 to 1707, interpretive dance spread to religious dancers at Alwar, Jaipur, and Murshidabad in the northeast. Cultic worship of the mischievous Krishna, the supreme god, and his lover Radha involved kathak dancers in miming before a holy idol.

In a commentary on *Bhaktamal* (The devout, 1712), the critic Priyadas described an Islamic preference for refined, lyrical Lucknow kathak. Under ruler Muhammad Shah Rangila of Delhi after 1719, the Mughal Empire declined during his twenty-nine-year dalliance with luxury, sex, and aestheticism, including kathak presentations in the bazaars. At Awadh in west central India following the Carnatic Wars, the storytelling dance flourished after 1775 during the twenty-two-year rule of Asaf-ud-Daula, who built a new capital at Lucknow. Nurturance of music and folk dance for men and women radiated outward from his court across castes to street buskers, who hybridized the kathak with puppetry, juggling, fiddling, and mime.

By 1825, more than one hundred hereditary kathak clans functioned in Benares. Art historians proposed a connection between Roma migrations from central India west through Turkey, Romania, and Hungary. During the diaspora of nomads, strains of kathak music introduced Indian harmonies to Hungarian composers. The Roma trek west through Slovakia and France reached Andalusia, where the kathak influenced the flamenco.

After 1847 in Awadh, the voluptuary Wajid Ali Shah, the last nawab of Lucknow, hosted musicians, singers, and folk dance troupes. The nawab favored folk performances with financing of musical instruments and costumes and offered the lawns of courtyards at Kaiser Baug Palace as dance floors for his concubines to join in. In an atmosphere of Indo-Islamic refinement, he patronized the arts by studying as a kathak dancer under trainer Thakur Prasadji and developed a graceful, hypnotic foot stamp. Wajid imported folk dancers to mime the romances of milkmaids with Krishna, whom the troupes portrayed with restrained sensuality.

At annual royal fairs, boy companies who apprenticed under their parents in hereditary dance clans played a starring role for their rhythm. In contrast to the precise standards and tripled tempo of Jaipur dance farther north and Rajasthan on the western border, Lucknow folk dance developed flow and subtle sex appeal fostered by an era of great dance idols. With accompaniment by the best instrumentalists, costly presentations flourished in the city until the English exiled the nawab to Calcutta in 1856.

The Outside World

Under the judgmental British after 1856, Indian folk dancers abandoned kathak and the eclectic presentations of courtesans, who sometimes incorporated balancing acts and juggling. At the Royal Asiatic Society in June 1865, the Reverend James Long, an Anglican priest from Ireland, proposed that kathak dancers instruct the illiterate on Christian stories and European tales as they once had taught Hindu lore. In an 1893 edition of *Church Missionary Review*, an English moralist felt insulted by applause for kathak presentations and spectator cries of "Ram, Ram."

In diverse strands, kathak mode survived in the seductive performances of nautch girls and the private tutoring of upper-class Hindu girls of Bengal and Rajasthan in pure family dance. In *The Wrongs of Indian Womanhood* (1900), reformer Jenny Frow Fuller, wife of Bombay missionary Marcus B. Fuller, castigated expressionistic temple dance to amuse Krishna's immobile statue. She raged that 120 kathak "harlots" debased themselves by enacting enslavement to a deity and serving priests and pilgrims as an erotic amusement. Fuller declared the adoption of illegitimate girls to train as dancers a "demoralization" of the Hindu home and launched an anti-dance movement.

Stage versions of kathak in London in 1924 and visits to Calcutta and the Lahore bazaars by professional dancers Anna Pavlova, Ted Shawn, and Ruth St. Denis restored respect to the neglected kathak. Poet and Nobelist Rabindranath Tagore of Calcutta arranged for St. Denis to teach the resilient religious style at his Bengali school, Visva-Bharati University. Around 1926, Madame Leila Roy Menaka, a Brahman choreographer from Bengal, revived the employment of dancing families among the social elite by reducing the monotonous repeated beats. A native dancer, Uday Shankar, traveled with Pavlova's troupe in the United States and, in 1929, returned to India to assemble a folk dance company. The troupe toured Paris and returned to the United States featuring the instrumentalism and dance of Uday's brother, Ravi Shankar, who globalized Indian music.

During the emergence of modern kathak after 1930, training reintroduced the popular Lucknow storytelling dance throughout India and in tours of Europe. After the departure of British governors from India on August 15, 1947, middle-class Indians reclaimed the traditional kathak as a component of nationalism preserving a heritage of myth, legend, romance, and religious tale. In the postcolonial period, females danced in tight blouses and long gathered skirts edged in metallic thread.

The dance spread beyond Lahore in the Punjab to Kathmandu, Nepal, and Rangoon, Burma, and contributed to the development of tap dance from Roma percussive footwork. By 1955, the kathak underlay balletic dance drama, popularized on the stages in Delhi. Late in the twentieth century, exponents of heritage kathak foot patterns nurtured village group dance.

In 1979, soloist and educator Chitresh Das of Calcutta introduced the complex rhythms of the kathak at the Chhandam School of Kathak in San Francisco. On an advanced level, he taught the first accredited kathak dance classes at San Francisco State University and Stanford. At his death on January 4, 2015, his chain of ten schools had spread kathak solo work around the globe.

See also body art.

Sources: Chakravorty, Pallabi. *Bells of Change: Kathak Dance, Women, and Modernity in India.* Calcutta: Seagull Books, 2008. "Chitresh Das Dies at 70; Indian Classical Dancer Was Master of Kathak." *Los Angeles Times,* January 9, 2015. Fuller, Mrs. Marcus B. *The Wrongs of Indian Womanhood.* New York: Fleming H. Revell, 1900.

KURDISH DANCE

For millennia throughout Asia Minor, Kurdish dance has epitomized a complex nomadic culture of Caucasian mountain folk who have survived political chaos and diaspora. Their art incorporates symbolic green, red, and yellow costumes, shoulder-to-shoulder grouping, and heritage music into all special days, from marriage, births, and circumcisions to New Year's rituals. Out of exuberance for spirituality and tribal religions, Kurds dance during processions to shrines of saints, sometimes with daggers in their fists.

The Kurds, who derived from the Zagros highlands east of Iraq from 3000 BCE, retained the artistic elements of Armenian and Assyrian or Chaldean dance, but omitted veiling of women. Dancers differed from their conservative neighbors in Iran, northern Iraq, Armenia, Georgia, Israel, and Anatolia by mixing ages and genders and encouraging bent torsos, hand holding or little-finger linking, stamping, and ululation, the rapid vibration of the tongue. Women made a fashion statement in bright silks and gold buckles.

Like the dances of the nomadic Roma, performance of rustic choreography defined the geopolitical nation of Kurdistan and the long, difficult history of a marginalized and outcast people. The *delilo*, a hospitality ring dance of eastern Turkey, combined a simple three-step advance and three-step retreat representing welcome and invitation. For Newroz, the first day of spring or the vernal equinox on March 21, dancers moved outdoors to encircle the fireside, a communal symbol of Kawa, the Kurdish blacksmith. According to Firdowsi's Persian epic *Shahnama* (*The Book of Kings*, ca. 1000 CE), Kawa, a hero of illumination, assassinated the mythic villain king Dehak of Mesopotamia to liberate the Kurds. Their dancing expressed pride in resistance to a foreign monarch. Another example of medieval folk art, the *sexhani*, a face-to-back Kurdish line dance, dates to a Yezidi saint, Sheik Adi (or Hadi) ibn Musafir of Iraq, around 1100 CE.

Nuptial Dance

For traditional arranged marriages, Kurdish women hosted a bride's night for decorating her hands and feed with henna symbols. To entertain the future matron on Henna Night, women wearing belted caftans over tunics and loose trousers linked hands to the back. In unison, they performed boisterous choreography involving clapping, side-to-side neck movements, subtle hip rolls, and ululations. One favorite, the story dance of *zeyniko*, depicted a busy maiden passing flirtatious men on her way to the village well.

Meanwhile, Kurdish males honored the groom with exhilarating dances for men only, notably tribal skirmishes in the çepik and an allegro combination of bounds, knee bends, and lunges for the *xwarzani*. An athletic choreography required leaping over flames in the *simsimi*, for which male troupes dressed in the ancestral short-sleeved aba (cape) and round felt cap. The *beri*, a satiric dance by males, ridiculed ugly women and drudges at common chores. The *eylo* (eagle dance) elevated men for their prowess and strength with upper body posturing, bending from the waist, and limited footwork as they pretended to snatch up a fox or lamb with their talons.

Before the wedding ceremony, guests joined the *dilan* (or *halay*), a processional dance before and around the bride and groom along the way to the officiating chieftain. The national dance of Azerbaijan and Turkey, the dilan involved all attendees in a chain, semicircle, or ring to call-and-response lyrics. The lead dancer and the last participant twirled handkerchiefs while keeping time with the shoulders and performing a heel-and-toe step.

The dilan incorporated the melody of the *zurna* (flute) and frame drum and dated to the ancient encircling of bonfires at communal feasts. A variant placed an elderly couple performing a figure at the center. For Sunni Kurds, the three-day nuptial celebration violated Islamic isolation of females from mixed-gender activities in public.

Folk Arts and Politics

Events in the Middle East politicized the Newroz dance, facial tattoos, and songs, which Mustafa Kemal Ataturk, founder of modern Turkey, added to curricula from kindergarten to university in 1917. In a policy reversal, he prohibited Kurdish dance in March 1921. Denied an independent state, Kurds clung to folk arts as evidence of their heritage and their resistance to silencing of terminology and lyrics. As Turkey developed its self-awareness in 1929, ethnic dance proved popular with tourists, who photographed performances by Armenians, Assyrians, Arabs, Greeks, Jews, and Kurds.

In 1932, Ataturk dispatched ethnographers to inventory folk lyrics, story dance, and costuming for compilation in the book *Turkish Folklore*. With stress on a unified Turkish culture, in 1939, he added to the staff of Istanbul University a department of folklore, which assiduously excluded Kurdish music and dance. A plague of aphids in the mid-1940s at Urfa in north central Turkey supplied a text for the *kimil*, a history dance imitating the work of farm families at capturing aphids in jars. With the establishment of a Jewish state of Israel on May 14, 1948, rural Kurdish Jews preserved their dance songs in the vernacular and initiated the young into ancestral performances.

In 1955, Turkish arts purveyors amassed sixteen hundred traditional folk dances, six hundred, or 38 percent, of which retained prominence on dance programs and at competitions. The evolution of the *galuç* in the 1960s contributed an agrarian miming of sewing grain in furrows to a 6/4 tempo. A liturgical performance, the galuç incorporated kneeling, praying for rain, and the sharpening of scythes for the harvest. Coquettish girls brought water jars to the fields and flirted with thirsty reapers. The dance ended with a mime of courtship and marriage proposals.

In recent times, Kurds legitimized their ideology through singing, story dance, and peaceful protest by dancing the delilo. Over the passage of time and diaspora, they adulterated their original steps and tunes with elements assimilated from Arab and Turkish ethnicities. Violation of Islamic law earned Kurd dancers death threats in June 2015. On the Syrian-Turkish border in early February 2015, Kurdish fighters victorious over ISIS danced in uniform in the north Syrian streets of Kobanî. A form of visual propaganda, the impromptu figure defied conservative Muslims who sought to suppress free elements of culture.

Source: Karakeçili, Fethi. "Kurdish Dance Identity in Contemporary Turkey: The Examples of Delilo and Galuç." Master's thesis, York University, Toronto, 2008. www.academia.edu/6546183/Kurdish_Dance_Identity_In_Contemporary_Turkey.

LABYRINTHINE DANCE

A Bronze Age activity from the Mediterranean, labyrinthine dance invested worship with a special form of chain dance, as with the spiral church garniture by Corsicans on Good Friday. Maze processions have survived for millennia, involving congregations in north central Crete at Knossos Palace, a Minoan stronghold that dates to 2000 BCE. According to myth, King Minos, who lived around 1300 BCE, engaged the builder Daedalus to construct a labyrinth to imprison his monster stepson the Minotaur, a half-man and half-bull monster.

Daedalus laid out a tiered dancing space on the threshing floor for Princess Ariadne. During the annual feeding of the monster with sacrificial Athenian youths, the participants cleverly threaded the occluded hallways and blind alleys much as Theseus followed a ball of red twine to the heart of the maze and slew the man-beast. A palace fresco at Knossos pictured the Cretan dancers as leaping over the horns of a real bull, a celebration of a sacred union between the hero, Theseus, and Princess Ariadne, the mistress—and possibly priestess—of the dance. In the falling action of the myth, the surviving young men and women danced together in the labyrinth in exultation at their escape from death.

At the sacred isle of Delos, the death-slayer Theseus and the escapees held hands and reenacted the dance counterclockwise at the altar of Dionysus to strums of a lute. Unlike the initial performance, they reenacted the stalking myth, boy with girl, in full daylight and free of terrors of the Minotaur's dark underworld. In a sinuous chain, each clasped the waist of the youth in front and danced down the intricate halls of the labyrinth in the *geranos* (crane or stork dance). Another version depicts them grasping a rope in imitation of a serpent, an emblem of renewal for shedding its old skin and revealing the new. By depicting cranes soaring overhead to honor Aphrodite, goddess of passion, the Thesean troupe became the first Aegean men and women to dance in partnership.

A Traditional Pattern

Homer's *Iliad* (800 BCE) described a scene on Achilles's shield portraying Athenian foot soldiers gripping each other's wrists and wheeling and crisscrossing with joy. Unwinding the funerary steps in reverse of their advance, the performers negated the

171

death sentence by logic, which triumphed over confusion. The Homeric maze dance adorned Cretan coins and reached Marseilles via the Phoenicians in the 800s BCE; Tragliatella, Etruria, around 620 BCE; Vulci, Etruria, after 440 BCE; and Didyma, Ionia, after 300 BCE. According to the poet Lucian, author of *De saltu* (*On Dance*, ca. 160 CE), entwined figures remained popular in Crete among sailors, who emulated Theseus's talent for problem solving and relished his good fortune in combat and romance. The Greeks danced away evil with the maze dance and painted serpentine patterns on their homes as icons of good fortune. Representation of a chain of dancers resembling a garland suggested an ephemeral significance in contrast to a copy of the harmonious orbit of stars and planets around the heavens, a concept proposed by Plato around 400 BCE.

Roman dancers retained the Greek fundamentals, but added gendered complexities similar to those of the English maypole dance. According to Roman novelist Apuleius, boys and girls presented the Greek Pyrrhic war dance in elegant costumes. Unlike the partnering of the Cretan labyrinthine dance, the circling of Romans involved sideways moves and separations into boys' and girls' lines that continued until a trumpet finale ended the folk dance.

In Book 5 of Virgil's *Aeneid* (19 BCE), the epic hero, Aeneas, carried the labyrinthine mode from Troy to Italy, where games and amusements concluded the funeral for his father, Anchises. At Alba Longa, Aeneas's son Iulus Ascanius taught Albans the winding Troia (Trojan ride) dance, or *carouse*, as mock combat drill or cavalry tactics conducted in an invisible maze. Virgil compared the dazzling moves and countermoves to the playful swimming of dolphins off Carpathia or Libya. Augustus, Virgil's patron, acclaimed the Troia after his investiture as Rome's first emperor.

Interpreters of metaphysical folk imagery pictured the meandering spiral as winter engirdling the sun, which maze dancers awakened each spring. The Greek *syrtos* retained the cultic steps as a model of circuitous paths to the underworld and confinement of the dead at the center. The Kore cults applied the twisting steps to the chorus of maidens honoring Persephone/Proserpina and her springtime emergence on Earth from the kingdom of Hades as well as her return to the underworld each fall.

From Myth to Medieval Dance

Aegean maze myths influenced Christian architecture, which adapted the atavistic tales into the search for salvation and rebirth at the center, the symbolic residence of God. In 200 CE, Christ's devotees danced the first sacred ritual, "Hymn of Jesus." Churches adopted mosaic labyrinths in Africa around 400 and Italy after 1000. The Christian *bergerette* (little shepherd) paralleled the traversing of life, a forty-foot pattern incorporated into the portico of Lucca Cathedral after 1063 and the paved floor of Chartres Cathedral in north central France after 1194. To sacred chants, French clergy held hands with congregants and danced the entangled path on Easter Sunday, the one day that the sun danced.

Similar Italian geometric labyrinths in the nave of San Michele Maggiore at Pavia and San Vitale in Ravenna may have represented a pilgrimage to the holy city of

Jerusalem or a heroic reverence to Theseus, the Christ figure, the conqueror of chaos and evil, betokened by feeding the satanic Minotaur with human bodies. The customary Easter maze dances continued at Besançon in east central France until 1738. From 1396 at the Cathedral of St. Stephen at Auxerre, the ecclesiastical choreography of turn-halt-counter-turn followed twelve concentric circles each Easter Monday to Wipo of Burgundy's hymn "Victimae Paschali laudes" (Praises to the Easter victim). Mystic analysis saw the winding in and out as tracing the harmonious petals of a rose, symbol of the Virgin Mary and also alchemy and a magic mandala.

Ancient turf mazes, which appeared in Iceland, Germany, Poland, Serbia, England, Ukraine, and Siberia, may have entertained dancing children and outlined parade routes for May Day and Whitsuntide, the Monday after Pentecost on the Christian calendar. In Norway and Sweden, the choreography bore the names *Jungfrudans* (maidens' dance), *Troyaburg* (Troy town), and *Steintanz* (stone dance). Medieval Welsh *caerdroia* (mazes), called "Troy towns" or "shepherd's race," were the work of herders. Carved into hillcrests, the turf mazes served as pathways for a ritual procession to lead evil predators to entrapment.

Art historians surmised that rural people danced such medieval serpentine styles as the farandole on a dynamic, curved path at the spring equinox and midsummer's day to bring luck to the harvest. Barren women reputedly danced the same swerving, meandering route by the full moon to increase their chances of conceiving children. In the late Middle Ages, landscapers repeated the sinuous dance patterns in knot garden plots at castles and manors.

Into the Renaissance, the labyrinthine dances influenced the verse of French lyricist Pierre de Ronsard on the ins and outs of love. In the last half of the 1400s, Italian scholar Marsilio Ficino explained how music and dance served their purpose by imitating the soul's passions as well as their gestures, harmonics, and actions, which reflected both earthly affection and divine love. Similar allusions in the masques of Ben Jonson and William Shakespeare's *A Midsummer Night's Dream* (ca. 1590) and *The Tempest* (ca. 1610) reflected patterns of mingling and parting, which characterized Jacobean court amusements.

In the Valois era at the wedding of Henry III and Anne d'Argues in 1591, French maidens held hands and mastered the forty geometric interlaces of advance-pause-turn-turn again. During the Reformation and the Age of Reason, religious scholars rebutted the mystic thinking of past centuries by impugning the place of ecclesiastical dance in holy precincts. By 1690, the Auxerre labyrinth disappeared from the structure. In 1778, Canon Jacquemart ordered the labyrinth removed from Rheims Cathedral to halt the noise of children playing dance games along the shape. In the New World, Christian presentations of the *matachines* north of the Rio Grande united New Mexican dancers in a serpentine dance step suggesting a bull lost in a maze.

See also barn dance; farandole; maypole dance; polonaise; stomp dance.

Sources: Greene, Thomas M. "Labyrinth Dances in the French and English Renaissance." *Renaissance Quarterly* 54, no. 4.2 (Winter 2001): 1403–66. MacQueen, Gailand. *The Spirituality of Mazes and Labyrinths.* Kelowna, BC: Wood Lake Books, 2005.

LAMENTATION DANCE

Dances that lament unimaginable loss attest to the natural role of folk dance at pivotal moments in human fortune, as demonstrated by the dance dramas that mourners among the Gamberma of northern Togo and Benin perform for deceased elders, the Valencian *vetlatori* presented during mourning for a deceased infant, and the *moirologia* (mourning) that the encircling Byzantine laity presented in the church narthex at funerals. In Central Africa, the metempsychosis of the Angoni and Achewa dance aided the deceased to take the shape of a totemic animal. For the living, the Bechuana of South Africa arranged a monotone chant, crossed arms, and danced for orphans. The Bwiti of Gabon applied footwork to mourning, hexes, and healing. In West Africa, Yoruba mourners cared for a grieving family by sending a masked dancer to enact the meeting of the deceased with beloved ancestors.

Visceral acknowledgment of deep grief stands apart from a holiday spirit for its kinetic expression beyond the reach of keening and tears, as with the ring dance to repetitions of "*dan*" in Oman and "*ouf*" in Syria, the Druze dirge performance in Lebanon, and the West Sumatran *tari ilau* of grieving females. Through circumambulation of a fire pit, cairn, or altar, the grieving reconnect with infinity and the certainty of death, a philosophy of Gilbert Islanders and New Guineans and of Greeks in Homer's *Iliad* (800 BCE). In Mali, the Dogon orchestrate ceremonial masking of a secret brotherhood, which escorts the departed spirit into the afterlife with ritual and dance.

Prehistoric Mourning

In prehistoric Egypt, burial ritual swept the cemetery of evil spirits in the style of the god Bes, a protective deity over babies and women in childbirth. To honor a departed spirit, females processed at funerals and flourished palm branches before the tomb. While women clapped, men wearing tall caps woven of rushes stepped forward at a dignified pace. During the Middle Kingdom after 2000 BCE, dwarves performed gestures of grief in the funeral cortege, such as the dancers depicted on murals at the cemetery of Beni Hasan in Middle Egypt for princes Baqet III and his son Khety.

As a dance genre, lamentation has its roots in Egyptian liturgy and Hebrew scripture. It began after 1543 BCE with the mystic Egyptian dance of lamentation performed to Isis and Nephthys, complementary deities of the throne and housewifery. To plucks on the harp, the sister goddesses mourned the murder of their father/brother Osiris. For David, the founder of the Hebrew nation in the eighth century BCE, loss and death confirmed for Israelites the purpose of divine love. In Psalm 30, the shepherd poet rejoiced that a fearful and isolating turn of events revived choreography exalting a trust in Yahweh's grace to all humankind.

In Judges 11, Jephthah, the eighth-century BCE judge and war general of Israelites who lived at Tob east of Gilead and southeast of the Sea of Galilee, rashly pledged to burn on the sacrificial altar the first person who emerged from his house when he returned from a military victory over Ammon, a kingdom east of the Jordan River. Because Jephthah's unidentified daughter—and only child—emerged first from the front door, he carried out his oath. The results, similar in tone to the Achaean general

Agamemnon's sacrifice of Iphigenia at Aulis to gain fair winds before sailing to Troy, elicited a lamentation dance for the doomed girl.

During eight weeks' grace, Jephthah's little girl walked the highlands and wept for her womanhood, a pilgrimage that set the tone of a subsequent honorary choreography for all sacrificed maidens. In her honor, in Judges 11, Hebrew women observed an annual lamentation dance extending over four days. A grievous parable, the pattern story of the sacrificial virgin left generations of Old Testament and *Iliad* readers to account for so barbarous a slaughter of innocence.

Commemorating Loss

The motivation of the ancient mourning dance is unforeseeable suffering, the theme of the moralist Jeremiah's prophecy around 590 BCE. As recorded in chapter 31, he foresaw a liturgy of weeping and timbrel and flute playing upon Judah's exile, a deportation of 4,600 Hebrews to Babylon ordered by Nebuchadnezzar II in 589 BCE. The prophet's image of mortal grief incorporated the stereotypical sobbing woman, the progenitor of stirring restoration dance worldwide. Jeremiah predicted that a reversal of fortune would generate a triumphal gala to welcome the Hebrew repatriation to Israel, which came true a half century later in 539 BCE.

Egyptian sorrow dance foregrounded a Sudanese circle cortege of the Makaraka tribe repeated three times a day for three days after a funeral. The Anlo-Ewe of southeastern Ghana acted out sorrow with the *atsia-husago*, a lamentation for freedom fighters and deceased priests and priestesses. To drum accompaniment, troupes mimed the glories of the brave and regretted the loss of valiant heroes in the times to come. Among the Polynesians of the Gilbert Islands, dancing at funerals extended over eight days. During washing, oiling, and drying of corpses in the sun, mourners danced to anthems and chants and decked the remains in garlands.

Sorrow dances typically evolved from ineluctable fate, such as presentation of the all-female *caracolu* at an unexpected death in Corsica and Sardinia, the mourning *jota* for a Spanish child in the coastal town of Alicante, and the Tibetan and Bhutanese dance of many *raksa*, a festival commemorating the judgment of souls. Worldwide, ritual dance manifested the anxieties common to the perilous and poorly paid work of soldiers, miners, and sea folk. The fearful jobs of Middle Eastern fishers and pearl divers in dhows on the Arabian Gulf precipitated group solace among mothers, sisters, wives, and daughters. While singing mournful lyrics to the raksa circle dance, Arab females chanted to the almighty about the natural mortal cycle of giving and taking lives. Recalling absent males, the women formed parallel lines and danced the *murdah* with tiny advances and retreats.

In response to suffering, other peoples gravitated toward dance as the customary reaction to pain and heartache, as with a curative tarantella in southern Italy, the Aragonese *jota* at Christian vigils, and the mourning *cèilidh* or wake held all night at Croy, Scotland, in 1748. The *kolyacha* in India separated the genders, with fishermen pretending to row out to deep water and women fluttering handkerchiefs in gestures of parting and good fortune. Out of honor and affection for the dead, Muslims in India held a feast and dance. In central Australia, the Arunta burned the belongings and home of the deceased and danced and stamped around the embers to force the soul into the next world.

Diasporic Liturgy

The New World generated its own bereavement songs and dances, notably the funeral ritual of the Cree of the Canadian prairies and the graveside dancing of the galop by the Conibo of eastern Peru, the Arawak of Guiana, the Tarahumara of central Mexico, and the Osage of the pre-Columbian Mississippi Valley. On Futuna Island after 1841, dancers experienced penitence for the martyrdom of Father Peter Chanel. From the 1770s into the late 1800s, uncertainty in a new sect on the frontier precipitated the mournful chant of hymns accompanying American Shaker dances. At Watervliet, New York, and eight satellite compounds in the Midwest, dancers memorialized apprehension with circle and line dances to the hymn "Whither, O Whither on Earth Can I Roam?"

As a result of diaspora, sorrow expressed disconnection from the folk past, both memory and kinetic experience. Regret and yearning generated the elegiac ring and partnering choreography of the Irish lamentation dance imported by settlers of the Appalachian Mountains. Richard Henry Dana's *Two Years before the Mast* (1842) recorded a surprising scheduling of the fandango in California at a child's funeral in Monterey, then in Mexican possession. Within four years, the area passed to US ownership, another uprooting mourned in hymns and the *canción ranchera*, a string and accordion melody for waltzing.

In 1835, American portrait and sketch artist George Catlin captured for posterity the brave's medicine bag dance of the Fox and Sauk, a combination grief ritual, triumphant parade, and comfort to a war widow. To honor a dead brave who fell in battle during a great victory, his comrades performed an hour-long ritual in front of his family's tepee. For fifteen days, the lamentation dance assuaged the grieving wife and children while fellow braves brandished enemy scalps recalling the warrior's fortitude in combat. The commemoration of wartime courage and sacrifice concluded with gifts tossed to the bereft family to maintain their food stores.

Mortality Rituals

To solace Indian press gangs at silver mines in Potosí, Bolivia, and Quiruvilca, Peru, Catholic brotherhoods promoted spiritual dances to mournful melodies and hymns. For miners who risked accidents and malnutrition in the Andean colonies, story dance and mime exhilarated spirits from the everyday overwork and despair by means of folk music instantly retrievable whenever needed. At priestly ceremonies in Arequipa, *curanderos* (healers) comforted forced laborers through the Afro-Peruvian *alcatraz* (fire dance), a cosmic performance with lighted candles. Lifted feet and rotating hips turned hopelessness into a reclamation of libido and joy.

From October 31 to November 2, the Mexican and Filipino Día de los Muertos (Day of the Dead), a holiday listed by UNESCO as an Intangible Cultural Heritage, coincides with Halloween, All Saints' Day, and All Souls' Day. Based on an Aztec cult of deceased ancestors from 1000 BCE, the Mesoamerican skull festival coordinated the cleaning of grave markers and adorning graveyards with fruit and marigolds. Folk processions and zapateado performances featured traditional Amerindian feather headdresses and disguises of dancers as tricksters, skeletons, and demons.

The shaking of rattles and clackers and the stitching of shells on ghost costumes raised a clatter intended to awaken dead souls. The merrymaking incorporated Hispanic communities worldwide, including Ecuador, Bolivia, Guatemala, Texas, California, Arizona, Czechoslovakia, Italy, and New Zealand. The Day of the Dead echoed Korean ancestral ritual and the stick dancing of cultists in Nepal. Around 1850, a priest to the Guiana parish, Charles Daniel Dance, compiled *Recollections of Four Years in Venezuela* (1876) in which he marveled at the jig that a heartbroken mother performed around the corpse of her dead child. In the 1950s, the creation of the limbo added group competition to wakes in Trinidad and Tobago. Participants mimed the crouching of slaves whom ships' crews forced into the hold for the journey across the middle passage to New World slave pens.

Into the twenty-first century, a New Orleans custom, reverence to the dead with a jazz funeral parade and marching band, highlights a come-one, come-all street dance. In slow processional steps, mourners sashay to a step-close rhythm while flaunting straw hats and umbrellas to the sober hymn "Just a Closer Walk with Thee." As grief gives way to joy with trumpet riffs and drumming to "When the Saints Go Marching In," the retinue quickens struts, blows whistles, and individualizes arm gestures to display festive funeral garb and fringed sashes.

See also allemande; censorship; corroboree; Eskimo dance house; exorcism; fandango; film, folk dance in; galop; jig; *jota*; lion dance; nudity; Polynesian dance; processionals; sacrificial dance; Shaker dance; tarantella; *Totentanz*; zapateado.

Source: Woodman, Ross Greig, and Joel Faflak. *Sanity, Madness, Transformation: The Psyche in Romanticism.* Toronto: University of Toronto Press, 2005.

LÄNDLER

A hopping, skipping, turning love dance in open position, the *Ländler* (also *Laendler, Landler, Schleifer,* or Tyrolese) raised controversy for allowing men and women to snuggle bodies during two-handed turns. In Alpine Austria, Bavaria, Bohemia, Styria, and the Ziller Valley in the Tyrol, after 1690, the style retained the charm of a village wooing ritual dating before 1023. Fiddle and Alpine horn iterated the pastoral origins and accompanied the yodeling arpeggios from Landel in the Ens Valley of upper Austria.

The dance name indicates "country-like," an evocative metaphor recalling lederhosen, aprons over dirndl skirts, and hobnail shoes and boots striking rough-hewn wood floors. Gendered motifs retained the finale of Tyrolean shoe clapping, a rowdy folk style adapted from Bavarian cockfighting of black grouse. In the coda, the hen appeased the virtuoso rooster with feminine wiles.

According to agrarian legends about the Ländler and other German dances, by tossing the woman high above the floor in rapid turns, each man set a standard for a rich harvest of tall grain. Because the acrobatic gesture exposed female legs, moralists at Ulm southeast of Stuttgart banned the Ländler in 1404 and forced dancers to move in single file. During the Protestant Reformation after 1517, a censorious German pastor at Schellenwalde targeted the Ländler as an invitation to lewdness and lust. The Austrian folk choreography passed to upper-class patrons of Astor House in Bremen and, after 1637, to European royalty at the courts of Ferdinand III of Hungary and Croatia, Charles VI of Prussia, and Leopold I of Belgium.

Ländler Style

Integral to the Ländler figures lay the robust peasant custom of gripping the woman about the waist during spins around a large perimeter while she held her partner's shoulders. One rationale for intimate contact and deep gazing into the partner's eyes resided in the man's fear of a woman's tripping on long skirts from excessive spinning or fainting from disorientation or vertigo. These two reasons prefaced the banning of the Ländler in Bohemia on March 18, 1785, and the more strenuous *Langaus* in Vienna in 1791. Whatever the justification for the repeated embraces, the Ländler shocked refined urbanites, causing mothers to forbid their daughters to participate in an unseemly dance that involved a man's hands on the woman's midriff.

The Austro-German Ländler gained fans among folk youth for back-to-back courtship figures to triple meter, a personalized facet it shared with the French allemande and *volta*, German *Dreher* and *Weller*, Norwegian *halling*, Basque *arresku*, and Ukrainian *hopak*. As emigrants fostered the ebullient contradance in Hungary, Switzerland, Slovenia, and the Ukraine, skilled performers adapted the original turns with a gliding execution and increased speed on a par with the erotic *Deutscher Walzer*, a forerunner of the Viennese waltz. Individual dancers enacted solo sets before joining their partners to repeat the initial figure.

Mutating Customs

In the 1790s, music historians declared the Ländler a precursor of the waltz and a cousin of the wooing and acrobatic lifts of the *Schuhplattler*. The swaying motif influenced opening strains of Ludwig van Beethoven's *Eroica* (1804), a salute to Napoleon. At the Duchess of Richmond's ball at a coach house in Brussels, the dance brought couples to the floor on June 15, 1815. Amid polite socializing, princes, countesses, barons, and generals anticipated an invasion of Napoleon's forces, which ensued three days later at the Battle of Waterloo.

Austro-German spinning dance predisposed the compositions of the great baroque composers toward folk motifs. In 1824, the string quartet of Johann Strauss I fostered the Ländler at dances in taverns near the Danube River. Melodies for the Ländler by George Frideric Handel, Wolfgang Amadeus Mozart, Franz Schubert, and Johann Strauss II stimulated passion for the dance among Swiss peasants into the late 1800s.

In Munich dance halls in 1870, peasant instrumentalist Johann Petzmayer introduced Ländler tunes on the zither. During the decline of the courtly minuet and the rise of European nationalism in urbanized Vienna, aficionados of social dance promoted the waltz as more relevant. With its spinning disconnect from agrarian folk arts, the waltz rose above the bucolic Ländler in tone and sophistication.

See also allemande; contradance; *hopak*; *Schuhplattler*.

Sources: Grove, George, ed. *A Dictionary of Music and Musicians (A.D. 1450–1889)*. London: Macmillan, 1889. Mirka, Danuta. *The Oxford Handbook of Topic Theory*. Oxford, UK: Oxford University Press, 2014.

LINE DANCE

An inclusive celebration, recreation, or amusement, line dance orders participants separately in a row without regard to age or gender, a mode illustrated on Maui with Mexican *paniolo* (cowboy) dances and in 2007 by dancing to "You Can't Stop the Beat" in the film *Hairspray*. The linear mode shaped the hula in Hawaii, English morris dancing, and the movements and rhythms at Tewa Pueblo dances satirizing the Navajo of Arizona and New Mexico. Within Zulu villages outside of Mombasa, Kenya, the *ngoma* acknowledged nuptials and circumcisions with male line dance affirming masculine values and behavior. The Mbende of Zimbabwe broke from a straight line into individualized hip swinging and acrobatics for the *jerusarema*, a mimetic fertility dance.

Globally, line dance coordinates geometric rows in community galas, a facet of Bora choreography in the Amazonian rainforest, Guaraní men's dance to interlocking handholds in parts of Bolivia and Uruguay, and the Balkan *kolo* at hemp harvests. Bouncy, springy hops and kicks marked the French gavotte and the Galician *muñeires*, a variant of the Irish jig. At Skopje, Macedonia, Roma line dance headed by a leader generated exuberance at weddings and migrated with individuals resettling in Toronto. Males used the occasions as opportunities to invent virtuoso crouch-and-leap figures.

Regimented Dance

Linear formation supports groups visualizing a unified belief or theme. From Phoenicia or Canaan in the second millennium BCE, Turks, Palestinians, and Jordanians synchronized a *dabke* line to kick and stomp their ethnic oneness. The form influenced Jews to syncretize lines with their chain dances and women's solos. Seagoing families on the Arabian Gulf performed the *murdah*, an all-female line dance bewailing the perils their men faced while fishing and pearl diving. At Bahrain, Qatar, Oman, and the United Arab Emirates, the facing lines chanted lamentations acknowledging the possibility of death at sea.

Line dance inspired singing, instructional, and counting games for children and courtship rituals for teens. The creation of the *yang ge* during the Song Dynasty after 960 grouped maidens in a column for gesturing with handkerchiefs, which they tossed toward likely mates. Occasions for the yang ge ranged from a harvest thanksgiving and autumnal equinox at the Fall Moon Festival in China and Vietnam to folk socials in Chinatowns around the world.

In France, Belgium, and England, the *Carillon de Dunkerque* (Chimes of Dunkirk) welcomed young and old to a called set of clapping, stomping, and sashaying reminiscent of square dancing. Originally a peasant quadrille or contradance, from 1437 the Carillon developed into a line dance inviting any number of couples to join in the mimicry of bell ringing. The coordinated sets served physical education classes and the teaching of the deaf as models of playground rhythms and instruction in following directions. As a heritage dance, the lyrics and figures preserved an element of communal life—the assembling of parishioners for events and worship via village church bells. The grand round equalized dancers with repeated rearrangements of participants.

Emblematic Steps

North American folk artists adapted line dance to a variety of themes and symbols, for example, the left-right gyrations of the Brazilian *alagoas* and the *batuque*, an ancient Cape Verde fertility ritual honoring brides. Back-and-forth steps energized the conga in southern Brazil, Paraguay, and Argentina. For the Northern Ute on the Colorado Plateau, the iron line dance moved via the swaying cross-front-cross-back (grapevine step), which imitated motions of the sun. On Southern plantations, slaves arranged themselves at harvest time for a chalk line dance, a disjointed array of reapers clapping and swaying to a banjo strum.

In west central China in the 2010s, educators at universities in Qinghai proposed introducing line dancing to class kinetics. For elementary school students, mastery of figures imparted awareness of the difference between a leader or caller and an independent performer, a concept of "Simon Says" routines and "This Old Man" mime. Into the present, the use of parallel rows enables fitness therapists to treat the elderly and victims of Parkinson's disease with pleasurable exercise.

See also Balkan dance; chain dance; contradance; gavotte; harvest dance; Jewish dance; jig; lamentation dance; mime; quadrille.

Source: Koskoff, Ellen, ed. *The Concise Garland Encyclopedia of World Music.* New York: Routledge, 2008.

LION DANCE

For their strength and grace, large felines—leopards, tigers, jaguars, cheetahs, cougars—influence secular and religious beast dances around the world. Before the arrival of Hindu missionaries in the first century CE, Indonesians on Bintan Island and in Gianyar, Bali, masked themselves as animals and performed a thanksgiving *barongan* (story dance) about a mythic white lion, portrayed by two dancers to a percussion orchestra. In the allegorical battle between good and evil, the lion represented beneficence by preventing the evil queen Rangda from devouring children.

The Ibo (or Igbo) of northern Nigeria scheduled their lion choreography for Christian holidays. Around 948, troupes cloaked their identities in shapeless suits rustling with seed pods and brass bells for presentations of the *agaba* (lion dance) to drumming. A traditional processional held at Christmas and Easter, the agaba performance starred a soloist clad in black and disguised with a carved mask. The improvisational steps of the masquerade projected the masculinity and power of the secret agaba cult, a holdover from indigenous West African warrior militias.

In China and Southeast Asia as well as Taiwan, Hong Kong, Malaysia, Singapore, Tibet, Sikkim, and Okinawa, the two-person lion dance ushers in the New Year with the closing Lantern Festival. Dancers in the lion's head and fabric body process to a Confucian or Taoist altar to the accompaniment of cymbals, gongs, and drums. The dotting of the lion features with cinnabar brings the figure to life to shield peasants from harm. As the animistic image gains vitality, it spreads green vegetables among spectators and awakens spirits of good fortune.

Adapted Folk Arts

Because China lacks predatory felines, bestial choreography, formed of martial arts poses and stylized figures, took shape during the Han Dynasty after 206 BCE to emulate the Persian concept of lions. During the Tang Dynasty after 618 CE, a variant lion art form coordinated the moves of five ten-foot-tall beasts of contrasting colors and ten attendants who led the lions on ropes and ribbons. For drama, custom-made wood lion heads and silk tails began and ended fuzzy torsos. By fitting the head with gilt eyes and silver teeth, costumers enhanced the dazzle of movable eyelids, ears, and tail and flexible jaws that snatched offerings of green vegetables, symbols of prosperity.

When the lion dance reached Japan, Buddhists supplied flute, shamisen, and taiko drum music and added horns to the costume. Performers adapted the mythic steps and occasion to Buddha's May 14 birthday as well as New Year's Day and Shinto commemorations. A festival favorite in the Song Dynasty, the lion dance reached Japan in the 700s. The Korean version, received from China in the Goryeo period after 918, directed a comic lion from house to house during the lunar New Year to exorcise sickness and ill fortune with its stunts.

The History of Lion Dance

More lion companies marked China's development of folk arts. During the Ming Dynasty after 960, a hybrid lion performance in Guangzhou grew out of tales about the monster Nian, which allegedly arose from the sea or the mountains each spring to gobble up children and devour crops before harvest. Folk participants warded off the attack by throwing firecrackers at the dance company. The northern lion tradition choreographed playful steps and acrobatics on platforms and capers on a high wire.

The funeral dance of the white lion, Ma Chao, presented a vengeful story and a lamentation for the father and brother executed by the emperor of Wei after 336 CE. During an excursion to Japan in October 1912 on the ocean liner *Manchuria*, crew entertained passengers with a lion dance. When native mimes presented the mummery at the International Exposition in San Francisco in 1915, the footwork amazed the crowds. The southern lion, decked in a papier-mâché head shaped over bamboo, cavorted to drumming to salute Sun Yat-Sen in 1921 upon his investiture at Guangzhou.

In the past half century, for performances at weddings and grand openings of businesses and in gym classes in Taiwan, a family of lion characters joined the traditional Chinese dance, ranging from a male and female couple to a lion cub. At a series of Chinatowns in Oceania, Europe, and Africa and in the Americas in Ontario, California, Texas, New York, Georgia, and Hawaii, each bore color coding to indicate age, rank, and symbolic meaning to spectators. In Malaysia in 1974, a lion performance saluted Prime Minister Abdul Razak Hussein upon his state visit to China and launched a plea from peasants for adding the dance to Malaysian culture. At Publai in 1987, government sponsorship recruited Malaysian youths to learn the lion's mime and steps that characterized their Chinese roots.

See also animal dances; comic dance; film, folk dance in; lamentation dance.

Source: Carstens, Sharon A. *Histories, Cultures, Identities: Studies in Malaysian Chinese Worlds*. Singapore: Singapore University Press, 2005.

LITERATURE, FOLK DANCE IN

Folk arts permeate each other with a single-mindedness expressive of peasant aims and the self-deceptions of the gentry, for example, maidens seeking dance partners in the Finnish *Kalevala* (1835) and the caste struggles in the plays and stories of Anton Chekhov and Nikolai Gogol. The social consequences of public folk performances created surprise at a funeral fandango in Monterey, California, in Richard Henry Dana's *Two Years before the Mast* (1842) and ominous overtones from the tarantella in Henrik Ibsen's *Hedda Gabler* (1890). Modes of performance generated speculation about immigrant morals in Willa Cather's *My Antonia* (1918), reactions to chain dancing in Jens Pauli Heinesen's Danish short stories from the 1970s, and unsettling reflections over the entrancing seduction dance in Senegalese author Mariama Bâ's feminist novel *So Long a Letter* (1980).

Griots, gleemen, storytellers, balladeers, and minstrels mastered a gamut of folk arts for entertaining banqueters and communities. Outstanding examples range from the Navajo narrators of the North American Four Corners and Tusitala (the name Robert Louis Stevenson adopted when he lived among Samoans) to the graybeard bards aboard Scandinavian whaling vessels and Scots-Irish *cèilidhs*. By alternating narrative and verse with repetitive dance rhythms, the performer rested his voice while giving listeners an opportunity to flex stiff joints and respond to the narrative.

Folk galas permeated global groups with a natural amalgam in medieval village dance plays about the heroine Ashima at Yunnan, China, where Sani residents joined a line dance to clapping and the sound of a flute. The water-pumping songs and harvest rituals of sixth-century Malayalam *kathakali* coalesced into a classical dance drama suite performed at Kerala in southern India. A more demanding jack-of-all-trades, the storyteller, puppeteer, singer, and dancer of Tamil Nadu *theru koothu* entranced shoppers in southeastern India with marketplace story dance from the Hindu epics, the Mahabharata (400 BCE) and Ramayana (300 BCE).

Extemporaneous Arts

Spontaneous singing of folk songs and a priest's recitation of local history and narrative verse formed a grab bag theatrical at Indian temples. Similarly unstructured, the *bhavai* folk theater from 1360 featured satire, puns, witty repartee, parables, and peasant dance intended to educate North Gujarati commoners about their ethnic ancestry. In northwestern China, the nomadic Tu (or Monguor) minority listened to legends, enacted rice god ritual, and joined the *anzhao* masked circle dance while waving incense in a boisterous procession stretching from 3:00 PM until after midnight.

In south central Asia, art forms blended seamlessly like stew. Nepali actor-dancers standardized sixteen gestures to present the legend of King Jai Singh and Queen Hemaiti, a prevalent theme in central Asian verse and drama from the mid-1600s. Manipuri writings featured Marathi plays of the 1840s based on social conditions in Hindu villages and on folk festivities from Uttar Pradesh in northeastern India and along the Burmese border. Late in the 1800s and the early 1900s, Bengali and Kashmiri dramatists incorporated Perso-Arabic folk dance from Sanskrit sources into theatrics.

Children's hero legends, beast tales, and episodic adventures typically intersperse the oral tradition of singing games, counting rhymes, and riddles with dancing, a pervasive scenario in Jamaican Anansi, the spider trickster lore, and the frontier family party in Laura Ingalls Wilder's *Little House in the Big Woods* (1932), set near Pepin, Wisconsin. From antiquity, Aesop's fables from 600 BCE equate dance with deception, as with the foolish capering that leads to downfall in "The Fox and the Monkey" and pursuit in "The Wolf and the Kid." Another animal parable juxtaposes folly with death in the mesmerizing four-legged whirling that precedes predation in "The Fox and the Pheasants." In a classic English fantasy, the spontaneous lobster quadrille in Lewis Carroll's *Alice in Wonderland* (1865) describes the partnering of Alice and the Mock Turtle in two lines and the advancing and retiring in a structured set that concludes with somersaults and antics, with occluded mention of lobster as a dinner entree. In 1972, English fabulist Richard Adams incorporated into the epic *Watership Down* the innocent moonlit galas of rabbits. The carefree mating, grazing, storytelling, and frolicking captured the optimism of naive animals beset by human and animal foes.

Literary Dances

Within European literature, dance is both performance and kinetic trope for authors in the rank of epic writers Miguel de Cervantes and John Milton, novelists Maria Edgeworth and Gustave Flaubert, storyteller Rudyard Kipling, and poets George Gordon Byron, Edith Sitwell, and William Butler Yeats. In William Shakespeare's comedy *Much Ado about Nothing* (1599), Beatrice, the protagonist, cited the Scots jig as a metaphor for hot, precipitate wooing that follows no floor pattern. In her comparison, the jig prefaces a more modest ancestral wedding dance, which visualizes the dignity of a traditional nuptial. The playwright concluded the trio of dances with a *cinquepace* or galliard, the quick, syncopated leaping that trips the rueful lover and sends him to his death.

With similar one-to-one ratio, William Wycherley marked his restoration play *The Country Wife* (1675) with descriptions of the cotillion, a French craze based on the eight-person square that emulates seventeenth-century baroque social norms. Poet Alexander Pope took up the contrast between peasant and social dance in *Essay on Criticism* (1711), in which he likened folk performances to the natural appeal of wit, a fluent extemporaneous expression, unadorned and unforced. For the main character of Johann von Goethe's *The Sorrows of Young Werther* (1774), the rhapsodic waltz enabled the male dancer to immerse himself in the beauty and grace of his partner.

During the romantic era, peasant choreography marked impromptu gatherings with fun and camaraderie. Into the lifestyles of commoners, Sir Walter Scott's historical novels wove folk steps, such as the sword dance in *The Pirate* (1831) and the Scots *branle*, as with the memories of Queen Mary's lady-in-waiting of a wedding masque in *The Abbot* (1820). To enact a caste schism, in an era of Gallic ballroom dancing, social novelist Jane Austen applied folk dance to the condescension of Lord Darcy in *Pride and Prejudice* (1813), in which he scorns the Scots reel as countrified and its devotees as homespun rubes. In 1846, Danish playwright Fredrik August Dahlgren joined composer Andreas Randel in adding the earthy Nordic *polska* to *Wärmlänningarne* (The people of Varmland), source of one of Sweden's early sound films. The variant from the parish of Jösse highlights the athleticism of a young male who poses in closed position before raising his feet to tap the ceiling.

Author George Eliot set dance amid character action as proof of faults and weaknesses. In the allegorical novel *Silas Marner* (1861), the exhibitionist hornpipe, jigs, fiddling, and hand clasping at Squire Cass's New Year's Eve party fail to lighten Godfrey's mood until he ventures out in the snow in his dancing slippers. The liberation he receives through the death of his laudanum-addled wife, Molly Farren, returns him to the dance floor to partner with the genteel Nancy Lammeter and propose marriage despite his abandonment of his only child, the as-yet-unnamed Hepzibah "Eppie" Marner. The dance symbolism depicts Godfrey as ostensibly shriven for his sin of marrying in secret and neglecting his first family.

In the tragic lines of the narrative vignette *The Spanish Gypsy* (1868), Eliot again juxtaposes innocence and lust by dramatizing an Andalusian rhythm as an unknown quality in Lady Fedalma. Imbued with the same sexual need that once gripped Godfrey Cass, Fedalma performs a carnal figure to the tambourine among Roma peasants in the streets of Bedmar, Spain. The fervor recalls the emotive Gypsy sword dance that enraptured Gringoire in Victor Hugo's *Notre Dame de Paris* (*The Hunchback of Notre Dame*, 1831).

Social novelist Thomas Hardy, himself a rural fiddler, stands out as a backcountry amateur reared in traditional Dorset jigs and reels and educated in string tunes immortalized by three generations of musicians. In *Under the Greenwood Tree* (1871), he orchestrates a three-couple dance at a Yule house party, concluding at midnight. At the festivities, a rivalry for Fancy Day, a pretty guest, sets the handsome Dick Dewey against Mr. Shinar during the swing, hands across, six-hands-round, and promenade up the middle. Within the courtesies of a peasant figure, the face-off concludes when the dance requires the two simmering males to join hands in an arch for Fancy to sashay under as though oblivious to the man-to-man duel for her favors.

For the medieval Norwegian folk at Jørundgaard in Sigrid Undset's three-part saga *Kristin Lavransdatter* (1919), an impromptu musicale and dance mobilizes young people and even convent maidens on vigil nights for a frolic to ballads and fiddle tunes. Assembled on the church green, the company demonstrates the spontaneous enjoyments of a close community. A reference to Lavrans's hospitality on St. John's Day pictures the householder leaping into the post-Yule dance and the poor accepting ale at a hearthside feast and joining in storytelling and an evening caper in the estate courtyard. Insidious discussions of propriety intertwine Erland's invitations to Kristin to dance and his advances in the dark corners of the dance floor, a contrast to the honest open-air steps to the music.

See also branle; *cèilidh*; cotillion; hornpipe; jig; Manipuri dance; morris dance; *polska*; reel; scripture, folk dance in; sword dance.

Source: Marcsek-Fuchs, Maria. *Dance and British Literature: An Intermedial Encounter.* Leiden: Brill Rodopi, 2015.

· *M* ·

MALAY DANCE

Indigenous and imported Malay dances anchor agrarian customs in Sumatra, the Malay Peninsula, Singapore, the Riau Archipelago, and Borneo. Contrasting types include the *saba*, a song-and-dance routine honoring the spirit of the coconut palm, and the miming of hoeing, reaping, and carrying rice in baskets, facets of the *balai*. From prehistory, dancers received outside influence, particularly Arab and Indian males performing the *hadrah*, a partnered choreography to drumming that limits performance to men and transvestites. Another mimetic men's dance, the *ayam didik*, imitated rooster struts and feints during cock fighting.

Early Malay dance emerged from folkways. For the shore villagers of Kedah, the *cinta sayang* bid farewell and blessing on family and friends departing by sea. Executed by men and women, the dance united locals in supporting mariner clans. For land-based dancers at Minang, the *endang* preserved farming costumes and kerchiefs for a tambourine dance mimicking field labor. Workers sat in a line while pretending to pluck tea leaves and mop their brows.

Malay artistry evolved the *asli* and *inang*. The asli acquired standardized grace, flow, and beat in the 1300s, when presentations featured females dancing to the tap of a gong. The slow postures interpreted emotional verse typifying romance, yearning, or grief. Instrumentation gradually added hand drums, violin, and accordion. An offshoot of court protocol, the inang, named for the royal nanny, began during the Malaccan sultanate and gained popularity after 1488 in the reign of Sultan Mahmud Shah. At nuptials, modest females swayed to a brisk meter. When the steps passed to the peasantry, men and women joined in separately and as couples.

Fusion Dance

In the early 1400s, Arab and Persian merchants and Muslim missionaries from Yemen introduced Malay men from Pahang, Johor, and Selangor to the *zapin*, a dignified presentation that opened on an acknowledgment of spectators. At first limited to palace audiences before the sultan, the richly interactive steps forward, backward, and diagonally followed the beat of bongo, hand drum, lute, and accordion. The choreography followed a strict pattern of paired dancers that included sudden torso rotations and concluded with a reverence.

Early in the 1500s, Portuguese shippers at Malacca introduced the *joget*. Derived from the Iberian *branjo* and *farapeirra*, the dance spread throughout Malaysia, Sumatra, Borneo, and the Riau Archipelago. A rapid, upbeat choreography coordinating hands and feet to the Portuguese tambour and harmonium, the joget dominated social functions and galas. In northern Sumatra in 1934, the joget became Indonesia's national dance after the choreographer Sayuti turned the folk dance into story dance featuring twelve levels of wooing from meeting to marriage. The couples increased touching of foot to foot to heightened drumming.

See also animal dances; comic dance; harvest dance; story dance; warrior dance.

Source: Yousof, Ghulam-Sarwar. *The Encyclopedia of Malaysia: Performing Arts*. Singapore: Archipelago Press, 2004.

MANIPURI DANCE

An ancient indigenous folk art form from Uttar Pradesh in northeastern India and along the Burmese border, Manipuri dance reflected the oral tradition and artistry of a diverse culture. The libretto derived from Hindu scripture, the *Bhāgavata Purāna* (Tales of the Supreme Lord, ca. 3000 BCE), written by Vyasa of Tanahun, Nepal. To revere the divine Hindu couple Krishna and Radha, female performers and one male representing the supreme god presented a modest devotional composed of soft steps, gracious gestures, and subtle facial expressions.

From 154 CE, the dance incorporated pliant choreography to percussion on the double-headed neat-skin drum and cymbals, the innovation of King Khuiyoi Tompok. Around 1400, the Manipuri dance exhibited the personal attachment of a devotee to the gods and served as the foundation of the dramatic *kathak*, another classic Indian dance. To maintain an air of modesty, dancers performed in glittering tunics over long skirts. All aristocratic girls learned the steps as elements of royal dignity before public spectators.

During hostilities with the Burmese in 1759, Maharaja Bhagya Chandra, a deeply religious monarch, standardized lavish Manipuri choreography, which dancers presented in a temple courtyard, annex, holy lodge, garden, or private home. After experiencing a vision of Krishna, the maharaja raised a shrine at Kaina Hill and began compiling music and making costumes to the god's specifications. With the aid of theologians and scholars, on November 23, 1779, Bhagya Chandra initiated the *Rasa lila* (or *Ras lila*, sweet act), a dance honoring the full moon with the dance of Radha and her ladies-in-waiting. According to mystic instructions, the maharaja based the lunar dance drama on a scriptural story of the supreme god, his consort, and her six handmaidens and their gambols south of central Nepal. For the part of Radha, Bhagya Chandra chose his eight-year-old daughter, Bimbavati. He set himself among the musicians as a drummer for the initial five-day performance.

Manipuri dance projected religiosity through body postures and moved the little princess so deeply that she devoted her life to Krishna. To spread regional culture, female royalty patronized stagings of the Rasa lila. Women at court took roles in the dance troupe for each presentation, whether in Assam in northeastern India or as far toward the Bay of Bengal as coastal Calcutta. Each performance lasted 150 minutes and consisted of standardized steps and extensive mimicry of romantic attraction.

Divine Merrymaking

In contrast to lascivious dances of the material world, Manipuri dance described an innocent nighttime caper of six milkmaids who slipped away from the Yamuna River to the forest under a full moon in spring to dance to the ecstatic music of Krishna's enchanted flute. In a sacred grove, the company of maidens carried the star actors to their thrones and reverenced them as though they were gods. Holding sticks, the women performed the dance tableau to lyric songs played on sitar and drum and sung in Hindi, the regional language and source of classical literature. As they danced, their eyes followed the tips of their fingers.

Womanly postures stressed poise and obeisance to the divine couple. The milkmaids executed a circle dance with lighted lamps on trays. The divine couple joined the maids in conjugal love play devoid of lust or coercion. The tempo doubled, concluding with maidenly pirouettes and obeisance to Krishna and Radha. Krishna kept the meter with his feet and leaped before his beloved. The maids linked arms and danced in pairs.

Manipuri dance featured a moving finale. At a dramatic moment, Krishna somersaulted before Radha. He knelt and mimed his love with hand and head gestures before executing the peacock dance on his knees. More singing and dancing involved duets and group hymns by the milkmaids. According to myth, the god honored his love for Radha by extending the night to 4.32 billion years.

Ecstatic Dance

For the dreamy lunar spectacle, the audience removed their shoes, sat on the ground, and avoided talking or smoking, two misbehaviors forbidden by swami ushers. Attendees sang along and clapped, swayed, and wept. Interpreting the dance as faith in action, worshippers sank into ecstasy and transcendent happiness. In bliss, they crept forward, prostrated themselves, and touched the bare feet of the lead dancers, to whom they offered coins.

Manipuri dance impressed the poet Rabindranath Tagore, winner of the 1913 Nobel Prize for literature. In November 1919, he brought Manipuri companies to western Bengal. In addition to creating a dance department at his university, he added the flute and stringed instruments to the accompaniment of the Rasa lila. Seven years later, Naba Kumar joined Tagore's experimental school and taught the curving limb, shoulder, and head movements and exaggerated finger posturing to students of dance drama. Manipuri dance developed into a global folk tableau popular in many nations.

See also circle dance; drumming; *kathak*; worship dance.

Source: Sanajaoba, Naorem, ed. *Manipur, Past and Present: The Heritage and Ordeals of a Civilization.* Vol. 4. New Delhi: Mittal, 2005.

MARTIAL DANCE

Military parades preserved the drama of rallying and drilling forces and extolling splendid victories and the cavalier's ambitions—the motivations for Persian clashing of shields as well as the grand polonaise of Eastern Europe. Other modes of troop dance mimed the shielding of kings and deities from harm and readying men's bodies and weapons for future invasions and combat, the purpose of the *takalo* performed on the island of Niue northeast of New Zealand to build esprit de corps. An Asian example, the *silambattam* modeled self-defense training that peasants practiced during the reign of Tamil kings of southeastern India from the sixth century CE.

Much of early martial dance enhanced male bonding, as with the Pyrrhic dance of Doric and Cretan soldiers and the Norwegian *halling*, an acrobatic display dating to 500 BCE. The Greek poet Hesiod admired Ethiopian males for dancing their way onto the battlefield. According to historian Xenophon's *Anabasis* (ca. 400 BCE), Macedonians reenacted a civil assault in the Carpaean dance, a duet that matched an unarmed plowman against a robber.

Bellicose choreography ranged around the globe, from the practice fields of Roman legionaries at Pompeii and winter quarters at Aquilea to Sioux enclaves in the Dakotas. In the Said of Upper Egypt, Arab men reenacted man-to-man fighting and hunting with a stick dance called the *tahtiyb*. Throughout Scandinavia, Nordic males danced in weapons rituals reverencing Thor, the god of war, by which squads warded off the faithless. In gestures of brotherhood and loyalty, at nuptial banquets, men executed steps honoring the drinking horn, a symbol of shared destiny.

Martial dance took the form of a human cavalcade in the Middle Ages with the chain dance, a linking of performers in a show of unity and egalitarianism. In 1621, Catalonian celebrants of Corpus Christi Day held dance dramas depicting the challenge of mighty aggressors—the Philistine giant Goliath and the Hebrew shepherd boy David. The mime playing Goliath balanced a papier-mâché head while stilt walking through Berga's crowded *plaça*. The addition of two set-tos—angels and St. Michael against eight demons and the battle of four Turkish infantrymen waving scimitars and daggers at a four-man crusader cavalry on hobbyhorses—roused dancers to historical reenactment of the reconquest of Spain from the Moors. While the bass drummer counted out beats from a balcony, the mock battle concluded with three Turks kneeling in submission to Christian insurgents while a third fled captors.

In an affirmation of manhood and combative temperament, the Macedonian *aramisko* imitated the arming and performance of the swordsman and artilleryman. By demonstrating the correct posture of a crouching, kneeling, or standing position, the dancer expressed manhood and devotion to country and family. One spontaneous martial dance, the *cibi* (club dance) of Bau Island in Fiji, erupted during a triumphal return from war in 1850. Another Polynesian martial dance, the *kailao*, involved Tongan males brandishing clubs and practicing battle tactics to a leader's call and the beat of a slit drum.

Typically, Malay dance taught young men *silat* (martial arts) through meticulous choreography. Males defended themselves from attackers by acting out sequences intended to prove strength and courage. To display nationalism, members of military dance companies dressed in traditional black jacket, headband, and sashed pants, a regional uniform.

For the edification of young Mediterranean men and the building of esprit de corps, Macedonian veterans sighted down the imaginary rifle barrel or raised the sword to display preparedness and training in weaponry. In reenactments of banditry, the home guard dramatized the pursuit of lurking predators and rustlers. Dancers accompanied dead comrades to their graves and honored their memory with chant and sober gestures and body postures.

Preparing Youth

Among the Ewe of Ghana, the *agbadza* ennobled youth and trained prospective fighters for the military. To prove readiness, each young man followed the signals of the main drum, which directed tactics to the left, right, and forward. During the *atsiagbekor*, new recruits formed squadrons and directed the rhythm toward a loyalty oath and vigorous obedience to orders. On return from first combat, the soldiers, acclaimed as veteran fighters, added to the dance scenarios of individual deeds and triumphs.

For the Fon-Ewe of Dahomey and Benin, a more devout form of dance drumming for the *adzohu* stirred manhood and patriotism. Dancers consecrated themselves to war gods and communed with the divine by invoking spirits and gesturing militant tactics and thanks. To the west on the Ivory Coast in francophone Africa, importation of the popular *coupé-décalé* (cheat and run) served the people during extensive political and military crises as a release of anguish over political debacles and state corruption.

Contemporaries of Scots leapers of the highland fling, Czech dancers of southern Moravia performed a recruitment dance dating to the 1700s. Town troupes in decorated vests, tight pants, and boots revived the performance for revels. Beginning with sedate steps, they increased the speed to spotlight individual dancers and showcase leaping competitions. The vivid presentation paralleled the *gayong otar*, a combatant preparation of Malay recruits that paired offensive and defensive sword thrusts and shield parries to gong and drum.

The Global Hakka

Among the precolonial Maori in New Zealand, war was a sacred duty and tattooing with red ochre scrolls and whirls a doctrinal obligation. Maori *hakka* dancers exaggerated their toughness by posturing threatening gestures to slaps of the chest and clenches of fists, an imitation of demonic carved idols. As a dirge over fallen soldiers, warriors whirled a bullroarer to overlay an eerie drone to chants and drumming. An ancient dance prop, the rolling hoop humiliated defeated enemies by displaying the tattooed thigh skin of a corpse stretched over the circle.

To a suite of mythic songs, tattooed faces grimaced furious hostility and vengeance with bulging, rolling eyes, militant taunts and grunts, goblinesque cries, hand vibrations, and tongue thrusts. For laughs, a buffoon mimicked the gestures with grotesque parodies. In 1820, a war chief at North Island composed the "Ka Mate," a hakka chant declaring the warrior's resolve to live life to the fullest and overcome the fear of death. By standing with feet wide apart and stamping aggressively in rhythm, the performers gave the impression of stolid, unshakeable defiance of the enemy, a stance Maori infantry took in Egypt in 1941 during World War II.

The *siva tau* compounded the hakka with a challenge or war dance. Children acquired a code of conduct and cultural skills by performing the hakka and siva tau at school and for holidays and memorials to fallen soldiers. Adult athletes in Kuala Lumpur, Australia, England, Wales, and the United States readied themselves and spectators for rugby and football matches and the Olympics by dancing a hakka choreographed for each sport. A seated hakka involved more swaying of the torso and arms and less militarism.

See also chain dance; *halling*; highland fling; *hopak*; morris dance; North African dance; Persian dance; polonaise; Pyrrhic dance; Roman dance; *tirabol*; sword dance.

Source: Barr, Amelia E. "Characteristic Dances of the World." *Lippincott's Magazine* 27, no. 4 (April 1881): 330–41.

MASKED DANCE

Masks hide the identity and transcend the humanity of dancers. Such costuming might take the form of an exaggerated helmet, false face, skull crest, or ritual horns, or it may be a whole-body disguise for shamanic ceremonies, mime, carnivals, parades, and masquerades. The covering of the true self with an imaginary physiognomy liberates the dancer for choreographic challenges, for instance, the long killer whale false face of the Kwakiutl shaman in the Pacific Northwest, where healing routines require manipulation of mandibles, dorsal fin, and tail with hidden strings and hinges. Reclaimed from the ordinary self, the disguised performer can mime comic as well as austere or malicious spirits.

Disguises enhanced shrine dancers to please nature gods, an integral part of animistic worship, such as that of the Dogon of southern Mali, the Baga of northern Guinea, and the dancing Beti-Pahuin sorcerers in the rainforests of Principe, São Tomé, Gabon, Congo, and Cameroon. Covering of features and sometimes torsos, hands, and feet altered the performer, such as a Cingalese devil dancer of Ceylon, Iroquois false-face wearers, and jesters in the Hopi kachina ritual and the Eskimo dance house. In a show of folk art, mask makers employed ochre powder, paint, raffia and leaves, metal, coconut hulls, seashells, fur and pelts, rawhide, horns and fangs, mud or clay, feathers and plumes, bark cloth, or wood.

Freed from human limitations, maskers could safely approach ancestral ghosts, the purpose of Pacific Coast dancers of British Columbia around 8000 BCE. For the Chinese holy man around 1500 BCE, facial obscurity facilitated healing therapies and transformative initiation rites of tribal youths. The addition of lion and bird mouths to the Bamenda of the Cameroon and movable jaws and wings to the North American Inuit and Andean Inca assisted presenters of imitative dances in replicating animal behaviors, such as the soar of the seabird or the gambol of the alpaca. Around 1000 BCE,

Mexican Indians characterized their ancestors in role playing, what later became known as Día de los Muertos (Day of the Dead), a dance drama common to heritage rituals in Australasia and Buddhist monasteries. By 425 BCE, Greek comedy writers aroused audiences with the *cordax*, a racy, ribald masked dance that Aristophanes incorporated into his comedy *The Clouds* (423 BCE), which lampooned the philosopher Socrates.

Medieval Masking

Late Roman and medieval false faces concealed real people while transforming them into foolish or sacred characters, a source of merriment in stage farce and early Christian processions for Advent and Lent. After 700 CE on the Ivory Coast, Fon stilt walkers topped their faces with clay and wood masks to broaden emotional expressions. In Dahomey, face covers enabled a Yoruba male to perform a female impersonation, a transformation establishing the magical power of the false face.

Eighth-century Bhutanese, Tibetan, and Nepalese dancers wore antlered demon and animal heads of carved wood in Buddhist morality pageants as a force for blessing the audience. Contributing to religiosity, instrumentalists played bells, cymbals, drums, horns, and conches to set the rhythms of peacemakers and wrathful deities. At monasteries and temples, monks and laymen danced annually in disguise to purify the soul and obtain consecration.

In medieval Venice, from December 26 to Shrove Tuesday, half and whole vizard masks hid the excesses of Christian miscreants before the holy rigors of Lent. Before beginning the required gustatory and sexual abstinence, dancers could caper in grotesque face coverings as though divorcing the self from absurd or sacrilegious actions. In contrast to nervous Italian Catholics, from 1150, a full cast of South Korean characters performed the traditional *hahoe byeolsingut* healing drama in Andong, where troupes restored psychological wholeness by portraying monks, a bride, butcher, aristocrat, or learned man.

In the rural hamlets of Hwanghae Province, North Korea, the *talchum* dance merged disguise, mime, comedy, and storytelling with elaborate bounding figures, kicks, hops, and knee bends. The cathartic dance, accented with pratfalls and the waving of whips and white scarves, derived from *goryeo* court ritual of 1130 to relieve the poor of despair and frustration. Performers rotated roles for the knife dance, hunchback dance, leper dance, and lion dance and involved youngsters in the children's company.

In the Joseon Dynasty of Korea after 1392, each New Year or holiday at an all-night gathering of the agrarian and slave classes, spectators assembled around a communal fire to depict human, divine, monstrous, aquatic, avian, and leonine characters. Grotesque masks identified each and drove off evil spirits and diseases. For differentiation, mask makers decked the carved wood bases and movable jaws with hair, fur, moss, gourds, paper, and yarn depicting smiles, grimaces, and physical deformities. At the shaman's shrine, enactors burned the masks at the end of a holiday dance to ward off misfortune from humans, herds, and crops.

By the 1400s, Korean talchum developed into fun folk dances performed by itinerant or homeless bands financed by the state. Improvisations at rituals, weddings, funerals, and exorcisms satirized human foibles as a source of social reform. Lower-class dancers concealed their humble identities in masks and jeered at the faults of snooty aristocrats, Confucian literati, fools, lepers, and privileged Buddhist monks. Domestic scenarios ridiculed the granny's battle with the most recent concubine to join the household by flaunting wide-mouthed false faces with slanted or bugged eyes, raised eyebrows, blemishes, and prominent noses with oversized nostrils. Dancers increased drollery with women posing as monks and men playing female roles. Many of the masks are preserved in the Hahoe Mask Museum in Andong.

Into the late Middle Ages, the Dayak of Kalimantan, Borneo, adopted masked ancestral *topeng* dance to tell a more respectable story—the cyclic myths of Prince Raden Panji, a heroic monarch represented by a white or green face covering. The plot line, narrated by an actor in half mask, required a unique disguise to identify the hero and two contrasting false faces to represent a soldier and a foolish old man, the comic relief in each tale. The martial dance moved to Bali and Java in the 1400s as an interpretation or caricature of anthropomorphic behaviors.

Disguise Makers

Throughout the fifteenth century, performers in Bali and Java concealed their human faces under exquisite masks mimicking the emotions in episodes from two Sanskrit scriptures, the Mahabharata (400 BCE) and Ramayana (300 BCE). After 1755, Indonesian sultan Hamengkubuwono added masked giants and monkeys to Hindu dance stories. Five-hour thanksgiving ceremonies in Borneo required Dayak dancers to craft faces of agrarian pests—crows, rodents, lions—by shaping banana bark and palm fronds into ugly helmets that terrified threats to the harvest.

At the height of European colonialism, disguise among slaves in the Western Hemisphere enabled black Africans to act out their hatred of planters and overseers in dancing and pageantry. Ironically, performers scheduled their outrageous rebellions on Christian holidays, the ritual days foisted on laborers by white missionaries. At the height of the Southern plantation system, maskers for Mardi Gras balls contributed grotesque expressions to dancing caricatures of the rich planter, simpering debutante, vicious slave driver, and overworked field hand.

Meanwhile, Europeans and Americans danced in disguise as innovative entertainment demonstrating adept use of fabric and makeup. Guests at court masquerades in 1764 chose tight-fitting vizard masks to conceal their frolics during the pavane, a stately processional. Among immigrants, holiday false faces recalled traditional folklore, for example, New Year masks of Chinese lion and dragon dancers in Chinatown and the praise rituals to the earth mother of the Gelede shaman in Nigeria.

Currently, plastic and molded masks enhance the ancient practice of obscuring dancers. Japanese performers of *torisashi odori* at Nagasaki cover scalps and noses with fabric to emulate bird hunters. In the *baile de los viejitos* (dance of the old men), a Mexican dance of the Purépecha of Michoacán, the shuffling and collapsing of masked male dancers deride the limitations of advanced age. For the January dance of the *parachicos* (street performers) in Chiapa de Corzo, wood masks accentuate the rejoicing of individual saint's days.

Among the Gouro of the Ivory Coast, each village honors a lead Zaouli dancer showcased at wakes and parties. The dance begins with repetitive flute and drum cadences, which summon the performer to a circle of spectators. A mask keeper unveils the traditional disguise, a loose collection of raffia and bangles dyed bright colors. After the audience admires the horned false face, the masker begins hopping on one or both legs and shaking fly whisks. His upper body remains still while ankle bells jingle to a pulsing rhythm.

See also coming of age; commedia dell'arte; disguise; dragon dance; Eskimo dance house; headdress; healing dance; *matachines*; mime; *odori*; pavane; scripture, folk dance in; Thai dance.

Sources: Aching, Gerard. *Masking and Power: Carnival and Popular Culture in the Caribbean.* Minneapolis: University of Minnesota Press, 2002. Bell, Deborah. *Mask Makers and Their Craft: An Illustrated Worldwide Study.* Jefferson, NC: McFarland, 2010. Johnson, James H. *Venice Incognito: Masks in the Serene Republic.* Berkeley: University of California Press, 2011. Seiji, CedarBough. "The Bawdy, Brawling, Boisterous World of Korean Mask Dance Dramas." *Cross-Currents: East Asian History and Culture Review* 4 (September 2012): 146–68.

MATACHINES

An allegorical dance performance of First Peoples of the Western Hemisphere, the *matachines*—from the Arabic for "false faces"—perform a rare combination of indigenous art. The original presentation, initiated by religious brotherhoods, combined elements of the North African Tuareg, Phoenician rain ritual, and Hispanic line dance. From its inception in Mexico in 1700, the mid-winter mummery derived energy from Tarahumara, Ocoroni, Mayo, Tewa, and Yaqui oral tradition and featured sequences danced in moccasins for wakes and plaza fiestas.

The matachines served the aims of New World proselytizers and took vows to dance for life whenever someone scheduled a Christian ritual. The Order of St. Francis proposed the Christian festivals in place of Aztec rituals and featured syncretic Hispanic saints and deities, notably Nuestra Señora de Guadalupe (the Virgin of Guadalupe), an icon of purity. Whether scheduled for Easter, Christmas, or both, the drama and its uniform costuming retained their significance from Belize to Bernalillo, New Mexico, and Pueblo, Colorado, west to Las Vegas, and south to Colombia and Peru.

Mexican Choreography

A religio-historical spectacle of hop–steps and crossovers to guitar and violin strains, the matachines retained strands of Roman rituals performed after 715 BCE by priestly *salii* (leapers) and the fifteenth-century *morisca* sword dance. In 1528, conquistador Hernán Cortés imported thirty matachines dancers to Spain. A year later in April, they presented their dance to Pope Clement VII. An Italian fool's dance from 1530 added pratfalls, tumbling, and obscene posturing to the sound of cornets and oboes. When

Anne of Austria entered Burgos, Spain, to marry Philip II in October 1570, a dozen muscular matachines acrobats performed for her.

The Mesoamerican pageant showcased beribboned and ruffled headdresses, masks, fan-like wands with three tines, and fringed Moorish disguises of the upper face and eyes. Blessed by Catholic priests, the overriding theme of good vs. evil (or Christianity vs. paganism) veneered the propaganda of European conquerors misrepresenting their exploitation of Central American Indians as a form of salvation. At Taos, New Mexico, iconography of conquest blurred the lines between the Moorish king in Iberia and Hernán Cortés in Tenochtitlán.

The first Hispanic masked dance in Mesoamerica, along the Rio Grande, the matachines featured Iberian religious conflict in the "Dance of the Moors and Christians" from the anti-Arab persecutions of 1492 and the "Dance of Cortés," a story dance reenacting the conquest of Spanish conquistadors from 1519 to 1521 over the Aztec, Maya, and surrounding Mexican tribes. Symbolism merged the triune gods of Quetzalcoatl, a Mayan feathered serpent, with the Christian trinity. Central to the dramatic interest, male performers played the parts of Montezuma II, Cortés, and his native mistress, La Malinche, the betrayer who interpreted for him in 1521 when he overran Tenochtitlán.

The matachines entertained audiences with atmospheric gestures and burlesque characters orchestrating a complex procession overlaying allegory with low comedy. The entrance of El Toro (the sacrificial bull) preceded diagonal crossings and a fast-paced finale in which whip cracks permeated kicking, crouching, and stamping. For comic relief, portrayers turned the bull into a satanic trickster, whom Montezuma killed. The dual slaughter/castration scene suggested triumph over pre-Columbian deities as well as fertility and the birth of a new abuelo (male elder), who called the dance figures and maintained order in the troupe.

Preserving Folk Art

As a morality or mystery play, at north central New Mexico's Picurís Pueblo, the matachines took shape in the 1980s with a formal procession of kick steps into the San Lorenzo church, a mud-floored sanctuary. The action gained speed and color with the second song, in which steps united Malinche and Montezuma with a female elder in stamping, kneeling, crouching, obeisances, and pirouettes. The dancers strutted fancy leggings to the gyrations of wands and sheathed gourd rattles.

Following a twelve-day rehearsal, the Christmas Eve pageant began in the afternoon and extended into the night. Players called, "Hoohoo," while winding steps through the luminarias around the plaza. The Picurís troupe maintained performer separation to clarify the dramatic uniqueness and innovations of each sequence. Presentations at various communities as far north as Wyoming, California, Kansas, and Colorado contained local idiosyncrasies:

Matachines Variations

Location	Monarch	Malinche	Evil	Totem	Elders	Addition
Aguascalientes	—	—	—	—	comics	drumming
Albuquerque	—	blonde Malinche	—	—	—	—
Alcalde	—	transvestite	—	bull	—	December 26 presentation
Arroyo Seco	—	one Malinche	—	—	midwives	maypole
Belize	—	four Malinches	Cortés	—	—	—
Bernalillo	Montezuma	many Malinches	—	bull	ogres	female dancers
Durango	Virgin of Guadeloupe	—	—	—	—	all female, one drummer
Huajuapan	Montezuma	—	devils	—	giants	European dance
Jeméz	—	two Malinches	—	bull	—	tunics and scarves
Juárez	—	three Malinches	—	—	—	white tunics
Pasqua	San José	young boys	—	—	—	sacred flowers, harp
Picurís	—	little girl	—	bull	—	maypole
Río Sucio	—	transvestite	—	—	—	prose narrative
Samachique	—	—	—	buffalo	chaperones	caped dancers
San Ildefonso	—	—	—	buffalo	—	Santa Claus
San Juan	—	little girl	—	—	comics	silk capes
Santa Clara	—	native Malinche	—	—	—	one drummer
Taos	Montezuma/Moorish king	little girl	Cortés	buffalo	chaperones	maypole
Tortugas	—	three Malinches	—	—	Juan Diego	blood drinking, maypole, aprons
Zacatecas	—	no female character	—	—	comics	drumming, native dance

A Peruvian version of the conquest dances illustrates the adaptations of Andean folk art to relevant history. At Cuzco, Quechua dancers replaced the overthrow of Montezuma with the *muerte de Atahualpa* (death of Atahualpa), the last Inca emperor, whom Francisco Pizarro's forces strangled on July 26, 1533. Highland companies typically performed the anti-European dance drama at the pre-Lenten carnaval.

See also sacrificial dance.

Source: Rodriguez, Sylvia. *The Matachines Dance: A Ritual Dance of the Indian Pueblos and Mexicano-Hispano Communities.* Santa Fe, NM: Southwest Heritage, 2009.

MATING DANCE

The alliance of human reproduction with dance modulates gestures, body language, and steps to aid one potential mate in alerting and courting another, as displayed in the West Indian *calenda* and the Spanish fandango. After 2000 BCE at Memphis in Egypt's Old Kingdom, bare flesh, tasseled attire, and short kilts announced to males the seductive intent of a female troupe. On Africa's east coast, permanent alliance foregrounded the *eunoto*, a vertical coming-of-age jump dance among Maasai youths in Kenya as they proved their strength and stamina to nubile girls in precopulative display.

In varied settings, mating dances legitimated the yearning of seducers by leading to a libidinous coda or finale. From the Tang Dynasty at Peking and west over the Silk Road, traders enriched themselves on the appeal of the translucent scarf, a mesmerizing fabric essential to African and Asian folk art from Morocco to Malaysia. The peek-a-boo style of Salomé in the lore of Galilee raised the scarf dance to an acme of sexuality, which belly dancers perpetuated in Turkey and among the nomadic Roma and in the *assiko*, or the Mankon shawl dance in the Cameroon and Guinea.

Dancers paid the high price of sheer fabric to add ephemeral touches to their choreography. The translucent veil betokened the fragility of youth and the emergence of fertility, two facets of the ancient *ballos*, a Greek flirtation figure executed to light music. For the Malay *endang*, couples exuded passion until they arrived at a basis for lifelong union. In pre-Columbian Peru, the *huayño* delineated human codes of behavior and courtship by imitating the spirited stamping and pawing of the Paso Fino stallion to impress a mare in estrus. After colonization of the Andes, Catholic missionaries curbed the spirited male-female scenarios by resetting the dances from Quechuan love ballads to hymns reverencing the Virgin of Carmen.

In Alpine Austria, Bavaria, Bohemia, Styria, and the Ziller Valley in the Tyrol before 1023, medieval entreaty dances imitated the cooing and feather preening of birds. In gendered bonding, males exhibited bravado while the females retreated into the cunning of stolid hens. When the dance evolved into the *Ländler*, folk performers poured themselves into stomping, clapping, and spinning. In outrage at the obvious physicality between the sexes, carping urbanites prohibited the dance.

Renaissance Pursuit

The introduction of social dance in the late 1300s prefaced an era of choreography restrained by courtesy and decorum, essentials of social intercourse at more refined social

For a Sensoji Temple Festival in Asakusa, Tokyo, dancers wear crane costumes and mime bird-like steps and wing and head gestures. *Wakako Imamura and Priscilla Portsmouth, Japanese Tourism Organization, www.ilovejapan.ca, Toronto, Ontario.*

An art poster depicts a Roma tambourinist in loose peasant blouse, fringed sash, and head scarf. *Lera Yanysheva, svenko70@ yandex.ru, Moscow, Russia.*

The flower dance to a sky folk ballad in Sado City, Niigata, demonstrates a ring sequence performed counterclockwise in typical Japanese costume—obi, tunic, sandals and socks, and straw hats. *Wakako Imamura and Priscilla Portsmouth, Japanese Tourism Organization, www.ilovejapan.ca, Toronto, Ontario.*

At Cuzco, Peru, a plaza performer demonstrates the use of handheld props, headdress, animal skins, and body paint. *David Knowlton, dcknowlton@gmail.com, Utah Valley University, Orem, Utah, www.cuzcoeats.com; photography by Walter Coraza Morveli.*

An ingenious burlesque of white superiority, from the 1860s to the 1920s, the cakewalk allowed black dancers to dress in style and strut in competition for a prize. *Library of Congress, www.npr.org/sections/codeswitch/ 2013/12/23/256566647/the-extraordinary-story-of-why-a-cakewalk-wasnt-always-easy.*

Early folk choreography featured organized community dances, as with this Croatian chain dance performed in heritage costumes. *Livija Zgurić, marketing, livija.zguric@lado.hr, National Folk Dance Ensemble of Croatia, Zagreb, Croatia.*

Clogging creates its own music from the rhythmic sound of wood- or metal-edged shoes. *Holly Ireland, photographer, info@ hollyireland.com, Carlsbad, California.*

Young Croatian girls express mature delight in dance that acknowledges their entry into womanhood. *Livija Zgurić, marketing, livija.zguric@lado.hr, National Folk Dance Ensemble of Croatia, Zagreb, Croatia.*

At the Inter-Celtic Festival in Peel, 2014, Manx women perform circle dances that display the Celtic figures on their skirts. *Chloe Woolley, Culture Vannin, Douglas, Isle of Man, chloe@culturevannin.im; photograph by Jiri Podobsky.*

At the summer Dynamism Festival in Tokushima City, Japanese children express their enthusiasm with gestures and fans. *Courtesy Wakako Imamura and Priscilla Portsmouth, Japanese Tourism Organization, www.ilovejapan.ca, Toronto, Ontario.*

Folk dancers accentuate theme and climactic action with grand finales, as with the last figure of a gavotte for four Scots couples in Glasgow, as illustrated on November 28, 1825, in the *Northern Looking Glass. Grove, Lilly.* Dancing. *London: Longmans, Green, and Company, 1895, 283.*

A jolting, improvised solo beloved around the globe, flamenco exhibits authentic folk-loric passions. *Silvia Salamanca, http://silviasalamanca.com/classes/, Houston, Texas.*

Ukrainian headdress for the *hopak* features primary colors in flowers and ribbons that flutter to the skipping steps. *Mikhail Smirnov, mikhail@barynya.com, www.barynya.com; photograph by Barynya Ensemble, New York.*

At the Japanese Gardens of the Morikami Museum in Delray Beach, Florida, performers synchronize steps and the waving of hand fans. *Monika Amar, marketing coordinator, Morikami Museum, www.morikami.org, Delray Beach, Florida.*

The handkerchief serves folk arts as a symbol of order and decorum, two components of refined dance by mixed genders. *British Library, http://resources42.kb.nl/MIMI/MIMI_120D13/MIMI_120D13_ 006V_MIN.JPG.*

The Ukrainian *hopak* stresses masculine bravado in solo parts and concludes with partnering to skipping steps. *Mikhail Smirnov, mikhail@barynya.com, www.barynya.com, Barynya Ensemble, New York*

Padmasree Kalamanadalam Gopi and Kalamandalam Vijayakumar perform in *kathakali* style featuring body art and jewelry. *Barbara Vijayakumar, barbaravijayakumar@yahoo.co.uk, Kerala, India; photograph by Garry Laybourn.*

Youthful Irish dancers perform jig steps by partnering in ring formation. *Margaret Evans, director, Kelly Irish Dancers www.thekellyirishdancers.com, Chattaroy, Washington.*

Children in Cuzco, Peru, in iconic skirts, shawls, and hats enjoy learning traditional folk dance. *David Knowlton, dcknowl*
on@gmail.com, Utah Valley University, Orem, Utah, www.cuzcoeats.com; photograph by Walter Coraza Morveli.

Kathak dancer Parul Gupta demonstrates the eye following the gesture of the left hand while she spins her skirt in the opposite direction. *Parul Gupta, artistic director, Infusion Dance, www.infusiondance.ca/parul-gupta, Toronto, Canada.*

Synchronized steps, body paint, and foliage tie harvest dancers to nature, the focus of a drawing of line dancers at the San Ildefonso Pueblo by Juan Cruz Roybal. *Alexander E. Anthony, owner, Adobe Gallery, www.adobegallery.com, info@adobegallery.com, Santa Fe, New Mexico.*

The Chinese lion dance, performed in traditional comic bamboo head, tufted pelt, and movable mouth, eyes, and ears, features folk dancer Citra Satria Ongkowijoyo. *Citra Satria Ongkowijoyo, founder, Ksatria Lion & Dragon Dance Troupe, University of Melbourne, Melbourne, Australia.*

For Roma dancers, skirt display recaptures the motion and attitude of Esmeralda, the barefoot dancer in Victor Hugo's *The Hunchback of Notre Dame. Lera Yanysheva, svenko70@yandex.ru, Moscow, Russia.*

The graceful, fluid movement and emotional expressions of Manipuri dance convey the nuances of romance between the Hindu deities Krishna and Radha. *Sohini Ray, Manipuri Dance Visions, www.manipuridancevisions.com, Los Angeles, California.*

The appeal of *kathakali* dance relies in part on mime and intensely colored and gilded headdress, jewelry, and mask. *Barbara Vijayakumar, barbaravijayakumar@yahoo.co.uk, Kala Chethena Kathakali Company, Kerala, India; photograph by Sarah Sturdy.*

The alliance of human reproduction with dance modulates gestures, body language, and steps to aid one potential mate in alerting and courting another, as displayed in this Croatian mating dance. *Livija Zgurić, marketing, livija.zguric@lado .hr, National Folk Dance Ensemble of Croatia, Zagreb, Croatia.*

For the *kitsune odori* in Hamejima Village, children perform with painted faces. *Wakako Imamura and Priscilla Portsmouth, Japanese Tourism Organization, www.ilovejapan.ca, Toronto, Ontario.*

Polynesian dance emphasizes the agility of waist and hips, a sinuous movement accentuated by grass skirts. *Lulu Tepaeru-Ariki, Anuanua Dance Groupe, Cook Islands, www.anuanuadance.com.*

A soloist performs a Russo-Roma dance in her bare feet to guitar music. *Lera Yanysheva, svenko70@yandex.ru, Moscow, Russia.*

A Tuscan musical introit to the Italian Renaissance, the saltarello (also *saltarelle* or *cascarda*) advanced leaping, walking steps to a solo or synchronized choreography. *"Il Saltarello,"* Penny Magazine *14, no. 3 (September 20, 1845): 364.*

The shawl dance, performed in Washington, D.C., in 2007 by Arikara/Comanche dancer Kelly Walker, demonstrates the butterfly motions of the arms and the flutter of fringe to vigorous footwork. *http://iipdigital.usembassy .gov/st/english/article/2007/08/20070814165217glnesnom0.6256525.html#axzz3jqkswWjG.*

Coordinated costumes and the suggestion of bridal attire contribute romance to story dance in Cuzco, Peru. *David Knowlton, dcknowlton@gmail.com, Utah Valley University, Orem, Utah, www.cuzcoeats.com; photograph by Walter Coraza Morveli.*

Awal Alhassan and Esinu Gbolonyo energize the *fume-fume*, a Ghanaian dance from sub-Saharan Africa. *Mya Photography, Curtis Andrews, co-director, Adanu Habobo, www.adanuhabobo.com, Vancouver, British Columbia.*

Whether solo or in groups, weapons dance in the Middle East, China, France, England, Spain, Germany, Italy, Austria, Switzerland, Czechoslovakia, Finland, and Sweden elevated the vigorous warrior to defender of nations and security guard of the gods. *Livija Zgurić, marketing, livija.zguric@lado .hr, National Folk Dance Ensemble of Croatia, Zagreb, Croatia.*

Neopagan and occult rituals from Celtic Britain and northwestern Europe energized devotees in tribal pageantry intended to invoke mystic gods and unite the individual with the divine self. *Anne Marie Greymoon, www.wiccanto ether.com/profile/AnneMarieGreymoon, greymoon@wiccanfest.com, Ontario, Canada.*

Mimi Rios and Valerie Amanda lift their skirts in a flirty performance of zapateado to stringed instrument accompaniment. *Gema Sandoval, floricanto@att.net, www.danzafloricantousa.com/about_director.php; photograph by Frank Sandoval, Los Angeles.*

levels. Teachers held practice sessions to introduce youths and the rising merchant class to the jig, galliard, and *volta*, a risqué couples dance involving a firm male grip on the female midriff. The adaptation of the French *branle* from a country ring dance into a sophisticated court figure introduced the branle gay, a brisk courtship figure in triple time, and other innovations involving scandalous lifts like the volta and the embraces and kisses at the finale of German dances.

In the late 1400s, Florentine engraver Baccio Baldini etched a scene of dance floor partnering that displayed not only fine steps but also fashionable couture and hair jewelry, both inducements to social and political advancement. His artistry anticipated the pavane, a sedate seduction metaphor that the Spanish took to Oaxaca after 1528. Mexicans enjoyed the enacting of European courtesies in a slow procession—the peacock stance of the military man in gold-trimmed uniform and saber and the overdressing of high-born ladies in finery, lace, and jeweled slippers. For women, the display of wealth and privilege implied willingness an attainable fiancée whose parentage offered social prominence and ample dowry.

In the second century of colonialism, Venezuelans and Colombians celebrated the birth of the *joropo*, a diasporic dance merging the jungle lifestyle of the Orinoco basin with Arabo-Andalusian equestrian dash. The vernacular dance reached into the past for the best in seafaring arts and the plaints of Iberian troubadours. At street festivals in Cuba, Mexico, Puerto Rico, Curaçao, St. Lucia, Trinidad, and Tobago, the aggressive joropo rhythm seized the male imagination as he eyed the whirling skirts of the arrogant but available female.

Baroque to Modern Wooing

Segregated from predictable Old World social orders, Creole dance expressed the mixed heritage of slaves and Amerindians who relied on instinct rather than religious dogma or social canon. To the insistence of the goatskin drum at Grenada, Dominica, and Martinique, couples spoke with eyes, hands, and postures the carnality of the *bélé* (from the French "*belle aire*"), a pure African mating and fertility rite. At Congo Square in New Orleans, swarthy people of improbable ethnic mix expressed a yearning for liberty and equality in the daring pelvic thrusts of ritual mating. In both choreographies, aggressive dancing tended to leave performers panting with exhaustion rather than desire.

In the late eighteenth century, the Coca people of Cocula in western Mexico created the "Mexican hat dance" or *jarabe tapatío*, an archetypal seduction dance. Like paired doves, Mesoamerican men and women dramatized the eternal advance of the lusty male toward the shy or coy female. Named for the Aztec term for barter, the figures elongated the perky choreography with triumphs and setbacks in the unforeseeable tempo of human romance. The pas de deux reached a visual pact after the male tempted his potential mate with the gift of his sombrero. Her acceptance initiated greater intimacy consisting of a discreet kiss behind the uplifted hat.

Into the twentieth century, folk art reconfigured seduction dance to suit Christian expectations and post-Reformation mores. Among Muslims, the all-girl *khaleegy* compromised Sharia law by exuding skirt-lifting dalliance, supple midriff bends, and tosses of the hair while showcasing the troupe in tight dresses overlaid to the feet with diaphanous silk. In Huila, Colombia, revelers at the Fiesta de San Pedro joined in twos for the *sanjuanero*, by which they won their sweethearts according to canon restraints. Costumes stressed gendering, with the males flaunting hats and neckerchiefs and women swishing wide skirts without revealing too much leg.

See also belly dance; *branle*; *calenda*; fandango; *huayño*; *jarabe tapatío*; jig; *joropo*; *Ländler*; Manipuri dance; pavane; Polynesian dance; scarf dance.

Source: Anon. *The Dance: Historic Illustrations of Dancing from 3300 B.C. to 1911 A.D.* London: John Bale, Sons & Danielsson, 1911.

MAYIM MAYIM

Performed like seaside undulations to a joyous pulse, the Israeli *mayim mayim* (literally "water water" in Hebrew) epitomizes the emergence of folk art from a pervasive commitment to agriculture. One of the first Israeli intersections of art with religion, the dance coordinates hops, skips, and left-right-left toe taps during a clockwise circling. Individuals hold hands, clap, and advance in the epitome of frontier farm zeal.

Integral to the mayim mayim, a cross-front-cross-back grapevine pattern produces visual intricacy on a par with the pioneer settlement of Israel. The woven figure, a facet imported by Yemenite Jews, derived from the Middle Eastern route of the diaspora and suggested the appeal of rippling water to a desert people. For the elastic drive of the mayim mayim in affirmation of Israeli unity, large numbers of dancers broke into concentric circles, either all facing inward or some circles inward and some outward.

The Water Dance

Based on the style and motifs of Eurasian dance, the choreography by German-trained dancer Else I. Dublon to music by Ukrainian composer Yehuda Sharett dates to a water festival in August 1937. The water dance immortalizes the location of water at Kibbutz Beit Ha-shita in the Negev Desert at Na'an near Mount Gilboa. At the Emek kibbutz in Jewish Palestine west of the Sea of Galilee, dancing pioneers sang the verses of Russian lyricist Emanuel Amiran-Pougatchov, who rephrased a prophecy from Isaiah 12 into a source of esprit de corps.

Like the nationalistic dances of the Austro-Hungarian Empire, mayim mayim vivified a culture that reverenced survival against heavy odds, yet avoided the exacting dogma of orthodox Jewry. In an era that idealized permanent Jewish sovereignty, performers elevated a desert well into a symbol of a booming Semite state founded on scripture and prophecy. Because of a festival performance at Dalia on July 14–15, 1944, the dynamic swaying cross-front-cross-back (grapevine or mayim) pattern passed among massed dancers at kibbutzim throughout the Jordan Valley.

Dancing as One

As Zionists pressed world leaders for an independent Israel, performances of mayim mayim resonated throughout the Jewish diaspora as a call for solidarity. Groups executed the circle dance as a coda to the Sabbath and high holy days. On flute, violin, cello, and drum or accordion, instrumentalists accompanied the ring dancers and their repeated shouts of "mayim, mayim, mayim, mayim."

At the Japanese surrender on September 2, 1945, the US high command introduced the iconic mayim mayim at nursery school gym classes and labor recruitment meetings as a means of rebuilding Japanese community. Another postwar initiative acquainted folk dance circles in Taiwan with the Israeli tune, which raised cardiac rates among the unemployed along with hope. Into the 1950s, the folk dance movement spread the effervescent mayim mayim among amateurs of all ages and backgrounds. Hasidic innovators added leaps, rocking, swaying, hands raised to Yahweh, and scarves fluttering between individuals, an authentic touch by female troupes at bar mitzvahs and weddings.

See also Jewish dance.

Sources: Dublon, Else I. "The Origins of 'Mayim, Mayim.'" *Jerusalem Post*, December 25, 1972, 10. Ingber, Judith Brin. *Seeing Israeli and Jewish Dance.* Detroit, MI: Wayne State University Press, 2011.

MAYPOLE DANCE

A procreation symbol and organizing place for May Day, Pentecost (Whitsuntide), or midsummer pageantry, the maypole dates to Germanic and Scandic tribes of tree cultists from 1200 BCE. During the third century BCE, Romans observed Ludi Florales, the cultic flower dances and feasting that extended from April 28 to May 2 in honor of the goddess Flora. The Celtic veneration of the oak tree, a Druidic sacrament at the Feast of Bel or Beltane, preceded the reverence for Yggdrasil, a Norse ash tree that centered the universe and linked earth with sky. The web of ribbons radiating from the pole top symbolized the multiple pathways of destiny, similar in meaning to the Tarot's Wheel of Fortune. Dances to quick-paced music echoed the exuberance of the first outing of the year, when unmarried males and females could join hands without the approbation of the church.

On the June 24 midsummer day solstice festivities, Swedish maypole figures to "Klappdans," "The Little Frogs," and "Hopp, Mor Annika" (Jump, Mother Annika) stressed hands on hips, schottische steps, and slaps of the hand on the opposite foot similar to the German *Schuhplattler*. Boisterous fertility rituals ushered in the medieval courting season with flowered coronets adorning the heads of maidens, whom church fathers chaperoned. Girls who spent the night dancing and appeared with grass stains on their skirts suffered the derisive taunt of "the green gown."

Spring customs of Welsh and Scots-Irish highlanders began with "Mayers" raising the birch maypole and topping it with garlands, symbols of seasonal renewal. Scots dressed in tartans and sashes and individualized dance figures with the sharp kicks and springs of the highland fling to bagpipe renderings of "Strathspey" and "The Prince of Orange." For the skit the "Romance of Kyng Alisaunder," Cheltenham chimney sweeps dressed in tatters and blackened their faces before prancing around a may bush. St. George and the Dragon, Robin Hood, and Jack-o'-the-Green, a jester disguised as the Green Man, added history and mysticism to the May ritual by cavorting among the company to improvised steps.

In the Northern Hemisphere, the spring dance thrived in the Middle Ages with processions and squares and circle dances around the anthropomorphic centerpiece, an element of May ritual in the Tyrolean Alps and egg dancing in Austria. Troupes mimed the lyrics of songs, with children leaping like frogs and girls pretending to scrub the winter laundry for a spring airing. In 1147, the Church of St. Andrew Undershaft in London took its nickname from the height of the May post, which exceeded the spire. Churchwardens stored the annual maypole under the eaves. The traditional post survived Puritan fanaticism for four centuries until a mob destroyed it, an ominous prelude to suppressions to come. Under the Plantagenets after 1154, maypole dancing freed milkmaids from chores. In 1170, mummers painted faces and disguised themselves as bears and wolves before stamping with sword dancers around the maypole in a crisscross figure.

The Renaissance Maypole

In the 1500s in Austria and Germany, Frisians, Bavarians, and Swabians centered the village green with a *maibaum* (maypole) as the locus for joyful post-winter frolics. Censorious Anglicans and Scots Presbyterians declared May Fair symbols idolatrous and pagan. Authorities ordered the poles cut down until the rule of Mary I in 1553, when Catholics reclaimed the emblem. The London festival held on May 30, 1557, included among the performers the May king and queen and morris dancers, members of an informal court. To the tunes of "The Weaving Dance" and "The Shepherdess Dance," the company wielded crooks and crowned their springtime royalty in the style of the Wiccan observance of Beltane.

In Scotland in 1560, post-Reformation lawmakers banned spring dancing around a central post. In contrast, Tudor queen Elizabeth I promoted maypole dancing to the tune of "Sellinger's Round" (1590), featuring a step-step-pause rhythm. Her courtiers decked themselves in laces, ribbons, and scarves tied with bells. To drumming and piping, the May troupe entertained the queen with a colorful flurry of stamping, jingling, and pirouettes. Music of "The Foresters' Dance" mimed the actions of Robin Hood and his band in Sherwood Forest.

By the early 1600s, English parishes erected central poles as a source of unity, for example, the permanent centerpiece of Offenham, Worcestershire. Planters exported the traditions to Barbados, Jamaica, Nevis, and Yucatán, where Mexican couples plaited ribbons around a pole for the *baile de las cintas* (ribbon dance). At New Plymouth in Massachusetts Bay Colony in 1628, indentured servants held a brief midsummer fling by raising a maypole, disguising themselves as deer and wolves, and executing nuptial round dances before the May king and queen. In 1633, James I introduced the Jacobean amusements in *Declaration to His Subjects Concerning Lawful Sports to Bee Used,* which officially legalized maypole dancing.

In Massachusetts, drinking and licentiousness scandalized Magistrate John Endecott, a dour Puritan who charged the Salem Episcopalians with profanity and, in 1630, ordered the maypole axed. In 1644, mounting Puritan control in Britain banned both the maypole and spring dancing. After the execution of Charles I in London on January 30, 1649, to flout the pious Puritans headed by Oliver Cromwell, the gladsome continued holding village dances in secluded meadows. The Scots of East Ayrshire observed the tradition for another 140 years.

According to English writer John Aubrey, the restoration of Charles II to the throne on May 29, 1660, returned peasants to joyful heritage dance, a physical release from Puritan persecution. Children carried small maypoles to school and competed for the most eye-catching garlands. In central London, fans of spring dances raised the largest post—130 feet—in the Strand, some 42 feet higher than the model in Nun Monkton, North Yorkshire.

The Massachusetts Bay maypole dancing resumed at Charlestown on May 26, 1687, as an emblem of anti-Puritanical sentiment. By the 1770s, the Sons of Liberty in Boston, New York, and Philadelphia erected maypoles as rallying points for clashes with British occupation forces. In Edinburgh in the late 1700s, John Knox opposed the maypole pageantry as sacrilege. In contrast to his diatribe, the winding and unwinding of the maypole among the Yaqui of Mexico provided a dawn finale to the Easter *matachines* dance.

English watercolorist Joseph Nash depicted a seventeenth-century maypole around which men and women welcomed spring at a community festival. *Grove, Lilly.* Dancing. *London: Longmans, Green, and Company, 1895, 147.*

Historic Maypoles

In the Napoleonic era in Friuli, Marche, and Umbria, Italian maypole frolickers hoisted a liberty tree honoring the French Revolution of July 14, 1789, and attached ribbons matching the colors of the dancers' dresses. For the choreography, boys and girls paired in a circle and grasped pastel ribbons. By moving in opposite directions, they danced the ribbons into a colorful plait. As demonstrated in labyrinthine figures, by reversing patterns, the performers extended the spectacle with weaving and raveling of the mesh.

By 1845, Canadians were arranging maypole dances and picnics every May 24 for the birthday of Queen Victoria, who ruled until her death in 1901. Despite the modernizations of the Industrial Revolution, British Columbia maintained the record for continuing maypole traditions from 1870 to the present. In 1909, an English pageant commemorating the visit of Queen Elizabeth I to Bath in 1590 concluded with a traditional Roman dance and a minuet around a twenty-five-foot central post. Children clad in white formed the queen's canopy with streamers and pennants. A symbolic court in 1914 at Frackville, Pennsylvania, decked a parade float on which Daughters of Liberty surrounded a maypole.

The playground movement in the early 1900s provided US children with a space for country dances and musical games around the maypole. Diagrams pictured the skipping of wreath bearers and milkmaids to the pole and the entry of the queen's retinue for a graceful waltz. More intricate performances scheduled a five-pole figure, a Dutch windmill, a four-circle spider web, and a "How Do You Do," a circle dance in which couples skipped together. Musicians played "London Bridge Is Falling Down," "Gretchen Mine," and "Pop Goes the Weasel," an American folk classic based on the winding of wool onto a spindle. The peasants' dance to "Comin' Thro' the Rye" featured curtsies and bows.

German, Canadian, and English dancers continue to raise the maypole, especially in the Rhineland, Toronto, Edmonton, and Cornwall. The Tamil Nadu have their own version of the weaving dance, the *kolattam*, an interlacing of colored ropes around a pole by female dancers, a new moon veneration that involves unweaving and reweaving. At spring posts in Spain, Basques carry swords during the jumps and kicks of the *cinta dantza* and animate a puppet at the top of the pole for the *dominguillua*. Galicians encircle a decorated May tree and clap sticks to set the rhythm of their pageantry. In the United States, maypole activities flourish at women's colleges, where participants plait a daisy chain reflecting the theme of weaving a sisterhood.

See also circle dance; labyrinthine dance; *matachines*; morris dance; Roman dance; Wiccan dance.

Source: Diehl, Daniel, and Mark P. Donnelly. *Medieval Celebrations: Your Guide to Planning and Hosting Spectacular Feasts, Parties, Weddings, and Renaissance Fairs.* Mechanicsburg, PA: Stackpole, 2011.

MAZURKA

A traditional Polish, Filipino, Irish, and Swedish peasant dance, the mazurka energized participants with its triple time set by the *dudy* (bagpipe). The improvisational choreography of promenades, running steps, hops, glides, and clicks of metal heel taps on boots gained interest first in the 1500s as the war dance of Mazovia due north of Warsaw in central Poland. A century later at Poland's pinnacle of nationalism, the spirited dance acquired devotees across the country and into neighboring states for the accented second beat, which made the galloping rhythm easy to learn and fun to execute. Couples varied steps with lifts and a double spin, once clockwise and again counterclockwise.

Around 1697 after musicians added the violin, accordion, clarinet, and bass drum, Augustus II of Saxony, a noted womanizer and arts patron, imported the vivacious dance to Germany. The Parisian elite mastered the steps before Londoners learned them. Two years following Poland's defeat by Prussia and the dissection of the country by Austria and Russia, the gallant form provided homeless Poles with a national anthem, "The Dabrowski Mazurka" (1797) by patriot and poet Józef Wybicki of Pomerania.

The mazurka's martial air inspired Napoleon and his nobly uniformed Hussars, who courted village girls with the dance during the army's march across Europe. European émigrés carried the dance across the Atlantic to the West Indies. At Dominica, dancers graced the "mazook" or "mazouk" with easy slides and shuffles ending with cross steps. For a finale, they elevated the feet and clicked heels in figures that formed the island's national dance.

Evolution of the Mazurka

The mazurka evolved with the composition of the *kujawiak*, a slow, sentimental partners dance initiated in the 1820s, and advanced to the national dance of Hungary and Poland. When the steps combined with the repetitive quickstep of the *oberek*, the alliance yielded the standard mazurka. In 1825, Warsaw pianist Maria Szymanowska published the first collection of stylized dances in *25 Mazurkas*, an impetus for European sympathy with displaced Poles. At Montparnasse in 1830, Parisian dancers revved up the mazurka and galop into the high-energy cancan, an exhibitionist routine of high kicks to display lacy drawers and titillate night clubbers.

On November 29, 1830, the doomed November Uprising of Poles against the Russians inspired deeply patriotic composer Frédéric Chopin to produce more urban mazurkas. Over the next nineteen years, he wrote sixty-two moody pieces intended for soulful piano solos rather than dance. Of the main collection, twenty-seven, or 44 percent, of his mazurkas featured a minor key. During the Polish diaspora and the flowering of romantic nationalism, the mazurka epitomized the gay dance style and the disconsolate folk plaints of the expunged Polish homeland.

While competing with the schottische, reel, galop, polka, and waltz, the mazurka found favor with the lowest and highest classes of Russians in St. Petersburg. At court, dancers embraced the optimistic air and the rhythm as a victor's meter. In the 1830s, the Grand Duchess Maria "Masha" Nikolaevna, the arts-loving daughter of Nicholas I of Russia and Charlotte of Prussia, improvised the polka *mazur*, a variation that foregrounded the waltz.

Influenced by William Cavendish, the Duke of Devonshire, in 1845, the British embraced Polish folk arts. The English danced in ballrooms to Chopin's piano pieces, while the Irish preferred smoky pubs and renditions of "Shoe the Donkey," a two-hand dance in semi-open position. Although the Catholic hierarchy censured partnering, hip Parisians seized on the new steps in 1848, when waves of immigrants brought the mazurka and the musette (accordion) to riverbank *guinguettes* (dance halls) along the Marne. In competition with the *varsouvienne* from Warsaw, the mazurka also appealed to French folk groups in Nice and Languedoc and passed through Spanish colonials to Bohol, Philippines. In the same period, Americans in Chicago and California learned the dance from immigrant East European brewers and miners.

A mazurka charmed Emperor Napoleon III and Empress Eugénie at the 1870 debut of *Coppélia* at the Paris Opera, where composer Leo Delibes legitimized the first folk repertoire in classical ballet. Into the last quarter of the nineteenth century, Russian composers Alexander Scriabin and Alexander Borodin and Spanish pianist Enrique Granados retained the form, which Czech musician Antonín Dvořák added to his *Slavonic Dances* (1878). At the height of story ballet, Peter Ilyich Tchaikovsky showcased the dance in *Swan Lake* (1876), *Eugene Onegin* (1879), and *Sleeping Beauty* (1890).

The twentieth century produced long-trained designer dresses called mazurkas, Finnish classes exercising to Polish steps, and resurgences of dance studios and YMCA classes in the mid-1930s teaching the Eastern European rhythm. Sergei Prokofiev composed a mazurka for part two of the ballet *Cinderella* (1943). Two years later, when debutante and cotillion clubs taught Polish social dance to teens and children, skater Carol Lynne added a mazurka to her rink show. Into the modern age, bands in Nepal practiced the mazurka rhythms for accompanying Gurkha dancers. Jerome Robbins's *Dances at a Gathering* (1969) featured the innovations of Patricia McBride and Anthony Blum to the Polish dance.

The mazurka returned to dance floors in 1989, when the National Folk Ballet of Poland exhibited precise partnering in New York. In 1998, couples vied for awards at the French dance hall on l'Ile du Martin-Pêcheur. The dance retained its appeal on the Cape Verde island of Brava, at Bohol in the Philippines outside Cebu City, in Creole clubs in Guadeloupe and Martinique, and at Portuguese festivals. In Latin America, dance groups in Brazil, Mexico, Cuba, Nicaragua, and Curaçao performed the original rhythm and steps and assimilated them into Mexican folk art.

See also galop; polka; reel; schottische; story dance; *varsouvienne*; waltz.

Source: Grosby, Steven Elliot, and Athena S. Leoussi. *Nationalism and Ethnosymbolism: History, Culture, and Ethnicity in the Formation of Nations.* Edinburgh: Edinburgh University Press, 2007.

MERENGUE

A Dominican and Puerto Rican folk dance in closed position, the merengue expressed island gestures in circular hip thrusts, raised elbows, and right-to-left crossovers. Following in the wake of the *tumba*, an African beat from Aruba and Curaçao, and the Berber influence on the Cuban habanera, the merengue earned the name of foamy egg whites whipped with sugar, a dialect reference to the sweetness and frivolity of consensual sex. After Saint Domingue separated from Haitian rule in 1844, the merengue entered folk history as a risqué entertainment at the Perico Ripiao (ripped parrot) brothel.

In executing a stick-fence step, a side-to-side chassé (chase step), and Congo-Caribbean hip roll of the jungle lizard, folk performers dragged one leg to symbolize the impediment of plantation slaves chained together while they cut sugarcane or possibly to salute a buccaneer or war hero with a wooden right leg. As a stimulus to patriotism, Spanish lyrics belittled Tomás Torres, a deserter from the Battle of Talanquera, which the Dominicans won. The Haitian adaptation, called *"méringue,"* contributed elements of the European contradance and merged the choreography with the *calenda* and the *chica*. The gentler, guitar-based Haitian variant showcased antiphonal singing in French and mimicry of bourgeois colonial dance.

Diaspora Dance

Merengue steps from West African dance and aboriginal Taíno gestures followed a fast meter set by the *güira* (scraper), accordion, and two-ended tambora drum. While heel taps counted out the syncopated 2/4 beat, partners engaged and disengaged in backbends and close torso hugs, which conservative activist Ulises Francisco Espaillat charged as immoral in 1875. Individual experiments in Cuba and other Hispanic enclaves—call-and-response stanzas, stylized pirouettes—kept the merengue in a constant state of change.

Art historians identified the dance as an icon of miners and farmers of Santiago in the Cibao region in the north, dubbed the "cradle of the merengue." The trade in accordions for tobacco in the 1880s by German merchants added keyboarding on the squeezebox to the strum of stringed instruments. To simplify Caribbean rhythms for American occupation troops after 1905, innovators choreographed the *pambiche* (literally "Palm Beach"), a slower version easily mastered by US Marines.

Propaganda Dance

Upon the advance of Rafael Trujillo to the presidency of the Dominican Republic, on August 16, 1930, his campaigners refuted the Creole origins of the merengue to back racist denials of Trujillo's black ancestry. He forced instrumentalists to play merengue music over the radio and on television because the crisp, dazzling dance epitomized his lower-class upbringing and the comeuppance meted out to aristocrats.

With the promotion of the dictator and his brother, Petán Trujillo, the merengue progressed to the national Dominican dance, a priority it held for more than three decades. The marimba (thumb piano) coordinated with conga drums and other instruments to yield a unique island ambience. At Trujillo's assassination on May 30, 1961, salsa and rock and roll flooded the island, permeating merengue rhythms and choreography with erotic dips, winding-unwinding sets, and coiled hand twists.

In the 1970s, the "black is beautiful" movement forced a reexamination of Eurocentrism in art history, especially of the Bara of Madagascar, who may have introduced the merengue to the Caribbean. Dominican immigrants to Miami, the Bronx, and Manhattan introduced slick versions of the merengue in nightclubs and stage shows. As a result, all-female orchestral variations embroidered folk origins with pop adaptations that peaked in popularity in the 1990s during an influx of salsa bands.

See also bamboula; *calenda*; contradance; Creole dance.

Source: Sellers, Julie A. *Merengue and Dominican Identity: Music as National Unifier.* Jefferson, NC: McFarland, 2004.

MIME

A form of folk art and street theater, mime enlarges on dance by enhancing footwork with facial expression, body language, props, and mummery, the elements of the aboriginal Australian corroboree, the galloping steps of the sixteenth-century Polish *krakowiak*, and arm and shoulder motions of the Saami rowing dance from northern Norway. Beginners get their turn at learning the apprentice steps to the Norwegian Yulebokker and the Bavarian *Schuhplattler*. Imitation incorporates the bobbing and courtship of doves in the Mexican *jarabe tapatío*, the flutter of fans in the Korean *buchea-chum* (fan dance), and the harrumphing and tottering of the *baile de los viejitos* (dance of the old men), a Mexican dance from the Purépecha of Michoacán. To the monotonous tunes and rooster crows of the *murga*, Pakistani dancers replicate the cock's posturing over the hen and ensuing wing flaps and pelvic thrusts of mating.

In the ancient world, mime won the hearts of folk art lovers for its variety and agility, for example, the imitation of plowing and sowing in the Persian Carpaean dance, which takes a militant turn after a robber attacks the farmer. In the early Roman Empire under Augustus after 27 BCE, two skilled performers, Bathyllus and Pylades, amassed fans for their verve in spinning and slowing down to static schemata (poses) as well as for their intensity of gesture and emotion. According to Greek rhetorician Libanius around 360 CE, viewers of Roman mimes regarded the silent mask and the quick clacks of the *scabilla* (tap shoes) as essentials of story dance.

Masks and Disguises

Attire and equipment enabled dancers to mimic attitudes and scenarios, for example, the stilt walkers at Renaissance fairs playing the pranks of court jesters. From the 1600s in Zambia, Malawi, and Mozambique, the Chewa matriarchal society assuaged the insecurities of males by affirming secret men's societies. For the coming of age of youths, the brotherhood danced each July in straw and wood costumes consisting of oversized heads and whisks. The disguised figures enacted dishonorable behaviors in a morality pageant intended to terrify preteens and teach ethical and social values. After the colonization of the Chewa by Britain, in the 1860s, dancers in Mozambique and Zambia had to conceal the animistic source of their pageantry to escape the bans of Christian churchmen and the state.

Mime visualized common denominators of ethnic survival, for example, building an adobe roof in the Middle East, sawing logs into planks in Scandinavia, planting rice paddies in Southeast Asia, stalking birds in Pakistan, and gathering wheat to tie into sheaves in central Canada. Along the shores of Malaysia, villagers honored fisher folk with a costumed dance. As boats left from the coast, performers imitated the crew's united labor in casting nets and hauling in seafood.

Realistic Action

Natural phenomena and historical events supplied themes and topics for folk choreography, for example, moonrise in the hula, human bondage on the merengue, conquest in the Sioux scalp dance, and the battle of Moors and Christians in the *matachines*. Following the first encounters between European seamen and Tahitian islanders, Polynesian dancers turned shipboard slang into a circle dance. In imitation of the officers' yelling, "Heave now!" to rotations of the anchor chain, Tahitians encircled instrumentalists to form a wheel and chanted, "Havinau." Couples meeting on each pull faced each other and yelled to quivers of knees and hips, evidence of exhausting labor.

A daintier form of mime, the Swedish weaving dance incorporated a whole community in representing common fiber work. Two lines of dancers symbolized the alliance of warp and woof threads on a loom. To illustrate patterns, the lines crossed and recrossed, altering their stance with upraised hands and heads lowered to pass under the opposing line like threads in finished fabric. In a model of shuttle operation, children skittered between paired dancers.

See also animal dances; *branle*; commedia dell'arte; corroboree; cotton-eye Joe; dragon dance; Eskimo dance house; fan dance; highland fling; hornpipe; hula; hunting dance; *jarabe tapatío*; *kathak*; *matachines*; merengue; morris dance; *odori*; Persian dance; pipe dance; planting dance; scalp dance; *Schuhplattler*; *tanko bushi*.

Source: Hall, Edith, and Rosie Wyles, eds. *New Directions in Ancient Pantomime.* New York: Oxford University Press, 2008.

MORRIS DANCE

An Anglo-Welsh specialty from 1448, the morris dance derived from ancient sacrificial sword dance and the *morisca*, an ancient Moroccan fool's caper from farm to farm around agrarian boundaries. Originally, face blackening with fireplace ash retained the blessings of the Yule log, a Celtic custom of Irish mimes. From Iberia around 1300, late medieval morris dancers claimed pan-European rural customs and seasonal spectacle as ethnic expressions of unity and belonging.

In the gendered style of the Norwegian *halling*, the English morris dance highlighted the power and audacity of male exhibitionism. By the mid-fifteenth century, the Goldsmiths' Company in London received seven shillings for a presentation that contained three or four partner dances and single and double jigs. Moorish costuming retained the history of the struggle between Muslims and Catholics in Iberia until the ouster of Islam in 1492. On December 25, 1494, folk companies entertained Henry VII, who paid more than six pounds to obtain a dancer's disguise. An oak panel at Lancaster Castle captured the spirit of the era with a bas-relief of the dysard (fool), the key figure in morris revelry.

The Spanish victory over Islam injected strong pro-Christian sympathies and iconography into sixteenth-century mummery, for example, the face blacking of morris torchbearers at a banquet for Henry VIII in 1509. The following year, a juvenile company mimed a morris antic for the king's amusement. Costuming in 1584 at Shrewsbury, Herefordshire, for the Anglo-Welsh border morris showcased stick fighting, a hobby horseman, and a transvestite version of Maid Marian, a favorite heroine from the legends of Robin Hood.

Mumming and Royalty

During the reign of Elizabeth I, dancers in Coventry reenacted the 1012 war of Scots king Malcolm II against the Danes at Cruden Bay by trotting a four-hoofed gambade (caper) with hobbyhorses rather than real mounts. Drawing on the traditional Feast of Fools, morris costumes streamed parti-color ribbons and tinkled bells tied to the knee. The major sequence aped sword fights with clashing sticks and an indeterminate number of repetitions.

At London in 1600, actor William Kempe, a member of the Lord Chamberlain's Men, performed an unarmed version of morris mummery featuring sashes dangling from his elbows. As the laboring class took over morris companies from amateurs, they scheduled paired dancers and solos at Whitsuntide (Pentecost) on the Christian calendar. Because beggars emulated morris dancers by blackening their faces and pleading for coins, the morris disguise became a public nuisance, much as Halloween and carnival masks conceal thieves.

Pub and street appearances thrived until the formation of the English Commonwealth under Oliver Cromwell in January 1649. Under ultra-conservative leadership, fastidious Puritans suppressed tippling and street pageantry for disturbing the peace, especially on Sundays and church holidays. For justification, they denounced the dancing for having satanic sources. In London into the mid-1600s, morris travesties added comic touches to the lord mayor's procession to take the oath of office. By the restoration of Charles II to the throne on May 29, 1660, English peasants reclaimed morris performances in Chipping Campden, Grampton, Abingdon, and Headington Quarry.

Colonial Horseplay

Morris companies carried the mumming tradition around the colonial world to Hong Kong, New Zealand, Australia, Singapore, and Canada. Pageantry influenced the Philadelphia mummers' parade, also presented in blackface, and anticipated minstrel shows and the cakewalk, an exaggerated cortege created by slaves. In 1779, a morris dance theatrical from Revesby, Lincolnshire, reinstated a Christmas spectacle performed by plowboys. The following year, two more texts from Truro, Cornwall, and Islip, Oxfordshire, recorded japery and choreography. A Welsh version dating to 1788 confirmed morris dancing from Cheshire.

On the North American frontier, facets of the morris dance influenced the barn dance, clogging, and the neighborhood hoedown. As the British lower classes took over morris miming in the 1800s, performances took on a martial air, a quality they shared with the Norwegian *halling*, the Spanish *matachines*, and the Scots *lanciers* (lancers). Dancers wore white shirts with dark trousers, baldrics crossed over the chest, and bells attached to shin pads. Troupes of six men executed stick and handkerchief dances. Soloists added jigs. At Bromsberrow Heath, Gloucestershire, additional artistry from concertina players and hornpipe dancers varied the traditional steps and figures.

The morris dance passed through near death and resurrection. On December 26, 1899, a British revival of the pageantry initiated scholarly research into melodies and choreography that had lapsed over a quarter century. Amateur ethnographers

Ella Mary Leather of Herefordshire and Mary Neal of Birmingham retrieved dance history from obscure sources. Neal formed female morris troupes and promoted performances in the United States.

    See also barn dance; cakewalk; clogging; disguise; *halling*; handkerchief dance; hornpipe; jig; *matachines*; maypole dance; mime.

    Source: Cutting, John. *History and the Morris Dance: A Look at Morris Dancing from Its Earliest Days until 1850.* Alton, UK: Dance Books, 2005.

MUSIC, FOLK DANCE

Musicianship undergirds most folkloric dance, for example, the religio-historic *matachines* performed to drumming in Aguascalientes, Mexico; the whirling of bullroarers and shaking of nutshell rattles by the Mabuiag of the Torres Strait south of Papua New Guinea; and the Moroccan *ahwash*, for which lines of Berber men and women encircle drummers. The choice of instrumentation epitomizes sound and rhythm of choreography, a factor individualizing Trinidadian dance with bells, Spanish fandango with castanets and snapping fingers, Irish and Dutch cloggers with wood shoes, and the *terah taali* of Rajasthan, India, with the ting of finger cymbals. For the Kuy people of northern Cambodia, Laos, and Thailand, dancers performing the *robam kom areak* reduce their musical needs to the clatter of several bamboo poles.

    Percussive sound dominated primitive dance, an aural factor of Cheyenne ring dance and the Hindu *kathak* of 1200 CE, when dancers followed the metallic ring of cymbals and the meter of the table drum. In salute to the appearance of a rainbow or a four-master merchant vessel in the Tongan horizon, quartets of islanders performed the *soke*, a drum cadence setting the rhythm of sticks against each other. Rhythmic variations synchronized hitting sticks together at top or bottom, rotating the stick, and a finale, a thud of stick ends on the ground.

Diverse Music

Medieval celebrations involved gleemen, tumblers, stilt walkers, and reciters to the sounds of lyre, pipes, and rattles. The minstrels of Normandy orchestrated bones and spoons as well as trumpet, viol, and hand drum, the musical instruments that flourished as far south as Iberia, Majorca, Sardinia, Sicily, and southern Italy. By the 1300s, the bagpipe and harmonium altered both rhythm and tone of traditional instrumentation for the highland fling, sword dance, and *lanciers* (lancers).

    An array of sounds and timbres marked folk choreography that prefaced the Renaissance, as with the singing during the farandole and labyrinthine church dances. In the fourteenth century, Chaucer and others wrote of the mix of gymnastics with leaps through a hoop, lifts, walking on hands, and steps on stilts by men and women, a vigor that flourished in Rouen, France, and Ely and Lincoln, England. The Feast of Fools required skill at moving the head to jingly bells on the cap and rhythmic steps sometimes set to a hurdy-gurdy, a stringed instrument cranked with a handle to pluck a melody or activate a drone.

At Sheik Ali's outside Luxor, Egypt, in 1982, Khairiyya and Redja Maazin perform to the *rebaba*, a one-string instrument made from horsehair strung over a spike nail driven into a coconut shell. *Carolina Varga "Morocco" Dinicu, morocco@casbahdance.org, New York City.*

Music and Nationalism

Instrumentation set the tone and character of baroque folk dance, as with the frame drum and *zurna* (flute) accompanying the Kurdish *dilan*, the *raks baladi* to African flute and drums at Tehran, shoe and thigh slaps of the German *Schuhplattler* and clogging, and the lute, pipe, and tambourine backing a Palestinian or Jordanian *dabke*. After 1682, Tsar Peter the Great forced modernization on Russian folk arts. To raise the level of creativity to French and German standards for the harpsichord and harp, he prohibited dancing to traditional balalaika and zither. To outwit the edict, villagers reduced their usual folk presentations to singing rather than instrumental accompaniment.

In southern Mozambique, the Chopi arranged extravagant musicales to support a dance troupe of twelve performers. While the dancers sang, chanted, and recited pastoral verse, an orchestra of some thirty wood *timbila* (xylophones) accompanied the community sing. Each instrument required the placement of sneezewort wood slats over resonating gourds. The instrumentalist, whether child or adult, tuned the percussion scale by sealing the gourds with beeswax and tempering the vibrations with *nkuso* fruit oil.

In North America, painter George Catlin immortalized a threatened folk art, the discovery dance of the Fox and Sauk, which required no music. In 1835, he witnessed a tuneless pantomime fleshed out with drollery to the patting of bare feet. The figures set two or four males forward at a time. Skulking and surveying the country, the men mimicked spying on enemies or the tracking of deer. At the height of the silent dance, hunters signaled their reports to the dance leader. In contrast to the quiet pat-pat of feet, the Lakota Sioux beggar's dance, which Catlin sketched in 1832 outside Fort Pierre, South Dakota, at the mouth of the Teton River, advanced to loud drumming, hallooing, singing, and rattles of young men in quilled breechcloths encouraging the tribe to donate to the poor and helpless.

Square dancing and the Hispanic *jota* and fandango followed whatever instruments immigrants and pioneers brought with them as they crossed the frontier. In the South, call-and-response singing, juice harp, and banjo backed up the juba and *calenda*. For the cotton-eye Joe and cotillion, barn dancers on the plains of Canada and the United States shaped figures to fiddle, guitar, organite (barrel organ), and accordion or concertina. For holidays, particularly carnival throughout the Caribbean and South America, whistles, drums, horns, clapping, and chant vied for the lead.

See also barn dance; *calenda*; circle dance; clogging; cotillion; cotton-eye Joe; drumming; fandango; farandole; highland fling; *jota*; juba; *kathak*; labyrinthine dance; *matachines*; *Schuhplattler*; sword dance.

Source: Anon. *The Dance: Historic Illustrations of Dancing from 3300 B.C. to 1911 A.D.* London: John Bale, Sons & Danielsson, 1911.

· *N* ·

NORTH AFRICAN DANCE

North Africans produced the original folk rhythms and choreographed the first set figures. According to stylized pictorial evidence, after 4400 BCE, predynastic Egyptian folk dance followed musical meter, as presented in Amratian art from El Amrah in which the trainer counted the oldest four-beat cadence in history. Presentations advanced from solo choreography in propitiation of the sun to precisely symmetrical woman-with-woman or man-with-man ranks and processional dance at temple festivals and around the sacred sun barge. No image suggests man-to-woman partnering.

In a style that prefigured Greco-Roman dramatic chorus of tragedy and comedy, Egyptian groups characterized emotions, events, or ideals. Expressions focused on yearning, loss, abduction, emancipation, fertility, and abundance. Food security dominated rites to the lioness deity Bast after 2890 BCE and the dancing goddess Hathor at agrarian thanksgivings. After 2686 BCE, worshippers propitiated the mother goddess Mut in village group dances.

Intricate Egyptian figures, gymnastic *salto mortales* (somersaults), lyrical combinations, processional steps, and imitations of stork, ostrich, and crocodile movements took their cues from the percussion of wood castanets, tambourines, and cymbals and the phrasing of flutes, harps, lutes, single and double pipes, and the magical *sistrum*, a branched metal shaker believed to dispel evil. Street performers limited accompaniment to snapping fingers and drumming. The peasant class indulged in pantomimes of the rich and prominent and grotesque satires of human foibles and handicaps, often performed by court dwarves, such as the pygmy that Governor Harkhuf of Aswan dispatched from the Nile island of Elephantine to ten-year-old Pharaoh Pepi II Neferkare in 2274 BCE.

For banquet entertainment from 2000 BCE, paired dancers of the Old Kingdom appeared in bare feet and bodies adorned with jewels, tasseled girdles, aprons or short skirts, and handheld canes. The troupe's line, encouraged by female hand clappers, continued into the street, where spectators tossed coins. In a dining hall at Memphis, male and female dancers clacked hollow wood castanets and acted out a lyrical seduction scene marked by female pirouettes and balanced postures. More sophisticated attire featured the transparent linen caftan. After 1700 BCE, company attire consisted of collar, toe rings, wig, pigtail or braids, garlands, and head cone, a perfumed emollient that gradually melted, spreading a heady scent over the dance floor.

Standardized Dance

The ancient Egyptians were the first choreographers. They codified pirouettes and vibrant finger snaps, which survive from 1000 BCE on painted walls and papyrus scrolls and in bas-relief. The two-dimensional displays capture the essence of honor to royalty performed by palace slaves and imported black Nubian leapers; tomb art glorified religious rites governing death and rebirth, two Egyptian obsessions. The exodus of Hebrew slaves from bondage around 1446 BCE impacted Hebrew temple sacrifice and thanksgiving with Egyptian-style dance and praise to Yahweh for a safe flight of the Israelites from the pharaoh, perhaps Thutmose III.

During the rise of Persia to an Asian superpower, priests cultivated soma, a sacramental drink that fueled cultic dance among royal magi. In Egypt, gymnosophists, in the style of monastic Brahmans, followed similar patterns of stimulation before the ceremony. The Greeks learned firsthand about holy drink and dance from Alexander the Great, who met the magi in India. After 300 BCE, monks quartered outside Alexandria perpetuated the rituals, which passed to Romans at Ostia, Greeks at Piraeus, and Hebraic Essenes living in caverns along the Dead Sea.

With the arrival of the Fatimids in 973, Egyptian male *darawish* (Sufi dancers) adopted the *tanoura*, a counterclockwise physical meditation featuring a tall cylindrical hat, black robe, short jacket, and long white tunic topped with a long skirt adorned with geometrics or Islamic cultic symbols. For more than two centuries, the kaleidoscopic whirling skirt dance captured the cyclical seasons and the spirituality of the Sufist as he merged into nature. By stripping colored layers from the spinning skirt, the solo performer illustrated the mystic shedding of earthly ties. Chanting "La illa-ha ill llah," the dancer glorified and merged with Allah in a trance-like state of purity. He lifted his right hand and pointed down with his left to indicate a mystic fusion of heaven with earth.

The Western Mediterranean

Algerian dance heritage, as recorded on cave walls of the Mahgreb, commemorates the originality and wisdom of ancestors. On the desert border with Niger, the nomadic male Tuareg of the Sahel emulated hunting and combat movements with the *tergui*, a dance performed to a small frame drum, stringed instruments, and female ululations generated by tongue flutters. Performers at weddings and feasts dressed in black and white turbans and loose robes and brandished shields and swords. For a symbolic version, they presented a stick dance similar to the Tunisian saber dance or united villagers to act out historic combat to the singing and drumming of female backup groups.

For weddings and social gatherings farther inland at Timbuktu, Mali, women of the Tuareg Kel Tagelmousse (blue people) shuffled to the repetitive *guedra* trance dance, a blessing from the Moroccan Sahara arousing spiritual joy. The indigo powder of the one-piece *haik* (robe) tinted the skin and kept it moist in an arid environment. The headdress consisted of braids and cowrie shells, which symbolized the power and fecundity of female genitalia.

A performance lasting hours throbbed to drumming on a cauldron topped by animal skin. In the matriarchal culture, women displayed their sexual experience and wooed their mates at courtship dances where a circle of females clapped, swayed, and chanted gratitude for life to ancestors and the universe. Until 1956, they performed the traditional gliding steps bare breasted with kohl-edged eyes flashing, cheeks and fore-heads whitened with clay from Agades, and hennaed hands flicking from head to torso.

A gendered dance in western Morocco, the *dans el alaoui* coordinated steps to a shrill flute repeating the same musical phrase. Clutching a thin stick, male soloists made small steps while flexing back and shoulders. The focus of movement on shoulders flaunted the male physique. From 1810, the *chaouia* (or *shawiya*) and the *rahaba* of the northeast expressed the hospitality of Berber desert dwellers, who welcomed strangers and guests with song and a shoulder- and belly-shaking dance to the flute and frame drum.

At Tan-Tan in southern Morocco from the 1930s, some thirty itinerant tribes gathered in May for the *moussem*, an annual agricultural and camel- and horse-trading fair. Nomads celebrated marriages with dance, games, chant, poetry contests, and instrumental presentations. Security threats ended the moussem from 1979 to 2004. When it resumed, celebrants chose September to display their cultural arts.

At Gourara, Algeria, the Zenete observe the all-night *ahellil*, an arts fest derived from Berber, Arab, and Sudanese homage to holy days and pilgrimages. Through polyphonic music, dance, and chant to the flute, participants shoulder in to a tight circle and shuffle around the lead singer. The lengthy religious ceremony reaches a climactic coda sung at a crescendo. The conclusion emphasizes the power the tribe gains from harmony and shared Islamic beliefs.

Tunisian women display reed skirts, feather and shell accessories, and multihued paper crowns as they sing and dance the *bou saada*. Integral to current folk art in Tunisia and Libya are limited head and shoulder involvement, swift sways of the hips, and intricate twists and slides of bare feet to singing and flute and bagpipe accompaniment. For public presentation, acrobatic slides and rolls at street level to the frame drum demonstrate male agility and grace. Women clasp ends of head scarves and twirl them overhead while keeping up a strong beat with bare feet.

Barefoot Mauritanian dance in voluminous embroidered robes creates an air of swirling and an uplift from gravity. While women ululate and clap on the offbeat, turbaned male dancers lift the edges of their robes to suggest wings in bold solo improvisation to flute, drum, and cymbals. Leg swings and acrobatic leaps take precedence over hand and head movement. A mock militaristic version coordinates leg swings while both hands grip a piece of wood shaped like a rifle.

Less chaste than Mauritanian coverings, the bulbous breast and upper hips of female Moroccan belly dancers display fleshy bodies as elements of femininity. At nuptial festivities, skin-topped frame drums thunder while dancers' ululations release bursts of joy. For displays of manhood in the *ghiayta* dance, Haha Berber boys in the Atlas Mountains stamp their feet and enact battles by pretending to shoot rifles. Women prefer fluidity and grace for the *ouai*, which vaunts belted silk caftans to performances of fiddle and mandolin music. For the *houara*, Berber men and women join a close-packed circle and claim the honor of a solo dance to exhibit intricate footwork.

In the highlands, dancers of the *ahidus* shouldered in for a circle or parabolic lines and moved to the music of performers in the center. Another version involved wedding parties in the *bendir*, a rhythmic dance devoid of improvisation. For the *ahwash*, Berbers form men's and women's circles that enwrap the drummer. As the circles rotate, each group makes up poems to recite as a gendered competition, males against females. For a more physical test of stamina and endurance, males and females try to outdance each other in the *dukkala*, the Moroccan version of the Phoenician *dabke*.

See also belly dance; circle dance; martial dance; nuptial dance; propitiation.

Sources: Lexová, Irena. *Ancient Egyptian Dances.* Mineola, NY: Dover, 2000. Welsh, Karlamu. *World of Dance: African Dance.* New York: Infobase, 2010.

NUDITY

The shedding of clothes for pageantry demonstrates joie de vivre (joy of living), health, and removal of social barriers between performers and spectators. The liberation of spirit became the dominant motivation for the Germanic Walpurgis Night excesses and nude Korean fan dance and the purpose of Cheyenne war chief Roman Nose for an Iowa scalp dance in London in fall 1845. From the Neolithic Age, naked figures honored Mesopotamian deities with processions to taps on the tambourine. In bas-relief, one impression of nudity on the Fertile Crescent enhances the importance of a conical headdress and lauds the juggler who keeps a ball in motion while performing sacred choreography. After 2000 BCE, Babylonians adopted religious nudity and striptease, a temple dance gradually disclosing intimate body parts to honor Ishtar, goddess of love and procreation.

The Body as Art

Egyptians performed ritual and private choreography in the nude or in minimal wraps, a display of physique and articulated motion that shamed their conservative Hebrew slaves around 800 BCE. The Egyptian *bedleh* (belly dance costume) featured the bare midriff undulations of soloists coordinated with processions of bare-chested male and female performers in belts and aprons. After the migration of the Lapita over Oceania in this same period, aborigines introduced island choreography at Fiji, Samoa, and the Marquesas. Following combat, nude Marquesan widows performed lamentation dances for dead husbands as a way to arouse vengeance against the enemy.

In folk arts on the Peloponnesus, Greeks claimed bare musculature as evidence of human excellence, a tenet expressed by bare girls commemorating Theseus's slaying of the Minotaur on Crete and young men honoring the festivals of Apollo with circle and line formations. In 765 BCE, Lycurgus of Sparta exonerated elite females performing the *hormos* for bodybuilding and ignoring the criticism of commoners. Around 650 BCE, Spartans organized bare soldiers into military processions for unified steps to marches. Descriptions of Queen Helen of Sparta depicted her dancing bare in the custom of her people.

At Rome each February 15, the Lupercalia honored the mothering of city founders Romulus and Remus by a she-wolf. To cleanse the city of winter's staleness, priests stripped to a goatskin belt before loping through the streets to summon fertility and health with dances and lashes of their whips. The Roman introduction to Germania impressed the historian Tacitus with the nude dance of the Alemanni (or Swabians) of the upper Rhine Valley. According to his chronicle of 98 CE, young soldiers disrobed to perform steps on the tips of javelins and spears in a daring style similar to the highland fling.

Throughout the Roman Empire, nude choreography became the province of the lower-class entertainer. The *saltatrix* (dancing girl) mesmerized guests at banquets with glinting torso belts, anklets, and garlands in her hair. She enticed roguish glances by flirting with her *coa vestis*, a sheer veil or transparent bit of linen drapery that floated behind her, offering limited glimpses of her limbs and torso. Proper matrons watched the dance, but distanced themselves personally and socially from so tawdry a performance.

Naturalism and Christianity

Christian dogma wavered on issues of pagan exhibitionism. In Algeria after 100 CE, the cult of Adamites, sensual mystics, retained the chastity and innocence of Adam and Eve from the book of Genesis by conducting processions and ceremonies that flaunted bare flesh. In Byzantium, Christian converts gradually accepted dance into Eastern Greek Orthodox culture. Pageantry included the exotic components of Gothic dance performed by naked troupes. Turkish males with uncovered chests partnered with female belly dancers.

After Charlemagne, King of the Franks, and Pope Stephen III prohibited dance in 768, female devotees of Saxon goddess cults retreated to Brocken (or Blocksberg) Mountain, the highest peak in northern Germany. In seclusion, votaries danced naked or cloaked in animal skins. On May Eve, university students in Finland, Denmark, Germany, Czech Republic, Latvia, Lithuania, Estonia, France, Belgium, Holland, and Spain reclaimed the nude ring dance, which they performed until sunrise as a form of nature worship.

The height of the bubonic plague (1347–1353) in Germany evoked the pagan in survivors. Unimaginable grief yielded funeral processions and the stripping of mourners for the *Totentanz*, a nude lamentation dance atop tumuli and cairns. For the sake of satire, in the late Middle Ages, dancers introduced an orgiastic nude caricature for *The Comedy of Katablattas* (1433), a mockery of Demetrios Katadokeinos of Thessalonica, a former infantryman at Bursa and political hack guilty of impiety and sybaritism.

Social Rarities

By the baroque era, bare flesh became the exception rather than the rule in folk arts. In Devon, East Anglia, and the Lake District of England, male cloggers danced their arguments by performing naked and settling their tiffs by kicking opponents in the head. In this same period in Oceania, Captain James Cook toured the Hervey Islands and Tahiti in 1773 and 1774, where the Areois, a secret brotherhood of celibate warriors, held all-night dances. Wearing only red facial paint, black body markings, and coconut oil, they performed scenarios of combat and passion.

The seminude Etruscan dance from 600 BCE anticipated the flagrant nudity of performers during the Roman Empire. *Anon.* The Dance: Historic Illustrations of Dancing from 3300 B.C. to 1911 A.D. *London: John Bale, Sons & Danielsson, 1911.*

According to explorers, a male-female choreography executed by the Bora of the Amazonian rainforest involved dancing in a short fig-bark kilt below a naked torso. In a village ceremony held in a community pavilion, new mothers shielded their milk-engorged breasts by cuddling their infants as they danced. Late nineteenth-century victory songs of the Omaha and Ponca of Nebraska changed during the conversion of northern plains tribes to Christianity. In place of scalp dances, warriors created the nude grass dance, during which participants imitated the sway of prairie grass. Mimetic figures illustrated methods of stalking the enemy through waving green expanses. From Australia, aboriginal dancer David Gulpilil performed balletic moves and painted bare flesh for the film *Walkabout* (1970).

See also belly dance; body art; circle dance; fan dance; line dance; North African dance; Polynesian dance; scalp dance; *Totentanz*; Walpurgis dance.

Sources: Collon, Dominique. "Dance in Ancient Mesopotamia," *Near Eastern Archaeology* 66, no. 3 (September 2003): 96–102. Crowe, Felicity, Emily Hill, and Ben Hollingum, eds. *Sex and Society.* Tarrytown, NY: Marshall Cavendish, 2010.

NUPTIAL DANCE

The choice of dances to grace betrothals and weddings preserved in art chronicles the rise of folkloric choreography, as with the obligatory Jewish dance honoring brides, Hawaiian hulas performed by brides for their new mates, and the Chinese lion dance, which spread through diaspora across the Asian world and to global Chinatowns. Diverse examples ranged from the dance of Isaiah that Byzantine guests performed at weddings to the fandango that honored newlyweds in Richard Henry Dana's *Two Years before the Mast* (1842). At Europe's feudal courts, guests formed a chain for the torch dance, a nuptial tradition that filled the great hall with light, laughter, footsteps, and singing.

Late medieval weddings incorporated dance as a stimulus to community. A royal model, the highland fling, unified all social levels on November 1, 1285, at Jedburgh Abbey for the wedding of Scots king Alexander III to Yolande de Dreux, the Countess of Montfort. Roving troubadours led the festivities as part of their duties as hired entertainers and dance instructors to the young, who boarded in baronial castles to acquire the manners and courtesies of pages, grooms, valets, and ladies-in-waiting.

A Social Leveler

During the Renaissance, wedding directors scheduled the dances of the day—the reel, pavane, galliard, gavotte, hora, sarabande, *branle*, polonaise, and saltarello—as exercise and entertainment for freedmen, servants, children, and artisans. In the late 1500s, church prelates concurred that dance offered clean, structured fun that stabilized society and accorded dignity to weddings as well as funerals. In central Poland around 1679, the *oberek* challenged merrymakers to twirl with partners and sing ribald verses to marriage songs.

In Suriname, an Afro-Caribbean *kaseko* troupe follows the wedding party through the streets as a form of blessing and good wishes. In the style of seventeenth-century Ghana and Ivory Coast Maroons in French Guiana, dancers shuffled, marched, and dipped to drumming, whistles, and brass riffs in syncopated 3/4 time. Dutch colonists transported the soothing Creole calypso strains to Holland radio broadcasts, preserving in part the *kawina* and *winti* religious call and response and Yoruba and Akan choreography of Creole Latin America.

Innovative Dance

A simple but enlivening dance of the eighteenth century, the Aragonese *jota* set toe taps and bounds to songs of love, courting, intimacy, and wedlock. Late in the 1700s, Dalmatian wedding receptions at Dubrovnik incorporated the *lindo* (also *lindjo*). A lively duet of stamping boots and arms held overhead, the nuptial lindo combined figures and rhythms from Greece and the Ottoman coast. A leader announced sets and coaxed soloists to create new figures. A more structured choreography governed Swedish weddings, where the bride danced first with the minister, then the groom and her father and father-in-law. The series ended with a ring dance around the groom, whom men in the wedding party saluted by raising him to their shoulders.

At Assyrian weddings, guests grasped hands in a line or ring for the *khigga*, a reception dance. After the honored couple completed their vows, they passed through a clutch of dancers whose fancy footwork expressed joy and merriment. The leader raised a cane or sounded bells and rattled beads in a gesture of good will and luck. A parallel view of Turkish wedding ritual in the film *Before Your Eyes* (2009) emphasized the simplicity and unity of family dance.

See also branle; chain dance; circle dance; diaspora; film, folk dance in; galliard; gavotte; highland fling; hora; hula; Jewish dance; *jota*; lion dance; martial dance; *oberek*; pavane; polonaise; *polska*; reel; saltarello.

Source: Barr, Amelia E. "Characteristic Dances of the World." *Lippincott's Magazine* 27, no. 4 (April 1881): 330–41.

· *O* ·

OBEREK

A national couples dance of Poland, around 1679, the *oberek* (also *obertas* or *ober*) introduced frenzied spinning and bouncing among the peasants of Mazowsze, Mazovia. A type of mazurka for the harvest celebrations of feudal times, the oberek exhibited a variety of whirling, twisting, springing, and rolling moves common to gatherings on village greens. Suites of fast and slow footwork followed the phrasing of violin, accordion or harmonium, and jingle drum played with both ends of a mallet in 3/8 meter. The pulse-raising execution served multiple purposes, including celebration and educating the young in the kinetic skills that remained in practice for centuries.

Less dignified than the polonaise and the sedate walking step of the pavane, the dizzying oberek migrated from farmland to urban areas. During a century and a half of statelessness for Poles from 1772 to 1918, the dance preserved ethnic memory of social traditions and buoyed patriotism. In the hope of regaining sovereignty, dancers at eighteenth-century pre-Lenten carnivals flourished from the rise of romanticism and appreciation of folk arts. Amid masking and hobbyhorses, oberek dancers bonded in virtuoso showmanship of counterclockwise turns while revolving clockwise around a circle.

A Blend of Folkways

From ethnic pluralism, the oberek gained embellishments and hybrid blends with the Hungarian-Roma czardas, German *Ländler*, and Czech *sedska* (also *sousedska* or *svedska*), a slow, swaying dance in 3/4 meter. Beginning with hand clasping, Polish pairs stamped, hooted, and set a heart-pounding pace that reached its height in the 1830s. Innovators added teasing duets, two-footed bounds, double stomps, kneeling, heel clicks, and lifts equal in power and daring to the World War II jitterbug. Oscillations and reversals set braids and aprons flying and revealed ruffled underskirts, which reflected the impeccable white of female blouses under torso-hugging vests.

During the uncertainty of nineteenth-century power politics, Poles entered a diaspora eased by the transport of music and dance to new lands. The one hundred Silesian families who fled Russian oppression in Poland and settled Panna Maria and Bandera in southern Texas in 1854 imported a dichotomy of folk music—their

Catholic hymns and the rural melodies of the oberek and polka. By October 1855, some seven hundred Poles established their folkways and music in Bremen, Texas, featuring the mazurka tunes of native son Frédéric Chopin. The singing of Bohemian dancers accentuated nonsense syllables along with jibes and sexual innuendo, particularly for wedding receptions.

Dance and Assimilation

At the peak of immigration from Poland to the plains states of North America in the 1880s, the Catholic Church balanced worship with the ethnic gaiety of dance. At the parish hall, clubs and fraternal organizations held socials that taught children the steps and rhythms of the fatherland. The national costume—loose red trousers above shiny black boots for men and boots and striped red skirts for women—shaped a kaleidoscope of color and vigor to wide leg swings and heel lifts.

By the 1900s, the oberek progressed from folk genre to stage and recreational application among Polish-American youth in Chicago and Milwaukee and farther north at Halifax, Nova Scotia; Calgary, Alberta; Regina, Saskatchewan; and Elmira, Ontario. In the 1920s, Polish rule of Polissia, Ukraine, promoted the oberek north of the Black Sea. The jubilant sound thrived into the post–World War II era through radio broadcasts from Detroit.

Under the Marxism of the 1930s, folk dance supported socialist ideology as an assertion of nationalism, which dancers executed in Berlin at the 1936 International Dance Festival. For Polish-Americans of Orange County, Florida, the oberek retained its feudal connection to the onion harvest. In the 1970s, the folk arts movement incorporated the oberek into elementary school physical education in Louisiana and into wedding receptions in Utica, New York.

See also acrobatic dance; circle dance; czardas; diaspora; *Ländler*; masked dance; mazurka; pavane; polka; polonaise.

Sources: Carlos-Machej, Klaudia. "Polish National Dance as a Value of Culture." *Philosophical Education* 48 (2009): 219–40. Rinaldi, Robin, Elizabeth A. Hanley, and Jacques d'Amboise. *European Dance: Ireland, Poland, Spain, and Greece*. New York: Infobase, 2010.

ODORI

A traditional summer circle dance, Japanese *odori* derived from a late twelfth-century all-night community festival commemorating souls. First mentioned as a dance of joy in a Buddhist sutra, the superstition derived from 657, when peasants adopted a ritual choreography from India welcoming the dead to their homes with lamps lighting the route from cemeteries to towns. Dance steps from grave to front door raised the spirits of ghosts and dispelled fears. After 1185, rural families performed the *kumi* odori for several days to give thanks to ancestors for ample stores.

In Shinto style, from the 1200s, rural dancers honored clan spirits at the same time that they warded off demons. To welcome the New Year, *honen* odori thanked deities for abundant food. Steps set to roundelays and hymns to Buddha requested rebirth in paradise. Presentations took on a secular meaning at coastal Tokushima in 1586, when free sake and the *awa* odori dance of the dead involved all citizens in the opening of Lord Hachisuka Iemasa's feudal castle.

Odori by children, youths, adults, and elders reflected everyday life, animism, and folk sociability. Nimble dancers performed to the familiar *minyo* (call and response) songs, plowing and planting melodies, children's tunes, and sea chanties of Hokkaido country folk in the far north. In the Edo period after 1603, the choreography took on localized elements of raised arms, clapping, quick gliding and shuffling, and exaggerated triangular gestures as well as the lyrics of foolish taunts.

A more spiritual version from the southern midland city of Ochiai, *shishi* odori, danced in deer masks, demanded chanting of Buddhist prayers at shrines to complete the transformation from human spirit to mammal. By manipulating deer bones, from ancient times, performers predicted the rice-growing season. To create contact between the living and dead, performers dressed in antlers, beat drums, and mimed the life of a deer in leaps and stalking.

Music and Mime

In coastal Tottori, odori dancers honored the dragon god and king and wielded paper parasols to combat drought. The arrival of the rainy season required more choreography in thanksgiving. To the song "Soran bushi," dancers moved in unison mimicking ocean waves, seagull flutters, and fishermen's chores of lifting and tugging ropes and pulling in nets. In fishing communities, odori instruction became part of school curricula. In 1657, the witty, folksy spirit of odori permeated the Yaeyama Islands as *angama*, a masked samurai dance for celebrations and funerals in which questions and answers probed the mysteries of death.

Other dance exports included *jiruku* on Kohama Island and *eisa* among Okinawa's seasonal laborers, who danced behind a procession of drummers making high steps, turns, and stomps to the beats. In the Kyushu coal mining region, dance to "Tanko bushi" derived from the Kyoto era after 1716. Dance mime imitated the miner entering a lower level carrying a lantern and performing his tasks of digging, loading a cart, and pushing it to the surface.

Farther south in Shiga, Japan, dancers improvised odori to "Goshu ondo," lyrical music from the Meiji era after 1868. Played on taiko drum and shamisen on a central platform, the tune, originally a religious game song, accompanied story dance and elicited exuberant audience participation. A jester mocked serious dance with somersaults and cartwheels and imitations of a soaring kite.

Dance Contests

In the early 1900s, block parties from July to September introduced child and adult competition for awards in group cohesion and costumes. To perpetuate Asian culture and maintain contact with deceased relatives, diasporic odori replicated summer festivals and street dancing in California, France, and coastal Argentina; Maui, Hawaii;

Traditional Japanese dance sets rhythms to the koto and samisen. *Eastlake, W. Delano. "Japanese Home Life." Popular Science 43 (May 1893): 8.*

Penang, Malaysia; and São Paulo, Brazil. Masked dancers presented the Korean version, known as *baekjung*, and fostered friendship by inviting other villages to join the fun.

Odori attire coordinated the display of summer kimonos, head wraps, fans, wood clackers, and colorful hand towels. While dancing with bent knees, men led with right arms and feet and crossed the left legs, then repeated on the other side. Women in tight kimonos minced along, accentuating their advance with kicks to the rear, the only open part of the skirt. The all-girl *hanagasa* odori incorporated V-shaped straw hats tied under the chin.

In 2005 in the style of a Christian All Souls' Day in San Francisco and San Jose, Buddhist priests led a memorial assembly of taiko drummers and dancers in kimonos and *happi* coats. The performers followed patterned steps to release suffering ghosts from torment. At parks, temple ponds, and shores, lanterns floating on water escorted the spirits back to the afterlife. Currently, performers of *torisashi* odori at Nagasaki carry mock spears and wear cloth beaks to emulate prehistoric bird hunters.

See also circle dance; drumming; parasol dance; *tanko bushi*.

Source: Lancashire, Terence A. *An Introduction to Japanese Folk Performing Arts.* Farnham, UK: Ashgate, 2011.

· 𝒫 ·

PARASOL DANCE

The Japanese *hiyori kasa* (literally "nice day") or parasol dance builds delicacy and gentility within children's games and ethnic figures performed by little girls and women. From the second century BCE, the accoutrements of parasol dancing derived from *hakka* inventors in northern China and dramatized prop manipulation as a part of choreographed figures intended to amuse Japanese farmers. The giddy steps and trivial motifs convey patriarchal social prohibitions ensuring the chastity of girls and women as far east as Malaysia and west to Persia.

The female bauble emerged in the 500s during the Tang Dynasty from oiled paper coverings manufactured in China, Korea, and Japan. From the late Middle Ages, the Japanese umbrella dance prefaced summer activities with dance steps set to plucks on the samisen. First executed with mincing steps and frozen facial expressions, the dance gained favor during the reign of Emperor Ashikaya Shogun beginning in 1368. Because of a ban on female dancing in 1635, male performers learned female coquetry and executed a transvestite version of the choreography that further trivialized the role of women in society and the folk arts.

Enacting Vulnerability

A standard image of Japanese female attire, the paper umbrella over sashed kimono with wide lapels and block-heeled wood clogs suggests the insignificance of submissive women throughout East and Southeast Asian history, a facet shared with the Korean fan dance. Just as foot binding of Chinese toddlers crippled women over time, the parasol dance in Thailand and southeastern Cambodia visualized the educational and socioeconomic handicaps of females, especially preteens. For symbolic reasons, female guests at weddings performed with umbrellas to mirror the bride's limited expectations under a domineering head of household.

During assertions of femininity from the 1400s, parasol dancers struggled with gendered barriers to self-expression by adding umbrella raising and lowering to folk music. In Okinawa, women evolved from Kabuki dance drama the *higasa odori*, a late twelfth-century community spirit dance reflecting Ryukyuan court protocols of the 1700s. Imaginative gestures—recessive shuffles of tabi-swathed feet, dexterous twirling of handles, hiding behind figured silk tops, standing or sitting under the floral umbrella—illustrated the stagnation and monotony of female artistry and lifestyle. While peeping out from behind the facade, presenters typified both impediments to a full life and curiosity about what they were missing.

In the late 1800s, North American performances idealized the unfettered lives of nubile girls in the outdoors with elaborate mime, such as the Asian umbrella-themed musicale delivered in Pasadena, California, in 1899. Dance school recitals and welcome-to-Japan tableaus at Yokosuka harbor in Honshu acknowledged modernization of the arts with umbrellas that lit up. Still, the nature of clogs, kimonos, and parasols remained shackled to the patriarchal past.

A Japanese parasol dance features a geisha soloist performing on elevated shoes. *Eastlake, W. Delano. "Japanese Home Life."* Popular Science *43 (May 1893): 10.*

Parasol Lampoons

On early twentieth-century stages and in taverns in the Philippines, United States, and Europe, stripper shows and burlesque versions parodied the parasol dance with mock modesty and coarse pratfalls. In contrast to the effete thirteenth-century choreography of androcentric Japan, black American exhibitionist Josephine Baker subverted ultra-girlish dance poses in Paris in the 1920s. When she swung an umbrella to high kicks, she evoked female liberation and self-determination. Czech-American watercolorist Jan Matulka replicated the audacious dance idiom in the gouache painting "Dancing Woman with Parasol" (1929), a modernist depiction of raised umbrella and parallel leg lift.

The Amerindian form of umbrella attitudinizing contrasted with the precision and poise of the more common Asian parasol dance. In recent times on the Andean border of Bolivia and Peru at Lake Titicaca, a sinuous Aymara dancer executed long strides and twirls of the parasol handle with feminine self-possession. Her self-indulgent turns and twists to a rhapsodic flute, bongo, and string melody redirected feminine posturing toward a suggestive eroticism.

See also fan dance; *odori*; scarf dance.

Source: Udall, Sharyn R. *Dance and American Art: A Long Embrace.* Madison: University of Wisconsin Press, 2012.

PARTNERING

An advance from prehistoric fire dances and processions, partnering displayed a higher state of civilization as choreography acquired the cachet of interethnic gender mixing. Examples exist worldwide in the *marinera norteña* and *huayño* courtship duos of pre-Columbian Andeans of Peru, the Swedish three-beat *hambo*, the Norwegian *samdans* and *gammeldans*, and the Hispano-Mayan *baile de las cintas* (ribbon dance), a couples pageant around the maypole in Yucatán, Mexico. Open position preceded partnering with male-female pairs standing side by side or holding hands, as for a Polish *oberek* and the undulating *siva* Samoa of Oceania.

Ancient literature recorded pairing around 800 BCE, when the Greek poet Homer admired the *hormos*, an interweaving of maidens and youths in a modest geometric figure. Much as acrobatic pairs enlivened the circus, the union of dancers dramatized the harmonic momentum, coordination, and comparative strengths of opposite genders, the focus of the Hispanic fandango. To the rhythm of drumming, chanting, singing, and instrumental music, synchrony enabled pairs to interpret figures that joined yin and yang in a visual and kinetic spectacle. The result pleased both performers and viewers and influenced sculpture, bas-relief, painting, mural, and verse with the idealized dancing duo.

Censorship of Twosomes

In the late Middle Ages and early Renaissance, couples dances manifested improved social mobility, as with the partner changes in the French cotillion and the Polish *chodzony*. As a result, the contact of male with female aroused controversy in some societies and beliefs, particularly Islam, Catholicism, and Protestant Puritanism. Couples dances—the attitudinal Gypsy *romalis* and the whirling *polska* in Finland and Sweden—acquired satanic connections to devil dancing and the black magic of the fiddler's bow.

Exuberance combined with pride in ancestry among the Kurds, a nomadic people spread over Turkey, Iraq, Iran, Yemen, and Israel. By celebrating unity and resistance, dancers typically violated Islamic law in the mixing of men with women and the invitation to all to join the lines, semicircles, chains, or circles of the hospitality dance. Inclusion sometimes enlarged the catenation of dancers to thousands. For sub-Saharan dancers, pairing remained taboo until the coming of the colonial English, French, Portuguese, and Germans. A rare exception, tribes in the Cameroon and Guinea mimicked male-female seduction with the *assiko*, Mankon bottle dance, and Guinean *macru*, a scarf dance featuring a shawl that the chooser placed on the chosen partner.

Partnering generated situations demanding rules of deportment, for example, the European custom of signing dance cards and the Swedish protocol for polska twosomes at wedding receptions. Upon the arrival of Danes to Danebod, Minnesota, in 1780, newcomers imported a courteous couples dance. Performed in a ring to mixed meters, the circling began with a staid promenade and advanced to a Viennese waltz figure in closed and open position before giving way to a jubilant stamping and vigorous frolic. The emergence of the polka in the early 1800s became the second couples dance in closed position. In São Paulo, Brazil, in 1848, young men complained that the master of ceremonies matched duos for the polka or mazurka, deliberately saving maidens for older men and allotting matrons to feistier young males.

In the late 1840s, slave and Creole dance in the Mississippi Delta introduced the *bamboula*, a frenetic mating dance consisting of made-up figures and gymnastic contortions. Pairs executing the cakewalk created an outlet for repressed hatred of slavery and the desire to satirize pompous whites. In this same era, Finns adopted the waltz, which lost its refinement when performed in rural areas and reflected the innocent exuberance of the polska. In other parts of Scandinavia, couples favored the *varsouvienne*, a partners dance from Warsaw, Poland.

Liberal Attitudes

For the Islamic realm, partnering remained taboo under Sharia law. In 1920, Mustafa Kemal Ataturk, founder of modern Turkey, updated the old Ottoman Empire in part with European dance. By dispatching Selim Tarcan as cultural ambassador to Sweden, Ataturk intended to import to Turkey male-female duets, a foreign notion to conservative Muslims. Tarcan initiated the *sari zeybek*, a stomping, skipping, and leaping men's ring dance before a line of swaying women. The segregated dance made no inroads in a culture devoted to the nationalistic spectacle of traditional solos. The rejection underscored an ethnic distaste for touching and grasping between men and women.

For the value of rhythm and coordination to grown-up poise, in northern Europe and the United States, physical education classes in schools and settlement houses adopted the ring dance and choreography for two, such as the schottische and the Virginia reel. Beginning in the 1970s, global reclamation of folk dancing restored vitality to leisure and national identity among ethnic groups. Partnering reduced the loneliness and rootlessness of working-class immigrants, such as Cajun Louisianans and elderly retirees. In the 2000s, couples dancing in industrialized nations set the tone of therapy for handicapped people. For patients suffering from mental retardation and dementia, physical contact in quadrilles, reels, rumba, salsa, and waltzes restored the center of gravity and revived a sense of self and heterosexual relations.

See also allemande; *bamboula*; *branle*; Cajun dance; cakewalk; chain dance; circle dance; cotillion; fandango; *huayño*; *Ländler*; mating dance; maypole dance; mazurka; *oberek*; *pasodoble*; pavane; polka; *polska*; Polynesian dance; processionals; quadrille; reel; schottische; *varsouvienne*; *volta*; waltz.

Source: Lee, Carol. *Ballet in Western Culture: A History of Its Origins and Evolution.* New York: Routledge, 2002.

PASODOBLE

A passionate late Renaissance couples dance from the south of France, the *pasodoble* (double step) has the fastest execution in Latin folk choreography. Classified with the bolero, cha-cha, rumba, merengue, and samba, the pasodoble claims ancient Cretan and Syrian village roots as well as kinship with twelfth-century motets and the hybridized zarzuela (operetta), a lyrical alternative. For the pasodoble, the couple favors an open position for spot dance, a series of steps performed on one point of the street or dance arena.

To pulsing horns, reeds, maracas, and acoustic guitar chords, after 1726, crowds at Spanish bullrings calmed from shouting and swearing to listen to forceful music registering 112 beats per minute. The dance appealed to the social elite, laboring class, and Roma. At after-fight revelry, the man-woman melodrama progressed by enacting the matador and shadow, the matador and cape, the torero and bull, and the prototypical flamenco dancer and partner.

The pasodoble yielded a miniature theatrical of the libido. Flirtation in closed and semi-open stance built suspense. Dramatic pauses separated precise phrasing that the couple set off by pronounced heel clicks, sharp rising and sinking on the balls of the feet, and quick staccato clapping *gitana* (Gypsy) style.

Stylistic Details

For pageantry, peasant blouses and slit skirts edged in fringe for women and skin-tight men's pants below vests or bare chests enhanced sexual tensions and sensuous, sultry attitudes. Impeccably upright carriage required a tight derriere and abdominal muscles, forward chest, lowered shoulders, and elongated spine. Key to the spectacle, the eyes stayed on the partner in the style of a torero calmly monitoring the bull for signs of aggression.

Beginning *sur place* (in place), the double-time chassé (pursuit), drag or slide, heel stamps, and straight and circular promenade showcased the dynamics of a female eluding an arrogant, dominating nobleman, but with less man-on-woman violence than the French *apache*, an underworld reenactment of pimp with prostitute. In the pasodoble, the mock stabbing motions of the *coup de pique* required bold, aggressive gestures with arm and hand. Twisting out of range demanded pelvic rotations and a diminished profile.

Dance History

Upon popularizing the glamorous dance in Granada in the 1700s, Andalusian choreographers articulated the steps for staged comedy and into a Spanish infantrymen's march rhythm. In the 1800s, the dramatic 2/4 beat of pasodoble music opened on the trumpet blast of the corrida (bullring). The genre provided the cadence for Iberian matadors during their *paseo* (procession) into the arena and during *faena* (passes) preceding the lethal stroke that felled the bull.

The appeal of Spanish folk dance in the 1890s in the Dominican Republic raised the pasodoble in competition with Cuban and Puerto Rican *danza* and bolero and rural Afro-Caribbean merengue. During Filipino resistance to American insurgents after 1898, dancers adopted Iberian dance rhythms—habanera, pasodoble, fandango—urging island patriotism and Spanish identity. Until 1902 on promenades and at concerts, the pasodoble earned renown among campesinos (peasants) in pre-Republican Cuba during occupation by Spanish soldiers.

Throughout the Mexican Revolution (1910–1920), indigenous composers wrote salutes to Spain in the form of the schottische and pasodoble, which brought lower-class couples to the dance floor as far north as Chihuahua, Sonora, and Texas. The pasodoble found favor in Oaxaca along with the fox-trot and *danzón* as a type of sport. After World War I, Russian composer Igor Stravinsky adopted the nuances of the Spanish 2/2 march along with the Argentine tango. Throughout North America, the popularity of the rumba, fox-trot, Charleston, Lindy hop, black bottom, and pasodoble created a demand for appropriate ballroom outfits and shoes and for five- and six-member dance bands to entertain social gatherings.

Venezuelans reserved the stylized folk pantomime and rich musical modulations of the pasodoble for parties and nuptials. For silent film, collections of background music allied the pasodoble with the fox-trot, waltz, and tango. In the film *The Four Horsemen of the Apocalypse* (1921), Argentine filmgoers remarked on Rudolf Valentino's exaggerated tango, which appeared to synthesize parts of the rumba and pasodoble with the male-on-female violence of the French apache dance.

In Germany, France, Spain, Costa Rica, Colombia, and Vietnam, the pasodoble suited the mood of refined Latin social dance. An anglicized version marked Sir William Walton's *Façade*, an opera performed in June 1923 at London's Aeolian Hall. The dance impacted female folk designs of the 1920s with asymmetric ruffled skirts long in back and reaching the upper thigh on the short side in the style of a matador's cape. By 1930, the wild, palpitating partner duo provoked rejection by Basque Catholics. Parochial school staff vilified the electric physicality between boy and girl as a possible prelude to illicit intimacies, social disease, and pregnancy.

In Paris in the 1930s, Pierre Zurcher-Margolle and Doris Lavelle popularized the rumba, samba, Argentine tango, and pasodoble at the Cabine Cubaine nightclub, which drew patrons seeking to learn the hottest dances. In London, Zurcher-Margolle opened a dance studio in Soho and hosted exhibitions at the Café de Paris. A brisk flamenco variation added the clack of castanets, syncopation common to radio and gramophone dance tunes in Malaysia.

The Mexican-American poet Américo Paredes from Brownsville, Texas, emulated the pasodoble in verse depicting themes of memory, romance, and death. During the Spanish Civil War (1936–1939), the cochineal red of the bullfighter's cape colored the dancer's dress, subtly supporting the "reds" that fascist dictator Francisco Franco battled. The couples dance also flourished from the late 1930s into present times as a duet for ice skaters.

The pasodoble enticed middle-class couples to Colombian dance halls in the 1950s. To the music of full orchestras, French dance masters revived the steps in England in the 1960s at Latin American clubs. In the Western Hemisphere in the 1990s, while the pasodoble thrived at fiestas on saints' days, the Latin American diaspora transported the pasodoble to Australia. Weight watchers applauded the vivacious, sexy rhythm for varying less vigorous ballroom dance and burning more than four hundred calories in an intense aerobic workout.

See also bolero; fandango; merengue; schottische; tango; *tirabol*; waltz.

Source: Ramirez, Abel Saldivar. "The Art of Performing the Spanish Paso Doble." *Bandmasters Review* (June 2008): 27–28.

PAVANE

One of the oldest dances extant, during the high Italian Renaissance, the pavane consisted of a columnar or circular procession of upper-class couples. An outgrowth of the Spanish Inquisition, the dance exhibited the incontrovertibility of the divine right of kings and the arrogance of Catholic priests. Around 1320, the stately steps replaced the egalitarian peasant circle dance with a presentational advance to a throne, altar, or dais.

The pavane belongs to the *basse danse* (low dance) genre or the *branle* for its dignified gliding over the floor in 2/2 meter. The Italian version possibly took its name from Paduana, indicating a dance from Padua, or more likely from the Latin *pavo* (peacock) for its strutting gait. Catherine of Aragon, the future wife of Henry VIII, reputedly introduced a restrained pavane to the English in 1501, when the death of Prince Arthur left her a sixteen-year-old widow.

With a hesitation step, grandly dressed partners advanced on the balls of the feet and paused to rock back or side to side and lift both heels before moving to the next step. The processional became a common rhythmic approach of bridal parties during wedding rituals. It also served congregations on such solemn occasions as confirmations and ordinations and dignified the advance of university graduates at commencement ceremonies.

The pavane first appeared in print by prolific Venetian bookmaker Ottaviano Petrucci, who specialized in polyphonic music. In Italian lute composer Joan Ambrosia Dalza's *Intabolatura de lauto libro quarto* (Arrangements for the lute, book 4, 1508), variations on nine pavanes stressed Iberian influence. With the male participant on the left escorting his partner, the majesty, pride, and sobriety of the pavane's long gliding steps mimicked courtly mannerisms in the same spirit as the polonaise. The showy walking dance reached Germany in 1523. Spaniards living in Paris fostered the pavane in France in 1529.

The Pavane in History

On returning from his conquest of the Aztecs in 1528, Spanish explorer Hernán Cortés, newly advanced to Marquis of Oaxaca, adopted the *pavane d'Espagne* as a proclamation of his success. Knights in coats of mail and women draped in the Native American manta acted out the strict gendering and circumspection of inner court behaviors. As a wooing dance, the pompous movements encouraged men to demonstrate their military posture and rank and women to preen in jewels and finery attesting to their fathers' wealth and possible dowry.

A series of even curtsies and bows and slip steps in retreat and advance influenced state or funereal retinues for royalty in France. The pavane gained popularity in Tudor England in the 1540s during the physical decline of Henry VIII, who could no longer execute fast footwork. In Italy, popularity ebbed in 1546, when the *passamezzo*, galliard, and *volta* replaced the pavane. As mentioned in Thoinot Arbeau's *Orchésographie* (1589), an annotated handbook to ballroom footwork and mannerisms, the repetitive march announced the beginning of a grand ball. Arbeau described the solemn pavane as a noble performance at masquerades to highlight the entrance of costumed gods and goddesses and as an interlude in the play *La pellegrina* (The pilgrimage, 1589), performed at the nuptials of Christine of Lorraine to Ferdinando de' Medici.

Dance Style

As summarized in Fabritio Caroso da Sermoneta's treatise *Il ballarino* (1581), while circling the dance floor, marchers in the pavane chanted a litany or sang to the music. The staid rhythm allowed men to display shoulder capes, feathered hats, and jeweled swords and enabled women in jeweled stomachers and brocaded satin gowns to flirt with hand fans and the long trains trailing behind them. For maximum presentation, women preceded pages lifting their trains from the floor.

Less chivalric versions of the pavane added affectations with the back-and-forth caper and flourish of men and with the *fleuret* (skip), a hint of lift or thrust in the advancing foot of either partner. After the initial cavalcade of couples, the dance sometimes gave way to a leaping galliard, the favorite dance of Queen Elizabeth I. In 1587, she promoted Sir Christopher Hatton to Lord Chancellor for his splendid performance of a presentational pavane in shoes topped by green bows. For the sake of her oldest and least agile staff, the queen kept the pavane as the opening dance of a morning physical workout in triple time.

As a symbol of order and respect, the pavane—also called the *cinque pas* (five step)—coordinated the gestures and tone of large group gatherings before royalty or prelates. By the end of the sixteenth century, the peasant class added their own versions of the pavane to their repertoire of saltarello or *cascarda*, a hopping, twirling dance

One of the oldest Western dances extant, the pavane of the high Italian
Renaissance consisted of a columnar or circular procession of upper-
class couples. *Grove, Lilly. Dancing. London: Longmans, Green, and
Company, 1895, 255.*

based on side-to-side steps. Nathan Bailey's etymological dictionary noted that William
Shakespeare's comedies *The Merry Wives of Windsor* (1597) and *Twelfth Night* (1601)
reserved the pavane for Sir John Falstaff, Doll Tearsheet, Sir Toby Belch's surgeon, and
other vulgar characters.

For the marriage of Henry IV of France to Marie de' Medici at Chambord Castle
on October 5, 1600, a special pavane for the nuptial "Belle qui tiens ma vie" (The beauty
that holds my life) marked the rise of the dance as an occasional piece. A pinnacle of
grand airs, the pavane flourished among dancers at the court of Louis XIII in Paris after

1610. In 1617, German composer Johann Hermann Schein of Dresden inserted a ceremonious pavane in his baroque dinner suite, written in imitation of secular Italian music.

In the mid-1600s, Louis XIV abandoned the pavane and replaced it with the livelier courante, but the slower, more contemplative spectacle of the pavane remained popular in Spain until 1676. For drama, the male Spaniard kept his right hand on the hilt of his dagger and left his left hand inert. In 1723, a Dutch-English dictionary described the addition of robed judges to the pavane processions. Still performed at masked balls in 1764, according to the *Tatler,* the pavane figured in a description of a royal entertainment for Hanoverian king George III at which performers donned vizard masks.

The Marquis de Paulmy's *Mélanges tirés d'une grande bibliothèque* (A miscellany drawn from a great list of books, 1782) substantiated regard for the pavane for its grandeur and beauty, but a Scots text from 1792 declared it too serious to please young dancers. In the French-Italian dictionary definition of Giuseppe Filippo Barberi in 1838, the dance seemed vainglorious. In 1897, American muralist Edwin Austin Abbey completed *Une Pavane,* an over-mantel painting of dancers featuring Renaissance garments and postures against a Venetian backdrop. Classical composers Gabriel Fauré, Camille Saint-Saëns, Ralph Vaughn Williams, and Maurice Ravel adapted the pavane to elegant orchestral and choral suites as cradlesongs and introspective mood pieces.

See also branle; polonaise; processionals; saltarello.

Source: Meri, La. *Spanish Dancing.* Northampton, MA: Interlink Books, 2011.

PERSIAN DANCE

Because much of the history of Persian folk arts survives in brief glimpses from architecture, monuments, and texts, including Chinese sources from the Qin Dynasty, most descriptions of authentic dance rely on visuals. Historians feature Persian folk dance in a standard procession to propitiate the gods. On less formal occasions, choreography pleased male guests as an after-dinner amusement and strength builder.

At their military height, when Persia's empire spread from India west to Egypt, both folkloric and refined dance marked personal and group triumphs, as with the battlefield capering and flaunting of a head lopped from the enemy. From around 560 BCE, Cyrus the Great led armored men in the *persica*, a joyous expression of manhood and might through crouching and clashing of bronze shields as though warding off multiple attackers. Court dance limited female presence to the performance of girls imported from Ionia and Greece, a gendered custom still in effect under Tahmasp II, one of the last kings of the Safavid Dynasty.

As Persia rose to prominence and political influence, royal magi (advisers) drank sacred soma, an intoxicant that stimulated ritual dance. For the Carpaean dance, men mimed plowing with an ox, sowing grain, and fighting a thief. After 404 BCE, a cultic solo by King Artaxerxes II at Persepolis venerated Mithra, the soldier's deity and the god of truth and harvests. When Roxanna, a Sogdian princess, danced at a banquet for Macedonian general Alexander the Great at a fort north of Bactria in 327 BCE, she sealed her destiny as the conqueror's wife.

Joy and Welcome

Outside the capital city of Persepolis, the nomadic Qashqai performed the *raks-e dastmal* (scarf dance), a village display of color and movement. In the third century BCE, Seuthes, king of Thrace, received a state welcome at Athens from the historian Xenophon, who entertained foreign legates with Persian peasant dance. According to frescoes and murals in a thousand caves in Gansu Province, China, during the Sassanid period after 226 CE, Persian music and folk dance acquired Buddhist facets of self-expression from residents of the oasis at Dunhuang, the gateway to the Silk Road. The route became the conduit by which Persian Orientalism and elegance traveled east and west.

Transported by nomadic Roma entertainers for five centuries, elements of Kurdish, Turkish, Jewish, Armenian, and Uzbek arts permeated Middle Eastern choreography, notably the evolution of *kathak* interpretive dance in the Indus-Gangetic belt of north and east India. In the 700s during the Golden Age of Islam, Persian dance featured lines, solos, worship ritual, harvest thanksgiving, and martial dance. At the Persian Gulf, heritage *bandari* (harbor) dance stressed Arabic rhythms and African kinetics. The creation of the tarantella in Apulia on the Ionian Gulf at Taranto eventually diffused to Persia. Imported figures also featured the Greek *antikrystos* (face-to-face), a choreographed model of eastern Mediterranean hospitality.

Dance in Diaspora

Persian migrants carried their styles to surrounding cultures. In 1273, the Persian *sema* dance permeated religious music education of the Mevlevi, a brotherhood of Sufi dancers at Konya in Anatolia. To escape worldliness, the men whirled in place to fuse their spirits with the almighty. On the Malay Peninsula in the early 1400s, Persian traders and Muslim missionaries introduced the *zapin*. A presentational figure meant to honor the sultan, the choreography synchronized rapid body turns and diagonal moves to lute, bongo, and frame drum. The zapin ended with reverence to the dignitary.

Four centuries later, Malay folk arts adopted the Persian *boria*, a humorous skit dance similar in tone to the Italian commedia dell'arte. After 1526, a migration of Persian tastes, refined mannerisms, and Sufi whirls on straight legs set the tone of the Mughal Empire. Into the 1800s, the Persian penchant for dance and song to tambourine accompaniment survived in travel writings focusing on Circassian women.

See also commedia dell'arte; diaspora; harvest dance; *kathak*; line dance; lion dance; martial dance; propitiation; Roma dance; Sufi dance; tarantella.

Source: Curtis, John, and Nigel Tallis. *Forgotten Empire: The World of Ancient Persia.* Berkeley: University of California Press, 2005.

PIPE DANCE

Native Americans revered the pipe ritual as a transformative experience uniting humankind with the spirit world. The most potent rite, the peace pipe dance symbolized harmony with the souls of ancestors and brotherhood on earth. The choreography forced the dancer to crouch in the shape of a peace pipe. As the drum beat a 3/4 rhythm, the performer changed his posture back and forth and held it during a long pause until the next drumbeat. In addition to yelps, the dancer inserted boasts of virility and hardihood.

Among the Iroquois Confederacy of Albany, New York, after 1570, an elaborate calumet dance commemorated respect for peace among the Mohawk, Cayuga, Oneida, Seneca, and Onondaga member tribes. West of Green Bay, Wisconsin, the Pawnee calumet ceremony derived from sun worship and involved the daughters of chiefs in a series of hopping steps emulating eagles feeding on the ground. Diffused in all directions in 1680, the dance influenced the medicine pipe ritual of other plains tribes, beginning with the Omaha and Kansa and spreading to the Blackfoot, Gros Ventre, Cree, Teton Dakota, Cheyenne, Caddo, and Ponca and the Sarsi of Alberta, Canada.

Pipe Dance Rites

In New York in 1770, the Seneca, led by War Chief Ganon, performed a pipe dance, which they accented with eagle fans made from maple, ash, or hickory handles dyed red and three or four eagle feathers from birds trapped in pits. To promote peace, the Seneca presented the steps at stockaded Cherokee villages, where residents chose Seneca individuals to adopt. In Canada around the Great Lakes, the Iroquois formulated their own pipe bundle dance as part of the eagle dance and sealed adoption rituals with gifts of wampum belts. Similarly, the Cree of Minnesota reverenced the creator during the bear ceremony with a presentation of medicine pipes, a ritual they abandoned in the twentieth century.

In southwestern Wisconsin on August 19, 1825, James Otto Lewis painted an Ojibwa pipe dance that marked the Treaty of Prairie du Chien. The art commission began his career recording the portraits of some sixty prominent Midwestern leaders from the Ottawa, Potawatomi, Iowa, Menominee, Sauk, Fox, Winnebago, and Sioux. An ominous performance, the dance of four Ojibwa warriors with sword, rifle, and battle-axes clustered around a drum pounded by another warrior holding a pipe. Dancers stressed the balance of peace in one hand and readiness for war in the other.

Among the Upper Missouri tribes at the juncture of the Missouri and Platte rivers south of Omaha, Nebraska, in 1825, the Crow adopted the Hidatsa or Mandan sacred pipe dance, a remnant from Arikara culture. In Montana in 1832, painter George Catlin immortalized the Assiniboine pipe dance performed by seven young males in feathered trailers, whom a chief inaugurated with smoke from the pipe. After circling several times, performers dragged others into the circle one by one until all spectators were dancing, yelping, and barking like dogs. Farther south among the Pueblo Indians of the Great Basin, the San Juan of north central New Mexico created a calumet ceremony that never gained the prominence of northern plains pipe dances. While holding their peace pipes perpendicular to their torsos, a couple performed the dance to drumming.

Another pipe dance tradition of the Fox and Sauk passed to the Winnebago of Nebraska and the Abenaki outside Montreal. For performers of the traditional steps, elders named males who best performed the war dance. Clockwise figures coordinated with iambic drumming, cries, and shakes of the rattle in the right hand, a posture identical to the Blackfoot dance in Montana and the Meskwaki version in Iowa. While crouching on one knee, each dancer flourished the rattle before hopping back to a standing position. With a straddling crouch, the dancers bent their heads to the ground and swayed to the rhythm of the pipe song. The choreography ended with a hop on the left foot and heel and toe touches with the right.

Adoption Ritual

As a factor of medicine culture from the Yellowstone River valley east to North Dakota, the Crow pipe ritual enabled the pipe owner to adopt up to four couples into his clan. At a banquet in winter or early summer, members met to sing, dance, and offer gifts, notably a medicine bundle wrapped in buffalo calf hide and containing a redstone bowl, sweetgrass, corncobs, and two pipe stems. At tribal dances, the owners revered the stems as sacred artifacts and stored them apart from the bowls as symbols of male and female.

Following a ritual adoption before a buffalo skull, two Crow participants clad in deer tail headdresses and bustles clutched a pipe stem and tufted rattle and moved them rhythmically with the steps. Special guests kept time by swaying like birds in flight. During the steps to four songs, dancers stooped humbly, crossed their arms, and deposited the stems on a new blanket. The ceremony continued with a procession leading the adoptee to his new father's tent.

The adoptive parents mimed the cutting of the umbilical cord and the piercing of the infant's ears. The adoptee's receipt of the medicine bundle and group smoking of sacred tobacco united the new family. The rising smoke emerged from the mouth as truth and connected earth and sky before spreading to all nature. While other plains dances disappeared from Indian culture, the pipe ritual remained viable into the early 1900s.

In the Dakotas, Nebraska, and Montana, the Sioux treasured a pipe dance as part of the *yuwipi* ceremony, a segment of an ancient healing rite in which dancers gestured to the four directions with smoke from the sacred pipe. They created a new pipe dance in 1954 to support Sioux soldiers fighting in the Korean War. In Wisconsin, the Menominee singled out the man who lighted the pipe with his own song and dance. In Wyoming and Colorado, the Arapaho version of the pipe dance involved a shuffling circle dance that encompassed the entire tribe in a blessing.

See also circle dance; processionals; worship dance.

Source: Keillor, Elaine, Tim Archambault, and John M. H. Kelly. *Encyclopedia of Native American Music of North America.* Santa Barbara, CA: ABC-Clio, 2013.

PLANTING DANCE

A natural adjunct to liturgy and prayer to prevent starvation, planting dances enabled agricultural communities to please deities with their steps and songs. Forms feature the guiding of the plow in the Russian *khorovod* (choral dance), a welcoming of water in the Israeli *mayim mayim*, dancing a corn ritual in an ox mask among the Hausa of West

Africa, and the swinging of baskets and spreading of seeds by Ecuadorian girls in the Amazonian jungle. Extended farm families worked and danced as a unit to complete the essential tasks of the seasons, as demonstrated by the reforestation of Zimbabwe with a tree-planting dance each December 3 and the soil-tamping step of Breton women in Rennes, France.

From 1600 BCE, the Chinese dragon dance encouraged celestial support for farm families by disguising rain bringers as mythic flying dragons. From 1200 CE, Japanese folk art venerated ancestors in Shinto style with the *odori*, a traditional summer circle dance reflecting everyday life and nature. Employing *minyo* (call and response) that regulated depth and coverage, performers mimicked plowing and seeding rice fields.

In the Aegean islands from prehistory, graphic gestures and choreography on threshing floors and in grape arbors rid farmers of hubris (pride) while blessing grain seeds and vine cuttings, the focus of the Gallic farandole after 800 BCE. After humbly offering seeds and slips to the earth mother Gaea, planters covered the garden beginnings with soil, a kinesthetic ritual commemorated on bas-relief and clayware. The dancing influenced the Roman Floralia, a spring holiday preceding the breaking of ground. After formation of the Roman Empire in 27 BCE, Rome's priests performed synchronized steps before praying for ample herbs, vegetables, grain, wine, and honey.

Into the Middle Ages, dancers in Great Britain abandoned the grain deity Ceres and the winemaker Bacchus, the agrarian gods of Roman occupational legions. Celts returned to the soil with primeval dibbles (digging sticks). The propitiation of nature operated on two levels—the production of edibles and the conception of healthy babies, whose growth depended on a diet based on the essentials of legionary cookery.

On the Continent, planting choreography involved juvenile participants. French children mimed Chinese and Roman horticultural methods with a ring dance asking, "Savez-vous planter des choux?" (Do you know how to plant cabbage?). After 1650, British children formed rings and frolicked to an appropriate tune, "Oats, Peas, Beans, and Barley Grow," a reflection of their agri-musical heritage.

Action Dance

Adult mime turned the Filipino rice-planting dance into a theatrical. Performers carried their seeds in baskets and stepped lightly among rows while thrusting their hands up and down as though hoeing. They expressed homage to the heavens before filing among rows, using their hands to cover seeds with imaginary soil. From the colonial era, Creole Filipinas in Hispanic dress reduced the peasant mimesis to an abstract reflection of sowing by waving their hand fans in the *magtanim hindi biro* (rice-planting dance). The choreography progressed to germination with arm gestures toward sunlight.

Among the Kainai and Siksika of southern Alberta, the tobacco dance sustained agrarian families until the Canadian government banned the ceremony. Sustained in the 1960s by custodian Amos Leather of the Blackfoot Confederacy of Alberta and Montana, the ritual retained 230 songs and artifacts. Through museum archives and films of the planting dance, subsequent performers revived the symbolism and released sacred smoke and fragrance to carry to heaven prayers for peace and harmony. Although presentations honored no edibles, they increased wellness and awakened spirits.

A traditional Pueblo planting dance featured rattles, anklets, masking, and representations of the seasonal cycle. *Vance, Lee J. "The Evolution of Dancing." Popular Science 41, no. 52 (October 1892): 746.*

Labor and Propitiation

At Teerangore in southern Sudan adjacent to Uganda, children and adults of the Lopit Latuka tribe implore the heavens for rain with a circle dance, the annual *nalam*. Around the hereditary rain-men, dancers form a field procession to propitiate nutrition for the children from rich harvests of peanuts, cassava, sorghum, sugarcane, coffee, cotton, peas, sesame, maize, and millet. The dance incorporates a curse on weeds, fungi, and stalk-chewing predators. For home vegetable plots, Ugandans dance the *ayomana* at preharvest rites in late summer.

For the Bhil of central India, the *sherdi charo* (sugarcane dance) stresses cooperative agriculture, a common feature of ecofeminism. In a land where females often superintend fieldwork, women begin their spring dances with imitations of plowing. In a line, they pass one to another through their legs the slips that go into each furrow, a parallel to the yam slip-planting scenario on Vanuatu. One by one, dancers stand and complete the covering of seedlings. With percussive accompaniment, the Banjara women of Rajasthan raise their hands and step to the beat of the frame drum during the *lambadi* (sowing dance).

Outside Jakarta, Indonesian farmers mask their faces and dress in banana leaves and bark to perform the five-hour *hudoq* dance. A ring dance follows, ridding the field of leaf-destroying insects, rats, crows, and lions. The women of Aichi, Japan, anticipate bounty by topping their costumes with a woven hat similar in shape to a winnowing bowl. Japanese planters at Tadano in western Koriyama enhance agrarian dance with the *kyuroku* (trickster), who adds fun to the serious work of tenant farmers. Before a shrine at Fukushima in 2014, female survivors of the tsunami on March 11, 2011, joined for a rice-planting ritual. A boost to the spirits of elderly women, the dance performed in heritage dress—belted kimonos, sandals, and socks—displayed national fervor.

See also barn dance; circle dance; disguise; farandole; harvest dance; Kurdish dance; *mayim mayim*; Siberian dance; sub-Saharan dance; totemic dance.

Source: Miller, Denise. "Our Tobacco Is Sacred." *Windspeaker* 23, no. 6 (2005): 26.

POLKA

An early nineteenth-century craze, the polka (also *krakowiak*), a pumping Bohemian couples dance, followed the cheerful patterns of the galop, hornpipe, bourrée, and schottische. The world's second partner dance in closed position after the waltz, the easy hop-step-close-step in 2/4 meter originated among Czech peasants to upbeat melodies. The polka took the Czech title *"pulka"* (half), a reference to a dominant half step.

Preceding the polka, the migration of Roma performers through the Balkans in 1100 carried Turkish steps from Anatolia and a brisk *moresca* sword dance from the islands of Corsica and Korcula off southern Croatia. In the early 1300s, Dutch fishers, farmers, and animal slaughterers shod in low-heeled ash wood *klompen* (safety shoes) enjoyed the *klompendansen* (also called the *boerendansen* or farmer dancing) to polka rhythms.

Liberated from the pomp of the high-toned minuet and grave polonaise, polka steps influenced the *nuevo leon*, a heady choreography from Mexican folk art that throbbed with emotional intensity and loud music. The clog polka prospered in Scotland in 1819 and permeated steps and figures of the Irish *cèilidh* at Cork and Kerry under the geographical names Sligo polka and Clare polka. After delighting Berlin and Vienna in 1822, the polka drifted to dancers in Prague, London, Paris, and Sydney, Australia.

In the 1830s, the Grand Duchess Maria "Masha" Nikolaevna, the arts-loving daughter of Charlotte of Prussia and Nicholas I of Russia, created the polka *mazur*, a forerunner of the waltz. A string of variants included the heel and toe polka, polka coquette, polka waltz, polka *redowa*, schottische polka, and Esmeralda, a dance named for the Roma protagonist of Victor Hugo's *The Hunchback of Notre Dame* (1831). Nightspots and dance halls profited from polkamania, which increased business at the Prado and Ranelagh in Paris and Almacks and Vauxhall in London, a surge reported in the *London Times* and *Punch Magazine*.

The American Polka

In 1844, the polka migrated to the New World along with other Eastern European folk arts. In New York City, an observer for *New Peterson Magazine* compared the craze to cholera. Slovenian immigrants arranged socials at union halls and ethnic brotherhoods in Chicago and Cleveland, Ohio. Across the United States, Saskatchewan, Quebec, Ontario, Nova Scotia, and Newfoundland, the polka evolved into the cotton-eye Joe, a spunky rhythm reflecting elements of the schottische. Scandinavians adapted the choreography into the *varsouvienne*, a couples dance from Warsaw, Poland. At Salt Lake City, Utah, in 1852, prophet Brigham Young stimulated hardihood among Mormon pioneers by arranging folk dances to the quadrille and glide (or slide) polka, a smooth technique that presented the elevated left foot in a downward point.

Upper Silesians settling Panna Maria in southeastern Texas on December 24, 1854, brought with them the concertinas and accordions that accompanied the *oberek* and polka. In Acadiana, Louisiana, zydeco musicians played a variety of rhythms for the cotillion, galop, varsouvienne, and polka, the basis for Creole folk music. The heel and toe steps of the Bahamian polka to rake and scrape bands clearly defined the island style. In Paraguay, the melancholy *guarania* channeled folk dance into urban locales while the polka flourished in the countryside. Aficionados calmed the up-and-down performance by cutting the initial hop to a rise of the torso.

A European Fad

In the late eighteenth century, Norwegians, Swedes, and Danes developed their own polka form, the *gammeldans* (or *gammaldans*), a gentle hop–slide and turn. The choreography did not reach Finland until the 1860s, when polka fans fostered innovation. Western Norwegians diversified the original rhythm to two beats per measure for the *rull* (or *rudl*) and in 4/4 time for the *ganglat/snoa*, a more fluid rotating dance that kept feet grounded on a smooth floor. The rapidity of newer melodies increased the polka turn to a snappy clockwise pivot.

Vying for attention in the realm of Franz Joseph I in 1860, the Magyar ardor of the czardas began edging out the waltz, quadrille, mazurka, and polka. At a harvest home in West Loathly, Sussex, in 1869, musicians balanced the program, but lessened the number of polkas compared to marches, galops, quadrilles, and waltzes. By the 1890s, the languorous tango supplanted the polka and waltz in sophisticated settings.

After American duos popularized "Roll Out the Barrel" (aka "Beer Barrel Polka," 1927), a wave of interest in folk arts in the 1930s brought unschooled youth into the diversion of East European couples dance. For the new generation, Czech, Croatian, and Slovak troupes demonstrated the rhythms of the motherland. During World War II, the polka returned to fame among troops of many nations—Balkan, Scandinavian, Dutch, Iberian, Italian, Eastern European, Russian, and Japanese.

See also cèilidh; clogging; cotillion; cotton-eye Joe; Creole dance; czardas; galop; hornpipe; mazurka; *oberek*; polonaise; quadrille; schottische; sword dance; tango; *varsouvienne*; waltz.

Source: Gunkel, Ann Hetzel. "The Polka Alternative: Polka as Counterhegemonic Ethnic Practice." *Popular Music and Society* 27, no. 4 (2004): 407–27.

POLONAISE

A self-conscious presentational figure in earnest, martial posture, the polonaise (also *polonez*, *polski*, or *chodzony*) directed couples in rows and circles that separated and re-formed to a 3/4 meter. A Slavonic peasant dance foregrounded by chivalric formations and altar rituals, the "*danse aux lumières*" (dance of lights) followed the sedate Venetian pavane and the four-beat allemande from southern Germany. From Poznan, Poland, in the late 1500s, the polonaise aligned step-step-thrust on the ball of the foot to the stiff three-beat meter of ancient folk songs. The third beat incorporated a *ballon* (dip or bounce) on the working leg as the alternate foot pointed ahead.

Echoing the style of the Moorish sarabande, the Eastern European polonaise synchronized the approach of proud-booted veterans on parade and moderated the slides of gentrified duos as they filed through court pageants. The French initiated the militaristic stride at Cracow on February 21, 1574, at the welcome of Henry III of Anjou to the Polish Diet to receive the title of king of Poland. By 1645, women joined the lofty procession of men in martial dress, balancing male vainglory with softer female gestures and steps.

Dance and Caste

In a welcome to spring, peasant variations of the polonaise moved majestically through villages to escort winter to the borders. On a higher social level, couples greeted their hosts and, two by two, joined the growing line of participants in a social event. Within a quarter century, the pomp of unbending body language influenced the compositions of major composers—Johann Sebastian Bach, Georg Philipp Telemann, Wilhelm Friedemann Bach, Carl Philipp Emanuel Bach, and Wolfgang Amadeus Mozart. The polonaise set the atmosphere of weddings in St. Petersburg, Russia, including the marriage at Trinity Church on May 21, 1725, of Princess Anna Petrovna, daughter of Peter the Great, to Karl Friedrich, Duke of Holstein-Gottorp.

At salons in Poland in 1790, ambitious social climbers claimed the polonaise as a national dance. Ensembles stepped martial measures to piccolo, trumpet, and tympani. Suites moved directly from processions to duos for the mazurka, sarabande, or polka. During the rise of nationalism in the romantic era, piano composer Frédéric Chopin initiated a softer, more poignant polonaise reflecting Poland's partition on January 23, 1793, at the order of Catherine the Great and her elimination of the royal dynasty of Stanislaw II. In Austria, Switzerland, and Hungary and across Western Europe, an evening of dancing concluded with the reversal of the original polonaise as couples said good-byes to their hosts.

While Napoleon's forces occupied Warsaw after 1811, the polonaise influenced fashion, which featured men in striped military pants and sabers escorting women in fitted bodices and flounced petticoats, a duo that couturiers called a "polonaise." Into the next decade, the constrained promenade to the music of Mikhail Glinka and Joseph Mazilier opened masquerades and civic balls in Vienna. At garden parties, a torchbearer led the winding line around fountains and through mazes, a retreat into the medieval mode of labyrinthine dance.

In mid-nineteenth-century Warsaw, the *varsouvienne* adapted the 3/4 beat of the polonaise for a fashionable couples dance blending the promenade with toe taps and crossovers. After 1859 in Croatia at Zagreb, where locals rejected the waltz as too German, Venetian dance master Pietro Coronelli taught students the polonaise along with the quadrille, polka, mazurka, and *kolo*, a hop-turn style easily adapted into circle, line, and chain dance in Bosnia, Dubrovnik, and Budapest. When Peter Ilyich Tchaikovsky perused themes of snobbery and classism in St. Petersburg for *Eugene Onegin* (1879), he began act III with a polonaise, the same dance that opened grand balls in Victorian England. In 1885, a conservative congregation in Vaszkai, Lithuania, recoiled from the organist's choice of a polonaise for a prelude.

In the United States, the impressive three-beat polonaise stanza acquired more utilitarian purposes than presentations and obeisance to the powerful. Tourists in the White House followed the 3/4 beat of march king John Philip Sousa's "Presidential Polonaise" (1886), an upbeat introit featuring horns, woodwinds, and percussion. After World War I, the same music and choreography gained popularity at weddings in South Africa.

To "The Happy Wanderer," a World War II tune originally named "Der fröhliche Wanderer" or "Mein Vater war ein Wandersmann" by Friedrich Wilhelm Möller, children trod the polonaise in gym class while caroling, "Valderi-valdera." Teen partners stepped to the gallant cadence at debutante balls. The reclamation of 734 Polish orphans after 1944 resulted in housing in New Zealand, where the polonaise reminded the young survivors of home. After 1954, folk maven Amalia Hernández introduced the polonaise to Ballet Moderno de México, a coordination of folk rhythms and body language. For the rehabilitation of schizophrenics, therapy in the 1960s employed baroque dances—minuet and polonaise—as mental models of order.

See also allemande; circle dance; labyrinthine dance; mazurka; pavane; polka; sarabande.

Sources: Barr, Amelia E. "Characteristic Dances of the World." *Lippincott's Magazine* 27, no. 4 (April 1881): 330–41. Cowgill, Rachel, David Cooper, and Clive Brown, eds. *Art and Ideology in European Opera: Essays in Honor of Julian Rushton.* Rochester, NY: Boydell Press, 2010.

POLSKA

A patchwork of Slavic heritage choreography, the *polska* evolved from the *langdans* in the late 1500s into the original Nordic couples dance that replaced medieval ring dance. The term, derived from the Czech for "Polish girl," named a left-pause-right step that traveled around the room. In Poland, southern Finland, Denmark, and Sweden, the bubbly polska rhythm replaced the more sedate minuet and somber polonaise with a promenade and turns in waist-shoulder hand positions or a more intimate, tightly clasped closed position.

In 3/4 or 2/4 time, the suave partner dance set steps to singing, ornamented fiddle tunes, and bagpipe music in a minor key. After 1587 at Warsaw, the choreography derived a two-part standard from the Polish court of Sigismund III Vasa and Anna of Austria. Priests dubbed the snuggly duet "the devil's dance" for its suggestive alliance of male and female bodies and adoption into nomadic Roma street performances. Clerical suspicions of satanic influence extended to the fiddler as well for improvising the devil's tunes, which rural folk linked to the medieval mania of St. Vitus' Dance and the black magic of the southern Italian tarantella.

During a period of interethnic and social transformation, seventeenth-century musical suites in a contrast of rhythms paired the polska with a minuet. Over time and much flirting and ale drinking, diverse populations formulated steps with the gladsome character of a Polish mazurka. As the polska acquired the vigor of a Scots reel, young couples spilled over from indoors to whirl their duets in the streets.

Evolutionary Dance

Poles created a national dance from the intoxicating sixteenth-note polska, but aficionados of the Scandinavian polska refused a standard structure. Innovators generated the ring polska, cross polska, spin polska, polonaise polska, *halling* polska, *radspolska*, four-step polska, and the acrobatic Jösseh polska, a cartwheeling, ceiling-touching couples dance reflecting antics of the *Schuhplattler*. After the polska revitalized the folk arts of the countryside and mining towns, it exhibited the melding of other common rhythms and steps, for example, Danish ring dance marked by dramatic heel stamps to each side. At all social levels, the Danish polska flourished for a century, acquiring gymnastic figures. In 1650, French choreography replaced the former national dance.

The polska diversified in eastern Norway to the *pols*, eighth-note polska, and triplet polska, all participatory choreographies that invited spectators at all levels to join in. At Røros, Trøndelag, Østerdal, and Gudbrandsdalen, Norwegians favored the *springleik*, which encompassed the whole dance floor with slow treads begun on the left foot and turns in either direction. The intense folk character of the dance duplicated peasant choreography worldwide, including elements of the Aragonese *jota*.

Sweden's Polska

Swedes adopted the polska as their national dance. The Swedish *hambopolska* from Föllinge set rapid turns to traditional fiddle melodies; the *bodapolska* marked partner turns with bent knees. For the polska at Smaland, partners remained in one spot on the dance floor; Varmland, Harjedalen, and Jamtland performers preferred detailed promenades. At Hälsingland near Mount Harga, participants created the *Hälsinghambon*, an offshoot of the polska that drew thousands of contestants to global championships. During the imprisonment of Swedish oboist Gustaf Blidström at Tobolsk, Russia, in 1715, he compiled three hundred polskas in a single volume that differentiated the earthy peasant steps from the more formal polonaise.

At Swedish weddings in the 1770s, the minister claimed the first dance, the priest polska, with the bride before joining the hands of the newlyweds for their first dance as man and wife. Protocol passed the bride to her father and father-in-law while the groom partnered the matron-of-honor and the rest of the female bridal party. The evening ended with "dancing out the groom," the encircling of the groom, whom male members of the nuptial party lifted onto their shoulders.

A parallel "dancing out the wreath" began with Swedish female guests and attendants placing a flower tiara on the bride's head and blindfolding her. As everyone danced the polska, the bride passed the wreath to another maiden. In the 1800s, the women's honor to the bride ended with "dancing the bride to the ceiling" on a chair while guests continued the polska around the floor of the reception hall.

The polska retained its cultural appeal in Sweden for performing around the Christmas tree. The tunes dominated folk music in the 1910s in part as a component of elementary school physical education in northern Europe and the United States, where students learned two flirting dances, the Sicilian tarantella and the Swedish Fjällnäs *polska*, a set pattern of hopping, stamping, and kicks to left and right. Finnish weddings in the 1920s incorporated the polska at receptions that lasted until sunrise. Through arts exchanges between Scandinavia and dance clubs in Hungary, Estonia, and Soviet Russia, transnational influence hybridized the polska. In the 1970s, a resurgence of *bygdedans* (ethnic dances) introduced the younger generation of Swedes and Finns to fiddle music and the polska.

See also halling; literature, folk dance in; *jota*; mazurka; nuptial dance; reel; *Schuhplattler*; tarantella.

Source: Hoppu, Petri, and Karen Vedel. *Nordic Dance Spaces: Practicing and Imagining a Region*. Farnham, UK: Ashgate, 2014.

POLYNESIAN DANCE

From prehistory, rhythmic and presentational dance in the Pacific islands epitomized solidarity and cross-cultural exchange. Aboriginal posturing accompanied monotonic percussive music and worship, but lacked the melody and harmony of secular European styles. Upper body thrusts, especially of males, dominated forward and backward steps, which suggested an approach to a shrine, the main characteristic of the Marquesas breadfruit harvest dance at Nukuhiva. Coordinating moves of arms, torso, head, fingers, and eyes by moonlight, Marquesas girls performed solos outside their dwellings.

The dancers of Oceania emulated human interaction with earth, air, fire, and water and taught their young children dance ceremonies. After 800 BCE, the Lapita, the aboriginal settlers of Fiji and Samoa, introduced the *siva* Samoa, a couples dance to a gentle rhythm emulating the slap of waves on shore. Unlike the warrior dance of the Maori, male and female Samoans extended hands and arms in gracious sways, a contrast to the stomps and grunts of wartime choreography. With faces painted red and bodies coated in black, they shuffled their feet, but made no aggressive moves. As a mark of hatred for treachery or crime, a vengeful male refused to dance until he had extracted recompense from an enemy.

Farther east, the stilt dancers of the Marquesas Islands entertained villagers in amphitheaters by posing above spotless mats atop intricately carved posts. Men made ungainly leaps to drum and bamboo pipe music and brandished fiber finger rings decked with feathers. War widows danced naked to express grief and summon vengeance from fellow islanders. The use of stilts suggested commemoration of aboriginal ancestors, whom the tall wood legs elevated above mortals.

Across Oceania, island dancers created distinctive innovations in choreography and gestures. Among Easter Islanders west of Chile and the Malagasy Islands off the east coast of Africa, a hind kick emulated the backlash of four-footed beasts. At Rarotonga, reenacting a victory in a wrestling match entertained Cook Islanders with a balletic version of youthful sport. Female Maori added a cheerleader-like routine by swinging *poi*, weighted spheres of knotted flax or cattails attached to tasseled tethers. Advanced nighttime presentations featured flaming poi twirled in fiery circles like stars in the heavens.

When the elegant siva Samoa spread north to Hawaii after 300 CE, Marquesas dancers served as arts ambassadors for luau galas and ended after dark with torchlight processions. Similarly, the *otea*, a precolonial Tahitian spectacle, involved men and women in a tremor of grass-skirted knees and hips that moved in mesmerizing circles. To syncopated drumbeats, barefoot performers diversified poses from crouching to standing or formed a circle around a soloist. Up to five minutes in length, the choreography of the otea harmonized arcs, circles, quadrangles, and figure eights to the rapid throbs of a sharkskin hand drum.

Dance in Recorded History

When English sea captain James Cook arrived at Tonga aboard the HMS *Resolution* on October 2, 1773, he recorded for Europeans an eyewitness account of the *me'etu'upaki*, mimicry of paddling a canoe that originated in the 1100s on Uvea Island. Rows of bare-chested men cloaked in bark cloth and encircled with leaves stepped sideways while synchronizing arm movements and maneuvers of stylized paddle boards to choral singing and the thump of a slit drum. The stand-up dance illustrated cooperative skills, which required organization and discipline.

When Tongan canoes arrived at hostile islands, the outsiders had to perform the me'etu'upaki as proof of their provenance. When Cook toured the Herveys and Tahiti in 1773 and 1774, he commented on the Areois, a secret society of celibate warrior-performers. After erecting miniature temples in sixty canoes and praying to the war god 'Oro, members traveled to neighboring islands to display their all-night dances.

To the flickers of candlenut lights, the Areois presented their choreography nude with red paint on their faces and blackening on their bodies and a sweet waft of coconut oil. Exhausting gestures exhibited passion and violence, which alarmed the English until they saw kind expressions and smiles. On the third voyage of the *Resolution* in 1776, Cook described Polynesian accompaniment, which tended toward idiophonic thumps on chests, bamboo poles, or sticks gripped in the teeth.

With the arrival of seventeen London Missionary Society evangelists from Woolwich around Cape Horn to Tahiti aboard the HMS *Duff* on March 6, 1797, the sensuous *'upa'upa* shocked and dismayed puritanical sensibilities. Christian observers credited a warm climate and Polynesian idleness as the cause of degeneracy. By denouncing the hip-shaking figure as lascivious, in 1819 the outsiders banned tattooing of flesh and sexually suggestive mating dances. Islanders withdrew from villages and perpetuated their culture in secret. A similar suppression of vice on Tonga outlawed the *lakalaka*, the national dance, because pairs completed the ritual amours in the thick outback.

At Tuvalu, villagers commemorated the rule of royalty and skill of a builder or fisher with the innovative *fakaseasea*, a spiritual dance of thanksgiving and pleas for intervention in suffering and the passage of spirits to the afterlife. Evangelists prohibited the slow undulations of the fakaseasea, which they considered carnally titillating, and also forbade a quicker variation, the *fakanau*, a ritual of gratitude for ample turtle eggs and island fruit. Out of favor with Europeans, the folk dances vanished from the island culture.

In salute to the appearance of a rainbow or a four-master on the island horizon, quartets of Futuna islanders performed the *soke*, a drum cadence ranging the blows of sticks against each other. Rhythmic variations synchronized hitting sticks together at top or bottom, rotating the stick, and a finale, a thud of sticks on the ground. As a gesture of penitence, the person-to-person aggression commemorated the martyrdom of Father Peter Chanel, whom an island ax murderer assassinated on April 28, 1841.

During the reign of Queen Pomare IV over Tahiti, French advisers restored the 'upa'upa in 1849, but disallowed gestures toward genitals. By the 1900s, district companies and church troupes limited their hip gyrations to commemorations of Bastille Day each July 14, the source of interisland competition in the 1920s. Companies costumed themselves in hibiscus fiber skirts, with men stripped to the waist for saber and fire dances on the shore by torchlight.

A warlike Samoan folk dance, the *siva afi* armed a solo male with up to four knives. In San Francisco in 1946, Freddie Letuli of Nu'uuli, Samoa, emulated a Hindu fire spectacle by pouring gasoline on flaming machetes, tokens of military might. He toured with folk dancers who performed with fiery blades in the United States, Australia, and Europe and at world fire knife competitions among Hawaiians, Tahitians,

Floridians, and Cook Islanders. In retirement, Letuli taught Polynesian folk dance at public schools and promoted the siva afi as a tourist attraction.

In 1956, the first Tahitian troupe revived the *tamure*, a heritage dance that appealed to tourists and amateur performers for the agitation of the knees while feet and shoulders remained stationary. Males encircled female dancers, who rotated grass-skirted hips to an increasing tempo. On land and tourist cruises, the reclamation of island folk art modes restored precolonial pride and unity. The success of distinctive dance troupes on each island enlivened the economy through set and costume design; instrumental music; hotel entertainment; and the sale of photos, paintings and sculpture, recordings, pareus, handicrafts, and bark cloth to tourists.

Mime Dance

Polynesian dance features actions resulting in success, victory, or everyday satisfaction. A Tongan group activity, the *sasa* involved seated or standing villagers in a follow-the-leader imitation game synchronizing fish swimming, birds soaring, paddling outriggers, weaving tapa cloth, hoeing roots, netting fish, and stirring and straining cauldrons of kava, a ritual pepper drink. Another Tongan group dance seated boys and girls in alternating positions around a circle or concentric circles for the *ma'ulu'ulu*. The drummer set the pace with a huge drum and initiated miming to a familiar song. The presentation by rows sitting, kneeling, and standing ended with heightened speeds and spectator applause. For elderly Tongans, the *'otuhaka*, performed from a seated position, limited motion to swaying head and body and hand and arm maneuvers to the rhythm of sticks beating bamboo poles.

At Tonga, Polynesian dancers mimed the completion of heavy tasks with the *taualuga*, a choreography similar to the mythic Tahitian *'aparima*. As a finale to feasting and amusements for weddings and holidays, royal or aristocratic children dressed in lory feathers and woven skirts and executed the refined conclusion, a sacred gesture toward hospitality and generosity. Coconut oil diffused a natural fragrance from the performers to spectators. Tahitian jesters turned the dance into merriment by exaggerating hand patterns.

For the taualuga, accessories on ankles and upper arms coordinated ti leaves with carved bone, shells, and boars' tusks. Men brandished hooked cane-cutting blades, blubber knives, and goat horns and mimicked an assault with war clubs. Outstanding dancers received coins and praise. The core activity in Samoan culture, the taualuga involved congregations in religious processions to strikes on a log gong. A later variant, the *ula*, danced by young girls, followed elderly women's presentation of the 'otuhaka, a kava drinking song to the thrum of bamboo sticks.

At Rotuma Island in Fiji, youthful beach musicales yielded a *fara*, a house-to-house processional dance by which performers invited residents to join the fun. To preserve female reputations, Methodist missionaries chaperoned shore parties and courting dances executed to the music of guitar, ukulele, and drums. Hosts passed fruit platters and beverages and sprinkled the dancers with powder and scent.

A sedate Rotuman *tautoga* coordinated the moves of large numbers of villagers in phalanx formation. Garbed in sarongs or leafy overskirts, feathers, and flower necklaces, women undulated arms to the slow, delicate shifting of feet. To stick percussion counted out by elders, men performed shuffles and leaps on feet set shoulder width apart, sometimes with bent knees. Chanting to gendered syllables preceded harmonics and clapping. Completion of the first verse initiated a shift of the front row to the back of the quadrant.

See also censorship; circle dance; drumming; mime.

Source: Danver, Steven L. *Native Peoples of the World: An Encyclopedia of Groups.* New York: Routledge, 2015.

PROCESSIONALS

From early history, a parade or promenade of measured footwork and flourishing of pennants, masks, and garlands preceded worship, funerals, sports, military victory, and rejoicing. Examples are the Día de los Muertos (Day of the Dead) ensembles performing the zapateado in Mexico, a holiday cortege to a Confucian or Taoist altar by the Chinese lion dancers, and jazz funeral parades in New Orleans. Notable examples include the python dance of Amazonian tribes in Peru, the Egyptian *shemadan*, a nuptial march adopted by Coptic Christians to lead wedding guests to the groom's house, and the jubilant steps of Algerian celebrants of the Muslim bride borne on a camel howdah. At Agia Triada, Crete, in 1500 BCE, dance to singing and a rattle brought Minoan harvesters from the fields to store grain and venerate agrarian deities, a common folk thanksgiving worldwide. In the same spirit of gratitude and reverence, with steps metered by lyre and timbrel, the Hebrews followed the Ark of the Covenant from Mount Sinai and Jericho to the tabernacle, a sacred mobile tent, and on to Zion, the mythic name for Jerusalem.

Greek communities honored the dead with comic mime and competitive sports that involved a funeral cortege to altars and arenas. Recessionals resumed the tone and atmosphere of daily life with a more spirited column. At the height of rejoicing, every four years after 776 BCE, Greek athletes synchronized steps to the lighting of the Olympic torch at the shrine of Zeus in Olympia before the Pan-Hellenic Games.

In 500 BCE, the ceremonial litanies to Kali, the Hindu goddess of empowerment, expressed the pinnacle of civilization among the Aryans of northwestern India. In her honor, the lead dancer painted his body black. For a post-midnight spectacle, he dressed in black robes as he supported a ewer of holy water on his head. The precise dance took the director and a cadre of marchers from the Ganges River to the temple of Siva, the dancing god, in whose honor attendants buried the urn at the holy altar.

Historical Cavalcades

During the Byzantine Empire, the suppression of pagan dances in Macedonia, Pontus, and Cappadocia by the Eastern Greek Orthodox hierarchy proved too regulatory. To accommodate Greek converts to Christianity, in 381 CE, the church allowed stylized processions honoring Christmas and Easter and torch-lit vigils memorializing the dead, saints, and martyrs. Enamelware from 1050 depicted a flag corps of noblewomen making long strides and expressing emotion with hands raised over their heads to flutter woven banners.

From 618 to 1000, dragon dancers at Zhejiang marked the Chinese New Year with a colorful propitiation of harvest gods. Parades synchronized the steps of participants under the textured paper or cloth body of a mythic beast figure as long as 70 meters (230 feet). For the remainder of the Middle Ages, the multiethnic street procession spread to other locales as a festive entertainment in Iberia, for beauty contests pleasing to a Japanese lord during the Edo period, and at Jewish weddings, where guests raised the chuppah (canopy) over rabbi, bride, and groom. At Tai Hang near Hong Kong, a militaristic *hakka* troupe of 120 strode to the gait of a 220-foot straw fire dragon, a sinuous, crouching figure that shielded locals from typhoons and contagion.

Following the Hundred Years War, which began in 1337, the French promoted the processional *basse danse* as a hierarchical show of rank and captured treasure. After the immolation of Jews in Brussels in 1370, Dutch and Flemish patriots introduced the *kermess*, a church parade preceding dances and sports. As events at street fairs, the dance thrived in Ghent and Antwerp and passed to Maine, Indiana, and Wisconsin with low-country immigrants. Another late fourteenth-century procession, Europe's dance of death disported ghastly disguises through the streets. Their ghoulish walk and linen costumes, painted with skeletons, reminded spectators of mortality.

Renaissance processions extended parades into street theater featuring icons of saints, formal blessings, and the strutting of triumphant regiments, mummers, and trade guilds. In late May 1454 at Berga north of Barcelona, Catalonian troupes took sacred vows to march in the Patum, a five-day Corpus Christi allegory miming the battle between good and evil. In the sixteenth century, the allemande introduced the ritual advance of pairs in southern Germany to lute music. The step-step-plié and thrust pattern marked the February 1540 reception at Ghent, Belgium, for Charles V, the Holy Roman Emperor, arranged by Francis I of France. The sedate march foretokened the polonaise, a presentational dance for monarchs and church hierarchy and a subsequent stage entrance for ballets.

Purposeful Parades

Processions often coordinated steps that blossomed into more diverse choreography, a transformation in seventeenth-century Spain that turned a cavalcade honoring St. Sebastian into the zapateado or masked *parachico*. A parade of males and females partnered for the *jarana Yucateca*, a courting folk dance executed in pairs. In this same era, the Provençal *rigaudon* took on aristocratic airs at the French court under Louis XIII and became a processional figure for ballet. After 1669, Louis XIV favored the grave sarabande, a stately presentation of the chassé, bourrée, and repetitions of toe-in, toe-out.

In the Americas, processions enabled slaves to caper through streets to observe holidays and toss candy and flowers to spectators. An Afro-Brazilian character dance, the *maracatu* directed revelers at carnaval through the streets of Fortaleza, Olinda, and Recife for the investiture of the Kings of Congo, black leaders of the enslaved community. Before emancipation in 1884, marchers adapted liberation figures to call-and-response song and the cowbell, drum, and *shakere*. From Portuguese colonists, Brazilians at Manaus and São Luis evolved the *bumba-meu-boi*, an ornately costumed

For the Shinto night *kagura* dance in Takachiho Town, Miyazaki, costumed dancers form a two-line procession behind a leader. *Wakako Imamura and Priscilla Portsmouth, Japanese Tourism Organization, www.ilovejapan.ca, Toronto, Ontario.*

resurrection drama miming the death and revival of the bull. The Afro-Iberian parade choreography of the *congada* featured marchers and dancers disguised as royalty, ambassadors, and palace guards. The pageant honored Ginga, an Angolan queen martyred in 1663 while fighting Portuguese insurgents.

In St. Croix, the *bamboula* replicated African body postures and bold gyrations that epitomized defiance of bondage. A police ban in Louisiana in 1886 limited parades to the pre-Lenten Mardi Gras, but crowds continued to dance through streets into the mid-1910s in St. Lucia, Dominica, Martinique, Haiti, St. Thomas, and Trinidad. In the post-slavery era, black couples ridiculed white masters of the American South with the cakewalk, a soldierly strut that coordinated hat tilts, cane twirls, and backbends representing resistance to Jim Crow humiliations.

See also allemande; attire; *bamboula*; cakewalk; dance drama; diaspora; dragon dance; Jewish dance; lamentation dance; lion dance; *matachines*; pavane; polonaise; *rigaudon*; stomp dance; Sufi dance; *tirabol*; zapateado.

Source: Gallini, Giovanni Andrea. *A Treatise on the Art of Dancing.* London: R. Dodsley, 1772.

PROPITIATION

Before recorded history, pleas to deities involved dancers and shamans in attention-getting body language, clamor, steps, antics, props, costuming, and the precise lifting of legs, factors in the procession to a Confucian or Taoist altar before the Chinese lion dance and the precise lifting of legs. The stepping forward and back for the Khmer propitiation ritual in 2015 in Angkor Wat, Cambodia, affirmed victims of the Nepal Gorkha earthquake. For the Malay *hala*, a rice paddy ritual, seven communities dance to invoke the almighty to feed an agrarian people for another year. Music spills out from the finger cymbals and shin bells, frame drums, bone whistles, bullroarers, rattles, and vocal lamentation during conciliation of mystic powers, the focus of Day of the Dead street performance of the zapateado in Mexico and the Philippines.

Ancient propitiation typically arranged circle and line dance at an altar or holy shrine for confession and thanksgiving. From the Shang Dynasty after 1600 BCE, Chinese serpentine dance ritual honored a snake totem and begged the gods to favor the farmer with good weather and an ample harvest. Along the Bering Strait of eastern Siberia after 1000 BCE, the aboriginal Khanty and Mansi disguised themselves as the brown bear, a totemic spirit they mollified through dance and mime of tracking and skinning. In South Africa from the fifth century CE, the Sotho dressed in blanket cloaks and black ostrich feathers for praying for rain by gesticulating toward the sky while bounding in place.

Community Appeasement

As demonstrated by devout Sotho, worshipful spectacle required teamwork and unified motivation. A fire dragon dance on the coast of Hong Kong in 1880 set a *hakka* troupe in a reverent gesture to Buddha and an ancestral cult that arranged exhumation of family from inland China for reburial on the coast. For three nights, fireworks and joss sticks (incense) warded off disease and typhoons by calling on the heavens for good fortune. Propelled by 120 dancers, a 200-foot straw dragon fluttered his tongue, twisted his middle, and lunged at danger. The elaborate synchrony concluded with an annual sacrifice, the drowning of the dragon in the harbor at Causeway Bay.

To stave off similar fears in the Western Hemisphere, First Nations traditionally called on deities to intercede in inauspicious times and stave off looming disaster. Along the Bering Strait between Siberia and Alaska, the Kingikmiut Eskimo spent five wintry months assuaging the weather gods to bless whales, bear, seal, and walrus populations to ensure human sustenance for the coming spring. In the Eskimo dance house, preparations began with assigned seating around the circle and gift giving before the performers appeared in black face paint and deerskin to sway and execute ritual figures.

New challenges restored vernacular dance to use. Because of outbreaks of loss, greed, depression, fear, juvenile crime, and drug abuse on the North American plains, in 1950, the Canadian Cree, Sioux, Blackfoot, and Ojibwa revived an ancient healing spectacle to drumming as a force for good. A Crow dance rite in 1955 called on the Great Spirit to end the Korean War and rid veterans of post-traumatic depression and guilt. The dance revivals broadened communication between the generations and taught youths songs and choreography that soothed the damaged spirit.

Post-Modern Reconciliation

Diasporas and shifts in world power structures continue to inspire folk ceremonies in placation of divinities, a trait shared by the massive migrations from Syria into central and Western Europe and the United States in fall 2015. In San Francisco's Chinatown, folk specialist Corey Chan's lion storytellers perform ancient masked dances to beg the gods' blessing. The lead dancer engages spectators in mock struggle, an allegorical religious drama pitting humankind against the unknown.

With more color and gesture, dragon dancers honor the emergence of the Chinese from dragon ancestors. Movable jaws and eyelids and the rolls, squats, and martial arts gestures of dancers hidden under the cloth body usher in the Chinese New Year. In massive masks painted yellow, green, orange, and red, the dragon cavorts to gong and drum over the dance space to bring rain and control floods and unforeseen calamities. The progression of steps displays fealty, humility, and Asian piety.

For the totemic dancers on the island of Yam in the Torres Straits, honors to the hammerhead shark and crocodile require an annual dance by two parallel lines of men. On holy environs of a temple, males sing and perform in red or black body paint and feathers. The holy pageant involves extending the arms with palms out and waving hands to entreat heaven for good weather. A third row reverencing the sea snake guides the troupe's steps around a shrine to request protection in battle.

See also attire; circle dance; community dance; dragon dance; Eskimo dance house; Greek dance; lamentation dance; line dance; lion dance; North African dance; pipe dance; planting dance; sacrificial dance; shamanic dance; sub-Saharan dance; totemic dance; zapateado.

Source: Eiss, Harry. *The Mythology of Dance.* Newcastle, UK: Cambridge Scholars, 2013.

PYRRHIC DANCE

A lightly stepped Doric choreography also performed on Crete, the Pyrrhic war dance derived from structured honoraria to semi-divine heroes Hercules and Theseus and from Homer's hoplite (infantry) dance. Exaggerated anger and growls accompanied the pounding of javelins on shields and patterned movements replicating the dodging of fists, weapons, and missiles. Practice by Dorian recruits stimulated the appetite for attack and conquest.

The scheduling of a Greek Gymnopaedia sent males as young as five years old into staged battle to the piping of the double flute. At the Panathenaea, Athenian recruits gave less-martial versions of Pyrrhic dance in commemoration of Athena's mustering of Olympian powers to defeat a race of giants, emblematic of precivilization. According to Plato early in the fourth century BCE, Athena herself, the goddess of wisdom and war, delighted in the sportive choreography, which she mounted in full armor. In 500 BCE, sculpture captured the grace and musculature of an Amazon performing a war dance.

Alterations to Pyrrhic dance illustrated shifts in Mediterranean societies, particularly after the Peloponnesian War (431–404 BCE) and the heroics of Alexander the Great from 338 BCE to his death on June 10, 323 BCE. Gendered adaptations to headdress and martial boots and armor enabled females to dance soldiers' routines. In contrast, among mountaineers in Macedonia and Thessaly, the Pyrrhic dance remained an androcentric swagger of swordsmanship.

In 50 BCE, Julius Caesar, the remodeler of the Circus Maximus, introduced the Pyrrhic dance to Rome, where Bithynian children from western Anatolia modeled the steps. Sometimes performed by troupes of condemned felons, the dance dramatized myths of Dionysus, Icarus, and Paris. Into the early Roman Empire, Caligula and Nero expanded on the Pyrrhic dance as a form of self-adulation. The tradition continued under Emperor Hadrian until 138 CE and, in the second century, at Sparta as training for male teens. By 200, religious votaries replaced weaponry with torches and thyrsi, ritual staffs wrapped in ivy and topped with pinecones in reverence to Dionysus, the god of wine.

See also labyrinthine dance.

Source: Anon. *The Dance: Historic Illustrations of Dancing from 3300 B.C. to 1911 A.D.* London: John Bale, Sons & Danielsson, 1911.

· 2 ·

QUADRILLE

A four- or eight-person square dance, the quadrille epitomizes the rise of a European social dance that evolved into a Caribbean folk tradition. The original figures emerged in 1740 in France as an alternative to the slower, less invigorating minuet. The name derived from the seventeenth-century parade figure exhibiting the horsemanship of four cavalry officers and their steeds. The Scots became enthusiasts of the orderly figure in the 1780s.

In Puerto Rico, Martinique, Guadeloupe, St. Lucia, Dominica, Grenada, Carriacou, Montserrat, St. Croix, and Madagascar around 1779, African gestures and rhythms to drum, shakere, banjo, and violin creolized the figures that harbor slaves learned from Scots boat builders. Upon mastering the quadrille, bondsmen turned the original decorum into a mockery of owners of West Indian sugar plantations. For leisure and dancing at seasonal fairs and observances of Easter Monday, Empire Day, and Emancipation Day (August 1), Jamaican islanders abandoned their masters' English mode and created the camp-style quadrille, a patchwork of the original squares and flamboyant improvisations. Companies performed in bright Madras skirts, flounced petticoats, red sashes, and *tignons* (turbans) for women and white shirts, red sashes, and plaid vests for men.

French Mode

Among the French, Germans, and Italians in the 1790s, the court of Napoleon I set an unhurried pace for the European quadrille, which appealed to high and low social classes alike. An offshoot of the cotillion and the folksy contradance, the quadrille consisted of five parts—*le pantalon* (pants), *l'été* (summer), *la poule* (hen), *la frenis* (reins), and *le final* (conclusion). The promenades, two-hand turns, chains, and courtesies observed during changing of partners impressed the English in 1808 at a gathering at Buxton hosted by William Cavendish, the 5th Duke of Devonshire. The choreography reached fashionable status with social climbers in 1813 and appeared on dance class schedules three years later, even among Quakers. A prisoner of the Napoleonic Wars, Moritz von Kotzebue, a lieutenant in the Imperial Russian Army in 1816, attempted to join a quadrille square in Soissons, France, and discovered that the figures varied from the adaptations he had learned in Russia.

The plain quadrille altered further under the mincing Caledonians, Irish set dancers, and Finnish square dancers. For the *vendsyssel,* Danes added a shout and raised fist as well as a clapping game. In 1817, the quadrille developed into its most prevalent hybrid, the *lanciers* (lancers), a pattern marked by the military formality of marching, bowing, and saluting. The original quadrille received standardization as well as notoriety from English dance teacher Thomas Wilson's *Quadrille and Cotillion Panorama* (1817) and a Scots choreography manual, Barclay Dun's *A Translation of Nine of the Most Fashionable Quadrilles* (1818). A year later, *Blackwood's Magazine* revealed the ingenuity of Scots maidens who outlined a guide to confusing dance figures on the back of their fans.

The Global Quadrille

For middle-class Italians, colonists of Australia and New Zealand, and Bahamians of the Caribbean, as noted in an 1825 issue of *Harmonicon,* the quadrille was easy to learn and execute without special lessons or practice. At St. James Palace in London on June 11, 1829, Princess Maria Theresia Esterhazy turned a royal ball into a dancing lesson on the galop, which she alternated with waltzes and quadrilles. By 1856, the lanciers, with its romanticized cavalry air, surpassed the quadrille in popularity in France, Sweden, Germany, Austria, Ireland, and North America. On the rowdy American frontier, the pairing into couples to form squares produced square dance.

In *The Fitz-Boodle Papers* (1842), social satirist William Makepeace Thackeray noted the decline of the orderly quadrille because young people had not learned the figures. By World War I, the dance waned in elite European society, but not the Caribbean. The original pattern and camp-style quadrille served physical education classes in Jamaica, Guadeloupe, and St. Lucia by modeling patterns and preparation for competition. The figures remained a popular twenty-first-century folk genre in Franco-American New England and Canada.

See also chain dance; contradance; cotillion; galop; quadrille; square dance; waltz.

Sources: Louzioti, Dafne. "Introduction to Quadrille." *Caribbean Communities in Europe.* Accessed October 20, 2015. www.caribbeancommunities.eu/CACOEU_investigates.pdf. Miller, Rebecca S. *Carriacou String Band Serenade: Performing Identity in the Eastern Caribbean.* Middletown, CT: Wesleyan University Press, 2007.

· ℛ ·

REEL

An Old Norse rhythm in 2/2 or 4/4 time, the reel (or *reill*), Scotland's national dance, predates history in the Isle of Mann, Hebrides, Orkneys, Shetlands, and Scots highlands. Set to such clan marches as "The Campbells Are Coming," the traveling, interlacing figures foregrounded the highland fling, a martial sword dance that imitated a stag's capers, and the Virginia reel, an English contradance from the 1600s. Called a *ril* in Norway and Denmark, the fixed order of low, bouncy, whirling figures in precise time flourished within the lower class as a gay amusement.

After the Danish invasion of Britannia at Ipswich in early August 991 CE, folk musicians blended Celtic and Scandinavian fiddle tunes with reel choreography. The intricate figure dance, performed in soft shoes, became the Danish national dance. In the thirteenth century across rural Ireland, Scotland, Wales, and Northumberland, England, reels uplifted the folk gatherings at *cèilidhs* (house parties), where dancers stepped lightly on the balls of the feet.

An Evolving Dance

With the addition of spoons, juice harp, flute, accordion, dulcimer, and bodhran (frame drum), Celtic community members surrounded a peat fire to vary reels with jigs, schottisches, hornpipes, and polkas along with ring dances directed by a caller. By winding around partners, into the early English Renaissance, the folkloric farandole (also hay or hey) lent sparkle and animation to the Irish *lanciers* (lancers) reel. For weddings, the turning dance concluded with a couples promenade.

British sailors introduced the reel in Finland in the early 1700s, when the penny whistle carried the melody. Conservative Presbyterians in the Scots Highlands prohibited the dance in the mid–1600s, when reel fans took their fun into hiding. By 1750, sheet music for reels reached the public in London and Edinburgh, notably John Bowie's compilation *A Collection of Strathspey Reels and Country Dances* (1789). Dance masters migrated from village to village to instruct peasants on reel arches, four-hands-across, and partner changes.

In the late 1700s as far from urban areas as the Isle of Skye, the Irish made late public claim on the circular reel, which they danced with their whole hearts. For learning new faces, callers instructed participants to glide to the next partner and exchange names, a learning ploy later adopted by elementary school teachers. At Oatlands, Surrey, on May 30, 1800, Frederica Charlotte of Prussia, the Duchess of York, requested that local folk arrange an authentic demonstration reel.

Celtic and Cornish emigrants carried the tunes and figures to North America, where maritime dancers at Cape Breton, Nova Scotia, customized the steps to New World melodies. At the tsarist court of Nicholas I in St. Petersburg, noble Russians added reels to the polka, mazurka, and waltz, all of which appealed to peasants for socials and weddings. At informal "Virginia hops" in 1772, Governor John Murray, the 4th Earl of Dunmore, chose the reel as a figure to energize stately visitors at Williamsburg Palace. In 1774, Nicholas Cresswell, an English visitor of the Scots governor, noted that frequent cutting in kept the dance in motion until the musician collapsed from exhaustion.

The North American Reel

Barn dancers and square dancers in the United States, Saskatchewan, Quebec, Ontario, and Newfoundland adapted the four-hand reel into the cotton-eye Joe, a line dance performed with arms over shoulders or around waists. In North Carolina in the 1840s, suites paired the reel with the cotillion, schottische, or a rowdy galop. In Louisiana and the Caribbean, Creole folk artists made the reel the basis of the lanciers and the French quadrille. The adaptation of the reel into an invocation of spirits at Tobago and Trinidad resulted in Africanized trance dances similar to those performed in Haiti and holiday frolics on the streets of St. Croix in the Virgin Islands.

The amiable sound and visuals of the reel suited disparate peoples who settled Canada. With a jolly spirit, Canadian Mounties on the Macleod Trail at Calgary, Alberta, claimed the reel and schottische for pioneer galas, wintertime escapes from snowed-in cabins and forts. Throughout the Northwest Territories, immigrants taught the reel to the Hare Dené at Fort Good Hope.

US claimants of the reel valued its historical significance to folk arts, for example, as a facet of physical education overlapping classroom lectures on culture. Into the 1890s, the Daughters of the American Revolution saluted folk dance by introducing the Virginia reel at colonial-themed masquerade balls and parties saluting the birthdays of George Washington and Abraham Lincoln. At the Century of Progress fair in Chicago in 1933, Irish-Americans presented a *claibh* (sword dance) and reel set to the striking of wood sticks.

See also barn dance; *cèilidh*; censorship; circle dance; contradance; cotton-eye Joe; farandole; galop; highland fling; hornpipe; jig; literature, folk dance in; mazurka; polka; reel; quadrille; schottische; square dance; sword dance; technique; waltz.

Source: Henry, Lori. *Dancing through History: In Search of the Stories That Define Canada.* Vancouver, BC: Dancing Traveller, 2012.

RIGAUDON

The *rigaudon* (also rigadoon, *rigadone*, or *rigadon*), a springy solo or capricious couples quickstep in 2/2 or 4/4 time, dates to Mediterranean sailors or the agrarian French from 1485 at the village of Gap (or Gavots), Dauphiné, in southeastern France. Peasant performance featured sentimental tunes and gestures of head and arms to taps on the tambourine, a relief from the more sober gavotte. Dancers accentuated diagonal and lateral capers in the style of the Hungarian czardas. Filled with repeats of the basic choreography, around 1500, the rigaudon stirred appreciation in southern France, encompassing farm folk in Provençal, Dauphiné, Languedoc, and Vavarais.

Numbered among nationalistic figures and playful contradances, the rigaudon resembled the contradance *Anglaise* (English) and contradance écossaise (Scots). The joyous figures reached popularity in Germany, at England's Jacobean court after 1603, and throughout central and northern France in the 1640s, late in the rule of Louis XIII. Italian composers rounded out theatricals with rigaudon finales. For its frivolous nature, the French added the figure to suites of the pavane, galliard, and *furlana* and a chorus of ariettas.

The Standard Rigaudon

Around 1630, the baroque style took its name from either a Marseillaise dance teacher named Rigaud, who brought it to Paris from the southeast, or the English "rig go down" or the Scots "rig-a-down-daisy," a vernacular description of merrymaking. Other possibilities of etymology link the rigaudon with the Italian *rigolone*, a circle dance, and the Latin *gaudere* ("to rejoice"). With a hopping step, couples standing side by side joined hands and tiptoed forward to the cadences of a harpsichord. The pair switched feet in a pas de bourrée and executed glissades (gliding steps), *eschappés* (leaps from feet together to feet apart), *entrechats quatres* (leaps and front-to-back swaps of feet in the air), and *sissones* (scissors kicks) before skipping in a circle.

The rigaudon flourished in Paris after 1643 in a more aristocratic style of Louis XIV, the father of classical ballet, and became a standard part, along with the minuet, of aristocratic children's education in the arts. Court refinement in the *ballet l'ecole* (textbook dance) of Pierre Beauchamp, the king's dance master, prefaced use of the rigaudon as a ballet processional. As a stylistic detail, dancers stressed a catlike definition to each hop.

At a low point in dance history, the parliament at Grasse acted on the complaint of Louis de Bernage, Bishop of Grasse, by banning the dance on April 3, 1664. Lawmakers censured the figure for venturing from genteel folk performance into vulgar embracing, indecent posturing, and lustful kissing. In 1669, Antoine Godeau, the Bishop of Vence northwest of Nice, preferred that legislators outlaw public presentations in the piazzas in front of churches. Nonetheless, author Marie de Sévigné approved the dance in 1672 for gatherings of young nobles at Grasse.

At the same time that the North American colonists of Quebec learned the rigaudon, in 1680, Jacques Favier, dancing master to the dauphine Marie-Anne Christine-Victoire of Bavaria, daughter-in-law of Louis XIV, taught her the seductive hopping dance until advanced pregnancy limited her participation. Composer Jean-Baptiste Lully introduced the figure at the Paris Opera on September 6, 1686, in *Acis et Galatée*. As described by Edward Isaac, dance teacher to English royalty at White Hall in the 1680s, the rigaudon developed a range of variations. By the late seventeenth century, the rigaudon reached Filipino–Spanish dance floors in Manila as the "*rigodón d'honneur*," a patriotic quadrille, and served Scots highland soldiers as a limbering exercise performed on the crossed blades of swords.

Refined Folk Dance

According to baroque arts theorist Santiago de Murcia of Madrid, the dance advanced from a peasant figure to a courtly art by 1700. In England, court dancers performed the steps for the birthday of Queen Anne. Composers Henry Purcell, André Campra, Johann Sebastian Bach, and François Couperin wrote pieces to accompany the dance. On stage, foppish characters tiptoed about in rigaudon steps to illustrate effeminacy. The figure appeared in a benefit presentation on May 10, 1716, at Lincoln's Inn Fields performed by Diane Schoolding-Moreau and John Topham and offered comic relief to George Frideric Handel's serious opera *Radamisto* (1720), set in the second century of imperial Rome.

English arts critic Soame Jenyns, a proponent of individualized steps, applauded the rigaudon in *The Art of Dancing* (1727) for its nimble, sprightly air. In the latter 1700s, French musical scholar Pierre Alexandre Monsigny composed numerous rigaudons for the comic opera. In this same period, when French mountain families sent wives and children south to the Riviera for the winter, the dance provided a seasonal diversion, especially for New Year's Day, pre-Lenten carnival, and cafe entertainment.

In Italian impresario Giovanni Andrea Gallini's *A Treatise on the Art of Dancing* (1762), he reported the rigaudon much in demand for piano and dance. The Paris Opera performed choreographer Gaëtano Vestris's *Dardanus* (1767), which featured a march and rigaudon. The folk dance remained a Gallic favorite until the French Revolution of July 14, 1789, and appeared as a pastime of the New Orleans elite in arts critic Moreau de St.-Méry's *Danse* (1796), the first book on the art published in the United States.

Still stylish in the Pyrenees in 1844, the dance also appeared in Italian arts theorist Carlo Blasis's *Notes upon Dancing: Historical and Practical* (1847). On March 19, 1892, a benefit performance of composer Jean-Philippe Rameau's "Rigaudon" coordinated Moorish maskers, pages, wait staff, and gardeners in an effort to ease the Russian famine and raise cash for the Paris ambulance service.

In 1926, Filipinas at the Philippine Women's University retained the dance for its national symbolism. The term "rigaudon" took on political significance in January 1990 to describe a bureaucratic shuffle in the Filipino cabinet of President Corazon Aquino. The rigodón d'honneur remains a favorite quadrille in the Philippines.

See also contradance; czardas; *furlana*; galliard; gavotte; pavane.

Source: Villaruz, Basilio Esteban. *Treading through: 45 Years of Philippine Dance.* Quezon City: University of the Philippines Press, 2006.

ROMA DANCE

The Roma or Romani artisans and entertainers emerged as an identifiable culture in Rajasthan in northern India around 3000 BCE. The nomadic Kalbeliya tribe, an untouchable caste of snake catchers, maintained worship of the mother goddess Kali, whom they later called Sara. In ecstasy, devotees presented the *sapera*, a sensuous cobra dance performed with serpentine movements.

While Kalbeliyan men played the reed *poongi* (snake charmer's pipe) and percussion instruments to spontaneous tunes, women joined the rapid dance in ornate black robes that flared to exhibit embroidery, silvery ribbons, and beading. Tattoos, metallic stitchery, and mirrors on garments added allure to the hypnotic pirouettes. The tent dance concluded with a braiding of ribbon suggestive of a maypole frolic.

Another version of Rajasthani female dance at Jaipur, the *ghoomar*, retained the whirling of the sapera and added a veil in bright colors over layered skirts. In central India, a circle of girls and women from the rural Bhil tribe, including the bride at weddings, snapped their fingers and slapped palms while singing worship hymns in Hindi to praise Saraswati, the goddess of knowledge. At all-night festivals, the circle revolved and reversed to express historical inclusion of the self over time in world culture.

In a darkened space, the Indian *shavenu* (wise woman) chanted and gestured while holding devotional oil lamps in each hand. Designs on dance dresses conjured kundalini (serpent power), an emblematic recognition of energy coiled at the human coccyx (tailbone). To dispel disapproval, persecution, and disempowerment by surrounding peoples, Romani dancers awakened their reptilian powers and worded mantras and curses reputed to menace victims forever.

On the Move

In 250 BCE, the migratory Roma crossed the Punjab into northern Baluchistan and Sindh (western Pakistan) with their campfire dances. Under the name Lori, they lived among the lowly and supported themselves as midwives, carpenters, goldsmiths, and blacksmiths. Their entertainments ranged from juggling and sleight of hand tricks to palmistry and fortune telling, the source of a modern stereotype of Romani as superstitious charlatans. The wealthy employed them to arrange nuptial banquets and provide background music and dance for receptions.

Around 600 CE, the Roma continued their migratory existence across western Asia and Europe and began acquiring the musical and dance elements of Arabs, Persians, Serbs, Czechs, Slavs, and Romanians. After 1000 among Turks in the bars and clubs of Anatolia and taverns in Greece and Macedonia, the Romani developed rhapsodic violin music. For informal occasions, musicians accompanied a working-class dance on the bouzouki (mandolin) as performers joined hands and encircled tables. In tight spaces, they gyrated to rhythmic, melodic *fasil* music played on clarinet, autoharp, drum, lute, and violin, the fount of modern klezmer music and Gypsy jazz.

In the Sulukule section of the European side of Istanbul, Romani performances punctuated dance moves with comic gestures, belly rolls, torso twists, hip undulations, and sudden sinking to the knees with heads bent back to encourage tips from spectators. The earthy, cathartic dance to 9/8 rhythm incorporated sly facial expressions, improvised footwork, voluptuous shoulder tremors, and raised arms. In 1060, upheaval in the Ghaznavid Empire under the rule of Ibrahim of Ghazna forced the Roma farther west from Persia over the Caucasus into Armenia and Georgia, where they wove baskets, soldered tinware, and performed in circuses the stylized line and circle dances for male troupes. Men's exertions reflected the influence of Ukrainian dance, a show of athleticism, masculinity, and stamina.

Syncretic Dance

Over the Romani trail, itinerant groups dispersed from Turkey northeast to the Balkans in 1100 and Crete in 1322, where migrants added Aegean layered skirts and handkerchief manipulation to their festive solos. Spectators gathered at street puppet shows and dances and hired performers for weddings, bachelor parties, baptisms, funerals, and memorials. Romani caravans migrated into late medieval Germany and Austria in 1440, where locals called them "Sinti" for "people of Sindh," a reflection of disapproval for dance modes from the Indian subcontinent.

The Roma journeyed on to France and Iberia in the late 1400s, when they acquired the names Gitan/Gitano-Gitana from the Greek for "untouchable." In Paris, the travelers performed their specialties in the Batignolle District. Because of their nonconformist lifestyle, the Spanish Inquisition and the Pragmática of 1499 from Louis XII expelled Iberian Roma, who carried their polyglot songs, comedic gags, and erotic dances to the northeast.

The Roma found no haven in England, where the British named them Gypsies, a Middle English corruption of "Egyptian" from the erroneous belief that the first Roma came from Egypt. In 1554, Queen Mary I, known as Bloody Mary, condemned to death any Roma entertainers or citizens attending their musicales. A parallel ouster from Scotland by James VI in the 1570s sent the nomads southwest to Wales.

In the early 1600s, the Romani diaspora crossed Great Britain, where hanging awaited rural squatters and street and pier buskers, who drew audiences by adding Eastern exotica to their dances. The wanderers reached Scandinavia, Poland, and the Ukraine, introducing both soulful and fast *polska* tunes danced to clapping, thigh slaps, and wood clackers. In the Austro-Hungarian Empire in the mid- to late 1700s, the Roma became the interpreters of tenth-century Magyar dance.

Performers treasured the original songs of Hungarian violinist Panna Czinka, Bratislavan musicians Janos Bihari and Janos Lavotta, and beggar-cabaret composer Antal Csennak. Royalty invited Romani dancers and instrumentalists to palace entertainments, the employment of Hungarian violinist Belo Laci on the Danube River at Pest castle. A popular Roma original, the czardas flourished along the nomads' diaspora to Serbia, Croatia, Ukraine, Poland, Slovenia, Moravia, Bulgaria, and Transylvania.

In Skopje, Macedonia, female Roma dancers presented the *jeni jol*, a line dance performed slowly to brass duos or trios. European artists fetishized the wild, passionate dances in murals and paintings, which accentuated unusual body postures and heavy-lidded eyes. By the 1860s, strands of Roma carried their music and dance to Canada, the United States, Australia, Chile, and Brazil. The Roma style suffused the modern stage work of the era's experimental dancers—Isadora Duncan, Martha Graham, and Ruth St. Denis. Vitiated styles omitted the true Romani movements, which white audiences interpreted as threatening.

Bulgarian Roma

Roma presence in Bulgaria fused a minority folk strand to the ethnic music of Sofia. Called *chalga*, the sound and hedonistic lyrics interwove Greek and Byzantine arts heritage with references to drugs and genital manipulation between lovers. At public squares and Romani balls, the majestic bearing of couples displaying dark makeup, baggy blouses and trousers, open sandals, and heavy jewelry resulted in high pay from non-Roma and would-be Roma fans. Despite the demand, conservative Bulgarians banned bare-midriff performances as decadent and too Middle Eastern for their tastes.

At Balkan banquets and weddings in the early nineteenth century, the *cocek*, a popular Croat-Serb chain dance for cross-dressing males, derived from Muslim Roma belly dance tradition and Ottoman military brass bands. Some historians trace the cocek's pumping rhythm to the Vedic dances of 1700 BCE honoring Hindu gods. The original cocek linked community dance to Bulgarian healing rituals bringing rain and promoting fertility in herd animals.

With precise back-and-forth skips to drumming, tambourine, and flute, a line or circle of cocek dancers held hands and advanced, crouched, and retreated in the direction of the leader, who fluttered a handkerchief. The absence of cultural constraints over the lower torso, macabre posturing, and hints of incest in the nuptial song "Usti Usti Baba" shocked and offended religious communities. During solo renderings of the cocek, Bulgarian-Romani performers welcomed the atmosphere of a forbidden dance performed with zesty, oversexed abandon.

Romanian Roma

On the Danube Plain outside Bucharest in the mid-1500s, Romani adults taught their sons and daughters as well as local children partnering, circle dances, and the popular ti-sane (or *kurtisane*), a solo associated with opium consumption. Repertoires coordinated leaps, stamps, claps on thighs and torso, crouches, and rolling on the floor. Significant Romani tastes added hip and shoulder vibrations, backbends, and curving, revolving motions of arms and hands to syncopated beats. Instrumentalists from the artisanal class provided *lautari* (lute) music for southern Moldavian festivities. However, Romanians who danced to Romani music preferred not to intermingle with Romani hirelings.

In reflection of the troubled Romani existence, emotional gestures depicted fierceness, rage, joy, passion, pain, yearning, and sorrow, the overriding tone of the Gitana national anthem, "Djelem, djelem" (I went, I went, 1949), composed by Serb-Romani Zarko Jovanovic. Around 1775, Romani musicians formed guilds to manage artisanal dances to violin, lute, and pan flute music. In the late eighteenth century, Boyars, the upper-class Slavs, hired Gypsy quartets to accompany folk weddings and festival dances with rich harmonies and solo presentations of easy-listening doings to accordion, panpipes, or clarinet.

Ornamental techniques accompanied the plaintive Turkish *manele* ballads from the late 1700s; the acrobatic running steps, kicks, and two-footed leaps of the *calusul*; and the hora and fast-paced *sârba* circle dances, a spirited rhythm in 6/8 time alternating quick and slow steps. The counterclockwise hora spun the circle three steps ahead and one step back. Another version of the hora involved parallel lines of dancers in simple Roma nuptial revelry, which extended over two days the community dance and liberal consumption of alcohol.

Russian Roma

To the strum of balalaika, violin, and guitar, *tsingane*, a Russian-style Roma dance, energized holidays and weddings with fast footwork, spinning, dumb show, and flourishing skirts of red, orange, yellow, and blue. By increasing speed, dancers drew spectators' attention to a frenzied completion, eliciting a wave of Gypsyphilia anticipating the romantic era. In the 1770s, soloist Ivan Sokolov of St. Petersburg led a Romani choir at Count Alexei Orlov's estate outside Moscow in true Roma waltz tunes. The eclectic costumes ranged from bare feet, head scarves tied tightly over braids, and flounced skirts to loose-necked peasant blouses slipping down to reveal breasts. The main features of Russian Romani attire—mixed patterns and comfort—yielded a loose outfit that allowed full body engagement in dance.

In 1956, Soviet bans on wandering lifestyles threatened Romani culture. Few nomads continued to practice blacksmithing and midwifery or raise their families in vans or tents. Primitive ballads of their travails and artistry waned, as did fireside dancing, colorful posters, and the atmosphere of independence from governments, church dogma, and community mores. After passage of the older generation, younger Roma had only pop culture to emulate.

Spanish Roma

Spanish Gitano or Calo music and dance, lionized as the archetypal Andalusian *romalis* or flamenco, bore traces of the northern Indian *kathak*, a storytelling dance punctuated by stamps of heel and toe, raised legs, elongated necks, and whip turns. Some nomads reached Iberia by passing across Africa and through Gibraltar, reaching Barcelona and Zaragoza in 1425. The wanderers merged with Sephardic Jews and Moriscos (Muslim Spaniards), the least Hispanic population in Granada, Cádiz, and Seville. In the late 1500s, Spanish repression forced the Gitanos into ghettos, where their folk arts, including the flamenco, remained relatively free of other cultural strands.

In the coming centuries, among a diverse population, idiosyncratic dance and instrumental music in grottoes, caves, and patios provided comfort and cohesion as an antidote to dispersal and prohibition of Gitano settlement. The Roma fled from church and state expulsion and ghettoization in France. Passage of the edict of Henry of Navarre on April 13, 1598, labeled the nomads rogues and vagabonds and condemned them to galley slavery or deportation to distant colonies.

The coercive law thrust the travelers southwest into mountainous Basque territory, where they dwelled apart and made little effort at acculturation. The Roma language acquired a Basque term, *dantzari* (dancer), and added the fringed shawl and cane to audacious Spanish steps. Roma performers developed vibrant footwork to the *alegría*, a lively ballad performed to graceful moves and guitar strums exalting the Gypsy and the bullfighter.

In contrast to life in the Pyrenees, the nomads merged comfortably into communities farther south in Spain. A thorough fusion of Spanish and Gitano elements invested Castilian folk steps and rhythms with sybaritic abandon, the hallmark of Romani music. Bohemians danced at street fairs and religious festivals, adding Roma flair to traditional Spanish folk dance by balancing trays and flaming swords on their heads while tapping a tambourine or brass finger cymbals. Persecution worsened during the Great Gypsy Round-up of July 30, 1749, when Ferdinand VI attempted to purify the arts and lifestyle of Spain of Roma influence. Spanish raiders dispatched by Gaspar Tablada, Bishop of Oviedo, incarcerated some twelve thousand Gitanos in labor camps, mines, factories, and prisons.

Until the release of husbands and fathers in 1763, free-ranging Gitanos formed refuge towns, where they could perform wedding dances throughout their traditional three-day nuptials. After the newlyweds withdrew, guests danced the *bulería*, a cacophonous twelve-count stomping, clapping dance later replaced by the rumba. To firm heel taps, the intricate, mesmerizing hand patterns summoned *duende* (magic), which substantiated the rumor that Gitanas cast spells with a sweep of the hands.

For pair dancing of the bulería, men held out arms and grasped their partners in fiery embrace before the women surged away in rapid whirls. As though readying for combat, the males expressed fierce retaliation and ardor with pelvic thrusts toward their partners, who arched their necks and cast hateful looks. The finale resulted in a cry of brutal conquest and rhapsodic union, a technique that Giovanni Giacomo Casanova learned from a Romani instructor in the mid-1700s. Prudish Britons, bug-eyed with admiration of the bulería, termed the dance the "olé."

Each Easter after 1847, the Seville April Fair interspersed bullfights and parades with Gitano dance and extended into all-night fiestas the exuberant *sevillanas*, a couples presentation in 3/4 time in brilliant costume displaying arched back and arrogant head postures. Authentic Gitanas clacked castanets, clapped or tapped tables to a syncopated beat, and flaunted flowers in their hair, handheld fans, and layered ruffles on flamenco dresses. The women mastered rapid turns while partnering with Gitanos in short bolero jackets, tight pants, and boots. According to traveler's guides, in the mid-1800s, the voluptuous pairing and dizzying tempos and the romance and excess of Andalusian-Gitano rhythms provided a licentious tourist attraction for the prurient. The style and technique continued to draw audiences for the film *Train of Life* (1998), which showcased jubilant Jewish and Roma dance to klezmer music.

See also Arab dance; Balkan dance; belly dance; bolero; *cachucha*; clogging; czardas; fandango; flamenco; *huayño*; *kathak*; *polska*.

Source: Charnon-Deutsch, Lou. *The Spanish Gypsy: The History of a European Obsession.* University Park: Pennsylvania State University Press, 2004.

ROMAN DANCE

Amusements in ancient Rome derived from the rural Greek Dionysian wine frenzies and the fertility dances to Pan and Echo as well as Corsican, Oscan, Sabellian, Sardinian, and Sicilian folk dance. On first view of the residents of Alba Longa, the Romans observed their victory dance on the riverbanks. From 800 BCE, Etruscan funereal dance influenced bas-relief on tombs as proof that the deceased could expect a joyous reception in the afterlife. Musicians wearing fools' caps accompanied the mourners' cortege with the sounds of the double pipe; lyre; and brass, steel, and wood castanets. Similarly, stately Samnite dances around the altars in Campania and southern Italy displayed tasteful steps and worship decorum.

For disporting women, Roman friends joined hands to form a ring for the idiophonic *chorea*, an impromptu revel set to the sound of their voices. Maidenly circle dances exulted at marriage processions. A *citharistria* (female string player) accompanied the ring presentation. For exercise, women danced while lifting dumbbells. For the *deductio* (marriage by capture), guests led the nuptial couple from the temple to their home with much rejoicing and folk figures. At taverns and snack shops, plebeians of easy virtue performed "*discinctus*" (ungirdled) among the tables for tips. On the streets, the *ludius* (strolling player) performed in the same impromptu style as a busker.

Romulus, the mythic first king after 758 BCE, instituted a history dance, the *saltatio bellicrepa*, commemorating the rape of the Sabine women in 750 BCE and the origination of the nuclear family within the pagan all-male camp on the Tiber. Early cultic choreography observed the pastoral festival of the Lupercal on February 13 and the agrarian Ambarvalia fertility rite each May 29 with a line dance through settlements and croplands. Other patterns ranged from choreographed interweaving in the Greek crane dance, presentations to the Great Mother Goddess Cybele, farm purification, and spectacular state parades to scandalous tap dance, cavorting on a slanted rope, and striptease in theatrical comedies. As trade brought sea traffic and overland commerce, the growth of multiculturalism introduced exotic forms from Egypt, Carthage, and Iberia performed by itinerant troupes.

The College of Salii

Under the rule of Numa Pompilius, Rome's second king, from 714 to 670 BCE, the college of *salii* (leapers) presented in the streets and on the army's drilling field a cultic martial dance derived from the Etruscans and Albans who preceded Rome's founding. Each spring and fall, twelve priests of the patrician class performed while they intoned a hymn to Jupiter, god of light and thunder. Each votary wore a short red cloak, embroidered tunic, bronze belt, and pointed skullcap tied under the chin. Each dancer carried a wand or sword for striking a sacred Bronze Age shield suspended from a pole borne by a pair of worthy ministers.

By coordinating a warlike tread with feints and assaults while banging their swords on the shields, the twelve salii processed noisily around the city walls as though driving away invaders. The choreography venerated the sacred state and the war god Mars,

Rome's patron and the father of Romulus, the founding king. Seneca compared the leaping and antics to the work of fullers, who cleaned laundry by jumping on it to force clay into the fibers.

The ritual of leapers drew spectators on March 1, the Roman New Year, and again on March 9. On March 19, dancing accompanied the Quinquatrus or festival of Mars. At the Armilustrium on October 19, the end of the military season that preceded withdrawal into the barracks for the winter, the priests repeated their ceremonial dance to the sound of trumpets for the purification and storage of weapons atop the Aventine hill, the place where Romulus gave the city its name.

Public Dance

Preceding state-sponsored games in the Circus Maximus, from around 578 BCE, the *pompa circensis* (circus parade) included a dance company performing to the lyre and panpipes along the Sacred Way from the Capitolium to the forum. Consisting of children, teens, and men dressed in crested helmets and tunics dyed royal purple, the company danced to martial steps and brandished spears and swords as gestures of fealty to Mars and the state. Trailing behind, a comic troupe outrageously costumed with goat tails and loincloths satirized the soldier dancers.

In obedience to a sibyl's command in 263 BCE, from April 27 to May 2, the Romans danced a joyous Floralia. The six-day adoration of the life-renewing goddess Flora contrasted martial dance with garlanded performers glorifying fecundity, nature, and spring. Tossing chickpeas for good luck, revelers dressed in bright colors and processed to shrines at the Circus Maximus with libations of honey and milk and gifts of nanny goats and rabbits. By torchlight, dancers stripped naked and pantomimed bawdy skits.

After 190 BCE, author Quintus Ennius promoted sensual Greek amusements in Rome. Under Cato the Censor, however, opinions changed toward immigrant deities, especially Apollo and Dionysus of the pompous Greeks and Serapis and Osiris, goddess of the supercilious Egyptians. In 184 BCE, the Senate banned all foreign arts that Cato judged to be immoral, particularly the ecstatic belly dancing to the shaking of the *sistrum* at the mystery cult of Isis, the Egyptian mother goddess.

Neglect of the Floralia dance ended in 173 BCE after torrential rain and hail ravaged croplands, vineyards, and flower gardens. The restored blossom dance revived grain harvests, apiaries, olive groves, and winemaking and anticipated maypole dances and rituals of Beltane and the Christian Easter. At the end of the Second Punic War in 146 BCE, curriculum for Roman youths incorporated ritual dance for teaching grace and stamina.

Imperial Dance

At the decline of the Republic, two dancers—the rebel arts maven Sempronia around 75 BCE and the mime Dionysia around 60 BCE—gained renown for promoting folk dance. The judgmental orator Cicero dismissed public participation as the pastime of drunks and lunatics. His critique censured the *cordax*, a ridiculous low buffoonery derived from Greek comedy. Performers identified themselves by wearing *soce* (slippers), an affectation that called attention to the rapid crisscrossing of feet.

In the novel *The First Man in Rome* (1991), Colleen McCullough characterized the patrician fashion in taking lessons in lascivious dance, the ploy of Gaius Marius's dowdy wife Grania to retain his affection. She built on the idea of exotic dance mesmerizing Romans in *Antony and Cleopatra* (2008), in which Mark Antony moves in a street milieu at Alexandria of musicians, dwarfs, freaks, magicians, gymnasts, clowns, mimes, and dancers from the Middle East. McCullough describes his enemy Octavian fantasizing about the Roman general's addiction to eunuchs and half-naked girls cavorting in the Egyptian manner.

Unlike the more censorious Roman, Augustus, the first emperor in 27 BCE, admitted being moved by story dance, which entered a new era of popularity in imperial Rome. He introduced public festivals gratis to citizens as a promotion of civil legislation and political campaigns. Under his patronage, the Alexandrian freedman Bathyllus performed comic narrative dance that appealed to aristocratic matrons. Around 18 BCE, Bathyllus's associate, the freedman Pylades of Cilicia, composed a manual on character dance, which described masks with closed mouths.

Under Augustus's conservative rule, patricians devalued libretti and rejected dance as an activity suitable for the dignified Roman to execute in public. The wealthy hired foreign dancers and *saltatores* (mimes) to amuse guests at dinner parties, weddings, and receptions. At Herculaneum and Pompeii, muralists decorated atrium frescoes with portraits of dancers, some of whom were enslaved performers from Africa, Iberia, and Greece. Grave markers bore the praise of respected dancing girls—nine-year-old Julia Nemesis, fourteen-year-old Thyas, and twenty-two-year-old Terentia.

After 14 CE, the emperor Tiberius carried gimmickry to extremes by having armored riders mount elephants that danced on ropes. Under the influence of Nero's dissolute behavior after 54, companies performed in public in scanty garments and depicted sexual acts, a violation of early Christian standards. According to the satirist Martial, around 65 CE, the Phoenicians imported the nautch dance from India to Gades (Cádiz) in Hispania. The languid waving of limbs to tinkling finger cymbals resembled the bas-relief on royal tombs of idealized Egyptian females and tempted Roman maidens to learn the gestures and posturing.

The imperial patronage of folk dance continued against the denunciation of Christian bishops and popes. Descriptions of hypnotic cultic dance revering Dionysus on Rhodes reflected the vast contrasts in the god's mythic moods. During the reign of the emperor Marcus Aurelius, an aficionado of the dance after 161, feather quilts and cushions reduced the dangers of rope dancing by breaking a fall. By the 300s, the Byzantine Empire imported Roman dance to Constantinople, but stripped it of pagan exotica.

See also matachines; Pyrrhic dance.

Source: Rich, Anthony. *A Dictionary of Roman and Greek Antiquities.* New York: D. Appleton & Company, 1873.

· ʃ ·

SACRIFICIAL DANCE

Sacrificial dance connects myriad ethnic groups with primeval needs for expiation, blessing, purification, and spiritual transfiguration, the aim of Manchu trance dance and the offering derives from Emperor Wu De after 403 BCE and subsequent honoraria to Confucius each September 28 on Teacher's Day, a holiday commemorated with sacrifice, music, and dance. Varieties of ritual dance preceded or followed the killing of a gift animal, as with Arab steps encircling the sacrificial white camel in Kazakhstan and the Naxi rooster boiling and chain dance to flute music in Daan, Tibet. New World models include the cannibal dances of the Kwakiutl of coastal British Columbia, the symbolic bull sacrifice during the *matachines* in the Hispanic Southwest, rain dances of the Moki Pueblo clans of prehistoric Colorado, and the sun dance of the Teton Sioux of South Dakota.

The type of offering ranged in type and purpose, reaching barbaric extremes in Mesoamerica with Olmec, Toltec, and Aztec eviscerations and skinning of human victims. In a less sanguine form, the West Indian Carib presented gifts of pepper, crab, fish, manatees, iguanas, ducks, and seabirds to departed relatives to ward off sickness and accidents. In Oceania, Balinese dancers presented baskets of mangosteen, soursop, bananas, papayas, and rambutan fruit at temple rituals. Bakene fathers in Uganda announced the birth of a child and rejoiced with folk dance and the drying of the afterbirth as a gift to the gods.

In Alberta, Manitoba, and Saskatchewan, Cree and Ojibwa males pled for rain at the annual "thirsting dance." To obtain a vision or beg for healing, participants fasted, presented gifts of tobacco and cloth, and smudged with burning sage or sweetgrass to rid the air of negative energy. After processing to the dance lodge and assembling clockwise around a totem pole marked with a symbolic thunderbird, performers rehearsed raising arms to the totemic image and bobbing on flexed knees. To the rhythm of rattles and hand drums, a dozen dancers participated in sacrifices over four days in booths erected on the periphery.

Ancient Offering Dances

In south central Asia around 1200 BCE along the Indus and Ganges riverbanks, Aryan wanderers, in obedience to the Rigveda, accepted a caste system that placed a priestly hierarchy of Brahmins over family sacrifice. The suttee (or sati), a particularly grim offering to patriarchy dating to 400 BCE, forced widows to join a thrumming mourning dance at a Hindu temple and climb their husband's funeral pyre as living testimonials to the subjugation of women. For ancient Phoenicians and Carthaginians, song and chain dance to pipe, lyre, and tambourine followed the offerings of their infants at the Tophet (roasting place). Devotees placed the small bodies on metal idols of Moloch stoked like furnaces.

In the ancient Dionysian mystery cult that originated in Thrace or Crete after 800 BCE, Greek maenads (or Bacchae), the female revelers who worshipped the wine god, drank intoxicants that revived primeval emotions. In ecstasy, they grasped snakes and wrapped asps around their heads before dismembering a bull or deer sacrifice, drinking its blood, and devouring its raw flesh. Blood sacrifice set the tone of orgiastic body arching and hand flourishes. The dance with mythic satyrs channeled passions and acclaimed ocean waves and nature cycles by moonlight.

According to the Pentateuch, chapters 1 and 66 by the prophet Isaiah condemned the barbarism of human sacrifice and the superficiality of animal offerings by the residents of Sodom and Gomorrah. As written in II Kings, after 715 BCE, the prophet's medium, Hezekiah, king of Judah, reformed temple ritual after the Assyrian king Sennacherib invaded Jerusalem in 701 BCE. Hezekiah's new regulations purged the holy of holies of cultic dance and ritual by smashing a brass snake idol to Moloch at the center of obeisance.

Iconic Dance

Symbolic sacrifice reset world dance ritual with a less pagan form of thanksgiving, a custom at the ritual circle dances of the Anacostia and Piscataway of Maryland. After 221 BCE, the Qiang of Sichuan, China, and Tibet performed the *buzila* sacrifice ritual to pounding on a sheepskin frame drum, the dispenser of sacred insight among Himalayan tribes. The syncretic story dance reenacted the founding of central Asian culture by a monkey. The dance activated nature worship with cycles of innovative figures rather than standard choreography.

In the Amur River basin after 500 CE, the Nanai and Evenk of Russia and China limited sacrificial dance drama to shamanic presenters and extended feasting for hours after the ritual. Performers dressed in ceremonial belts with metal pendants for a jingling choreography to drumming and the offering of vodka, tea, and rooster blood to repel snakes. During the night, dancers assumed that the shamanic deities left unsatisfied by the ritual continued drumming, eating sacrificial dishes, and dancing until dawn. In dreams from the invisible spirits, the Nanai learned the authentic facets of sacrificial dance, the source of priestly healing.

For ancient Phoenicians and Carthaginians, song and chain dance to pipe, lyre, and tambourine followed the offerings of their infants at the Tophet (roasting place). *Anon.* The Dance: Historic Illustrations of Dancing from 3300 B.C. to 1911 A.D. *London: John Bale, Sons & Danielsson, 1911.*

After 1835, American sketch artist and portraitist George Catlin detailed a Hidatsa green corn dance. At the center of male participants moving clockwise around a boiling kettle, four medicine men at the center filled the water with fresh ears as a gift to the Great Spirit. While rattling a shaker in one hand and lifting a corn stalk in the other, the quartet executed dance steps, thanksgiving songs, and bodies spread with white clay. Outside the concentric rings, villagers observed the ritual and awaited a feast with wood bowls and spoons carved from mountain sheep or buffalo horns.

Currently, the cohesive Lhomwe communities of southern Malawi sacrifice via the *tchopa* drum dance to ensure good hunting and propitiate spirits to protect performers from disease, grief, bleak harvests, and drought. Shuffling clockwise, line dancers blow whistles and pat the dust with bare feet. Clad in rags, raffia kilts, feathers, mango seed ankle wraps, and animal pelts, the performers brandish axes, fly whisks, farm tools, and spears as symbols of shared efforts to protect their clans. In 2012, UNESCO declared the tchopa an Intangible Cultural Heritage of Humanity.

See also ghurei dance; labyrinthine dance; *matachines*; morris dance; shamanic dance; sun dance; sword dance.

Sources: Bulgakova, Tatiana. *Nanai Shamanic Culture in Indigenous Discourse*. Frankfurt, Germany: Books on Demand, 2013. Rodriguez, Sylvia. *The Matachines Dance: A Ritual Dance of the Indian Pueblos and Mexicano-Hispano Communities*. Santa Fe, NM: Southwest Heritage, 2009.

SALTARELLO

A Tuscan musical introit to the Italian Renaissance, the saltarello (also *saltarelle* or *cascarda*) advanced leaping, walking steps to a solo or synchronized choreography similar in style to the tarantella and the *furlana*, a Venetian couples dance. In a double-time variation on the more sedate *basse danse*, pairs moved along an arc in rapid triple time, either 6/8, 3/8, or 3/4, to lute strums. Like the antique German *hoppertanz* and *springdantze*, the French *pas de brabante*, and the Iberian *alta danza*, in the late 1300s, the unsophisticated saltarello turned vertical step-hop or step-step-step-hop into a popular devil-may-care court dance.

An October gala in Italy in 1415 began with issuance of six hundred invitations to women to even out pairing with men for the entrance saltarello, accompanied by the shawm (oboe) and viola. Neapolitan presenters often footed it with the merry *estampie* from Provençal and ended a session with a breather and sip of ice water. For the fall festival, Roman women laced themselves into new national costumes and paused at St. Peter's Basilica for a prayer before launching into frisky dance mode.

Groups favored a faster saltarello *misura* and the lively saltarello *doppi*, which Spaniards called the *segue trenchant*. For variance, the male partner stood still while the female performed a fickle advance-retreat or skipped around him flapping her apron, enticing with large arm sweeps, or rattling a tambourine. At Pergola on the northern Adriatic coast, dancers performed the simple steps to honor the town's martyred patron, St. Secundus, whom Hadrian ordered beheaded in 119.

High Form

In the high Renaissance, the saltarello sometimes preceded and followed jousting, such as the game held at Florence in 1459 in honor of a visit from newly crowned Pope Pius II and Galeazzo Maria Sforza, the fifteen-year-old duke of Milan. Galeazzo also enjoyed watching women dance the saltarello at the country villa at Careggi of the elderly Cosimo de' Medici, a banker and power wielder. A year later, the same dance opened a state visit by Luigi III Gonzaga, the Marquis of Mantua and mercenary in a crusade against the Ottoman Turks. In Florence, a panel of judges observed a saltarello performance at the *festa di danzare*, a competition staged at the Piazza del Signori at Verona before the 1460 carnival, the preface to self-denial during Lent.

Near the Ponte Vecchio at the Mercato Nuovo before a state dinner, Florentine noblemen used the saltarello in precise protocol as an opportunity to dance with pairs of maidens and married women, one on each side. After a bow to each male attendee, the noble led his ladies in a promenade of the dance floor and concluded with a grand reverence. A post-prandial saltarello preceded more festive dancing with women spiraling around a line of men.

Sprightly saltarello hops energized other fifteenth-century choreography, a fact established by Milanese dance master Antonio Cornazzano's *Libro dell'arte del danzare* (Dance manual, 1455). A century later, courtesans turned the unsophisticated saltarello into a droll cross-dressing masquerade presented to the music of the button accordion, frame drum, and bagpipe. Men exaggerated their timing with finger snaps.

In France in 1546, innovators added slapping of left-to-left hands and right-to-right hands and fused the saltarello and its numerous repetitions with the more vigorous galliard. Outside Rome, rural folk popularized the skipping, bouncing dance at village diversions. Within the city limits of Rome and Venice, saltarello dancers executed the ebullient step-hops in *osterias* (inns). Puglian art critic Giacomo Gorzanis's commentary in 1564 indicated that a varied form from northern Italy acquired the name saltarello Bergamasco, which shared pavilion scheduling with the *gigo*, *curenta*, and *sbrando*, a left-right circle dance from the Piedmont to concertina tunes.

A Folk Favorite

By the 1600s, royalty and aristocracy moved on to the more intricate *tourdion* and other Burgundian couples choreography, leaving the saltarello to Italian folk gatherings at Abruzzi and Romagna for the next two centuries. Lack of documentation from the period left much in doubt about figures and patterns for the dances, particularly the composition of the baroque suite and the introductory pavane that preceded brisk hopping and the steps of the furlana, a syncopated wooing dance. Fortunately, sketches and oil paintings preserved footwork and over-the-head arm lifts and castanet clacking of dancers in Campagna, Urbino, and Tivoli, where spectators joined the gaiety.

In 1821, Bartolomeo Pinelli, an illustrator from Trastevere, the raffish across-the-Tiber section of Rome, painted the unconstrained leg lifts and canted torso of the saltarello Romano, sometimes performed by two women. He substantiated the forceful role of dance in cafe life, as seen in the sketch "Saltarello del mese di Octobre" (Saltarello in the middle of October). Dresden artist Adrian Ludwig Richter's *Saltarello* (1825) also set peasant dance in open air among revelers in Trastevere. In 1827, landscape artist Dietrich Wilhelm Lindau of Dresden painted another exuberant peasant version of the dance with the lute player emulating the hops of the lead female.

Danish imitators adopted the saltarello, for example, in the 1810s at Frederikke Brun's salon for his daughter Ida at Sophienholm, a country house in the Copenhagen suburbs. Scandinavian fascination with the hopping dance from the Renaissance colored Danish art. At Copenhagen, painter Wilhelm Marstrand characterized additional aspects of the saltarello, posing body language and eroticism as metaphors for Italian joie de vivre. Choreographer August Bournonville contributed a stage vision of Italy's golden era of saltarello with the ballet *The Festival in Albano* (1839). The dance maintained a presence in European art and silent films.

See also furlana; galliard; pavane; tarantella.

Sources: "Il Saltarello." *Penny Magazine* 14, no. 3 (September 20, 1845): 364–65. Neville, Jennifer. *Dance, Spectacle, and the Body Politick, 1250–1750.* Bloomington: Indiana University Press, 2008.

SARABANDE

A colonial folk mime marked by light springs, brushes, half pirouettes, knee bends, and *tombés,* the sarabande (or *zarabanda*) emerged in Panama in 1539. Technique called for a Mozarabic stylistic gusto recovered from twelfth-century Spain. The naming of the secular dance by Spaniards at the port of Seville connected the mesmerizing line dance with a female demon. Other etymologies declared that the Mesoamerican dance named a Persian city.

Little detail survived to delineate the sarabande from the Spanish *chacona* or French *chaconne,* a mocking, coquettish quickstep in triple time to the clack of castanets. In *The History of the Indies of New Spain* (1581), Dominican friar Diego Durán accounted for the notoriety of the sarabande as titillating sport filled with wiggles and prurient female flirtation. The choreography crossed the Atlantic to Portugal and Spain, where, in 1583, the conservative king Philip II prohibited execution of the sarabande at Barcelona and Madrid socials.

Gaining Respect

Despite disparagement, the chassé, bourrée, drags, and toe-in, toe-out flourished in Guatemala to a triple tap on the tambourine. In Western Europe, the sarabande shape-shifted into an effete polonaise processional witnessed at Barcelona in 1599. Still taking the conservative tack, Spanish epicist Miguel de Cervantes vilified the sarabande in 1600 as an unseemly solo dance to castanets. Playwright Lope de Vega sneered at the dance in 1618 as a "zambo" (mestizo) folk art.

The transposition of the New World sarabande to Old World sensibilities stressed small steps, posture, and poise. Low to the ground, the subdued footwork pleased Anne of Austria in 1635 when Cardinal Richelieu danced for her. Sarabande compositions by Jean Baptiste Lully accommodated the obesity and gout of Louis XIV, who retired from professional ballet in 1669. An amalgam of the allemande and gigue, sarabande suites articulated the walking, gliding, and left-right-left figures in open position and concluded with a simple bow to phrases of the lute or clavichord. The grace and flow of elided steps exhibited women's farthingale skirts and the ornate sleeves of men's hip-length jackets and flashing finger rings.

From Folk to Court

Into the baroque era, when the European dancing master set standards of decorum and artistry for the young, the sarabande acquired a balletic ball-of-the-foot style for court performances to homorhythmic music. In Italy and France, wedding guests joined in the dance at the Duke of Burgundy's marriage to Marie Adelaide of Savoy at Versailles on December 7, 1697. Musical suites juxtaposed the choreography with the knee bends of the courante, a running, bounding figure in triple time. In 1700, French choreographer Pierre Beauchamp recorded the only extant notation of the dance figures.

The sarabande achieved status among classical composers, who tinkered with its original form. When George Frideric Handel wrote a sarabande in 1703, he adapted the figures to harpsichord phrases drawn from the Western world's most ancient tune "La Folia," a shepherd's melody in minor mode. In 1723, German musicologist Johann Gottfried Walther of Leipzig typified the steps as serious and brief. At Hamburg in 1739, music theorist Johann Mattheson characterized the choreography as a dispirited showpiece for the ambitious.

Late nineteenth-century retrospect returned the sarabande to music history as a relic of baroque art. In 1884, three decades after composer Johannes Brahms declared the dance monotonous, Norwegian musician Edvard Grieg incorporated a sarabande in the *Holberg Suite*. In 1905, impressionist composer Claude Debussy retained the unhurried folk dance in *Suite Bergamasque*, which paired the sarabande with a *passepied*, a flowing Breton *branle*.

See also branle; Creole dance; nuptial dance; polonaise; processionals.

Source: Pierce, Ken. "Uncommon Steps and Notation in the *Sarabande de Mr. de Beauchamp*." Accessed October 3, 2015. http://web.mit.edu/kpierce/www/sdhs2003/beauchamps.pdf.

SCALP DANCE

Scalp dances epitomized the outrage of forest and Plains Indians toward any insurgent, Indian or European, on ancestral hunting grounds. The Amerindian concept of venerating enemy scalps appeared in the reports of French explorer Samuel de Champlain, who observed the rites of the Huron, Algonquin, and Montagnais of Maine in summer 1609. Jesuit missionary Claude Jean Allouez wrote in 1667 about the completion of a Miami scalp dance with smoking of a community pipe. According to the journals of explorers Meriwether Lewis and William Clark, in September 1804, their party attended an indoor scalp dance performed by the Teton Dakota.

Typically, Amerindian boys began learning the counterclockwise choreography and chants of ritual and victory dances in toddlerhood. Before the all-male assembly, men hunted for tobacco to smoke and meat to roast and devour after the exhausting scalp dance. At trophy displays, warriors of allied tribes preceded a circle dance around a fire with boasts of capturing wives and hacking scalps from dead enemies after marking the hairline with a bowstring. Of particular value were the red and blond hair of Europeans.

Vengeance and Warfare

In surveys of high plains warfare preceding the American Civil War, ethnographers claimed that such ritualized vengeance extended intertribal wars. Combat along the Columbia, Missouri, Yellowstone, and Snake rivers remained fierce among the

Ojibwa, Shoshone, Bannock, Snake, Shawnee, Hidatsa, Crow, and Assiniboine. In Missouri after 1809, Scots botanist John Bradbury observed an all-female Arikara scalp dance in men's clothing and armaments.

For pleasing Wakanta, the Iowa god, fifteen nights after a battle near Liberty in Missouri Territory against the Osage, warriors vaunted trophies at a torch-lit war and scalp dance. On the Des Moines River in fall 1809, participants brandished tomahawks and scalping knives while reenacting battle and singing of victory. While White Cloud recuperated from combat wounds, he appointed Big Ax, a war hero, as a proxy dancer to display Osage scalps on netted hoops from the tip of a lance. After the presentation, women took charge of lifting the lances while men executed ritual steps before Otoe guests. After signing a peace treaty in 1833, as a tribal elder, White Cloud refused to participate in any more war parties or scalp dances.

On the east bank of the Columbia River near Wallula, Washington, in July 1818, Scots fur trader Alexander Ross and Donald MacKenzie observed line dancing of Nez Perce in parallel rows alongside poles hoisting scalps for all to see. The six-day dance began with a series of leaps and shuffling to left and right. Entertainment incorporated feasting, horse races, and gambling for both genders. Braves forced prisoners of war to take part in the ritual and flaunt the scalps of their comrades while enduring knife cuts, stabbing with awls, beatings with sticks and stones, and hair pulling, all perpetrated by women.

After American portraitist and sketch artist George Catlin visited the Mandan of North Dakota in 1832, he described tribal choreography with guttural yelps, leaps, and starts superintended by a medicine man. A Lakota ritual the painter observed in 1835 near Fort Pierre, South Dakota, at the mouth of the Teton River gathered a war party by torchlight for the first of fifteen nights of dancing and boasting of combat prowess. The rare role for women enlisted females to stand at the center of the ring dance to hold up scalps while the men repeated two-footed jumps, bared teeth, hissed through nostrils, glared, and thrust bows and war clubs in imitation of combat against their enemies, the Arikara.

Other eyewitness accounts survive from this same decade. In Montana near Fort Alexander, Belgian priest Pierre Jean de Smet reviewed a Blackfoot scalp dance performed by women. In the painting of a Minataree scalp dance in 1834 at Fort Clark, Missouri, artist Karl Bodmer pictured men and women moving freely amid drummers and warriors. Among the Cheyenne of Colorado, men tethered women together before females executed the steps with men.

The Dance of Roman Nose

In London in 1845, Roman Nose, a distinguished teenaged warrior of the Northern Cheyenne, led the scalp dance of fourteen Iowa, who used a bowstring to mark the head of the corpse before slicing around the edge and ripping the scalp free. For the presentation of combat trophies, warriors exhibited Indian iconography on tomahawk, shield, and quiver. Below a red crest and bare chest, Roman Nose danced in kilt, sash, leggings, and moccasins. The ceremonial ring dance typically proceeded over fifteen days and ensured young braves of tribal influence, position, glory, and wealth.

Performed in a counterclockwise direction, the scalp dance of Plains Indians featured gestures proving prowess with weapons and fearlessness in the face of the enemy. *Index to* The Miscellaneous Documents of the House of Representatives for the First Session of the Forty-Ninth Congress, 1885–86. *Washington, D.C.: Government Printing Office, 1886, 308.*

Costumes for Roman Nose and the other males limited body covering to paint, moccasins, breechcloths, and feathered headdress. Before fighters could claim the title of hero, their testimony of battlefield exploits detailed the hacking and sawing at the top of the victim's cranium and the tanning of scalps for preservation. Pride in war prizes explained punctures in front of blond and red braids and auburn ringlets by which dancers tied them to display poles to substantiate Caucasian kills.

Englishwomen pinpointed Roman Nose among the performers for his great height and handsome profile. The tall Cheyenne youth considered the performance a presentation to please the Great Spirit rather than entertainment for Europeans. To explain his combat methods, he gesticulated before spectators with scalping knife and tomahawk. He elevated two scalps on his lance until relieved of his trophy by two squaws, who joined the dance circle in the style of Ute and Crow women.

Varied Choreography

Settlers, hunters, and soldiers submitted eyewitness accounts of scalp veneration at White Stone Hill in Dakota Territory on September 5, 1863; in Kansas after 1867; and during the Great Sioux War of 1876 in Montana and western Dakota. Among the Sioux, after a night of drumming and prayer by lighted firebrands, warriors cleansed themselves of bloodguilt in the sweat lodge to prepare for circle dancing to a female chorus. As the

Plains warriors danced, they brandished deer hoof rattles and mimicked the birdsong, snarls, and growls of crows, coyotes, and wildcats in a litany of self-glorification.

Sioux women, elders, and children surrounded the circle dance and joined in the victory cries and rhythmic stamping. Some performers sounded captured cavalry bugles; others drummed with double sticks. Attendants stoked the fire for a spiritual catharsis that lasted all night. Enemy victims secured to stakes during war dances survived skinning until death ended their mutilation.

Among the Omaha and Ponca of Nebraska, girls and women executed the steps of the *we-watchi*. A sacred ring of dancers formed in a clearing around a single pole-bearer displaying the featured scalp. Only victorious males could join the victory song, which they repeated over three days. After missionaries and ghost dance conversions persuaded Plains Indians to give up displays of revenge, the nude grass dance replaced the scalp dance.

See also body art; circle dance; ghost dance; warrior dance.

Source: Catlin, George. *Notes of Eight Years' Travels and Residence in Europe.* New York: Burgess, Stringer & Company, 1848.

SCARF DANCE

Because of their diaphanous movements and translucent weave, scarves have served choreography from antiquity, beginning with the floating lengths of linen that eroticized predynastic Egyptian dance and the silk wraps dancers fluttered at imperial Roman soirees. All along the Silk Road from China to the West, gauzy fabrics added a dreamy, hypnotic touch to folk dance, from a long scarf solo at Peking in the Tang Dynasty to a northern Cree wooing dance north of the Great Lakes. After 600 BCE, outside Persepolis, the Iranian Qashqai performed the *halay* (also *divan* or *yalli*), a chain dance featuring waftures of whirling silk around a bonfire. The romantic flourishes spread to Kurds, Pashtuns, Anatolians, Assyrians, and southern Slavs.

Pictured on carvings, reliefs, and cave art from 207 BCE, Chinese dancers of the Han Dynasty sported long sleeves and scarves. At the far end of the Silk Road, the Magyar *kendostanc*, a Slavic dance, carried scarf dancing west into Europe. To the south in Cyprus, head scarves brightened Mediterranean dances with Roma insouciance. The custom continued to the east in China into the tenth century CE and to the west along North Africa's seacoast with the Tunisian, Moroccan, and Libyan performances of scarf twirling for the *bou saada*, a buoyant female solo involving skips and hops to a upraised arm gestures.

From Goryeo court ritual of 1130 in Hwanghae Province, North Korea, the *talchum* dance melded white scarf flickers with ribald leaps and kicks. Korean, Chinese, and Japanese shamans exorcised evil spirits and demons through *salpuri* (soul cleansing), a dance ritual that used a white stole as an icon of the departing soul. A Guinean courtship dance, the *macru* scarf dance featured a length of fabric that the pursuer placed on his sweetheart as a sign of a committed relationship. Similarly romantic, the Renaissance *jarana* in Yucatán flaunted wheeling scarves as models of Mexican passion and fertility.

National Identity

Scarf dances typically displayed colors, fringes, and patterns that enhanced identity, especially for Bulgarians and the homeless Roma. Costumes topped daring peasant chemises and ruffled skirts with bright head kerchiefs over plaits that highlighted Roma chic. Unlike the eroticism of hip wraps in Arab and Turkish belly dance or the Italian saltarello, in the 1300s, folk arts in Indonesia and Malaysia learned from Persian and Arabic traders how to costume dancers in head scarves for the *endang* (also *indang* or *badindin*), an Islamic tutorial supported by hand crossing, clapping, and taps on the tambourine.

The Renaissance embellishment of handkerchiefs and shawls added new dimensions to folk dance. In the late sixteenth century, the English queen Elizabeth I urged her courtiers and ladies-in-waiting to tie bells to scarves for a maypole dance, an outdoor spring frolic especially dear to the English. The idiophonic accompaniment foregrounded merry sport that bid farewell to winter.

When the full-length ruana came in fashion in the 1700s in place of coats and jackets, Russian dancers stressed their heritage in the folk patterns of fringed shoulder mantles over peasant dresses and boots. In the 1770s, at Count Alexei Orlov's mansion outside Moscow, soloist Ivan Sokolov of St. Petersburg directed Roma singers in engaging Roma waltzes. In Jemez, New Mexico, ponchos, rebozos, and shawls served dancers as disguises for the *matachines*, a Mesoamerican religio-historical dance celebrating the Christmas season. In St. Vincent and Dominica, Roman painter Agostino Brunias stylized Afro-Caribbean dance by characterizing mating dances performed with scarves or handkerchiefs.

The Womanly Arts

Worldwide, feminine grace and allure from manipulations of fabric and veiling inspired paintings, murals, and sculpture focused on dance. Malay couples dramatized the heightening of romance with the *siti payung*, a mimed seduction between unattached males and females. The enticement of aristocratic maidens began with men waving expanses of silk over their shoulders. The flirtation engaged reticent girls with coy advances. The finale depicted the boy and girl united at last.

For the Tet New Year in Hanoi on February 9, 1929, the Vietnamese Nationalist Party chose model soldiers from the Red Guard to perform a dragon dance. The men cavorted in red tie-up shirts and red scarves, icons of revolution. In this same era, Polish women entertained wedding guests in the Łowicz region west of Warsaw with a slow *chodzony* (scarf dance), the introit to nuptial rituals. In the mid-1950s, the *sa'dawi*, a Tunisian cafe dance, took on political meaning with the exposition of red and white scarves, which represented Arab-Berber peasant demands for independence from France.

Religious groups turned fabric undulations into symbols of water for the Israeli *mayim mayim* and sanctuary dance featuring Christian altar and vestment colors of red for martyrdom, gold for divinity, white for purity and sanctity, and purple, the tone depicting royalty, mourning, and penitence suited to Advent and Lent. For Filipina concubines of the sultan at Mindanao, lone ladies-in-waiting sought forgiveness for affronts by decking themselves with beads, metal fingernails, parasols, and long mantillas for the *asik*, an earnest outpouring of regret emphasizing subservient posturing. Tibetan Buddhists employed blue scarves in children's dance of the sorcerers, in which they swung the fabric in a symbol of infinity. Globally, teachers introduced folk kinetics to school children by encouraging free-form dance with scarves.

See also art, folk dance in; belly dance; chain dance; *mayim mayim*; tarantella.

Source: Malborg, Kim. *Korean Dance*. Seoul, Korea: Ewha Womans University Press, 2005.

SCHOTTISCHE

A fetching descendant of the hornpipe and the saloon polka, the schottische (also Rheinländer or Bavarian polka) retains fame as one of Europe's oldest couples dances. Performed lightly on the balls of the feet, the choreography applied partnering to a popular Bohemian rural dance in 2/4 or 4/4 meter. In the form of a slow polka, the dance spread among Gaelic performers at Irish *cèilidhs* (house parties) and enlivened maypole processions to lilting melodies and upbeat footwork.

Dance masters taught the back-and-forth trots of the German peasant dance to Scots children in Edinburgh in 1819. The side-to-side figure with a hopping foot lift to the back influenced the Norwegian *gammeldans* and the strathspey, which added more hops in place of glides. For the French, the dynamic contrasts of pianissimo and fortissimo impacted footwork of the écossaise as dancers performed it on the Riviera at Nice.

The schottische first appeared in history in 1844 and confused art historians, who claimed its origin as Celtic, Danish, Scots, and Polish. Throughout the 1840s, the intricate twirls, pivots, and promenades found willing performers in Scandinavia, Iberia, Tuscan Italy, Poland, Russia, and Greece. In Berlin, the hopping figure acquired the name "hunter's schottische." At Table Rock, North Carolina, an Appalachian mountaineers' ball featured the schottische in suites alongside the reel and cotillion.

By the mid-1800s, Mormon pioneers and settlers of Texas and California adopted the faddish schottische figures and their hypnotic melodies. To the familiar tune "Go In and Out the Window" (1762), dancers blended the schottische with the glide polka, cotton-eye Joe, promenade, quadrille, and the high kicks of the galop. The first dance manuals to feature the schottische reached print in 1850, contemporaneous with the hopping step of the *varsouvienne*, a partners dance from Warsaw, Poland.

Dance on the Move

In southern South America after 1851, Volga German immigrants from European Russia spread the schottische dance more throughout northern Argentina and southern Brazil, especially at the court of Emperor Pedro II at the Palace of São Cristóvão in Rio de Janeiro. In the Hispanic schottische, the novel steps and turns merged with the *chamamé* and the *xote*, a dance olio that later fused the versatile choreography with the salsa, mambo, and rumba. In Spain, composers of zarzuelas (operettas) incorporated new versions of the schottische for the stage.

A mixed reception followed fascination with the schottische, notably the availability of sheet music for only pennies a copy and the questionable behaviors of dancers at private balls and public venues. German dance floors grew so crowded that the host separated dancing couples with a rope over the entrance to hold in reserve the next couples waiting to try the new schottische. In 1857, priests prohibited the vain dance in France and fined hosts of house parties for encouraging "voluptuousness." After Edward, the Prince of Wales, arrived in Nova Scotia on July 23, 1860, he attended a ball in St. Johns at the Colonial House, where the program featured the schottische in 10 percent of the dances. He had such a good time that he continued dancing until 3:00 AM.

During the joyless days of the American Civil War, the schottische revived gaiety and sparkle among soldiers on leave and within the covered wagon camps along the Oregon Trail and the Bozeman–Virginia City route. Postwar migrations to Texas spread interest in a variety of choreography—*lanciers* (lancers), polka mazurka, and the schottische, which private instructors taught in Cherokee County. Diarist Ellen McGowan Biddle, wife of a US infantry major, reported a social at Fort Lyon, Missouri, where she enjoyed a schottische, a relief from the tedium of being pent up behind tall ramparts.

Farther north, the schottische and reels entertained the North West Mounted Police at galas along the Macleod Trail in Calgary, Alberta. In 1878, anonymous lyrics to a lively schottische tune in South Lake Tahoe, Nevada, preserved the heroics of stage driver Hank Monk and invigorated schottische performers at barn dances. At Newcastle, Northumberland, in 1880, preparatory to deployment to Cape Town, South Africa, English troops partnered their wives and sweethearts in the step-step-hop figure at a courthouse dance while babies slept next to the bandstand. By the 1890s, the closed position shifted to open in the first bars and back to closed at the finale, the regimen of the Swedish schottische.

Variants and Adaptations

In the early twentieth century, the cheery step-step-hop-based dance acquired new adaptations. British folk dancers turned the schottische into the quickstep; the French adapted the basic figure to seven steps. Locals in Blair, Wisconsin, raised $100 for the library by hosting an evening of schottische. At dances at Chihuahua, Sonora, and Texas during the Mexican Revolution (1910–1920), local music honored Spain with versions of contrasting figures—the sultry *pasodoble* and the schottische, a favorite peasant caper.

Among the American elite, the vigor and peasant air of the schottische made it too low class for ballroom functions. Meanwhile, in rural areas, the choreography adapted to elementary gym classes in the 1920s and country-western line dance and the newly imported Austrian ski waltz in the 1930s. In the manual *Good Morning: After a Sleep of Twenty-Five Years, Old-Fashioned Dancing Is Being Revived* (1926), folk art collectors Henry Ford, his wife, Clara Bryant Ford, and Benjamin Lovett reclaimed the old-fashioned schottische as a cultural relic. In Illinois during the Great Depression, the Works Projects Administration archived directions to the dance. After World War II, the original figures acquired the two-armed turns of the sweetheart schottische.

See also barn dance; galop; hornpipe; line dance; *pasodoble*; *varsouvienne*.

Source: Hulot, Henri Louis. *Balls and Dancing Parties Condemned by the Scriptures, Holy Fathers, Holy Councils, and Most Renowned Theologians of the Church*. Boston: P. Donahue, 1857.

SCHUHPLATTLER

A zestful forerunner of clogging and the hopping, skipping Austrian *Ländler*, the *Schuhplattler* (also *Schuhplatder*)—literally "shoe clapper"—expressed the idiophonic vitality of males in the Bavarian Tyrol. Bohemian, Austrian, and northern Italian youths used their bodies to make music. Syncopated stomping, knee lifts, tongue clicks, and clapping along with yelping and yodeling followed a 3/4 meter. Traditionalists accented the promenade and unregimented steps with acoustic smacks on lederhosen, toe taps, and slaps on backside, thighs, knees, ankles, floor, and shoe soles to accordion, cowbell, and alpenhorn tunes.

Described in Latin essays from 1000 CE, the Schuhplattler may have originated as ritualized aggression among hunters during the Neolithic Age before 3000 BCE. As such, clap dancers preserved Europe's oldest surviving *Volkstanz* (folk dance). A parallel of the Norwegian *halling*, bouncy horseplay and shoe smacking derived from the winter body warm-ups of woodcutters at isolated mountain cabins. An animal version, the *Gamerlsprung* (mountain goat bound) mimicked the leap of high-country quadrupeds.

As *Burschenplattler* (male competition), the noisy dance delighted guests at Alpine socials and before the Wittelsbach court at Scheyern Castle near Aichach in Bavarian Swabia. In 1023, mountaineers used the sharp thwacks and angular gestures to mimic the strutting and wing drumming of the amorous male black grouse. The anonymous author of the *Ruodlieb* (1050), a knight's tale, described the choreographic thunderclaps after he witnessed a solo near Tegernsee Abbey, a Benedictine cultural center south of Munich under the patronage of Holy Roman Emperor Henry III.

Evolving Dance

In the 1600s, a partnered adaptation, the *Gruppenpreisplattln*, introduced nonaggressive hen gestures and skirt lifts from women who encircled male soloists with pirouettes. The twosomes concluded their individual choreography with the men lifting the females high in the air and twirling them into an affectionate rotation of the Ländler, another love dance from central Europe. Late in the eighteenth century, English nobles sneered at Bavarian affection for a high-country rhythm lacking the glides and poise of court dance.

By adding shoulder mounts, headstands, and stamps on the ceiling, in the 1820s, hardy males synchronized clap steps and bounds as an exhibition intended to impress women. The sets attested to gymnastic strength and stamina similar in style to the Norwegian *halling*, Afro-American juba, and Ukrainian *hopak*. Apprentices invented gestures from their professions for the *Glockenplattler* (bell clapper), *Ambosstanz* (blacksmith's dance), and *Bergknabenetanz* (salt miner's dance), and additional tropes for herders, skiers, and coopers. For the *Mühlradl* (miller's dance), soloists acted out the gears on a mill wheel with a ring dance; for the *Holzhackertanz* (woodchopper's dance), performers chopped, sawed, and clap danced to the beat. In the *Mahder* (hay harvester), soloists mimed sharpening a scythe and cutting hay.

German peasant displays for royalty offered shoe clapping as a token of respect. On a spa respite in 1838, the Russian empress Alexandra Feodorovna viewed Schuh-plattlers at Wildbad Kreuth southeast of Munich, where females whirled around the hand-slapping men and maintained a bell shape in flashing dirndl skirts. In honor of a royal progress of Maximilian II of Upper Bavaria through the Alps on July 15, 1858, villagers entertained his entourage with exhibitions of the Schuhplattler.

Ethnochoreography

Between the 1860s and 1880s, costumed folk clubs east of the Jura range promoted improvisational and synchronized percussive dancing at Miesbach, Bayrischzell, and Ramsau. For May Volksfests, midsummer dancing, and Oktoberfest, costumes featuring chamois leather shorts and knitted knee hose echoed body whacks and contextualized ethnicity much as the czardas identified Hungarians. To expand the tourist industry in the Tyrol and Vorarlberg, at Swiss inns, and in Salzburg and Munich cabarets, in 1890, the clap dancers heightened commercial attractions with comic presentations in which males peeked under their partners' skirts. A less humorous version, the *Haberertanz* mim-icked fistfighting and knife attacks with gestures that occasionally drew blood.

The original Schuhplattler retained its nonviolent gestures. At Breslau in January 1906, the Alpine Club accommodated Jews and gentiles for founder's day, which danc-ers commemorated with a clap dance. In 1910, lampoons of the clapping and yodeling incorporated the *Watschenplattler*, a mock slapping fight between men. An official ban ended the miming in 1925, but the slap dance continued in private at teen parties.

In the heady days of the Weimar Republic (1918–1933), Berlin's Löwenbräu Bar featured Schuplattler juxtaposed with cowboy and Negro dance allegedly from Arizona. During the Third Reich from 1933 to 1945, the clap dance took on a politi-cal aura after Adolf Hitler and the Nazi party identified the smacking and stamping as hyper-virile evidence of their superior-race ideology. Unsmiling performers came to attention on the dance floor and struck and slapped themselves and other males. A pro-Nazi dance society met weekly in the Yorkville section of New York City.

In the Alps at Oetz, Austrian girls filled in for militarized males in 1938 and stud-ied the raucous dance steps and yodels at the Cafe Tyrol. The gendered performance of Bavarians at Ruhpolding hosted Captain Joachim Schepke and the U-boat crew of the *U-100* at Kurhaus, Switzerland, in February 1941. German Dada artist Hannah Höch lampooned the awkward, primitive foot stomping in a collage as proof that Germans were unwise to reawaken indigenous culture as proof of ethnic superiority.

To differentiate from Nazi symbolism the nonviolent folk art of the Tyrol, refugees to Great Britain, Australia, and North America took their Schuhplattler with them. By the late 1940s, postwar soccer training camps taught crossover arm and leg coordination with body-smacking lessons, which stimulated both hemispheres of the brain. Physical education programs; ski compounds at Stratton, Vermont; and adult culture clubs in Canada at Ottawa, Toronto, Calgary, and Vancouver featured the Schuhplattler as holistic exercise and a model of central European folk art. A work slowdown in Canberra in 1952 gave immigrant German builders free time to form a Schuhplattler team. On August 26, 1972, Chancellor Willy Brandt approved the Schuhplattler to alpenhorns and a brass band as part of the summer Olympics opening ceremonies at Munich.

See also animal dances; czardas; clogging; *halling*; *hopak*; juba; *Ländler*.

Source: Kolb, Alexandra. "The Migration and Globalization of *Schuhplattler* Dance: A Sociological Analysis." *Cultural Sociology* 7, no. 1 (March 2013): 39–55.

SCRIPTURE, FOLK DANCE IN

In discreet crevices of holy writ, references to dancing authenticate views of God's people as jubilant, physically engaged worshippers who flourished at weddings, circumcisions, baptisms, harvests, burials, processions, and military victories. In the *Li Chi* (Book of Rites, ca. 900 CE), Chinese writings from the Han Dynasty pictured the harmonic dancer with shield and battle-ax as virtuous and serene. From a more spiritual perspective in the *Guru Granth* (after 1469), the scripture of Sikhism, verses by Amar Das denounced Hindu dancing to honor Krishna and urged Sikhs to dance in their hearts for God.

In "Becoming the Child," chapter 45 of the *Egyptian Book of the Dead* (after 1550 BCE), an elegant essay in the first person described the possibilities living in a child's imagination as an antidote to chaos. The imagery pictured the newborn entering life with song and whirling into darkness to spit flames that became stars in the night sky. The poet urged all to dance in the moment, to grasp melody and to spin and chant to overcome mortal sorrow. A parallel passage in the *Ethiopian Book of the Dead* (400 CE) invoked ancestral dancers to return to Earth and spread primitive magic as a source of new inspiration.

The subject of creative arts bore an intimate, personal significance among the Aryans who founded Hinduism. The chant, music, and dance of devotees became inseparable liturgies for expressing hope, need, and pent-up fears. From around 2000 BCE, the warrior-herdsmen of central Asia carried the Vedas to India as the basis of Hindu culture. The prime volume, the *Rig Veda* (Praise stanzas, ca. 1200 BCE), typified Indian religious dance as vigorous and physical in the clasping of worshippers to each other. The *Yajur Veda* (Sacrificial prayers, 1000–600 BCE) formulated hand blandishments devised to arouse spiritual moods.

Specifics of Hindu story dancers and jubilant war ritual pictured body paint on storytellers, fighters in gold breastplates, and gorgeously clad and ornamented women honoring victory. In 500 BCE, the *Nata Sutras* (Dance verses) compiled the principles and regulations of theatrical dance, which focused on epic events and heroism. The height of Hindu civilization, as described in the *Mahabharata* (400 BCE) and *Ramayana* (300 BCE), pictured the hero Arjuna disguised as a dance instructor to the women in the mythic king Virata's palace near Jaypur. The dramas took root in Asia and passed to Cambodia, Thailand, and Java as sources of folk choreography. Under Emperor Chandra Gupta after

376 CE, poetry lauded temple dancers at Mahakala northeast of Bombay for the tinkling ornaments on their sashes and the jeweled fans that they waved.

To the south of the Indian subcontinent, Shiva, the "Lord of the Cosmic Dance," became the apotheosis of mythic science, religion, and the arts, a divinity repeated in *The Tibetan Book of the Dead* (ca. 775 CE). Sculpture and murals pictured Shiva in the Himalayas with a hand drum and an hourglass in two of his four hands and one foot extended. The pose indicated the readiness of the supreme deity to join in graceful kinetic activity attuned to the order of the stars, waves of the ocean, currents of the rivers, and flutter of leaves and branches. Poems described his countenance as shining and his locks of hair as vibrating to the blissful choreography that never ends.

Hebrew Dancers

Allusive references in the King James Bible (1611) attest to the prevalence of dance in Hebraic culture before the first millennium BCE. Biblical dance integrates male and female among celebrants. Of the few identified Judeo-Christian participants, after 1220 BCE, Jephthah's daughter danced with gladness at her father's victory in Judges 11. In I Samuel 18, the women of Israel sang and presented a victory parade after 1050 BCE because Saul and David overcame the Philistines in the Valley of Elah west of the Dead Sea. After the Israelites crossed the Red Sea in Exodus 15, composed around 950 BCE, the prophet, tambourinist, and drummer Miriam led women in a dance of joy at liberation from the pharaoh. In Song of Songs 6, around 600 BCE, the sensuous black Shulamite expressed passion in her dance for the "right man."

Because disobedience to Yahweh oppressed the people of Zion in Lamentations 5 after the Babylonians sacked Jerusalem in 586 BCE, the faithful ceased dancing and turned to mourning for their shortcomings. In Job 21, from around 400 BCE, the wealthy dispatched their children in a flock to dance. In Jeremiah 31, after 300 BCE, the Lord promised that Israel would overcome sorrow and again make merry. The *Mishnah* (Commentary, after 100 CE), the first volume of rabbinic literature, notes in Sukkot 5 the performance of Rabbi Simeon bar Yochai, a sage of ancient Israel who juggled eight lighted torches while the Levites played lyre, harp, cymbals, and trumpets. More familiar characters danced for individual reasons—the widow Judith to free herself of sexism in Judith 15, written in the late second century BCE; Salome in girlish eroticism at Galilee in Mark 6 about 70 CE and Matthew 14 a decade later; and, in 67 CE, the Acts of John 96, Jesus at the center of a ring dance of rejoicing disciples at Gethsemane.

The Hebrew chronicler Josephus's *History of the Jews* (75 CE) added commentary on David's ecstatic dance at the placement of the Ark of the Covenant in the temple at Jerusalem in Psalms 149 and 150. The patriarch's first wife, the princess Michal and daughter of King Saul, scolded David for nudity in front of servants and handmaidens, an unseemly behavior for a monarch. David's retort legitimized prayer dance as acceptable to God, even if female observers disapproved. From a more conservative perspective, in the New Testament, in 54 CE, Paul banned instrumental music and women's songs and preferred instead simple chants and psalms. When Christianity reached Ethiopia in the first century CE, priests rattled the sistra, chanted, and drummed to choreography known as "King David's dance," the finale of Christmas festivities.

Technical Terminology

Translation of scriptural choreographic terms reveals that the Hebrew *yadah* (praise) contains an element of reaching and gesturing with the hands that influenced twenty-first-century evangelicals. Another common Bible term, *barak* (praise) incorporated kneeling and saluting. A third, *shachah* (worship), named a posture of bowing, prostrating, and adoring. In addition, the Torah imparted specific references to circle dance (*hagag*), circular procession (*sabab*), skipping like four-footed herd animals or deer (*raqad* and *pizzez*), and jumping (*qippus* and *dillug*), more energetic facets of worship dance.

The involvement of holistic movement in Hebrew worship leaves no question that the ancients merged dance with reverence to God. Precise instructions on whirling (*kirker* and *mahol*), playful dance (*siheq*), leaping (*kafotz*), and limping (*pasah* and *zala*) suggest distinct choreography or mime dance. A complete image in Judges 21 from the period describes the dancing place in each vineyard at Shiloh northwest of the Dead Sea, where maidens saluted the harvest twice annually with circle dances and accepted as life partners the men who danced with them. In Song of Songs 7, two troupes of guests honored a wedding. From the Greek New Testament came additional nuanced terms for dance: *proskuneo* (bow) and *agallio* (springing). Minority sects revived the reclamation of the body as a source of glorifying the divine.

The fragmentary Dead Sea Scrolls specified choreographic concepts of biblical drama. The War Scroll glorified the apocryphal battle between the sons of light and the sons of darkness with a victory ritual and the emergence of the Davidic Dynasty. According to directions in Exodus 15 and Judges 21, after intense slaughter, Israel's high priest took charge of the revelers, timbrels, and dances. The ceremony concluded with the purification of all from the blood of conquest. More specifically, the paean to joy in the Apostrophe to Judah called for happy dancing, feasting, and the raising of the right hand in a sign of praise. Similar in exuberance to David's musical psalms, the passage urged full participation in life's pleasures.

See also gendered dance; Jewish dance; *mayim mayim*; Sufi dance.

Source: Yarber, Angela. *Dance in Scripture: How Biblical Dancers Can Revolutionize Worship Today.* Eugene, OR: Wipf and Stock, 2013.

SHAKER DANCE

Earnest English millennialist Ann Lee founded the Shakers, the common name for the United Society of Believers in Christ's Second Appearing, a society of spontaneous charismatics. From her conversion in 1758, she joined in ecstatic worship based on the model of Miriam and David in the book of II Samuel in the Old Testament, where King David exulted in Yahweh by escorting the Ark of the Covenant through the city gates of Jerusalem to the entrance of the holy of holies. Through physical and emotional spirituality, Lee formulated a transcendent theology based on equality by caste, gender, and race.

Advancing from silent meditation, Ann Lee solicited vows of commitment from each disciple, who saluted her as "Mother." As a spiritual exercise, she promoted celibacy and healing through shouting, twitching, shivering, waving her arms, and rapturous dance, a trance-like means of relieving sexual urges without coitus. The demonstration of faith lasted until dancers sank from exhaustion.

Because of the sect's persecution and jailing in Manchester, England, in July 1772 for breaking the Sabbath with dancing, Mother Ann Lee led eight disciples from Liverpool to New York City in mid-May 1774. Aboard the brig *Mariah* until their arrival on August 6, the bizarre religious gyrations annoyed Captain Smith, who rebuked their dancing up and down and collapsing in convulsions on the deck. By skipping, whirling, and shaking, they divested themselves of the creeds and dogma of Anglicanism.

New World Dancers

To maintain their nontraditional lifestyle, Ann Lee and the Shakers founded a sectarian commune in September 1776 at Watervliet, New York, the first of eight religious compounds. They commemorated a difficult past by singing and dancing to the hymn "Whither, O Whither on Earth Can I Roam?" Through evangelism and communal living, cultists drew widows, orphans, and the poor, homeless, and disaffected to their vigorous, uplifting liturgy.

During weekly services, some members experienced visions and vibrated to the Holy Spirit within. As emotional outlets, they brandished fists to expel Satan, breathed love into each other's faces, and genuflected humbly before God to the hymn "Who Will Bow and Bend Like a Willow." To create an atmosphere of worship, which they called "square order shuffle," women lined up into columns along pegs driven into the plank floor. Led by three male elders, the female Shakers faced lines of men, tucked elbows to their sides, and held hands out with palms up as though offering themselves as gifts to God.

In addition to line dance, Shakers practiced patterned and circle dance and innovative frenzy, an aberration from traditional worship that sparked controversy among non-Shakers. Spectators, including French historian Alexis De Tocqueville, jostled to enter the worship hall. They stood dumbfounded to watch the sin-killing agitation, evidence of belief in Adventism, or the coming of a savior, a nineteenth-century belief. While singing, praying, and barking in unison, Shaker brethren and sisters synchronized their choreography by stepping or marching forward, tapping toes, and treading back.

According to Mother Ann, the rolling, turning, roaring, twisting, tramping, clapping, stomping, and shaking of hands relieved Shaker bodies of carnal urges and rid them of evil. Lyrics of mournful hymns sung full voice on only four notes stressed the nature of Christian love and prophecy of a "new light." When congregants manifested their joy in a pounding rhythm, extravagant flailing, and shouting a cadence, neighbors called the charismatic sect the "merry dancers" and the "shaking Quakers."

An American Dance Phenomenon

Contributing to conviviality, members rang hand bells and devised complex patterns of steps and gestures for more upbeat round dance. At Turtle Creek, Ohio, in 1804, they kept writhing and encircling the lectern for more than an hour, intoning glory to the Holy Spirit. By 1807, the sect had spread their sectarian dance style to the Carolinas,

Connecticut, Florida, Georgia, Kentucky, Maine, Massachusetts, New Hampshire, Pennsylvania, Tennessee, and Virginia.

Religious innovators continued to collect aphoristic hymns and steps, introducing the Shaker quick dance in 1811. However, the aging of members required more marches and less lively, intricate footwork. During the Era of Manifestations from 1830 to 1850, celestial zeal filled young Shaker women, who experienced glossolalia (speaking in tongues), drew mystic pictures, and whirled like dervishes to "'Tis a Gift to Be Simple" and "Lord of the Dance," signature tunes by hymnographer Joseph Brackett and lyricist Sydney Bertram Carter.

By 1846, there flourished some six thousand Shaker converts, among whom the New Lebanon commune in central New York numbered four hundred. In 1920, *The Spatula* magazine published an article on the Shaker method of kinetic healing through precision dance. In the twenty-first century, art historians ranked Shaker dance among memorable forms of American folk art.

See also circle dance; healing dance; lamentation dance; line dance; shamanic dance; worship dance.

Source: Williams, Emily. "Spirituality as Expressed in Song," *Connecticut Magazine* 9, no. 4 (1905): 745–51.

SHAMANIC DANCE

In holistic acts of curing, shamanic story dance codifies ritual invocation with theatrics, acrobatics, fire handling, and wonder working, an essential of Shaker dance. Miracles motivated the frenzied, convulsive performances by a Polynesian priestess at Rotuma, Saami ritual in northern Finland, and the uplifting Afro-Peruvian *alcatraz* (fire dance), a native ritual in Arequipa that relieved the despair of press gangs working in underground mines.

Currently, performers intend a shamanic ritual to heal and bless aboriginal tribes, such as the Bambara of Guinea, Hausa females of Nigeria, the !Kung and San of the Kalahari Desert, the Evenki peoples of Siberia, and the Saulteaux of Eagle Lake, Ontario. Among Malay dancers in Kelantan, the *hala* unites seven villagers before the shaman to pray for the harvest. Set in a paddy, the dance propitiates spirits to grant food bounty for the community from rice, their staple food.

Examples of shamanic ritual include the traversal of burning embers by young Manchu mediums in China and, from the 1850s, the rites of the north Malawian Tumbuka, who restored mental stability with the *vimbuza*, a mystic therapy-inducing spiritual possession. The components of the dance created consternation in Scots Presbyterian missionaries Thomas Cullen Young and Robert Laws at the Livingstonia compound, where, in 1899, they declared the dance repugnant. Shamans continued the practice, cloaking it as a caricature of precolonial paganism.

Through transcendent states of consciousness, other ceremonies conferred healing. Mongolian spiritualists glared, gyrated, and wrestled evil to rid the body of disease. At the culmination, mediums envisioned the patient restored to wholeness. In the Ural Mountains of Uzbekistan and the Ukraine, Bashkir shamans danced away evil that prevented female uterine labors from resulting in a healthy birth. The Hunza spirit channeler of north Pakistan performed a blood sacrifice and breathed the smoke of burning juniper before whirling in a frenzy-causing syncope. More complex ceremonies among the Garifuna in the temples of Belize began with percussion on conch and turtle shells and drums and proceeded to a shuffle step echoing with a rattle coordinated with the shaman's heartbeat.

In Korea, to an hourglass-shaped drum copied from models in India and Tibet, healing companies presented mythic story dance to rural fishers and farmers as a communal form of divination, séance, empathy, and entertainment. Trance clairvoyants of Bali and the Tuareg dancers of Niger, Mali, Algeria, Libya, and Burkina Faso performed acrobatic mimicry that originated in ancient Canaan. They gestured from a seated position before lapsing into euphoria. A source of self-directed therapy, the grounded dance stripped the afflicted self of anxiety, envy, insecurity, powerlessness, pride, and arrogance.

Dance History

From prehistory, as exemplified in the Paleolithic cave art and pictograms at Zion Canyon, Utah; Acacus, Libya; and Arequipa, Peru, shamanism guided the despairing and suffering into more positive states of mind through choreography and mime, such as the salmon or deer shaman of the Coeur d'Alene of Idaho and the medium's ancestral dance in Seoul, Korea. Sometimes hyperventilation and highly charged emotions threatened the sanity and survival of the performer. Overexertion combined with psychotropic drugs generated the Saami medium's catalepsy in Finland, the Kazakh sorcerer's convulsions in central Asia, the Koryak mania from ingesting fly agaric fungus in Siberia, and the death-like stupor of the Huichol and Mescalero Apache shaman from hallucinogenic peyote, which linked the Durangan or New Mexican priest with the underworld.

From 206 BCE in the Han Dynasty of eastern China, the Taoist *wu* (invoker) danced to summon rain. Her steps worked magic to control the floods common in China's lowlands. Priestly movements jangled jade pendants from a sash to the beat of drums and the music of zithers and pipes. In an altered state, she made a spirit journey to receive a deity, which possessed her body and empowered her performance. In competition with the folk priesthood, Taoist schools taught shamanic divination, exorcism, and dance throughout southern China and Taiwan. The concept flourished in northern Norway around 1170, when the Saami shaman performed steps, sang, and drummed to free his soul for extensive travel.

Isolated examples of shamanic dance tended to flourish in isolation, out of the ken of religious or anthropological evaluation. In 1692, Nicolaas Witsen, a Dutch explorer and shipbuilder, summarized the all-night work of the practitioner in *North and East Tartary*, a groundbreaking survey of exorcism in northern Siberia and Mongolia. He illustrated the text with an antlered shaman chanting to a drumbeat to drive out demons. Additional pictures attested to the necessity for disguises and dance costuming with a magical wand, spirit bells, cap, belt, gloves, or boots.

Nicolaas Witsen's ethnography of northeastern Siberia incorporated distinct dances, notably a Yakut imitation of a wild horse with attendants holding the reins clipped to the shaman's robe. One example of a Russian shamanic service along the Taldu River in the Altai range on the border of Kazakhstan described a sinuous snake dance that required priestly agility and grace. As the pantomime of an animal double became less frenetic, the dancer slowed his leaps to impose peace and wholeness on the patient. In another example, a weeping priestess encircled the fire pit and hurled sacrificial food into the flames as payment for healing.

New World Shamanism

Shamanic dance displayed great powers of stamina, especially for student rainmakers at Creek and Choctaw schools in precolonial Georgia, the Pueblo practitioner wearing a coyote pelt and headdress, and Guaraní and Tupí pilgrims escaping slave labor in colonial sugar mills by leaving Brazil in 1539 to scale the Peruvian Andes. After 1760, black Africans kidnapped by slavers from Benin, Ibo, Mandinka, and Yoruba enclaves for sale in the New World reprised cultic and ecstatic dance in colonial Haiti and Louisiana as a means of preserving shamanic faith. Dance at Congo Square in New Orleans imitated the priestly healing rituals of Santeria as well as courtship and fertility dances for nuptials. In 1820, observation of a Salish prophet dance at Puget Sound and the straits of Georgia and Juan de Fuca introduced missionaries and traders to Amerindian shamanic therapies.

From Saskatchewan to Texas, the messianic medium promulgated rhythmic prayer, bird and animal mimesis, and meditative smoke inhalation and army marches to the positive energy of drums. A Lakota or Teton Sioux priest superintended the sun dance that involved devotees in spiritual cleansing through self-mortification and incantations to the earth mother. Alaskan Inuit clustered around a demonstration in the dance house of a masked shaman, who defeated harmful spirits and chased them away through a nonverbal catharsis. The emergence of the prophet Wovoka and the circular ghost dance in Nevada in 1890 reunited reservation Indians with their epic heroes while prophesying a calamity to the white world.

Shamanic services continued mediating health and healing into the late twentieth century. Before the eradication of Yoruba folk culture in southern Montserrat by a volcanic eruption on July 18, 1995, cult followers danced the *jombee*, a revival of ancestral souls. To the ting of triangles and the pairing of drums with concertina, teams of mediums repeated the waltz, quadrille, and polka until they lapsed into hallucinations. Spirits spoke through shamans to reveal the cause of sickness and personal crises.

See also Andean dance; animal dances; exorcism; fan dance; ghost dance; healing dance; juba; polka; quadrille; sacrificial dance; shawl dance; Sufi dance; sun dance; waltz; worship dance.

Source: Hutton, Ronald. *Shamans: Siberian Spirituality and the Western Imagination.* London: Bloomsbury, 2001.

SHAWL DANCE

Like the handkerchief and parasol dances, shawl dancing manipulates attire in varied global settings, particularly China, Indonesia, Mesoamerica, and European parts in the Roma diaspora, home of the Iberian flamenco. The concept of mediating womanhood and ritual with the triangular or rectangular shawl dates to ancient Egypt, Greece, and Rome. Illusions of concealment and exposure created by all sizes of shoulder wear enhanced the standing of women in societies dominated by aggressive males.

Colonialism carried the Aragonese *jota* to the Philippines, where men added the clack of bamboo castanets and women waved shawls. Among Afro-Uruguayans, the shawl created drama as well as ethnic identity. In Bolivia, the Aymara combined a female shawl dance with men in ponchos performing a counterclockwise circle dance to drum and flute. The isolationist Chipaya and the dwindling Uru of Lake Titicaca promoted freestyle configuration of the female flaunting her shoulder wrap to flute melodies.

In Sri Lanka, Asian performers combined holistic medicine with humor. A shawled shaman performs a comic exorcism in the *salupaliya*, a dance drama of the Sinhalese aborigines. Clapping and cavorting to the drumbeat, the masked shaman flips the shawl and minces in a transvestite routine intended to heal and restore whole body wellness. In contrasting mode, at the sacred brown bear ritual, the Khanty of Siberia charge their shawl dances with mystery by manipulating the fabric to cover the upper body. The Javanese *yogyakarta* dance also stressed dramatic moves of the *sampur* (shawl).

Among Indians of the Southern United States, female Ponca performers evolved the contemporary shawl dance from the original jingle dance. The style paid tribute to the healing of homebound war widows and to the ancestral female costume topped with a modest wool blanket. By adorning buckskin costumes with lightweight shoulder wraps and topping their hair with beaded bands, shawl dancers displayed a burst of painted cosmological symbols on cloth or buckskin. As they extended their arms in an iconic "coming out" from grief, the appliquéd beads, ribbons, and sequins suggested butterfly wings emerging from a cocoon to celebrate beauty and joy.

Dance as Protest

By creating the shawl dance and performing in public, female Indians resisted US laws from the 1880s banning religious ritual by refining new steps for routines. From 1928, participants at the White Eagle arena in north central Oklahoma preserved Ponca culture with the basic crow hop, a double-beat bird movement that kept fringe aloft in imitation of the men's warrior dance. Through balanced, innovative combinations to left and right, by 1950, the women competed with male presenters. Within the decade, the floating, dipping, jig-like female style and fanning spins compared in panache and poise to that of male fancy dancers.

Native shawl dancer routines fluttered, twirled, and soared with light steps. Wingspans stretched gracefully to display color and fringe. The regalia coordinated capelets and yokes on shawls, elegant needlework on leggings and moccasins, and flashy beads on earrings and wristlets. As second-wave feminism freed women of outmoded social restraints, in the 1970s, female dancers of the Wind River Shoshone accentuated athleticism with leaps and kicks. For the Kiowa gourd dance, women added the shawl as a symbol of tribal revitalization. Homosexual Indians adopted the dance as an emblem of "coming out" of closeted duplicity to embrace their true sexual nature.

Fluid Folk Art

Across North America as far west as Kauai, the shawl dance maintains a female presence at pan-tribal summer powwows, tourist exhibitions, Mexican folkloric dances, and reservation and Wild West shows. The choreography flourishes among the Osage and as a demonstration of loyalties professed by the Tigua of El Paso, Texas. For the Haliwa-Saponi of eastern North Carolina, gestures of extra-long fringe reflect female leadership of a tribe that the state government has denied official ethnic status.

Educators teach Lakota and Winnebago girls as young as age five to dance on their toes, crisscross feet, sway to the beat, and lift legs high while maintaining dignity and humility. Elderly women participate as a form of exercise, therapy, and social support for the younger generation. To symbolize pride in heritage and assuage the afflicted, girls and women bob their cloaked bodies up and down from bent knees and strenuous footwork in time to drumming and chant.

Shawl dance technique requires a conscious control of attire. At Mille Lacs Reservation in Minnesota, slight shifts of pirouettes, swaying, gliding, and nodding of plumes on the head articulate phrasing of Ojibwa figures. A skilled shawl dancer halts on the final beat and remains unmoving to display control. Middle school curriculum in Albuquerque in 2000 incorporated shawl dancing at the Jemez Pueblo Feast Day to develop modesty and ethnic pride in Amerindian girls. On February 12, 2010, the opening ceremony of the Vancouver Olympic Winter Games coordinated intertribal shawl dancing as a salute to First Peoples.

See also flamenco; handkerchief dance; *jarabe tapatío*; *jota*; shamanic dance; veiled dance.

Source: Miller, Heather Andrews. "Dance Reflects Tradition and History." *Windspeaker* 24, no. 3 (2006).

SIBERIAN DANCE

The agrarian and religious calendars of Siberia scheduled a choreographic cycle of indigenous folk art. From 33,000 BCE, animal masking disguised the humanity of Arctic-Siberian shamans and allowed them to merge with animistic deities and totemic beasts. According to rock carvings, Siberia, the cradle of shamanism, nurtured the dance ritual that may have sustained migrants around 18,000 BCE across the Beringia land bridge to North America and furthered the passage of Siberian folk art into Amerindian culture.

From 5000 BCE, consumption of psychogenic mushrooms enhanced ritual autosuggestion with a physical inebriation that influenced the miming of story dance. After 1000 BCE, totemic dances along the Bering Strait engaged aboriginal Khanty and Mansi in propitiation of the brown bear. Masked performers donned birch-bark false faces and mimed stalking, hunting, and skinning.

Mime and Ring Dance

Along the Tunguska River in the game-rich expanses of the taiga and tundra areas, shamans of the Tungus disguised themselves as birds, bears, or deer to perform trickster capers and magic rituals that cured mental unrest and disease. The Tungus shamans and the Ket priests in the Yenisei River basin enhanced their ritual figures with antlers, tambourines, bells, and hobbyhorses. In the far north, aboriginal Samoyed dance involved youths encircling the shaman's tent during trances and his unseen communication with the spirit realm.

Around a tepee of logs flaming fifty feet in the air, participants in the traditional *yohor* ring dance twirled and sang. Into the dawn, they celebrated herding, horsemanship, planting, and harvests from the steppes and Mongolian plateau. In fealty to the khans, troupes from the Khentii steppe on the northern border of Mongolia synchronized figures that displayed silk and peacock feather costumes. Comic wrestlers executed toe balances in boots and bounded upward before collapsing on their knees.

Religion and Politics

In 770, the migration of the hypnotic *tsam* (or *cham*), a military story dance from monasteries in India, followed a meandering diaspora across the Himalayas from Tibet, Bhutan, and Mongolia to Siberia. Over several days, the grotesque silk robes and aprons, bulging-eyed masks, gestures, and figures waged physical and psychological combat against enemies of Buddha and restored the faithful to spiritual purity. After Siberians converted to Christianity, steps choreographed along turf labyrinths celebrated May Day and Whitsuntide.

In the eighteenth century, shamanic ritual and Belarusian trance dancing permeated the arts after an influx of immigrants from the Ukraine and eastern Russia. At Irkutsk in south central Siberia in the 1780s, dinner dances to gay and somber melodies provided social outlets for cultural life. During the 1850s, 1890s, and again in the 1930s, appeals to young girls to move to Siberia initiated amusements and parties, as with the wooing dances in the Amur area to the Far East arranged to balalaika and accordion.

Tsam dancing became one of the first choreographies to disappear under Soviet Russian ethnic prohibitions. Presented to frame drumming and the discordant sound of cymbals and horns, the striding, bounding leg extensions and heel-and-toe steps remained integral to tantric worship ritual until Communist bans on Buddhist lamas. The hard line from Moscow resulted in death for eighteen thousand Buryat monks. A contemporaneous onslaught under Vladimir Lenin suppressed shamanic ritual among the Chukchi, the aborigines on the Arctic Circle.

To increase the formation of families among single men in Siberia, in February 1937, Valentina Khetagurova distributed flyers inviting girls to come to the Far East. Into 1939 at Khabarovsk, the largest city on the Chinese border, some twenty thousand unmarried women joined dancers at a pavilion outside the five-domed Dormition Cathedral, one of the largest churches in the Russian Far East. To win potential mates, the newcomers performed folk dances in display of vigor and health suited to the settlement of a harsh land.

See also attire; circle dance; community dance; *hopak*; hunting dance; mime; shawl dance; totemic dance.

Source: Hartley, Janet M. *Siberia: A History of the People.* New Haven, CT: Yale University Press, 2014.

SQUARE DANCE

Uniquely American, square dance, the US national dance, follows a caller, a controlling figure in children's games and the medieval farandole. With the fundamental geometrics of contradance, from the 1600s, the called figures of square dance—promenade home, allemande, birdie in the cage, do-si-do, ocean wave, star—altered at the will of the leader. Without boundaries, in France and England, the dance decreased or increased complexity and opportunities for individualizing. For instruction in configurations, London arts publisher John Playford compiled *The English Dancing Master* (1651), which remained in print until 1728.

Among isolated French Canadians, New Englanders, and mountaineers in the Appalachian chain, from the seventeenth century, community gatherings gave dwellers an opportunity to blend Scots-Irish reels and jigs with quadrilles. At the Scots *cèilidh* (house party), partnering and called figures anticipated structured ring dance, such as the Gay Gordons, a highlands combination of walking, pivoting, and polka steps that a leader announced. In contrast, the quadrille, more patterned than the Scots and Western square dances, required no caller.

Adaptable Figures

Guests at parties requested the Virginia reel, another forerunner of square dance to fiddle, guitar, banjo, and accordion tunes and jug band music. On Maui, Hawaiian *paniolo* (cowboys) from Mexico and Puerto Rico added the slack key guitar to accompaniment of square dance. At "play parties" and house, church, and barn raisings in rural North Carolina, Tennessee, and Kentucky in the eighteenth century, residents developed square dancing into the "hillbilly tap dance," a local term for clogging. Skipping steps to Scots-Irish fiddle melodies reflected the influence of the Scots *lanciers* (lancers) and German step dance and *Schuhplattler*, an energetic rhythm of slaps on the chest, backside, thighs, and feet and smacks on lederhosen.

Beginning square dancers needed demonstrations of the eight-person square and practice to master the shifts in circling and partnering. In Franco-American New England and Quebec, callers aided newcomers by announcing figures in English and/or French. By the 1800s, the unruly square dance and hoedowns began replacing the more refined cotillion with robust swings and shouted "yee haws," the language of farmers and ranchers. To please fifty thousand settlers, in 1868, the California legislature honored the country folk dance with its own week, September 8–15.

Vassar College gym teachers adopted square dancing in 1877 for indoor training in calisthenics. During a fad in Kobe, Japan, for all things foreign, in October 1886, consuls celebrated the birthday of Emperor Meiji with square dancing. The November 1889 issues of *Autumn Leaves*, a Mormon magazine published in Lamoni, Iowa, applauded young women who preferred square dancing to partnering in intimate holds with any men who invited them. In January 1903, the *Young Women's Journal* concurred by questioning the morality and ethics of "round" as opposed to square dancing.

Square Dance Fads

In the 1930s and 1940s, a surge of American patriotism during the Great Depression and World War II initiated elementary classroom lessons in square dance to develop motor skills. On June 8, 1939, the Soco Gap square dance team from Asheville, North Carolina, and the Skyline Farms dancers from Scottsboro, Alabama, performed at the Roosevelt White House for a state visit by England's King George VI and Queen Elizabeth. Over WPTF-Raleigh radio in 1948, the Foggy Mountain Boys, led by Lester Flatt and Earl Scruggs, popularized bluegrass songs that square dancers preferred—"Your Love Is Like a Flower," "Foggy Mountain Breakdown," and "Reunion in Heaven."

To homemade harmonica "quill music" and banjo picking, rural couples thronged public dances at Midwestern grange halls and Southern and New England barn dances. In the postwar years, callers scheduled dances at Rhode Island corn huskings and harvest homes, Southwestern county fairs, parish house wakes, and veteran rehabilitation centers. Across the United States, Ontario, Saskatchewan, Quebec, and Newfoundland, square dancers varied their patterns with the cotton-eye Joe, a line dance performed in 2/4 meter to fiddles and banjos at Cajun hoedowns, Western saloons, and Southern roadhouses.

Cowboy movies and television series, such as *Duel in the Sun* (1946) and the *Dr. Quinn* episode "Best Friends" on December 4, 1993, spread square dancing globally by romanticizing men's boots, wrangler work clothes, bandanas, and Stetsons. Women's fashions adopted gingham dresses, pinafores, and prairie skirts raised a few inches above lacy petticoats, which dancers flourished in sashays and promenades. For fun and exercise, recreation programs suited square dance therapy to the needs of the elderly and the handicapped.

See also allemande; barn dance; *cèilidh*; clogging; contradance; cotton-eye Joe; farandole; jig; line dance; quadrille; reel; *Schuhplattler*; step dance.

Source: Pittman, Anne M., Marlys S. Waller, and Cathy L. Dark. *Dance a While: A Handbook for Folk, Square, Contra, and Social Dance.* Long Grove, IL: Waveland Press, 2009.

STEP DANCE

A percussive dance of African, Latino, and British invention, step dance flourished in disparate parts of the globe as an idiophonic folk art that made its own music. A vibrant ancestor of tap dance and soft-shoe, the folk art incorporates gymnastic stunts, marching, clapping and body slapping, knee lifts, and complex call-and-response routines. The combination sets the atmosphere of rigorous footwork using the body as an instrument.

The Celtic Original

Along with Celtic sword dancing, ring dance, jigs, and reels, step dance began in the British Isles after 1200 BCE. Influenced by Druidic ritual after 350 BCE, stepping featured leaps over *dúidíns* (clay smoking pipes) and harvesters' flails. At a regional *feis* (arts fair), notably the Aonach (great festival) at Tara in east central Ireland, participants vied at hopping, body percussion, and switching feet for the longest nonstop performance. In monasteries after 500 CE, including Kells Abbey, Bangor Abbey, and Kilroot Monastery, Christian illustrators of religious manuscripts pictured Irish step dance in illuminations.

From the late Middle Ages among Gaelic speakers in rural Ireland, Scotland, Wales, and Northumberland, England, the *cèilidh* (dance party) incorporated step dance in 4/4 or 2/2 meter. For a varied evening pleasing a variety of tastes, the energetic footwork paired with the polka, eightsome reel, jig, schottische, waltz, military two-step, hornpipe, and strathspey. In Scotland, street step dancers adapted their choreography into folk clogging, shepherd's dance, schottische, slip jig, clog rag, clog polka or waltz, Scots hard-shoe, and clog-hornpipe, all intended to draw audiences.

Early sixteenth-century Irish dance developed panache from transient dance instructors headquartered in Munster to spread gestures and figures of the hornpipe, reel, and jig among young boys. Over a six-week period throughout Northern Ireland, the expert taught "battering," the fundamental step dance, as a skill requiring stiff carriage and arms straight at the sides. Into the Tudor and Jacobean eras, the popular amusement earned the name of Irish or native dancing on the common.

Post-Renaissance Dance

In Argentina after 1600, dancers and drummers evolved the malambo, a Hispanic step dance mimicking gaucho postures and folkways. Whether in ring form or line dance, clomping steps from the Pampas emphasized wide strides, front and back slides, and rapid turns flashing tall black work boots. Crescendos to drumming, spur jingling, and swings of paired bolas accentuated both the romance and proficiency of an androcentric culture. Colonists to North America carried step dance to Kentucky, Tennessee, and the Carolinas along with the German *Schuhplattler* executed to fiddle melodies. In Mexico, the focus on footwork evolved into the zapateado.

The step dance acquired fame as Ireland's national dance, but met with censorship from conservative Methodists around 1750. To learn the steps, beginners concealed their lessons in barns and backcountry shanties. In limited space—on an abandoned door or in a goat-milking shed—dancers learned to direct their rhythms in the same spot. To increase idiophonics, they drove nails into shoes. As a showpiece for the Gaelic League, the fancy footwork flourished in London and Glasgow.

In the 1700s, the steps and rhythms traveled the globe with British sailors and migrated to Quebec, Ontario, the Canadian Maritimes, and down the Appalachian chain with Scots-Irish and French colonists and missionaries. In cramped cabins and on saloon tables, performers learned to make the most of small spaces. During transmission of Celtic step dance, basic moves acquired elevated steps, arms akimbo, rocks, leg swings, and heel clicks. The adapted version became known as Canada's national dance, which an instructor introduced in Philadelphia in 1789.

Afro Step Dance

Like West African juba, work hollers, and ring shout, step dance enabled slaves to retain tribal dance culture and traditional rhythms, the source of minstrel shows. In southern Africa, in the 1880s during Apartheid, step dance derived from Tembu and Zulu stick-fighting choreography as communication. Whether seated or standing in a line, South African miners at Durban and Johannesburg advanced life-enhancing chain rattling and gumboot stepping routines (also *isicathulo*) as a replacement for drumming and the source of a wordless loyalty oath. Overworked migrant crews shackled in gold mines turned the steps and gestures into nonviolent satire of the guards and staff who threatened them with beatings and firing. During tense harborage in men-only industrial hostels and barracks, laborers danced away their doldrums.

A popular genre in Franco-American New England and Canada, step dance infiltrated black fraternity socials at Howard University in Washington, D.C., and Lincoln University in Philadelphia. In 1911 and 1914, among members of Omega Psi Phi and by Ghanaian pledge Kwame Nkrumah of Phi Beta Sigma, step dancing evolved into a competitive showpiece for churches and charity and pledge drives. For variety, Nkrumah introduced the cane as a prop.

After World War II, black military veterans seeking college degrees introduced close order drills into fraternity stepping. Other originators extracted the idiosyncratic motions of R&B classic groups the Temptations and the Four Tops. In 2006, dance instructor Jessica Saul established the step arts, or "soul stepping," which she taught to after-school groups and Girl Scouts in California and Indiana.

See also circle dance; highland fling; hornpipe; jig; line dance; polka; reel; schottische; *Schuhplattler*; sword dance; waltz; zapateado.

Source: Foley, Catherine E. *Step Dancing in Ireland: Culture and History.* Farnham, UK: Ashgate, 2013.

STOMP DANCE

A healing tradition among Eastern Woodland First Peoples and tribes in the Mississippi Valley, the stomp dance (also jump or leading dance) links clans with a multitribal community that shares beliefs and values. The performance involves congregations on a square platform that faces the four directions. To encourage participation, the Muskogee-Creek arrive early to clear the ground of weeds and brush, which they pile around a pole.

Like medieval labyrinthine dance, the stomp dance figure coils around the sacred fire in counterclockwise direction, causing feathered hair adornments to bob and spin. Steps take their meter from the women's gourd or shell leg rattles, which the Creek and Seminole make from box turtles or terrapins. A procession of participants, children, and guests follows in synchronized toe-heel jog-trot either in single file or Choctaw fashion, in a chain with right arm entwined with the left arm of the person in front. The second figure initiates left-right hopping in place as participants face the fire and raise arms left-right to the beat.

Rules of the Dance

The stomp ceremony begins at the direction of an elder, who announces regulations for proper deportment and attitude. After 11:00 PM, male soloists take their turn presenting antiphonal call-and-response songs and chants of words and sounds for the men's chorus to comment on. Lyrics tell animal fables and express abstract thoughts on friendship and love. Tribes support each other by attending rituals at other stomp grounds and, in summer, offering prizes for the best percussionist.

During the ritual, women may speak only to other women. Pregnant and menstruating females take no part in activities. At nightfall around a sacred fire, dancers abstain from drugs, alcohol, and sleep through the all-night ritual and eat none of the barbecued meat served at gatherings. The reverent atmosphere and expectations of good health and prosperity from the creator derive from the mixing of cleansing medicine from roots and herbs.

Dance History

As a result of the forced removal of the Cherokee, Chickasaw, Choctaw, Creek, Delaware, Miami, Ottawa, Peoria, Seminole, Shawnee, Seneca-Cayuga, and Yuchi from their lands in the United States and Canada, tribes bore ceremonial customs to new locations in eastern Oklahoma. After their deracination from Florida in January 1851, the Seminole initiated the stomp dance by incorporating the traditional spiral into the green corn ritual. The Shawnee performed their dances at grounds outside Tulsa, where they celebrated July Fourth. In winter, schedulers moved the ceremony indoors.

More nations acclimated to new surroundings, but retained their cultural stomp dance, which took place amid a semicircle of shady brush arbors, the retreats for spiritual leaders. In 1867, the Miami revived their dance in Ottawa County, Oklahoma. The Cherokee decided to restore ancestral practices in 1889. In 1897, they established their stomp grounds at Collinsville while maintaining performance grounds at Big Cove, North Carolina.

Change was inevitable. The Caddo, Ottawa, Peoria, Miami, Quapaw, and Delaware extended their stomp dance to secular gatherings. By the 1900s, prairie and Plains Indians—Arapaho, Ponca, Omaha, Winnebago, Kickapoo, Sauk, Oglala, and Pawnee—had adopted the woodlands stomp dance or merged the ritual with the warrior dance. In the mid-twentieth century, Delaware-Shawnee-Peoria artist Ruthe Blalock Jones began painting native women in the stomp dance dresses.

See also chain dance; community dance; labyrinthine dance.

Source: "Oklahoma Historical Society," www.okhistory.org/publications. Accessed November 9, 2015.

STORY DANCE

Dance compounded with mime creates a powerful nonverbal narrative as gay and unrestrained as the Congo *bamboula* or as tense as the wrangle over a young maiden in the *moresca*, the traditional folk dance on the island of Korcula. Art historians value demonstrations by the Scots-Gaelic farmer impersonators in the wren's croft and Tamil Nadu presenters of ancient episodes and myths in the *oyil kummi* dance from southeastern India. More specific lifeways emerge from Vietnamese fishing tale mimes and the Cambodian *yike*, a dance narrative of Khmer rural life derived from Malay choreography.

Story dance retains scriptural, legendary, and historic elements, as found in the reclamation of Aztec heritage by the Concheros dancers of Mexico City and the itinerant White Roots of Peace company, a coterie of First Peoples formed by the Mohawk Nation in honor of the Iroquois League, a confederacy of six nations. From 1150, balladeers in the Faroe Islands, Lapland, and Iceland pantomimed the gothic lore of "Wolfemaiden," "Holger the Dane," and dramatic scenes from knighthood. Story dance conferred on refugees and stateless peoples both identity and healing, a necessity for Kurds, Hmong, and Roma. In the late 1800s, Danish and Swedish immigrants to Norway introduced the *songleik*, a dance dramatizing a recitation of rhymes.

Altered Lives

As a source of religious history, narrative dance re-created cause and effect of permanent change, as with the emergence of mestizo choreography in Chile, Uruguay, and Argentina. Malay Muslims at Johor reenacted the Islamic proselytizing of primitive local people with the *kuda kepang*. The drama depicted nine Javanese evangelists who carried scriptural narrative into the island interior. Mounted on horses made from rattan and hide, actors posing as Islamic missionaries fought their way through apostates to the sound of gongs and tambourines.

With a more sentimental tone, Malay soloists performed the *lilin*, a candle dance from Sumatra requiring a female performer to balance on her palms lighted candles in shallow dishes. The nighttime choreography dramatized a romantic legend of the grief of an abandoned maiden after her lover departed to seek his fortune. The loss of her engagement ring forced her to search into the night by two flickering lights, a delicate choreography requiring poise.

Current Story Dance

Narrative choreography remains a stable part of folk art. The Uyghur, an ethnic minority in Xinjiang, China, perform *mugam*, a lengthy program of song and dance. One variety, the "Twelve Mugam," consisting of three hundred tunes, takes some twenty hours to perform. To enhance narrative texture, dancers vary style and steps to various rhythms and poetic themes and content. Musicians accompany the presentation on string and reed instruments.

In 2005, UNESCO designated the Garifuna drum dance and *punta* hen-and-rooster mating ritual of St. Vincent, Dominica, Belize, Guatemala, and Punta Gorda, Honduras, a Global Treasure of Oral and Intangible Heritage marking holidays and wakes preceding reincarnation. The *achi* dance preserves from Mayan beginnings a four-act creation myth presented on January 25 for Saint Paul's Day. In like manner, the Nicaraguan palo de Mayo tinges a maypole festival with Afro-Caribbean agrarian lore. Choreography consists of female slap dance gestures around a fruit tree to the sounds of bongos, washboard, and percussive taps on a donkey jawbone. These honoraria to prehistoric myth display the wise choice of sixteenth-century Catholic missionaries to promote past memories as a foundation for conversion to Christianity.

See also Balkan dance; *bamboula*; Concheros dance; fan dance; *matachines*; maypole dance.

Source: Lee, Jonathan H. X., and Kathleen M. Nadeau. *Encyclopedia of Asian American Folklore and Folklife.* Santa Barbara, CA: ABC-Clio, 2011.

SUB-SAHARAN DANCE

In traditional activities devoid of male-female pairing, sub-Saharan dance stresses community solidarity and collective devotion to oral culture. Involvement expresses admiration for human capabilities through mastery of technique, for example, balancing objects on their heads. Infants begin imitating the musical rhythms of their mothers during fieldwork, cooking, and weaving. Nigerian natives set complex rhythms, typically polyrhythmic—two-against-three syncopated beats—for head, torso, hips, shoulders, and limbs. The Kalabari accentuate pelvic thrusts and sways; the Agbor alternate hip and chest articulation.

In contrast to torso rhythms, in southwestern Nigeria, the *agovu* in Yeve ritual propitiates gods to allow a human to enter the spiritual realm. In contrast, more dynamic spirituality in the *adavu* and the *sovu* presents the concentration of the spirit-possessed along with cries of blessedness. As an introit to worship, dancers follow the polyrhythmic beats of the *husago*, a common part of funerals. The *fofui*, an energizing figure, incorporates fast footwork as a boost to well-being.

During a recreational dance called *kpanlogo*, the Akan of Ghana gesture wildly with extremities to the beat of conga drums, while the Ga of Accra angle the arms from the chest and swing in unison to poses on alternating feet. While crouching and bending the back, dancers imitate coital movement. The innovative, explosive energy coordinates with spirited singing and skits depicting the actions of liberators. An individualized dance involves Ghanaians in a week-long tramp through the village. The complaints and grudges that burden their spirits motivate their exertions. Through nonstop gyrations, they release frustrations.

As a form of coming of age, the Anlo-Ewe and Fon embrace the *kinka* drum dance as a youthful defiance of adult control. They consecrate themselves and their deeds with the sacred *afa* and reserve the *agbekor* for mourning, oath-taking, or cultural activities exemplifying interdependence. In preparation for war, participants alternate allegro dancing with adagio segments containing ancient interludes and ritual songs. By allying full body turns with steps of the *takada* patterned to barrel drumming, female dancers assert empowerment. The dance mocks the warrior's reconnaissance, surprise ambush, hand-to-hand grappling, and stabs at enemies with horsetails on sticks.

In gendered style, Ewe maidens in southern Togo perform the *atsia*, a stylized exhibition of female comeliness, pride, and virtue and dramatization of women's views on village issues. In the 1950s, Togan women demanded their rights by drumming, wielding horsetails, and performing the takada. Their dignified dances became exemplars of equity, peace, and social unity. In Benin, women dance the *agahu*, a circle dance that guides them around stationary males who extend a bent knee for women to perch on.

Yoruban group activities tend to separate youth and adults by gender, thus introducing the young to the values and tribal regulations governing the distinctive gestures, movements, and stylized interaction of men and women. For a coronation, a new king conducts dancers on a procession through the village. Zambian males stress exertion and stamina; Lundan girls from the Congo learn the guile of womanhood by studying in secret the dances related to menarche.

Nigeria's Egun people observe social occasions with the agahu, a double ring dance that segregates men from women. Both perform percussive steps to beats of an oversized drum. In Angola, men blow whistles while women gyrate to the side with arms and bent legs. Angolan women rotate their hips and thighs to set in motion thin raffia skirts, an essential for expressing the exuberance of carnival season.

The Dogon of southern Mali perform a skipping, leaping *dama* dance for funerals of respected elders. Costumed in raffia wristlets, tunics, cowrie shell suspenders, and masks, the all-male troupe brandish sticks, whirl flywhisks, and nod their heads to activate ritual horns and totemic shapes, which they secure with their teeth. Drum and cowbell accompany solo dance, two-man skirmishes, and the antics of stilt walkers. The ritual ends with the placement of skull and bones in cliffside caverns.

Among the Baga of northern Guinea and Mali, until the Islamic-communist dictator Ahmed Sèkou Toutré ousted traditional religious dance in Guinea in 1960, the *kakilambè* blessed nature and praised an ample harvest and safe childbirth. Village dancers consulted a stilt-walking seer, who maneuvered around the dance space with his elongated legs and tall raffia mask and skirt. As village guardian, he predicted tribal health and full silos. As the tempo tripled, the seer spoke through the sacred mask to reassure participants of protection of a supreme power and good fortune to come. Dancers expressed their gladness, awe, and homage to the earth with humble gestures. At the dictator's death in 1984, the Baga reinstituted their annual tribute dance.

The Horn of Africa

Like the female troupes of Angola, Ethiopian dancers top long dresses with thin raffia skirts, a natural attire woven from palm fronds common to the tropical zone of East Africa. Their skipping steps align a short beat with the raised foot. For the *eskesta*, the waggling of shoulders accentuates the breasts. Men keep time to the beat with similar undulations of upper chest and arms and gestures reflecting a pastoral heritage.

The Somali favor clapping, beating of feet, drumming, and the buttocks-swaying night dances of women who wrap their hips in scarves. To direct attention to the motion, women and girls glance over the shoulder at the undulations and flirt with males in the audience. Beginning in 2006, Islamic courts established their authority by attempting to stifle musicians and dancers. On November 14, 2008, a Muslim militia invaded a folkloric dance, arrested thirty-two participants for the mixing of male and female dancers, and flogged them in front of hundreds of observers.

Despite protests from Muslims in the north, in Teerangore in southern Sudan along the Ugandan border, children and adults of the Lopit Latuka tribe hold the annual *nalam*, a rainmaking ritual. Warriors decked in ivory armbands, copper torques, and brass helmets topped with white and black ostrich plumes dust their heads and chests with clay and brandish long poles as symbols of authority. Women limit their dance finery to ostrich feathers and beads. All shuffle in a circular agrarian procession around the hereditary rainmaker. Before cultivating fields in spring and planting peanuts, cassava, sorghum, tobacco, hemp, sugarcane, coffee, cotton, peas, sesame, maize, and millet, participants form a circle and summon heavenly blessing and luck from the rainmaker to protect their produce from crop diseases and pests and their children from malnutrition.

Another annual Sudanese dance, the *ayomana* involves pleading for the gardens in August and September. After six days of bell ringing alternated with three days of silence, a crop magician appears to kill pests living in maturing millet and sorghum. Women dressed in cow or goat leather skirts and beads assemble at the entrance to the fields. Around two vertical poles, they dance a curse on weeds, diseases, and insects. Their crop blessings require two more performances of a monotonous drum dance in tight formation.

In October and November, Sudanese villagers perform the *etobok* warrior dance, which serves the double purpose of giving thanks for steady rains during planting. Before the December and January harvest, the *ekanga* ritual celebrates Latuka prosperity. The *alam* dance during the dry season of February involves the making of beer from flour before the afternoon festivities. A second alam in March honors the rainmaker and requests rain from the gods. The ritual ends with a new contract for the rainmaker's services.

Before a hunt, the Latuka village mayor arranges a dance on sacred ground. A similar ceremonial ritual drives away epidemics. When the mayor or rainmaker dies, villagers commemorate them with a two-day drumming and funereal *aburio tulo* dance around a grass and stick figure wrapped in skins. Attendants toss the stick figure into the bush and bury the human remains in the dance ground. After a year of dancing over the graves, villagers dig up the bones and honor the deceased with reburial in a sacred site.

Central Africa

The influence of Islamic modesty in Chad limits male dancers to long-sleeved caftans and head wraps, which conceal musculature. Along the border with the Central African Republic, women abandon chaste coverings to perform a circle dance of laid-back steps around males. Forest peoples decked in broad leaves vary from line to circle dance. In the south central region, the Bakala initiation dance involves feet close together and rhythmic bobbling of heads to drumming. West of the Ubangi River, the Babinga of the Central African Republic choose banana leaves for dance costumes swathing shoulders, neck, and head. Before an elephant hunt, a chosen soloist performs to bring luck to trackers.

To the south of Chad in the Cameroon, the Beti inject animism into their dances, which salute sorcery as a source of healing and wellness. In the highlands, the Bamenda top their heads with animal masks and imitate the movements of forest lions and birds. During weeklong ceremonies at the capital of Yaoundé, the Ewondo dance the *bi-kutsi*, a lyric performance evolved from Beti and Ewondo traditions. At social events, weddings, and funerals, performers mark the tempo of harp and calabash by stomping the ground. For the Wolof of Senegal, a similar wedding feast dance accompanies the phrases of the griot or storyteller. The neighboring Mandinka also dignify the chant of a traditional oral historian with drumming and dance to plucks on the twenty-one-string kora, a combination lute and harp.

In a stark departure from Ewondo technique, the Aizi of the Ivory Coast feature fleshy women in the *mapouka*, a suggestive bending of the waist and presentation of the posterior in wiggly motions in imitation of a traditional tribal dance. In the Congo, the soukous presents a less lascivious swaying of the buttocks, usually performed by females dancing alone. Among French-speaking nations, the choreography spread rapidly after a 1998 government ban of dance from television. Into the twenty-first century the appeal of plump buttocks weaned young African girls from the American craze for thinness and back to traditional rounded hips, which Africans respect as evidence of fertility.

For Rwandans and southern Ugandans, gendered social events separate women into the cow dance and males into the *intore* or heroes' dance. The latter, an intricate choreography performed with slender dance sticks, features costumes with waist-length raffia wigs, wrap skirts, and ankle bells. At festive performances, men measure their barefoot steps to drumming, clapping, and singing and leap with up-drawn feet to demonstrate the triumph of returning warriors. Other gestures imitate the motions of the cow, gazelle, and elephant.

On the boundary between Kenya and Uganda, the Bugisu dance and process for three days in preparation for the annual circumcision ritual of teen boys, who stand out from other villagers because of a smearing of yeast over the skin. The exertion and significant beer drinking sedate each boy and rid him of panic at the first sign of the priest's knife. In cold months, the Bakiga of southwestern Uganda and northeastern Rwanda use dance as a warm-up exercise before leaving for work in the frosty hill country. With jumping and stamping, they locate underground water supplies.

Throughout northern Tanzania and southern Kenya, the mood dances of the Maasai display the uniqueness of a nomadic life. For courtship, Maasai boys and girls form parallel lines and chant while directing pelvic thrusts at each other. Only one voice droning on a single tone accompanies the dance, typically in the style of call and response. For the Akamba of Kitui in south central Kenya, healing dance, initiation ritual, and pleasure dancing incorporate a steady beat on the goatskin top of the *kithembe* drum. The Mbeere of Mount Kenya add ankle bells and horns, while the Kikuyu prefer portable idiophones.

During the *eunoto*, a coming-of-age ritual, Maasai men execute high jumps to flaunt the physical height that sets the tribesmen apart from shorter Kenyans. For maturing males, the jump dance lifts thin-braided locks in the youthful period preceding adult head shaving and dyeing of the skull with red ocher. The height of leaps attests to competition among potential warriors, who align their limbs vertically and push upward from the balls of the feet. Admiring tones from spectators accompany an impressive leap. While mothers applaud their sons for strength and prowess, marriageable girls process around the circle to display seductive red costumes and woven beaded earrings that stretch the lobes.

Off the east coast in Madagascar, ancestral and worship dances call on forebears for inspiration. In the 1880s, the Malagasy of Sakalava and Merina invoked spirits through subtle pulsations to cure illness and relieve stress. A more elaborate production number in the midlands, the *hira gasy* compounded drumming with singing, chanting, whistling, clapping, horns, and reeds to accompany exhumation of the ancient dead and circumcision of young men.

Southern Africa

Across Southern Africa, heritage dance survives in the petroglyphs of the San, who relive ancestral imagery through mimicry. Namibian paintings picture hunter-gatherers dancing as early as 25,000 BCE. On the Comoros Islands, women dress in high-waisted fashions and clap or bang rhythm sticks on the offbeat while shaking their hips. By barely moving their feet and holding their head and shoulders still, they focus folk artistry on the lower torso, a style that young girls imitate. For the samba, Comoros men in solid-colored caftans and flattop caps are similarly sedate.

The Bantu so treasured dance that they questioned strangers with "what do you dance," an indication of tribe and religion. Rather than preach spirituality, the Bantu ritualized it. They set figures and musical phrasing to asymmetrical footwork and syncopated cross-beats. The djembe drum, a symbolic heartbeat, allied with double bells, rhythm sticks, and shakers to unify participants in clashing thumps emulating emotional unease, self-doubt, and impending difficulties. The skilled dancer attained fearlessness by drum dancing, an exercise in character building.

The Xhosa of southeastern South Africa perform a shaking dance to spinal ripples, whistles, rattles, and hand claps. Farther north, the tribes of Lesotho cultivate a glissade or gliding motion punctuated by jumps, kicks, twists, and stylized giant strides. On the South African border of Zimbabwe, the Venda recognize menarche with the *domba* (python dance), a close-packed row of unwed girls, each holding the elbow of the one in front. The winding initiation ritual fills the night with exertions that promise female fertility and rains to support crops.

Farther north, Zimbabwean dance coordinates steps with a variety of panpipes, open-ended drums, mouth bows, gourd leg rattles, and choreographies. The Korekore specialize in the ritual mbira, performed to the tinkly music of the thumb piano. Into Botswana from 1896, Ndebele and Shona warriors professed nationalism and diversionary strategies through the *mbende/jerusarema*, a defiance of colonialism through a fertility dance that outraged Christian missionaries.

To drums and rattles, female Zimbabweans observed the fertility ritual with yodeling, clapping, and whistling. Male troupes mimicked the tracking of the mole by kicking the right foot at the ground and imitating the hunter by surging outward from a crouch. Likewise in Mozambique, hunters cloaked in lion pelts and adorned with primate tails dance with long shields and spears.

For the Zulu and migratory Nguni of South Africa, exaggerated leg lifts and the stamping of feet to the music coordinate vigorous trampling of the ground and gestures with dance sticks. By hammering packed earth and stirring up dust, participants pay homage to the land, which coats their sweaty bodies. With uncontainable zeal, dancers act out spiritual oneness with nature.

See also circle dance; healing dance; hunting dance; line dance; music, folk dance; planting dance; warrior dance.

Source: Welsh, Karlamu. *World of Dance: African Dance.* New York: Infobase, 2010.

SUFI DANCE

In a culture not inclined toward couples dance or touching, Sufi spinning (or *dhamal*) demonstrates the extremes of quasi-metaphysical release from the body through counterclockwise dance-meditation. Called *tanoura* in Dubai and Egypt, ritual whirling performed by a *darawish* (or dervish), a male suppliant, activated vows to asceticism, poverty, devotion, and service. The rotations, like planets in the heavens, buoyed long paneled skirts, with each design representing an order of Sufis. Some performances were strenuous enough to cause stress fractures of the pelvis.

The Sufi brotherhoods dated to the 300s CE in Baghdad and ninth-century Persia (modern Iran). In opposition, conservatives at an urban mosque ordered the hanging of mystic dancer Mansur al-Hallaj on March 26, 922, for blasphemy after he declared himself "the truth." Derived from these Persian and Anatolian traditions, the *sema* (worship) dance of the Mevlevi mystics began in Konya, Anatolia, in the late thirteenth century to the reed flute, tympani, and cymbals.

According to legend, the Islamic scholar, lawgiver, and poet Mevlevi Jalaluddin Rumi of Afghanistan performed the first dance in the artisanal center of Konya, Turkey. He regulated his steps spontaneously to the hammering of goldsmiths. In the ring of the hammer, he heard the Muslim call to prayer, "There is no god but Allah." Free of dogma, Rumi's philosophy centered godhood in the natural cycles of living plants and animals, the harmony of the planets, and the throbs of his own heart.

The Whirling Sect

When Rumi died on December 17, 1273, his oldest son, Sultan Walad, formed a Sufi dance society of the founder's disciples. The Mevlevi (guided ones) lived in cloisters during training while praying and studying ethics, theology, and liturgical music. After fasting, Sufis took their places around the sheikh in a round room, removed their black cloaks from their white, shroud-like tunics, and placed a domed brown wool cylinder on their heads in preparation for prayerful whirling.

Each postulant extended both arms and posed on the ball of the left foot in constant contact with earth. With a restrained beginning, he directed whirls with the right foot while praising the prophet Muhammad. The initial rite preceded a procession of disciples around the sanctuary. By crossing wrists over the chest and controlling breathing, the darawish became a moving icon of purity and transcendental oneness with God.

The heavy skirts of Sufi dancers highlight the drama of trance dance. *Photographer Yigit Atakli, Jale Nejdet Erzen, erzen@metu.edu.tr, Middle East Technical University, Ankara, Turkey.*

Body language of the Sufi dancer turned posture into a sacramental emblem of the mortal stripped of earthly trappings and yearning for God. The disciple reached one palm to the heavens and pointed the other hand at the ground, a symbol of a living conduit conveying godly passion to humankind. As the tempo of mystic Turkish hymns increased from slow to rapid, the Sufi's unfocused glance introduced a trance state. Nuances from the cosmos filled the soul with silence, sanctity, and truth, which the dancer sealed with Koranic scripture and prayer. At the end of the rite, dancers kissed the floor and blessed spectators with God's peace.

Sufi Dance in History

Through advances in verse and hymnography, the idiorhythmic tradition thrived during nearly three years of training and discipline at a noncelibate monastery in Istanbul and through family instruction by father to son. From writings in Urdu, Bengali, and Persian, the sect spread to Syria, Lebanon, Palestine, Egypt, and the Balkans as well as England, France, Sweden, India, Morocco, Indonesia, Singapore, China, Kashmir, Australia, Senegal, Nigeria, Ethiopia, and South Africa. In 1413, darawishes attained prestige by their kinship with Sultan Mehmed I Celebi, head of the Ottoman Dynasty. Around 1550, Turks and Persians added more hymns to the Mevlevi dance repertoire.

Sufi dance reached Constantinople in the 1600s. Near the end of the Safavid Dynasty, in 1678, Muhammad Baqir Majlesi, an Iranian clergyman, initiated suppression of darawish dance for insufficient respect toward Islamic law. Turkish president Mustafa Kemal Ataturk's modernization laws declared the brotherhood pagan. He forced a twenty-nine-year halt to public Sufist dance from September 30, 1925, to 1954, when adherents commemorated Rumi's anniversary. Some dancers reclaimed the tradition by exiling themselves to Syria.

Dishonored by the Turkish government, Sufi ritual dance continued in the mid-twentieth century as a public tourist attraction rather than a private centering of the heart on remembrance of God. The Spanish compared the whirling to the atheistic worship of the golden calf described in Exodus 32:4. Undeterred, the disciples performed ecstatic dance in London in 1971 and visited France, the United States, and Canada. In 1990, a revival of Sufi spiritualism returned devotees to the sema ritual. Moroccan authorities restored Sufism to school curricula in 2003 as an alternative to militant Islam.

In March and May 2005, Islamic terrorists directed twenty-nine assaults on Sufis in Pakistan, killing 209 and wounding 560. In 2008, UNESCO named the Mevlevi whirling dance a Masterpiece of the Oral and Intangible Heritage of Humanity. More conservative activism in Egypt in May 2010 resulted in a ban on Sufi whirling, followed in September 2012 by the assassination of practitioners and the destruction of Sufi shrines in Libya and Russia and, in 2013, in Tunisia.

See also kathak; North African dance; Persian dance; processionals; worship dance.

Sources: Mojaddedi, Jawid. *Beyond Dogma: Rumi's Teachings on Friendship with God and Early Sufi Theories.* New York: Oxford University Press, 2012. Singh, Karan. "Istanbul: Dance of the Dervishes." *India International Centre Quarterly* 30, nos. 3–4 (Winter 2003–Spring 2004): 169–73.

SUN DANCE

For Plains Indians from Saskatchewan to Texas, purification and reconnection to identity and the Earth required participation in the sun dance. As the pinnacle of ceremonies, the Teton Sioux of Pierre, South Dakota, began the ritual in the first quarter of the 1700s at the end of buffalo hunts. Held on the banks of the Missouri River, the observance featured "Song of the Braves' Dance," "I Have Conquered Them," and "Black Face Paint He Grants Me," reflecting elements of ancestral warrior initiation.

As a welcome to the summer solstice between June 20 and 22 and as an antidote to incarceration at residential schools, from four to eight days, the Lakota, Ojibwa, Métis, Cree, Potawatomi, Algonquin, Mississauga, Inuit, Oneida, Cayuga, Tuscarora, Seneca, Iroquois-Mohawk, Arapaho, Piegan, Assiniboine, Ponca, Omaha, Shoshone, Kiowa, Blackfoot, Ute, Cheyenne, Crow, Arikara, Gros Ventre, Hidatsa, Mandan, and Pawnee dancers displayed traditional regalia, blew eagle whistles, and moved about a circle to reclaim native values and spirituality. Called the "sun-gazing dance," the choreography relied on self-sacrifice, piercing the flesh, fasting, body ornamentation, signing, and singing to restorative drumbeats to enable participants to merge self with nature.

For the classic sun dance, the supervising shaman chose the arena and appointed twelve men of pure heart and mind to locate an appropriate centerpiece. At the core of a warrior dance, men attacked a thirty-five-foot cottonwood as though killing an enemy. They raised a tepee over twelve poles that surrounded the central sun pole, a trunk with a forked top sanctified by placement of a buffalo skull. A medicine bundle anchored at the fork secured buffalo hide, tobacco, fetish dolls, and sacred eagle feathers, symbols of wisdom. The pole epitomized Earth's center and directed songs and prayers to heaven.

A firekeeper kindled the holy fire and tended it throughout the ritual. Chiefs and elders removed leggings and moccasins and danced around the lodge before directing their steps to the arena. A crier preceded the dancers, brandishing a five-foot pole adorned with beading and horsehair tufts. In the surrounding encampment, tribes gave gifts of food and clothing to the poor.

From the lodge and spectators under an arbor, entreaties arose to Wakan-Tanka, the primordial spirit worshipped by buffalo hunters. Males seeking a personal dream vision or healing from the Great Spirit pledged themselves to suffering. Adorned with wild sage (*Artemisia absinthium*) garlands around heads, wrists, and ankles, they attached rawhide tethers to the pole and the bone slivers piercing their chests. Each suppliant continually faced the sun, a sacrificial pose that Utes called *tagu-wuni* (standing thirsty).

The Steps

As sun dancers bent at the waist, blew wood or wing bone whistles, and double-stepped in time to the drum, they shuffled about the mystic hoop of life (perimeter). By leaning outward to tighten the tether, they envisioned themselves becoming one with the herd. Those who ripped free and collapsed in symbolic death received visions permeated with insights into self and wisdom to perpetuate the tribe. In late May 1880, the Ponca of Oklahoma danced to assuage their sorrow at loss of territory through the treaties of 1851 and 1865 and lopped off flesh to offer to the sun in exchange for life and health.

After the ordeal, participants rested from shock and pain on pallets of aromatic sage and recited to the priest the visions and prophecy that arose during the dance from the sacred grandfathers (ancestors). The scars on men's chests conferred permanent honor to courage, self-sacrifice, endurance, and integrity. The Kiowa added the howl of the red wolf as a salute to spiritual transformation and oneness with nature. After dancers made offerings of tobacco or blankets to priests, the tribes abandoned the sun dance lodge, leaving the holy space for nature to reclaim.

Because of the solidarity of intertribal sun dancers at the Kiowa ritual after 1844, following the Fetterman Massacre near Fort Phil Kearny, Wyoming, on December 6, 1866, the US government grew uneasy with native homage to the ordeal. Indian agents suppressed native dance as a means of Westernizing tribes. Hunkpapa Lakota chief Sitting Bull increased tensions after the Fort Laramie Treaty of 1868 by leading a sun dance in the Black Hills of South Dakota, a sacred space overrun by white gold prospectors. Following the 1882 sun dance held by the Teton and Yankton Sioux at the Red Cloud Agency, South Dakota, Secretary of the Interior Henry Moore Teller issued the Religious Crimes Code on April 10, 1883, outlawing the mutilation element and targeting the Kiowa ritual for suppression. Canada passed its own ban on April 19, 1884.

Across the Great Plains, enforcement of federal laws and Bureau of Indian Affairs policies relied on religious teachers, Indian agents, Royal Canadian Mounted Police, and the US cavalry. Typically, whites recoiled from the sun dancers' suffering without learning its religious significance. By 1887, the Kiowa held their last sun dance on reservation land in southwestern Oklahoma. Priests hid the fetish doll Tai-Me in 1888 and renounced the dance tradition in 1890.

The Modern Sun Dance

Because the sacrificial elements of the sun dance appeared to mock Jesus' crucifixion, Jesuit and Episcopalian missionaries persuaded Christianized Indians to chop down totems and burn regalia, drums, and sacred fetishes in a profound cultural genocide. Nonetheless, Black Elk, a Lakota holy man at the Pine Ridge Reservation in southwestern South Dakota, continued his involvement with the sun dance in 1890 in defiance of white persecutors. At Fort Washakie, Wyoming, the Shoshone retrieved the sun dance from ignominy. In 1911 at Fort Yates, South Dakota, on the Standing Rock Reservation, viewers recorded thirty-three of the Teton and Yankton Sioux sun ritual songs.

Spurious sun dancing replaced authentic ancestral observances. In March 1916, the Seminole of West Palm Beach, Florida, initiated a three-day commercial sun dance festival as a tourist attraction. At the Wind River Reservation in Wyoming, the Southern Arapaho performed an altered ritual for seven days in 1923 by removing flesh piercing from the performance. After the Lakota, Cheyenne, and Shoshone took the solemnities underground in 1934 through night dances, some sun dancers obscured the ritual as part of Fourth of July observances. To cultivate divine favor, the Sioux revived the ceremony in 1938. At the Crow Reservation in Pryor, Montana, holy men renewed the cosmic dance in 1941.

In 1950, the Canadian Cree, Sioux, Blackfoot, and Ojibwa revived the healing spectacle to treat trauma, materialism, despair, anxiety, juvenile delinquency, and substance abuse among First Nations. A Crow ceremony in 1955 propitiated the Great Spirit to end the Korean War and cleanse veterans of post-traumatic stress. To preserve the tradition from corruption or loss, the Kainai of southern Alberta filmed the ritual in *Circle of the Sun* (1960), a Boards of Canada documentary featuring narration by Pete Standing Alone.

The Canadian documentary coincided with a resurgence of native pride during the American Indian Movement, founded in Minneapolis in July 1968. In June 1971, Wallace Black Elk began mustering tribes to Wounded Knee, South Dakota, for a shared sun dance featuring native activists John Lame Deer and Leonard Crow Dog. The American Indian Religious Freedom Act of 1978 rescinded the ban, freeing the Blackfoot to perform the sun dance once more at Badger-Two, Montana.

Through regalia, body paint, and circle movements, the sun dance maintains its plea for peace, especially following the Vietnam War, Desert Storm, and the Afghan War. Extending from sunset to sunset, the communal dance relieves fears of death and the loss of First Nations' heritage. As an affirmation of clan unity, along the periphery of the arena, family members support each seeker by drumming and dancing in place. On March 9, 2003, Chief Arvol Looking Horse announced the Lakota closure of the sun dance to outsiders.

See also sacrificial dance.

Sources: Crawford, Suzanne J. *American Indian Religious Traditions.* Santa Barbara, CA: ABC-Clio, 2005. Densmore, Frances, ed. "Songs of the Sioux." Library of Congress (1951). Accessed July 8, 2015. www.loc.gov/folklife/LP/AFSL23Sioux.pdf.

SWORD DANCE

Whether solo or in groups, weapons dance dramas in the Middle East, China, France, England, Spain, Germany, Italy, Austria, Switzerland, Czechoslovakia, Finland, and Sweden elevated the vigorous warrior to defender of nations and security guard of the gods. Exaltation was the purpose of the Greatham sword dance from Durham, England, performed in Westminster Abbey on June 2, 1953, at the coronation of Elizabeth II. The figures accentuated her role as symbolic defender of the faith and monarch of the British people.

Dances derived significance and sobriety from ancient magical ceremonies allegorizing the fight of good over evil, such as the Egyptian *tahtiyb* (stick fight) from 2500 BCE, the pagan goat sacrifice at Yorkshire, and the blackface sword dance of the coconut performers in Bacup, England. In the Iron Age after 1200 BCE, Scots highlanders evolved a sword ritual contemporaneous with Celtic ring dance, jigs, and step dance, the basis of reels. For maximum rakishness, each Scot twirled his brat (cloak) above kilt, sash, vest, and lace-up ghillies. A parallel to Scots reverence for the sword began in 660 CE in Korea with the *geommu*, a deft performance of footwork and blade slashes to flute and drum music.

In contrast to the romanticized dance figure, athletic Arab males in Iran eschewed exhibitionism in favor of physical agility, intricacy, and flexibility. Like the *jian wu* (military training exercise) in Chinese opera, Arab dancers performed mock duels and skirmishes with *shamshir* (sword dance), a form of martial arts preparation. A hopping, gesturing display of sword and shield, the choreography pitted two males in a semblance of swordplay and fancy footwork to drum and flute. In Tunisia, a militia pageant synchronized clashing saber gestures with unison steps. Turks at Bursa on the Sea of Marmora commemorated Ottoman might with clashing blades and choreographed body language.

Dance Motivations

Specifics of sword dances revealed the use of a short or long sword and its symbolism, for example, the rivalry over a female in the Serbian and Montenegran *rugovu*, stick dancing among American slaves from Angola and the Congo, and the fertility rite of the Romanian *calus*, an acrobatic performance of a tribal brotherhood of horsemen. *Morisca* (also *moreska*) dancers on the island of Korcula dramatized the centuries-old struggle between Christians and Muslims. Each July 29 on the Feast of Saint Theodore the Martyr, dancers backed up a drama depicting two kings and the courtship of a veiled maiden. The tense conflict launched the maiden's father into a male-dominated competition for possession of a young female who had no voice in settling her future, a common tragic theme in medieval literature and stagecraft.

The control of trade guilds in the Middle Ages predisposed feudal communities to economic unions, as with the cutlers of Nuremberg in 1350. Among burghers and artisans, guilds superintended occupational dance, an enterprising method of displaying skills and competencies. To boost sales, in Norway and Sweden, metalworkers organized a theatrical sword dance illustrating parts of the armoring process rather than the maneuvering of weapons in combat.

Polished Folk Arts

Into the Renaissance in northern Europe, salutes to blades and preparedness perpetuated sword spectacle in Germany, the Orkneys and Shetlands, Hebrides, Denmark, and Saxony. At Ulm northwest of Munich in 1551, an athletic sword spectacle encircled a pool and concluded with one performer climbing to the tip of a blade. Olaus Magnus, author of *De gentibus septentrionalibus* (On Northern Peoples, 1555), described a Shrovetide ritual that gradually increased danger, from sheathed to unsheathed blades and steps that increased from a walk to frantic treads.

In Segovia on November 14, 1570, a folk troupe performed the Burgos sword dance for the wedding of Anne of Austria to Philip II of Spain. At Tarragona, a regional sword dance in 1693 presented steps now lost to history. In the Carpathian Mountains in Austria and Slovakia, the bending of hazel limbs into arcs preceded the replacement of real blades with garlands, a natural progression to spare dancers a slip of honed edges.

Off the west coast of Shetland, the sword dance from the island of Papa Stour introduced a period religious theme in musical spectacle. Seven men representing national Christian champions—St. Andrew of Scotland, St. George of England, St. David of Wales, St. Patrick of Ireland, St. Denis of France, St. James of Spain, and St. Anthony of Italy—mastered intricate footwork in rings and arches. With St. Andrew setting the pace to bagpipes, the men vaulted, crossed blades, and paired up back to back. While holding the hilt in the right hand and the point of the sword to the left, each man raised a blade into a seven-point figure. A comic version of British sword dances survived in Yorkshire at Bellerby, where men armed with wood swords interacted with jesters bearing broom handles, the epitome of the antiheroic.

See also circle dance; highland fling; jig; martial dance; *matachines*; reel; *rigaudon*; warrior dance.

Sources: Barr, Amelia E. "Characteristic Dances of the World." *Lippincott's Magazine* 27, no. 4 (April 1881): 330–41. Park, Ga Young. "Androgyny of Sword Dance Costumes in the Joseon Dynasty." *International Journal of Human Ecology* 15, no. 1 (2014): 23–31.

· 𝒯 ·

TANGO

A deft, elegant duet to torchy music, the tango followed the waltz and polka as the craze of the late 1800s–early 1900s. Steps to the *baile con corte* (dance with a rest) originated in the working-class brothels, slaughterhouse districts, and barrios of Buenos Aires, Argentina. The choreography visualized a kinetic trope of the poverty and social ills besetting underprivileged blacks and mestizos. Sensuous contact between torsos and suggestive intermingling of legs derived from the seventeenth-century Afro-Cuban habanera and the *candombe* procession in blackface to barrel drumming on St. John's Eve each June 23 in Argentina.

Steeped in the folk rhythms of enslaved Yoruba, Fon, Dahomey, Kongo, and Hausa, the tango embellished the syncopated Afro-Caribbean *milonga*, a relaxed rural folk choreography in 2/4 time performed as a duet in closed or open position. In bars, knife-wielding males acted out hand-to-hand fighting with a balletic two-man tango to the music a busker cranked out on the organite (barrel organ). In seedy port dives, prostitutes offered to partner clients in the disreputable dance—a signifier of the outcast, dead-end culture of harbor slums.

The Male Partner

The nostalgic couples tango set a distinctly gendered pattern of the male in cocked hat navigating the female across the floor like a tomcat stalking a wren. With raised left arm, he improvised stops, hesitations, and body language exuding passion and ulterior designs. The stylized embrace and gliding promenade drew tourists to Argentine red-light districts and backstreet dance clubs. Facets added to the Argentine tango in the 1860s by Italian, Spanish, British, Russian, and Polish immigrants gave form to the cha-cha and the mambo.

At first repulsed by the intimacy of the male thigh lowered for the woman to sit or kneel on, the upper class boycotted the tango for its "negroid origin." The privileged class eventually shushed the racist labeling by claiming that Theban tomb relics and Greek sculptures in the British Museum pictured girls executing tango steps. Respectable people adopted the torrid posturing, which spread to elite socials in Montevideo and Rio de la Plata, Uruguay. Art historians compared the graceful steps to figures of the minuet.

311

In 1886, the importation of the German accordion altered tango melodies with gentler chording than that of the guitar. Within three years, the smoldering dance marked street gatherings in Tampa, Florida, and Tenerife, Canary Islands. By 1896, the tango Andalus had replaced the *sevillanas*, an outgrowth of flamenco in Seville, Cádiz, and Málaga. From April to August 1898, men fighting the Spanish-American War gravitated to the habanera del cafe, a variation popular with barmaids in the close but easy atmosphere of Caribbean nightspots and Honduran dance halls.

The Tango Fad

Ignited in the port of Marseilles by Argentine sailors in 1907, tangomania swept Montmartre five years later as the first improvisational dance in Paris, where innovators created more than one hundred romantic and acrobatic figures. By summer 1912, the dance involved bold Frenchmen and their dates in the patrician circles of the Grands Boulevards and the Avenue de l'Opéra. In October 1912, Londoners indulged in a sedate form of tango at tea dances. In Spain, journalists credited the Roma with injecting titillation, pursuit, and surrender into the fad dance at cafes and hotels.

The questionable taste of intimate partnering in a hip-centered closed position aroused scandal and condemnation among conservative churchgoers. While fans embraced the tango in Budapest and São Paulo, Brazil, prohibitions among the military hierarchy of Kaiser Wilhelm II and at the court of Victor Emmanuel III in Italy denied new partners a chance to learn the steps. In April 1913, Mayor William Jay Gaynor of New York City launched an investigation into tango cabarets, liquor consumption, and the debauchery of young girls.

More enquiries of after-hours immorality involved Chicago, Cleveland, and Panama. In London, Queen Mary, consort of George V, opposed intimate dance. On January 16, 1914, a formal censure from the antimodernist pope Pius X declared the tango damaging to the soul. His charge of a "new paganism" included a request that dancers reclaim the energetic *furlana*, a flirtatious folk dance from northeastern Italy. A papal ban on the tango in Rome and all Protestant countries preceded a condemnation six days later from Cardinal Aristide Cavallari, the patriarch of Venice, who shamed dancers for "moral turpitude."

Proper Tango

The outcry over the tango caused European and North American dance masters to formulate standards for partner positions and steps. The intoxicating choreography with its dramatic head snaps continued to thrive in London, Berlin, and New York, filling dance venues until the outbreak of World War I. At British tango teas, the long strides of female dancers required a more alluring skirt design, a replacement of the Victorian hoop with a tulip or pencil skirt slit to the thigh to reveal rayon stockings clocked with geometric and floral designs.

By the Golden Age of Argentina in the 1930s, studios acclaimed the flamboyant tango a social and competitive dance surpassing the melodrama and sizzle of the *pasodoble*. Song lyrics boasted the verve of the swarthy gaucho and his captivating rock step, leg extensions, and quick changes of rhythm. Feature films—Al Pacino's poignant dance-floor philosophy in *The Scent of a Woman* (1992); *Assassination Tango* (2002), depicting Robert Duvall in a comic underworld role; the cell block tango in *Chicago* (2002); and a seductive Antonio Banderas partnering Catherine Zeta-Jones in *The Mask of Zorro* (1998) and as a dance teacher in *Take the Lead* (2006)—glamorized the male exhibitionism begun by the stevedores of Buenos Aires. Argentineans saluted the more stylish ballroom tango with a national day each December 11. On April 20, 2013, Pope Francis I, an Argentinean by birth, enjoyed an Italian-Argentine festival that Rome's Mayor Gianni Alemanno held in the Piazza del Popolo to celebrate the tango.

   See also cakewalk; film, folk dance in; *furlana*; polka; waltz.

   Sources: Denniston, Christine. "The Hidden History of Tango." *History of Tango.* Accessed October 9, 2015. www.history-of-tango.com. Kinney, Troy, and Margaret West Kinney. *The Dance: Its Place in Art and Life.* New York: Frederick A. Stokes Company, 1914.

TANKO BUSHI

A simple Japanese work song to a stolid melody in 2/2 meter, the *tanko bushi* (coal miners' song) gained fame as the most popular *bon odori* (ancestral) song recognizing the perseverance of miners and a major pillar of energy and the national economy. Evolved in the Chikuho region, the folk choreography features female line dancers in a regular pattern of two steps to the right, two to the left, and one rock step forward in a counterclockwise ring. Toe and heel taps and quick–quick–slow claps complement bent backs, shaded eyes, and arm flexing.

   The folk dance imitates the underground toil of digging by lantern light, tossing rock over the shoulders, and scooping and sieving lump coal from black dust. The day's tasks end with pushing the mining cart, wiping sweat, and loading coal in sacks for the overseer, a universal working-class theme similar in tone to medieval guild processions. Since composition of the dialect lyrics by Ono Hoko in 1910, the beginner's dance drama saluted two forty-five-meter smokestacks of the Miike Coal Mine in Ibaraga Prefecture northeast of Tokyo in Kyushu. From heightened productivity, output rose from 1.3 million tons in 1885 to 40 million tons during World War II, when Miike yielded 12 percent of the nation's total.

Dance Drama

To the singing and swaying of miners and the countermelody of nonsense syllables, the narrative reflects the separation anxiety of the sweetheart of a female miner who wants to join her in the crew's barracks. Added stanzas contrast labor to life's pleasures and invite the lonely boyfriend to leave the mountains and visit the mine. Folk troupes at Seoul, Tokyo, Honolulu, Sydney, Los Angeles, Seattle, Sacramento, and other Asian enclaves scheduled the dance at the mid-August O-Bon, a Buddhist Festival of Souls, a feast for the dead at which the faithful anticipate reunion with deceased family members. The coal miners' lanterns symbolically lit the path for spirits to follow back to Earth.

In May 1942, the internment of 120,000 Japanese-Americans preceded performances of the tanko bushi at Manzanar and nine other camps—Gila River, Topaz, Amache, Heart Mountain, Jerome, Minidoka, Poston, Rohwer, and Tule Lake—in California, Arizona, North Dakota, Idaho, Texas, New Mexico, and Montana. Following World War II, American occupation forces scheduled the folk dance as a gesture of good will. Mine foremen revived the ballad and lock steps to encourage laborer cooperation and a rise in coal removal. After the influx of issei (first-generation) Japanese immigrants to North American, the choreography developed into a global folk performance in the 1950s honoring inmate resilience. During the Cold War, politicians stressed the value of ethnic cooperation in the iconic dance for the sake of peace.

Holiday Dance

For people of Japanese extraction, the tanko bushi flourished at memorial services, bon dances, and annual pilgrimages to the internment camps and as a training exercise for girls learning *odori* technique. Performers wielded oilpaper fans as their shovels. For the energetic leg bends, clapping, and crossed arms, the tanko bushi, like the fisherman's *soran bushi*, the comic unemployed worker's *yatton bushi*, and the iron scooper's *yasugi bushi*, became a curriculum staple of elementary school physical education classes and mixed groups at Shin Buddhist temples and multiethnic street festivals.

As a finale, the provincial tanko bushi sympathizes with the subterranean female worker, who welcomes a glimpse of the moon upon her emergence from the mine pit. In 2008, a festival in Tagawa, Fukuoka, commemorated the centennial of the Miike mine with presentations of the mime dance. Reset to the tune of "Guantanamera," the tanko bushi remains part of Japanese-American festivals in Mexico, the Caribbean, Canada, and the United States, notably the 125th anniversary of Japantown in San Jose, California, and 2015 reunion of Terminal Island residents in Los Angeles Harbor.

See also circle dance; line dance; *odori*.

Sources: Sweeting, Terry, Peter Werner, Lori H. Williams, and Alyssa Crump. "Tanko Bushi: Designing a Japanese-American Dance Experience." *Journal of Physical Education, Recreation & Dance* 83, no. 1 (2012): 15–31. "Tanko-Bushi Inspiration Honored." *Japan Times*, November 8, 2008.

TARANTELLA

A family of fast tambourine jigs common to Calabria, Abruzzo, and Apulia in central and southern Italy, the tarantella combines pathologic choreography with exorcism. Derived from the ecstatic dance of female religious devotees in the ancient Mediterranean, the peasant phenomenon began during wolf spider bite hysteria in Apulia on the Ionian Gulf at Taranto around 1100 BCE, when dancers called the pirouettes and skips the *pizzica pizzica* (bite bite). The disease manifested its control over victims stereotyped as criminal, ignorant, and neurotic types or in love-obsessed females seeking to fascinate potential lovers.

Each summer, the onset of tarantism produced stupefaction, limb contortions, blackened limbs and face, and profuse sweating. Complacency progressed into vomiting, quaking, weeping, swooning, and making animal cries. Finally, rapid dancing to drum, whistle, and flute was performed in 6/8 meter. The Gothic spectacle of swaying, knee walking, bounding, and whirling to tarantella music migrated to Sicily, Sardinia, Albania, the Troad of northeastern Turkey, Spain, Germany, Persia, Ethiopia, and Argentina.

Therapies

Dancers skipped and leaped in lines or clockwise in concentric circles and lifted joined hands in unison. Victims seized on red handkerchiefs as a comfort to the convulsions and extreme muscular spasms. Spectators dressed in bright clothing, wrapped themselves in vines, and joined the seductive crossover and heel-and-toe steps as though in fun. Charlatans used annual recurrences as justification for seeking charitable donations to pay musicians and dancers. An influx of musicians ensured the annual summer outbreak of tarantism.

Without music as an antidote, tarantism threatened exhaustion, madness, suicide, or death, a possibility noted by eleventh-century physician Gariopontus of Salerno and late medieval poison authority Santes de Ardoynis of Venice. Out of fear for the vulnerable, mothers hummed the jouncy melodies while dancing with their babies. Doctors treated the distraught with blistering, cupping, cautery, purging, hydrotherapy, and bleeding. Musicians clapped their tambourines and adjusted rhythms to the patient's need.

The Tarantella in History

In the finale to the harum-scarum plots of the commedia dell'arte, transalpine tarantella influenced a group farandole. Into the late 1400s, Italian tarantellas emulated knot garden mazes, Albanian sword dances, and religious labyrinth liturgy featuring geometric repetitions of advance-pause-turn-turn again. An outbreak of mass hysteria begun in the 1400s terrorized Italians for three centuries with agitation and nameless terrors, especially at Galatina in the southeastern tip of Italy.

The medical wisdom of the late Middle Ages recommended marathon dancing and shrieks as therapeutic relief from the obsession. On the Feast of Saints Peter and Paul each June 29, women attired themselves as St. Paul's brides for the exorcism. The dancing plague reached new heights in the 1600s. In the 1700s, the dance received a positive comparison to the Spanish fandango for its vivacity and speech. In 1817, Italian academician Francesco Cancellieri summarized the range of symptoms manifested by the anomaly. Subsequent descriptions of the tarantella described the dancing victims as all females afflicted with psychosomatic stress and anxiety.

Purely as a folk art, the tarantella delighted English dancers in 1844. Distinctive group patterns and dorsal foot flexion injected into theatrical choreography the energy and symbolism of the tarantella. The dance figured in Norwegian playwright Henrik Ibsen's ominous dance in *Hedda Gabler* (1890) and Russian composer Peter Ilyich

Tchaikovsky's classic ballet *The Nutcracker* (1892). To pipes, trumpets, fiddles, and concertinas, the tarantella flourished in the mid–1900s in Sicily, Capri, and Sorrento.

See also circle dance; fandango; farandole; labyrinthine dance; line dance; sword dance.

Source: Loudon, Rebecca. *Tarantella.* Edmonds, WA: Ravenna Press, 2004.

TECHNIQUE

Dance mastery requires coordination of disparate elements, such as the muscle memory essential to the manipulation of two metal rods in the elastic *danza de las tijiras* (scissors dance) of the Peruvian Quechua and in reverse steps of medieval Walpurgis Night celebrants moving back to back. In solo performance, the coordination of footwork in rapid order determines the expertise of the West African juba and hornpipe performer and the clogger, whose wood or metal-edged shoes generate the music of the dance. Only the best clogger can maintain an uninterrupted rhythm. Similarly, the Scots soloist leaping and raising an arm in a highland fling mimics the stag's capers and the curved antlers overhead. The best technique establishes accuracy and timing of the precise Celtic reel.

From the Middle Ages, the tarantella of southern Italy simulated exorcism of frenzies and death throes caused by the bite of the wolf spider. Dancers maintained a fierce psychosomatic expulsion of pain and venom by head jerks and finger thrusts to characteristic tarantella music. Unlike secular ring and line dance, melodramatic figures and motions followed the physical manifestations of suffering and convulsion and acted out a war against a lethal poison. The finale plunged the dancer/patient into exhaustion and a collapse followed by lethargy and sleep until an annual reemergence of the dance mania revived the folk art phenomenon.

Renaissance Choreography

French arts writer Thoinot Arbeau's manual *Orchésographie* (1589) recorded the techniques of Renaissance dance, including the allemande, a smooth figure highlighted by elided, side-to-side steps. For a unique version, he outlined the *branle du chandelier* (torch dance), for which men carried lighted candles as a dramatic facet of couples dancing. Such annotated textbook commentary continued in the nineteenth century with the dance notebooks of Frenchman Arthur Michel St. Léon, who observed styles and innovations of the Württemberg court in southern Germany. More valuable to visual study, the Flemish presentations of the branle and farandole in the paintings of Pieter Brueghel the Elder and his son, Pieter Brueghel the Younger, offer studied views of body language and individualized footwork by dancers enjoying outdoor folk fairs.

For the *tirabol* of Catalonia, throughout a five-day fiesta, performers of counterclockwise steps to the beat of a drum balanced the bobble of papier-mâché heads of angels, demons, giants, Turks, and crusaders. For the observance of Corpus Christi Day each May 26, the figureheads, some over a century old, preserved southeastern Spanish artistry and holiday significance. In the late 1700s, the depiction of David and Goliath required skill in stilt dancing for the oversized Philistine warrior.

Visual Characteristics

In the wake of a disastrous exile in 1755, Acadians from Nova Scotia clung to the distinctions of Franco-American folk style, which added panache to the standard quadrille or contradance. In Quebec, the Caribbean, southeastern Texas, and the delta region of Louisiana, a characteristic hip waggle and shoulder roll in the Cajun waltz identified its origins. The Canadian traits marked other cultural genres, including the Cajun jig and jitterbug and the quadrille, a four- or eight-person dance drama depicting wooing. Unlike Western square dance, Franco-American performers memorized a five-stage courtship figure and presented the dance with theatrical touches and facial expressions.

As the tango developed from folk rhythms adopted from enslaved Yoruba, Fon, Dahomey, Kongo, and Hausa into an aesthetically appealing Argentine fad, by the 1800s, the display of male navigation of the female partner enhanced the seductive appeal. Without standardized patterns to emulate, the man communicated through a firm grip on the woman's midsection. The typical finale—the female posed on his raised knee—demanded full partner control concealed by grace and a commanding posture.

See also allemande; art, folk dance in; *branle*; Cajun dance; clogging; contradance; farandole; highland fling; hornpipe; juba; partnering; polka; quadrille; square dance; tarantella; tango; Walpurgis dance.

Source: McCutchen, Brenda Pugh. *Teaching Dance as Art in Education*. Champaign, IL: Human Kinetics, 2006.

TERMINOLOGY

Folk dance terminology incorporates age-old peasant descriptors as well as precise terms from professional music and ballet, for example, the chain hold of the farandole and the *ballon* (dip or bounce) of the polonaise. Kinetics typify physical involvement of core muscles, as with the athletic exuberance of the *hopak*, the formal step-step-thrust of the three-beat Eastern European polonaise, the svelte gestures of the Hawaiian hula and Japanese *odori*, and the fluidity of the in-step for the sixteenth-century *tombé* or the sinking step of the secular Hispano-Panamanian sarabande. Meter quantifies the speed by which patterns take shape, as with the medium beat of the African American *calenda* and the rapid exhibitionism of the West African juba, a slave-era showpiece of thigh and torso pats at Congo Square in nineteenth-century New Orleans.

Terms may particularize sounds, as with the strophe or metered verse of Greek theatrical dance and the call and response of South African step dance and Maasai mood dances among bounding Kenyan and Tanzanian nomads. For Middle Eastern performers, ululations, or tongue flutters, of women enhance drumming and the excitement of the belly dance, which emanates from jingling jewelry and midriff undulations. Polyphonic music grounds choreography of sung or orchestrated harmony, a feature of the Polish mazurka.

Specific dance figures acquire metaphoric names for coordinated, flexible combinations, as with the knots of labyrinthine Cretan dance, the glissades of the courtly pavane, the pas de deux of the mazurka in closed position, and swaying cross-front-cross-back (grapevine step) that Yemenite Jews added to the *mayim mayim* (water water), a twentieth-century Israeli celebration of a well in the desert. For stagy performances, the trickster identifies a character who deceives or ridicules other figures, as with the earnest performers of Pueblo rain ceremonies and the portrayer of Satan in Spanish Corpus Christi Day *matachines* processions each May 26. Other types of allegorical or representational dance portray propitiation or summoning of divinities, the purpose of Celtic grain planting ceremonies and Bechuana harvesting rituals in South Africa.

Choreographic categories identify by gesture and step different genres of folk dance, for example, the European dance of death, or *Totentanz*, that characterized terrors of imminent death and damnation from the plague during the fourteenth-century Black Death. Similarly, the tarantella and carmagnole fit the definition of death dance mania brought on by social chaos and economic deprivation. In northern Africa, the Tuareg trance rhythm of the Tuareg Kel Tagelmousse (blue people) presses individuals toward cosmic peace and a union with nature.

From the late 1500s, gendered dance further categorized choreography by the placement of men, women, and mixed partners in set figures, as with the man flanked by two females in the Russian troika of the early 1800s, the male-only Sufi whirling in central Turkey, and the intimate contact of torsos for the Viennese waltz, an outgrowth of the Tyrolean *Ländler*. Gendering accounts for the limitation of martial arts in the stick dance to young Japanese males and the building of camaraderie and attack strategy in the *hakka* warrior rituals of New Zealand. The female circle and line dances that solace wives and sweethearts initiate the choreographed welcome of fishers, hunters, and victorious soldiers during war, particularly Scots infantrymen who trod the first highland fling atop spiked shields.

Integral to gendered dance terms, indications of open, semi-open, and closed position name the amount of physical contact between performers. The precise terms standardize the expectations of dancers during formal instruction. Amerindian ritual of the Great Lakes typically separates men and women of the Cree and Sioux into solos executed in rings to honor bear and buffalo hunts. For powwows, fancy dancing features the soloist as a star performer, including the female presenter of the shawl dance. In contrast to strict configurations, zydeco dancers alternate clasps of one or both hands and pull partners into body contact for closed figures.

Choreographic terms identify specific segments of dance figures, particularly the coda and finale. A coda alters the final measures to indicate the falling action of dance drama, as with the indoctrination of young males into the thrumming, singing brotherhood of Australian aborigines, the coy affectations of Danish flirtation dances, and the stylized mime of a medieval Gallic planting dance executed in a ring by Franco-American children. A finale differs from a coda by emphasizing a grand conclusion, for instance, the exorcism of evil from a child with the Thai candle dance. Essentials of the theatrical coda range from the facial mobility and theatrical disappearance of the Inuit shaman down a trapdoor of the dance house following a healing ritual to the maypole figure at the end of the Hispanic *matachines* on Christmas Eve. For most European dances and the Japanese *odori*, a polite reverence or bow extends thanks to spectators.

See also farandole; finales; healing dance; highland fling; juba; *matachines*; mime; *odori*; polonaise; sarabande; shamanic dance; shawl dance; step dance; *Totentanz*; zydeco.

Source: McCutchen, Brenda Pugh. *Teaching Dance as Art in Education*. Champaign, IL: Human Kinetics, 2006.

THAI DANCE

Folk dance in Thailand incorporates a disparity of styles, from country circle types to ritual boxing matches and the rigid masked performances for royal courts. Influences on instrumentation and costuming from Burma and the Cambodian Khmer preceded the importation of Indian philosophy and religion. To the north, a test of agility involves dancers in leaping between bamboo poles beaten in time to the music. To the northeast, animists exorcise evil from children with a candle dance.

As early as 1431, Siam's ancestral worship involved stylized reverence of saints and former monarchs drawn from the sermons of monks. Based on Hindu traditions from India and presented in dance forms preserved from the Ayutthayan kingdom (1351–1767) in the southwest, episodes drew on the three-thousand-page Ramakien, the Siamese national epic adapted from the Indian Ramayana (300 BCE). Given in rural fields or open-air stages with bamboo benches, segments featured the Thai version of the god Shiva and Hanuman, a flying monkey. However, the downfall of Ayutthaya to the Burmese army in April 1767 resulted in the murder of members of folk troupes and the destruction of historic evidence of age-old inaugural dance and song.

Dancing for the King

Beginning with Rama I after 1782, Siam's monarchs legitimized their rule by importing Indian concepts of kingship to fill the cultural void and dignify the Siamese state. Choreographers recovered much of the legendary cycles from the memories of elders and engravings at the Angkor temple of masked soldier dancers. Court mime involved armed warriors in a rough, virile *khon* (royal) dance drama, which the treasury sponsored until the end of the Thai monarchy with a revolt against the Chakri Dynasty and the exile of Rama VII and Queen Rambhi Barni on June 28, 1932.

To choral narration and the music of xylophones, gongs, tympani, and flutes in the piphat orchestra, troupes danced scenarios for weddings, funerals, and births or at community gatherings in public squares. For nuptials, troupes followed the bride to her new home, singing and dancing as a blessing on the new family. Masks formed of rice flour, sumac resin, and koi bark paper exaggerated dancers' smiles, snarls, and grimaces on oversized mouths with protruding teeth. Dancers honored the masks before each presentation and stored them in sacred space.

The 311 character parts involved the hero Rama; his wife, Sita; his brother, Lakshaman; the holy man Rusi; and acrobatic monkey soldiers dressed in white. Children mastered the dance roles as a standard part of school curricula. Headpieces featured ornate tiaras and tall gilt crowns suggestive of towering temples. Together, the lead dancers defeated evil and recovered the kidnapped Sita or an abducted princess, roles acted by men. A southern version of khon, called *norah*, adapted the stolen princess into a bird-woman.

Folk Mime Standards

Colors identified the fire god Nilanol in red and the death deity Nilapat in black. Additional mimes played angels, goddesses, and ogres in ornate gilt shirts and ankle-length pants over bare feet. The demon king appeared in green for war and gold for peace. With metallic lines reflecting actual garments of the royal family, patterned fabric that juxtaposed geometric and floral motifs accented the swirl of dance figures. Wardrobe agents kept garments, fur bodices, and masks in repair with touchups and restitching.

To enhance spectacle, the characteristic Thai posturing required gold and silver nail extenders on fingers, hands turned back at the wrist, and graceful bows of the head. Flexed knees and feet perpendicular to the body axis enabled performers to leap, stamp, and frolic while holding the torso erect. Heavy eye makeup outlined hostile glances between enemies. Mock sword fights incorporated fencing thrusts and parries, counterweighted flying forays, and a victorious finale. Comic interludes presented jesters recapping the plot and predicting the next scenarios.

The artistic accomplishments of khon dance expanded after 1809 during the fifteen-year reign of Rama II, who initiated greater recovery of heritage dances. More restructuring under Rama IV after 1851 and Rama VI after 1910 allied the khon ritual with original Sanskrit texts. Under Rama IX after 1946, a scholarly analysis of khon dance continued the search for sources of national musical arts. For surrounding peoples, khon dance influenced the folk styles of Cambodia, Laos, and Myanmar.

See also story dance; sword dance.

Source: Kislenko, Arne. *Culture and Customs of Thailand.* Westport, CT: Greenwood, 2004.

TINIKLING

In Filipino mimicry of long-legged birds, the lowland Waray evolved *tinikling* by adapting foot maneuvers between ten- to twelve-foot poles one foot apart and smacked together or beaten to the rhythm medieval string serenades. Tinikling emerged as both a game and a dance in rural Leyte on the Visayan Islands during colonial rule of the Philippines, which began on March 16, 1521, with the arrival of Portuguese explorer Ferdinand Magellan aboard the carrack *Victoria*. The athletic hops and leaps dodged the clap of parallel bamboo poles as though delicate feet of the heron were eluding snares set by rice farmers. Percussionists banged or slid the poles together, against the ground, or on a wood block to establish a rhythm demanding synchrony and eye-foot coordination.

Legend-makers surmised that European planters may have tormented native laborers by shackling them between poles riddled with thorns. To the click–click–clack, peasant workers hopped in-in-out to prevent being pierced in the foot or ankle. A more esoteric explanation of the iconic dance is the political dodging and avoiding of clashes between Asian, Hispanic, and American invaders and Filipinos demanding sovereignty of the island cluster.

The Filipino National Dance

Similar to the actions of Ukrainian *hopak* dances and double Dutch jump rope introduced in New York by immigrants from Holland in 1609, the athletic moves outlined an energetic dance loved by adult villagers and children for parties and fiestas. During the Filipino diaspora to South America, Mexico, the Caribbean, Hawaii, California, Texas, and New Orleans, immigrants introduced the intricate tinikling to fun gatherings and school physical education curricula to improve eye-foot coordination. The iconic leaps and hops with alternating feet came to represent the culture of displaced Filipinos amid the entrapments of assimilation.

By the 1940s, the slow serenades and erect posture gave place to faster bends and more challenging tempos that demanded gymnastic skill from American soldiers billeted in the islands. To avoid embarrassing tourists, in the 1950s, male Filipino dancers began wearing trunks rather than the *bahag* (g-string). On April 17, 1958, the Bayanihan Philippine Folk Company entertained spectators at the Universal Exposition in Brussels before the dance appeared in the United States on *The Ed Sullivan Show*. In the 1980s, drag shows updated tinikling music with disco recordings and pulsing lights.

Concentration and Skill

Execution of the dance features barefoot hops and rhythmic patterns below torso and arm moves in 3/4 meter. Couples perform single and double hops shin high in semi-open position or alone with hands on hips or arced above the head. To increase complexity of the national bamboo dance of the Philippines, competitors at contests leap over multiple poles in a line, among four poles at right angles, or in and out of a star or other geometric figure. For nighttime scheduling, dancers execute the hops and leaps in the dark while swinging lanterns.

A more demanding pose places dancers on benches between poles. Costumes—tunic, kerchief, and loose cotton pants for men and dress with arched sleeves and sash for women—underscore the patriotic appeal of tinikling. The addition of fans and umbrellas adds color and shape to balancing and timing tricks. Elementary school pupils learn tinikling as an object lesson in grace and rhythm. When dancers fail to clear the poles, they switch positions with the pair banging the bamboo. The Maranao on Mindanao apply tinikling steps over two or four clapping poles to performance of the *singkil*, a skilled folk rhythm reflecting the ability to overstep vines and tree limbs without jostling them.

See also acrobatic dance; fan dance; parasol dance.

Source: Lopez, Melli Leandicho. *A Handbook of Philippine Folklore.* Quezon City: University of the Philippines Press, 2006.

TIRABOL

Children and adults in Berga perform an annual Catalonian street revelry sixty days after Easter between May 21 and June 24. As a pagan welcome to summer grazing season and a thirteenth-century religious observance originally called *bulla*, the allegorical *tirabol* epitomized hometown solidarity, conviviality, and Christianity with a spiral figure formed by skipping feet. The name *tirabol* derived from "pull the ox," a reference to a version of crack-the-whip danced respectably arm in arm on Wednesday noon and by a juvenile company the next day. A rowdier skipping dance and mock jousting filled Saturday night in spite of vertigo, inebriation, and sleep deprivation.

The provincial tirabol began in 1454 as the conclusion on May 26 to Corpus Christi processions known as La Patum. North of Barcelona, the annual masquerade featured papier-mâché hobbyhorses, dragons, giant Saracens, and horned demons armed with maces and whips. An irregular rhythm of acrobatics concluded with the tirabol, an exuberant leaping dance. A single percussionist garbed in period red velvet livery and plumed hat beat the *tabal* (bass drum) in a single cadence of pa-tum', pa-tum'.

In a biblical dumb show of good vs. evil in 1621, the pairing of David and Goliath presented the huge Philistine warrior on stilts. An immense eagle bobbed in place and stepped to a slow, elegant choreography as a dual symbol of John the Baptist and Catalonian pride. As a framing of self-determination, hobbyhorses formed an outer circle and moved clockwise around dwarves miming a farce of pigtailed municipal officers wearing tricorn hats while they waltzed and spun.

Historical Dance

North of Barcelona, even after Catalonia's loss of independence to King Philip V on September 11, 1714, the five-day folk theater maintained the Dionysian joie de vivre of ancient Greece. By 1723, revelers performed the eagle dance and some one-act plays, applauded by gangs of children. In the late 1700s, the Corpus Christi holiday began with a formal opening and procession featuring papier-mâché hobbyhorses, fire-breathing mule-dragons with giraffe necks, and peasant dwarfs, symbols of lowly agrarian status.

In darkness, dancers paraded from the parish church to Casa de la Ciutat (city hall) and brandished torches, an emblem of flame illuminating primitivism and heat overcoming sin. The choreography characterized opposition through the skirmishes of angels against some one hundred twenty horned demons, huge false faces that performers preserved in municipal storage. Berga residents anticipated the devil dance, which flaunted green (nature) and red (fire) felt suits and armed conflict with maces and whips. The iconography reflected the constant battle of farmers against weeds, which they combated with swiddens, the burning off of fields to incinerate unwanted seeds.

A mock crusade between giant Turks and Christian knights ended with the deus ex machina of triumphant angels and a crowned St. Michael clutching shield and spear. An uninhibited rhythm of acrobatics concluded with the tirabol, an exuberant leaping dance presented more than twenty times to repetitions of "La banya de bou" (The ox horn). The steps moved counterclockwise around the Plaça de Sant Joan and the Plaça de Sant Pere with the giant robed kings and queens on wood frames spinning to the addictive beat and demons jumping and loping with riders on their backs.

Changing Meanings

The tirabol developed social satire in 1890 with the introduction of another mule and four new dwarfs, effigies parodying the egotism of the privileged bourgeoisie with a complex clapping-skipping-spinning configuration. Berga citizens canceled the dance during revolutionary upheaval in December 1938. The festival met the disapproval of Francisco Franco's dictatorship from 1939 to his death on November 20, 1975. In defiance, pageant performers "resisted hell" by combatting devils, the icons of Franco's military.

In the decline of the dictatorship after 1970, the tirabol was revived as a sociopolitical collective. Devoid of the procession of the sacraments, the folk pageant extended throughout the Pyrenees and through Andorra to Trent, France. As outsiders crowded in and chased the oversized masqueraders, purists announced in vain over loudspeakers the need to respect the mystic holiday dance and its traditional regalia.

As a framework for Catalonian rejuvenation, whirlpools of dance rhythms ranged from the original 6/8 meter to a *jota* and *pasodoble*. The snap of firecrackers and the lighting of sparklers filled the night sky with an explosive orgy of flame and smoke. Dancers warded off self-immolation by wearing long-sleeved shirts. Despite the lack of room for grand choreography, bands assembled on the cathedral's stone steps and kept the shuffling crowd in motion to "La Patumaire." On November 25, 2005, UNESCO declared the Corpus Christi festival a Masterpiece of the Oral and Intangible Heritage of Humanity.

See also disguise; *jota*; mime; *pasodoble*; processionals; sword dance.

Source: Noyes, Dorothy. *Fire in the Plaça: Catalan Festival Politics after Franco.* Philadelphia: University of Pennsylvania Press, 2003.

TOTEMIC DANCE

An amalgam of ancestor worship, ritual sacrifice, and mystic transformational dance characterizes global totemic art in concrete animal, plant, or mineral form, a practice among the Aztec, Egyptians, Apache, Ojibwa, Maori, Norse, Celts, Zulu, Haitians, Australian aborigines, and Finns. The list of magical models includes yak maskers in Tibet, Malay dancers reverencing mythic hybrid animals, the praying mantis dance of South African San, and the Dogon raffia shapes in southern Mali that mourners don for the burial of elders. During planting, the Hausa of West Africa perform a corn dance that features a horned ox mask, a symbol of strength and endurance. For the Arunta of central Australia, concealment shielded totemic magic of female dancers from outside scrutiny until the 1930s, when white colonists obtained direct knowledge of the continent's mythic and folk art and destroyed the secret basis for initiation rites.

Among children in Papua New Guinea, identification with a totemic mammal or fish precedes a coming-of-age ritual to sacred flutes conferring love and protection on initiates. For community dances, clans paint totem effigies on chest or back with clay and colored pigments to declare their fealty to a sept, as with the Mawatta, southern Papuans who honor both the cassowary and the crocodile. Among the Toro along the Bensbach River of south central New Guinea, boys dance their coming-of-age rites with bullroarers, weights that they swing to create an insistent hum to summon beneficent spirits. Farther east at the village of Iasa on Kiwai Island, grateful residents acclaim the annual yam and banana crop at a clan longhouse. On a dance floor elevated some six feet above ground, the headman organizes ritual thanksgiving choreography.

Shape-Shifting

Most totemic dance begins with a badge or disguise, such as a feather crest of the cockatoo, fins of a swordfish, walrus tusks, or a staff and stilts representing a long-necked stork. Dancers perform a real-life imitation of waddling bears, spitting camels, snorting bulls, capering baboons, a stalking lion, or the leaping eland or hartebeest revered by Bechuana tribes in central South Africa. Among the Bantu of the Angoniland plateau in Mozambique, a secret brotherhood of dancers wears animal disguises and frolics on stilts while the company performs a funeral rite on a moonless night. The purpose of the spectacle is to reveal the animal shape that the deceased has taken.

More exotic totemic dance invokes birds, particularly the eagle and the owl, as well as plants, fish, and reptiles, such as the sago palm, mangrove, yam, hammerhead shark, crab, turtle, and boa constrictor. In the sacraments of the Shang Dynasty after 1600 BCE, snake totem worship preceded dragon dancing. The mystic masking and choreography esteemed Chinese resilience, dignity, and wisdom. The steps and gestures warded off ghosts and plagues while securing a bounty of rice and grain. In Hong Kong, the animal dance concluded with the tossing of the dragon image into the sea, a preservation of magic in a water element.

In a comic circle dance to a moderate or rapid 2/4 tempo, the medieval Armenian, Assyrian, Kurdish, Pontine Greek-Georgian, Macedonian, and Azerbaijani kochari (or kotsari) mimed the bounding, crouching, and butting of heads like goats. By grasping shoulders and vibrating their bodies to lateral steps, from 1000 CE, goat pantomime illustrated the solidarity of survivors of war and social chaos. Children learned the steps and goat behaviors as a means of preserving medieval heritage.

Rhythmic Mimicry

In dance houses to the beating of drums each January during the Inviting-In Feast, the Greenland Inuit imitated the idiosyncrasies and rhythms of emblematic spirit beings that gave purpose and significance to clan members. The repetitive, hypnotic thumps linked the dancer's heartbeat with that of the mythic animal and created an illusion of shape-shifting, a power to defeat mortality. At Kingikmiut Eskimo dances along the Bering Strait between Siberia and Alaska, the shaman created three-dimensional totem puppets with pelts, feathers, and driftwood. Totemic masks with hinged jaws vibrated along feathered surfaces, giving the impression of the utterance of a living beast.

Upon conversion to Christianity, Eskimo priests destroyed and burned totemic dance regalia in obedience to Protestant missionaries. Among Mesoamericans, Catholic proselytizers took the opposite approach to totemic dance by encouraging the "Dance of the Moors and Christians" from the anti-Arab persecutions of 1492 and the "Dance of Cortés," a history dance reenacting the conquest of Spanish conquistadors from 1519 to 1521 over the Aztec, Maya, and surrounding Mexican tribes. To Christians, animal slaughter or castration of a capering bull affirmed the meaning of sacrifice.

See also animal dances; corroboree; disguise; lamentation dance; *matachines*; mime; sacrificial dance.

Source: Galenorn, Yasmine. *Totem Magic: Dance of the Shapeshifter.* Berkeley, CA: Ten Speed Press, 2004.

TOTENTANZ

Mystic mania dance followed Europe's conversion to Christianity, when believers experienced the collision of the concrete body with the abstract concept of nonbeing. Often funeral processions preceded nude dancing of the bereaved on cairns and raised tombs and along labyrinthine paths in and out of cemetery rows. Frenzied steps and gestures denied death its claim on the human imagination.

In the decline of feudalism in the late 1300s, the German danse macabre (dance of death) expressed the agitation and despair of survivors of famines and the Black Plague (1347–1353). Similar in hysteria to the Italian tarantella, from Provence to Normandy, the ring dance figured in late medieval paintings, woodcuts, frescoes, tales, symphonies, passion plays, and tableaus. Dialogue between the briskly striding Grim Reaper and his next victim revealed the magical footwork by which the living sought to elude death.

Equalizing Mortality

One example of dance drama, the anonymous Spanish morality play *La danza general de la muerte* (The general dance of death, 1360), equalized the future for all humankind regardless of caste. In a procession to the underworld, costumed dancers faced annihilation and decay. The rhythm emulated suspension between body and spirit, life and death, time and space.

Totentanz performances marked a transcendent state between mortality and doom. Joining hands with Satan or a skeleton, the living formed a configuration that sometimes featured maskers dressed as Adam and Eve or the Seven Deadly Sins—pride, greed, lust, envy, gluttony, wrath, and sloth. While the remorseful lashed themselves with whips, performers acted out the Dies Irae (Day of Wrath) and the hell-march of the doomed via two steps forward and one step back.

Historical Totentanz

In the Rhine Valley in summer 1374, mass hysteria emerged at Aachen, Hennegau, and Liège, where impromptu wickedness seized individuals. Fearing damnation, they grasped hands, quivered, and sprang across village greens and meadows in a dire farandole to a piper or fiddler's tune. While recoiling from visions of gore and orgasmic extremes, they

In the decline of feudalistic repression and the aftermath of the Black Death, mass hysteria seized individuals in Germany and France in summer 1374 in a dance of death. *Hartmann, Schedel.* Liber Cronicarum. *Nuremberg, Ger.: Koberger, 1493.*

followed a path of dance drama to holy precincts for rescue by exorcists. The unprecedented frenzy at Cologne, Trier, Ghent, Metz, Zurich, and Flanders developed into convulsions, which Swiss occultist Theophrastus Paracelsus called St. Vitus' Dance.

At Corpus Christi festivals each May 26 and the pre-Lenten carnivals into the mid-1400s, spectacle dances aligned performers in England, France, Flanders, Holland, Brussels, Austria, Switzerland, Sweden, and Italy. In a lesson to the vulnerable, as with the frieze by Pomeranian painter Bernt Notke at Marienkirche in Lübeck in 1463, allegorical corpses and death figures mounted ox carts. As the devout trod a town street by torchlight, the cortege sang *Miserere* (Have mercy). With trembling steps, the tragic processional passed mortuary chambers, church ossuaries, scaffolds, cloisters, vaults, and churchyards. The visual terrors survived around 1500 in the facade of the Austrian bone house at Metnitz, Carinthia, and in a ballad by Goethe.

See also circle dance; exorcism; farandole; labyrinthine dance; lamentation dance; *matachines*; *polska*; processionals; tarantella; *tirabol*.

Source: Bryant, Clifton D., and Dennis L. Peck, eds. *Encyclopedia of Death and Human Experience.* Thousand Oaks, CA: SAGE, 2009.

· 𝒱 ·

VARSOUVIENNE

A Pomeranian folk dance to accordion music during turmoil in German states, the *varsouvienne* (also *varsovienne*, *souvienne*, or *varsoviana*) treated couples to a slow, elegant partners dance to skipping rhythms in 3/4 meter. Emulating figures from contradance and square dance, the varsouvienne opens on a promenade hold with the man standing behind the woman and grasping both her hands at shoulder height. Counterclockwise footwork alternated glissades, pauses, and step-step-step-point with restrained hops and rotations similar to the waltz.

Originated in Warsaw, Poland, in 1850, the dance resembled the Bohemian polka *redowa*, hop waltz, and mazurka in its smooth continuity. The name referred to a "woman from Warsaw" and emphasized the swish of petticoats in swaying skirt flourishes. Critics noted that the dance suited slender women for showing off their willowy waistlines, an asset to Cajun dance in Louisiana and Quebec and the seamstresses who designed dresses.

A Global Dance

Following the 1849 Gold Rush, in Catholic Spanish California, the varsouvienne flourished in immigrant Polish communities for St. Anthony's Feast Day (June 13). Parents and Protestant ministers at first questioned the suitability of closed-position round dance for their children, who were more comfortable with square dance. The varsouvienne spread to cowboys and Mormons over New Mexico, Arizona, Utah, Colorado, the Tex-Mex border, Canada, and Argentina. Missourians identified the dance as the heel-and-toe polka. In Texas, schedulers substituted the song title "Put Your Little Foot" or just "Little Foot" for the original dance name.

The varsouvienne pleased folk dancers in Prussia, Holland, Austria, France, England, Scotland, Ireland, Spain, Russia, South Africa, and New South Wales, Australia. By 1853, Swedes, Finns, and French courtiers of Napoleon III and the Empress Eugénie adopted the genteel figures, which reflected influence from the schottische. Dance instructor Charles Durang outlined the Polish figures in *The Fashionable Dancer's Casket; or, the Ball-Room Instructor* (1856). Choreographer Edward Ferrero recommended in

1859 that parents introduce children to the varsouvienne, which guided them in cour-teous body language and gracious movements of limbs.

After 1864, the travels of the empress Carlota and Maximilian I, Emperor of Mexico, to Paris introduced the empress to the dance at the Tuileries. Carlota copied Eugénie's evening gatherings with Monday-night socials of her own, at which guests interspersed the galop and quadrille with the varsouvienne. As a refined dance, the latter received negative criticism in *The Habits of Good Society: A Handbook for Ladies and Gentlemen* (1867).

A Change of Class

Cachet of the varsouvienne declined in 1870, when folk dancers claimed the steps from royalty and the privileged class. In *The Gentlemen's Book of Etiquette and Manual of Polite-ness* (1876), American frontier biographer and compiler Cecil B. Hartley declared the gliding and hopping figures "ridiculous" for refined society. By 1883, *Collier's Cyclope-dia* proclaimed the dance passé, yet the term *varsouvienne* attached to Franco-American menu items, racehorses, dresses, and men's hats. Because the lower class elaborated on the visual appeal of the original Polish figures, in the 1890s, critics complained that the varsouvienne had adopted vulgar gestures.

In 1906, the varsouvienne sank from a mark of social savoir faire to a reduced status among Swedish peasant dances performed by ice skaters and taught to school children in lessons on continental folk arts. The dance survived in 1908 as a relic of past civility suitable for a debutante ball at Government House in Annapolis, Maryland. To revive the country dance genre—waltz, varsouvienne, quadrille, polka, contradance—in the United States in the 1920s, Clara Bryant Ford urged her husband, automaker Henry Ford, to locate an instructor in Dearborn, Michigan, and offer lessons to middle-aged couples. The plaintive music figured in the atmosphere of Tennessee Williams's play *A Streetcar Named Desire* (1947) and the recreational curriculum of Phoenix College and post–World War I educational programs in Tokyo, Japan, and Seoul Korea.

See also Cajun dance; contradance; galop; mazurka; partnering; polka; quadrille; schottische; square dance; waltz.

Sources: Gifford, Paul M. "Henry Ford's Dance Revival and Fiddle Contests: Myth and Reality." *Journal of the Society for American Music* 4, no. 3 (August 2010): 307–38. Marshall, Howard Wright. *Play Me Something Quick and Devilish: Old-Time Fiddlers in Missouri*. Columbia: University of Missouri Press, 2012.

VEILED DANCE

Veiling of female dancers under patriarchal supervision obeyed customary modesty reg-ulations while accentuating the fragility and fertility of the virgin and the propriety of the pious wife. From 3000 BCE, Roma entertainers at Rajasthan and Jaipur in north-ern India imported the mysticism of the *sapera* (cobra dance) to an adaptation of the *ghoomar*, a veiled synchronized pirouette in honor of the goddess Saraswati, the fount of wisdom and the arts. Gypsy women ornamented costumes with bright rectangles and shawls that framed the facial expression and floated in the air behind statuesque posturing. Under wispy weaving grasped lightly between thumb and index finger, dancers displayed backbends and arms curving into the fabric, which draped naturally from their limbs. The concealment magnified tempestuous exotic dance, a disguising of the figure and symbol of the impenetrability of the female persona.

East of Iraq after the third millennium BCE, Kurdish dancers rejected the regional veiling of Anatolian women under muslin in favor of full self-expression in Armenian and Assyrian or Chaldean dance. In Egypt after 1570 BCE, female mastery of the belly dance used to advantage the illusory *bedleh* (belly dance costume), a dual vision of outside and inside. The ephemeral veils and hand and head scarves elicited spectator fascination with undulating muscles of the bare midriff and the ting of finger cymbals. Dreamlike, the veiled female beckoned viewers into the fantasy of stripping bare a private aesthetic.

Classic and Religious Dance

In the style of the Greek Primavera and the Three Graces, the iconic translucent textile in the ancient *ballos* enhanced a flirtation dance executed to light string music at Ionia, Byzantium, Smyrna, and the Aegean Islands. After 300 BCE, a Hellenistic bronze statue of a veil-enveloped dancer at Alexandria, Egypt, illustrated the femininity of the lower face in niqab and the raised hip shrouded in sheer folds. Into the Roman Empire after 27 BCE, the muffling of the *saltatrix* (dancing girl) in thin linen or imported silk augmented rather than diminished titillation by turning glimpses of her contoured arms and bosom into an elevated peep show.

In obeisance to the prophet Muhammad's ministry begun in 610, at Arab enclaves from Libya to Egypt, veiled brides-to-be at weddings clapped, swayed, and chanted to the playful *hagallah*. Encircled by men, the bride validated female maturity and acceptance of wifely duties by brandishing a stick against any male who tried to swipe her head covering. For public presentations along the Arabian Gulf at Arabia, Bahrain, Kuwait, Oman, and Yemen, female cafe dancers flaunted sensuality with the tossing of fluid veils and hair over shoulders and enticing hip rolls. Liberal application of body covering prevailed until the rise of the Almohad Dynasty in 1121, when Moroccan traditionalists enforced strict rules of concealment, especially for eyes and breasts.

One exemption allowed Bedouin entertainers to dance without concealing their movements. At Goulimine in the Sahara Desert, the Tuareg Kel Tagelmousse (blue people) of the Berber incorporated veiling into the *guedra*, a hypnotic ceremony projecting a transcendent peace. To the throb of a pot drum, clapping, and chanting, the female soloist, immured in a black veil, lapsed into an altered state that invoked the almighty. Gesturing to north, south, east, and west, gradually she materialized out of her body mask and lifted an index finger heavenward to bless the assemblage.

On the island of Korcula west of Dalmatia in the twelfth century, the medieval *moresca* dramatized males sparring for the attentions of a veiled woman, a symbol of the impenetrable feminine mystique. Late in the Middle Ages, the fashionable veil of Gallic women limited their capering in the farandole, a community chain dance that a leader directed through homes and churches and under copses and orchard trees that could entangle fine chiffon. After 1556 at Delhi, India, *kathak* dancers honored Hindu and Muslim customs by draping the female soloist in a filmy tissue that diminished the outlines of bare midriff musculature.

Oriental Dance

During the Victorian fad of Orientalism in France and England, painters and sculptors chose dance as a provocative motif, as with transformations of images of the Babylonian love goddess Ishtar and Italian silversmith Luigi Pampaloni's graceful, discreet statue *Beatrice di Tenda* (1838) at Santa Croce in Florence. French artist Armand Point's 1898 oil painting of the mythic Salomé of Galilee pictured her gesturing with her costume scarf toward King Herod Antipas and his wife Miriamne. Art deco forerunner Aubrey Beardsley violated Eastern codes of chastity by drawing a bare-breasted dancer scarcely swathed by a lowered veil.

The American stereotype of the seductive siren slithering to the fictitious "Dance of the Seven Veils" marked formulaic photography of the 1920s and late nineteenth-century film. Exotic dancing generated the first case of cinema censorship, which halted viewings of *Fatima's Dance* (1896) on the shores of Atlantic City, New Jersey. Into the twentieth century, examples of sleazy non-history depicted Rita Hayworth stripping her mantle in *Salome* (1953) and an alluring Brigid Bazlen reduced to semi-nudity for *King of Kings* (1961). The Coasters further cheapened Middle Eastern dance with the pop song "Little Egypt" (1962).

See also belly dance; coming of age; farandole; film, folk dance in; nudity; sword dance.

Sources: Heath, Jennifer, ed. *The Veil: Women Writers on Its History, Lore, and Politics*. Berkeley: University of California Press, 2008. Rutherford, Annabel. "The Triumph of the Veiled Dance: The Influence of Oscar Wilde and Aubrey Beardsley on Serge Diaghilev's Creation of the Ballets Russes." *Dance Research* 27, no. 1 (May 2009): 93–107.

VOLTA

An early Renaissance crossover from impromptu hopping folk figures to choreographed social dance, in the early 1500s, the *volta* (also the turning or the *cinquepace*) introduced a coda to the galliard in closed position. In the teasing mating dance, with its left-right swapping of pointed toes, a dramatic turn and lift of the female partner excited spectators with its sudden intimacy. At the climactic moment in the execution, the female partner lifted her hand and sprang toward the male partner's left side.

The placement of male hands on his partner turned the volta into a social and courtly controversy. For the caper or pivot, the man lifted the woman by the waist under the busk (corset) and left hip in the style of the French *branle*. Reaching from left to right, he positioned her on his left thigh or knee while she anchored her near hand on his shoulder and steadied her skirts with the other hand.

The obscure origins of the volta suggest that late eleventh-century troubadours and their poems of courtly love initiated the intimate dance in southeastern France, making it the first folk dance in 3/4 tempo. After 1137, the volta intrigued Louis VII, the first husband of arts lover Eleanor of Aquitaine. During the 1210s, the diaspora of troubadours from France during the Albigensian Crusades introduced the steps to northern Italy.

The Historic Volta

As wealth provided leisure during the Renaissance, the rural dance found fans among the rising merchant class of Provençal, Germany, Austria, Switzerland, and Italy, notably at Westphalia as the subject of an engraving in 1538. In the late 1540s, the joyful steps and centrifugal turns moved up in respectability from village plazas to royal courts. In 6/8 or 6/4 meter, the leaping and trio of high lifts delighted Louise Borgia, the Duchess de Valentinois, a lover of court dance.

The volta reached the Parisian court of Catherine de' Medici, wife of Henry II, in 1556 during socials at Versailles, which restored her to court after her near death in the birth of twin daughters. Under the queen's influence, unwed maidens and ambitious males exhibited their skill at turns, vaults, and lifts to advance their sociopolitical standing. To increase participation, the queen's tutors provided dance instruction in both Italian and French.

After the crowning of Elizabeth I in 1558, the English queen bypassed the stately pavane and raised the galliard, the allemande, and the provocative volta in court approval. Each morning for exercise, she performed the galliard to the sentimental melodies of John Dowland of London. She preferred the tassel kick and aimed her foot at a decoration on her dress. Her regimen ended the galliard with the volta, an athletic figure often danced to pipe, tabor, and woodwinds.

A court favorite, Robert Dudley, the Earl of Leicester, achieved mastery of the volta. He and other partners stripped their raiment of cape and saber to free their limbs for the strenuous dance. The rapid pivot of at the climactic moment shocked courtiers by revealing the queen's feet and lower legs up to the knees. The dance passed to Basque peasant girls in Provence at the 1565 Fêtes de Bayonne, a major European fair where, over five days in August, performers executed a pattern of three quarter turns and a leap.

The Volta in Disrepute

By 1582, Henry III of France, one of Elizabeth's royal suitors, welcomed the dance among his courtiers, as did his successor, Henry IV. Although the censorious Puritan pamphleteer Philip Stubbes predicted in 1583 that the dance would lead to lust, whoring, and fornication, Italian dance masters instructed teens in northwestern Europe and the British Isles in the jig, galliard, and volta. The alluring volta choreography prospered at the 1596 Montpellier carnival on the southeastern coast of France and developed polished glissades. After 1610, the prudish prince Louis XIII banished the volta from his court.

The volta prefaced the Nordic *polska* and Norwegian waltz, German *Ländler* and *springtanz*, Bavarian *schleifer*, Italian *nizzarda*, and nineteenth-century Viennese waltz, another couples dance that shocked prim society. To the detriment of history, abstemious arts critics tended to omit the optimism and spirit of the volta steps. According to French arts writer Thoinot Arbeau's manual *Orchésographie* (1589), the intimate figure concluded with a pivot of the woman in three separate arcs before returning to the galliard steps.

The athletic volta lost its athletic motifs in the early 1600s and presented a tamer air with feet on the floor for polished glissades. Female dance aficionados accommodated the changing style with broad skirts, millstone ruffs, and the wide-brimmed Rembrandt hat, a shield to blushing cheeks. The dance faded from ballrooms by 1636 as the minuet replaced exhibitionism with mincing steps and a codified formality more suited to baroque tastes.

In 1668, German writer Johannes Praetorius repeated past condemnations of lewdness and indecency in the volta. He made rash allegations based on the male dancer's placement of one hand upon his partner's buttocks, a dance posture he accused—without proof—of causing miscarriages and murder. The volta continued to appear on programs until the early 1800s and, in 1807, pleased couples at the Zum Sperl dance hall, Vienna's most famous evening venue.

See also allemande; *branle*; diaspora; film, folk dance in; galliard; jig; *Ländler*; mating dance; *polska*; waltz.

Source: Knowles, Mark. *The Wicked Waltz and Other Scandalous Dances: Outrage at Couple Dancing in the 19th and Early 20th Centuries.* Jefferson, NC: McFarland, 2009.

· 𝒲 ·

WALPURGIS DANCE

A diabolical Celtic holiday, Walpurgisnacht (also Walpurgis Night, Hexennacht, or Beltane) encouraged free-spirited enjoyment of company, mead, bell ringing, candlelit processions, and cavorting on the waning days of winter. The holiday originated in the eighth century in the Harz Mountains in honor of St. Walpurga, an English abbess from Devonshire posted at Heidenheim in southern Germany. Walpurgis dances retained the excesses of Brocken (or Blocksberg) Mountain, where witches pranced at the Hexentranzplatz (witches' dance floor). Among the magic glades sheltering stone circles around the *menhir* or standing stone, witches reputedly rode their brooms or long ladles into the night sky and twirled with imps and satanic black goats to the fiddler's tune.

A mythic interpretation of the dance linked Walpurga's Day with the birth of Venus on the summer solstice, an orgiastic night of desire and metamorphosis generated by "dancing in May." The goddess of passion preserved her nubile youth and purity by surrounding herself with wisewomen, the female sages/midwives devoted to the protection of pregnant women and the delivery of newborns. Through sensual ring dance and the chaotic noise of stone clapping, animal calls, and rattles, the defenders drove away ghouls and devils who longed to violate the maidenhood of Venus.

Good vs. Evil

From the Middle Ages, Vatican edicts failed to stymy peasant divination and observances of witch dances, the washing of hands and face in dew, fire and broom leaping, and the mad practices that constituted high heathenism. In defiance of church strictures and the bans of Pope Stephen III and the Frankish king Charlemagne in 768 CE, women's goddess frolics still flourished among Saxon shepherdesses. They prized their heritage and liberty to caper through the night at Brocken Mountain, the highest peak in northern Germany. Along the paths to their occult shrines in the cliffs, dancers painted their bodies, wrapped themselves in animal pelts, and carried firebrands to terrorize the Frankish sentinels.

On May Eve at the crest, female pagans used brooms to sweep away the snow and ready the clearing for a witches' Sabbath. To the suspicious, showers of sparks and odd-shaped shadows on the slopes gave the illusion of supernatural phenomena. The revelry spread over Finland, Denmark, Germany, Czech Republic, Latvia, Lithuania, Estonia, France, Belgium, Holland, and Spain in celebration of mystic forces. To dispel wolves from livestock, at Luxembourg, the enchantresses rang bells before dancing. Profane entertainment lured youths and European university students to clasp hands and dance naked in a ring until dawn on May Day.

On Walpurgis Night in northern Europe, crazed frolics involved mead drinking, flying goats, hexes, and nude dancing, all facets of an unholy witches' sabbath. *Pearson, Karl. The Chances of Death and Other Studies in Evolution. London: Edward Arnold, 1897, 30.*

Current Dances

In Germany six months after Halloween in 1896, the first organized Walpurgis dance occurred with only men in attendance. At Roodmas (or Holy Cross Day) on May 3, the English welcomed the mating of the May queen with a follow-the-leader dance and the nocturnal mumming of the horned greenman, a masculine nature spirit configured from leaves, vines, nuts, berries, and fruit. Participants joined arms and moved left in a circle. At a climactic point in the choreography, they stood back to back, danced in reverse, and pretended to be crazed.

The Austrian version of Walpurgis dance depicted a black man grabbing maidens of the May queen's court and rubbing soot on their bodies as they danced away snow storms. Southern and midland Swedes celebrated the return of spring simultaneously with Walpurgis Night, a pageant pitting Christianity against Satanism. While kindling and stoking bonfires on hillsides on April 30, revelers from Uppsala, Lund, Stockholm, and Gothenburg universities danced the galop and sang seasonal songs. In the twentieth century, the town of Thale in north central Germany drew tourists to the carnivalesque holiday.

See also circle dance; galop; holiday dance; maypole dance; processionals.

Source: Cooper, John Michael. *Mendelssohn, Goethe, and the Walpurgis Night: The Heathen Muse in European Culture, 1700–1850.* Rochester, NY: University of Rochester Press, 2007.

WALTZ

A family of working-class or servant-class dances common in Styria, Bavaria, and Tyrol from 1750, the waltz (also *Weller, Dreher,* or spinner) predated a millennium of pleasurable social dance. The close partnering that brought torsos and cheeks in contact retained from 1023 an open-ended courtship figure, yodeling melodies, and the spinning and tight embraces of *Deutscher* (German) dances from Alpine Austria, Bavaria, Bohemia, Styria, and the Ziller Valley in the Tyrol. From France, choreographers added balancing on the toes to the gliding turns of the allemande, a skipping, hopping figure in 2/4 meter. Picturesque facets of the Portuguese fado expressed the love plaints of the twelfth-century Provençal troubadour.

From Bohemia, Bavaria, and Austria, urban youth popularized the kaleidoscopic shifting of the waltz to a 3/4 meter and spread it across Europe, the Americas, and Australia. Unlike the community revelry in the farandole and the presentational polonaise and pavane for audiences, duos enjoyed the waltz for their personal enjoyment and an inclination toward ardent bonding with a partner, an intimacy found in the sixteenth-century Italian *volta*. At Augsburg from 1580, dancers indulged in hug dancing, an innovation in partnering that became a favorite among Hapsburg courtiers. When the box step and its left-right pendulum balance reached colonial Cuba, Mexico, Brazil, Venezuela, and Peru, the glamour of bodies touching and lingering energized dance drama and promoted the tango, samba, and Dominican merengue.

An Emerging Craze

Because the waltz captivated Russians in the 1770s during the winter months and Lent, in St. Petersburg, the grandeur of close partnering outclassed the mazurka among aristocrats and peasants. Workers sought relief from dreary jobs with evening diversions in dance halls. In the 1770s outside Moscow, Roma instrumentalists and a choir accompanied a passionate session of Gypsy waltz at Count Alexei Orlov's estate. As the large-scale pattern infiltrated opera and stage performance, conservative parents reviled the fad as a violation of good breeding and feared an endangerment of young girls from fainting or falling. Johann von Goethe's novel *The Sorrows of Young Werther* (1774) corroborated parental premonitions that rhapsodic whirling across the dance floor stimulated fantasies of romance and carnal embrace.

While the restrained minuet lost fans, the advance of European nationalism swept the waltz to Vienna in the 1780s. Wolfgang Amadeus Mozart summarized the shift in dance style in the opera *Don Giovanni* (1787), which progressed through a trio—the mincing minuet, democratic contradance, and more daring *Deutscher Walzer*. By 1800, the Irish middle class hired itinerant dancing masters to teach the delirious waltz. The figures burst into the social scene at the 1800 Warsaw pre-Lenten carnival and influenced the curricula of public and military academies.

By 1804, a wild frenzy of waltzing seized French ballrooms, the Prado club in Paris, and the glades of Tivoli Gardens in Italy. After 1807, two Viennese nightclubs, Zum Sperl and the Apollo, extended their dance floors to accommodate revolving partners and women's long gowns and seat more viewers in the balconies. The graceful gestures set the tone of class identification and the rousing tempo for the ambitious, a pairing during the Napoleonic Wars that social novelist William Makepeace Thackeray satirized in *Vanity Fair* (1848).

In London in 1812, Princess Dorothea Benckendorff von Lieven, wife of the Russian legate to England, risked her reputation by waltzing with interesting men. Her dance with Prince Pyotr Borisovich Kozlovsky encountered ridicule in a cartoon by satirist George Cruikshank. By 1813, the waltz was all the rage in England. From September 1814 to June 1815, the dance set conventions at the Congress of Vienna, where international peacekeepers from Iberia to Russia thronged ballroom galleries to watch the fascinating rotations. In post-Napoleonic Berlin, Prussian censors forbade the waltz until public pressures triumphed in 1818.

The Waltz and Change

Throughout the regency period, Austrian, German, and Scandinavian couples reset dance norms by turning away from spectators toward each other and progressing around the room in a steady circuit. In Edinburgh in 1819, Scots innovators modified clogging with fluent waltz mannerisms. By 1825, the reduction of interest in the bucolic *Ländler* buoyed the crowds at urban ballrooms, where orchestras accompanied romantic steps with the faster meters of Johann Strauss I, the Napoleon of Austrian dance, and the moderate three-beat rhythm preferred by Johann Strauss II. In 1829, waltzes jostled with the Czechoslovakian *redowa*, a folk dance that violated placid rotations with leaps and heartier turns.

At the Strauss Festival in Elk Grove, California, the sleek tuxedo of Stan Dunn accommodates the voluminous skirt of Popi Rizzi, exhibiting how the Viennese waltz impacted Edwardian fashions. *Stan Dunn, manager, www.tempoparknews.org/2_BYU_flyer_2PG.pdf, Brigham Young University International Folk Dance Ensemble, Salt Lake City, Utah.*

Modified figures and meters added dips, promenades, chassés, twinkles (lateral crossovers), drags, hesitations, and *fleckerls* (spot rotations). Because religious tenets forbade Turkish males from partnering with Islamic females, in the 1830s, men in Istanbul danced the dynamic, rhapsodic waltz only with Christian women. In Mexico, missionaries prohibited the closed position in 1834 and replaced cheek-to-cheek dancing with the Spanish waltz, a staid presentation by two couples. Utah's Mormon mogul Brigham Young took the same negative stance in Salt Lake City, but he abandoned his rebuke of waltzers in 1854. In the Northwest Territories, the Hare Dené at Fort Good Hope adopted the Scots reel and waltz from European immigrants.

In competition with the *varsouvienne* from Warsaw, Poland, the Viennese waltz doubled the tempo of the original set in the 1850s. Partnering required rapid turns while each couple circled the floor counterclockwise. To save hemlines from tears and women from falls, seamstresses added wrist tethers that elevated the skirt from the floor. In Peru, skirt lifts, hip sways, and inviting shoulder dips separated couples for execution of the Creole waltz. In raffish sections of Paris in the 1880s, Italian instrumentalists promoted *bal-musette*, polka, java, and waltz to the hurdy-gurdy, bagpipes, and accordion.

The accompaniment of silent movies in the early 1900s placed the tango, *pasodoble*, and waltz in daily performances in the United States as background music for screen dancers. Children learned the courtesies of the box step in gym classes across North America as an introduction to dancing around the maypole in spring. In the

1930s, Viennese waltzing returned to fame among folk troupes in Austria and Germany and Slovenians in Ohio. In the fifteen years following World War II, a similar revival of the bal-musette in France altered the sounds of Strauss waltzes from strings to accordions. In 2007, the Chinese flirted with the liberation of social dance by scheduling cross-step waltzing in a public park at Beijing.

See also clogging; fado; farandole; *Ländler*; maypole dance; mazurka; merengue; partnering; *pasodoble*; polonaise; shamanic dance; tango; *varsouvienne*.

Source: McKee, Eric. *Decorum of the Minuet, Delirium of the Waltz*. Bloomington: Indiana University Press, 2012.

WARRIOR DANCE

Over history, spontaneous warrior dances abstracted the elements of strife into art, the source of the Spanish *morisca*, highland fling, a war and peace ritual of the Yut-yunto of Australia, and the Peruvian *muerte de Atahualpa* (death of Atahualpa). In ancient Egypt, Greece, Morocco, Iberia, Mexico, and Brazil, choreography and war mime evoked virility among military men. In Egypt under Pharaoh Rameses II during the New Kingdom after 1300 BCE, undeployed squadrons of mercenaries—Nubian Medjai, coastal Libyans, Semitic sea-going Pedtiu, and Philistine Shardans—exercised through nationalistic folk dance and shouted combat slogans over the throb of the drum. Libyan troops danced to the clap of curved wood boomerangs and imitated attack, feint, and triumph as well as retreat.

For the Tamil Nadu of southeastern India, combative dancing delineated male and female roles. The return of the king from the battlefield involved soldiers and the king's marshals in long dance lines replicating tactical alignment. While the king danced around his chariot, women formed parallel lines behind the wheels and joined in the gala, illustrating their subservience to both their ruler and all males.

In ancient Hungary, officials among Kazars, Turks, and Bulgarians merged a death ritual to ancestors with war games performed in churchyards and burial grounds to drum, fiddle, and pipe. Attendees at Moravian funerals lauded heroes with the *aldomás*, an existential blessing dance acknowledging the risk of death in combat. At sacred shrines to the Scythian god Isten, priests sacrificed oxen, sheep, and white stallions and burned the remains. At a banquet, the prelates directed thanks to the almighty for the generosity of the valiant in giving their lives for their tribe. Dancers shared a loving cup of animal blood retrieved from a pit and raised a group toast to victory.

Historical War Dance

At the monastery of St. Gallen in Switzerland in 917 CE, Magyar warriors, led by the hero Arpad, combined dance with wrestling while grasping weapons in their hands. The Hungarian penchant for dance reached a pinnacle at Vienna on August 26, 1278, when King Ladislaus IV commemorated the combat death of the Czech king Ottokar II of Bohemia with a whole day of dance. The ebullient songs and steps survived until Christian authorities at Budapest in 1279 banned ancestral warrior dance from graveyards for its savagery. From sixteenth-century Peru, the *huayño* dance to "Ollanta" extolled an Inca fighter who set an example of nobility and courage.

In the 1700s, Malay men performed the *dabus*, a training spectacle that readied them to attack enemies of Islam. A form of proselytizing, the dance reached Malaysia from Sumatran merchants and evangelists. The effort to terrify attackers evolved into a healing ritual in which performers dodged stones and stabbed themselves with a mock sword. A more cordial version, the Bavarian *Haberertanz* from the 1890s involved male duos in a menacing *Schuhplattler*. Gestures mounted to fistfighting and knife attacks, some of which turned lethal.

Among North American Plains Indians, men of Shuswap, Sioux, Blackfoot, Inuit, Navajo, Ojibwa, Mohawk, Cherokee, Potawatomi, and Seneca warrior societies danced purposeful narratives. A powwow began with a grand entry in which elders led a retinue with staffs and flags into the arena. The solemn advance recognized a color guard of veterans with prayer and noble songs. The holiest icon, eagle feathers in headpieces, elevated the warrior's sanctity. A fallen feather received immediate attention for symbolizing death in battle.

Warrior Technique

Attire affirmed Amerindian dance style. Fighting men enhanced choreographic movements with headbands, anklets, armbands, bustles, dance sticks, and hackles. Through complex kinetic storytelling, jumps and leaps expressed personal adventures and fights. Bent backs and delicate footwork to drumbeats mimicked stalking elk and deer and tracking enemies.

In a glimpse of Lakota Sioux choreography in 1832, American oil painter George Catlin detailed the nighttime war dance of fighting men around a fire. During the counterclockwise moves, braves jumped through the flames, boasted of past kills, and swore a loyalty oath while striking a reddened post, an emblem of the bloodied enemy. Additional episodes represented the galloping horse, fleeing buffalo, or soaring hawk as well as accuracy with the bow and spear. The powwows renewed spirits, released the inner warrior, and restored unity and heritage values among participants and spectators.

In Algeria, male groups danced in parallel lines or a circle. While Muslim singers intoned calls to Allah, performers hoisted loaded muskets. At the sudden finale, riflemen pointed their weapons toward the dirt and discharged them in unison, releasing noise and smoke for a dramatic conclusion.

Tunisian militiamen presented a similar dance with sabers. A Maghreb horse dance derived from racing and stylized swordplay set to drumming. The Tuareg choreographed a similar dance with camels moving to a galloping cadence set by female singing and drumming.

See also circle dance; highland fling; martial dance; mazurka; North African dance; nudity; Persian dance; pipe dance; scalp dance; *Schuhplattler*; Siberian dance; sword dance.

Sources: Koskoff, Ellen, ed. *The Concise Garland Encyclopedia of World Music.* New York: Routledge, 2008. Miller, Heather Andrews. "Dance Reflects Tradition and History." *Windspeaker* 24, no 3 (2006).

WICCAN DANCE

Neopagan and occult ritual from Celtic Britain and northwestern Europe energized devotees in tribal pageantry intended to invoke mystic gods and unite the individual with the divine self. At nightly spirit gatherings, Wiccans of all ages, both clothed and skyclad (nude), joined the bonfire circle or chain and transformed their everyday selves through group energy, a common theme in the German symbolist art of Franz von Stuck. Until sunup, adherents synchronized steps of the ring dance, ecstasy, and belly dance from Africa, the Middle East, Mesoamerica, and Celtic and Hindu enclaves in a jubilation of universal oneness. Deep meditation and repetition of a mantra during the dance could result in a trance state.

A common feature of the cycle of seasons, the welcoming of spring incorporated the medieval maypole fertility rite for Beltane on May 1 or Roodmas on May 3. The central pole, the axis mundi (world axis), represented the divine phallus as it entered a symbolic womb woven of ribbons in the seven colors of the rainbow. Around a central bonfire to the rhythm of the Maychant or Mayrune, a high priestess and high priest led the *carole* (ring dance), a symbol of infinite regeneration.

Light and Dark

In the United States in the mid-1950s, as a form of self-determination, feminists reclaimed worship of the mother or moon, alternately identified as the Greek Artemis and Hecate, the Roman Bona Dea or Diana, the Egyptian Isis, the Mesopotamian Astarte or Inanna, the Babylonian Ishtar, or the Hindu Kali. Participants embraced rebirth by performing the spiral dance, also called the weaver or grapevine. To honor mystic writer Starhawk's publication of *The Spiral Dance: A Rebirth of the Ancient Religion of the Great Goddess* in 1979, the first Wiccan pageant occurred at Samhain (Halloween), the Druidic New Year. To perform the grapevine step, dancers crossed one foot over the other, first to the front, then a side step by the back foot, and a cross to the back.

In observances worldwide, darkness enveloped Wiccans as fire dancers twirled flaming batons, juggled fire sticks, or swirled Polynesian poi. An extended configuration between double bonfires purified body and spirit. For luck, dancers leaped the balefire (sacrificial flame), taking into their bodies the power of flame to ensure health, love, and fertility.

Between Life and Death

By holding hands in sacred space and coiling widdershins (counterclockwise) toward a bonfire or centralized altar, the devout exalted spirits of deceased ancestors as well as the fallow earth stripped by foodstuffs during the harvest. Throughout the pageant, a leader intoned the liturgy and named the infants born since the previous Samhain. Parallel to Christian ritual for All Souls' Day, a sonorous voice called the names of the dead since the last October 31, including beloved pets.

Graces (priestesses) comforted the grieving, who often wept or wailed. Steps allied to drumming or chanting reached the center altar before reversing and dancing deosil (clockwise) to the perimeter. The reversal placed worshippers face to face, where they sometimes exchanged a kiss of unity or peace. The focus of dancers on pardon and mercy ended quarrels and buried grudges.

Wiccan choreography revived Celtic seasonal occasions as elements of the eternal wheel of the year. Subsequent spiral dancing honored Litha or Whitsunday (June 21), an observation of midsummer or the summer solstice, for which dancers decked themselves with flowers and bright colors in a style similar to the Slavic revelry at the Kupalo festival. Mummers disguised themselves in the leafy mask and costume of the greenman, also called Jack in the Green. At Lammastide or Lughnassadh each August 1, Wiccan dancing praised wheat or maize, the heritage food of American Indians.

See also belly dance; circle dance; labyrinthine dance; mime; shamanic dance; worship dance.

Source: Starhawk. *The Spiral Dance.* New York: Harper & Row, 1979.

WORSHIP DANCE

From prehistoric times, prayer, sacrifice, and adoration of deities incorporated processions and dance composed of traditional footwork, attitudes, and postures. Examples include the *kagura*, which preserves the pantheistic Shinto faith of Japan, and the *kavadi aattam*, a dance of the Tamil Natu of southeastern India in which they balanced shoulder poles with milk and coconut on each end while singing deity stories along walks to the temple. Egyptian worship incorporated choreography, as depicted at Abydos by dance dramatists reenacting the overthrow of the enemies of Osiris. Ancient Magyars in Moldavia reverenced the Scythian god Isten at the *aldomás*, a blessing dance involving the holy sacrifice of animals and the drinking of blood.

In the mid-200s CE, Gregory Thaumaturges, the bishop of Pontus, introduced dance to joyful music as a form of spirituality suited to praise and worship. A century later, Saint Basil of Cappadocia urged dancing on Earth as a preparation for heavenly rejoicing. In imitation of the processionals of Miriam and David in the Torah, Jews performed the hora during the Middle Ages in the dance halls of France, Germany, and Poland.

Devout gestures and body language sacralized medieval worship dance with representations of sacred acts, including thanksgiving, veneration, and repentance. At Iurreta, Spain, the Basque *hildakoarena* enacted an unusual theme of resurrection by lowering to the floor an inert troupe member, who revived and returned to action. Among Kurds, the *sema* (prayer dance), presented at Islamic worship centers, allied male and female in lines and circles. Participants placed hands over hearts and performed the stages of a dignified worship rite. The liturgy concluded with kneeling on prayer rugs in a meditative trance.

South of Morocco at Goulimine in the Sahara Desert, the Tuareg Berber, descendants of ancient Canaanites, introduced the *guedra*, a spiritual ritual projecting inclusion and peace. A hypnotic dance of the Tuareg Kel Tagelmousse (blue people), named for the dye of their caftans, the guedra took its meter from a pot drum and lulled a solo performer into a trance. Chants and clapping accompanied the steady choreography, a kinetic blessing or invocation to God. Slowly, the dancer emerged from a black veil and raised an index finger to the heavens as she undulated to the four directions.

Historical Worship Dance

The rise of Christianity in an age of crusades and plague required solace for people beset by northeastern invaders and cyclical epidemics. To comfort and uplift Christendom, monasteries permeated the traditional mass with processional dance and added mime and choreography to miracle and morality plays. For poor communities, lay brother-hoods supplied wigs, musical instruments, and costumes to members of folk troupes.

Into the Middle Ages at Byzantium, Eastern Greek Orthodoxy conceded to Greeks the edification and ecclesiastical value of gendered ring dance. Events com-memorated legends and allegorized holiday emblems with maze dances and proces-sions. Specific choreography epitomized in chronicles included taking of the habit, a ritual at convents, and the Dance of Miriam, acclaiming the Israelite prophet. In Aragon, Spanish Christians welcomed the grape harvest and held vigils for the dead with presentations of the *jota*.

In thirteenth-century Japan, Buddhist evangelist Ippen Shonin journeyed to mountain shrines and honored the kami (nature spirits) with the ecstatic footwork. His outgoing style appealed to peasants, who joined his pilgrimages and dancing. In central Turkey, the presentations of Sufi hymns from the 1400s stressed liberation from dogma by gathering singers and dancers outdoors.

After the conquest of Venezuela by Spain, from 1650, the conversion of natives at Aragua and Vargas introduced them to Christian pageantry taught by the Sociedades del Santísimo (Societies of the Holiest). A papal censure of dance at Iberian cathedrals generated an uproar and supplication in 1685 to Pope Innocent XI, who lifted the ban for Corpus Christi Day in Seville.

At Yare near Madrid in 1742, African slave groups joined whites in venerating San Francisco on Corpus Christi Day. The choreography pitted the evil *diablos danzantes* (devil dancers) in battle against good. Christian forces fought the grotesquely masked red devils that clustered around Satan and snapped leather whips.

Each May 26, Corpus Christi choreography set in motion ornamented horns, rosaries, amulets, crucifixes, palm leaves, and scapulars, creating varied sounds to con-tribute to flute, maracas, and drums. The back-and-forth sequences continued all day until the expected victory of good over evil at sundown. The panoply recognizing the transubstantiation of Christ's body into the Eucharist won an Intangible Cultural Heritage of Humanity designation from UNESCO.

The spread of Islam to Malaysia in the 1700s involved folk worshippers in the *dikir barat*, a call-and-response ritual to clapping and gong taps glorifying Allah and the prophet Muhammad. In the 1850s in Acre and Haifa, Israel, the establishment of the Bahá'i faith, the most recent of the world's religions, introduced a wedding ceremony featuring vows, music, and dance. In the late 1800s in Bangladesh and western Bengal, mystical Baul minstrels taught the spiritual residence of God in the human body by performing verse, song, and dance for the poor from village to village. The itinerant trainers accompanied their syncretic Hindu-Buddhist devotions on a drum and a one-string *ektara*.

At a 1976 folk festival in Marrakesh, Morocco, a Tuareg "blue people" dancer performs the *guedra*, a trance blessing ritual from the Moroccan Sahara arousing spiritual joy. The indigo powder of her *haik* (robe) tints the skin and keeps it moist. The headdress consists of cowrie shells and braids. *Carolina Varga "Morocco" Dinicu, morocco@casbahdance.org, New York City.*

West African Reverence

Among the Dagarti/Lobi of northern Ghana, dancing the *bawa* directed thanks, prayer, and humility toward divinity. Performed to marimba music, the figures centered worship within a village and heightened local awareness of belonging to Earth, the community, and a supreme being. By presenting steps with humility and reverence, the performers gave thanks for ample fishing and farming as well as the blessing of a successful hunt.

For the Gelede of Nigeria, a solo performance by a masked shaman praised a maternal earth goddess. In contrast, the *egungun* dancers of Benin communed with past heroes much as the Sioux and the Magyars of Moldavia reverenced their war dead. To escape reality, performers in Benin balanced baskets on their heads and dressed in face cloths and skirts formed of twenty to thirty disconnected panels. As they whirled the panels in repetitive, hypnotic motions, their minds lapsed into a trance state that received communications from ancestors in the afterlife.

See also hora; *jota*; labyrinthine dance; Manipuri dance; North African dance; pipe dance; Siberian dance; Sufi dance; warrior dance; Wiccan dance.

Sources: Barr, Amelia E. "Characteristic Dances of the World." *Lippincott's Magazine* 27, no. 4 (April 1881): 330–41. Karakeçili, Fethi. "Kurdish Dance Identity in Contemporary Turkey: The Examples of Delilo and Galuç." Master's thesis, York University, Toronto, 2008. www.academia.edu/6546183/Kurdish_Dance_Identity _In_Contemporary_Turkey.

· Z ·

ZAPATEADO

An Andalusian solo or couples dance common to rural get-togethers from the 1500s, the zapateado (or zapateo) features pliant limbs and a brisk syncopated footwork varying in tone and rapidity. Imitating the striking hooves of a galloping horse, the 6/8 percussions to harp, violin, guitar and bandola, and accordion reflected the capers of a stamping dance from the Roman Empire. The choreography paralleled the Andean *huayño*, a stomp dance emulating gambols of the Peruvian Paso Fino stallion.

According to Spanish composer Manuel de Falla, the influence of the Moors of Granada linked the zapateado to the Arab styles of Morocco, Tunis, and Algiers. Like the French *anglaise* and *sabotière* and the Breton *jabadao*, the zapateado footwork combined heel tapping with graceful turns and bows for either a male or female soloist or partners. The French aristocracy sneered at the steps for their provincial joie de vivre without offering due praise of the Q&A of one dancer tapping a pattern and a second dancer answering.

Spanish epicist Miguel de Cervantes dramatized a throbbing evening of the zapateado in *Don Quixote* (1615). In one episode, the roving knight observed entertainment at a wedding at Don Antonio's farm. After 10:00 PM, the knight jolted himself to exhaustion with his "shoe-clattering" on the floor. Through his protagonist, Cervantes honored Spanish dance for inciting laughter and stimulating the five senses. Among the young, the clacking of rustic clogs and the striking of the shoe with the palm of the hand embodied a zest for life. Don Quixote's salute to dance credited the zapateado with uplifting the soul and relieving the body's restlessness, a state he knew well from his mock epic wanderings.

As a courtship ritual in seventeenth-century Spain and Lower Brittany, the vivacious zapateado incited passionate mixing on the dance floor after the departure of censorious priests and chaperones. The dance typically began with a promenade and continued with such improvisations as slides, shuffles, pauses, and strikes against a hollow *tarima* (wood platform). Women accented variations of right-left-right, left-right-left with individual flicks of the fan, passes of the hands over the head, or flirtatious lifts and dips of their long skirts. Men performed skipping steps and flings of the heels to the back while holding their chests in an arrogant posture and elbows close to the ribs as though grasping the reins of a horse. Slight sways of the hips presented a cocksure air.

344

Zapateado in New Settings

The dance migrated to the New World as the colonial zapateado Chicano, a standard presentation at Día de los Muertos (Day of the Dead) observances each November 1. In Guatemala, the steps matched the brio of ritual and social dance by Arawak and Carib Indians and African slaves. When Gallo-Scots explorer and spy Amédée François Frézier reconnoitered Lima, Peru, in spring 1714, he was surprised by the postures of Andean performers, called *zapateadores*. Instead of gesturing with head or arms in the French style, throughout saucy foot stamps, they held their upper limbs slack and concentrated on striking the floor with both heels.

Central American campesinos omitted the Spanish hauteur of the dons and damas and reveled barefoot for joy and earthy fun. The interplay of heel and toe became a favorite step of Yaqui Indians in Jalisco, Vera Cruz, and Yucatán and the basis of the Mexican flamenco and Afro-American tap dance. Striking with abandon before a booth during a religious festival in Santiago, Chile, in 1822, the performers held the arms tightly to the chest and kept time with the heels and twitches of the shoulders.

Promoted to tourists as an authentic folk art, the zapateado flourished in nineteenth-century fiestas and cafes, especially in Granada, Spain. In 1831, a summary of a Castilian version described the pairing of the violin to clacks of a dancer's castanets and the slap of one man's hand against the opposing palm. At the London Opera in January 1834, four zapateadores from Madrid debuted the exhibitionist folk dance among the English gentry to the jingle of a tambourine.

At the feast of St. John on June 24, 1835, a visitor to Lima, Peru, witnessed a biracial assemblage where black rancho cowboys stamped the zapateado at a public hall. That same year at a Sunday evening *tertúlia* (musicale) in Lima, William Samuel Ruschenberger, a US naval surgeon from New Jersey, noted advances and retreats of the dancers, who leaned forward while holding eyes downcast and arms akimbo. A dos-à-dos (back-to-back) figure varied the steady advance and retreat. To cries of "*otra, otra*" (another, another), the retiring dancers returned to allegro tapping on the floor with their heels, increasing speed toward the finale.

In colonial Cuba in the 1840s, bicultural groups featured the zapateado at every festival and entertainment. Africanized versions in the Dominican Republic emphasized the shuffle step rather than heel stamps. In 1847, French lithographer Frédéric Miahle pictured the zapateado as a rural couples dance favored by Afro-Caribbean and Afro-mestizo Creoles. In New Orleans and other urban settings, to the shout of "ole" from spectators, a youthful pair of zapateadores competed in a choreographed argument until one missed a beat or collapsed in exhaustion.

When a male spectator admired a female *zapateadora*, he rewarded her skill by draping his handkerchief over her arm or tossing his straw hat onto her head. At the end of the set, men redeemed their tokens with coins. A superb zapateador sometimes collected one hundred gold rials. An awkward male dancer received the same tokens in mockery of his inept steps. Droll spectators rewarded the bungler with nutshells, orange and banana peels, and cigar butts.

Gallo-Danish soloist August Bournonville fostered eclecticism in Scandinavian stage performances by incorporating the zapateado into his ballet *The Toreador* (1840), for which he earned a hero's reception in Copenhagen. For the masked *parachico* in

Chiapas, a festival rhythm accompanying processions honoring St. Sebastian and other holy icons, dancers presented a double zapateado with the left hand extended and the right hand shaking a rattle streaming with colored ribbons. The exertion tested endurance, especially for females.

Toward a Staged Dance

Exalted by Spanish dramatist Federico García Lorca in the early 1900s, the zapateado retained its social grace as a display of macho drumming of the heels and seduction via an invitation to partners. By the 1920s, ballroom customs reduced virtuosity and stressed a gentle advance and retreat. In fiery flamenco, dancers added sets of zapateado to their footwork. In the 1960s from Mexico north into Santa Fe, New Mexico, zapateadores accented their steps with wood-soled sandals. Along the Rio Grande, men dressed in guayaberas and held palm hats in the right hand. Women preferred the pre-Columbian wrapped skirt, apron, cape, and regal headdress dating to Nahuatl attire.

When the rural choreography progressed to the ballet folklórico, staged choreography arranged dancers in a single line facing spectators or parallel lines, *la cruz* (a cross), and *el saludo* (a greeting), a face-to-face pairing of man and woman. In Cuzco, Peru, in the late 1990s, a marked racial difference in performances set native Andean zapateadores into a stooped posture and hopping pattern of steps while mestizos danced upright with swaying motions.

In the twenty-first century, men and women performed the zapateado in rancher's dress, usually ruffled shirt and vest with pants or slit skirt, boots, and hat. The grasp of the lower vest with both hands contributed to a stiffened upper body and focused eyes on the footwork. A cockier version posed the dancer with tilted head, lifted chin, sensuous back curve, and one arm arced above the shoulder. In the Mexican village of Jarácuaro, little boys turned the zapateado into the "dance of the old men," a character mime, by carrying canes and bending their bodies like an arthritic senior male. Because of the steady pounding of the heels into the floor, folkloric dancers often suffered knee or hip injury from repetitive flexion and stress on the joints.

See also Creole dance; flamenco; *huayño*; *jota*; lamentation dance; mime.

Sources: Hellier-Tinioco, Ruth. *Embodying Mexico: Tourism, Nationalism, and Performance.* New York: Oxford University Press, 2010. Nájera-Ramírez, Olga, Norma Elía Cantú, and Brenda M. Romero. *Dancing across Borders: Danzas y Balles Mexicanos.* Chicago: University of Illinois Press, 2009.

ZYDECO

A diasporic music and dance of Acadia in southwestern Louisiana, zydeco may derive from the Afro-Atakapa Indian residents of the Gulf of Mexico in the early 1700s. According to Southern author George Washington Cable, enslaved field hands—Mandinka, Senegalese, Ibos, Angolan, Bambara, Foulah, Guinean—spent Sundays at Congo Square in New Orleans. Free of labor, they postured and cavorted to attitudinal *bamboula* accompanied by African wood horns, juice harp, bones, banjos, and goatskin drums played with cattle bones, hands, fists, and feet. To circumvent insurrections, urban whites suppressed the frenzied dancing in 1843 by police order.

After the British exiled Acadian Catholics from Nova Scotia in 1764, zydeco emerged from a chaotic period of Cajun adaptation to the coastal bayous and swamps and black slavery, the sources of racial intermarriage and Creole culture. The term corrupted the French *les haricots* (green beans), the meatless food of the poor. The illiterate Cajuns recorded narratives in songs describing the alienation, separation, and yearning of exiles. Fiddlers accompanied the steps, which derived from a mix of European *varsouvienne*, cotillion, polka, galop, waltz, and mazurka, dances that babies learned by standing on their grandfathers' feet.

Transcultural Dance

By the late 1800s, German immigrants contributed a major shift in instrumentation with the squeezebox accordion. In closed, open, or hand-to-hand push-pull position, zydeco dancing in tight jeans and cowboy boots and hats flourished at house and yard dances in Lafayette, Louisiana, and west in Beaumont, Galveston, and Port Arthur, Texas. Foot slides, thigh pats, and fast turns moved quick-quick-slow to the throbbing, heavily syncopated beat, accented by the claps and stomps of slave worship services. Amid mixtures of race and culture, folk bands played the *frottoir* (washboard vest) and button accordion to accompany satires of stiffly arrogant whites, a hip-to-hip two-step, and inventions to ballad singing in patois (Creole French).

In a defiance of the banning of Creole French from schools, in 1928, radio and jukeboxes popularized the first zydeco recordings of "Joli Blon" and "Allons à Lafayette." An influx of American oil derrick roughnecks contributed country-western dances to smooth, subtle ballads. Saturday-night cane cutter and cattle workers' dances at plank-floored roadhouses, bars, and clubs comprised the crawfish circuit, a parallel to the Mississippi juke joint. On a dusting of cornstarch and under colored lights, sweaty dancers waltzed, stomped, and jitterbugged for hours.

The Zydeco Aficionado

Following World War II, dancers reclaimed the zydeco to a new form of washboard after barn builders and roofers turned corrugated tin into a new sound punctuated by stroking and scraping the ridges with spoons and bottle openers. Texas instrumentalists added steel guitar, bass, and drums for a revised dance of quick-quick-slow-slow. The merger of bouncy zydeco with rhythm and blues, country-western, and rock and roll in the 1950s expanded the original sound and varied rhythms, including the swing and the hobble step of the Cajun jitterbug.

The 1964 Newport Folk Festival spread zydeco to younger dancers and musicians. In the 1980s, the typically upright partnering gave place to bent knees and crouches, a style popularized by Boozoo Chavis and dubbed the Boozoo evolution. By the twenty-first century, transnational zydeco welcomed soul, rap, hip-hop, salsa, and reggae.

See also bamboula; *calenda*; cotillion; Creole dance; mazurka; polka; waltz.

Source: Cable, George Washington. "Creole Slave Dances: The Dance in Place Congo." *Century Magazine* (February 1886): 517–31.

Appendix

National and State Dances

bélé	Martinique
chain dance	Faroe Islands
choro	Brazil
clogging	Holland, Kentucky, North Carolina
contradance	England
corroboree	Australia
cotton-eye Joe	Texas
cueca	Chile
czardas	Hungary, Poland
dabke	Iraq, Jordan, Lebanon, Palestine, Syria
danzón	Cuba
delilo	Kurdistan
dilan	Azerbaijan, Turkey
fado	Portugal
flamenco	Spain
gavotte	Brittany
gnawa	Algeria, Morocco
hakka	New Zealand
highland fling	Scotland
hopak	Ukraine
hora	Israel, Moldova, Romania
hornpipe	England
horo	Bulgaria
huayño	Bolivia
jarabe tapatío	Mexico
jenkka	Finland
jig	Ireland
joget	Indonesia
joropo	Venezuela
jota	Aragon, Spain
kathak	India, Pakistan
khaleegy	Bahrain, Iraq, Kuwait, Oman, Qatar, Saudi Arabia, United Arab Emirates
kolo	Croatia, Serbia
lakalaka	Tonga

lamvong	Laos
Ländler	Austria
limbo	Trinidad, Tobago
lundu	Brazil
manipuri	Bangladesh
marinera norteña	Peru
maringa	Sierra Leone
mazouk	Dominica
mazurka	Hungary, Poland
meke	Fiji
merengue	Dominican Republic
méringue	Haiti
morris dance	England
muchongolo	Zimbabwe
oberek	Poland
oro	Macedonia
polka	Germany, Paraguay, Wisconsin
polonaise	Poland
polska	Denmark, Finland, Norway, Sweden
quadrille	Dominica, St. Lucia
reel	Denmark, Scotland
rumba	Cuba
samba	Brazil
sega	Mauritius, Reuníon
shag	North Carolina, South Carolina
square dance	Alabama, Arkansas, California, Colorado, Connecticut, Georgia, Idaho, Louisiana, Maryland, Massachusetts, Mississippi, Missouri, Nebraska, New Jersey, North Dakota, Oklahoma, Oregon, South Carolina, Tennessee, Texas, Utah, Virginia, Washington
step dance	Canada, Ireland
Sufi dance	Turkey
swing	California
syrtos	Greece
tamborito	Panama
tamure	Cook Islands
tango	Argentina, Uruguay
tarantella	Italy
thie bou dien	Senegal
tinikling	Philippines
waltz	Germany, South Carolina
zapin	Brunei, Malaysia

Glossary

allegory   artistry permeated with a hidden moral or political overtones, for example, suggestions of triumph in the thanksgiving dances of ancient Celts, Danes, Picts, and Saxons and in the Catalonian Corpus Christi Day Patum processionals and *tirabol*, Chinese lion dance, Egyptian *tahtiyb*, German *Totentanz*, Judeo-Christian worship dance, and pre-Lenten carnival antics of Venetian troupes.

allegro   quick-paced, lively, as in the precombat dance mode of the Anlo-Ewe and Fon in Ghana, bounds and lunges of the Kurdish *xwarzani*, Russian and Romanian rondo, and the staccato heel taps of the Peruvian zapateado.

assemble   an alliance of the feet before execution of dance steps, a stylized air-borne feature of gavotte.

attitude   a dance pose on one leg to support elevation of the second leg, as in the deep backbends that mark the Aragonese *jota*, Mexican *jarabe tapatío*, Spanish *cachucha*, and the *moresca*, a segment of the commedia dell'arte.

bas-relief   a sculptural technique giving the allusion of three-dimensional presentation, a source of historical analysis of dances in Egypt, Persia, Greece, Rome, India, and Cambodia.

bel canto   artistic or operatic singing, such as the style of fado presentations in nineteenth-century Coimbra, Portugal.

bourrée   a French gliding of feet side to side, an aspect of the sarabande as performed to the tambourine in Guatemala.

breakdown   a slave-era plantation caper involving jumping with both feet crossed, a facet of eighteenth-century juba performances at Congo Square in New Orleans. Also, a musical term for an instrumental solo in barn dance, cotton-eye Joe, Métis jigs in Alberta, and country-western square dance.

cabriole   a quick snap of the support leg to the elevated working leg, a virtuoso caper of the sixteenth-century galliard and *la guerre branle*.

call and response   paired phrases of music or dance, as in the glorification of Allah and the prophet Muhammad in eighteenth-century Malaysian Islamic dance, suggestive back-and-forth during the Caribbean *calenda*, antiroyalist song and victory ronde of the eighteenth-century carmagnole, North Carolina *jonkonnu*, French farandole, Serbo-Croatian and Bulgarian *chorovod*, Peruvian Zamacueca, slave-era juba, Turkish *dilan*, Cuban merengue, Afro-Brazilian *maracatu*, Creek stomp dance, and Malaysian *dikir barat*.

carole   a progression of left-right steps to singing, a facet of the medieval Catalonian or Provençal farandole, Danish church dance, Wiccan Maychant, and an Irish or Finnish after-tournament amusement.

catharsis   a release of anxiety or suffering as a result of exorcism or healing dance, such as the shamanic dance of the San and !Kung in Botswana and Namibia, the Saami of northern Finland, Evanki of Siberia, Saulteaux of Ontario, Uzbeks of the Ural Mountains, Mescalero Apache of New Mexico, Guaraní and Tupí of the Peruvian Andes, Salish of Puget Sound, ghost dancers of Nevada, and the Alaskan Malemiut of Kotzebue Sound.

chassé   a chasing or pursuit step, for example, the step-together-step modifying the basic German waltz in the early 1800s, French *pasodoble*, Dominican and Puerto Rican merengue, German *Ländler*, Hungarian galop, and the Guatemalan sarabande.

closed position   a grasp of arms or contact of torsos between facing partners, two features of the mazurka, polka, *volta*, quadrille, czardas, Danish *polska*, Dominican and Puerto Rican merengue, *pasodoble*, Swedish schottische, Argentinean tango, *varsouvienne*, zydeco dance, and Cajun and Viennese waltz. *See also* open position; semi-closed position.

coda   a closing dance passage different in style or cadence from preceding steps, such as the whip turns that men added to the sixteenth-century galliard to draw attention to their artistry and the Dominican and West Antillean cotillion added to a quadrille. Other examples marked the Catalonian *tirabol*, Yaqui *danza del venado*, Tyrolean *Ländler*, Aztec dance in Mazatlan and Cancun, *assiko* mating dance of Cameroon and Guinea, Thai candle dance, and Berber, Arab, and Sudanese *ahallil*.

counterpoint   a complex merger of independent dance meters, an African mode of the eighteenth-century juba, French gigue, sixteenth-century English allemande, Arabo-Andalusian *joropo* and *cachucha*, and the Seminole hunting/harvest dance.

crossover   a chain of two steps performed by shuffling the feet, a facet of the fifteenth-century Spanish bolero, French gavotte, Napoleonic mazurka, Pueblo hoop dance, Dominican and Puerto Rican merengue, Polish *varsouvienne*, Australian and British *Schuhplattler*, Italian tarantella, French *volta*, and Czech *redowa*.

diaspora   the flight or forced emigration of an ethnic or racial group, as with West African and Chinese slaves to the Western Hemisphere, Anatolian Kurds to Syria, Japanese and Filipinos to Hawaii and New Zealand, Tibetans to China, Sikkim immigrants to India, Armenians and Iranians to Canada, Haitians to Cuba and New Orleans, and the Jews and nomadic Roma to the Austro-Hungarian Empire and Israel.

divertissement   a dance interlude during a long, serious work, as with the Australian insertion of the hornpipe in eighteenth-century theatrical drama, the *joropo* into stage shows in Trinidad and Tobago, the *hopak* to *The Nutcracker*, the flamenco to *Carmen*, the galop into *Giselle, kathak* into dance dramas in India, mazurka into *Coppélia* and *Sleeping Beauty*, polonaise in Ballet Moderno de México, *rigaudon* in *Acis et Galatée*, saltarello in *The Festival in Albano*, and the bolero and cakewalk in Italian ballet.

en pointe   on the toes, a performance mode for the cakewalk when dancers performed it in 1903 in a San Francisco ballet.

figure   a pattern of steps, for example, the two steps forward and two back of the labyrinthine dance and the geometric figures composing a contradance, quadrille, cotillion, square dance, barn dance, New England May Day ritual, Crow and Assiniboine scalp dance, English *volta*, Scots highland fling, Samoan coming-of-age ritual, Central African Republic circumcision ceremony, Caribbean *quinceañera* dance, commedia dell'arte *moresca*, and cotton-eye Joe.

gendered   designated for male, female, or heterogeneous partnering for dance, a determinant of presentation of the all-male Ukrainian *hopak*, Sioux buffalo dance, Chinese dragon dance, the *zaffan* in Oman, Persian Carpaean dance, Norwegian *halling*, Spartan *hormos*, Burundi nuptial dance, Serbian and Montenegran *rugovu*, Hunkpapa Lakota sun dance, Crow shawl dance, Mevlevi Sufi dance, Botswana *jerusarema*, Maasai *eunoto*, Sudanese *etobok* warrior dance, and the maidenly Greek circle dance to the goddess Cybele.

glissades   gliding steps against the floor, a stylistic detail of the Pomeranian *varsouvienne*, French allemande, Romanian *floricica*, Cuban *cachucha*, Mozarabic contradance in Andalusia, Korean fan dance, Parisian *rigaudon*, Xhosa shading dance, and Viennese waltz.

grapevine   a traditional weaver step that troubadours introduced in the 1100s. Dancers crossed one foot over the other, first to the front, then a side step by the back foot, and a cross to the back. The grapevine grounds the serpentine chain, *carole*, *branle*, Muslim line dances, Ute and Wiccan circle dance, and the Israeli hora and *mayim mayim*.

homorhythmic   a sameness of texture, a feature of the baroque-era sarabande and in Shaker and Australian aboriginal dance, Ivory Coast *mapouka*, Congo *soukous*, Ethiopian *eskesta*, and Ponca fancy dance.

idiophonic   a percussive accompaniment to dance from body movements and sound arising from attire or props, particularly the rattles of Pueblo dance, terrapin shell shakers of Seminole dance, the stamping of the Croatian *kolo*, the tinkling jewelry of Armenian *tamzara*, and the foot taps and hand slaps to thighs and torso for hornpipe, *Schuhplattler*, and clogging. *See also* ululation.

idiorhythmic   a dancer's self-generated movement stressing weak and strong beats, the source of religious immersion and trance in Turkish Sufi dance, Chinese lion dance, and the Sioux sun dance.

kinetics   anatomical motion or fluidity emerging from response to rhythm or music, the focus of Arab, Polynesian, Norse, and Malay dance and specifically of Egyptian belly dance, Spanish *jota*, African lamentation dance, Chinese line dance, Shaker healing dance, tarantella, sinuous labyrinthine dance, and hula.

knot   a tight interweaving or spiraling of dancers, a result of coiled figures of the labyrinthine Cretan dance and the medieval European hay, in which a leader wound among the other dancers in an S or Z pattern.

legato   smooth and connected, a quality of the Tuvaluan *fatele*, Viennese waltz, Polish *varsouvienne*, Ionian and Macedonian *syrtos*, Norwegian *ganglat/snoa*, French allemande, zydeco ballads, and Hawaiian hula.

libation   the ritual gift of liquid as a propitiation of deities, a segment of ancient Aztec blood sacrifice, Nubian and Tibetan ancestor ritual, and Roman ceremonial dance in the Circus Maximus, which preceded the pouring of honey or milk on altars.

meter   a rhythmic structure or pattern of stressed and unstressed beats, for example, the hop-step-close-step of the Czech polka, the fast syncopation of the Dominican and Puerto Rican merengue, the springy quickstep of contradance, Japanese *torisashi odori* to stringed accompaniment, and the three-beat legato of the courtly pavane.

open position   the connection of hands between dancers without close contact of bodies, a feature of Cajun dance and the czardas, *polska*, and *Ländler*. *See also* closed position; semi-open position.

pas de deux   a duet, as in the partnering of the gigue, mazurka, *carabine* scarf dance, tango, flamenco, and Mexican *jarabe tapatío*.

plié   a simultaneous bending of both knees, a feature of the gavotte, allemande, and polonaise.

polonaise   a self-conscious Eastern European processional or formal parade before a royal court. The precise march rhythm advanced prim couples in two steps on arched feet. The third step involved the flexed knee on the working leg and a forward thrust of the opposite leg. By 1790, the smooth, self-assured polonaise reflected the nationalism of proud Poles.

polyphonic   coordinating two or more musical lines, an element of accompaniment for the Venezuelan *joropo*, Algerian circle dance, Italian pavane, barn dance, and Polish mazurka.

propitiate   to conciliate or win the attention of a deity, a purpose of the Chinese lion dance, Egyptian and Persian thanksgiving processions, Malawi *tchopa* sacrifice ritual, Laotian ring dance, and Khmer rituals in Cambodia.

reverence   a dancer's gesture of thanks to spectators, a conclusion to medieval English maypole figures, Japanese *odori* and parasol dance, and fifteenth-century Italian saltarello.

semi-open position   the grasp of arms and shoulders, but distancing of torsos from each other, a partnering common to Filipino *tinikling* and the Polish mazurka. *See also* closed position; open position.

staccato   sharply precise and separated, a style of sounds generated by the heels and toes of a flamenco, performer of the *Schuhplattler* or juba, South African step dancer, Maasai leap dancer, Muskogee-Creek stomp dancer, and hornpipe soloist or clogger.

strophe   a structural unit or division of Greek stage choreography, scriptural dance from the Song of Songs, and Choctaw-Chickasaw dance.

tombé   a sinking step, a visual facet of the secular Hispano-Panamanian sarabande.

trickster   a comic mischief maker or devious figure in character or story dance, for example, the dragon-headed peacock/tiger in Balinese *barongan*, clown in commedia dell'arte, coyote in the Amerindian hoop dance, mocker in the Malayalam *attam* of India, Anansi the spider in Jamaican narrative dance, Tungus animal jokers of Siberian dance, Japanese *kyuroku*, Colombian *joropo*, or the intruder in the flirtatious *calenda* of Angola and Zambia and the Mexican zapateado.

troubadour   an itinerant European musician or disseminator of folk arts during the late Middle Ages, for example, the introducer of the Iberian fado, Italian *volta*, and the grapevine step in the French *branle*, *carole*, nuptial choreography, and serpentine chain dance.

ululation   a tongue flutter and high-pitched wail common to Tuareg *tergui* presentations in the Sahel, Mauritanian acrobatic performances, and Roma belly dance in the Balkans. In the geopolitical region of Kurdistan within the Turkish state, bans on tongue vibrations prevent Kurdish dancers from expressing nationalistic exuberance and unity. *See also* idiophonic.

Bibliography

PRIMARY SOURCES

Books

Alexander, Hartley B. *The Religious Spirit of the American Indian*. Chicago: Open Court, 1919.

Anon. *The Dance: Historic Illustrations of Dancing from 3300 B.C. to 1911 A.D.* London: John Bale, Sons & Danielsson, 1911.

Castellanos, Henry C. *New Orleans As It Was: Episodes of Louisiana Life*. New Orleans, LA: L. Graham & Son, 1895.

Catlin, George. *Life among the Indians*. London: Gall and Inglis, 1861.

———. *Notes of Eight Years' Travels and Residence in Europe*. New York: Burgess, Stringer & Company, 1848.

Dinicu, Carolina Varga. *You Asked Aunt Rocky: Answers and Advice about Raqs Sharqi and Raqs Shaabi*. Virginia Beach, VA: RDI Publications, 2011.

Ditchfield, P. H. *Old English Customs: Extant at the Present Time*. London: George Redway, 1896.

Dubois-Maisonneuve. *Introduction à l'étude des vases antiques d'argile peints*. Paris: P. Didot, 1817.

Fuller, Mrs. Marcus B. *The Wrongs of Indian Womanhood*. New York: Fleming H. Revell, 1900.

Gallini, Giovanni Andrea. *A Treatise on the Art of Dancing*. London: R. Dodsley, 1772.

Grant, Horatio N. *The Highland Fling and How to Teach It*. Buffalo, NY: Electric City Press, 1892.

Grove, George, ed. *A Dictionary of Music and Musicians (A.D. 1450–1889)*. London: Macmillan, 1889.

Grove, Lilly. *Dancing*. London: Longmans, Green, and Company, 1895.

Harris, William Torrey, Edward Everett Hale, Oscar Phelps Austin, and Nelson Appleton Miles. *The United States of America: A Pictorial History*. New York: Imperial Publishing, 1906.

Hartmann, Schedel. *Liber Cronicarum*. Nuremberg, Germany: Koberger, 1493.

Haskett, William J. *Shakerism Unmasked; or, The History of the Shakers*. Pittsfield, MA: self-published, 1828.

Hawkes, E. W. *The Dance Festivals of the Alaskan Eskimo*. Philadelphia: University of Pennsylvania Museum, 1914.

———. *The Labrador Eskimo*. Ottawa: Government Printing Bureau, 1916.

Howe, Henry. *Historical Collections of Ohio: An Encyclopedia of the State*. Vols. 2–3. Columbus, OH: H. Howe & Son, 1894.

Hulot, Henri Louis. *Balls and Dancing Parties Condemned by the Scriptures, Holy Fathers, Holy Councils, and Most Renowned Theologians of the Church*. Boston: P. Donahue, 1857.

Kinney, Troy, and Margaret West Kinney. *The Dance: Its Place in Art and Life*. New York: Frederick A. Stokes Company, 1914.

Kippis, Andrew. *The New Annual Register; or, General Repository of History, Politics, and Literature for the Year 1801*. London: T. Davison, 1802.

Matthews, W. H. *Mazes and Labyrinths: A General Account of Their History and Development*. London: Longmans, Green, and Company, 1922.

The Miscellaneous Documents of the House of Representatives for the Second Session of the Fifty-Third Congress, 1893–94. Washington: Government Printing Office, 1895.

Pearson, Karl. *The Chances of Death and Other Studies in Evolution*. London: Edward Arnold, 1897.

Powell, J. W. *Fourteenth Annual Report of the Bureau of Ethnology to the Secretary of the Smithsonian Institution, 1892–93*. Washington: Government Printing Office, 1896.

Randall-MacIver, D. *El Amrah and Abydos, 1899–1901*. London: Kegan Paul, Trench, Turner & Co., 1902.

Rich, Anthony. *A Dictionary of Roman and Greek Antiquities*. New York: D. Appleton & Company, 1873.

Schmidtmeyer, Peter. *Travels into Chile, over the Andes*. London: S. McDowall, 1824.

Smith, William. *A Dictionary of Greek and Roman Antiquities*. London: John Murray, 1875.

Starhawk. *The Spiral Dance*. New York: Harper & Row, 1979.

Strutt, Joseph. *The Sports and Pastimes of the People of England*. London: V. Methuen and Company, 1801.

Tucker, Henry. *Clog Dancing Made Easy*. New York: R.M. DeWitt, 1874.

Visser, Marinus Willem de. *The Dragon in China and Japan*. Amsterdam: J. Müller, 1913.

Vuillier, Gaston. *A History of Dancing from the Earliest Ages to Our Own Times*. New York: D. Appleton and Company, 1898.

Weule, Karl. *Native Life in East Africa*. London: Sir Isaac Pitman & Sons, 1909.

Williams, Joseph J. *Voodoos and Obeahs: Phases of West Indian Witchcraft*. New York: Dial Press, 1932.

Witsen, Nicolaas. *North and East Tartary*. Amsterdam: Schalekamp, 1785.

Wood, John George. *The Uncivilized Races, or Natural History of Man*. London: George Routledge and Sons, 1868.

Periodicals

"American Home Scenes: The Breakdown." *Harper's Weekly*, April 13, 1861, 232.

Barr, Amelia E. "Characteristic Dances of the World." *Lippincott's Magazine* 27, no. 4 (April 1881): 330–41.

Brainerd, Mary Bale. "Dinky." *Atlantic Monthly* 53, no. 8 (August 1884): 206–12.

Cable, George Washington. "Creole Slave Dances: The Dance in Place Congo." *Century Magazine* (February 1886): 517–31.

"The Cakewalk." *Our Paper* (Concord, MA), December 3, 1904, 780.

Dickens, Charles. "A Tale of Two Cities." *All the Year Round*, November 1859.

Dublon, Else I. "The Origins of 'Mayim, Mayim.'" *Jerusalem Post*, December 25, 1972, 10.

Eastlake, W. Delano, "Japanese Home Life." *Popular Science* 43 (May 1893): 10.

Ellis, Havelock. "The Philosophy of Dancing." *Atlantic Monthly* (February 1914): 197–207.

Elson, Arthur. "Musical Thought and Action in the Old World." *The Etude* (January 1914): 418.

"Il Saltarello." *Penny Magazine* 14, no. 3 (September 20, 1845): 364–65.

Moore-Willson, Minnie. "Seminole Indian Feast Days." *Forest and Stream* 66, no. 5 (February 3, 1906): 176–77.

Starr, Frederick, "Dress and Adornment." *Popular Science* (December 1891): 199.

Vance, Lee J. "The Evolution of Dancing." *Popular Science* 41, no. 52 (October 1892): 739–56.

Venedey, Jacob. "Twaddling Tourists in Ireland." *Dublin University Magazine* 143, no. 24 (November 1844): 505–26.

Wickersham, James. "The Eskimo Dance House." *The American Antiquarian and Oriental Journal* 24–25 (1902): 221–23.

Williams, Emily. "Spirituality as Expressed in Song." *Connecticut Quarterly Magazine* 9, no. 4 (1905): 745–51.

Electronic

Densmore, Frances, ed. "Songs of the Sioux." Library of Congress. (1951). Accessed July 8, 2015. www.loc.gov/folklife/LP/AFSL23Sioux.pdf.

Dunmur, Ian. "Traditional Step Dancing." *Chris J. Brady*. (1984). Accessed September 3, 2015. http://chrisbrady.itgo.com/dance/stepdance/trad_step_dancing.htm.

Petrie, Tom. "Early Reminiscences of Early Queensland." (1904). Accessed October 9, 2015. www.seqhistory.com/index.php/aboriginals-south-east-queensland/thomas-petrie.

SECONDARY SOURCES

Books

Aching, Gerard. *Masking and Power: Carnival and Popular Culture in the Caribbean*. Minneapolis: University of Minnesota Press, 2002.

Alvarez, Julia. *Once Upon a Quinceañera: Coming of Age in the USA*. New York: Viking Penguin, 2007.

Bailey, Diane. *History of Dance*. Minneapolis, MN: Abdo, 2015.

Bell, Deborah. *Mask Makers and Their Craft: An Illustrated Worldwide Study*. Jefferson, NC: McFarland, 2010.

Browner, Tara. *Heartbeat of the People: Music and Dance of the Northern Powwow*. Chicago: University of Illinois Press, 2002.

Bryant, Clifton D., and Dennis L. Peck, eds. *Encyclopedia of Death and Human Experience*. Thousand Oaks, CA: Sage, 2009.

Bulgakova, Tatiana. *Nanai Shamanic Culture in Indigenous Discourse*. Frankfurt, Germany: Books on Demand, 2013.

Carey, Peter. *True History of the Kelly Gang*. St. Lucia, Australia: University of Queensland Press, 2000.

Carstens, Sharon A. *Histories, Cultures, Identities: Studies in Malaysian Chinese Worlds*. Singapore: Singapore University Press, 2005.

Carter, Alexandra. *Rethinking Dance History: A Reader*. New York: Routledge, 2004.

Chakravorty, Pallabi. *Bells of Change: Kathak Dance, Women, and Modernity in India*. Calcutta: Seagull Books, 2008.

Charnon-Deutsch, Lou. *The Spanish Gypsy: The History of a European Obsession*. University Park: Pennsylvania State University Press, 2004.

Chico, Beverly. *Hats and Headwear around the World: A Cultural Encyclopedia*. Santa Barbara, CA: ABC-Clio, 2013.

Cooper, John Michael. *Mendelssohn, Goethe, and the Walpurgis Night: The Heathen Muse in European Culture, 1700–1850*. Rochester, NY: University of Rochester Press, 2007.

Cosman, Madeleine Pelner. *Handbook to Life in the Medieval World*. New York: Facts on File, 2008.

Cowgill, Rachel, David Cooper, and Clive Brown, eds. *Art and Ideology in European Opera: Essays in Honor of Julian Rushton*. Rochester, NY: Boydell Press, 2010.

Craine, Debra, and Judith Mackrell. *The Oxford Dictionary of Dance*. Oxford, UK: Oxford University Press, 2010.

Crawford, Suzanne J. *American Indian Religious Traditions*. Santa Barbara, CA: ABC-Clio, 2005.

Crowe, Felicity, Emily Hill, and Ben Hollingum, eds. *Sex and Society*. Tarrytown, NY: Marshall Cavendish, 2010.

Curtis, John, and Nigel Tallis. *Forgotten Empire: The World of Ancient Persia*. Berkeley: University of California Press, 2005.

Cutting, John. *History and the Morris Dance: A Look at Morris Dancing from Its Earliest Days until 1850*. Alton, UK: Dance Books, 2005.

Daniel, Yvonne. *Caribbean and Atlantic Diaspora Dance: Igniting Citizenship*. Champaign: University of Illinois Press, 2011.

Dankworth, Linda E., and Ann R. David. *Dance Ethnography and Global Perspectives: Identity, Embodiment and Culture*. Basingstoke, UK: Palgrave Macmillan, 2014.

Danver, Steven L. *Native Peoples of the World: An Encyclopedia of Groups*. New York: Routledge, 2015.

DeFrantz, Thomas F. *Dancing Many Drums: Excavations in African American Dance*. Madison: University of Wisconsin Press, 2002.

DeMello, Margo. *Encyclopedia of Body Adornment*. Westport, CT: Greenwood, 2007.

Diehl, Daniel, and Mark P. Donnelly. *Medieval Celebrations: Your Guide to Planning and Hosting Spectacular Feasts, Parties, Weddings, and Renaissance Fairs*. Mechanicsburg, PA: Stackpole, 2011.

Dills, Ann, and Ann Cooper Albright. *Moving History / Dancing Cultures: A Dance History Reader*. Middletown, CT: Wesleyan University Press, 2001.

Dodds, Sherrill, and Susan C. Cook, eds. *Bodies of Sound: Studies across Popular Music and Dance*. Farnham, UK: Ashgate, 2013.

Eiss, Harry. *The Mythology of Dance*. Newcastle, UK: Cambridge Scholars, 2013.

Foley, Catherine E. *Step Dancing in Ireland: Culture and History*. Farnham, UK: Ashgate, 2013.

Francis, Dale. *The Quelbe Commentary, 1672–2012*. Bloomington, IN: iUniverse, 2014.

Fraser, Kathleen W. *Before They Were Belly Dancers: European Accounts of Female Entertainers in Egypt, 1760–1870*. Jefferson, NC: McFarland, 2013.

Fulemille, Agnes. *Magyar Orokseg Washingtonban: Hungarian Heritage: Roots to Revival*. Budapest: Balassi Intezet, 2014.

Galenorn, Yasmine. *Totem Magic: Dance of the Shapeshifter*. Berkeley, CA: Ten Speed Press, 2004.

Grosby, Steven Elliot, and Athena S. Leoussi. *Nationalism and Ethnosymbolism: History, Culture, and Ethnicity in the Formation of Nations*. Edinburgh: Edinburgh University Press, 2007.

Hall, Edith, and Rosie Wyles, eds. *New Directions in Ancient Pantomime*. New York: Oxford University Press, 2008.

Hanna, Judith Lynne. *Dancing for Health: Conquering and Preventing Stress*. Lanham, MD: AltaMira, 2006.

Harkleroad, Leon. *The Math behind the Music*. Cambridge: Cambridge University Press, 2006.

Harrison, Paul Carter, Victor Leo Walker, and Gus Edwards, eds. *Black Theatre: Ritual Performance in the African Diaspora*. Philadelphia: Temple University Press, 2002.

Hartley, Janet M. *Siberia: A History of the People*. New Haven, CT: Yale University Press, 2014.

Heath, Jennifer, ed. *The Veil: Women Writers on Its History, Lore, and Politics*. Berkeley: University of California Press, 2008.

Hellier-Tinioco, Ruth. *Embodying Mexico: Tourism, Nationalism, and Performance*. New York: Oxford University Press, 2010.

Henry, Lori. *Dancing through History: In Search of the Stories That Define Canada*. Vancouver: Dancing Traveller, 2012.

Higgins, James. *Lima: A Cultural History*. New York: Oxford University Press, 2005.

Hill, Constance Valis. *Tap Dancing America: A Cultural History*. New York: Oxford University Press, 2010.

Hoppu, Petri, and Karen Vedel. *Nordic Dance Spaces: Practicing and Imagining a Region*. Farnham, UK: Ashgate, 2014.

Horn, David, Heidi Feldman, Mona-Lynn Courteau, Pamela Narbona Jerez, and Hettie Malcomson. *Bloomsbury Encyclopedia of Popular Music of the World*. Vol. 9. London: Bloomsbury, 2014.

Howitt, Alfred William. *The Native Tribes of South-East Australia*. Cambridge: Cambridge University Press, 2010.

Hutton, Ronald. *Shamans: Siberian Spirituality and the Western Imagination*. London: Bloomsbury, 2001.

Ingber, Judith Brin. *Seeing Israeli and Jewish Dance*. Detroit, MI: Wayne State University Press, 2011.

Jablonski, Nina G. *Skin: A Natural History*. Berkeley: University of California Press, 2006.

Johnson, James H. *Venice Incognito: Masks in the Serene Republic*. Berkeley: University of California Press, 2011.

Jones, Derek, ed. *Censorship: A World Encyclopedia*. New York: Routledge, 2015.

Jones, Susan. *Literature, Modernism, and Dance*. Oxford: Oxford University Press, 2013.

Kaschi, Elke. *Dance and Authenticity in Israel and Palestine*. Leiden: Brill, 2003.

Kassing, Gayle. *Discovering Dance*. Champaign, IL: Human Kinetics, 2014.

————. *History of Dance: An Interactive Arts Approach*. Champaign, IL: Human Kinetics, 2007.

Katritzky, M. A. *The Art of Commedia: A Study in the Commedia dell'Arte 1560–1620 with Special Reference to the Visual Records*. Amsterdam: Rodopi, 2006.

Keillor, Elaine, Tim Archambault, and John M. H. Kelly. *Encyclopedia of Native American Music of North America*. Santa Barbara, CA: ABC-Clio, 2013.

King, Jonathan C. H., Birgit Pauksztat, and Robert Storrie, eds. *Arctic Clothing*. Quebec: British Museum, 2005.

Kislenko, Arne. *Culture and Customs of Thailand*. Westport, CT: Greenwood, 2004.

Knowles, Mark. *The Wicked Waltz and Other Scandalous Dances: Outrage at Couple Dancing in the 19th and Early 20th Centuries*. Jefferson, NC: McFarland, 2009.

Koskoff, Ellen, ed. *The Concise Garland Encyclopedia of World Music*. New York: Routledge, 2008.

Krishnan, Usha R. Bala, Meera Sushil Kumar, and Bharath Ramamrutham. *Indian Jewellery: Dance of the Peacock*. Mumbai: India Book House, 2004.

Lancashire, Terence A. *An Introduction to Japanese Folk Performing Arts*. Farnham, UK: Ashgate, 2011.

Laufman, Dudley, and Jacqueline Laufman. *Traditional Barn Dances with Calls and Fiddling*. Champaign, IL: Human Kinetics, 2009.

Lee, Carol. *Ballet in Western Culture: A History of Its Origins and Evolution*. New York: Routledge, 2002.

Lee, Jonathan H. X., and Kathleen M. Nadeau. *Encyclopedia of Asian American Folklore and Folklife*. Santa Barbara, CA: ABC-Clio, 2011.

Lexová, Irena. *Ancient Egyptian Dances*. Mineola, NY: Dover, 2000.

Looper, Matthew G. *To Be Like Gods: Dance in Ancient Maya Civilization*. Austin: University of Texas Press, 2009.

Lopez, Melli Leandicho. *A Handbook of Philippine Folklore*. Quezon City: University of the Philippines Press, 2006.

Lord, Suzanne, and David Brinkman. *Music from the Age of Shakespeare: A Cultural History*. Westport, CT: Greenwood, 2003.

Loudon, Rebecca. *Tarantella*. Edmonds, WA: Ravenna Press, 2004.

MacQueen, Gailand. *The Spirituality of Mazes and Labyrinths*. Kelowna, BC: Wood Lake Books, 2005.

Malborg, Kim. *Korean Dance*. Seoul, Korea: Ewha Womans University Press, 2005.

Manuel, Peter, ed. *Creolizing Contradance in the Caribbean*. Philadelphia: Temple University Press, 2009.

March, Richard. *The Tamburitza Tradition*. Madison: University of Wisconsin Press, 2013.

Marcsek-Fuchs, Maria. *Dance and British Literature: An Intermedial Encounter*. Leiden: Brill Rodopi, 2015.

Marshall, Howard Wright. *Play Me Something Quick and Devilish: Old-Time Fiddlers in Missouri*. Columbia: University of Missouri Press, 2012.

Matteo, Carola Goya. *The Language of Spanish Dance: A Dictionary and Reference Manual*. Hightstown, NJ: Princeton Book Company, 2003.

McCutchen, Brenda Pugh. *Teaching Dance as Art in Education*. Champaign, IL: Human Kinetics, 2006.

McKee, Eric. *Decorum of the Minuet, Delirium of the Waltz*. Bloomington: Indiana University Press, 2012.

Meri, La. *Spanish Dancing*. Northampton, MA: Interlink Books, 2011.

Miller, Rebecca S. *Carriacou String Band Serenade: Performing Identity in the Eastern Caribbean*. Middletown, CT: Wesleyan University Press, 2007.

Mirka, Danuta. *The Oxford Handbook of Topic Theory*. Oxford, UK: Oxford University Press, 2014.

Mojaddedi, Jawid. *Beyond Dogma: Rumi's Teachings on Friendship with God and Early Sufi Theories*. New York: Oxford University Press, 2012.

Mullally, Robert. *The Carole: A Study of a Medieval Dance*. Farnham, UK: Ashgate, 2011.

Nahachewsky, Andriy. *Ukrainian Dance: A Cross-Cultural Approach*. Jefferson, NC: McFarland, 2012.

Nájera-Ramírez, Olga, Norma Elía Cantú, and Brenda M. Romero. *Dancing across Borders: Danzas y Balles Mexicanos*. Chicago: University of Illinois Press, 2009.

Neich, Roger, and Fuli Pereira. *Pacific Jewelry and Adornment*. Honolulu: University of Hawaii Press, 2004.

Neville, Jennifer. *Dance, Spectacle, and the Body Politick, 1250–1750*. Bloomington: Indiana University Press, 2008.

Nielsen, Erica. *Folk Dancing*. Santa Barbara, CA: ABC-Clio, 2011.

Noyes, Dorothy. *Fire in the Plaça: Catalan Festival Politics after Franco*. Philadelphia: University of Pennsylvania Press, 2003.

Pittman, Anne M., Marlys S. Waller, and Cathy L. Dark. *Dance a While: A Handbook for Folk, Square, Contra, and Social Dance*. Long Grove, IL: Waveland Press, 2009.

Qian, Gonglin. *Chinese Fans: Artistry and Aesthetics*. San Francisco: Long River Press, 2004.

Rinaldi, Robin, Elizabeth A. Hanley, and Jacques d'Amboise. *European Dance: Ireland, Poland, Spain, and Greece*. New York: Infobase, 2010.

Rodriguez, Sylvia. *The Matachines Dance: A Ritual Dance of the Indian Pueblos and Mexicano-Hispano Communities*. Santa Fe, NM: Southwest Heritage, 2009.

Rostas, Susanna. *Carrying the Word*. Boulder: University Press of Colorado, 2009.

Royce, Anya Peterson. *Anthropology of the Performing Arts: Artistry, Virtuosity, and Interpretation in a Cross-Cultural Perspective*. Walnut Creek, CA: AltaMira, 2004.

Sanajaoba, Naorem, ed. *Manipur, Past and Present: The Heritage and Ordeals of a Civilization*. Vol. 4. New Delhi: Mittal, 2005.

Schaff, Helene, Marty Sprague, and Susan McGreevy-Nichols. *Exploring Dance Forms and Styles*. Champaign, IL: Human Kinetics, 2010.

Sellers, Julie A. *Merengue and Dominican Identity: Music as National Unifier.* Jefferson, NC: Mc-Farland, 2004.

Sharma, Kamal Prashad. *Folk Dances of Chamba.* New Delhi, India: Indus Publishing, 2004.

Solway, Andrew. *Country and Folk Dance.* Chicago: Heinemann, 2009.

Udall, Sharyn R. *Dance and American Art: A Long Embrace.* Madison: University of Wisconsin Press, 2012.

Villaruz, Basilio Esteban. *Treading through: 45 Years of Philippine Dance.* Quezon City: University of the Philippines Press, 2006.

Watts, June. *Circle Dancing: Celebrating the Sacred in Dance.* Mallet, UK: Green Magic, 2006.

Welsh, Karlamu. *World of Dance: African Dance.* New York: Infobase, 2010.

Woodman, Ross Greig, and Joel Faflak. *Sanity, Madness, Transformation: The Psyche in Romanticism.* Toronto: University of Toronto Press, 2005.

Yang, Lihui, and Deming An. *Handbook of Chinese Mythology.* New York: Oxford University Press, 2005.

Yarber, Angela. *Dance in Scripture: How Biblical Dancers Can Revolutionize Worship Today.* Eugene, OR: Wipf and Stock, 2013.

Yousof, Ghulam-Sarwar. *The Encyclopedia of Malaysia: Performing Arts.* Singapore: Archipelago Press, 2004.

Zarrilli, Phillip. *Kathakali Dance-Drama: Where Gods and Demons Come to Play.* London: Routledge, 2000.

Zhao, Xiaojian, and Edward J. W. Park. *Asian Americans: An Encyclopedia of Social, Cultural, Economic, and Political History.* Santa Barbara, CA: ABC-Clio, 2013.

Periodicals

Bellman, Jonathan D. "*Ongherese*, Fandango, and Polonaise: National Dance as Classical-Era Topic." *Journal of Musicological Research* 31, nos. 2–3 (2012): 70–96.

Carlos-Machej, Klaudia. "Polish National Dance as a Value of Culture." *Philosophical Education* 48 (2009): 219–40.

"Chitresh Das Dies at 70; Indian Classical Dancer Was Master of Kathak." *Los Angeles Times,* January 9, 2015.

Collon, Dominique. "Dance in Ancient Mesopotamia." *Near Eastern Archaeology* 66, no. 3 (September 2003): 96–102.

Dragomir, Corneliu. "The Sun: Profane Meanings in the Romanian Hora Dances in Northern Mehedinti." *Revista Romana de Sociologie* 1–2 (2012): 133–40.

Gifford, Paul M. "Henry Ford's Dance Revival and Fiddle Contests: Myth and Reality." *Journal of the Society for American Music* 4, no. 3 (August 2010): 307–38.

Greene, Thomas M. "Labyrinth Dances in the French and English Renaissance." *Renaissance Quarterly* 54, no. 4.2 (Winter 2001): 1403–66.

Gunkel, Ann Hetzel. "The Polka Alternative: Polka as Counterhegemonic Ethnic Practice." *Popular Music and Society* 27, no. 4 (2004): 407–27.

Hyatt, Ashley. "Healing through Culture for Incarcerated Aboriginal People." *First Peoples Child & Family Review* 8, no. 2 (2013): 40–53.

Knudsen, Jan Sverre. "Dancing *Cueca* 'with Your Coat On': The Role of Traditional Chilean Dance in an Immigrant Community." *British Journal of Ethnomusicology* 10, no. 2 (2001): 61–83.

Knutsson, Gunilla K. "The Wedding of Solo's King." *New York Times,* September 11, 1983.

Kolb, Alexandra. "The Migration and Globalization of *Schuhplattler* Dance: A Sociological Analysis." *Cultural Sociology* 7, no. 1 (March 2013): 39–55.

Miller, Denise. "Our Tobacco Is Sacred." *Windspeaker* 23, no. 6 (2005): 26.

Miller, Heather Andrews. "Dance Reflects Tradition and History." *Windspeaker* 24, no. 3 (2006).

Park, Ga Young. "Androgyny of Sword Dance Costumes in the Joseon Dynasty." *International Journal of Human Ecology* 15, no. 2 (2014): 23–31.

Pierce, Ken. "Coarse, Odd, and Comic: A New Study of Jigs." *Dance Chronicle* 38 (2015): 81–86.

Ramirez, Abel Saldivar. "The Art of Performing the Spanish Paso Doble." *Bandmasters Review* (June 2008): 27–28.

Rohter, Larry. "Carving Out a Bold Destiny for Fado." *New York Times*, March 25, 2011.

Rutherford, Annabel. "The Triumph of the Veiled Dance: The Influence of Oscar Wilde and Aubrey Beardsley on Serge Diaghilev's Creation of the Ballets Russes." *Dance Research* 27, no. 1 (May 2009): 93–107.

Schlacter, Ron. "Protest Music Appearing in Bolivian Nightsports, Labels." *Billboard*, October 9, 1971, 40.

Seiji, CedarBough. "The Bawdy, Brawling, Boisterous World of Korean Mask Dance Dramas." *Cross-Currents: East Asian History and Culture Review* 4 (September 2012): 146–68.

Sexsmith, Pamela. "The Healing Gift of the Jingle Dance." *Windspeaker* 21, no. 5 (2003): 28.

Singh, Karan. "Istanbul: Dance of the Dervishes." *India International Centre Quarterly* 30, nos. 3–4 (Winter 2003–Spring 2004): 169–73.

Sweeting, Terry, Peter Werner, Lori H. Williams, and Alyssa Crump. "Tanko Bushi: Designing a Japanese-American Dance Experience." *Journal of Physical Education, Recreation & Dance* 83, no. 1 (2012): 15–31.

"Tanko-Bushi Inspiration Honored." *Japan Times*, November 8, 2008.

Thorp, Jennifer. "Pecour's *L'Allemande*, 1702–1765: How 'German' Was It?" *Eighteenth Century Music* 1, no. 102 (September 2004): 183–204.

Zotigh, Dennis. "History of the Modern Hoop Dance." *Indian Country*, May 30, 2007.

Electronic

Brady, Chris, ed. "The Hornpipe National Early Music Association." *Chris J. Brady*. Accessed July 1, 2015. http://chrisbrady.itgo.com/dance/stepdance/hornpipe_conference.htm.

Denniston, Christine. "The Hidden History of Tango." *History of Tango*. Accessed October 9, 2015. www.history-of-tango.com.

"Ghost Dance." *Ghost Dance*. Accessed November 21, 2015. www.ghostdance.us/history/history-messiahletter.html.

Karakeçili, Fethi. "Kurdish Dance Identity in Contemporary Turkey: The Examples of Delilo and Galuç." Master's thesis, York University, Toronto, 2008. Accessed September 16, 2015. www.academia.edu/6546183/Kurdish_Dance_Identity_In_Contemporary_Turkey.

Lorenz, Roberto. "Flamenco Page." *Roberto Lorenz, Flamenco Guitarist*. Accessed October 18, 2015. www.timenet.org/roberto.html.

Louzioti, Dafne. "Introduction to Quadrille." *Caribbean Communities in Europe*. Accessed October 20, 2015. www.caribbeancommunities.eu/CACOEU_investigates.pdf.

Mendoza-Garcia, Gabriela. "Bodily Renderings of the Jarabe Tapatío in Early Twentieth-Century Mexico and the Millennial United States: Race, Nation, Class, and Gender." PhD diss., University of California–Riverside, 2013. Accessed September 16, 2015 http://escholarship.org/uc/item/8c47k3gm#page-6.

"Oklahoma Historical Society." Accessed November 9, 2015. www.okhistory.org/publications.

Pierce, Ken. "Uncommon Steps and Notation in the *Sarabande de Mr. de Beauchamp*." Accessed October 3, 2015. http://web.mit.edu/kpierce/www/sdhs2003/beauchamps.pdf.

Index

Note: Boldface indicates major topics. Illustrations appear in brackets.

About the Author

Mary Ellen Snodgrass of Hickory, North Carolina, writes and reviews reference books. A member of Phi Beta Kappa, she holds degrees in English and classics from the University of North Carolina at Greensboro and Appalachian State University and certification in gifted education from Lenoir Rhyne University. She taught high school and university classes for twenty-three years, reared six foster children, produced a column for the *Charlotte Observer*, and served as a state humanities lecturer and member of the NC Library Commission.

Snodgrass's honoraria for published works include New York Public Library Choice awards for *Japan vs. U.S.A.* (1993) and *Encyclopedia of Feminist Literature* (2006). Her *Encyclopedia of Utopian Literature* (1995) earned reference book of the year citations from *Choice* magazine, American Library Association, and *Library Journal*. For *Encyclopedia of Fable* (1998), she won a second *Library Journal* reference book of the year, followed by a *Booklist* Editors Choice for *Encyclopedia of the Underground Railroad* (2007) and a *Library Journal* award for *Encyclopedia of Clothing and Fashion* (2013). Her most recent work, *Encyclopedia of World Ballet* (Rowman & Littlefield, 2015) was lauded by *Booklist* and *Library Journal*.